EMERGENT FORMS OF LIFE AND

THE ANTHROPOLOGICAL VOICE

MICHAEL M. J. FISCHER

Emergent Forms of Life and

the Anthropological Voice

Duke University Press   Durham and London 2003

© 2003 Duke University Press
All rights reserved
Printed in the United States of
America on acid-free paper ∞
Designed by Rebecca Giménez
Typeset in Adobe Minion by Tseng
Information Systems, Inc.
Library of Congress Cataloging-
in-Publication Data appear on the
last printed page of this book.

FOR IRENE,

whose amazing intellect, willpower,

and grace in each new stage of life

continue to inspire, as does her love,

AND FOR SUSANN,

whose companionship in building the

communities of students and colleagues

from which these essays grow, and whose

abundant love, energize my life.

CONTENTS

New Pedagogies and Ethics

ACKNOWLEDGMENTS

I have been fortunate as a teacher in having students again in the 1980s and 1990s who have helped enrich and expand the intellectual, experiential, cross-cultural, generational, and cross-disciplinary delights of ethnography and anthropology. I thank in particular Mehdi Abedi, Lenore Anderson, Babak Ashrafi, Tajiana Bajuk, Jamila Bargach, Pat Bentley, Ryan Bishop, Roberta Brawer, Brenda Bright, Candis Callison, Melissa Cefkin, Anita Chan, Mousumi Roy Chowdhury, Greg Clancey, Mitra Emad, Linda Endersby, Kim Fortun, Laurel Georges, Slava Gerovitch, Yaakov Garb, Bruce Grant, Diane Greco, Stella Grigorian, Verle Harrop, Wenke He, Laura Helper, Meg Hiesinger, Rebecca Herzig, Chris Kelty, Wen-Hua Kuo, Hannah Landecker, David Mindell, Mayanna Lahsen, Judy Lentz, Mazyar Lotfalian, Rob Martelo, Ted Medcalfe, Jennifer Mnookin, Esra Ozun, Jeff Petry, Ben Pinney, Chris Pound, David Prater, Aswin Punathambekar, Eric Sievers, Naghmeh Sohrabi, Kaushik Sunder Rajan, Aslihan Sanal, Heinrich Schwarz, Pam Smart, Tulasi Srinivas, David Syring, Beth Tudor, Santiago Villavecces, Priscilla Weeks, Livia Wick, and Christopher York for having made the past few years so intellectually and personally rewarding. Many others in the graduate programs at Rice and MIT have contributed to this community of feeling—postdoctoral fellows in the STS Program Rich Doyle, Mike Fortun, and Adriana Petryna, visting scholars Constance Perin, Ricardo Ventura Santos, and Patricia Seed, visiting RPI students Virginia Eubanks and Patrick Feng, visiting ETH Zurich student Regula Burri, visiting Humboldt University student Axel Roch, the exchange students with Sweden, colleagues and graduate students in the Comparative Media Studies Program, and the colleagues and Rockefeller Postdoctoral Fellows of the Center for Cultural Studies at Rice—as did all the many contributors to the investigative and editorial experiments of the *Late Editions* project piloted by George Marcus, the members of the network of the Center for Transcultural Studies piloted by Ben Lee and Dilip Gaonkar and the separate but allied journal *Public*

Culture led by Carol Breckenridge and Arjun Appadurai, and the members of the Friday Morning Seminar piloted by Byron Good and Mary-Jo Del Vecchio Good.

Joe Dumit and Joao Biehl have been invaluable readers of a number of these essays. I am also grateful to the anonymous readers for Duke University Press, both for their enthusiasm and for their suggestions.

Hal Abelson deserves a special note of thanks for involving me in the fast-changing front lines of the "Law and Ethics on the Electronic Frontier" course, of which the law section of chapter 8 hearkens back to the very first iteration. The discussion group and subsequent joint MIT-Harvard Health, Science, and Technology (HST) course that Mary-Jo DelVecchio Good and Byron Good and I have been running for the past eight years has been a constant companion to the thinking of many of the essays here, and I thank all the luminous scientists, physicians, and engineers who have participated in that course, some of whose names appear in the essays, but I will save naming them for a more appropriate place in the near future. Charlie Weiner has been not only an inspirational colleague in tapping his contacts in the activist and regulatory worlds for our "Down and Dirty" course with a group of wonderful Parsons Lab graduate students—Nicole Keon, David Senn, Scott Hassel, Winston Yu—but has been and continues to be the kind of dream colleague and friend of which academia is ideally composed. Charlie single-handedly seems to have interviewed everyone in American science and is more than willing to energize and guide students and colleagues such as myself to all sorts of insights, troves of material, and ways of linking issues. Lily Kay was another such colleague who loved to introduce people across disciplinary barriers, and loved nothing better than a good intellectual debate, and I thank her for her friendship and for being one of the early supporters and coteachers of the "integrative seminar" that was one kernel of the later core course. Evelynn Hammonds has been another such wonderful colleague linking the worlds of history, medicine, anthropology, active social responsibility, academia, and the world beyond. She and Deborah Fitzgerald were the historians who helped me put on the core course. Sherry Turkle cotaught an iteration of the integrative seminar and helped with the core course. Almost all the active members of the core faculty of the Program in Science, Technology, and Society (STS) participated in the core course and the loosely coupled weekly colloquium, and I thank Dave Mindell, Hugh Gusterson, Ted Postal, and the historians Peter Perdue and Harriet Ritvo for lending their expertise to particular modules, as did Jed Buchwald and Evelyn Fox Keller. Thanks to Leo Marx, Ken Keniston, and Roe Smith for good-natured support from the sidelines, and to Loren Graham for always well timed and strategic active support and being such a model of scholarship, cross-cultural commitment, and *Menschlichkeit*. To Judith Stein, Chris Bates, and especially Debbie Meinbresse, more thanks than I can express in helping keep me sane even through the most turbulent of seas.

All the essays here have been reworked from previous venues. Longer versions of chapters 4, 7, and 9 appeared in volumes 4 (1997), 7 (2000), and 8 (2000), respectively, of the *Late Editions* project, edited by George Marcus, and published by the University of Chicago Press, a quite remarkable series both for its content and for the collaborative relationships it nurtured. (A version of chapter 9.2 also appeared in *Culture + Science*, ed. Roddy Reid and Sharon Traweek [New York: Routledge, 2000].) For a brief review of the eight volumes of *Late Editions* and the ways retrospectively I thought they had reflected the changing media, academic, and social environment over the course of the 1990s, see my "Before Going Digital/Double Digit/Y2000, A Retrospective of *Late Editions*," in *Late Editions*, vol. 8 (2000).

Chapter 1 was printed in the EASST *Review*, the journal of the European Association for the Study of Science and Technology, vol. 20(1) (March 2001). Chapter 2 is a review essay that appeared in the *Annual Reviews of Anthropology*, vol. 28 (1999). Chapter 3 appeared in *Religion and Media*, ed. Hent de Vries and Samuel Weber (Stanford: Stanford University Press, 2001), which was dedicated in part to exploring the recent writings of Jacques Derrida on the media in transnational contexts. Chapter 5 appeared in *Culture, Medicine, and Psychiatry* (2001). Chapter 6 appeared in *Autobiography and Postmodernism*, ed. Kathleen Ashley, Leigh Gilmore, and Gerald Peters (Amherst: University of Massachusetts Press, 1994), and was originally part of a quite wonderful conference that Kathleen, Leigh, and Gerry hosted at the University of Southern Maine in Portland. Chapter 8 appeared in the School for American Research volume *Critical Anthropology Now*, ed. George Marcus (1999). That volume was the outcome of an extraordinary weeklong workshop held five years earlier at the School of American Research in Santa Fe, New Mexico, and was conceived in part as revisiting some of the issues initiated in an SAR workshop held a decade earlier and published as *Writing Culture*, ed. Jim Clifford and George Marcus (1986). Written just as the Internet and World Wide Web were beginning to take off, some of the ethnographic material in sections of chapter 8 are now historical illuminations on a new technology's initiatory period. The theoretical and methodological issues remain, and I see a continuity between this chapter, the subsequent computer module in chapter 9.2, the reflections in "Before Going Digital," and another essay on the Y2K panic referred to in the prologue. Chapter 10 appeared in *Anthropology Today*, a journal of the Royal Anthropological Society, in issues 17(4–5) (August–October 2001).

I am very grateful to a number of wonderful editors and their reviewers, as well as to audiences and readers of earlier versions. Many thanks especially to Kathleen Ashley, Leigh Gilmore, and Gerald Peters; Hent de Vries; Mary-Jo Del Vecchio Good and Byron Good; Gustaaf Houtman; Chunglin Kwa; George Marcus; Roddy Reid and Sharon Traweek. Each made the writing, review procedures, and revisions go smoothly and communicated joy and a sense of reward in participating in larger and ongoing collaborations. To my newest editor, Ken Wissoker, and his staff, Christine Dahlin, Pam Morrison, my warmest thanks for making the process go so smoothly, and for taking such care. From the Someday Café in Davis Square, more cappuccinos await.

At the beginning of the year 2000 (Y2K), there was a now largely forgotten panic that there would be massive computer infrastructure breakdown because embedded legacy systems had only two digits for the year: the rollover to 00 might be read as 1900. Consultants made money devising scenarios of possible dangers and analogizing emergency planning to hurricane and natural disaster preparedness. Computer programmers were hired in droves to diagnose and patch complex computer systems that needed to remain robust and reliable but were layered with bugs and patches, work-arounds, and other things that are not simple rationalities. Although this was a peculiar millennial occasion for business hype and panic, it provided a small exemplar of settings in which the scenario form had come to be a central tool for dealing with risk and uncertainty—both a new tool of business preparedness for alternative contingencies and also a theatrical or performance space in which interactive gaming is used to engage, mobilize, and generate new clients, as well as model future complex organizational relations. The Y2K scare provided a microcosm of a more general interplay between hype and pragmatics: between the hype constitutive of much e-commerce in the new service and consulting economy, and in bioinformatics and genomics in the life science industries; and the pragmatic maintenance of the infrastructure (hardware, software, and social organization) of all organizations, public and private, a type of work that is critical and intensive, if often invisible and unrecognized. Hype is essential to getting venture capital and consumer demand, without which the creation of speculative new technologies would not occur; of course, many projects fail even with hype and capital.[1]

Third Spaces: Strategic Terrains, Ethical Topologies, and Dramaturgical Arenas

The panic surrounding Y2K was among other things a querying of the texture of contemporary life that eludes reduction to notions like calculated risk, and that also eludes memory (e.g., of the layered patches lost within legacy systems). The panic fanned by consultants was not just self-interested recruitment of business, or a convenient excuse for businesses to justify their spending on long-desired upgrades of their computer systems (a *strategic terrain* of business gaming), but a kind of *moral entrepreneurship* or *dramaturgical play* on a cat's cradle kind of *topological space*, where every action, twist, or turn of the lay of the land reorients all the other players. Moral entrepreneurship, the directing of attention to matters about which something ought to be done, is, as Donald MacKenzie points out regarding Y2K, a technique of reflexivity that can have a self-correcting, and often paradoxical, function in social action. Publicizing danger can be a self-negating prophecy because it often leads to actions that reduce danger; conversely perception of safety leads to complacency that can be dangerous in safety-critical computing (MacKenzie 2001: 302). The Y2K panic, further, was a crystallization of a visceral understanding of a new world order, of the uneven connectedness of global systems, of an awareness of how much of the world, especially money, was digital and could shift suddenly, massively, with accelerating speed, and via invisible capillary-like networks, and yet how much of the world remains outside such networks, operating on different, outpaced speeds, or with blocked access entirely. To follow and understand these differentials of connectedness and their fragilities requires an ethnographic sensibility. To map and critique these technoscientific worlds requires an anthropology attentive to an expanding variety of cultural differences that go far beyond traditionally understood cultural differences.

The last quarter of the twentieth century more generally was a time of developing new narratives, models, and scenarios to capture in useful ways the uncertainties, contingencies, and calculations of risk that complex technologies and interactions inherently generate. These include (1) scenarios as new tools of national security and business forecasting (Chakrabarti and Strauss 2002; Davis-Floyd and Dumit 1998; M. Fischer 1999b; Ghamari-Tabrizi 2000a, 2000b, 2001; Ringland 1998; Schwartz 1996); (2) explicit theories of risk regarding high-hazard industries from aeronautics, spaceflight, and chemical industries to nuclear reactors and medicine (Perrow 1984, 1999) and the need for social institutions of second-order, or reflexive, modernization that incorporate knowledge from more places in the social structure than, as too often in the past, only from experts isolated in their labs or offices (Beck 1986/1992, 1997/2000); (3) ethnographies and accounts of high-hazard work environments and their management (Chouhan 1994; Vaughan 1997; Gawande 2002; Perin 2004); (4) imaginative devices such as novels, films, and artworks; and (5) innovative social spaces for negotiation in constructing regulatory structures and precautionary care (e.g., citizen panels in environmental remediation; hospital ethics panels to mediate patients' rights to care and physicians' rights not to extend suffering and futile care; deliberative democratic tools for deciding whether society should take on technologies such as xenotransplantation; and deliberative ethics rounds for health care practitioners to review options, procedures, and separations between doctor-patient fiduciary relations and hospital or state welfare system imperatives).

In this volume, I juxtapose essays that combine and reflect on a number of these narratives, models, scenarios, media, and organizational spaces of the last quarter of the twentieth century, including novelistic technique, film, artwork, autobiographical figuration, and ethnographic investigation. I am interested, as an anthropologist, in exploring the tapestry of media that society uses to think through issues of uncertainty and complexity, not only as technical, business, and policy issues but also as ethical, political, social, cultural, and philosophical ones.

The challenge in renewing the ethnographic and anthropological voice in the twenty-first century is not the disappearance of difference, of different cultures, or of ways of organizing society any more than it is not the disappearance of class, capital, unequal exchange, power, or gender relations. On the contrary, the challenge is that the interactions of various kinds of cultures are becoming more complex and differentiated at the same time as new forms of globalization and modernization are bringing all parts of the earth into greater, uneven, polycentric interaction. The distinctive anthropological voice—the aspiration for cross-culturally comparative, socially grounded, linguistically and culturally attentive perspectives—continues to be valuable amid the pressures to simply turn to statistical indices for all policies and judgments.

Anthropology operates in a set of third spaces: where new multicultural ethics are evolving out of demands that cultures attend to one another, and within technoscientific networks where the demands of the face of the other, history, and autobiographical figurations counter the reduction of all to the same. Anthropology's challenge is to develop translation and mediation tools for helping make visible the differences of interests, access, power, needs, desire, and philosophical perspective. Above all, as we begin to face new kinds of ethical dilemmas stemming from developments in biotechnologies, expansive information databases, and ecological interactions, ethnography provides the groundings on which to develop tools for analysis, not just slot developments into the categories of the past, and to observe and help articulate new social institutions for an evolving civil society.

These third spaces are terrains and topologies of analysis, of cultural critique, of ethical plateaus. They are dramaturgical processes, fields of action, and deep plays of reason and emotion, compulsion and desire, meaning making and sensuality, paralogics and deep sense, social action and constraints of overpowering social forces. The following essays invoke Homi Bhabha's call to rewrite the history of modernity from the sites — Vienna, Poland, Texas, Amazonia; biology laboratories, computer infrastructures, ecological interactions — where modernity has eviscerated itself in ways that are not only the corrosive forces of capital dissolving the old social fabric and building new social relations. These new narrations are not lamentations or jeremiads but narrations of the peopling of technologies, of visual teletechnologies that reposition our points of view and modes of judgment, of stories to live by in ethically uncertain worlds that are composed in different ways from the moral worlds of the past. The following essays explore the deployments of various tools of cultural critique, ranging from Polish *odkłamane* and Iranian teletechnologies of social reconstruction after revolution and war to deliberative democratic tools to protect science and new technological inventiveness not just from misuse but from the delegitimizations that come through isolation and assertions of disconnected expertise. The following essays invoke visual as well as textual tools of reflexive representing, modeling, and simulating moral and ethical as well as social and political terrains that do not simply conform to the casuistries (arguing from precedents and cases) or religiosities (theologies, dreamings, or mythopoeic understandings) of the past.

Contexts

In 1993 I moved from an anthropology program pioneering ethnographic cultural critique in an interdisciplinary context to an interdisciplinary program focused on science, technology, and society. The earlier interdisciplinary context included directing a center for cultural studies, one in which anthropology interacted with history, literature, philosophy, religious studies, film and media studies, and other disciplines in the humanities and social sciences. More generally the 1980s and early 1990s were an era in which feminist, gender, media, postcolonial, and multicultural studies were experiencing a flush of creativity and reaction. The move into an interdisciplinary program that focused on science, technology, and society proved fortuitous: in the 1990s science studies became one of the key arenas of public discussion and contestation in academia and, more importantly, in civil society at large over issues having to do with biomedical research, the environment, and the creation of new social infrastructures and databases using networked computerized information technologies.

In the smaller arena of academia, in the aftermath of the failure by physicists to get the Texas supercollider funded, a few scientists turned their anger against the small and weak field of science studies in what became known as the "science wars." The anger came in part at least from a powerful symbolic wounding: the feeling that the defunding of the supercollider was a public exposure of the decline in the premier power and status of high-energy physicists. This power had been exercised over the previous forty years since the Manhattan Project by being able to shepherd their projects through the Washington funding labyrinth. The so-called science wars were loosely connected to previous and ongoing "culture wars" over the expansion of the humanities curriculum to incorporate work and research agendas from cultural studies, media studies, postcolonial studies, feminism, and gender studies. The claim of those reacting against any expansion of perspectives or questions was that these new initiatives constituted attacks on the intellectual foundations of knowledge. But as physicist and Nobel laureate Steven Weinberg noted (to the displeasure of his audience at the 1994 national meetings of the right-wing National Association of Scholars), this was a displaced direction for anger, for the real enemies of science and scientists were elsewhere and actually had money, power, and votes (including the fights in Texas with the schoolbook adoption committees that affected the national markets for textbooks, and the spectacle later in the decade in Kansas of creationists voting Darwinian theories of evolution out of the schools). Moreover, although often defending an idealist vision of science in a series of essays in the *New York Review of Books*, Weinberg quite freely argued at that 1994 meeting that there is no single scientific method, that much of what happens in science comes about for reasons that have little to do with the canons of philosophies of science that many scientists learned in school and to which they subsequently pay little attention. (To the ears of science studies scholars, this sounds like their own call to explore what communities of scientists and engineers actually do.)

Among that era's celebrated scandals was the blocking by mathematicians at the Institute for Advanced Studies in Princeton of the appointment of anthropologist Bruno Latour, one of science studies' leading lights. Another was the overheated attention given to an article by Alan Sokal in the journal *Social Text*. Submitted under false pretenses, Sokal's article was intended to parody and protest the scientific illiteracy of many in cultural studies writing about science by getting the *Social Text* collective to accept a piece that, while metaphorically aligned with the more extreme relativist claims of some in cultural studies and written under the credentials of a physicist lending his expertise, when read nonmetaphorically should have drawn attention to the nonsense being perpetrated. (Behind the scenes was a buzz of corridor talk that the article's references to the cultural studies literature were actually informed by a cultural studies colleague engaged in an internal feud in West Coast environmental and science studies that had little to do with the conservative-liberal, traditionalist-postmodern cast that the press gleefully gave the Sokal affair in their staging of the "science wars," and rather more to do with a "more Marxist or 'leftist' than thou" scuffle.)

But the real action in the 1990s and the first years of the twenty-first century was not in these minor academic skirmishes. Rather, it was in the growth of social movements demanding transparency and public accountability for work done in the technosciences as crucial to the development of more complex civil society in the twenty-first century. In the medical sciences, patient support groups, by using the Internet, began to shift the power of doctor-patient relations and insurance–medical system relations. HIV/AIDS patients forced the pace of new drug clinical trials. In environmental affairs, alliances stemming from Love Canal, Three Mile Island, and the Woburn water wells contamination (which became the subject of a bestselling book by Jonathan Harr and a Hollywood film, *A Civil Action*) forced Superfund cleanup legislation in the United States that included citizen action panels (CAPs) and funding for independent expert research, intended both to get information into the public arena and to create more democratic decision making and community control of environmental affairs. And in computer privacy and First Amendment rights cases over the course of the 1990s, industry, academics, hackers, and others fought out the way in which we will configure the legal, market, technical, and social infrastructure for the coming decades. All three of these broad domains of technoscientific restructurings—the way in which biology and medical research is funded and regulated, the way in which infrastructures are being reconfigured, and the ways in which the environment has come onto the agendas of civil society— are transnational and global, forcing planners with homogenizing visions to rethink their aims as local contexts make their differences felt.

Challenges and Third Spaces of Anthropology

In this context, the challenge in renewing the ethnographic and anthropological voice in the twenty-first century is not the disappearance of difference, of different cultures, or of ways of organizing society (the periodically claimed disappearance of the subject matters of anthropology), but rather that the interactions of various kinds of cultures (indigenous, ethnic, occupational, expert, linguistic, local-regional) are becoming more complex and differentiated at the same time as new forms of globalization and modernization are bringing all parts of the earth into greater, but uneven, polycentric, interaction. Nor is the current age (contra Fredric Jameson's suggestion) one of the erasure of the past through the various postmodern tactics of late capitalism: legacies of the past continue to haunt, constrain, reroute, and interact with the present.

The anthropological voice—the aspiration for cross-culturally comparative, socially grounded, linguistically and culturally attentive perspectives —remains a rare jewel among the contemporary social sciences. Anthropology's use of "culture" as a kind of touchstone has stood for the ability to do work in places where all the variables change at the same time, where (as Clifford Geertz noted long ago in *The Interpretation of Culture*) one cannot experiment by treating culture as a single variable that changes while all else is held stable. Yet one is able to observe patterns that are reliable and contestable on empirical grounds (positive knowledge), that are robust enough to contribute to policy formulation or correction often by pointing out the cleavages and differences among populations and their interests, needs, and perspectives (contributions to the polity), and that most importantly enrich cultural, philosophical, ethical, and moral discourses by exploring other ways of seeing and accounting the world (cultural critique). Culture is not a variable; culture is relational, it is elsewhere, it is in passage, it is where meaning is woven and renewed, often through gaps and silences, and forces beyond the conscious control of individuals, and yet the space where individual and institutional social responsibility and ethical struggle take place. (While many appropriations of the "culture" concept by other disciplines and efforts to adapt ethnographic techniques are salutary complements to the reach and philosophy of in-depth anthropology, the recent use of "culture" as a fixed variable by political scientists such as Samuel Huntington, and by the authors of the recycling of early modernization theory, and misreadings of Max Weber in particular, in the volume *Culture Matters*, is precisely the sort of thing to which anthropological notions of culture cannot be reduced and that lead to the promotion of stereotype thinking and invidious forms of comparative research. Nor is the quixotic proposal by some anthropologists to ban the word "culture," as if a word so widely used in ordinary language could be banned by a local guild, very promising. Better than to reify and censor the word is to allow it to continue as mobile, relational, adjectival, sub-versive. Better to acknowledge that culture is configured historically and that the coming into form, the work of maintenance, and the processes of decay, the dynamics of the weaving, are what are of interest.)

Anthropology is a third space: If anthropology was in part a creation of the colonial enterprise, its formation has increasingly been a third space between the desires of empire (of control) and the defense of the oppressed (of subaltern voices, interests, values, and perspectives), a third space of helping evolve new multicultural ethics, with translation and mediation tools for helping make visible the differences of interests, access, power, needs, desire, and philosophical perspective. If in the 1960s American anthropology was riven with contentious debates about the primacy of political economy versus cultural explanations, by the 1980s a more sophisticated third space had evolved, paying attention to the politics of economy as well as the politics of epistemology, a third space—not unlike the one facing Marx, Dilthey, Weber, Durkheim, Freud, Fleck, Mannheim, and the founders of social and cultural anthropology—in which new social formations challenged analysts to develop tools for analysis, not just slot developments into the categories of the past.

Ethnographic fieldwork and case study methods have been primary tools of anthropology as a third space. This tradition of ethnography has always been oriented toward the production of heuristically valuable social theory, drawing on—testing and contesting—older social theory grounded in older social formations, and claiming to build new theory empirically, comparatively, with attention to different worlds that languages and cultures produce, as well as to local social structures and their embedded (and conflictual) position in global systems. In the last twenty years, ethnography has been testing and contesting the social theory of the emergent forms of postmodernities, and increasingly becoming a distinctive contributor to the studies of computer-networked society, the life sciences revolutions, and environmental issues.

If in the 1980s and early 1990s a great deal of theoretical and methodological preparatory retooling and disciplinary self-questioning was done (e.g., *Anthropology as Cultural Critique: An Experimental Moment in the Human Sciences*, which I wrote with George Marcus; *Writing Culture*, edited by James Clifford and George Marcus; the journals *Cultural Anthropology, Public Culture, Positions*, and *Late Editions*), the payoff has now begun to manifest itself. There has been an efflorescence of new ethnographic writing in the 1990s that takes as its purview the changed world in which we live. Such efflorescence manifests itself in the many writings that contribute to the three arenas of challenge to ethnography that I sketch in the essay

"Emergent Forms of Life." My own interests at the moment lead me to read particularly for the lively new sets of engagements in the interfaces between anthropology and biology (medical anthropology; culture, medicine, and psychiatry; biotechnologies both medical and agricultural); anthropology, geography, and environmental studies (including risk and high-hazard technologies); anthropology and information-data-bank-networked infrastructures (virtual reality technologies, database generation and use, organizational studies, distributed production, digital media). The essays collected here register this shift.

Deep Play, Social Responsibility, and Emergent Forms of Life

We live (again) in an era in which there is a pervasive claim, or native model, asserted by practitioners in many contemporary arenas of life (law, the sciences, political economy, computer technologies, etc.) that traditional concepts and ways of doing things no longer work, that life is outrunning the pedagogies in which we were trained. This is perhaps clearest in (1) the new biotechnologies (new life-forms; cyborgian, hybrid cross-species; nanotechnologies and new materials), (2) expanding information-data-bank-networked infrastructures, (3) environmental or ecological changes, and (4) the legal, economic, psychological, and social institutional innovations that these three overlapping arenas require. Call this an ethnographic datum. We live therefore (again) in an era in which new ethical and political spaces are thrown up that require action and have serious consequences, but for which the possibilities for giving grounds quickly run out. Traditional ethical and moral guides seem not always helpful, and we are often left to negotiate multiplicities of interests and trade-offs in legal or other tournaments of decision making over time. For example, at a May 2000 MIT Whitehead Institute conference on the implications of research on the human genome, U.S. Supreme Court associate justice Steven Breyer encapsulated the point when he noted that the Supreme Court is not a good place to decide the advisability of action in contested areas of new biological research that some feel cross moral taboos. The Supreme Court, he argued, does better after many lower court decisions have been made, and petitions of many different interest groups have been filed, allowing the Supreme Court to then review the various outcomes and interests in a differentiated *terrain*, a terrain something like what I will call an *ethical plateau*. Call this a philosophical stance toward ethics and politics, one that Ludwig Wittgenstein formulated, noting that "giving grounds" for beliefs comes to an end somewhere and that "the end is not an ungrounded presupposition; it is an ungrounded way of act-ing" or a "form of life," a sociality of action that always contains within it ethical dilemmas, or, in the idiom of Emmanuel Levinas, "the face of the other."

In the book's opening essay, "Deep Play and Social Responsibility in Vienna," I introduce and explain a series of terms—forms of life, biopoli-tics, phantasmagoria, deep play, ethical plateaus, autobiographical voices—that, together with the shifts in social theory over the past century that are sketched in the second essay, work themselves throughout the rest of the volume.

This opening short and personally inflected essay was originally drafted in response to an invitation to address the theme of social responsibility, science, and science studies at a joint meeting of the Society for the Social Study of Science ("4s") and the European Association for the Study of Sci-ence and Technology (EASST) held in Vienna on the Jewish New Year, 2000. I would like to think that in its three examples, this essay addresses both the shifting challenges of the contemporary world (to anthropology, to sci-ence studies, and also to the construction of civil societies for the twenty-first century) and also the ethical questions formulated in the citations from Wittgenstein and Levinas. The invitation was issued because of the inclu-sion in the Austrian national government of Jörg Haider's Semitic-baiting, immigrant-baiting, populist-right-wing "Freedom Party." It so happened that the meetings occurred just after the member countries of the European Union lifted their mild sanctions on Austria. I reflect on this recent history as one form of an effort to create codes of conduct for transnational civil society institutions of the twenty-first century, and that for the time being was at least working to help keep Austria to its human rights commitments (Aus-tria has in fact accepted more immigrants than most European countries). I use two other examples that are elaborated further in two other essays in this volume, on the regulation of biotechnologies transnationally and on ethical codes for, and oversight of, transnational scientific research. There is always a concern about the form of such a piece: that it be dismissed as merely per-sonal or tokenized as a merely particularistic experience; that its intended ethical structure (of encouraging other stories, other perspectives, of admit-ting to uncertainty and ethical struggle, of asking for colleagueship in new projects, of neither moralizing nor asking for polite acknowledgment) be lost; and that its form is most powerful in face-to-face interpersonal rela-tions (the face of the Other) rather than through print or other distanced mediations.

Perhaps the most radical part of the essay is the call—adapting an interesting formulation from the literary critic Homi Bhabha—for rewriting the normative stories of modernity "from a position in which the very discourse of modernity is eviscerated and needs to be rewritten from a place other than its enlightened or civilizational origins." This is meant not so much as a harsh judgment on the recent history of Vienna but as an effort to reformulate in a more positive and productive fashion the kinds of critiques that Max Horkheimer and Theodor Adorno made in *The Dialectic of Enlightenment*, and that the multicultural efforts of the 1980s and 1990s attempted to foster. That is, the aim of the next generation and its children—my parents are refugees from Vienna—should be to find new narratives to live by, new modes of critique that can help establish ethical signposts and queries for an age of more complex institutions, cultural diversity, and reconfigured modalities of agency.

As I read back over these essays, I sense an effort to puzzle out the ways in which the situated perspectives of the individual person (the locus of the ethical struggle) interact with moral systems of larger societies or segments of society, how institutional spaces are created to negotiate conflicts between personal obligations and system requirements, as well as how moral systems interrogate one another (the locus of cultural critique). The ethical is often an anthropological third space between the individual and society. Hospital and cross-hospital ethics rounds provide exemplars. These are forums where discussions of evolving procedures, their degree of publicness and legitimacy, and the need to advocate for, and even bend the rules for, particular face-to-face medical urgencies are reviewed over and over, again and again, month after month, year after year. Levinas's figure of the "face of the other" and the "infinite" call for response (i.e., overflowing immediate bounded conditions) is a useful figure for the peopling (and institution forging) of technologies and the technosciences, but it needs to be understood as including the struggle to provide for long-term sustainability of the means of care for other urgencies. Justice and the law are another such third space of struggle between ideals of justice and the exigencies of the law.

The "individual" as ethical agent here is not only historically layered and (only partially) socialized, as classical social theory would have it, but now also configured within technoscientific systems, assemblages, and ecologies that complicate, implicate, embed, co-opt, and leverage the individual. Although I value the urgings of Bruno Latour and Donna Haraway to consider nonhuman agents and cyborgian machine-human hybrids (particularly Haraway's ironic and fictive use of these as figures for utopian or dystopian aspirations and warnings)—to not blinker ourselves with archaic anthropocentric perspectives, and to focus on the assemblages and systems that embed and transform human agency—I am unwilling to give up individual ethical agency and struggle, even when such agency needs to be thought of in new ways that acknowledge, for instance, how the agency of the surgeon may become redeployed as a form of near technician operating through virtual-reality-enhanced telesurgical systems, dependent on rapid recalculations from real time imaging of the operation in process and from distributed databases elsewhere. But agency and decision making still need to be exercised, especially if the system is not to become a runaway monitoring and control system (Garfinkle 2000; Lenoir 2001). Similarly, that genetically engineered oncomice may have human genes and diseases, and in that sense be our relatives, does not really take the questions of agency and social responsibility out of the hands of the human community. There remains thus in these essays an interesting tension surrounding the ways in which the autobiographical voice and the life history are both palimpsests of historical consciousness as well as haunted by traces of the other (other human beings, cultural forms, ways of thinking and accounting, institutional and incentive structurings, but also the other that exists in biological continuities with other species and with ecological interactions).

This "haunted," doppelgänger, often psychodynamic nature of the individual is perhaps what has made me hesitant about the easy rhetorical forms of personal "reflexivity" that some ethnographers adopted in the 1990s, often justifying themselves by citing *Anthropology as Cultural Critique*'s chapters on reflexivity, and *Writing Culture*. But *Anthropology as Cultural Critique* rejected that interpretation of reflexivity, insisting on reflexivity as a form of critique by juxtaposition between cultural, moral, or social discourses, where the juxtaposition would recognize that these were socially situated, that they required further inquiry about their formation, efficacy, and place among contesting perspectives. Similarly, *Writing Culture* was an interdisciplinary effort to draw attention to the complex rhetorical forms that professionals adopt, both to encourage inquiry into the formation of expert cultures and to encourage experimentation with a wider range of disciplinary tools to heighten the multidimensionality of anthropological inquiry and analysis.

Walter Benjamin, Emmanuel Levinas, Paul Celan, Edmond Jabès, and Jacques Derrida are among authors widely cited in the late twentieth century who challenged the pieties of "ontological" (or merely asserted) traditions of looking for ultimate Being (special philosophical aptitude between Greek and German, looking for "phenomenological" essences that are obscured by the veilings of technology, or wanting to find connections between identity, forest, blood, and soil—the "clearings" and *Holtzschnitten*, blazes on trees) and reasserted the centrality of infinite commentary and questioning, of nonfinite interaction with the other (other person, other culture, other gender, other class or status, relation to the "divine," relation to the biological, relation to all that is beyond the finitude of the momentarily given forms of life and life-forms, and relation to technologies, assemblages, networks of human and nonhuman actors). Benjamin in particular wrote with an intense interest in objects, images, and technologies, with historical specificities and the ways these were invested with double meanings derived from the different historical horizons in which they partook. All these authors wrote with a concern for the specific and the personal, the human and the relational, that is also a hallmark of ethnography and is missing from more abstract forms of philosophical writing, which at best acknowledge their revisionary work on a relatively small corpus of written texts. Anthropology adds to this a social and institutional analytic, concern for multiple media circuits and interferences, and a cross-cultural polycentric perspective, constantly scanning for comparison and difference.

This cross-cultural perspective is no longer a binary logic (us/them, civilized/primitive, Europe/the rest, Christian/savage, developed/underdeveloped) but, like most contemporary information matrices, a constantly comparative and difference-scanning perspective. As with an Affimetrix chip for testing many cells against multiple biological probes, so too cultural, institutional, and political economic scanning proceeds in many dimensions, many cells simultaneously. This chip array metaphor captures one key dimension, but only one: multidimensionality. Anyone who watches television or film no longer operates in a binary, us-them world, except under the extreme and atavistic conditions of reduction to civil war and ethnic conflict (Rwanda, the Balkans, Ireland, Kashmir, Palestine). Indeed, anyone who looks around in a First World hospital, staffing of a residence for senior citizens, science laboratory, high-tech corporation, or bank will notice a considerable cultural diversity as compared with even twenty years ago. The Affimetrix chip metaphor is misleading, however, insofar as it suggests that culture can be reduced to mechanical present/absent indicators. Another contemporary metaphor might be the development of virtual reality caves (as developed at Brown University and the University of Illinois) — rooms or cubes in which visualizations are projected onto three to five walls, ceilings, and floors, where one can experience an immersive, 3-D, and kinesthetic interaction with multiple virtual spaces and realities, theoretically as many as are archived in the cave's libraries (Richard Powers's *Plowing in the Dark* provides a novelistic version of three such realities). The metaphor here might function to draw on comparisons that are multidimensional and experiential, drawing on the prior experiences, biographies, and associations of the people doing the experiencing and comparison.

I find it intriguing in this puzzling out of the relation between the individual, the social, and the technoscientific that my father, trained as a historian and geographer at the University of Vienna, should have written his last version of a series of family histories in the form of fragmentary anecdotes. His first English-language book, *The Passing of the European Age* (Fischer 1943), which he wrote as an emigrant on the deck of the ship that brought him to America around Africa, across the Atlantic to Brazil and then north to the United States, during the submarine warfare of World War II (the ship was sunk on its return voyage), exhibited a comparativist social analysis, and he always saw my becoming an anthropologist as doing pretty much the same thing he had always done as a historian and geographer. What I find intriguing about his compendium of anecdotes is that, for me at least, they have a quite special textual power, one that does more than simply capture the stories he would periodically tell around the dinner table.

Just a few of these anecdotes for flavor: There are the stories of his failing to make sergeant in World War I because he couldn't shout loudly enough to command a polyglot group of Austro-Hungarian recruits. So he was sent to clerk in a draft board office, and he tells a hilarious shaggy-dog story of how they saved several Moravian or Bohemian peasant boys from being shot for failing to register for the army (thus being guilty of treason) using "Good Soldier Schweick" bureaucratic tactics of stalling and sending to their home-towns for more and more documentation until the war ended. There is the story of his former student who greeted him on a tram in 1930s Vienna and admitted to joining the Nazi Party, but it was just being rebellious, as he had always been in class, too, and reassured him not to worry about Hitler: "As soon as we get into power, we will get rid of Hitler."

There are the stories of my father's arrest on *Kristallnacht*, and his miraculous release, and my parents' and sister's hurried departure by train to Italy, and thence to Palestine. There is the story of my parents being sent to Tennessee their first summer in the United States and being greeted warmly by the local Baptist minister, who invited them to come to church on Sundays. But we are Jewish, my father pointed out. Yes, I know, replied the minister, but you are alone here, and this would be a way to meet people and have some community fellowship. So they went one Sunday, only to be nonplussed by the minister's public greeting from the pulpit that in the Bible it says that at the end of time, a sign of the second coming of Christ will be the dispersal of the Jews to all corners of the earth, and so we too now have our first Jews. There is the story of my father being asked at various times who his favorite American president was, and learning not to blurt out "Herbert Hoover" (who was blamed by Americans for the Great Depression but had saved the Viennese from famine after World War I). And there is the story that on the day the bomb was dropped on Hiroshima, my father and two others sat aside in gloom while the others in their oss office celebrated.

When the next elections came, my father voted for the vegetarian candidate, as did the two others in their precinct of Charlottesville, Virginia; they figured it out because there were only three votes for the vegetarian candidate. One of these two became a close friend of the family. He owned a farm in central Pennsylvania, and when in the 1950s we had civil defense evacuation drills in my elementary school just outside Washington, D.C. (a presumptive prime target should there be a nuclear war), I was given detailed directions of how to make my way to this farm should the family be separated, as my parents worked some ten miles away from my school.

This last set of linked recollections served me powerfully during the Vietnam War, when I not only protested the war but deliberated with my graduate school cohort at the University of Chicago whether and how to actively refuse the draft if called. My father was of the opinion that if called, I had a duty to serve the country that, albeit after long delays in granting visas (more stories), had finally saved the family and admitted us to a land of liberty. But I had his own example to use to stake out my own position.

Many allusions and perspectival differences get packed into these anecdotes. Their power, for me, arises both from an immigrant's comparative perspective—a comparative perspective that has become part of so many people's lives in the massive population movements of the twentieth century—and also from the rhetoric of what Homi Bhabha calls the "affiliative anecdote": the use of the personal and historically situated to engage the listener or reader in issues that have larger stakes. When it works well, the affiliative anecdote opens the discourse to the creation of an inclusive, self-critical community that can recognize one another's interests, experiences, and stakes, rather than a moralizing, exclusive community. Hence the interest in earlier centuries in character sketches, portrait painting (which fascinated my father), and the semiopen parabolic story, with moral conclusions adjustable to the specific conditions of the audience, as Walter Benjamin analyzed in his essay "The Story Teller" and deployed in his radio addresses for children (Mehlman 1993). In many of these forms, Bhabha points out, the perspective of the first-person narrator is one of uncertainty providing material, albeit fragmentary, for the reflection of the third-person listener. I try to draw on this ethical sensibility in "Deep Play and Social Responsibility in Vienna."[2]

In the second essay, "Emergent Forms of Life: Anthropologies of Late or Post Modernities," I first sketch the shift from classical social theory based on the experiences of the late nineteenth century and the early twentieth to the social theory formulated in the last quarter of the twentieth century on the basis of quite different generational and social structural experiences of massive social change. I think it is important that one have some working macrosocial theories to do good ethnographic work; and vice versa, ethnographies, strategically pursued, can provide building blocks for new social theory. I do not think that classical social theory is passé or superseded, but Marx, Weber, Dilthey, Freud, Durkheim, Fleck, Mauss, and the others did not experience or analyze the kinds of shifts that have become focal for post–Algerian independence French theory (Cixous, Deleuze and Guattari, Derrida, Foucault, Lyotard, et al.), post-Green social movements theory in Germany (Beck, Habermas, Kittler, Luhmann), post-"second industrial divide" Italy (Agamben, Cacciari, Melucci, Negri, Vattimo [Piore and Sabel 1984]), or post-cost-benefit analysis theories of risk and hazard in the United States (Perrow).

Second, I attempt to sketch out three arenas of prime challenge to anthropological ethnographic skills that became particularly strong in the 1990s: work on the reconstruction of society after massive disruption by war, ethnic violence, displacements of population, and various forms of social trauma; work on the key technologies that mediate the contemporary analogues of what Durkheim might have called the *conscience collective*, in their new, more differentiated, telemediated, transnationally diffusive, and multiculturally promoted and resisted guises; and work on the sciences and technologies that construct the changing infrastructures of the worlds we live and die by. In this essay, I have stressed the degree to which these challenges should have been taken up more centrally by earlier anthropology. It is an odd factoid, for instance, that film was disseminated in places such as India long before modern fieldwork anthropology, but the anthropology of India until recently paid little attention, writing about India as if film were not ever shown in Indian villages, much less to urban working classes, or were not a technology in the struggles against caste and communalism. This is a complex factoid that cannot be used against village studies or Indian anthropology per se, but it is indexical of shifting disciplinary interests and why different questions come to the fore. Today there is no longer any need to urge the broadening of the anthropological purview; it is happening with great energy and in many interesting ways. At issue now is bringing these expansions into interaction with processes of building useful social theory and cultural critique, useful for further academic work, for contributing to the construction of new civil societies, and for contributing to policy formulation.

Critique, Authorship, and Ethical Voice in the Age of Teletechnologies and Technoscience

The second set of three essays brings together the notion of critique, sites "from which the very discourse of modernity is eviscerated and needs to be rewritten," and the tensions surrounding individual agency or the autobiographical, authorial voice as a palimpsest vehicle of ethical sensibilities and historical consciousness extended into new settings.

"Filmic Judgment and Cultural Critique: Iranian Cinema in a Teletechnological World" is about the teletechnology represented by film, in a siting of the Islamic world, Iran and its diaspora, where the struggles over modernity are acute, and where an auteurial voice is acknowledged in the local discourses of film criticism and reception as mediating between traditional commentary and what Derrida calls "autoimmune" mechanisms of the filmic medium. If the teletechnology of cyberspace was the cynosure of attention in the 1990s as the space of speculation about emergent new forms of life (as biology has become since the late 1990s), film has been such a space over the entire course of the twentieth century. In the 1990s film became the subject of inquiry not so much as a medium in itself but as one medium within interacting threads of a tapestry of tele-media, including especially television, video and audio recordings, popular music, and the Internet. This particular essay is about film, the transformations of religion, and the challenge that has Jacques Derrida, among others, worried: the challenge that the power of corporate First World Christian or American media has in homogenizing the world. Derrida suggests that the Islamic world is a strategic site for observing these dynamics, which he describes not in the terms of invasion and resistance but as a more complex tension analogized to diseases of the autoimmune system. Thus the new media are deployed by various Islamicist groups, and others, to disseminate their points of view in both national and transnational markets. But the very media forms themselves may have a Trojan horse or autoimmune potential for undoing the very perspectives and ideologies that they are deployed to extend. Derrida, half joking, worries if this means the "end of commentary" in the traditional senses of oral and literate authorship and face-to-face community. I use the example of Iranian postrevolutionary films to explore this tension in a transnational niche where commentary work is intense, disruptive, and uses the modern media. Hauntings from the past are central to the work of commentary and identity, and to the structure of the postmodern, where "post" is understood as postal, as sendings between past and present, among multiple and alternative modernities. The specters of Marx are not lessening in intensity: on the contrary, the spectralization of abstraction and speed of circulation are intensifying. Hence both the questions raised by Derrida and the counter of the Iranian example to any simple stranded conquest by concentrated capital.

"Cultural Critique with a Hammer, Gouge, and Woodblock: Art and Medicine in the Age of Social Retraumatization" is about visual and medical technologies—photography, printmaking; surgery, psychiatry—at sites of a leading edge of primary modernities (modernity, late modernity, postmodernities, alternative modernities), the United States. The essay collages a life history and autobiographical voice as refracting a generational experience—in fact, three generations—of U.S. cultural history. The collaging technique explores the ways in which, and degree to which, the psychiatrist and artist Eric Avery's career and his artwork tactics operate as cultural critique in American society. These tactics include (1) overlaying historical visual images (from European art history; Mexican *calavera, retablo, papel picado,* and other vernacular forms; as well as North American art history from Gilbert Stuart, J. S. Copley, and George Bingham to Robert Mapplethorpe) with contemporary ones; (2) trying to perform therapy on institutions of art circulation (galleries, museums), medical education (clinics, medical humanities institutes), and advocacy groups (Amnesty International U.S.A.) that fail to see what is going on at home in their efforts to deal with problems elsewhere; and (3) inserting art actions and installations into the networks of the electronic media through news coverage and through videotape recording. The collaging technique (my commentaries, excerpts from interviews with Avery, and token images, unfortunately in black and white, of the artworks) deploys a layering of ethnographic and historical details intended to provide analytic reference points into the social fabric beyond the essay. Avery's printmaking technology is both a psychological technique of Freudian "working through" the body, transmuting anxiety and stress, and a Benjaminian dialectical visual technology bringing into the operating network of post-twentieth-century technologies—postfilm, postphotography, postradiological and PET imaging systems—a reworked, if centuries old, artistic technology using materials of our times (handmade paper from surgical gowns, woodblocks from Qur'an boards, old and new presses and papermaking techniques). Avery's commentaries deploy a situated set of gender, regional, and generational alternative perspectives to rewrite the dominant codes of 1950s Norman Rockwell America ("from which the very discourse of modernity . . . needs to be rewritten"). Part of this re-writing includes Avery's further commentary and effort to illustrate through his artwork that visual literacy is in fact underdeveloped in the medical humanities despite the new technologies of visualization and medical prac-titioners living in an age of visual proliferation. Images can exercise a histori-cal doubleness, a haunting of the present by various pasts and experiences elsewhere. Retraumatization, a psychiatric concept, suggests something not only about trauma in an individual life but also about chains of transmission more generally, and about dynamics beyond the conscious or political.

"Ethnographic Critique and Technoscientific Narratives: The Old Mole, Ethical Plateaus, and the Governance of Emergent Biosocial Polities" pro-vides an elaboration of the second example in "Deep Play and Social Respon-sibility in Vienna." Sited primarily in Vienna with transnational threads in the United States, this essay provides a reading of the puzzle novel *Vienna Blood*, by Adrian Mathews, juxtaposed to three ethnographic sketches of contemporary ethical plateaus or domains of ethical challenge—the chal-lenges of informed public consent to new technologies, the seductions to do whatever is medically possible (sometimes at the expense of quality of life or the "good death"), and the power of money in driving the biotech industries. *Vienna Blood* deals with precautionary germ plasm modification and chemi-cal camouflage justified as protection against ethnically targeted biological warfare, and touches on a series of technologies such as new reproductive technologies, genetic engineering, and cryptographic attacks and defenses, as well as the ability to evade regulatory controls. Such technoscientifically informed novels are useful as cautionary tales in exploring the complexity and interaction among new technologies and the phantasmagorias that help drive new technologies. They are not so good at thinking through insti-tutional development: a challenge for ethnography and new social theory. Ethnography, like novels, can function as checks on the mechanisms of ab-straction and universalization that frequently bedevil the nonanthropologi-cal, non-cross-culturally or cross-temporally comparative social sciences. Questions are raised about new or emergent biosocialities, forms of gov-ernance, and forms of cultural critique. I also reflect on the modalities of critique represented by the nineteenth-century old mole (my father, born in 1898, always claimed to be a nineteenth-century man living in the twenti-eth) and new juxtapositions of Foucauldian discourses, interests, and power configurations, embedded in new infrastructures, biopolitics, and ecologies, within which we twentieth-century ethical agents make our way into the twenty-first century. At issue are the ways in which regulatory agencies are subverted in an age of cryptographic attacks and defenses, and where amusingly the highest forms of security of a heavily defended computer and institutional system return to orality. At issue are how to deal with risk, hype, and secrecy in our current technoscientific worlds, and how we can build institutions that promote legitimacy for scientific research, done in socially responsible ways, accountable to the publics it is intended to serve.

Subjectivities in an Age of Diversity and Global Connectivity

Emergent new forms of life in the last quarter of the twentieth century included new ethnicities, religiosities, and scientific communities. Over the course of the twentieth century, there was an increase of knowledge and interaction among others' ethnicities, religiosities, and knowledge systems, and these often functioned as a form of immanent critique for individuals and new communities in "self-fashioning" their own intercultural new identities and creating new social forms.

In the 1970s, ethnic autobiographies in the United States flourished in a way that illuminated processes not registered in earlier sociological literatures on immigration and assimilation. Instead these autobiographically figured texts — often written by children of parents of different backgrounds, or by American children whose immigrant parents had left voids in their knowledge that needed to be worked through — generated ethnicities that came from somewhere outside conscious desire, often unbidden and unwanted, but insistent and very different from the identities of the parents. These texts often worked through mirroring tools of fantasies, trying on or interacting with a different ethnicity, or creating a new third space of ethnicity that acted not unlike crucibles for experimenting with multicultural identities. The techniques of these autobiographically figured texts expand on the affiliative anecdote mentioned earlier: dream-work and talk-stories; transference; alternative selves and bifocality; interreference and bilingualism; and ironic humor. The first essay in which I analyzed these texts by both male and female writers, "Ethnicity and the (Post)modern Arts of Memory," is available in the collection *Writing Culture*, edited by James Clifford and George Marcus. Instead here I have chosen a companion essay, "Autobiographical Voices (1,2,3) and Mosaic Memory," which expands the use of strategic life histories in spaces of social change to explore not only ethnicity but also religious identity and science as a vocation. The conceit of single-voiced, double-voiced, and triple- or multiple-voiced textualities is used to explore these three domains.

In the double-voiced textual domain of religion, a long essay on "torn religions" remains to be completed, but its outlines are presented in this essay. Several extraordinary biographies have been written in recent years in which the dilemmas of the historical horizon of the subject of the biography are refracted in the dilemmas of the historical horizon of the biographer, and in which both biographer and subject of biography are major figures in reshaping the understandings of their coreligionists. Gershom Scholem's biography of Shabbatai Zevi presents one such pair, as does Arthur Green's biography of R. Nahman of Bratislav. So does Henri Massignon's wonderful multivolume biography of al-Hallaj, and the biography of the Jain monk and social worker Santabalji by Navalbhai Shah, Gandhian social worker and former minister of education of Gujarat. Other texts that fit into this pattern include Fuad Ajami's book on Musa Sadr, and the various genre and discourse approaches to the biography of Imam Khomeini that I have surveyed in an essay called "Imam Khomeini: Four Levels of Understanding" (in the volume *Voices of Islamic Resurgence*, edited by John Esposito).

The third part of the essay turns to science as a complex arena where individual contributions are mediated by a constant routing through a third, beyond the kind of double textuality exploring religious change. Again this section draws on a longer essay entitled "Eye(I)ing the Sciences and Their Signifiers," in *Technoscientific Imaginaries*, volume 1 of *Late Editions*, edited by George Marcus. The suggestion here is that many scientists narrate their lives in ways that are formally isomorphic with the ways in which they narrate their science. For instance, whereas the biologist Rita Levi-Montalcini did not keep notes on her life, insisting that all the important events are thrown up and kept in her memory by a kind of Darwinian selection, the geometer and geodesist Irene Fischer, involved in a mapping enterprise, carefully charted her professional career against journals, letters, and documentary files, tracking historical changes of geodesy, of government science, and of creating a matrilineal structure within a male world.

"Post-Avant-Garde Tasks of Polish Film: Ethnographic *Odkłamane*" uses the films of Maria Zmarz Koczanowicz to explore a form of ethnographic cultural critique that was proposed during the 1990s as a direction for Polish film after the fall of communism and the transition into the global economy. The challenges for film parallel those for anthropology. The essay thematizes the visual techniques of hauntings by the past (in the replay of the early-twentieth-century modernist play *The Wedding* in a contemporary setting, and renewed concerns about how to reunify a divided society), and of the ways in which visual icons can both exhibit historical and cultural specificity *(The Edge of the World)* and erase specificity as in the journalistic use of photo archives of war, famine, and disaster, where it is hard to tell if an image is actually from the Balkans today or from World War II. This essay originally appeared as the second of a pair; an earlier one, based on interviews with Maria's husband Leszek Koczanowicz, a philosopher and analyst of postcommunist Poland, explored the absent/present place of Jews and the others in Polish cultural identity, and the end of the use of the romantic tropes that had powered Polish resistance to Russian, Austrian, and German rule but now seem irrelevant to, and impotent against, the spread of American and world pop culture (M. Fischer 1993).

That essay too begins with a commentary on the anthropological voice and media and mediation technologies that holds for many of the essays in this volume as well. The opening lines are a refrain in both essays.

Anthropological accounts step into an ongoing stream of representations. Anthropology in the late twentieth century is no longer the "discovery" of terra nova or undescribed cultures, but rather a method of informed critique, pursued often by placing into strategic and disjunctive juxtaposition different representations or perspectives so as to throw light upon the social context of their production and meaning, and to draw out their implications. . . . [Even the] story of the Holocaust is no longer a simple story of (re)discovery: a steady stream of newsreel footage, historical archival work, oral histories, survivors' accounts, novels, films, and investigative journalism continues to deepen both knowledge and ethical response to one of the most devastating upheavals in modern times. At issue now are reflections upon the rhetorics of narration and the ethics that ensue. . . . The heightened historical sense and ethical responsibility for the ways in which representations are treated has to do not only with the writing style but also with the ethics of daily life: [Marek] Edelman [the last living survivor of the Warsaw ghetto uprising] is a physician involved with a professor of cardiac surgery, and their contemporary interventions in the game of life against death are foregrounded. In attempting untried surgical procedures in cases where the patient is certain to die if the intervention is not attempted, the professor is afraid for all the normal reasons, but also, should he fail, "that his colleagues will say: *he is making experiments on human beings.*" Edelman's ethics are affected as well: he denies the elevation of death in battle, and the demeaning of death in the gas chambers: "the only undignified death is when one attempts to survive at the expense of someone else" (Krall 1986: 37); so too his theology:

— People have told me, Marek, that when you're taking care of simple and not terribly serious cases, you do it in a way out of sense of duty, that you only really light up when the game begins, when the race with death begins.

— That is, after all, my role. God is trying to blow out the candle and I'm quickly trying to shield the flame, taking advantage of His brief inattention. To keep the flame flickering, even if only for a little while longer than He would wish.

— It is important: He is not terribly just. It can also be very satisfying because whenever something does work out, it means you have, after all, fooled Him. (Krall 1986: 85)

Theologically this revolt, as Levinas's pun captures, *adieu/à Dieu*, is an important liberatory gesture, but as new dilemmas of biomedical pioneering and manipulation of physical bodies become possible, the ethics become problematic. Edelman and his colleagues are opening new, uncharted, and uncertain ethical terrain.

New Pedagogies and Ethics

The new infrastructures, ecologies, and technoscientific armatures of emergent forms of life also constitute what Foucault might call new discourses or here new pedagogies, new ways of doing things enforced by emergent new structures of life. These in turn raise ethical dilemmas and challenges that we have not yet encountered, but require attention for the creation of legitimation in emergent civil societies of the twenty-first century.

"Worlding Cyberspace" was written just as the Internet and World Wide Web were beginning to explode and transform the means of writing, exchange of information, and access to data banks. What would writing an ethnography of such a new environment look like? What would it mean for the writing of ethnographies of the future? Cyberspace provided a new infrastructure, with a material basis and an abstracted immaterial thought space (not unlike the abstraction of circulating paper forms of capital from steam power, electricity, machines, and labor power that Marx wrote about; and indeed cyberspace is part of that capital process). Cyberspace promised both to transform work and to discipline and downsize labor forces. It posed new legal questions about patents, privacy, First Amendment rights, state security versus freedom issues, and export control regulation versus national commercial competitiveness. In the mid-1990s, cyberspace was the premier space for speculation about emergent new forms of life, including even fantasies of otherwise sane computer scientists about the downloading of "carbon-based" information in the brain onto silicon chips, thus allowing the "self" to escape the body and achieve immortality. Less wild speculations about the ability to wire together nerve and muscle cells with silicon computerized components held out the promise of prostheses and micro- and nano-biotechnologies for repairing and enhancing the body. Other futuristic speculations and efforts at implementation included (ro)bots as electronic servants, doing everything from acting as personal assistants on the Web to creating smart banking cards, smart appliances, smart furniture, smart houses, and various forms of wearable computers. Cyborgian selves — avatars in computer games or chat rooms, prostheses from artificial limbs and pacemakers to surgical virtual reality robotic systems and medical record profiles — became relational objects of play and experimentation, including learning to think of humans as parts of larger networks or assemblages of human and nonhuman actants. This was truly a space of emergent life-forms and forms of life ranging from marketable commodities to speculative worlds in the process of coming into being. Learning to live in such emergent worlds was a form of pedagogy, of training mind and body to think and process information, work flow, and work organization, in new ways.

The fascinating histories/anthropologies of how experts form disciplines and create and defend platforms of knowledge are the subject of the essay "Calling the Future(s)." It is the kind of knowledge that new histories and anthropologies must engage as our worlds are transformed by modern biology, computer science, and environmental sciences. The specific focus of this essay was the effort to create a core course for a graduate program in science, technology, and society at MIT, and the effort to overcome a legacy of division within the faculty identified as historians or as social scientists. This was MIT, after all, and the institute prides itself in the sciences and engineering being interdisciplinary, in producing new knowledge by cultivating the interfaces between disciplines and by creating new centers and laboratories that bring together the tools of multiple disciplines. Moreover, this was in the 1990s, when new "emergent forms of life" were the talk of society at large. The essay describes a core course and pedagogical structure for a science, technology, and society (STS) program comprising a three-tiered set of courses and a matrix of disciplinary toolbox courses in historiography (of science, technology, and medicine), on one axis, and in anthropology (social theory, ethnography, social study of science and technology), on the other. In workshops, interdisciplinary interfaces with psychology, politics, and engineering proceeded as well. I tried as well to have "threads" through the course on the visual, the literary, and the cross-cultural. The essay can also serve as a platform for other experiments.

In the essay "*Las Meninas* and Robotic-Virtual Surgical Systems," which precedes the essay on the modules for an STS course, I pick out the visual thread. As we move into a world ever more dependent on informatics in all areas of knowledge, many employing visual techniques, it is perhaps useful to pause, and read back through the varied literature on the emergence of different scopic regimes. I pose the puzzle of whether a picture of an eye surgery system can serve as a meditative device about this new world we are entering with a similar richness to the way Foucault and others have used Velázquez's *Las Meninas* to meditate on the emergence of the epistemologies and disciplines of the modern era. When we began the STS core course, we began with a workshop on the new visual technologies in the humanities using the Web, both to think with as we went through the course and to suggest how STS could use the then still quite new Web platform for research and other projects.

The last essay, "In the Science Zone: The Yanomami and the Fight for Representation," picks up the third example of "Deep Play and Social Responsibility in Vienna." This final essay too is an occasional piece, solicited by *Anthropology Today* during the furor over journalist Patrick Tierney's *Darkness in El Dorado*. I attempted to use that debate to reflect on some of the changes between the 1960s and 1990s sciences as institutional enterprises, sketching three axes of difference: the ethics and institutional contexts of science; the way in which activists of all sorts, including scientists, become media players, complicating questions of who speaks for whom; and the palimpsest of continuities and differences between the human biology research projects (population genetics, sociobiology, human genome diversity project, health and epidemiological transition) of the 1960s and the 1990s. All three axes require attention to the importance of anthropology's interface with history on the one hand and biology on the other, and to an ethics of defending the Yanomami, science, and anthropology that depends on not turning the actors in any of these spheres into saints. The differences between the 1960s and the 1990s have to do as well with the increasing pressure for the participation of publics in decision making about scientific research that affects their welfare: a pressure toward accountability, if not transparency.

EMERGENT FORMS OF LIFE

1

Deep Play and Social Responsibility in Vienna

I was going to start (pause), and I will (pause), by saying *"l'shanah tova!"* (happy new year!).[1] We meet on the eve of the first new year *(rosh ha-shanah)* of a new century by the common era or Gregorian calendar count, the twenty-first century, but the year 5761 by the Jewish count (1379 by the Persian solar or *shamsi* calendar, 1421 *Hijri* by the Islamic lunar calendar; in a few days will be Mehregan, the fall new year of the Zoroastrian seasonal or *fasli* calendar used as the vernacular calendar in Iran).[2]

What happens in a few days, according to Jewish liturgy, is a very old ritual of social responsibility. We ask forgiveness from those we have wronged. God cannot forgive us for wrongs we have done to others; only those we have wronged can do so. We perform this act of sociality, of mutual recognition, before the Book is closed inscribing who shall live and who shall die.

L'shanah tova! May all of you and your loved ones be inscribed in the book of life.

Double Consciousness, Multiple Perspectives

Now, I was telling a member of the Jewish community of Vienna that in addition to the politics of coming to this conference in Vienna after the inclusion of the right-wing FPÖ (Freiheits Partei Österreich, the Freedom Party of Austria) in the government, coming to express solidarity with the University of Vienna (which has issued fine statements on tolerance and minority rights, and on freedom of research and expression), with the many demonstrators against the FPÖ (who have continued their demonstrations every Thursday evening now for eight months), and with the many Austrian intellectuals who have spoken and written against the FPÖ; that in addition to that politics, I also wanted — underscoring the Rosh Hashanah scheduling of a conference whose theme is social responsibility and whose venue, of all places, is Vienna — to take my grandfather's seat in the synagogue in which my parents were married, the only synagogue the Nazis did not destroy. He laughed and said that the scheduling of conferences on the high holidays has become not so unusual, the last was the dentists, that it is like a business: the Jewish community gets to sell a few tickets. A reminder, perhaps, that even memories, not to mention sentimentalities, can be commodified; and that life goes on and did not stop in 1939 even for the Jewish community in Vienna. But history is important, and experiences do affect subsequent choices.

Building Transnational Civil Societies

I understand the rationale and goal of this plenary to be to take note of our venue, of where and when we are meeting, and to underscore the themes of the conference: the role of technosciences in transnational social change, issues of equity and distribution regarding the knowledge and power that science and technology provide, the building of new social institutions for the more complex civil society of the twenty-first century, the ethics and politics of research, and thinking about who the audiences are for our research.

I savor the opportunity, and I thank Sheila Jasanoff, president of the Society for the Social Study of Sciences, and the other organizers, to speak in these halls of the University of Vienna where my father listened to Max Weber when he visited here for a term, where my mother studied with Moritz Schlick and Hans Hahn and others of the Vienna Circle, where an important foundation of socially committed ethnography began with the Marienthal study by Marie Jahoda (one of my mother's best friends in school), Paul Lazarsfeld, and Ernst Zeisel. All of these remain touchstones in my own intellectual formation.

Three Sites of Deep Play on the Ethical Plateaus of the Twenty-first Century

In my few remaining minutes I want to evoke three sites of "deep play" on what I have come to call "ethical plateaus." "Deep play," of course, is a nod to the essay by Clifford Geertz and to Jeremy Bentham; ethical plateaus are what I have come to call the strategic terrains on which multiple technologies interact, creating a complex topology for perception and decision making. The first of these deep plays is that of the politics of the FPÖ in Austria and more broadly in Europe, which was the original reason for this panel and poses questions about the building of transnational institutions for civil society, a first experimental effort for a Europe-wide construction of consensus on rights for minorities, refugees, and immigrants. The second deep play is that of the biosciences, which so many of the papers at this conference are about, which directly pose questions of who shall live and who shall die; implicate both of the other two deep plays; and exert pressure toward new institutions of reflexive modernization or deliberative democracy in some of the most difficult areas of human experimental trials, informed consent, privacy and surveillance, patents and ownership of biological information, and the power of huge amounts of investments, not just of money and power but also of ideology and fantasy (see further chapter 5). The example I will invoke here is xenotransplantation. The third deep play is a brief acknowledgment or alert—acknowledgment for many of you who have been part of its dissemination across the Internet, and alert for others—about the furor over new allegations regarding the studies of the Yanomami by the American geneticist James Neel and the American anthropologist Napoleon Chagnon, a furor breaking over my own discipline of anthropology, which will include other fields, and threatens to reopen the science wars and the sociobiology debates, but may potentially also affect the oversight demanded by institutional review boards and other regulatory bodies on the research that we all do (see also chapter 10).

"Deep play" refers to cultural sites where multiple levels of structure, explanation, and meaning intersect and condense, including the cultural phantasmagoria that ground and structure the terrain on which reason, will, and language operate but cannot contain.

Deep Play in Europe: Local, Regional, and Global Coalitions in Wars of Position

First, then, regarding the Austrian deep play. I want mainly to reaffirm our purpose in this panel, still now, even in the aftermath of the report of the "three Wise Men" (led by Marti Ahtisaari, former president of Finland, with Jochen Fowein and Marcelina Oreja), which ended the mild sanctions on Austria by the member states of the European Union (Ahtisaari, Fowein, and Oreja 2000). I wish that I had been here enough ahead of time to get and to be able to show slides of the wicked cartoons by the Austrian artist Manfred Deix, which are still on display at the Wiener Kunst Haus, on Oberer Weisgerberstrasse, across the street from my grandfather's house. In several of the cartoons, he takes on election slogans of the FPÖ such as Überfremdung (overrun by foreigners), and his caricatures work by exaggerating the anxieties of certain parts of the Austrian population (Deix 2000).

In one cartoon, he depicts an American Indian in war paint, an African, and a Chinese person all in lederhosen. In another he draws a Turk in red fez and harem pants skiing down the Alps, in charge of a skiing school while unemployed Austrians hold up signs asking for jobs. The best, perhaps, is a cartoon of a "Right Wing Extremist Opinion Poll," which has a series of questions and boxes to check asking about one's attitudes toward Jews, the *Kriegesgeneration* (the generation of World War II, "ordinary folks who did nothing wrong"), immigrants, and patriotism. The cartoons are an effective format for getting at displacements, denials, and the behind-the-scenes anxieties, complex psychological and ethical plateaus.

I want to pay tribute here to the many Austrian analysts who have done superb dissections of the rhetoric and tactics of the FPÖ and of Jorg Haider: the linguist Ruth Wodak and her colleagues (Wodak et al. 1990, 1993, 1995), the political scientist Johnny Bunzl (1997, 2000), the anthropologist Andre Gingrich (2000), the political theorist Hakkan Gürses (2000), the social psychologist Klaus Ottomeyer (2000), the political economist Otto Ötsch (2000), and many others. The tactics of the FPÖ remain — even now after the dropping of the sanctions — a serious political issue, but also a fascinating cultural site of deep play not only for Austria but for Europe and the global stage.

The report of the "three Wise Ones" (the ironic New Testament resonance would be in English unfortunately gendered; the pluralized German avoids this) says that the Austrian government has lived up to its legal commitments to protect the rights of minorities, refugees, and immigrants. Indeed, as the report acknowledges, Austria has accepted more immigrants than most European countries. But the report also takes as its mandate to evaluate the political evolution of the FPÖ, and here it says that although the FPÖ may yet evolve into a responsible democratic party, to date it remains (in the words of the report) "a right wing populist party with radical elements" that requires monitoring. The report cites the language of Haider calling extermination camps *Straflager* (punishment camps), as if those condemned were being punished for things they had done; and his tactics such as using libel actions to silence opponents, including the case of Professor Anton Pelinka, about which the protest letter to the president of Austria, being circulated at this meeting for signatures, appeals. (The European Union office for monitoring the rights of immigrants, refugees, and minorities is in fact located in Vienna.)

It is a deep play because it is at the same time psychodrama and politics, and it is also about the neoliberal or neoconservative restructuring of the economy that is happening not only in Austria but throughout Europe and across the globe, involving serious dislocations. Indeed, on hearing of the report of the three Wise Ones and the dropping of sanctions, members of the FPÖ renewed their call for the launching of a Europe-wide Freedom Party. The Hungarian philosopher G. M. Tamas has described the FPÖ as part of a much wider movement of postfascism, a series of policies, practices, and ideologies that have little to do, except in Central Europe, with the legacies of Nazism. In Central Europe, he says, familiar phrases have different echoes, and vigilance is needed, "since, historically speaking, innocence cannot be presumed" (Tamas 2000).

The report of the three Wise Ones, and the long series of treaties and legal conventions and commitments cited in it to which Austria continues to adhere, are part of an effort to build transnational codes and institutions. In this case, at least for now, it *is* working.

Deep Play in the Life Sciences™:
Markets versus Deliberative Democracy

The second deep play, regarding biotechnologies, has to do with fantasies of abolishing disease and immortalizing life, sometimes at the expense of human rights, informed consent, equity, and access. The American physicists went ahead with the bomb for Nagasaki, as Oppenheimer memorably put it, because it was "technically sweet." So too today physicians and patients often go ahead with heroic experimental trials because they are caught up in what Mary-Jo Good calls the biotechnical embrace, doing what technically can be done under the Hippocratic formulation of preserving and extending life, because it can be done, sometimes at the expense of the good death. Again Manfred Deix captures some of the fantasies, as in his cartoon of a genetically engineered pig, altered to be already a huge sausage, or his cartoons of various monsters—think post-Chernobyl fantasies of mutants—but monsters who have voting rights.

Xenotransplantation is one site among the new biotechnologies, where, because the science is so hard, there is some time to experiment with some creative thinking toward new institutions and new ways of bringing into being an informed citizenry on a global scale that can provide civil society oversight, accountability, and decision making. I have been watching in particular the efforts of Dr. Fritz Bach, the Lewis Thomas Professor of Medicine at Harvard, who incidentally is also Viennese born—his grandfather and mine, I'm sure, knew each other, both being prominent Viennese rabbis—and has directed genetics and immunology research labs in Wisconsin, Minnesota, and Boston, but also for five years here in Vienna, and has called for a moratorium on clinical trials in xenotransplantation. Xenotransplantation, like toxic waste, is a transnational issue. Old institutions of medical ethics are insufficient. The threat of xenosis that could unleash a pandemic like HIV/AIDS, however small the risk, is not something that can be dealt with in medical ethics models of doctor-patient relations, or hospital ethics committees, or even national-level regulatory institutions. Older methods of self-regulation by scientists in the Asilomar style of dealing with the fears about recombinant DNA in the 1970s seem no longer possible or adequate, and the recent experience of Monsanto with the "terminator seed" in the controversies over genetically engineered crops shows that the refusal to engage in public consultation can lead at minimum to public relations fiascoes. Dr. Bach has been experimenting not only with education modules at the high school, church, and grassroots levels, and with national committee structures at the political level in several countries in both the First and Third World, but also with new modes of global Web-based public consultation seeded with a network of opinion leaders in various countries. It will be interesting to watch this and other experiments in new institution and public critical knowledge building, especially in an environment in which calls for even limited moratoriums draw the ire of those who find it harder to raise research money and venture capital to push the science further.

Deep Play in South America: Media, Science, and the Politics of Representation

Finally, a brief word about the Yanomami, and the forthcoming publication of *Darkness in El Dorado*, by the investigative journalist Patrick Tierney (Norton, 2000). We have known for a long time that Napoleon Chagnon's accounts of warfare and its sociobiological basis in the linkage of male aggression to reproductive success was contested by many other ethnographers of the Yanomami. We have known for a long time that the documentary films of Tim Asch, if not exactly staged, were done on occasions and settings that Chagnon and Asch helped to set up. And we have known for a long time that James Neel's work with the Yanomami was funded by the U.S. Atomic Energy Commission; that he was interested in Amazonian populations as models for population, genetic, and disease studies; that he had earlier led the American investigations on the effects of radiation after Hiroshima and Nagasaki in Japan; and that the United States conducted a number of investigations on low-level radiation accumulation in human populations in the Marshall and Aleutian Islands, through radiation experimental releases over Midwestern populations, and other radiation experiments in hospitals, including ones that Neel did for the Manhattan Project in Rochester. The new allegations are first that the Yanomami may have been used as an experimental population in ways different from, but reminiscent of, the Tuskegee syphilis experiment; that Neel inoculated the Yanomami with live attenuated Edmonton B measles vaccine, a vaccine being phased out in the United States, donated by two pharmaceutical companies (an issue, still very much alive today, of pharmaceutical companies taking philanthropic tax benefits for donations of medicines being phased out or near expiry to Third World populations) and known to be dangerous and counterindicated for previously unexposed populations; that whether or not the inoculations unintentionally helped exacerbate a measles outbreak into the 1968 epidemic, the medical care he and his team provided was too little; and that (not in itself reprehensible) he opportunistically seized the occasion to observe the natural course of an epidemic among a previously unexposed population, among other reasons to test hypotheses about the immunological superiority of headmen over others in small populations by looking for their reproductive success. Second, in more sustained fashion, the allegations are that Chagnon's intervention into the local political dynamics with trade goods, and bringing together feuding groups for purposes of filming rituals, led to much of the violence that he portrayed as natural or primordial, and had unintended but further political fallout, including helping mining interests and the military interests in Brazil resist giving to the Yanomami constitutionally promised land rights and territorial demarcation.

It is too early to make any judgments on these allegations, but in the end they may turn not only on intent — charges that Neel's crew caused or exacerbated the 1968 measles epidemic may well be overdrawn, and they are not the center of Tierney's book — but on the interactive effects of what one might call the hidden machineries of technologies of large-scale multidisciplinary research projects with cargo planes bringing crates of medical, trade, and film equipment and descending on small populations, recruiting large numbers of them as porters and stage crews, as well as medical subjects, usually without concern for the pathogens that the outsiders might be carrying with their bodies. This should give us pause and cause for reflection on not only how we deploy research projects but also how we represent them, that is, the relation between research results and how we collect information, and the conventions of erasing the apparatus of the scientific collection process to present descriptions of societies and data sets as primordial or natural. Tierney's book, even if seriously flawed, is a fascinating account of such a large-scale research project combining genetics, filming, and ethnography, using many personnel, both outsiders and natives. Tierney's book is also an advocacy effort to intervene in a media war on behalf of Yanomami be-leaguered by miners, disease, and unfulfilled land rights commitments and social benefits. It has been at least one of the fastest disseminations of a call for reflection on science and ethics across the Internet, which many of you have already participated in.

The passion, as well as the name-calling, that the American and interna-tional press has delighted in fanning, signals that like the Austrian deep play, and those surrounding new biomedical technologies and agro-biotechnolo-gies, there is deep play here: psychodrama of antagonisms among scien-tists, deep passion, fantasy, status, and monetary investments beyond merely rational arguments and differences of perspective.

Ethical Plateaus: Places from Which to Renarrate the Normative Stories of Modernity

I want to end with a reflexive thought. I have tried to suggest deep play as an analytic device to explore charged sites of multiple levels of causation, explanation, and meaning, and ethical plateaus as sites where multiple tech-nologies interact to create a complex terrain or topology of perception and decision making. I have also tried, albeit not enough and perhaps not suc-cessfully, to invoke humor via cartoons, paradoxes, ironies, ambivalences, and what the literary critic Homi Bhabha has called affiliative anecdotes as tools toward creating and sustaining a self-critical community. Bhabha com-ments on the rhetoric of these forms, saying, "The uncertainty that the joke and affiliative anecdote casts on the production of knowledge goes beyond mimetic or epistemological paradoxes. It attaches to the very mode of ad-dress of modern thought in which the first person witness or teller feels un-certainty in judgment [that's my position here], and the third person hearer has the freedom to speculate with what is only partial, piecemeal, and frag-mented" (that is, the ethical moment). This, he suggests, is an effort to re-narrate the normative stories of modernity "from a position in which the very discourse of modernity is eviscerated and needs to be rewritten from a place other than its enlightened or civilizational origins."

What better place than Vienna to initiate such a practice?

2

Emergent Forms of Life:

Anthropologies of Late or Post Modernities

"Emergent forms of life" acknowledges an ethnographic datum, a social theoretic heuristic, and a philosophical stance regarding ethics. The ethnographic datum is the pervasive claim (or native models) by practitioners in many contemporary arenas of life (law, the sciences, political economy, computer technologies, etc.) that traditional concepts and ways of doing things no longer work, that life is outrunning the pedagogies in which we have been trained. The social theoretic heuristic is that complex societies, including the globalized regimes under which late and post modernities operate, are always compromise formations among, in Raymond Williams's salutary formulation, emergent, dominant, and fading historical horizons. The philosophical stance toward ethics is that "giving grounds" for belief comes to an end somewhere, and that "the end is not an ungrounded presupposition; it is an ungrounded way of acting" (Wittgenstein 1969: 17e) or a "form of life," a sociality of action, that always contains within it ethical dilemmas, or, in the idiom of Emmanuel Levinas, the face of the other.

Challenges for Theory and Practice

For example: the university. Universities—where much, if neither all, nor even most, anthropology is written and debated—are being set adrift from their past modernist moorings in cultural projects of maintaining their nation-states. Instead, it is argued, they are becoming transnational bureaucratic corporations regulated under administrative metrics of "excellence" and productivity (Readings 1996). The late Bill Readings argues further that feminism and race/ethnic scholarship, symptomatically, are targets of so much rancor and moral fervor precisely because they remind so forcefully, through the fact that bodies are differentially marked, that it is no longer possible for universities to create unmarked, universalistic subjects of reason, culture, and republican politics in the metonymic way envisioned by J. G. Fichte and Wilhelm von Humboldt, the architects of the modern university in Berlin. Similarly, Readings argues, teaching attracts much current rancor because of the "simple contradiction between the time it takes to teach and an administrative logic that privileges the efficient [measurable] transmission of information. . . . The transgressive force of teaching doesn't lie so much in matters of content as in the way pedagogy can hold open the temporality of questioning" (Readings 1996: 19). Readings argues that although the modernist ideal of the university as a model rational community, a pure public sphere, still exerts power on the imagination, the university is becoming, and should be celebrated as, "rather a place where the impossibility of such models can be thought—practically thought, rather than thought under ideal conditions . . . one site among others where the question of being-together is raised, raised with an urgency" (20).

Certainly many anthropologists are being challenged to teach outside anthropology, social science, and humanities departments, to situate our pedagogies within other worlds of students we seek to engage, not simply to teach them "where they live" but to puzzle out together with them, with their often quite sophisticated and engaged professional experiences, the new indeterminate emergent worlds within which we all now live. This is particularly true for anthropologists who teach within engineering or medical schools, who attempt to forge the emergent field of science studies in mutual exploration with practitioners (scientists, engineers, clinicians), or who wish to raise human rights issues in ways other than as distant objects of contemplation (Downey 1998; M. Fischer 1999a; Yoe 1998; K. Fortun 1999; M. Fortun and H. Bernstein 1998). These are spaces in which disciplinary assumptions are always subject to question, where tools of analysis from different disciplines are brought together, sometimes smoothly, more often in a kind of practical creolized urgency to solve real-world problems. For example, in a course taught in cooperation between MIT and the Harvard Law School, "Law and Ethics on the Electronic Frontier," lawyers and engineers learn to teach each other ways to think about alternatives through designing differently organized legal, technical, social-normative, and market "architectures" (http://swiss-ai.mit.edu/6095).

If universities are undergoing structural change of the sort Readings suggests, so too are other social institutions and cultural forms. Anthropology, with its empirical ethnographic methods, remains, arguably, still among the most useful of checks on theorizing becoming parochial, ethnocentric, generally uncomparative, uncosmopolitan, and sociologically ungrounded.

Three Strategic Terrains in Late or
Postmodern Sociocultural Formations

Anthropologies of late modernity (also called postmodernity, postindustrial society, knowledge society, or information society) provide challenges for all levels of social, cultural, and psychological theory, as well as for ethnographic field methods and genres of writing. There are three key overlapping arenas of attention.

1. The continuing transformation of modernities by science and technology, themselves understood to be mutating social and cultural institutions, rather than eternal Platonic "invisible colleges" of reason (Galison 1997; Haraway 1997; Kelty 1999; Landecker 1999; Marcus 1995; Martin 1987, 1994; Rabinow 1996; Rheinberger 1997; Sunder Rajan 2002; Traweek 1988).

2. The reconfiguration of perception and understanding, of the human and social sensorium, by computer-mediated and visual technologies and prostheses. This is often called the "third industrial revolution," with implications as profound as those of the first two industrial revolutions for interaction at all levels from the personal-psychological to the global political economy, ecology, and human rights (Dumit 1995; M. Fischer 1995b, 1998; Ginsburg, Abu-Lughod, and Larkin 2002; Kelty 1999; Landzelius 2003; MacKenzie 2001; Marcus 1996, 1997; Mnookin 1999; Morris 2000; Turkle 1995; Turner 1992).

3. The reconstruction of society in the wake of social trauma caused by world war, and civil and ethnic wars; collapse of command economies; massive demographic migrations and diasporas; and postcolonial and globalizing restructurings of the world economy, including the production of toxics and new modalities of long-term risk. All of these call into question the premises of social theory earlier in the century based on a more simple dialectic of social control versus social conflict (P. Cohen 1968; Parsons 1937, 1951), and they refocus social theory on questions of heterogeneities, differences, inequalities, competing discursive logics, and public memories; complex ethics of advocacy and complicity; and multiple interdigitated temporalities (Beck 1986, 1991/1995; Biehl 1999; Daniel 1996; Daniel and Knudsen 1995; Fabian 1996; E. Fischer 1943; M. Fischer and Abedi 1990; K. Fortun 1999; Geertz 1995; Honwana 1996; Malkki 1995; Marcus 1993, 1998, 1999a, 1999b, 1999c; Maybury-Lewis 2002; Nordstrom and Robben 1995; Petryna 1999; Tambiah 1986, 1996; Taussig 1987; Werbner 1991, 1998).

Ethnographic Challenges Posed by
These Three Strategic Terrains
The most important challenges for contemporary ethnographic practices include not merely (1) the techniques of multilocale or multisited ethnography for strategically accessing different points in geographically spread complex processes; (2) the techniques of multivocal or multi-audience-addressed texts for mapping and acknowledging the situatedness of knowledges; (3) the reworking of traditional notions of comparative work for a world that is increasingly aware of difference and interconnections; and (4) acknowledging that anthropological representations are interventions within a stream of representations, mediations, and unequal discourses, and always themselves contain, if not explicit acknowledgments of, sedimentations of prior representations (M. Fischer and Marcus 1999). Of equal importance are the challenges of juxtaposing, complementing, or supplementing other genres of writing: testing and contesting with historians, literary theorists, media critics, novelists, investigative or in-depth journalists, writers of insider accounts (e.g., autobiographers, scientists writing for the public), photographers, filmmakers, physician-activists, and others.

Metanarratives: Social Theory for Late or Post Modernities
The general social theories of modernity in the nineteenth century and the early twentieth have to do with the dynamics of class society and industrial processes (Karl Marx); bureaucratic, psychological, and cultural rationalization (Max Weber); repression and redirection of psychic energy from gendered and familial conflicts (Sigmund Freud, Max Horkheimer, and Theodor Adorno); abstraction of signs and tokens of exchange (C. S. Peirce, Ferdinand de Saussure, Georg Simmel, Thorstein Veblen); and the complexification of the conscience collective with the division of labor (Emile Durkheim, Marcel Mauss). In contrast, general theories of the postmodern or late modern era stress the processes and effects of the "third industrial revolution" (electronic media, silicon chip, molecular biology), as well as of decolonization, massive demographic shifts, and the cross-temporal and cross-cultural referentiality of cultural forms. These are transnational or global processes that thoroughly rework all local cultures. Some theorists stress the intensification of flexible capital accumulation, compression of space and time, growth of multinational organizational forms, and new forms of inegalitarian stratification (Harvey 1989; Jameson 1991). Others stress the massive demographic shifts resulting from decolonization and ideological warfare that are challenging the homogenizing efforts of nation-states into more heterogeneous cultural formations (Lyotard 1979/1984;

1983/1988). In Western Europe these are most tensely formulated through immigration politics; in the United States, they get coded as multicultural-ism. Still other theorists stress the information technology revolution that not only brings diverse parts of the world into daily contact but constitutes an intensification of postliterate, more mathematical, and graphic styles of generating, monitoring, and absorbing knowledge: simulations and model-ing replace direct experiential modes of knowing, a process with deep roots in the modernist experimental sciences (Benjamin 1968; Deleuze 1980/1987, 1983/1986, 1985; Poster 1990; Baudrillard 1981/1994; Ronell 1994; Emmeche 1994; MacKenzie 1995, 2001; Galison 1997). Other theorists stress the pro-duction of ecological hazards and risks by industrial capitalism, which ne-cessitates a new political dynamic and cultural logic. These in turn lead to systemic contradictions and pressures for reversal of centralizing control, as well as toward increased democratic participation by diverse agents in the complex division of knowledge and labor in what, during earlier phases of modernity, were nonpoliticized areas of business decision making and private entrepreneurship. That is, they lead toward a new "reflexive mod-ernization," which emerges out of the contradictions of industrial society in a manner parallel to the ways capitalism emerged out of the contradictions of feudal society (Beck 1986/1992, 1991/1995; Giddens 1990, 1991; Lash and Urry 1994; Perrow 1999; Perin 2003). Moreover, modernity can no longer be spoken of as a singular.

Working in Technoscientific Infrastructures and Imaginaries

The Sciences as Social and Cultural Institutions

Although science and technology have been central to social theory in a general way since the industrial revolution (A. Smith 1776; Malthus 1803; Marx 1928, 1971; M. Weber 1968; Merton 1938, 1973), it is only within the last two decades that ethnographic attention has been turned to the sites of production of scientific research and technoscientific commodities.

The one arena to which anthropology has long paid attention is that of medical settings, but usually primarily to health-care seeking by patients, to patient-doctor co-construction of illness and therapy, or to ethnosemantics of traditional materia medica, rather than to the biosciences and biotech-nologies proper. A second precursor to recent science studies was the con-cern about comparative rationalities and the ways in which systems of belief, including science, can be protected from falsification (Evans-Pritchard 1937; Kuhn 1962; Fleck 1935). A third precursor is the "sociology of science" studies of the 1980s (e.g., Barnes, Bloor, and Henry 1996; Latour and Woolgar 1979), but these took as their primary interlocutors philosophers of science rather than either science institutions in society or the cultural ramifications of science in general culture (as do Forman 1971; Galison 1997; and Hayles 1990).

The current anthropologies and ethnographies of science, technology, and society might be grouped loosely under three rubrics: (1) the comparative work of analyzing the different forms of social organization of science research settings from the beginnings of the "scientific revolution" to the present, and across different fields of the physical, biological, and other sciences and science-based technologies or technosciences, with attention to how these different ways of reorganizing both nature and social teamwork have connections and implications for wider society and culture, and especially to the diversity of such settings in the latter half of the twentieth century; (2) the historical structural transformations of the sciences, technosciences, and biosciences from small-scale to big science in the postwar period, involving new relations between the state, the academy, the market, and the public sphere (indexed lexically by the often felt need for neologisms such as bioscience, biotechnologies, bioengineering, information infrastructures, technosciences, and environmental sciences); and (3) the hermeneutic, literary, and cultural accounting work of the wider cultural groundings, implications, and deployments of technologies and science-derived theories, speculations, and models.

Since the mid-1980s a steady stream of social historical and ethnographic studies commenting on one another has begun to transform the field. One strand consists of ways in which communities of scientists form, find patronage, adjudicate truth, construct the appropriate forms of public demonstration and verification, and construct protective boundaries. The notion of a "modest witness," key to the experimental protocols of Robert Boyle and the Royal Society (Shapin and Schaffer 1985), for instance, has been taken up in a counterpoint fashion in essays by Haraway (1997) on the inherently compromised complicity we often find ourselves in concerning the complicated questions of today's technoscientific worlds of uncertain risk, testing, and pressures of the political economy.

Galileo's "courtier science" (Biagioli 1993), Boyle's seventeenth-century "gentlemanly science" (Shapin and Schaffer 1985), Pasteur's late-nineteenth-century "public scientist" (Latour 1988; Gieson 1995), and today's big science consisting of hundreds of scientists on a project (Galison 1997) are distinct social and cultural formations. In a review of Shapin and Schaffer, Bruno Latour (1990b) praised those authors' claims of viewing the procedures of scientific witnessing, adjudication, and construction of truth as simultaneously providing parallel processes in the growing arena of democratic politics and being hostile in both arenas to argument from authority (whether from the ancients in knowledge, or royal fiat in politics). Moreover, he praised their method of looking to a combination of material, literary, and social technologies to construct the institutions of both science and politics. This co-construction of the social and the scientific is an important thread in Latour's own work: how Pasteur shifted power ratios between the "on the ground" knowledge at the point of primary production (farmers) and central "obligatory points of passage" (the laboratory), and how Pasteur was able to harness or enroll the hygienics movement and make the bacteriological laboratory succeed to its position of authority. Both Latour (1988) and Gieson (1995) have analyzed how Pasteur carefully staged public demonstrations and deflected challenges from other experimenters. More recent studies have mapped how the Pasteur Institutes around the world were central components of the French empire, down to the way in which they set up plantation and quasi-industrial processing organizations to support their work. Latour's *Science in Action* (1987) dissects how scientists construct their various literary accounts (e.g., scientific papers), how rhetoric and citational strategies are used. His account (Latour 1993/1996) of the effort to build a utopian intelligent transportation system in Paris draws attention to the failure to sustain an expanding enrollment of institutional supports, and thus how the transportation system itself changed form depending on its changing set of supporters and their differing imaginaries, as well as on technical trade-offs. (This last account needs to be read in conjunction with—tested and contested against—accounts of other programs in building intelligent transportation systems, e.g., Klein 1996).

The account by Biagioli (1993) of Galileo's climb from low-status mathematician to high-status court philosopher under three different political regimes (Venetian republic, Florentine princely court, and Roman academies) builds explicitly on the logics of gift exchange and the economy of honor as an exercise in power (classically articulated in Mauss 1925/1954), as well as on Norbert Elias's 1982 excavation of the "civilizing process" of changing etiquette systems. The account by Hart (1997) of Chinese translators of Euclid looks to similar manipulations of the court and mandarin system. Newman's 1994 account of "the most widely read American scientist before Benjamin Franklin"—the Bermuda-born, Harvard-educated leading alchemist and Helmontian medical practitioner Eirenaeus Philalethes (George Starkey), patronized by Boyle—explores the tension between open exchange of information needed for scientific legitimation and the secrecy needed to protect pharmacological recipes, a situation not unlike the tension in today's patent regimes for molecular biology research funded by venture capital or pharmaceutical firms. Newman describes a transitional social formation between courtier science, seventeenth-century academies, and eighteenth-century salons (often organized in Paris by intellectual women where academicians could gain the polish needed to acquit themselves before the royal court [Biagioli 1994]) and the gentlemanly experimenter sciences of Boyle and the Royal Society, which is popularly taken as a direct precursor to modern experimental science institutions. (See also Principe's 1998 sleuthing/deciphering of the chemistry and alchemical language used by Robert Boyle and Philalethes.)

In work on science in the twentieth century, the borrowings back and forth between anthropology and history have continued. Ethnographers and historians have been working on physics (Traweek 1988; Galison 1997; Knorr-Cetina 1999) and the biological sciences (Cambrosio and Keating 1995; Fleck 1935; Fujimura 1996; Kay 1993; Keller 1995, 2002a, 2002b; Kohler 1994; Knorr-Cetina 1999; Löwy 1996; Martin 1987, 1994; Rabinow 1995; Rheinberger 1997; Rapp 1993, 1997); on material sciences (Nowotny and Felt 1997); on engineering (Bucciarelli 1994; Downey 1998; Henderson 1998; Kidder 1981; Latour 1993/1996; Mindell 1996; Clancey 1999); on nuclear weapons designers (Gusterson 1996; Broad 1985, 1992); on imaging instruments (Cartwright 1995; Dumit 1995; Rasmussen 1997; Waldby 2000); and on simulation technologies (Emmeche 1994; Helmreich 1998; Galison 1997; Kelly 1994; MacKenzie 1995, 2001).

Work by Traweek (1988, 1992, 1995, 1996) on high-energy physicists in the United States and Japan provides accounts of how the training of physicists screens out the merely technically proficient, how Americans and Japanese physicists relate differently to their machines, how mentoring lineages operate, how Japanese women physicists must strategize with international networks, and how the international division of labor in science operates a status hierarchy that requires confirmation and legitimation of work done in lower-status countries by leading countries. Peter Galison (1997) describes the transition between the "craft physics" of individual investigators before World War II and "big science" with particle accelerators in which hundreds of scientists are teamed into complex organizational forms. He describes a series of transitions from the nineteenth-century interest in mimicking the processes of nature in laboratory instruments such as the cloud chamber, to the relations between building instruments and the politics of the World War II period in Germany, England, and the United States (as in the development of radiation physics using film technologies held as secret patented materials by private firms), and then the transformation to truly large scale

government-funded science after the Manhattan Project. The struggle between strategies of seeking a "golden event" image of a hypothesized process and seeking statistical confirmation (image versus logic traditions in
physics) allowed Galison (1997) also to develop a notion of communication
among subfields of physics and engineering that utilize, borrowing from anthropology, "creoles" and "pigeon" languages in "contact zones"; some of
these creoles are material instruments and practices rather than language.
He thereby refines the problematic Kuhnian ideas about paradigm shifts in
science, allowing for observed ways that theory, instrumentation, and practices shift at different rates rather than as unified blocks (in which "paradigm
shifts" would generate "incommensurable" gestalt shifts) (Galison 1997).

Knorr-Cetina (1999) describes how the worldview generated in the large
high-energy physics organizational forms contrasts sharply with that of molecular biology. She describes how it is not only the natural world that is
reconfigured in the laboratory, but also the social. The large organizations of
physics experiments are like superorganisms, enforcing collaborative consensus, distributing credit among hundreds of authors, and engaged in a
semiological struggle of self-knowledge to separate "noise" from "information"—almost a "loss of the empirical" in "an alternative reality of signs
and simulations." In contrast, the small-team bench work of molecular biology laboratory organizations exists in individualistic, conflict-competitive
arenas, dependent on enhanced tacit skills inscribed in the body acquired in
interaction with blind variation and natural selection of biological materials—a kind of experience accumulation by the body that is quite different
from the cognitive knowledge of the mind.

Ethnographic accounts of the contemporary life sciences and biotechnologies engage with the changing relations of state, academia, and market
in a fashion as dramatic as the earlier transformations of physics and engineering underwent in dealing with the national security state. Rabinow's
1995 work on Cetus Corporation and the making of polymerase chain reaction (PCR), now a ubiquitous tool in molecular biology, is a historically
and strategically placed ethnography allowing a perspective on a number of
dimensions of the changing social organization of biological research: (1) the
shift in funding from philanthropic organizations such as the Rockefeller
Foundation in the pre–World War II period, to government funding (National Institutes of Health, Department of Defense) in the postwar period,
to venture capital and alliances with large pharmaceutical companies in the
1980s and 1990s; (2) the shift to recognition of patents on life-forms, and the
resultant increasing secrecy of research or closely monitored cross-licensing
agreements attendant to the market ("never publish before you patent");

(3) the resultant blurring of boundaries between academic, "pure or basic" research, and commercial research; and (4) the efforts to establish scientist-controlled "para-political" mechanisms to contain debates over social and ethical issues (for para-political mechanisms in Germany and the use of biotechnology as a national program to stimulate economic growth, see Gottweis 1998). Rabinow, as well, is interested in the "inner life" of scientists, for which he probes for their positioning in the general public sphere, their life experiences and their political concerns. He also separates out the different internal processes a biotech firm must foster, differentiating (1) the formulation of a *concept*, (2) actually getting an *experimental system* to work, and (3) the processes of managing and marketing *product*. The work on biotechnology products—interleukin-2, polymerase chain reaction, various kinds of diagnostic kits—has led into a growing nexus of anthropological studies ranging from how clinical trials are conducted, not in the abstract but in embedded institutional settings, negotiating between immunology laboratories and hematology laboratories as well as other subfields, and between basic science and clinical work (Löwy 1996; M. Good et al. 1995), to how the knowledges and imagery of medical sciences such as immunology circulate among laboratory, clinic, community center, and mass media (Martin 1994). The study by Dumit (1995) of the development of PET scan technology similarly shows how courtroom, patient-family interest groups, research interpretation, and engineering are mutually implicated. Hammonds's (1995, 1996, 1999) historical and contemporary work draws on parallel anthropological concerns: on the search for "perfect [social] control" (over uncontrollable bacteriological, viral, and immunological processes in public health and medicine), and "logics of difference" that make the history of gynecological surgery and the ethnically ("racially") unequally distributed incidences of diseases such as hypertension and HIV/AIDS issues of social justice and cultural categorization, that is, central anthropological problematics and not just medical scientific or technological ones.

The works cited are but a sampling of a growing literature that ethnographically is placing the sciences and new technologies into a central position in the understanding of the infrastructures and imaginaries of contemporary society. Among the contributions of such anthropological work are (1) putting universal claims about science and technical objectivity into their situated, comparative contexts, (2) insisting on the technical and scientific contextualization out of which cultural meanings often arise, (3) paying attention to the competition of strategies regarding representation, and (4) giving respect to the voices of scientists and technicians (as well as patients, insurance logics, and community-grounded activists and politicians), and paying attention to the inner lives of scientists and technicians (not re-ducing them to functionaries of the sciences).

After the changes in society and our cultural conceptions of ourselves wrought by physics (relativity theory, the Manhattan Project and the secu-rity state notions about hardball politics, space exploration with its *Star Trek* romance and spin-offs of materials science, along with the persistent public questioning about lost opportunities for better or alternative spend-ing of funds, and the social values implied by these decisions) and biology (green revolutions, genetically engineered crops, human gene therapies, ge-netically engineered pharmacologies, bioengineering products, the Human Genome Project), a third key arena that figures in contemporary "metanar-ratives" of late modernity and postmodernities is the environmental sci-ences. If quantum physics and relativity theory provided the basis for gen-eral cultural understandings that the world is not reducible to a mechanical single reference frame, and if biology has provided both open systems and notions of self-organizing complexity, environmental issues have provided the metanarratives of society becoming a risk society increasingly requiring more participatory and decentralized decision making while requiring more sophisticated modeling and regulatory regimes. As with the social organiza-tion of science, genealogies of knowledge about the environment are slowly being reconstructed, from the histories of acclimatization gardens estab-lished by the colonial empires (Grove 1995, 1997), and from ways in which "universal" botany and zoology were grounded in local knowledges (e.g., the Kerala toddy tappers who provided the knowledge for the texts by da Orta and van Reede that Linnaeus was later to study in Leiden [Grove 1995], or the way peasants provided the knowledges for savants such as Goethe in Europe [Koerner 1996]), to the histories of "ecology" as a discipline grounded in concerns about ecological succession in local landscapes (Bowler 1992) and in the dissemination of radiation, pesticides, and other toxics, and energy circulation in the environment (Winston 1997). Ethnographic studies are under way on climate-modeler communities (and the intense politics sur-rounding the petrochemical industries elicited by this research), and on how communities have dealt with toxic wastes (Lahsen 1998; Brown and Mikkel-sen 1990; Harr 1995; Crawford 1996; Reich 1991; K. Fortun 1999; George 2001; Allen 1999). Historical studies have shown how efforts at human control are "outfoxed" by the complexities of the ecological (and old anthropological functionalist) rule that you cannot change only one thing (see White 1995; M. Davis 1998), and on the equally complicated complicities that advocacy in seeking to correct wrongs, accidents, or injustices involve (K. Fortun 1999).

Risk society, and the various models of how risk is dealt with in industries from the airlines to medicine to environmental and health epidemiology, has become one of the more fruitful innovations in both ethnographic-empirical and theoretical work (Perrow 1999; Perin 2003). This is particularly true where the actuarial statistics of industrial accident calculation from the nineteenth-century mechanical industries no longer work (Beck 1986/1992) and governments and corporations therefore take on new, not always salutary, modes of behavior (Reich 1991; K. Fortun 1999; Wildavsky 1995; Graham and Hartwell 1997).

Cultural Readings of Technology

Given the attention that anthropology normally lavishes on the meaning structures of the objects, institutions, and symbolic systems of the societies it studies, it is curious how understudied by anthropologists the technoscientific worlds of the twentieth century have been. Arguably one of the most important transformations over the course of the twentieth century in cultural thought about technology has been from class-inflected politics over technological determinism (Marx, Heidegger, Adorno), to the midcentury technocratic systems-theoretic framework for contextualizing technology (Macey Conferences [Heims 1993]), to the more recent dynamically generative and often quasi-psychoanalytically figured analysis of the place of machines and technologies in the cultural imaginary. Anthropologists have and continue to participate in all three moments.

In the first moment, ethnography has been a valuable means of testing and contesting with historians such as Lynn White, with ecological culture area anthropologists such as Julian Steward, with philosophers such as Martin Heidegger (whose interpretations of modernity as nature transformed into quantified standing resources found little difference between industrial agriculture and genocide) or, with more interest in social relations, Theodor Adorno, Max Horkheimer, Walter Benjamin, and others of the Frankfurt school. Horkheimer and Adorno's interrogations of the culture industry and Benjamin's of arcades, films, irrigation levees on the Mississippi, and other material constructions extended Marx's challenge to view the products of industry and commodification as hieroglyphic texts to be read or decoded, texts that contain the secret of human alienation and suffering, lodged more in the (social) relations of production than in the forces of production (technology), social relations that can be exposed. Ethnography has deepened these inquiries (Taussig 1980, 1987; Tsing 1993; A. Ong 1987; J. Ferguson 1990; Escobar 1994; Gupta 1998).

In the second moment, ethnography has been a valuable means of testing-contesting first with political and development economists, sociologists, and ecologists (Parsons [1951] and the Harvard Social Relations Department, Geertz's agricultural involution [1963a] and the University of Chicago's New Nations Seminar [Geertz 1963b], quasi-cybernetic "materialist" or "ecological" studies of the 1960s Columbia-Michigan departments [Rappaport 1968; Sahlins 1972; Lansing 1991]). Secondly, ethnography (and ethnographic linguistics) has been a valuable means of testing-contesting with the Annales school in France of Marc Block, Fernand Braudel, Emmanuel Le Roy Ladurie, Jacques Le Goff, Jean-Pierre Vernant, and associated figures brought by Braudel into L'Ecole des Hautes Etudes such as Jacques Lacan, Claude Lévi-Strauss, Pierre Bourdieu, and Michel Foucault. This engagement with concepts of *la longue durée*, and the structuralisms that differentiate the logics of cultural *mentalités*, remains one of the most profound cultural discussions among the sciences, arts, humanities, and social sciences in the mid-twentieth century. More recently, arguably, the most interesting legacy of this facet of ethnographic questioning is the tracing out of the social implications and cultural effects of cyberspace, informatics, modeling, and simulation. Foucault's revisions (1963/1973, 1966/1970, 1975/1977, 1980) of Weberian accounts of modes of legitimate domination, and of Gramscian analyses for Italy of hegemonic compromise formations, along with Lyotard's provocations about the pragmatics and sociology of language games under early regimes of computerization, fit here via computers, micropractices, and new social movements focused on the transformation of everyday social relations extending far more diffuse, pervasive, and powerful disciplinary regimes than were conceivable in the early twentieth century. These new forms of power, as they have developed in the late twentieth century, depend in part on new thresholds of computer-mediated infrastructures, with all their attendant vulnerabilities for disruption (M. Fischer 1999b), and on new informatic databases that allow the deployment of biopower regulating both individual biologies and the social regulation of populations. This last has become a rich field of ethnographic investigations under the rubrics both of the new reproductive technologies (Strathern 1992; Franklin 1997; Clarke 1998; Davis-Floyd and Dumit 1998) and of the anthropology of biotechnology and the new life sciences (B. Good 1994; Rabinow 1995; Fujimura 1996; Biehl 1999; Landecker 1999; Lock, Cambrosio, and Young 2000; Sunder Rajan 2002).

In the third moment, ethnography has been a valuable means of testing-contesting with literary critics and philosophers (Taussig 1992, 1993; Ivy 1995; Turkle 1984, 1995; Ronell 1989, 1994; Kittler 1985/1990; Deleuze and Guattari 1980/1987; Guattari 1992/1995; S. Weber 1996). Cultural readings of technology are among the most innovative examples of this new work, drawing on a rich appreciation of changes in the media that disseminate cultural forms, and in a renewed cultural-hermeneutic (nonreductive) and psychodynamic exploration of the desires and anxieties invested in technologies. Although some authors claim to see a sharp break between hermeneutic attention to meaning and (post)structuralist play of semiotic tokens, what seems to be emerging is a renewed attention to the ways in which cultural analysis depends on chains of metaphor, semiosis/*écriture*, and even new forms of "automatic" writing via machines, discursive formations, and "machinic assemblages" of literary, material, and social technologies. In science studies, Bruno Latour's (1987, 1988, 1990a, 1993/1996, 1999) notion of instrumentation as machines that write inscriptions, which serve as "immutable mobiles" (transferring information across space, language, and subcultures of scientists) and can reverse or change ratios of power between centers of calculation (laboratories in the metropole) and field sites (where information is collected, tested, or produced), contests the older notion of individual scientists and gentlemanly colleges of science acting as "modest witnesses." Nor is it just instruments: the enrollment of heterogeneous actors in a "love" or passion for a large-scale utopian project, such as smart transportation systems, also takes on a kind of Durkheimian force of a social fact, without which technological projects will fail. Latour thus fits on the anti-hermeneutic side, along with Friedrich Kittler's readings of the difference between discourse formations in 1800 and 1900 (as the English title of one of his books would have it; but the German title *Aufschreibsysteme* [inscription systems] gives a different inflection). Kittler does a brilliant reading of Bram Stoker's *Dracula* as being about the machine worlds of typewriters in the early twentieth century, analogous to various appreciations of Nietzsche and Kafka as embedded similarly in telegraphic, postal, and rail networks (Shapiro 1989). Deleuze and Guattari too have mined this notion of machinic assemblages. And yet none of these texts can do entirely without meaning, without hermeneutics, without following out the play of metaphorics, semiotic analysis, and the transfer of meanings from setting to setting (as illustrated, for example, in Galison 1997; Ronell 1989, 1994; Haraway 1991, 1997).

Galison (1997), by showing the multiple genealogies of scientific instruments, is able to weave together arenas of cultural concern that are normally marginalized or even written out of histories of science, and thereby helps us to appreciate the multiplex technoscientific worlds that we all inhabit. For instance, the Victorian fascination with volcanoes, thunderstorms, and other dramas of nature is put together with the beginnings of modern instrumentation for modern particle physics, a story that involves as well the role of photographic film companies. Clancey (1998) shows the ways in which seismology arose in Japan and was buffeted by European teachings, Japanese and Italian empirical experiences, and the role of carpentry and architecture in both generating and being generated by those national expertises and experiences. Like Galison, Clancey has an unusual facility for showing how the formations of different disciplines intersect and are worked out in different national and cultural settings while being part of global interactions.

Ronell (1989) reinscribes into the histories of the telephone (1) fantasies and desires invested in new technologies, in this case desires to speak to the dead, and the spiritualist circles in which Alexander Graham Bell and his assistant Thomas Watson participated; (2) anxieties and pedagogies surrounding prostheses, stemming from work by Bell's father with the deaf and dumb, but also drawing on the widespread hesitations surrounding the use of telephones; (3) differences between what entrepreneurs envisioned for new technologies (business use only) and their actual uses (everyday communication); (4) differences between the rationality we retrospectively attribute to inventors and scientists, and the actual neuroticisms they often exhibited in life, as revealed through (5) readings of the autobiographical and biographical accounts of Bell and Watson. Ronell also experiments typographically and textually with ways to make us read differently, drawing attention to the physicality of the media in which our lives are embedded, beginning with her title, *The Telephone Book*, which claims one might use the text for random access the way one today does with the Internet. The typography of her text simulates in places the effect of "electric speech."

What makes Ronell's work truly engaging, however, is her philosophical rebuttal of the banalities of Heidegger's "philosophy of technology," which has become so mindlessly faddish among American students. Ronell rebuts in particular Heidegger's refusal to take responsibility ("to answer the call," or rather to only answer the call [of the Nazi Party] in blind obedience, as if technology were deterministic). She rebuts Heidegger's retreat to his mountain, to silence, arguing that we can neither blindly become cogs in whatever technological developments occur nor withdraw from any engagement. We are embedded, ethically, as well as existentially and materially, in technologies and technological prostheses. As the philosopher Jonas (1984) puts it, and as daily new debates about cloning, medical testing, and so on, demonstrate, our technological prostheses are also taking us into models of ethics with which our older moral traditions have little experience or guidance to offer; and despite the new professionalized fields of bioethics, we are again thrown, as Wittgenstein noted, beyond "grounds giving" to ungrounded ways of acting, to new forms of social life (1969: 17e).

Haraway (1991, 1997) espouses a similar philosophy, one that further draws on multiple — feminist, socialist, scientific — commitments, facing up to the contradictions that can occur among them. Whereas Ronell writes in the "lively language" of metaphoric deconstructive play (often as rigorously as Derrida), Haraway draws more explicit attention to the way in which certain names become implosive, excessively dense nodes of meaning: gene, seed, fetus, bomb, race, cyborg, nature as coyote. Haraway draws on science fiction, on a futurist sensibility with which to critique the imbroglios of the present day; but for anthropology, the global present is just as rich a scene to explore the idea of alternative modernities (see the section "Starting Over," hereafter).

Beyond Perception, Filmic Judgment, and Worlding Cyberspace

The late twentieth century is arguably undergoing a third industrial revolution (based on the silicon chip and computers) as profound as that of the first industrial revolution of textiles in the seventeenth and eighteenth centuries, or that of the science-based second industrial revolution of electricity, steel, and chemicals in the nineteenth century. Communicative and perceptual structures are being changed from worlds of direct experience to ones more accurately knowable through indirect play with structural coordinates and physical worlds available to human consciousness only through technological prostheses. In part this is merely a catching up by everyday experience and common sense to the movement of the sciences since the late nineteenth century, where direct experience has long been understood to be either misleading or at best a partial and supplementary access to the complexity of reality. But the world mediated by computers and simulation has taken us a step further yet, one that requires at least two kinds of knowledge simultaneously: the indirect structural precision of the sciences supplemented by the experiential, relational world of social relations and cultural mapping. We now live in a poststructuralist world, insofar as the world constructed in the 1940s by cybernetic control systems has evolved to the point where decentralized systems (such as the Internet) are necessary lest there be systemic breakdown.

Filmic technologies preceded and prepared the ground for computer-mediated communication. Earlier in the century, Benjamin (1968) argued that film was the gymnasium of the senses, teaching us to scan fragments in multiple channels of input. Virilio (1989) added that film (and trains and cars) not only taught us to deal with speed but also was a mass technology of derangement, which detached individuals from localities, mobilizing them to come to the bright lights of the city, marking them for war. And Deleuze (1983/1986, 1985/1989) argued that after World War II, when Sergei Eisenstein's montage techniques were no longer revolutionary and had been appropriated by fascists and mass advertising alike, the shock of the cinema was in the making of space-time increasingly virtual, that is, multiplying the number of dimensions of signifying systems to which "realism" pays attention (chronosigns, lectosigns or modes of inscription, noosigns or interior mental associations), including pointing to that which is out of the frame. For anthropology, I have argued elsewhere (M. Fischer 1984, 1995b, 1995c, 1998) that narrative films made by people about their own societies are often rich ethnographic registers, and increasingly in places like Poland and Iran, a filmic "Close Up" (the title of a film by Abbas Kiarostami) is staged as an alternative courtroom in which cultural critique can be unreeled into the public sphere.

Cyberspace and its virtual worlds have become increasingly strong sinews of our social worlds. If film taught us to deal with speed, fragmentation, and distraction early in the century, cyberspace has raised the bar on all these processes, adding to them information processing, mining and accessing information with a speed and analytic ability unimaginable only a few years ago. Worlds are being provided for psychologically learning to deal with ourselves as multiple and flexible (Turkle 1995). But we are also challenging community standards for moral codes, playing with traditional notions of intellectual property rights, forging new economics of (free) speech versus (commodifiable) texts. We are also finding potential tools for providing access around traditional deadened schools, local censorship, and bureaucratic stonewalling, new models for self-organizing systems (Emmeche 1994; Kelly 1994; Helmreich 1998), building object worlds with which to think about the changes of the late twentieth century ranging from the Internet as an icon of deterritorialization and decentralization of vital systems, and generating new humorous, fertile, and mind-shaping metaphors (Raymond 1993; Bukatman 1993) for dealing with culture, society, and personhood, reality and simulation, identity and multiplicity. In every practical sphere of life — law, economics, the sciences, engineering, music — computers are forging changes. The study of the worlds of computer scientists, software designers, and hardware techies has only just begun (Downey 1998; M. Fischer 1999b; Helmreich 1998; Kelty 1999), though many of them have written stories about themselves and their fantasies (Constantine 1993; Coupland 1995).

But computer-mediated communication also provides a design studio for social theory. It provides materials for thinking about a conjuncture of two kinds of science that can no longer do without each other: explanatory structures that are breaks with normal experience, which can only be arrived at through the prostheses of instruments, experiments, models, and simulations; and experiential, embodied, sensorial knowledge that acts as situated feedback. It also provides two charter mythologies of temporality that vie with each other: origin stories that shape hopes and fears about technological innovation, and cycles in the political economy of liberatory hopes for democratizing and decentralizing machines, hopes repeatedly disciplined by market processes of capital accumulation or redirected by patent and intellectual property law. Technological temporalities—origins and futures—are shifting complicities. Origins are ordinarily belated, existing in concept, desire, imagination, and linguistic metaphor before they are installed. And so the gap between expectation or fantasy and implementation can resonate with, and be used to provide openings to, alternative worlds. Such openings lie in multiple precursor genealogies, utopian hopes foreclosed, designers' inabilities to foresee users' appropriations. They lie in alternative styles of using a technology (Turkle 1995) and in the desires, family romances, and spirit worlds that power the obsessive urgency and dedication for the tedium of experimenting until invention is achieved (Ronell 1989). They lie in machinic assemblages that facilitate/enforce new subjectivities (Guattari 1992/1995), that speed up the flow of mutations (Virilio 1993/1995), that leverage displaced relations of power (Latour 1988), or that encourage a shift in thinking about technology as task-specific tools to technology as instruments of play and experimentation in social learning (Stone 1995; Turkle 1995).

There is much hype about cyberspace, but cyberspace continues to work behind the scenes when we space out, compiling our credit ratings, positioning our financial futures, restructuring our work lives and stratification systems, building new decentralized bureaucratic surveillance and security systems, providing scientific and pragmatic knowledges beyond ordinary perception, and keeping us distracted and suspended in complex temporal loops of partial knowledges, interactions, and circulating debts that merge and interact beyond individual responsibilities and control. We cannot afford to abandon responsibility, and we must therefore build new social forms of reflexive modernization that can make such systemic complexity and interactivity accountable. Hence the turn in much contemporary philosophy to questions of ethics within our new social prostheses of communication. Says Derrida (1992/1995: 116): "For philosophical or political reasons, this problem of communicating and receivability, in its new techno-economic givens, is more serious than ever for everyone; one can live it only with malaise, contradiction, and compromise."

Starting Over: Beyond Social Control and Social Conflict
No longer is it possible to speak of modernity in the singular. Social theories grow out of the experiences from which they are written. If German social theory in the early twentieth century was concerned with the defense of civil society against the rise of markets and mass politics, and was profoundly marked in the 1930s by the generational experience of the failures of struggles against fascism, French social theory in the post–World War II period was marked by a different generational experience: (1) of the Algerian War of Independence and the migration into France of North Africans who did not necessarily wish to become French (and hence pose the social issues in the terminology of Lyotard [1979/1984; 1983/1988] of "differends," of multiple, sometimes incommensurable value systems sharing the same social space); (2) of the expansion of computer-mediated communication in the 1970s; and (3) of the spread of American popular culture, mediated especially by Hollywood films. Postcolonial theory, similarly, grew out of Indian efforts to read between the lines of British colonial archives, providing a model generalized to other parts of the Third World colonized by European powers (parts of Asia and Africa), but less than fully acceptable to those parts of the Second and Third Worlds that had quite different experiences, for example, China, Taiwan, and the Chinese diaspora (A. Ong 1999; A. Ong and Nonini 1997). The rubric "alternative modernities" acknowledges the multiple different configurations that modernities have taken, and the recognition that modernization and globalization are not homogenizing processes. Indeed, much of the Islamic resurgence of the period since the 1979 revolution in Iran is one of a dialectical deconstruction of Western hegemony, and a search for alternative cultural groundings for technological society that would not subordinate the Islamic civilizational worlds to the imperatives of the Western metropoles. A similar search is signaled in the claims for a Confucian value system underpinning Chinese cultural positionings. In both cases, diasporic feedback transforms the traditionalist groundings of these culturalist claims, perhaps most dramatically seen in the 1998 arrest in Malaysia of the deputy prime minister Anwar Ibrahim and of some eight hundred others accused of trafficking in "America's Islam" (Lotfalian 1999).

Among the important makers of these alternative modernities are the tremendous disruptions of the second half of the twentieth century, of World War II, of the struggles for decolonization, of the collapse of the Soviet empire and its command economies, of civil wars in Africa and Cambodia, and the "disappeared" in Argentina. On the level of social theory, the old debates about whether it was more important to theorize "social change" or "social control" (P. Cohen 1968; Parsons 1937), or the modernization debates about new nation building, seem dated (Geertz ed., 1963). One can see in the writings of anthropologists working in societies such as Zimbabwe, Congo, Argentina, Ireland, and Cambodia a recent break in the ability to write about traditional topics such as religion and social organization (including kinship, family, socialization) as if they were a stable source of values and social integration. Werbner's (1991) and Honwana's (1996) accounts of the attempt to reshape the social integrative uses of witchcraft in southern Africa in the aftermath of civil war are poignant examples. So too is Hutchinson's 1996 account of the Nuer, after years of civil war, trying to deal with new modalities of killing that cannot publicly be acknowledged, as well as Daniel's 1996 accounts of the psychodynamic inability to recall to memory the witnessing of the torture of kin and friends in Sri Lanka. Relations of fieldwork change (Nordstrom and Robben 1995), but the challenges of analyzing social reconstruction remain beyond that of witnessing, requiring analytic frames beyond those of actor-witnesses (Werbner 1998; Malkki 1995; Marcus 1993; Tambiah 1996). Nor are such complicities, and challenges, only to be found in places torn by war and murderous repression.

Indeed, one might argue that the struggles over toxics and environmental issues — now indelibly symbolized by such names as Love Canal, Bhopal, Chernobyl, Minamata — are among the sites where the issues of long-term social reorganization are most exposed: to public view by various sorts of social movements and journalistic attention, to financial pressure on corporations and governments from legal and economic imperatives, to expanding populist ideologies and international treaties of rights to health and environmental justice. The chemical industries have been a focus of attention that raises the issues of doing multisited ethnographies in an industry that is worldwide and thinks nothing of shifting production or importing workers or recalculating risks from place to place; of the doubleness of technoscientific worlds, creating the necessities for contemporary life as well as the risks and vulnerabilities; of the ways in which technoscientific worlds draw in multiple worlds of expertise (medicine, law, economics, politics, engineering); of ways in which the sensorium and health are dependent on uncertain knowledges, and moral trust in others (Beck 1986/1992; K. Fortun 1999; George 2001; Hayes 1989; Petryna 1999).

The biotechnology industries — with genetically engineered crops and livestock — are a second such focus, not merely for panics over mad-cow disease but, in India, for the way in which the green revolution pushed people into cities such as Bhopal, or abroad into nonresident Indian diasporas, transforming the social and political relations of a country that is still too often dealt with in area studies programs and in the news media as merely a modernizing agrarian, religious, caste-ridden one (L. Cohen 1999; Sunder Rajan 2002). Not far behind as a growing ethnographic, history of technology, and political economy focus are the information technologies that increasingly provide the infrastructures of life to which not all have equal access (on India, Subramanian 1992; Kumar 2001; Rajora 2002; Kelty 2001; on Turkey, Ozan 2001; on Brazil, Schoonmaker 2002; on East Asia, Dedrick and Kraemer 1998; more globally, Castells 1996, 1997, 1998; Hardt and Negri 2000; Harvey 2001; Sassen 2001; see also chapter 8 in this volume).

The broad arena of reconstructing society after social trauma seems to be among the most important challenges for anthropology and social science generally. It challenges old area studies frameworks, as well as old-style social theory, and requires restudies of canonic anthropological societies to provide a sense of the transformations of the past century, as well as new ways of doing fieldwork, engaging colleagues and interlocutors in new relationships, and perhaps even generating new kinds of filmic and writing products, including the ability to deal with trauma itself as culturally psychodynamic. (A generation of anthropologists in South Asia, and elsewhere, has been forced to come to grips with what often emerges as a break and challenge to the kinds of studies with which they began their careers: Tambiah 1992, 1996; Kleinman, Das, and Lock 1997; Das 1990, 1995; Werbner 1991, 1998.) Here the literary and philosophical writers of the post-Holocaust and post-Algerian experiences have continuing relevance.

Conclusions

Composing ethnographically rich texts on emergent forms of life generated under late and post modernities, which can explore connections between changing subjectivities, social organization, modes of production, and symbolic or cultural forms, is a challenge that the anthropological archive is increasingly addressing. This challenge requires being able to work in technoscientific infrastructures and imaginaries; thinking through multiple temporalities, cycles of political economy, and reconstructions of social arrangements across local and global expanses; as well as deploying and critiquing new, lively, metaphor-rich languages and semiotic skeins that arise from and articulate new cultural expressions, understandings, and forms of mediation. Such ethnographic work can help clarify emergent forms of life for which conventional ethical guideposts from the past are not always sufficient, and while we may have run out of "giving grounds," we can nonetheless watch ourselves perform ungrounded ways of acting that have both social and ethical weight and consequences. The "new" is never without historical genealogies, but these often require reassessment and excavation of their multiplicity. For this and other layerings encrypted in emergent worlds, ethnographies are increasingly best done in partnership, conversation, and contestation with historians, insiders of all sorts, journalists, filmmakers, and others. The conditions of doing fieldwork, as well as of writing texts for multiple audiences, many of which have powerful interests in controlling the representations of the worlds in which they participate, have changed over the course of late and post modernities, not least because of new infrastructures of communication and information, including film and digital media.

Ethnographic accounts of these emergent worlds can be as rich as the best of new science- and technology-curious novels and similar genres that often partner ethnographic and historiographic efforts (Banville 1976, 1981; Bear 1985; Constantine 1993; Djerassi 1989, 1994, 1998; Malzberg 1985; Powers 1991, 1995, 1998; D. Smith 1993, 1994), including those which have stamped themselves on the broader public cultural self-understandings of the epistemological and ethical puzzles of late or post modernity (Pynchon 1973; Gibson 1984; Coupland 1995). Occasionally such novels are even written by anthropologists (Ghosh 1996).

CRITIQUE WITHIN

TECHNOSCIENTIFIC WORLDS

3

Filmic Judgment and Cultural Critique:
Iranian Cinema in a Teletechnological World

Truth in Painting

In the display window of Al-Hadi Bookstore in London, I notice a volume of Iranian revolutionary posters, collected on the occasion of the sixth anniversary of the revolution.[1] I enter and ask to see the book, ask its price. The shop assistant takes it out to show me but says it is not for sale, it is a shill, a device to bring customers like me into the shop. You know, he says, I'm an Iraqi; Iranians are supposed to be my enemies (the Iran-Iraq war is still not resolved); but look, I just have to show you, whatever the Iranians turn their hand to has high aesthetic production values.

So too with Iranian films. In the 1970s there was a small New Wave of Iranian films. With the revolution, cinema was among the key cultural tools identified as worth controlling. For a short period, production declined and turned propagandistic. But even the production of war films during the Iran-Iraq war had quite distinctive characteristics, rarely demonizing the enemy, but rather drawing on the moral themes of the Karbala story, of self-reliance, overcoming fear, and coping with the tearing of the social fabric among soldiers under stress and between the front and the society behind the lines (Sohrabi 1994). By the mid-1980s, Iranian New Wave filmmaking had revived, and by the 1990s, Iranian films were among the most highly regarded in international film festivals around the world.

On the Questions of Globalatinization
and the "End of Commentary"

At the end of the *Elementary Forms of Religious Life*, Emile Durkheim suggests that science and religion do not stand in a relation of replacement, but rather there will always be a shifting dialectical relation between what societies take as scientifically knowable and the puzzles at the limits of reason that generate religious responses (Durkheim 1912: 431). The return to center stage by religion in the age of teletechnologies raises questions about the relations between media and the forms of religion. In two rich and provocative essays, Jacques Derrida focuses attention on the transformative powers of teletechnologies toward which religions have double relations, both using and being undone by them (Derrida 1996/1998, 2001). Stressing the power of capital, and the concentration of media power, Derrida speaks of a "new war of religion" that "inscribes its seismic turbulence directly upon the fiduciary globality of the technoscientific, of the economic, of the political and of the juridical. It brings into play the latter's concepts of the political and of international right, of nationality, of the subjectivity of the citizenry, of the sovereignty of states." He invokes the Muslim world as a site par excellence of telecommunicative dissemination and of displacements of locality and tradition, warning that "the surge [*defurlement*] of 'Islam' will be neither understood nor answered as long as . . . one settles for an internal explanation (interior to the history of faith, of religion, of languages and cultures as such), as long as one does not define the passageways between this interior and all the apparently exterior dimensions (technoscientific, telebiotechnological, which is to say also political and socioeconomic, etc.)" (Derrida 1996/1998).

The "forms" of religion that are transformed by teletechnologies are various, and Derrida detours us first through an array of impossibilities and paradoxes of meaning ("at the limits of reason") as generative of religion and religiosities. Further, he suggests that teletechnological media and Christianity are currently allied and hegemonic in making all visible, incarnate, "brought to you live and direct" (thus "globalatinization" [*mondialatinisation*]), in contrast to Islam and Judaism, which refuse this iconicity and this presencing, insisting on infinite commentary, because God is never directly self-revealing. Yet as other religions attempt to use teletechnologies, they are drawn into this logic of globalatinization, of making visible/present and of spectralization long-distance. Teletechnologies can operate with a "terrible logic of autoimmunity," undoing them as well as extending their reach. And so he asks if globalatinization is the end of commentary in the Islamic and Judaic sense, while at the same time observing that globalatinization, while seeming ultrapowerful and hegemonic at the moment, is also in the process of exhausting itself. In the meantime, those who use it in a frenzy of outbidding for attention, for profits, and for followers generate a "maddening instability among positions" and the "madness" of "absolute anachrony of our times." (Derrida's primary examples are from television: evangelical

Protestant television in the United States, making miracles present, and Roman Catholic televisual reports on the travels of the pope, also imaging the transcendence of the dying/suffering body. Derrida notes that in contrast, Islamic and Jewish television tends to be of talking heads, discussion.)

Samuel Weber expands the discussion by invoking Walter Benjamin's initial understanding of mediality of language as *Mitteilbarkeit*, drawing out the German pun, both report-ability and im-part-ability, the possibility of a medium to divide and distribute itself, to im-part itself, its capacity to "come-going," to arrive-leaving, to with-draw (S. Weber 2001). Levinas's figure of religion as *adieu/à Dieu* fits here (a good-bye to dogma or received orthodoxy, as the movement toward God or the Other). Hent de Vries points also to the profound sedimentation of religious idiom in language that counters any easy ability to count religion as obsolete (de Vries 1999: 2). But he stresses that Derrida thinks of the return to religion not as a return to what is already there but as a movement after respiratory interruptions that bring one back to a renewal of spirit (4), and that the new teletechnologies are interruptive and new in their political economy configurations of nationalism and sovereignty issues, expansive capitalist and transnationalist mechanisms, and their technoscientific formats. Moreover, as de Vries also notes, again citing Derrida, successful religious performances seem always to be *perverformative*: "Any religious utterance, act or gesture, stands in the shadow of—more or less, but never totally avoidable—perversion, parody and kitsch, of blasphemy and idolatry" (11).

What Place Iranian Cinema on the Stage of Globalatinization?

A reader's hypothesis: nowhere today is teletechnology more revelatory *(Offenbarung)* or useful as access to revealability *(Offenbarkeit)* than in the films about and within the moral, ethical, and religious struggles of Iran.[2] Of course, one needs to read filmic technologies and telecommunications as Levinas understands the Book: "I understand Judaism as the possibility of giving the Bible a context, of keeping this book readable."[3] One needs, in other words, not to speculate from too much afar, or to grant too much too quickly to the forces of abstraction, capital, and specularization, but rather to engage ethnographically with directors, producers, distributors, and audiences, with their understandings, references, and allusions. It is not at all clear that globalatinization is the end of commentary, or that the forces of capital and concentration of media ownership merely suck all onto a

Christian-defined terrain or performativity, though it may well be that the Muslim world today is a site par excellence of telecommunicative dissemination and of displacements of locality and tradition.

Some forms of Derrida's worries were expressed twenty years ago by the leaders of the several factions of the Islamic revolution of 1977 to 1979, not only in the call to take cultural control of television and cinema, but more generally in Ayatullah S. Muhammad-Kazem Shariatmadari's warnings that should Islam become an instrument of the state, should clerics become government functionaries and official politicians engaging in the daily negotiations of power, should clerics completely control the media, Islam in Iran would become corrupt and destroy its own moral authority.[4] For Derrida's catalog of quintessentially televisual religious projections, one might think immediately of the demonstrations of the Islamic revolution staged for the camera, especially at the time of the seizure of the U.S. Embassy, which stopped on cue when the cameras were turned off. Perhaps the telephone and audiocassettes used by Ayatullah S. Ruhullah Khomeini from Paris in his campaign to oust the shah also fit the mold of globalatinization insofar as their geopolitical context was against the power of the Great Satan of the West. Television, radio, audiocassettes, sermons, pamphlets, and the dramatic poster campaigns of the revolution marked a kind of messianic space in which globalatinization and Islamic discourse agonistically generated multiple hybridizations of form and content, and in which a population was caught up in a heightened experiential regime in which everyday conflicting background assumptions became available for world-historical productivity, not only within Iran but, as the slogan of the times had it, also for the "export of the revolution." (Recall even the effort to export the revolution to African Americans, crystallized in a dramatic image on a stamp of the Islamic Republic, fusing together the image of Malcolm X and Bilal, the first muezzin [caller to prayer] of Islam.)

Throughout the course of the twentieth century, film has been one of the most powerful of media fostering a cross-cultural comparative understanding among peoples of the globe, borrowing and modifying genres, styles, consumption aspirations, sensibilities, affect, and recognition of difference. While cross-cultural referencing and awareness may be part of globalatinization, and part of what Walter Benjamin referred to as a loss of the naive parochial sense of original aura, a kind of captioning or reflexive indexing of art's social provenance, it need not be either a homogenizing process, or a wild frenzy of unstable positions driven merely by efforts to stake claims in the market. It can also work to establish niches in diasporic and transnational circuits.

Persian and Arabic have several words for religion: *mazhab* is the sect, legal school, or organized religious affiliation, *iman* faith, *deen* the noun for religion in general. *Dawa*, "invitation," religious missionary work, is the call to *deen*. Insofar as cinema "picturizes" (as the colorful South Asian English verb puts it) *deen* and provides a sound system for *deen* (not just the call to prayer but other religious sounds in poetry, music, and debating, arguing, deliberating voices), it performs calls to response and responsibility; it calls for community but also stages the struggles for ethical decision making against unthinking custom or tradition; it calls for translatability across languages and cultures and regions and class divisions; and it calls for ethical response to dramas of life, to the Other, and to the changing terrains of the moral and the ethical.

What is moral has to do with the social; the ethical is individual decision making: both are under pressure of change. It would be well to have windows and voices that open into the discussions and debates within the moral terrains of Iran and other Islamic worlds. The key terms of the Islamic revolution in Iran, after all, had to do with justice *(adelat)*, a central component of *deen*, not just religion in the institutional sense *(mazhab)*. Filmic judgment is a terrain, despite the state-constrained production facilities of the Islamic Republic of Iran, in which ethical as well as religious issues have been dramatized in ways that, while often deploying genre formats and cinematic borrowings and conventions, escape the stereotypic, and constitute an evolving moral discourse parallel to older poetic, Qur'anic, epic, literary, or theatrical ones.

The constraint on filmic production is a topic that very much needs exploration not only in terms of censorship but also in terms of audience demand. The number of theaters in Iran has declined from 417 before the revolution to 287, and there is now an effort to build more cinemas to support the industry. Meanwhile, however, the spectatorship for Iranian films has been declining, and some would argue that the state has supported films for export (rather than films for domestic consumption) precisely in order to pay the costs for production. In December 1998 a conference was convened in Tehran to consider the dilemmas of audience and film production.[5] There are at least four overlapping strands in discussions about audience: (1) the vulnerability of all national cinemas to Hollywood or global cinema; (2) the struggle of the Islamic state—in much the same way as the earlier Motion Picture Production Code (or Hays Code) in the United States—to set moral boundaries, which while felt as restrictive can also function, like the rules of a sonnet, as a creative game that can generate some excellent results; (3) the struggle between art cinema and commercial cinema even within a vigorous national cinema industry (as India and Hong Kong illustrate most dramatically, and independent films in the United States, as well); (4) the place of production for an international connoisseur niche, or for a diasporic audience. These considerations pose problems for claims about the effectivity of this medium in the general public sphere, but they do not constitute grounds for dismissal. Clearly in the late 1990s, newspapers were the prime medium for the cultural struggles in the Iranian domestic political arena, but film is in any case rarely such a directly instrumental medium. Nor is to recognize the cultural work of Persian films to disregard the role of Hollywood and other global film in the construction of fantasy within Iran, or even its role within Persian films as an interlocutor or vehicle for refashioning in local idiom.

For the Perso-Islamic world, the religious terrain of moral parabolic reason has included for centuries not just the Qur'an and its commentaries, or just the passion of Karbala (the exemplary stories used in sermons from the martyrdom of the third imam), but the *Shahnameh* (the national epic written down in Islamic times with pre-Islamic Zoroastrian diegetic content in a linguistically classic Persian, avoiding Arabic) and its recitations in the *zurkhaneh*s (traditional gymnasiums), the codes of *pahlevan*s and *javanmardi* (youthful heroism), the poetry of Hafez and of Rumi, and the codes of being a *darvish* (being unattached to the politesse and hypocrisies of the social world). Who (including clerics) would make a major decision in life without a quick divination (if only in jest) by opening Hafez or Rumi? Efforts in the most fundamentalist days of the Islamic Republic to downplay the Persian New Year (of Zoroastrian origin) have never succeeded.

But even taking the Qur'an itself, it might be worth at least one paragraph to remind ourselves of the hermeneutic richness that contests interpretations in the political arena in ways rarely reported by Western journalism (except insofar as journalists have reported on clerics who have defended the moral authority of Islam against what they felt were the political interpretations of the state). If, as is often asserted, Islam and the diasporic Muslim world are important to speculations about the social dynamics of globalization in the twenty-first century, one should understand the oral, textual, and telemedia modalities that operate both in parallel and as counterpoint to what Derrida worries as globalatinization. Derrida's call not to ignore the exterior forces for internal accounts of Islam is well taken, but at the same time one must not ignore the internal resources brought to the global stage: one needs to thicken the cultural accounting, as well as pay attention to the vectors of globalization. At the core of Islam is the recitation, the Qur'an, an oral form, ill captured by its textual transcript *(mushaf)*. Listen to recitations of Sura 96, considered the earliest revelation to Muhammad: it is clear that it is made up of different fragments. The rhythm or musicality changes, and the content indicates differences between the times the fragments occurred (in the cave during Muhammad's withdrawal from Mecca; in Mecca on Muhammad's return from the cave). In these two fragments, we already have several distinctive features of the Qur'an: (1) there is a dual order, for the first revelation chronologically does not come first sequentially (the suras or "chapters of verses" are ordered roughly by length, the shortest coming last); (2) the narrative unit is the fragment, not the sura; (3) meaning is conveyed by the sound and would be much more difficult to establish by the text alone ("taught by the pen; taught man, that he knew not"); (4) meaning is further established by a knowledge of the occasions or allusions of the fragments, without which the text is inscrutable, legible but unintelligible; (5) the fragments are of various genres, including dialogues with staged voices (e.g., between God and Abraham, Moses and Khidr, God and Satan, Moses and Pharaoh), implicit dialogues where Muhammad has been asked a question by Jews or unbelievers ("Say to them *qul!*"), and addresses from God to Muhammad and through him to Muslims; (6) only by recapturing the divine sound, as best one can, is one able to approach the presence of God and apprehend his divine words; as human speech is inadequate to the divine, so is the written text a poor transcript of the divine tablet *(lawh mahfuz, Umm al-Kitab)* of the seventh heaven.

So, too, cinema is writing with light and sound, involving multiple codes of signification. Cinematic discourse is constructed through films that cite one another, thereby creating a commentary tradition, a parallel ethical discursive arena to older poetic, Qur'anic, epic, parable, and theatrical forms. Iran's cinema addresses domestic, diasporic, and international audiences. And so we return to at least a heuristic readers' hypothesis: nowhere today is teletechnology more revelatory or useful as access to revealability than in the films about and within the moral, ethical, and religious conflicts of places undergoing sharp cultural struggle such as Iran, the Balkans (e.g., Emir Kusturica's *Underground*, Milcho Manchevski's *Before the Rain*), and India. In India, some commercial filmmakers are now making an effort to comment on contemporary problems such as religious communal riots (Mani Rathnam's *Bombay*, Aparna Sen's *Mr. And Mrs. Iyer*), Kashmir (Vinod Chopra's *Mission Kashmir*), and caste violence (Sheikur Kapur's *Phoolan Devi*). Moreover, many Indian films now incorporate relations with the diaspora, effectively turning Hindi film into a transnational form. Many Hindi films now make more money on their diasporic audiences than domestically. Although Iranian films do not have the same moneymaking draw, their dissemination to the diaspora via regular curated film festivals and via video is not insignificant.

Filmic Judgment and Cultural Critique

"Filmic judgment and cultural critique" is a double-voiced invocation. It refers in part to one of the key films of postrevolutionary Iran, Abbas Kiarostami's *Nema-ye Nazdik* (Close Up, 1990), which like Michaelangelo Antonioni's *Blowup* (1966) has as one of its themes the paradox that when one investigates something carefully, rather than simply clarifying the matter, further complexities are revealed. While *Blowup* refers to the literal blowing up of a photograph until the image becomes too grainy to make out, *Close Up* uses the self-reference to its filmic medium to contemplate cinema as an alternative space to the court system for critical reflection and judgment about social and cultural matters.

Based on a true incident, *Close Up* is the story of a man who tries to pass himself off as the filmmaker Mohsen Makhmalbaf. He is arrested and brought before an Islamic court; the film is framed in part through the story of the journalist who broke the story, and that of the filming of the documentary of the court trial, with director Kiarostami's voice on the sound track. It is a kind of psychodrama, in which a poor man unable to support his family is able to experience fragile moments of dignity and self-esteem by getting people to believe he is the famous director. It is like a narcotic, a kind of gambling or deep play, in which he is aware that he is not able to manage the pose yet is drawn back again and again to experience those moments of power. But it is not just a psychological story of dignity and self-esteem; it is also a social drama of Iranian society. In explaining himself, the man says that he posed as Makhmalbaf, not just any director, because Makhmalbaf's films are about people like himself, that they are the kinds of films he would go to see over and over, that they put people like himself on screen. The Islamic judge attempts to get the plaintiffs (a family who felt they had been taken in by the fraudulent pose) to settle with the defendant, and in this respect the film is a realistic portrayal of the work of an Islamic court, rather than the violent images of Islamic revolutionary courts that the Western press is fond of purveying.[6] In the courtroom, Kiarostami says to the defendant that there are two cameras, one focused on the courtroom proceedings as such, but the other aimed at the defendant, and it is to the latter that the defendant should speak those things which may not be admissible in court but he would like to be used to explain himself. The camera here is literally posed as an alternative court.

Filmic judgment stands here also as a general set of anthropological questions: the questions about how over the course of the twentieth century film and telemedia have changed (1) the ways we perceive and judge; (2) the shifting dia-logical, dialogic, and cross-cultural texture of ethical, moral, and religious discourses; and (3) the theatrical, performative, and political shapes of discursive power in public spheres that reflect, diffract, and contest institutional forms and conventions.

As an anthropologist, I am interested in film first as a vehicle of ethnography, as a kind of register, a descriptive medium, of cultural patterns, of patterned social dynamics, of the "present tense," and of the hybridities or the transnational negotiations of globalizing and localizing cultural processes. By "present tense" I mean the common intuition that there is something about film, even if often illusory, that gives an impression of being able to present the complexities of the present moment with an immediacy that is difficult to achieve through writing, in part, of course, because filmic media can present complexity through multiple musical, sound track, visual, and verbal means. When Walter Benjamin spoke of a new mode of perception that cinema taught through "distracted" scanning of multiple sensory channels, he suggested that it created an absentminded consciousness; but I would like to suggest that the subjectivities created are a more complex dialectic between absentmindedness and self-reflective consciousness, each side of this dialectic being itself a complex set of negotiations, especially under conditions of rapid and politically explicit social and cultural upheaval.

As an anthropologist, I am interested in film as a complex vehicle of cultural critique. At minimum, film over the course of the twentieth century has fostered a comparative perspective. Popular consciousness has moved from peep show or distanced views of the exotic other to cinema or closer views.[7] Film has become, in a manner similar to the role of the novel since the nineteenth century, a space for externalizing cultural and social patterns, dramas, dilemmas, and processes so that a society can see itself and reflect on itself. Involved here are both philosophical questions about the reconstruction of consciousness and sociological questions about the reconstruction of public spheres and the social functions of film.

Consciousness has had an important history since the nineteenth-century recognition that the brain does not just register perceptions but analyzes and reconstructs. Like the brain, so too the various apparatuses of perceptual prostheses such as the camera and projector. Like sociocultural understandings, so too the cinema is understood, as Walter Benjamin put it, as a gymnasium of the senses, where one is constantly checking one's reactions and understandings against those of others around one. Regarding cinema and telecommunications, let me telegraph with a few theoretical touchstones of the past century. First, as already indicated, there is Walter Benjamin's suggestion in the 1930s that film was a key technology of modernity, a place where people learned to deal with the shock of the new, learning a new mode of apperception, which he called "distraction," meaning the ability to scan and sample, to rapidly integrate fragmentary new information coming through multiple sensory channels.[8] At issue in any effort to think of the ways film functions as cultural critique is an inquiry into the double-sided relation between, on the one hand, film's "absentminded" functioning on the level of daydream or fantasy or even subliminal absorption of images and information that are but barely registered for later processing and integration, and, on the other, film's mirroring cultural work of making explicit, external, and available for conscious critique the patterns underlying everyday life that otherwise flow past in less available forms. Second, in the post–World War II era, Paul Virilio accounts film not only as a technology of speed but even more as one of "derangement," detaching populations from their localities, drawing them to the economic promises of the great cities, but also mobilizing them for war, marking them for destruction (Virilio 1989). Third, Slavoj Žižek, playing out late-twentieth-century psychological and Lacanian psychoanalytic perspectives, argues that film plays on processes of seduction not so much by picturing the objects of desire themselves as by staging the circuits of desire, the unending substitutions of desire, the circuits of obsession (Žižek 1991). Fourth, Wilhelm Wurzer provides a more cognitivist claim that the pleasure of film lies in the challenge of actually seeing the order of representation exposed, of watching displacements, detours of judgment, de-framings of power (Wurzer 1990). Fifth, Gilles Deleuze suggests not only that cinema is a kind of nomadic war machine, wherein the camera is able to move about in a deterritorialized fashion, seizing and remobilizing cultural bits for its own strategic purposes, but also that there has been an important break between pre–World War II film ("classical") and post–World War II film (Deleuze 1983/1986, 1985/1989).

Post–World War II film, Deleuze suggests, uses a different time-space image beginning with Italian neorealism and French New Wave, in which objects are more carefully observed than in classical "realism." Optical and sound elements, for instance, often take on autonomous existence, and multiple other sign systems can also be foregrounded: chronosigns, lectosigns (modes of inscription), noosigns (interior mental associations). Time-space becomes "virtual" rather than spatial, meaning that these various dimensions of signification can be foregrounded and interrelated in a variety of ways. At issue here is not merely an epistemological, but also a political, shift. Epistemologically more precision leads to a less easy realism, and what is usually being investigated in the postwar world are the powers of the false. This is perhaps what contemporary Polish filmmakers and critics call *odkłamane* (*od*, negative particle, + *kłamane*, "lies"), countering lies, myths, and conventional assumptions on which not only communist society was constructed but also the hopes and fears of the contemporary society are constructed on shifting sands of partial truths (see chapter 7 in this volume). The shock of the cinema, says Deleuze, can no longer be the forms of thought as in Sergei Eisenstein's montage techniques of the prewar era, not since both fascist and mass commercial art have appropriated modernist forms. The shock of the cinema, rather, as Ackbar Abbas felicitously puts it, is to show that we are not yet thinking, to point to what is out of the frame, to what is not present (Abbas 1992). Abbas's interpretation is suggestive of Lacan's understanding of the fantasies that motivate our neurotic behaviors, when through labile dreams or memories past events take on great significance in the absence of a therapist who can suggest that these are but dream figures and thus help them be integrated and desensitize them from their overweening power. Such psychodynamic or psychological readings of films can add to their interpretive richness. However, even without the psychological register, what is out of the frame often becomes as powerful a visual motivation "for the camera" or for the viewer's curious eye as is deferral of resolution in good narrative and storytelling.

Midrash 1. Mark Tansey's *The End of Painting* provides a parallel: it pictures an American cowboy shooting an image of himself in a framed mirror projected on a movie screen. As Mark Taylor comments, "the image is resolutely illusionistic, and implicitly narrative, functioning like a koan, simultaneously provoking and shattering reflection" (Taylor 1999).

If, then, we can in a preliminary way say that the new forms of consciousness or perception fostered by film have something to do with speed, multiple channels of information, scanning and sampling tactics, nonlinear attention, and pleasure in juxtaposing forms that shape and change informational perspectives or meaning, we can in similar fashion telegraph a series of anthropological-sociological functions of film that constitute the reconstruction of sociocultural consciousness. Studies of Hollywood in the 1920s point out how film performs future-oriented cognitive work, allowing immigrant working-class populations to think through new lifestyles. Larry May notes that one-third to one-half of the scriptwriters were young women, and the scripts reflected their interest in portraying new roles for women in balancing family and career (L. May 1980). Others have noted similar patterns as Betty Friedan did for stories in women's magazines contrasting the support for career women in the 1930s versus the insistence on shifting women back into the household in the 1950s (Friedan 1963).[9] Film has also been a vehicle for working through past social traumas: Pierre Sorlin's studies of European film industries show how films about World War I took more than a decade to emerge (much as there was a lag in American production of films about Vietnam), but then how the films of France and England thematized fears of espionage in democratic societies while those of Germany and Italy had different obsessions (Sorlin 1991). Sorlin also saw differences in World War II films, each country downplaying the help received from others and deepening the suspicions of others; at the same time, World War II films introduced cruelty and sadism in a new way and were deeply pessimistic about the partisans of the Resistance (they are usually killed). Films also help create national publics: Antonia Lant looks at the ways in which gender definitions create a British style of realism in contrast to American films in order to mobilize national identity and a national public during World War II (Lant 1991). Films, as already noted, introduced comparative perspectives to local populations all over the globe. They work as ethnographic writing machines, registering description (location, footage, modeling behavior, emotion, customs), registering hybrid forms in the present tense, and translating domestic differences within states trying to constitute themselves as coherent nations. The Iranian film *Bashu* does this in a particularly dramatic way.

Among the most visually striking of the postrevolutionary films, Bahram Beza'i's *Bashu, the Little Stranger* is an antiwar film about a little boy in southern Iran whose parents die in a fireball of Iraqi bombs, and who climbs on a truck to escape, emerging a day or two later in the totally different linguistic and physical environment of Gilan in northern Iran. A peasant woman takes him in and protects him against the xenophobia of the villagers, having in the process to come to terms with his different language and the fact that his dark complexion will not wash off. *Bashu* is a film about racial and cultural differences within Iran, as well as about the difficulties of the home front during the war with many of the menfolk away. It was a film that was banned until the end of the Iran-Iraq war, but is a powerful way for Iranians to view themselves. At the first North American Iranian film festival, *Bashu* elicited tears and cheers from a staunchly antirevolutionary Iranian audience, who suddenly found themselves confronted with evidence that not all that was happening in Iran was bad.

Although in some respects film is already becoming an archaic cultural form for thinking through the modalities of transnational cultural change—computer-mediated communication and digital media, it might be argued, provide the leading edge—in other respects, film continues to evolve as a central medium, along with television, for negotiating between the local and the global, for working through comparative perspectives in different national settings, and for reconstructing society and public spheres after social traumas of civil war, revolution, state collapse, earthquake, and other massive social disruptions. Film operates as one of the key modalities of insertions into popular culture (along with advertising) in amplifying, refracting, leveraging, and modifying the *sensus communis* (operating most effectively in Walter Benjamin's absentminded modality), but also with interruptive possibilities for response, reaction, talking back, and reflective critique.

The Work of Interruption in Pre- and Postrevolutionary Iranian Cinema

Indeed, the work of interruption is dramatic in the punctuations of cinema burnings, censorship, and political contestation over the freedom of cinematic production, and the commentary generated thereby—in Iran, and in many other countries undergoing reshaping of the public sphere (e.g., India, China). The work of interruption is ethical in the Levinasian sense: interrupting both spontaneity (unthinkingness) and totalizing (aestheticizing). The work of interruption is a stuttering, a halting speech, that dis- and re-articulates discourse segments into an immanent form of cultural critique.

Three sorts of work of interruption in pre- and postrevolutionary Iranian cinema might be distinguished: the politics of cinemagoing in prerevolutionary Iran, cinema burnings as part of the struggle for control over its means of production during the revolution proper and its aftermath in the dynamics of demand and availability of theaters and kinds of films, and the disruptions caused by the reception of films that struck a public nerve polarizing audiences.

Frame 1. The Politics of Cinemagoing in Prerevolutionary Iran,
1971, Yazd (Central Iran)

Defiant was how the womenfolk dressed to go to the movies. It was the opening night of a new film at Cinema Soheil. I was going with several families of the bureaucratic elite . . . not natives of Yazd. . . . This bureaucratic elite felt embattled. . . . The wives and daughters appeared unveiled at private receptions and parties, but dared to appear unveiled among the ordinary folk only when they went in groups to the movies protected by their menfolk. . . . In Yazd, the hostility to the cinema is chronicled in the closing of the first cinema, opened by a Zoroastrian in the 1930s. In the 1970s there were two functioning cinemas; a third had failed and many Yazdis complimented themselves on not wasting time going to the movies. . . . A ditty was composed contrasting Cinema Soheil with the nearby new Barkhorda Mosque:

Yeki sakht masjid, yeki cinema
Yeki gasht gom-ra, yeki rahnema
Tafavot bebin az koja ta koja
To khod dideye aql-ra baz kon

One built a mosque, one a cinema
One leads astray, one guides
You yourself, open the eye of your reason
Observe the difference from whence to where

Haj Mohammad Husain Barkhorda was persuaded to build a mosque rather than the hospital he had intended, as an architectural counter to the growth of a sinful part of town: the two cinemas and two cafés serving beer and arrack. Nonetheless, 70 percent of Yazd high school students chose movies as their favorite pastime (Naficy 1981: 283). Movie prices were kept low by government regulation to provide a popular entertainment outlet.

In the even more clerically dominated town of Qum, the first cinema was opened only in 1970 and then not in the center of town near the shrine, but across the river. The cinema burned down in 1975, possibly due to arson, and there was no hurry to rebuild it. A few religious leaders, recognizing the power of the cinema and the impossibility of denying it to the youth, urged that an alternative religious cinema be created. A similar debate had occurred earlier with the introduction of television, and the popular preacher Shaikh Mohammad-Taghi Falsafi is fondly remembered for a double entendre riddle: what is it that rises at night and sleeps during the day in Qum as well as elsewhere? — the television antenna. By the time of the 1977–79 revolution, control over television programming was a top priority of the religious revolutionary leadership.(M. Fischer 1984)

In the decade from 1968 to 1979, 480 feature films were produced in Iran. Many of these were *film-i abgushti*, in American idiom "grade B" (*abgusht* is the common man's stew). But the best of these films, the "New Wave," included a number of internationally acclaimed films, beginning in 1969 with

Dariush Mehrjui's *Gav* (The Cow), based on a story and screenplay by the renowned writer Gholam Hosain Sa'edi, a film variously interpreted at the time as perhaps having political innuendo but being centrally about ways of handling emotion, and as being a finely crafted intellectual puzzle that creates a mood of self-recognition and reflection.

Gav starkly and enigmatically presents an archetypal village through an episodic series of black-and-white images. It is the story of a poor village in which a cow dies, after which its owner goes mad with grief, much to the dismay of the villagers. Sa'edi, as well as being a writer, was a psychiatrist and wrote one of the best ethnographies to date of the Zar possession cults along the Persian Gulf. In *Gav*, the way he presents this case of pathological mourning illuminates much about the philosophical structure of Persian culture, transcending the rural setting of the story and the "harsh realism" of its ethnographic portraiture. Three sets of ambiguity serve as artistic guides. First, the central event is the death of Mashd Hasan's cow, but it is unclear if the death is due to an insider or to the three shadowy and threatening outside figures. We are never shown the killing of the cow, only a series of clues. We remain as mystified as the villagers, who suggest various possible causes: evil eye (i.e., something social and internal to the village), a snake (external natural causes), and the outsiders (external social causes). A second ambiguity critical to the mood of the film is the use of funeral and wedding images. The dark funeral images dominate, but there is a constant alternation with the lighter side of life, the sense of ongoing renewal, including at the end, when as the men discuss taking Mashd Hasan to a doctor in town and attempt to do so, preparations for a wedding are also in progress. The third ambiguity is the surrealistic turning of Mashd Hasan into a cow. Concerned that the outsiders will harm the cow, he sleeps with it, much to the amusement of the villagers. One day he goes on an errand without the cow and returns to find it dead. He goes into denial, then begins to bellow and rush about like a cow, then to eat at its fodder stall, insisting that he is the cow of Mashd Hasan. Such is the stuff of possession and insanity. Mashd Hasan becomes a cow, not one with four feet and a tail but one whose visage, behavior, and articulation take on definite bovine features, a portrait of a grief that has gone awry.

The loss of a cow is a serious matter in a poor village, and one can understand on the most literal level the obsession of Mashd Hasan: the cow is his existence, his essence. The cow may represent many things, from the fertile goodness of Zoroastrian legend and ritual, to the political conundrums of modernization and agricultural development plans, to the series of animal figures in modern Persian literature—along with Sadeq Hedayat's "abandoned dog" *(sag-e velgard)* and Samad Behrangi's "little black fish"—who challenge Iranians to think about the nature of their social ties, and to evaluate both internal and external sources of illness, decay, fear, and alienation. The threatening outside figures represent real danger but also the shadows of paranoia, the excessive fears that build up in Mashd Hasan and help trigger his displaced grief. The alternation of funeral and wedding images suggests that healthy life has ways of dealing with tragedy, death, and sadness, and the villagers attempt to channel Mashd Hasan's grief, and hope at the end that the town doctor can help transform denial and displacement into mature, realistic sadness. Sadness is not merely an appropriate feeling of loss but a central philosophical attitude, instilled through childhood teasing, cultivated through poetry as a companion to the soul, and elaborated in religion through *hadith* prayer and *rawza* (sermons and mourning ceremonies). Sadness is associated with depth of understanding, thoughtfulness, and awareness of the nature of reality, and with the cultivation of stoicism, patience, and inner strength.

Frame 2. The Revolution, 19 August 1978,
Abadan (Southern Iran)
On the twenty-fifth anniversary of the restoration of the monarchy in 1953, a stunning tragedy is perpetrated. Four hundred persons die in a fire in the Rex Cinema. It is a turning point in the revolutionary process of 1977 to 1979. Although five cinema theaters had been burned during the month of Ramadan (which had begun on 5 August) in protest against the import of foreign films purveying sex and Western materialism, this time people blamed the shah's secret police. The cinema was in a working-class section, not catering to foreigners or elites; the film being shown was Iranian, not foreign; the fire department was noticeably slow to respond, and the equipment would not function when it did arrive; and the police prevented citizen rescue efforts.

Control over cinema, over the means of production of a powerful cultural tool, was one of the goals of the revolution of 1977 to 1979. Some of the more avant-garde of the New Wave of Iranian films, although portraying themselves as politically engaged critics of the shah's tyranny, were rejected by the religious and popular classes as effete and nihilistic. It is said that films such as Parviz Kimiavi's *Moghul-ha* (1973) were received with tearing up the cinema seats by outraged audience members, not because of the content but out of frustration at not understanding the techniques. *Kulturkampf* existed not only between the state and dissidents; more tragically for the course of the revolution, there was *Kulturkampf* between the elite strata and the religious/popular strata who had different aesthetics and could not understand each other's form of discourse. The latter criticized the avant-garde elite for "nihilism," while they in turn accused the religious and popular classes of "repetition" of old religious stories.

Kimiavi's *Moghul-ha* (The Mongols, 1973) is a melancholy, if humorous, meditation on the unstoppable corrosion of Persian culture by Western technology, making Persian culture at best archaic. It is about the destruction by television not only of oral culture but also of film. It opens with scenes of the filmmaker studying a foreign French technology: turning the pages of a history of cinema, showing the various early forms of creating moving images. French technology is combined with Persian content: the filmmaker's wife reads from Juvaini's *History of the Mongols* as the filmmaker matches images of running Turkoman actors in traditional garb with the Muybridge stills of moving imagery. An old man asked about the past, about the Mongols, looks into a mirror. The film is composed in classic modernist montage fashion out of fragments of Persian visual icons — the illiterate Turkomans, a darvish, ruins of old mud forts, a caravanserai, windmills, the recitation of the epic *Shahnameh* — and contemporary references (a microwave relay tower, an intercom buzzer on a wrought iron gate, reference to European films). In the end, the filmmaker is not only not understood by his actors ("*Cinema chi-eh?*" [What is cinema?]), who want to go home, but is himself beheaded in a microwave tower figured as a guillotine, his head rolling off as a film canister.

Frame 3. Postrevolutionary Films That Touch a Social Nerve
Mohsen Makhmalbaf's films *The Peddler* (1986) and *The Marriage of the Blessed* (1988) were received by many in Iran as sharp criticisms of the Islamic revolution from one who had previously been the head of the Arts Center for the Islamic Propaganda Organization. Makhmalbaf was reported to have objected to the peace Khomeini concluded with Iraq as making a mockery of the sacrifices that Khomeini had demanded until then, of selling out a generation of young men who had given their lives in the war to fight via Karbala on to Jerusalem.

Marriage of the Blessed is the story of a war photographer who is traumatized and sent to an insane asylum. He is rescued by his fiancée, and they spend their time in Tehran photographing the social ills that the revolution promised, but failed, to solve. The camera here functions analogously to its role in Kiarostami's *Close Up. The Peddler* is a stylistically innovative film, a triptych of three interlinked stories. The first, set in the slums of south Tehran, is inspired by a short story by Albert Moravia and tells of a couple who have three children crippled by malnutrition. The wife is pregnant, and the husband begs her to abandon the child in the hospital so that it can have a decent life. She is unable to leave the child, and so they try to find other places to abandon it, where they can watch to ensure it is adopted by someone who will care for the child. The story is a series of heartbreaking failures, with some horrific scenes of an orphanage where they refuse to leave the child. The second segment seems to be a takeoff of *Psycho* but is about a crazy young man who takes care of his old mother. Made crazy by mechanical culture, he is obsessively driven by clocks and the routines of housekeeping. In a hilarious scene, he is unable to cross a busy street near the central Tehran bazaar. Toward the end of this segment, he is abducted in a car, robbed, and tossed out onto the street. Characters from all three segments of the film come together: the underworld characters of the third segment are his abductors, and the poor couple of the first segment scavenge from the grocery bag he drops as he is abducted. The third segment, shot in film noir style, takes place in the bazaar and a coffeehouse inhabited by the underworld and Afghan refugees. It is the story of a man who is intimidated by his Mafia bosses and therefore dies a pointless and animal-like death, suffering this death multiple times in his imagination long before he actually dies. Makhmalbaf himself argued at the time that the film was developing a distinctively Islamic filmic rhetoric about birth, middle life, and death, coded with color and light symbolism (divine blue frames an opening shot of a fetus as well as the final shots of merging into death), and that it was misread if taken as a social critique. But the richness of the footage and the testimony of his impostor in *Close Up* suggest that the social critique theme is one that does not go unnoticed by Iranian audiences, or by his fellow filmmakers.

In the late 1990s, two films stirred up audiences in Iran. Abbas Kiarostami's *A Taste of Cherries* (1997) pushed the envelope of Iranian morality in a story about a man who offers others money to bury him after he commits suicide. Dariush Mehrjui's *Leila* (1997) polarized Iranian audiences and touched a raw social nerve in a story of an infertile wife pressured by her mother-in-law to help her husband find a second wife, and the series of unhappy consequences that follow for all involved.

Kiarostami's *A Taste of Cherries* is a parable about three men who are offered money to bury the protagonist after he commits suicide, and their three different ethical and practical responses. A Kurdish peasant boy only two months in the army and far from home runs away from the dilemma, exercising fear; an Afghan *talabeh* (religious student) visiting a friend serving as a security guard at a construction site invokes Islamic rules and refuses to help; and a Turkish-speaking taxidermist who needs money for his daughter's operation tries to dissuade the protagonist by using humor and calling his bluff. There are various possible allusions to Sadeq Hedayat's famous novella *The Blind Owl* (being eaten up from the inside) and to Dariush Mehrjui's film based on Gholam Husain Sa'edi's story "*Gav*" (The Cow) (shadows, noir, isolation versus community). There is a play on the many ethnicities of Iran grounded in strong communal life, while the middle-class Persian Tehrani experiences anomie. The film is visually filled with the unfinished: building sites, the guard who makes tea that is never drunk. The film is also filled with icons from Kiarostami's earlier films: the single tree of life, the curving road, the Land Rover; and with icons of Iranian culture: the moon clouding over (from the Qur'an), the vultures and the dog (who sees into the next world and whimpers or barks at the demons of impurity and death). Institutions of society are figured: army (the Kurd), labor (Afghans), religion (the *talabeh*), and education (the taxidermist's university laboratory). The ambiguous ending of the film—vital to keeping it alive as parable—proved unsettling to the censors, who banned it until a video coda was added. For the censors, the suggestion that the suicide might have been completed was too un-Islamic to allow; the video coda makes it clear that it is all just a film, and things are actually or could be otherwise. The film itself does have an ambiguous ending. The gamble the protagonist plays with himself is a kind of Russian roulette, in which he needs a helper to have a clear outcome: to shake him awake if he is not going to die, and to bury him if he is dead.

Moreover, over the course of the film, the protagonist moves from being isolated and unable to talk to people: in the opening scenes, his questioning of a man in a telephone booth is peremptory; he is a little more humane in questioning a ragpicker, but a bit too prying in dealing with the soldier boy, and with the *talabeh* a bit more other oriented ("I know you will think, but . . ."), albeit still too instrumental ("I don't want your tongue or mind, only your hands"). With the Turk, the protagonist seems to have connected through the older man's recognition of his pain and anxiety, and this time it is not he who is doing the questioning but the Turk who is talking, trying to engage him. At the end, the protagonist runs back to reassure himself that the Turk will be with him, will accompany him to the Chinvat Bridge, will not abandon him, will be there, because he is not sure what he wants the outcome to be: it is a gamble; he wants God to decide, and someone to wake him if he is to live.

The opening scene is a brilliant invocation of the ambiguity that reigns throughout: we see him in his car slowly cruising the streets of Tehran, looking at groups of men: he might be looking for a laborer or two—many of the men standing around are looking for work and offer themselves to him ("*Kargar*? Worker? How many? Will you have two?"); he might be looking for a sexual pickup; he might be looking for a friend . . . In the poetic observation of Joao Biehl, the only scene of the protagonist's dwelling in the film is from the outside, in shadows; in the real world, as it were, he is but a shade, and it is only through the detours and refusals in the diegetic storytelling that his life continues. Everyday life is phantasmagoric, and hard to negotiate, and in this understanding, the film plays again with the thematics of *Gav* and *The Blind Owl*.

Midrash 2. It is not accidental that the most interesting filmic traditions for an exploration of contemporary religion should come from societies disrupted by social violence and nigh-Lyotardian differends of moral perspective. The question of art, ethics, and religion after the Holocaust is a central topos for the late twentieth century and the early twenty-first.

In the Haggadah for Passover, one of the central stories has to do with the questions of the four children: the wise one, the "evil" one, the simple one, and the one too young to be able to ask his or her own questions. On the philological level, the four children are a mnemonic for the four slightly differently formulated imperatives in the Bible to retell the story of the liberations from slavery and from idolatry. On the conventional homiletic level, the imperative of retelling (which falls ethically on all, whether or not one's ancestors actually were among those enslaved) is parsed psychologically: some ask to understand, some ask questions to start an argument, some are too simple to ask much, and some do not know how to formulate a question. Exoduses are many in Jewish history, and that history animates the telling for many families whose own lives have been marked by such involuntary displacements and resettlements. The word "simple" for the third child is *tam*, which also is the mystical state of union with God. This tip or trace has led me in recent years in my own retelling to invoke a historicized layering: that the question about ceremonies has to do with the Exodus from Egypt, through which much of the ritual structure of Jewish tradition was formulated; the question about rules and statutes and judgments has to do with the Babylonian captivity and the period in which the two Talmuds were written, establishing the constitutive hermeneutic tradition and active modality of Jewish intellectual self-understanding and renewal; the question represented by *tam* has to do with the expulsion from Spain and the dissemination of the cosmopolitanism of Jewish creativity as well as the flowering of the mystical tradition to which this usage of *tam* belongs; but most importantly, the child who is too young to ask has to do with the inability of post-Holocaust theology, philosophy, and art to know how to formulate the question.

It is here, perhaps, where not only the queries of Theodor Adorno, Paul Celan, and Emmanuel Levinas about the ethical dilemmas of art reside, but also the modality of film has come to supplement the previous modalities of ethical discourse traditionally represented by mythology, epic poetry, the plays of Shakespeare, and postromantic poetry. Film can work here not as image or direct representation (idolatry of the biblical idiom, the nonethical of Levinas) but as an écriture that deploys its modalities of semiosis, camera angling, and reframing to bring into question, into conversation (and the infinite commentary of midrashic work), and into a call across cultures, across local mythologizing, into expanding the imaginaries of the self, and the possibilities for response.

The Work of Ethics in Filming Iran

The films I have cited are only a few samples of a new filmic discourse. In the decade before the Islamic revolution of 1977–79, Iran had already developed an extraordinary film industry. In a 1984 article, I explored some of these films (along with some of the associated short story literature) as an access to the class-stratified cultural politics of Iran, arguing that the filmic and modernist literature had become a discourse parallel to earlier epic-parable, oral storytelling, poetry, and religious discourses built around the Karbala story of the martyrdom of the third imam, Husain (M. Fischer 1984). This new discourse was built around a kind of surrealist vocabulary initiated by the writer Sadeq Hedayat in the 1930s and 1940s. Like the older discourses, this one too served contemporary society as a vehicle for parables that help with moral evaluations of life's dilemmas. It was, however, a discourse understood by only parts of society and thus for an anthropologist was one point of access to competing cultural rhetorics. Much of the cultural politics of the 1970s were about Westernization, modernization, and technology being out of local control, being a means of subordinating Iran to the needs of the industrial West. There was a mutual disdain between the religious classes, who dismissed this newer filmic and literary discourse as nihilistic, and the intelligentsia, who dismissed the religious classes as merely repeating archaisms. Nonetheless, I perceived a common underlying philosophical structure of melancholia leading to stoicism and determination. With Derrida, one might question if this was but a step toward globalatinization, or if the richness in these local appropriations and commentary modalities continues.

With the revolution there was a short hiatus in filmmaking. But within four or five years, filmmaking reappeared. Some films were pure propaganda, either stolid productions of old religious stories or, increasingly, films directed at the rural youth to encourage them to "volunteer" for the war against Iraq in the irregular forces called the Baseej. Naghmeh Sohrabi has made a study of these films and points out that the better of them are quite remarkable in their own right (unlike American war films, for instance), not demonizing the enemy, in fact rarely portraying the enemy, but rather focusing on an almost Sufi-like aesthetic of self-sacrifice, of overcoming fear, of mutual support and care between commander and soldier, and of the alienation between the commitment of soldiers and the lack of commitment on the home front (Sohrabi 1994). War films continue as a genre to be made, disseminated through television. Many of these films were made by people who had served on the front and only then came to filmmaking. Sohrabi contrasts these with films by those who remained on the home front. But other films seemed to continue the traditions of the prerevolution New Wave. While these films affirmed the revolution by eschewing certain forms of fetishized sexuality of either the Hollywood male-gaze variety or the indigenous honor-revenge *abgushti*, or grade-B variety, they were capable of searing social criticism.

Two of the directors of the postrevolutionary period define some of its key parameters. One is Mohsen Makhmalbaf, who began as head of the Islamic Propaganda Organization's Center for the Arts but allegedly briefly went to jail for voicing criticism of Khomeini when the old man finally agreed to a cease-fire with Saddam Hussein. Makhmalbaf claimed that Khomeini had sold out his generation, had made the shedding of their blood meaningless, had given in to the man his generation had been taught to think of as a Satan with whom there could be no reconciliation. Makhmalbaf has made an astonishing variety of films, many of which are defining moments in the construction of the filmic discourse of postrevolutionary Iran, including *The Peddler, Marriage of the Blessed, Once Upon a Time Cinema, Boycott, A Time of Love*, and *Bread and Vase*. Interesting in his trajectory of filmmaking, in his own account, is that he moved from more instrumental uses of film to becoming increasingly involved with the techniques and possibilities of filmmaking as a rich medium of expression.

The other is Abbas Kiarostami, who employs a kind of cinema verité style, but with an economy of form that turns the everyday into parable. He often draws on the lives of children, uses nonprofessionals as actors, includes ambient sound, and deploys exquisite spare shots of living spaces and nearby landscapes. In prerevolutionary times there was a tradition of making films for and about children, and by the end of the 1990s it became fashionable to say that such films had become a staid genre form. And yet there is something powerful about viewing the complexity of adult life through the eyes and metaphors of childhood's ways of solving problems, finding one's place in institutions, and negotiating relationships. Kiarostami does it particularly well. Others such as Dariush Mehrjui and Bahram Beza'i are directors from the New Wave before the revolution who have stayed on and reemerged as key figures in the postrevolutionary filmic discourse.

It is a filmic discourse in the sense that films build on, and refer to, one another, constituting an intertextual fabric. This filmic discourse is highly self-conscious of its own medium, often incorporating commentary on the filmmaking within the film. Most importantly it is a cultural discourse in the sense that it constitutes a parabolic medium for discussions of ethical behavior, not in the fashion of dogma, preachments, or explicit religious invocations but rather in the fashion of posing dilemmas and working through their possibilities, constraints, and implications (parallel to the ways in which the poetry of Firdausi, Hafez, Sa'edi, and Rumi was and continues to be used). Often these films are politically, but also morally, controversial. One could argue that film has resurfaced as a key cultural idiom against the dogmatism of the conservative leaders of the state such as Hojat ul-Islam, Ali Khamenei, Khomeini's successor in the office of *velayat-I faqih*. It is important to remember that the current president of Iran, Muhammad Khatami, was for many years the liberal protector of the film industry in his role as minister of culture, and that his election to the presidency was on the basis of a campaign to build a liberal civil society.

I have already cited Kiarostami's *Close Up* to motivate the idea of filmic judgment. Another well-known film by Kiarostami, *And Life Goes On* (*Zendigi va Digar Hic*, literally, "Life and Nothing Else"), also begins from real life. In search of a boy who had starred in an earlier film of Kiarostami's, the director and his son set off in their car through the devastation of the earthquake that hit northern Iran. One sees mainly people stoically attempting to clean up shattered buildings, helping one another when they can, but often only able to be of partial help. The final scene is a kind of hieroglyph of this theme. Two boys whom Kiarostami has given a lift get out of the car and tell him that the next hill is very steep and that he will have to take a running start to make it. We see a long shot of the switchback road down one hill and up the next. Kiarostami's car does not make it up the hill, and he backs down to the bottom. A man carrying a gas canister stops to help him push-start the car, and Kiarostami guns the engine and makes the turn up the hill; near the top, he stops and waits for the man to catch up, gives him a lift, and they disappear together.

Both *And Life Goes On* and *Close Up* comment on the difficulties of life in Iran under the Islamic revolutionary regime. They have also woven themselves into the threads of the intertextual filmic discourse of a corpus of socially conscious films in the postrevolutionary era. Other early threads in this intertextual discourse are Makhmalbaf's *The Peddler* and *Marriage of the Blessed*; and Makhmalbaf's film *Once Upon a Time Cinema* (1992) provides a way of contrasting the place of film in the postrevolutionary era with that of the prerevolutionary era, by reading it against Kimiavi's 1973 *Moghul-ha*, a prerevolutionary film about the invasion of television. The Makhmalbaf film has a social critique subtext: it is widely seen by Iranians as a protest against the clerics' desire to control the cinema industry. Both *Once Upon a Time Cinema* and *Moghul-ha* present genealogies for cinema in Iran. *Moghul-ha*, as already described, sees television as a foreign technology that is corrosive to Persian culture, particularly to oral cultural forms, but also Persian film.

By contrast, Makhmalbaf's genealogy of film in Iran reflects a good-humored self-assurance that Iran is able to incorporate new technologies without losing cultural focus. It opens with the importation of camera technology by a Qajar prince, and a reprise of footage from turn-of-the-century Tehran. The film is then composed of famous scenes from the entire history of Persian filmmaking. The opening premise is of a Charlie Chaplin–like cinematographer whose beloved is Atiyeh ("the future"). He promises not to forget her, to remain true to the promise of cinema. He survives a death sentence by the Qajar prince, in a spoof of the guillotine scene from *Moghul-ha*, for filming things too intimate to the royal court; he makes a fool of the shah by turning him into a bovine (allowing him to act the part, a spoof on Mehrjui's famous *Gav*), thereby warning the rulers of Iran (clerics or shahs) not to meddle in things they do not fully understand lest they undo themselves; and the film ends in color with a sequence of clips from postrevolutionary films, all scenes of people embracing, including a signature zigzag run up a hill to a cypress tree from Kiarostami's *Where Is My Friend's House*, similar to the final scene of *And Life Goes On* (about the search for the boy actor of the former film). It is this last sequence of clips in color, as it were, that is the fulfillment of the promise not to forget the potential for using film for social good.

Everyday and Extraordinary Islamic Ethics

Four final "film clips" will serve to indicate some of the range of this post-revolutionary filmic discourse, in which religion is inserted in the background but is motivationally central; in which class and gender issues are foregrounded in a film by one of Iran's women directors; and in which the derangements from the Iran-Iraq war are figured as part of contemporary social problems. Global connections intrude everywhere, and one can perhaps question whether the moral abstractions in some of these plots might be responses to globalatinization, as if called forth in a world of unstable reference points, as displacements and assertions of principle in new social contexts.

Ali Reza Davudnezad's 1992 film *Niaz* (Need) is a morality play, which along the way portrays the hard work of sewing, construction labor, shoe-making, printing, and blacksmithing. Two boys in South Tehran need jobs to help support their desperately poor families. They are each brought to a print shop where there is only one job opening. For a trial period they are each given half a job. They initially act as rivals, have fights after work, which are broken up by passersby, but the rivalry is even more intense by others on their behalf. Mansur, the neighbor who is trying to help the one boy, Reza, ruins the work of the other, Ali. One day, Reza does not come to work, and Ali learns from Mansur that Reza has to care for a sick mother. Mansur uses the opportunity to show Ali his motives for his underhanded efforts to undermine Ali's work so that Reza will get to keep the job. Ali visits Reza and sees that Reza's circumstances are even poorer than his own. Ali quits the print job. The film began with a scene of the graveyard where Ali's father is buried, and throughout he tries to live up to the idealized values of the father. The final scene shows Ali working in a blacksmith's shop, where metal standards for the religious processions of Muharram are being made. In these *alamat* (standards, signs) the message of the film is embodied.

Rakhshan Bani-Etemad's 1995 film *Ru-sari Abi* (The Blue Veil) is a tale of oppressive class-based abstractions of morality, propriety, and honor, countered in an older man's search for giving and receiving human help. It is the story of a widower (played by the great actor Ezattollah Entezami), owner of a tomato growing and processing company, who through his own intense loneliness is sensitized to the loneliness of his employees. He hires and eventually takes as a mistress a woman from the slums, thereby violating the sense of propriety and honor *(abruh)* of his daughters, who invoke the cultural stereotype of widowers vulnerable to seduction by women who want their money. The tension between father and daughters results in a heart attack, a confrontation, and eventually the widower declaring his former self dead. The film ends with a boundary (a train crossing a road, the poor mistress and her siblings approaching on foot from one side, and the widower in his car approaching from the other) breached.

Ebrahim Hatamikia's 1997 film *Ajans Shishe-i* (The Glass Agency), a brilliant reworking of Sidney Lumet's 1975 *Dog Day Afternoon*, treats war veterans not just as being heroes or victims but as being able to mobilize their derangements from their war experiences in the service of ethical and moral intentions that nonetheless violate social norms, and in the process expose the ethical and moral ambiguities of normality. As in *Niaz*, much of the religious content is in the detailing, while the ethical content is in the negotiations of the plot. Hajji is the former commando leader who recognizes his ailing wartime group member, Abbas, now thin and sick with neurological problems, from the 1984 Iraq offensive Karbala 5. A third member of their commando team, a doctor, performs a series of tests — reflex tapping, x rays, CAT scan, spinal tap — and establishes that Abbas has shrapnel in his neck requiring delicate surgery best done by an Iranian specialist in London. The Fund for Disabled Soldiers is in bureaucratic disarray, and after long delays, when the fund finally agrees to pay for the surgery, the payment does not arrive at the travel agency. Desperate, Hajji takes the travel agency and its clients hostage, and the film turns into a psychological thriller, with members of the old commando unit arriving on motorcycles to help out their mates; the state's antiterrorist team, including another member of Hajji's old commando team, arriving with both force and talk; and of course CNN and BBC camera crews. Both inside and outside characters take many different positions, ranging from the travel agent who dismisses Hajji's sacrifice in the war ("I didn't ask you to fight for me"), and those who mock Hajji when he prays ("Prayers done in seized property are not acceptable"), to others who admire the former buddies for their loyalty to each other, and with the antiterrorist team member who joins Hajji in prayer, but with whom Hajji knows he cannot negotiate because there is too great a bond of trust. There are references to both Karbala and the Persian New Year, with a Hajji Firuz, the clown figure of the season, among the customers, and an old man who recites from Firdausi's *Shahnameh*. Hajji tries to use old storytelling parables ("Yeki bud, yeki nabud . . ." [Once there was, once there wasn't]) to further explain his intentions to the hostages. Throughout, personal loyalties often conflict with position taking, as in the case of the young antiterrorist police who was a commando with Hajji, or as when the police cut the electricity and phone lines, Hajji allows hostages to call out on a cell phone, giving again an opportunity for different opinions to be aired as they explain what they think is happening, or with the ill man who only wants to go home but will not abandon Hajji. As in Makhmalbaf's *Marriage of the Blessed*, there is not only a theme of purity/martyrdom struggling against the corruption of the world but also a critique of the reforms that the Islamic revolution failed to bring (Hajji snaps at a hostage who says "Who knows how much money you made out of the war," saying, "I was a farmer before the war and had a tractor; after the war, I returned to my farm, except now without a tractor and without medical insurance"). At issue, both in the diegetic story and just off screen in reality, is the struggle between the work of remembering the heroism of the Iran-Iraq war and its mobilization around the morals and ethics of Karbala versus the normalization of everyday and bureaucratic life. The ethical struggle is one that is complicated by potential misuses of abstract morality on both the sides of normalcy and of mobilization, with the ethics of what is appropriate to do revealed in ephemeral flashes of insight and action, negotiation, trust, and willingness to sacrifice self, and a brinkmanship of using imaginative threats while trying not to do harm. The film was a succès de scandale, causing much debate from both the Right and the Left about its portrayal of veterans.

Ahmad-Reza Darvish's 1995 *Kimia* is the story of the aftermath of Iraqi air attacks on Khoramshahr. A husband desperately trying to get his wife to the maternity hospital is strafed; the wife dies on the operating table, and the baby is abducted and adopted by the female doctor. When Reza, the husband, comes back after having been a prisoner of war, he tracks down his daughter to Mashhad, where amid the symbolism of the shrine of the eighth Imam and the flight of pigeons/doves, he eventually allows the doctor to continue to mother his child. Framed with technological means of life and death—film, tape recorders, medical devices—basic passions and ethical values are at issue in a postwar world where the pieties of traditional social and ascetic ideals must often be renegotiated.

Conclusions

Filmic discourse in Iran has six dimensions:

1. Cinema in Iran constitutes a discourse in the technical sense of being both intertextual (one film referring to others) and a moral resource for parables; it is not merely mindless and disconnected entertainment for either filmmakers or audiences.

2. There is a style to this discourse and filmmaking that we could call post-trauma realism, drawing on earlier Italian neorealist and East European absurdist-surrealist styles and focusing on the everyday, on the problems

and repair of society, and on the problematic cultural codes inherited from the past.

3. There is a transformed concern with desire and seduction, no longer in terms of sexuality either Hollywood style or the honor-revenge of pre-revolution *abgushti* films, but rather with the ends to which desire should be directed. Both *Close Up* and *Once Upon a Time Cinema* illustrate these concerns with the circuits of desire and obsession in Iranian society, and how they might be mediated and redirected through film.

4. There remain traces of the master narratives of the moral discourses of traditional Iran, such as the Karbala master narrative of Shiism. These are often not foregrounded but provide background, context. In *Niaz*'s final scene in the metal workshop making the *alamat* (metal standards) to be carried in the religious processions of Muharram, the visual allusion or trace invokes the entire moral apparatus of the Karbala story.

5. The films themselves provide an explicit discourse about the role of cinema in the public sphere: both *Close Up* and *Once Upon a Time Cinema* are centrally about the proper uses of cinema, *Marriage of the Blessed* also contains this theme, and the disjunctive collaging effects and symbolic codings of *The Peddler* also draw attention to the medium. The oeuvres of both Abbas Kiarostami and Mohsen Makhmalbaf have now included films about their own filmmaking (*Through the Olive Tree*; see also Abolfazl Jalili's *A True Story*, 1996), as well as in Makhmalbaf's case restaging events from earlier in his life and in the history of the revolution, using the actual characters from those times as coaches for nonprofessional actors in the restaging for the films (*Boycott, A Time of Innocence*).

6. Through their international circulation, these films have a chance to play a cultural ambassadorship of a kind that can cut across more stereotypical print and television journalism and provide some access where language blocks readerships of complex novels, stories, or essays that circulate within Persian-speaking worlds.

The Islamic revolution in Iran was fought, and continues to be fought, on many fronts. Film is among the most revelatory — critiquing, contesting, and negotiating the religious and ethical ideals of Islam and the Islamic revolution arguably more effectively than the philosophers or religious scholars to whom most in the West often turn for pronouncements on what Islam is or means for Muslim populations. Films perform a kind of "art captioning" to Iranian social life, externalizing the complexities of subjectivities formed in the interplay between various pedagogies and technologies, of which those of globalatinization and televisual formats are but one, if powerful, set. These religious and ethical modalities are lodged in a few discrete *alamat* (signs, metal standards carried in processions) at the end of *Niaz*, moral dilemmas *(A Taste of Cherry)*, clashes of moralities *(Leila, A Time of Love)*, and explorations of integrity *(Close Up, Boycott)*, moral duty *(Bashu)*, or social policy *(The Peddler, The Blessed Marriage)*. They are often explored in the parabolic lives of children, in the use of nonprofessional actors, and in the dilemmas of the everyday, the everyday as an anthropological and philosophical work space with multiple registers or cultural resource levels, filled with hybrid symbols, metaphors, parables, fantasies, desires, and other tools with which to fashion responsiveness and write life anew, renew life. If abstraction all too often is an evil in dogma and religious violence, and if the abstractive dynamics of an unregulated global market could sweep national cinemas into marginal corners, the commentary elicited by a filmic discursive medium of storytelling through a mosaic of detail and tropic redeployments can reenlighten, reorient ethics and religion, both *deen* and *mazhab*.

4

Cultural Critique with a Hammer,

Gouge, and Woodblock: Art and Medicine

in the Age of Social Retraumatization

Friedrich Nietzsche spoke of philosophy with a hammer, most concretely the hammers of his typewriter keys, both as prosthetic for his weakening eyesight and as part of an emergent new "postal" media environment of mechanical reproduction. Eric Avery's cultural critique is with a hammer, gouge, and woodblock. Avery brings into the operating systems of post-twentieth-century visual technologies—postfilm, postphotography, postradiological imaging systems—printmaking traditions together with materials of our times: paper made from surgical gowns (surgical greens, gynecological blues); woodblocks made from boards used for teaching literacy in Qur'anic schools in Somalia. He uses machines of different vintages (a 1940s Van der Kook letterpress, an etching press, a new Lee Mac-Donald paper press). He overprints and otherwise transmutes older images into powerful new dialectical ones, unfreezing old visual clichés, posing unsettling questions. Their dialectical form works through, somewhat in the manner of Walter Benjamin, flashes of recognition that flare in charged moments, redeeming past hopes that have been banalized in the present, or calling present atrocities to account in the context of pieties that attempt to cover them over. But wood- or linoleum-block printing works not through texts, the medium of the philosopher or the literary, art, or social critic, but through physicality, creating semiotic-material objects.

In Eric Avery's case, these semiotic-material objects circulate only partially through the veins or special spheres of exchange created by carefully tended and gated art world markets, galleries, and museums. They also disseminate through the alternative capillaries of small prints for demotic sale. More dramatically they disseminate through installations, unconventional performance spaces, and performance art in an effort to do therapy for institutions of art circulation (galleries, museums), medical educational spaces (clinics, medical humanities institutes), and advocacy organizations (Amnesty International) that fail to see what is going on at home in their efforts to deal with problems elsewhere.

The physicality of the work to produce this art operates also as a psychological technique of Freudian "working through" the body, transmuting anxiety and stress for the artist, but also tapping into more general cultural and generational anxieties. The language of emotional working through comes naturally to this artist, a physician and psychiatrist, who draws art out of the traumas of his own, and his generation's, experiences, and whose professional language is one of repeated "retraumatizations." In its full-blown psychiatric usage, retraumatization means recognizing psychodynamic patterns, from childhood on, of compulsion to place oneself in situations in which one is at risk of undergoing traumatic experiences. Many professionals narrate their lives as formal analogues of the narrative tropes of their sciences or professions (M. Fischer 1995a). For this physician-psychiatrist, working inside refugee camps created by global political forces (in Somalia, and among the Vietnamese boat people in Malaysia and Indonesia), inside the training of psychiatrists and surgeons (medical school as a traumatic space) as especially psychiatry has been swept by new ideologies and techniques, inside the political mobilization efforts to make visible the indifference of U.S. official institutions to those fleeing from torture, terror, and mass killings (to Texas from Central America), and inside prisons and clinics where persons whose histories of abuse and stigmatization have sucked them into the vortex of the AIDS epidemic (the Texas prison system served by the University of Texas Medical School in Galveston), the trope of retraumatization seems apt. These are the generational experiences of the post–World War II baby boom generation, focused here not on youth culture and consumer society (also part of this generational experience) but on the political consciousness formed by the Peace Corps (and its missionary analogues), the civil rights movement, the struggle to end the war in Vietnam, the sanctuary movement to help refugees from Central America, the anguish over the treatment of Haitian refugees, and the shock to the medical and public health systems as well as to the several "sexual revolutions" from the AIDS epidemic.

The resonances between an artist's life history and generational and social historical experiences are analogized in a lovely essay, "The Echo of the Subject," by Philippe Lacoue-Labarthe, to *catacoustis*, the inner echo "of a musical order," the return, in very precise circumstances, of a melodic fragment, like the "psychopathology of everyday life," of "a tune in one's head" that "keeps coming back," like the *Kol Nidre*.

1. Harvard Fogg Art Museum poster for World AIDS Day, 1997. Woodcut letterpress block print. Photo by UTMB Biocommunications.

If culture is your patient, or if immigration policy is your patient

Saturday afternoon, 28 November 1997, upstairs in the printmaking room at the Carpenter Center (Harvard): the place is deserted. Eric is using a Carpenter Center press to run off his woodblock print posters for his installation at Harvard's Fogg Art Museum. In stunning green, black, and white, the poster is a 1930s-style block print. Or even an older tradition back to Albrecht Dürer and Hans Holbein. The subject is like a poster from the Black Death in Europe, but there are also hints of other references: the *calavera* (skull, skeleton) tradition of Mexico, both the Day of the Dead imagery and the satirical political calavera prints and cartoons of José Guadalupe Posada; and William Blake's drawing *The Poet's Imagination*. The Fogg installation is part of the annual World AIDS Day art shows around the country, a cause with which Eric Avery has long been associated. Eric's installation is a brave insertion by the Fogg Museum's curator of prints, Marjorie Cohen, into a larger show of prints as functional rather than aesthetic objects — the life of art before it is excised and isolated in museums.

It is a brave act for the curator because Eric's installation breaches the institutional walls between the clinic and the museum: Eric is installing part of the Cambridge City Hospital's AIDS clinic in the Fogg Museum. He is putting it under a templelike wooden structure, wallpapered with his gorgeous three-by-six-foot black-and-white linocut print repeating design, which diagrams the life cycle of the HIV virus, superimposed on Giambattista Piranesi's *Prison VII* etching of a spiral staircase. In this clinical art space, clinicians will demonstrate AIDS testing and perform patient health care consultations. Eric notes that the treatment of the HIV-positive patient has so improved since 1993 that the levels of ramps and windings of stairs in the Piranesi print can be adapted into a metaphor of the staged administration of the new, effective drug complexes and complementary viral load testing. The schematic image of the life cycle of HIV "shows what happens inside a lymphocyte with the viruses entering on the left, sites of reverse transcriptase medication, protease inhibitors working on the right, the budding, and the virus receding underneath the wheel-like structure." Eric jokes, "There is a little guy standing there, that's me being ground into pulp by this process." Across the bottom are "some pictures that I draw frequently for my patients to help them understand the importance of viral load testing. We talk a lot to patients, but they don't actually know what a virus is. Certainly a lot of my patients in indigent clinics, nobody has ever looked through a microscope, so they don't even have a concept of the microscopic world" (interview by author, 2 December 1997).

If Eric's work is a challenge to the purpose of museums and how they function in society (and something of a challenge to Harvard lawyers worried about liability if clinical activities are carried out in a nonmedical space on campus), much more anxiety provoking for Eric is the sense that he might be breaking the taboo of the sacred doctor-patient relationship: "Managed care is violating the doctor-patient relation in such a big way, and I come along and do it even more. . . . What I am doing is moving the doctor-patient relation, the practice of medicine, into the public" (interview by author, 28 November 1997).

What he is doing has few, if any, precedents. "I don't know others doing anything similar. Sure . . . a lot of physicians do art as a hobby. But this is different. . . . there are no models to follow except reading in the history of medicine." In 1996 he did a show at the Mary Ryan Gallery in New York in which public HIV testing of volunteers was part of the installation. "It was the practice of medicine in an art space . . . medicine as art . . . a reminder of art's power to heal. There are the Navajo sand paintings, Tibetan uses of healing and the visual; but in the Western tradition, ritualized healing is less evident — one needs the historian to excavate it."

He reflects on the lineage of public demonstrations. Versalius's anatomy demonstrations provided the dialectical precursor that Eric transmuted in the poster for his 1982 show in Galveston *(After Versalius' Anatomy Les-*

2. *Life Cycle of HIV Showing Sites of Actions and Medications*, 1997. Linoleum block print. Photo by UTMB Biocommunications.

son). Surgical anatomy amphitheaters of the early-twentieth-century medical schools are another, and his home institution, UTMB (University of Texas Medical Branch) in Galveston, has a particularly well preserved one. Contemporary television programs showing surgical operations live might be another reference point. But Eric reflects, "A lawyer friend in Houston [who did not approve of Eric's public clinical art installation idea] said what I am doing is a violation of the very private doctor-patient relationship. He said that when you go to the doctor to talk about doing a late-term abortion, that is not something you want to talk about in a public setting. That is what I am doing. It is like asking a doctor in public about doing late-term abortions."

For the anthropologist, he immediately follows this with a challenge: "I don't know if I need to understand what I'm doing. I just need to keep doing it. My words have not kept up with my art. The art is a gift to me; maybe I need someone like you to analyze and explain" (interview by author, 28 November 1997). It is the nature of the gift that requires unpacking, a gift that can work socially, that can educate, that can operate as cultural critique if picked up by enough people, and that can perform institutional therapy.

Eric is challenging the museums, but his work is also a protest against certain trends in medicine: "I also got to layer this piece, because I moved the endangered practice of medicine into the protected aesthetic space of an art museum just the way you'd move other relics." In both directions, he practices a form of "institutional therapy." "I could explain what I do psychodynamically, or I could explain it in terms of the contemporary art world and what's happening, or I could talk about it in terms of changes in medicine and managed care. . . . One of the things I don't talk about very much is the institutional therapy that I do. . . . I would redefine medicine as different than just seeing patients. I mean, define the patient. If culture is your patient, or if immigration policy is your patient, or in my case [during the time in Laredo] it was really Amnesty International which was my patient, and it drove me absolutely crazy, all these middle-class people who were writing letters all over the world to stop bad things from happening didn't know what was happening down the road from their houses [in the Immigration and Naturalization Service detention centers]. My first crossover piece, where I actually walked into an art museum [the Houston Contemporary Arts Museum] dressed as a doctor with a nurse and another doctor along with me and a black bag, as if I was making a house call, and we set up and did HIV blood testing as an educational event—that felt really good to do because that was education.

"It was not about poor suffering people and all the loss and all this stuff.

That is just not what I do. Since I deal with all that stuff as a professional, I think I get to make [art]work about another part of it. And as it has evolved, this Fogg piece was an opportunity for me to move an entire clinic into an art museum to display a multidisciplinary approach to HIV care, to educate people about the importance of nutrition, about the roles of nurses, nurse practitioners, to highlight and really emphasize the social workers' role in dealing with the complexities of this disease, the importance of testing, of viral load testing. So I was able at this event, by moving this entire clinic, to show the contemporary practice of HIV medicine in ways that I think documented it. It is a historical document at this time. It will be a record of what was happening" (interview by author, 1 December 1997).

Eric explains some of the references in the Fogg exhibition poster. The palimpsest contains images from art history: an eighteenth-century German etching, *Interior of Saint Peter's at the 1700 Jubilee under Clement XII*, and Edvard Munch's *The Sick*. The green of the poster is the color of surgical scrubs and the glow of x-ray and computer screens. But the palimpsest also contains the artist's personal mythology, a stock of images and conflicts that reverberate through a maturing career and weave between the personal-experiential and the social-moral and political. The physician in the poster is Eric Coste, the medical director of the Zinberg HIV Clinic at Cambridge City Hospital, part of whose clinic is moved into the Fogg; but the physician is also Eric's father. "There is this little child (me) pointing at the skeleton in the shadow on the wall," says Eric, "or maybe the patient is me, as well. My father and me. Art and medicine. Father (the physician) and mother (the artist). My father was a pediatric hematologist. I am vulnerable here" (interview by author, 28 November 1997). The skeleton's hand grabs the child's wrist. Death grabs the child's hand.

Monsters lurking . . . myths of white America, twisting them,
making them more real

Eric's first influence as an artist was his Phoenix-bred mother; his first art teacher was a woman with muscular dystrophy. Linoleum-block printing was among his first art forms. At age thirteen he sold his block-printed cards in a local yarn store. In his lectures, Eric often begins with some of his childhood drawings and with the rueful psychiatrist's (and art historian's) quip "There were already monsters lurking in my past which I've been working on in my analysis" (interview by author, 30 November 1997). His first subjects were things his mother valued: ladybugs, insects, flowers: "Most of the insects, though, were walking out on limbs [that] were going to fall because of the snow on them. Or the ladybug was being chased by a very large insect with giant pincers that was ready to squash it" (interview by author, 11 December 1997). Eric followed his mother's trajectory to the University of Arizona, where his print teacher, Andrew Rush, cured him of "decorative" art. Rush had trained in Iowa with Mauricio Lasansky, a realist, if romantic, depicter of the human condition. Rush helped Eric sort out his conflicts between art and becoming "something more like Albert Schweitzer." Rush encouraged Eric to take science, lest he regret never having tried alternative routes. "When I went to college," Avery says, "my favorite artist was Norman Rockwell . . . I think I could do a whole second body of work, taking those myths of white America that I'd grown up with and just twist it and make them much more real" (interview by author, 1 December 1997).

His mother collected Southwest Indian paintings from the 1950s to the 1970s, what Eric thinks of as the transition in American Indian art of learning, in Anglo-staffed schools, to produce art on paper for the white tourist market. Eric challenged this Anglo market's—and his mother's—taste. "I asked her why none of the pictures she had showed any bad things that had happened to Indians. . . . And she said, 'Oh, I would never buy anything alike that' " (interview by author, 10 August 1998). Under Eric's prodding, she began to collect a few other kinds of Indian paintings. Eric reckons that her collection is quite valuable as a reflection of that particular moment of Indian art for the market.

"My mother is still living. I have a complicated and traumatic relationship with her." As also, befitting a psychiatrist, with his now deceased father. In a note attached to a 1962 *Life* magazine article featuring his father, Eric wrote, "I send it because my own involvement in 'social work' is in a tradition of service in my family. My powerful physician father was really mean to me—called me a little girl as I grew up, then 'porky pig' and he did not want any of his sons to become doctors. . . . We might not end up talking about any of this, but I felt it was important to ground our discussion in this psychological field." His mother is a fundamentalist Christian, and "a major focus of my psychoanalysis. She is totally and permanently a Bible literalist and a homophobic frightened creature whose overriding wish is for all her family to be reunited in heaven. She is very worried about me" (interview by author, 10 August 1998).

Just as Eric's mother is of interest in delineating changes in generational approaches to art and the operation of certain circuits of collection, Eric's father helps define the Texas politics against which Eric's art reacts, and at the same time invokes the contrasting New England worlds of Eric's grandfather, with which Eric's father broke.

The persona of grandfather Alfred Harlow Avery offers a model of the Yankee Protestant ethic—modulated, as so often in pre–World War II New England, with an Orientalist asceticism—as it merged into the twentieth-century military-industrial-academic complex. This was the Avery who gave $1.4 million to help establish the Maxwell-Avery Graduate School of Citizenship and Public Affairs at Syracuse University, and half a million dollars to Boston University. The same Avery also established the Parshad (Hindi for "gift of god") Charitable Foundation, which drew on the profits of some thirty businesses and supported some two thousand college students (selected for "scholarship, affiliation with their church ['character'], and interest in community service"), educated and fed some one hundred children around the world, bought and refurbished the Malden Youth Center, and put up foreign students in Avery's fourteen-room home. He had been a vice president of the Electronics Corporation of America (headquartered at 10 Memorial Drive, adjacent to MIT), where electronic eyes for automatic doors and heat-seeking missiles were developed, and photo eyes for geostationary satellites watching for missile launches. He had quit a top post at DuPont at age forty but stayed on as a consultant, putting his retainer checks into his scholarship pool. He shunned publicity, granting an interview four years before his death on condition it not be published until after his death. Descended from Plymouth Pilgrims (he still owned seven farms in Plymouth with handwritten deeds going back to the 1620s), trained as a chemist at Boston University, where he also taught before going into business, a member of Methodist churches in Plymouth, Boston, and Malden, he lived by a life plan formulated early in life that sounds like the Hindu stages of life: for the first twenty years (student) get the best education, for the second twenty years (householder) make as much money as possible, and for the rest of one's life (ascetic) give away as much money as possible. "My father's father was a happy man: my father described him sitting on his porch in Hingham giving away money" (interview by author, 28 November 1997). The obituary in the *Boston Globe* (29 May 1957) is headlined "Educational Godfather to Youth Being Buried from B.U. Today: Modest Avery Gave $5 million."

Harlow Fuller Avery, Eric's father, severed his ties to the Northeast, sold everything, divested the two family foundations, and moved to Pecos, Texas, the site of another culture and epic of twentieth-century American history. Trained as a physician and pediatric hematologist in Boston, he moved to Pecos, "a hard little racist town," and bought part of the semiweekly *Independent and Enterprise*, which became famous when it broke the Billie Sol Estes scandal in the early 1960s, winning its editor, Adam Griffiths, a Pulitzer Prize. Estes had connections to liberal senator Ralph Yarborough, and the scandal threatened Democrats in Washington. Estes had built a pyramid scheme of fraudulent chattel mortgages, asking cotton farmers, for what seemed like a good return, to give him their credit lines on fertilizer tank mortgages, then registering each of these mortgages in multiple courthouses, creating the illusion of hundreds of nonexistent tanks securing multiplying loans. Conservative Avery and his right-wing partner, surgeon John Dunn, would not be warned off the story, and when it broke, farms went bankrupt. For the little town, the event was traumatic. "Everything changed suddenly: people spit on my mother in the store. . . . John Dunn lost his hospital rights, but patients of my father organized and defended him, kept him there" (interview by author, 28 November 1997). A dramatic *Look* magazine article has a full-page portrait of Eric's father, phone in hand, along with sixteen photos of the local characters: an Anglo cotton farmer in cowboy hat; the fat police chief; the bald, cigar-chomping banker; the mustachioed and fedora-hatted mayor; the elderly justice of the peace; the anticorruption crusading right-wing John Bircher surgeon in hospital scrubs (John Dunn); and a series of more hieroglyphic photos of the bleakness of a dust storm swirling around a lanky young man in jeans by a barbed-wire fence holding on to his baseball cap; a silhouetted thin farmer in cowboy hat standing along an irrigation ditch; an older, heavier farmer with a fertilizer tanker in his fields (a victim of Estes); and a cowboy-hatted, Spanish-surnamed farmer with cigarette aggressively clenched in his teeth (he had spurned Estes).

These photos are really disturbing, but I want to show you how to see something that is very beautiful in these very traumatic situations . . . You [would] say, "You are taking down the tree"; they would say, "No, I am taking a piece." And slowly it shrank in pieces.

"Traumatic spaces . . . are for me places of overwhelming experience, and in trying to cope with that, you have to reconstruct your world, so your world of values is basically taken apart. That happened for me in medical school, and it happened again in Africa . . . working with AIDS . . . going into the prison. I continually put myself in these overwhelming experiences." "I have been retraumatizing all my life: I keep getting into situations incredibly overwhelming." Art became a mode of coping: "All my repressed anger that I have for all the bad stuff that has happened to me, you know, could be really destructive. So I channel all that stuff into my chopping and grinding and pounding and the type of stuff that I do with my art making" (interview by author, 1–2 December 1997).

In medical school, Eric underwent three very different waves of psychiatric pedagogy, so the current conflicts among professionals over how to treat in the prison, HIV, and transsexual clinics of the UTMB system are not new. Eric trained initially in Galveston, where both medical school and psychiatric training were traumatic, and ritualized, spaces that are supposed to transmute fears and anxieties about death, torture, and violence to the body. Eric thinks he handled dealing with cadavers in anatomy by the defense mechanism of dissociation, and he wonders if those who become surgeons do not have to deploy a kind of dissociation to be able to cut into the body or peel the skin of burn victims. He wonders about "the unconscious things that drive the choices that physicians make about what parts of medicine they go into." His analyst, "who does a great talk on the Marquis de Sade," argues that medical school is a "high patriarchal and hierarchical structure to control what is happening" (interview by author, 28 November 1997).

Psychiatry in Galveston at the time was "the last outpost of biological psychiatry to use electroshock in the South." Dr. Winston Martin ("We need to give you a little Houston Power and Light"), when asked by a resident how he knew when to stop, quipped that "he would keep going until the resident would refuse to give any more treatments for ethical reasons, and then he would go in and do one or two more himself. . . . Martin taught us that the most important thing for a psychiatrist was to believe in what you were doing among the competing approaches to treatment, and then do it. He believed in somatic treatments." For his residency, Eric went to Columbia Presbyterian in New York to train under Otto Kernberg, a psychoanalyst specializing in borderline patients. But Kernberg left when the psychoneuroendocrinologist Ed Sacher became chairman of the Psychiatric Institute and brought in a new group of psychiatrist-researchers. "We called them Ouitkin, Rifkin, and Klein. . . . Most of the residents had chosen PI [the Psychiatric Institute] to work with Dr. Kernberg. We had to represent our patients to the new psychiatrists, and many had their diagnoses changed— and their treatments changed also from long-term psychotherapy to some talking, but mainly drugs. . . . So, I experienced three phases of psychiatry. It was clear to me that psychiatry was a mess. It seemed to me that the same percentage of people got better with shock, Kernberg-style psychiatry, or drugs" (interview by author, 28 November 1997).

The alienations of medical school drove Eric back to art: to therapeutic photography of the trauma around him, and to Greenwich Village. "I met a photographer and later performance artist who still works with me [Karen Feinberg/Lily Pond]. I would take the A-train from Washington Square up to 168th Street and use that time to get myself into the frame of mind of a psychiatrist, this other world. . . . I joined a street band and played baritone sax for On the Lam Street Band. It was made up of people who had worked with the Bread and Puppet Theater, based in Vermont. . . . I learned you did not need money to live, only friends and sharing a way of life. This was the time of the Cambodian holocaust, and I wanted to volunteer to work as a physician there. Albert Schweitzer had been my dad's hero, so maybe there was a bit of that. I tried to volunteer various places; no one would have me. I was out of medical practice two years and a psychiatrist, but then World Vision said they were interested, but I would have to wait" (interview by author, 28 November 1997).

Photography became a way to intervene. He photographed the use of space by the elderly, hands of surgeons, and hospital scenes from birth to death: "rituals of surgery, family practice, pediatrics, pathology and still lifes of organs of the body, and cancer treatments of the 1970s."

Inspired by Gaston Bachelard's ideas about the poetics of space — space as an originator of images that express our intimate sense of private lives — the series of photographs of how the elderly use their spaces, especially their apartments, was premised on using the reactions of the photographed subjects as inputs for a more humane environment and system of care. The elderly would point out where sidewalk curbs were too high, or how they placed things in their apartments so that they could remember where items had been put. Although the project remained unfinished and unfunded, it attracted the attention of Al Vastyan, the director of the Hershey Medical Humanities Institute, the first such department in the United States (Galveston was the second). Vastyan invited Avery to Hershey. "During this period I also photographed orthopedic surgery in Galveston, made possible by [one of Eric's medical school teachers and continuing supporter of his art] Burke Evans [a pioneer of techniques for helping burn victims]. I photographed my father delivering a baby and working with patients, and a Mexican doctor in Puerto Progresso, Mexico, sewing up a child's hand" (interview by author, 10 August 1998). "Where is the art," Eric wrote in 1983, "in the seeing parts of medicine — patients in physical diagnosis, microscopic tissue slides in pathology, subtle changes in radio density in X rays, or computerized visual representations of sections of the body in the CAT scanner? . . . They illustrate but do not illuminate." They do not suggest infinite horizons the way art does (Avery 1983: 11, 138).

On the second day of his first three-day visit to Hershey, Eric met Jane Petro, a resident in plastic surgery. A dramatic series of photographs came out of the encounter that caused her to be unable to operate for a few days, the exemplar par excellence of the power of photography to disturb the medical gaze into a more mindful integration. "Her beeper goes off. She answers the phone. She says, 'Are they bringing the hand with?' She turns to me and says, 'Do you want to photograph a hand being sewn back on?' It turns out to be the first limb reattachment in Pennsylvania or at that medical center. A young Puerto Rican man chopping wood had cut himself with an ax right across his palm. All of this is just the normal doctor stuff. You know, it goes on every day. Cleaning, you know, the ritual of surgery, washing, draping, you know, all this removes the identity. It is, of course, for a lot of other reasons, but you know it depersonalizes everybody so we are all in this together. And what I was photographing, then, I got into this space. I'd been working with the space between art and medicine for a long, long time. And at this point, I was going to photograph the space of healing, this tiny little intimate space, that actually gets smaller when they go to the microscope and sew the blood vessels in this tiny little space. And now we are into what I was calling back in the late seventies the space of healing, a very small space where this transformation happens in the surgery. That's where all the drama happens. But at the same time, when I was making these photographs, my art training was clicking in, and I began almost having a religious experience as I watched this reattachment of a severed body part. So I made this set of photographs, a set of five.

"It became a metaphor. I'm not doing anything with the lighting, but I began to see this incredible connection. They ended up sacrificing the index finger, which I learned is the least important of your fingers because you can do this [gripping against the thumb] with any of your other fingers; you don't really need this one. But what you really need is the grip, so they sacrifice this finger to get the vessels that were used to anastomose across where the accident had happened. This was a ten-hour procedure, and what I began seeing in my mind were these images from art history: the Michelangelo image from the Sistine Chapel of God touching Adam's finger. As the surgery went on, and I clicked away at major transitions, I felt that the surgeons ritualized even more what they were doing. They put their instruments during the procedure like this [arranged on a tray]. It was an incredible and life-changing experience for me. Then they were finished. The instruments were put down and we came out of the space of healing, and the drapes came off and the patient went to the recovery room. The man had a functional hand, he had a fixed joint, he could not bend here, but he could actually grip.

"It was the first time that I had this experience of really seeing this art— that my art history brain began to really drive my image making" (interview by author, 1–2 December 1997). The photos of the surgeon's hands were put on display in a corridor of the Hershey hospital. Jane Petro saw her hands,

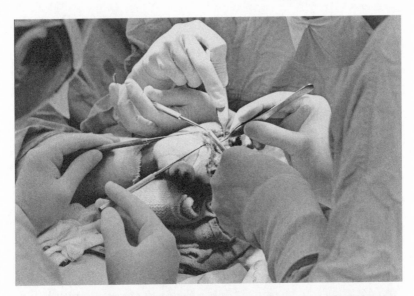

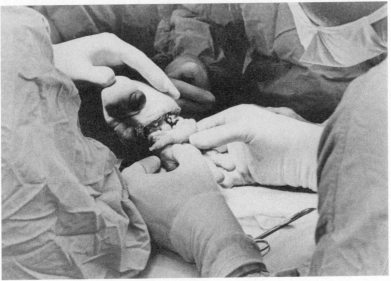

3, 4. *Hands Healing,* 1977. Photograph by Eric Avery.

and the experience did something to her: she found herself crying and unable to do more surgery. She called Eric in New York and asked him as a psychiatric resident what he thought he had done.

It took ten days or so until she recalled a long-repressed dream that she had in medical school while doing anatomy, of her cadaver sitting up and demanding she put it back together and her replying, "I can't. They take away the parts and burn them. They are gone," whereupon the parts began to chase her through the halls of the hospital. She could not continue, could not do the anatomy exam, until her professor went through the anatomy atlas with her, establishing that she knew the material, and passed her. Recalling the dream freed her to continue her surgery. It was a kind of integration, a sense of recognition of her identity as a plastic surgeon. She continues to the present to be a collector of Eric Avery's work, an important supporter, and a frequent participant in his art installations.

In 1977, when Eric returned to Hershey for three months, a photograph captured during an autopsy proved perennially haunting. There is constant tension between anxiety and beauty in Eric's accounting of his work, somewhat like the lotus of Buddhist philosophy, emerging out of the muck of suffering. It was only "at the very end of my time at Hershey [that] I photographed the death of a subject. I had a lot of anxiety about doing it. It is very difficult as a voyeur to go in and look at something just to be looking at it, not actually to be participating in the death process. So I left it until the very end. The person that I was working under at that point said, 'Go ahead and just do it.' So I photographed two autopsies while I was there. . . . After they had taken out the brain and had moved over to look at it, I turned to watch the gross part of that exam, to photograph that. Out of the corner of my eye I saw this body had taken on something. Out of the corner of my eye I saw this death's-head image just staring up at me. I turned around and made that photograph. I saw this image out of the corner of my eye while I was watching them slice the brain and just turned around and took that picture, and it haunted me forever. It was a woman who died of a stroke, the brain has been taken out, the head is tilted up, which created this picture of death [it looks like Edvard Munch's *The Scream*]. When I was on the ship working with Vietnamese refugees and had to do a destructive craniotomy to deliver a [dead fetus], as I was taking the brain out, I actually saw this image; this is a haunting image for me. Doctors look at this stuff all the time. So I think that is part of the medical gaze, how we detach ourselves from that" (interview by author, 1 December 1997).

"These photos are really disturbing. But as an artist, what I want to show you is how I am able to see something that is very beautiful in these very traumatic situations. This scene I call *Lazarus Up from the Dead* (1978). This [thirty-three-year-old] young man [who had fallen off a ladder a year before, broken his neck, and was paralyzed from the neck down] had not been properly cared for in a trailer house and had developed enormous bedsores, these large decubitus ulcers on both of his hips. Look at the nurse. You watch

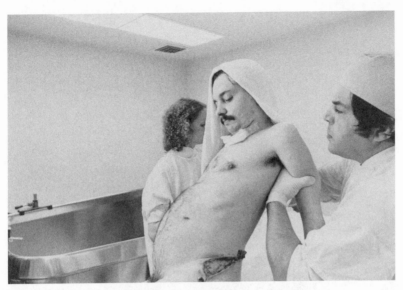

5. *Lazarus Up from the Dead*, 1978. Photograph by Eric Avery.

her drape him as they lift him up. For me, when I saw this happening, I have this background as a Presbyterian, so I have these religious images that come out, and I think this is one of the ways that I've been able to bind up and deal with the trauma that I've been exposed to" (interview by author, 1 December 1997).

Hands Healing demonstrates how photographs can disrupt the detachment of the medical gaze and can intervene in and reframe our self-reflexivity. *Lazarus Up from the Dead* and *Death's Head* demonstrate further how religious, soteriological, and aesthetic images can arise from, and give another meaning to, trauma and suffering. But even more profoundly, Eric cites his teacher Andrew Rush: "Images are not the point of the activity, but are debris, of a very special kind, left behind as artists, in the process of making art, become themselves. Very slowly this positioning has been taking place for me in medicine. Andrew Rush stressed that one puts one's life in a position to allow art to happen" (Avery 1983: 11).

Photography, however, proved to be a more troubled medium than other artwork. "I have a thousand photographic negatives from my Vietnamese work. . . . out in the Anambas Islands, the northernmost islands of Indonesia. We would sail out for ten days [on the World Vision aid boat *Sea Sweep*, based in Singapore] and collect refugees, bring them to the main camp in Penang, be in port four days, then go out for another ten. [MF: These are documentary photographs; did you do artwork there too?] Oh

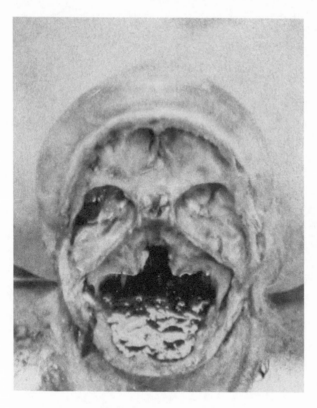

6. *Death's Head*, 1978. Photograph by Eric Avery.

yeah, I did artwork on the boat. I carved this picture of a standing figure, sort of a Gauguin-like image of a woman standing . . . idea of a tombstone or a stele as, you know, a memorial to this young woman who had died on, in my boat.

"[The death of this woman] was pretty soon after I got to [Southeast Asia], and I was on this ship to go out and get our first collection of refugees. . . . And they put me on a jet boat to go to a woman who has childbirth problems, and so I'm [crouched] down in this jet boat, and I'm in my obstetrics [book] going through it like this [mimics panic, flipping pages], and we got to this little island [where] they were drying dead sharks. We walked back to this [thatched hut on stilts], all these people were sitting in this dark room, and I was taken into the back room. And it was a girl about fourteen who had been in labor for three days, her membranes had ruptured, the baby had stopped moving, and it was, you could see it, it was just stuck beyond her pelvis and couldn't get out. And it was dead. . . . My dad had told me about destructive craniotomies that he had had to do a couple of times [saying it was the worst]. I thought, Shit, what am I going to do? . . . We put her on the ship . . . and headed toward an oil platform that had a helicopter that could take her to a hospital that was not too far. It would take a day to get there, so we had to keep her alive. We put her in our infirmary . . . but her blood pressure was really terrible. . . . There was an Indonesian doctor on the ship just for the ride, and he had his midwife with him, who was a man." They decided to do the destructive craniotomy on the dead child to get it out, and try to save the woman, and as they were doing it, Eric again saw "this picture of death I had done earlier at Hershey . . . the skull cut across where the brain had been lifted out, that looked like Edvard Munch's *The Scream*. Flipped me out completely! Just made me want to die." The woman hemorrhaged and died. They took her back home. "The Indonesian sea captain said I need to make a small speech, so I'm standing there with all these people saying how sad, we're sorry, we cried, and they thanked us and we left" (interview by author, 15 May 1998).

"And so by the time I got to Somalia, what I had learned was that in that world, they expect to die in situations like this, and that it was really traumatic for everyone to have her die away from them. . . . When I was in Somalia my experience with the Muslims, certainly in Somalia, was that they had this, I don't know, fatalism or acceptance; you know, it was a recycling of life, that Allah takes, and you know it will all come back. . . . They used to leave their babies under blankets, so we had teams going out, looking under blankets trying to find all these sick babies, because they would just quit feeding them and leave them, and they would just die. I didn't understand any of that. It's upsetting for me to think about all this, even today. . . . I wasn't trained to do this" (interview by author, 15 May 1998).

"A recycling of life, Allah takes, and you know it will all come back . . ." The third or fourth retelling of the trauma of the Indonesian death, amid the pointing out of pictures of people and places from the Indonesia experience, had been in part elicited by my questions about the Chinese-Vietnamese carpenter/contractor that Eric had recently hired to work on his Galveston house. "I would ask Vietnamese people when they came to the U.S., because at some point I [am going to ask], did you ever hear of a ship called *Sea Sweep*, which was the ship I worked on, and one of those people is going to tell me that they were on the ship. . . . He [the contractor] actually had come out of Vietnam early and had been on one of the early boats that was beached on this island called Kuku refugee camp. . . . He was thirteen or fourteen and had been put on a boat by himself. Of the thirty-three people who were on the boat, many had died; thirteen or fourteen were still alive when the boat was beached. . . . And so he told me these stories of this terrible stuff that can happen. He was an unaccompanied minor, so he had to stay in this town for a while, and he described the things he had seen. Terrible things. People had burned some guy on the beach because he was all infested and diseased. Anyway, so I felt there was some connection between this man and me. So he is my contractor." While working on Eric's house, this contractor's girlfriend was killed on a bike by a drunk driver, so Eric went through that with him as well. "We are bonded, makes it hard to complain about his work" (interview by author, 15 May 1998).

The work with the Vietnamese produced many photographs, few artworks. The work in Somalia produced some photos of Eric as a celebrity, a few photos by Eric, especially at the end of his stay, of the healthy children saved, and perhaps a dozen woodcuts done with bits of scavenged plank and Qur'an boards (in a land stripped bare of trees and wood), ranging in subject from landscapes of a famous mountain peak and the coast beyond to examinations of the hell of the refugee camp and its frustrations. Eric was in charge of a feeding program at Las Dhure, a camp near Hargesia with some 40,000 to 72,000 refugees. Some of Eric's most vivid images of Somalia are verbal, from his letters to friends back home, especially to the artists Michael Tracey and Karen Feinberg. "I didn't take pictures of the starving kids, I just couldn't do that, and I in fact did smash my camera and stopped taking photographs, because photographs really separated me from the experience I was having, and I felt I needed to process this whole thing through my body in another way. So I ended up making a lot of woodcuts in this place.... At about three months, I had a complete breakdown. I could barely survive. I had three more months to go. And the way I coped with this was really for the first time in my life making prints that had some connection to how I felt, the materiality of the wood, hammer, and chisel, pounding it out, and I could indulge my imagination and do this—*Nuclear Wish for Las Dhure* (1980)—my wish that this whole place would just be nuked, and just be wiped off the planet" (interview by author, 2 December 1997).

"Here is what I call *The Last Tree in Las Dhure* (1980). People were slowly taking this tree apart. You [would] say, 'You are taking down the tree'; they would say, 'No, I am taking a piece.' And slowly it shrank in pieces" (interview by author, 1 December 1997). The *Life* magazine photograph shows Eric, crouched in jeans, cowboy boots, and rolled-up work shirt, spoon in hand, holding the jaw of a tiny, protesting child, belly bloated, arms raised, skeletally thin legs stretched out on the ground. It was a joint effort by World Vision to raise contributions and *Life* and *National Geographic* to disseminate pictures of starving refugees saved by Western medical heroes. Eric was repelled by this sort of photography: "I did not need to humiliate the refu-

7. *Nuclear Wish for Las Dhure*,
1980. Woodcut on Qur'an
board. Photograph by UTMB
Biocommunications.

gees by capturing them on film in their desperate condition. So instead of
photography, I moved again into the print, the woodcut, and tried to carve
out my experience. Before I left Las Dhure, I spent several days with my camera, looking at aspects of the camp I felt captured some of the dignity and
life of the Somali refugees" (label from his 1982 Galveston show). "Mostly
I photographed the well children, the happy children" (Avery 1982b: 10).
He had a World Vision photographer take some beautiful pictures: of two
boys doing handstands, casting long shadows; two boys wrestling while four
others smile and wave; a striking geometric composition of a line of children walking through a neatly laid out cemetery, graves marked by piles of
stones in a grid pattern; a figure wrapped in a blanket silhouetted against
round huts in the camp against a hazy background.

A 1545 print . . . reminded me of my photograph . . . has a long history
. . . this presence growling out of this dead body with this open mouth

One of the most powerful experiences for many Americans of the postwar generation was living in a different civilizational context during formative early adult years: Peace Corps, anthropological fieldwork, and in Eric's case volunteer medical service, traumatizing work among traumatized people. Freud delineated the temporality of scenes that are recognized only in subsequent contexts, establishing a semiotic chain of reversed causality, the later event causing the imputation of a prior one. The *Death's Head* works in Eric's corpus in an analogous way. Upon his return to Texas, Eric saw a 1545 print from Charles Etienne's *De dissectione partium corporis humani* in a show at the de Menil–funded art gallery at Rice University. "It reminded me in some way about my own image . . . that had really haunted me. . . . I was really interested to find out that . . . [it] is an illustration not of the brain cavity . . . but of the ventricles. . . . [In the 1540s they] believed that animal spirits, animism, lived in these spaces. Then that made my reaction to this historical image clearer in relationship to my own, because this image I'm putting in the show, which I call the *Death's Head*, is a mask of death. It's almost as if there was this presence growling out of this dead body with this open mouth. . . . Posada has a print of a similar kind of large mouth of a beastlike thing. So at that point I began to see that the work I was doing in illustrating aspects of medicine . . . had a long history of illustrations of certain kinds of themes, death in this case" (Avery 1982b: 5). Not just themes but striking continuities of imagery, even if through displacements, as in Eric's San Antonio exhibition poster, *Images of Life and Death* (after Etienne's *De dissectione partium corporis humani*).

I couldn't show the work that I'm showing in the Moody Medical Library
in the public [Rosenberg] library because [a public library] is just not the
place to put up photographs of dead, dying people. . . . In Mexican
tradition, they used skeletons to communicate things about their social
concerns during the revolution.

The shock of returning to the United States was not merely that of leaving refugees, poverty, and strife to reenter a wealthy consumer society; it was intensified by another conflict, of Central American refugees being put into U.S. immigration detention centers in Texas and elsewhere, and by the distance that had grown between Eric and one of his erstwhile patrons and artist friends. Avery began to produce woodcuts using several techniques of

8. *Images of Life and Death*, 1982. San Antonio exhibition poster (after Etienne's *De dissectione partium corporis humani*). Offset print from linoleum cut. Photograph by UTMB Biocommunications.

overlay, transforming source images and struggling for a vision that does not accept the complacency of American perspectives on the world, or the ideologies of the Reagan-Bush policies. The images shift from intense melancholy (self-portrait), skeletons, and death images that invade and overprint

9. *Me*, 1983. Linoleum block print. Photograph by UTMB Biocommunications.

other, especially Renaissance, images; to a new run of documentary photographs — perhaps in the Jacob Riis tradition — exposing the Immigration and Naturalization Service's prisons and camps of poor refugees from war in Central America, invisible to the American majority population; to bitter satirical portraits of figures such as Jesse Helms, George Bush, and even George Washington; to brilliant multicolored prints that transform famous older paintings.

For a brief moment, the fourth group of these images seemed poised to catapult Eric Avery into the collectors' art market — and, indeed, his prints are in the Library of Congress, the Walker Art Center in Minneapolis, the Chase Manhattan Bank in New York, the Fogg Museum at Harvard, and elsewhere. Then the AIDS epidemic retraumatized the artistic process with images that people would rather not have in their living rooms or uptown galleries. Eric responded with a new form of action art, "institutional therapy" to provide public education in the maelstrom of the AIDS panic and

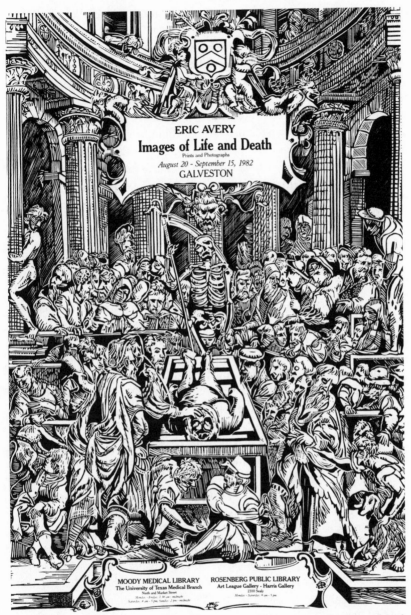

10. *After Vesalius' Anatomy Lesson*, 1982. Galveston exhibition poster for *Images of Life and Death*. Offset print from linoleum cut. Photograph by UTMB Biocommunications.

to protest the reduction of doctoring in the health system's managed care revolution.

In 1982 Eric did a split-location show in Galveston. In the Moody Medical Library, for a medical humanities audience, Eric created five sets of images for medical students, doctors, and other practitioners to meditate on their battles with death. The complementary Rosenberg Public Library exhibit was addressed to the civic politics of refugees. Triggered by the massacres in Central America, using linoleum prints but incorporating earlier photographs of medicine in Hershey, the poster for the double show was titled *After Vesalius' Anatomy Lesson* (1982). The image shows a classical rotunda with medieval folk crowding around a dissection table with the Grim Reaper at one end, and substituting for Vesalius's cadaver is the one from Hershey with its skull open *(Death's Head)*.

"Walk into the [Moody Medical Library]," Eric wrote to a friend, "and you are confronted with two 16-by-20 images of the *Death's Head* photos. . . . Around the corner are the black-and-white linocuts" (letter, 27 August 1982). "The first set, a group of linoleum prints, is images of skeletons: dancing skeletons, swimming skeletons that I've overprinted over reproductions of art by various people. Basically they are Renaissance paintings. . . . The start of this was really set off by reading about massacres in El Salvador. . . . *Rio Sumpul Massacre* . . . is something I read about in the press, about government forces going into a town, taking innocent people basically and shooting them in the village, but taking children to a cliff overlooking this river, and throwing the children off the cliff and using them for targets to shoot. . . . I thought, Well, I will just do a series of images of death, call it *Dance of Death* using Hans Holbein's series called *Dance of Death* as a model. But instead of turning more to a European example of art, I am using a Mexican printmaker from the early part of this century called Posada. . . . He worked in Mexico City doing zinc relief prints for newspapers, posters, and things like that. In the Mexican tradition they used skeletons to communicate things about their social concerns during the revolution. . . . The reason I put this first in the medical library is to just deal with the fact of art as image, art as picture, an image on a piece of paper, and to use the idea of social concern as a subject matter" (Avery 1982b: 2). The *Rio Sumpul Massacre* print takes a Christ on the Cross reproduction and overlays silhouettes of two men with rifles shooting men and women, a skeleton figure below.

"It was the first print I ever made where I worked on top of another image" (interview by author, 1 December 1998). Another linocut takes a bucolic scene of a canoe being paddled down the Missouri — George Bingham's painting *Fur Traders Descending the Missouri* — and overprints it with "skele-

11. *Rio Sumpul Massacre, El Salvador, 1981.* Linoleum block overprint. Photograph by UTMB Biocommunications.

tons coming up out of the water, going into the sky, and circling around the black sun." A third overprints Brueghel's *The Harvesters*. "I took the wheat and turned it into skeletons. It is a harvest of death. The people lying underneath the tree having their lunch in the painting, I've turned into skeletons. Then the tree: it is a tree of death. It is a tree that skeletons are springing out of and flying out into the sky" (Avery 1982b: 2). Juxtaposed to these prints, done in Vermont during the summer of 1981, are photographic images of death (from 1978 in Hershey).

But they do not show people in the act of dying. Rather, like the linoprints, they expose death's semiotic, syntactic, metaphoric, and symbolic structures: the "death's-head" of the stroke victim; the "shell of the body" left empty by a terminal lung cancer patient who had refused treatment; the

Lazarus Up from the Dead, paralyzed from a fall, being helped up from his bed. The death of a beloved pet provides another set of photographs: "I'm putting it [the *Dog Death* series] in the show [so] . . . a medical student can be reminded of his own experiences of, say, the death of a pet, and use that to reexamine some of his beliefs about death . . . as a humanistic tool that I'm trying to develop" (Avery 1982b: 7).

The Rosenberg Public Library exhibits focused instead on the plight of refugees from Ogaden province of Ethiopia in Somalia and from Central America in South Texas. "Get in your car and drive to the public library. Enter it and you see the open door to the downstairs gallery. Left turn and you've got a beautiful four-and-a-half-foot panorama of the Las Dhure refugee camp. . . . Then you proceed through the sick and dying, to the feces, to the roll of toilet paper reading 'Somali River' mounted in a Plexiglas box. Then through the trees to the cemetery, to the people. There is this beautiful sequence of five eleven-by-fourteen print images of the houses. . . . The last wall is two woodcuts, landscapes of the camp, with Qur'an board cuts mounted underneath. Then my three woodcuts of Lovers' Peak along the north coast. Next is nuclear blast large woodcut on pink paper. Last sequence shows my health education class and my interpreter. Then two portraits of me as honcho who survived" (letter, 27 August 1982).

"I'd love for some medical students to see my Somalia show and become interested in going out . . . and wanting to work in . . . some place foreign. . . . You gain a kind of understanding about other people and life that there's absolutely no way you can get if you go from college to John Sealy Hospital and then to Dickinson to work in your office" (Avery 1982b: 11–12).

Upstairs the show turns to America, continuing the skeleton motif, but gradually with more of a Posada-inspired style and biting political satire. The beauty of Eric's beloved house and grapefruit orchard on the Rio Grande in the town of San Ygnacio is figured by overprinting Picasso's *Demoiselles d'Avignon* with skeletons. Based on a Goya source image, *Tyranny* is depicted as a monstrous mouth in which a firing squad shoots a man as three figures cover their eyes and ears, a skull and crossbones nearby. A Mexican *papel picado* Day of the Dead silhouette format depicts five skeletons (Nicaragua, Honduras, El Salvador, Guatemala, Mexico) being dragged into hell by El Satano (the United States), with "Nicaragua" (the Sandanistas) broken away. *Death Gives Birth to Beauty* shows a skeletal Marilyn Monroe with a child descending headfirst under her billowing skirts (based on Botticelli's *Birth of Venus*). There are two striking self-portraits: one of Eric melting with melancholy; the other, done after this show, a mirror image of Goya's *Sleep of Reason Produces Monsters* showing the seated artist slumped over

12. *Demoiselles d'Avignon de San Ygnacio*, 1983. Linoleum block print. Photograph by UTMB Biocommunications.

13. *Tyranny* (after Goya's *The Third of May, 1808*), 1983. Linoleum block print. Photograph by UTMB Biocommunications.

14. *History*, 1983. Linoleum block print. Photograph by Adam Reich.

15. *Death Gives Birth to Beauty*, 1982. Linoleum block
print. Photograph by UTMB Biocommunications.

16. *The Sleep of Reason from Behind*, 1986. Linoleum block print over silk screen. Photograph by Roger Haile.

his table as bats fly up. In Eric's version, the viewer is positioned inside the Goya image, looking out at the monsters of our time.

These monsters would develop in two directions: angry satires of *The Face of Liberty* (Gilbert Stuart's portrait of George Washington overprinted with skeletal bones); of George Bush's mouth *(Read My Lips)*, produced in protest against the Immigration and Naturalization Service's incarceration and deportation of refugees back to face death; of Jesse Helms (*It's Your Turn, Jesse, Federally Funded Health Care for Senators* [1990]) being given the Robert Mapplethorpe treatment, an old-fashioned steel protoscope instead of a whip in the rectum. The other direction would be bold multicolored wood block prints that transform older images.

An attempt to get my artist friends to pay attention to this
social history of printmaking

A transitional yet signature piece is the 1984 *Massacre of the Innocents*, a three-by-six-foot linoleum cut, not yet in bold multiple prime colors. It is one of the pieces owned by Harvard's Fogg Museum. It is "a readaptation of a very small, very famous sixteenth-century print by Marcantonio Raimondi" (interview by author, 1 December 1997). Eric has replaced the Italian buildings on either side of a bridge in front of which the naked, vulnerable innocents are caught: on one side of the river border is a Mexican church; on the other, modern American skyscrapers. "It's what I started learning about when I moved back to the southern border: there was this huge refugee thing happening with people coming up from Central America, coming up through Mexico, and they began ending up in detention centers thirty miles from my house. So now I was next to a refugee camp in the U.S." (interview by author, 1 December 1997). The source image by Raimondi "is Herod killing all the male children, trying to kill Christ. . . . So I took this image and just recycled it into a print of a massacre in a more contemporary setting. I was going to put Central American clothes on these people and get a real contemporary scene of a massacre. But then since so few people knew the source image, and when I learned about this print, I learned that it was for about three hundred years one of the most important images in Western art. It was used as a model for structure, for expression in the body. It was used as a model for artists for three hundred years. Most everybody that I knew, all my artist friends, had never seen it. So I thought I'll just recycle this print so that contemporary people can get educated about this historical image that had a big function. I just switched the context a little bit, made it more current by changing the background scene. . . .

"Marcantonio Raimondi was Raphael's printmaker. Raphael set up the first print shop to make copies of things that could be sold to a large audience. This is one of the roots of printmaking: to make images that were available for middle-class people. So as the middle class developed, they needed ways to sell pictures of the saints and virgins, and stuff like that, that people

17. *Massacre of the Innocents* (after Raimondi), 1984. Linoleum block print. Photograph by Roger Haile.

couldn't afford to have the painters paint them pictures. So there is this industry developed to generate objects for a marketplace." The tactics of prints like *Rio Sumpul Massacre* (1981) and *Massacre of the Innocents* (1984) were "an attempt to get my artist friends to pay attention to this: I overprinted on a historical image which the artists were interested in" (interview by author, 2 December 1997).

She had this strategy for artwork that doesn't
really function in the art world.

One of the artists Eric failed to keep as a patron and friend was the well-known Texas artist Michael Tracey, "notorious [for] very large abstract paintings and for wild parties. . . . He had a big beard, [was] homosexual, a notorious drinker . . . [had a] reputation [for] throwing blood around on [canvases]. . . . He also owned a seaman's bar for commercial sex workers . . . he was just really notorious. . . . We became real close friends. . . . He is an incredible cook, an incredible entertainer, very successful in the art world, has traveled all over, knows everything about art, very strong ideas about things. . . . He was probably the last artist [the de Menils] really collected, because he's real Catholic, and he does these real tragic Mark Rothko sort of very abstract gold fields with blood." Tracey played an important mentoring role for Eric ever since they had been introduced by the surgeon Burke Evans

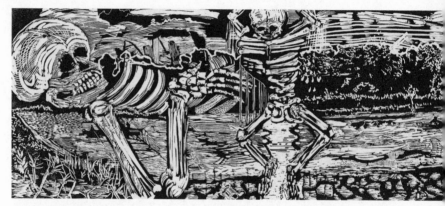

18. *View across the Rio Grande, the River of Death, from San Ygnacio, Tejas*, 1983. Linoleum block print. Photograph by Roger Haile.

when Eric was in medical school. Tracey left Galveston for San Ygnacio because "just too many people were visiting him. . . . He also wanted to live close to Mexico . . . his imagery is all infused with religious swords stabbed in hearts and bleeding open wounds. . . . When I needed to move out of New York and needed to move back to Texas, while I was waiting to work with World Vision, Michael had a house that I moved into. . . . When I left to go to Indonesia, I left from San Ygnacio. When I came back from Africa . . . I came back to San Ygnacio, all my stuff was there. . . . What actually happened when I got back to San Ygnacio, I went into a real deep depression . . . and Michael really helped me channel it into my art making. He encouraged me to take the work I'd made in Somalia and in Singapore and on the ship . . . and show it. So I took it down to Galveston, to my old medical school. . . . That was my first real show in Texas. . . . People in Houston became more interested in my work, and then I took my work to New York" (interview by author, 15 May 1998).

And yet Eric began to feel a kind of falseness in Tracey's relation to what was happening on the ground. Tracey "is an abstract artist . . . does big projects that involve a lot of people in large rituals. You know it is very high-romantic artist-hero kind of stuff: me against all the bad stuff happening in the Third World. . . . This was a big paradox, I couldn't understand it. During the whole Central American crisis, with all the refugees coming, the sanctuary movement, the murder of Archbishop Oscar Romero . . . Michael had this huge profile as an artist who was addressing that problem . . . his cross in the de Menil Museum: a gold leaf cross on a pyramid base, and the cross is penetrated with old Mexican and Spanish swords, and hanging from it are

all these *milagros*. That piece was in the installation dealing with the death of Oscar Romero, with the Stations of the Cross, painted with blood. . . . But he had absolutely no connection to what was really happening to these people who were coming across the border" (interview by author, 2 December 1997). Eric became involved in founding a Laredo chapter of Amnesty International but could not get Tracey involved. Their paths split in acrimony when Tracey felt that Eric's criticisms might threaten his image and his Texas art market.

So while Michael Tracey entertained the rich with neoexpressionist and ritualized art events, Eric and three Laredo activist women (Norma Cantu, Rosa Trevino, and Geri Sisco), joined shortly by the artist Anne Wallace, formed a chapter of Amnesty International U.S.A. in Laredo, and then the Laredo Refugee Assistance Council thirty miles from San Ygnacio. Eric had bought a two-room stone house in Ygnacio, Casa del los Cuates ("house of the twin sisters" who had made tortillas for the town). His front yard was a block from the Rio Grande. A photograph of the bend in the river shows a flat, desolate scrub horizon on both sides, but an arresting black-and-white woodcut shows a different reality. Called *View across the Rio Grande, the River of Death, from San Ygnacio, Tejas* (1983), it has two skeletons on the left and three figures with guns on the right, with Michael Tracey, Henry Estrada (Michael's lover), and Eric reclining and overlooking the river scene. One skeleton is prone, another is jumping in a *danse macabre*; the river is studded with dark shoals. Bodies would occasionally float down the Rio Grande and wash ashore in San Ygnacio. They were buried in the pauper section of the cemetery in unmarked graves.

In February 1989 the INS began rejecting all Salvadoran, Guatemalan, and Honduran political asylum applications and 96 percent of those from

Nicaraguans. Applicants were also not allowed to travel outside the border region. Within days, five thousand refugees were detained in a tent city in Bay View, further downriver from San Ygnacio, near Brownsville, Texas. Thousands of refugees were suddenly sleeping on the streets of Brownsville: 300 in cardboard and plastic garbage bag tents across from the Casa Oscar Romero—a sanctuary shelter where Stacy Merkt worked (arrested for moving refugees through an underground railroad)—until the owner of the field asked the sheriff to evict them; 250 in a condemned motel without heat, water, or sanitary facilities (until the city ordered the building sealed); hundreds more outside the INS building in Harlingen. Twelve hundred refugees were held in a former agricultural research laboratory (never tested for chemical residues from pesticides), and eight hundred in a Red Cross shelter (paid $3 million not to kick up a fuss about splitting families and preventing people from moving freely). In Laredo, four facilities were used for detention: a 270-bed facility was run by the Corrections Corporation of American (CCA), a private corporation registered in Tennessee; three were run by Webb County (beds for four hundred men on an old military radar station; two hundred places for Cuban refugees in the jail; a juvenile detention center for El Salvadoran youths). The bonds set were the highest in the nation ($7,500 for Central Americans; $20,000 for others), and there were almost no pro bono attorneys to help the refugees.

Conditions in these centers were not good, not in accord with legal regulations: Refugees were given no information about their legal or human rights or means of action for filing claims for political asylum. There was unpredictable access to immigration judges. Hearings were held, not individually but in groups of up to twenty-four by nationality. Telephone access was limited; library facilities either were lacking entirely or had no Spanish-language legal aid materials, only the Bible in Spanish. The food was poor. Beatings occurred. Released detainees were dropped six miles from Laredo with no telephone or transportation facilities.

Eric produced a series of documentary photographs and two important large woodblock prints. A few narrative threads can remind one of the intensity of the times: (1) dramatic events such as a hunger strike by forty-four Haitians and four Jamaicans at the CCA facility in January 1990; (2) case materials developed by Anne Wallace screening detainees with a paralegal assistant from Project Libertad for referral to organizations that could help them move to regions with better assistance, church sponsors, and chances for asylum (the Underground Railroad, the East San Francisco Bay Sanctuary Covenant, the Ano Program, Jubilee Partners), as well as psychiatric interviews done by Eric urging relief for those suffering from post-traumatic stress disorders; (3) legal actions such as the temporary restraining order against INS in February 1989 allowing ten days of emergency exodus of 2,500 Nicaraguans to Miami by Greyhound buses, and Salvadorans and Guatemalans to Houston, Los Angeles, and New York; the suit against INS by the Texas Department of Human Services to stop the illegal housing of minors in the CCA facility; and filings to block the use of Laredo by the INS as a fast-track deportation staging arena because of the lack of local pro bono legal representation; (4) the drama of the sanctuary movement's mobilization of churches to sponsor refugees; and (5) the dramatic statistics of refugees deported or turned back following the directives of the Reagan administration: 17,000 Central American refugees were arrested in 1986, a sixfold increase from 1982; $1,000 bonds were introduced in 1986, raised to $3,000 in 1987, and to $7,500 in 1988, while at the same time bonding companies withdrew until in 1988 only one was left and was charging a 50 percent fee. Even Nicaraguan asylum applications, which were more favorably treated, dropped from an 84 percent approval rate (1,867 granted, 357 denied) in 1987 to 53 percent (2,686 granted, 2,455 denied) in 1988, and to 24 percent in 1989. In fiscal year 1989, forced returnees to Central America included 199 Nicaraguans, 4,731 Salvadorans, 4,035 Guatemalans, 3,168 Hondurans, and 5,472 Haitians.

Eric produced a photographic record of what look like a gulag of prisons and concentration camps not just in Texas but reaching to Manhattan and across the United States. A map of Texas shows some thirty known refugee detention centers. In one photograph Eric captures a scene simultaneously stereotyped, comic, and sad: it is a portrait of *La Migra*, a very fat, double-chinned, uniformed INS officer holding the Amnesty International publication describing abuses of refugee rights in the United States, *Reasonable Fear: Human Rights and American Refugee Policy*. Another photo shows the CCA facility: a fenced, sterile, white, windowless building in the middle of nowhere.

"This was my local refugee camp. It looks like a prison. In fact, I think we have criminalized the treatment of refugees. Amnesty's concern wasn't really with the refugees per se, but with those fleeing for their lives, because if they would be deported ('refouled' in legalese) and tortured or extrajudicially mistreated or killed, they would become prisoners of conscience, thus our clients. You try to stop that. So this was our local detention center. I got to know the director really well ['a Mexican American man, we played golf together' (interview by author, 28 November 1997)], and he felt what he was doing was good and right and was very happy to show this place off. So we were able to tour almost the entire hierarchy of Amnesty International

U.S.A. through this facility, which really then began to wake people up to what was happening in our own country. We were also able to take Amnesty International U.S.A. members through this very large Port Isabel Processing Center down in the tip of Texas [called *El Corralon* by the inmates, it held 2,184 people]. These people, their crime was crossing the border. Of course, they didn't apply for asylum in their own countries because of the real discriminatory practice favoring refugee applicants from former Soviet client states. . . . How could refugees be fleeing a country where the U.S.A. was supporting the government and training the soldiers? . . .

"Driving down the road, you wouldn't know this, but this [another photo] was a children's detention center for unaccompanied minors, a former nursing home. . . . Most of Amnesty staff and members thought this was just a problem in the southern United States, so we did some investigation: seven blocks from Amnesty's office, on the seventh floor of this office building [another photo] on Varrick Street [across from the Houston Street stop], is the facility for Manhattan. So we began rubbing Amnesty's faces in it. Here's another facility in Brooklyn. We began organizing members of Amnesty in the United States to find out where refugees were being held, often in jails, and so we began making maps. I was living in Immigration District 14: we had nine facilities in 1989; there were seven facilities in District 40. So we started making maps. Jails were being used, private corporations, [one of which] was running [the one near my house]. . . . We toured these places with all these Amnesty volunteers, which is, of course, the best way to educate people, to take them in and show them. . . . Amnesty was part of the mobilization against those policies, and I think we did play a small part in changing them" (interview by author, 1 December 1997).

A contact sheet shows scenes from the Harlingen and Brownsville detention centers, taken during Asylum Summer, an effort to introduce university students who were members of the university Amnesty International U.S.A. chapters to refugee work. This was a first for Amnesty International U.S.A.: to do direct work with students in places where abuses were happening. Eric and Anne were involved in setting up and then training the students. They led workshops at these meetings, including art exhibits.

"A lot of cultural work was being done by artists . . . and refugees were also picturing their own stuff. So we did art shows for Amnesty at regional meetings, at national meetings. There was a big mobilization by artists around that, just as there has been around AIDS. And . . . I would exhibit my own work. I made these two big prints.

"One was about the death penalty, and the other was from work with the refugees. When the death penalty was restarted in Texas in the 1980s, I was present for the execution of Johnny Garrett. You know, it was this scene in Huntsville with a lot of local people standing under this big tree chanting, 'Kill, kill, kill the freak who killed the nun!' This was a mentally retarded person. The pope had actually gotten involved to try to stop the execution. . . . Mandy Bath, a researcher for Amnesty International, came from London and wrote about this event. And I did this large woodcut for the Fort Worth Museum of Art. I was commissioned with a group of artists to make a print for their museum for an exhibit. This would be another example where I felt I was making something really important, and as it turns out, I made something that nobody wanted, certainly at the high levels of the art world.

"But I had this print photographically reduced and made into a metal letterpress block, which I printed by hand in large numbers on my Van der Kook proofing press. I sold these for twenty dollars at Amnesty events to support our work. It continues to be sold. It is called *Johnny Garrett Is Dead*" (interview by author, 2 December 1997).

Eric attributes this tactic of selling reduced prints to Sue Coe, the Liverpool-born New York artist known for her animal rights work, especially the series *Dead Meat* (1996), her visual journalism for the *Village Voice*, and more recently for her work with *The X-Files* television series. "She had a strategy for taking artwork that doesn't really function in the art world. . . . The strategy that she taught me was when I do my talks, and when I travel around, I need to take my prints. Then I take the original image and photomechanically have a block made from it, or a reduced version, a smaller version, and then print those up in large editions that can be sold for ten or twenty dollars. What Sue does with hers is give half the money to the local causes that she is supporting. In my case, at the Fogg Museum, half of what I make is going to the Fogg, and the rest I am giving to my studio assistant who does the printing. . . . That puts the print in the hands of people who want this work. A rich person might not spend five hundred dollars for the piece, but the same image sells a lot at twenty to a whole different group of people who buy it and put it in their homes. . . . And so when I travel around . . . people will come up and say that they own a piece of mine, and how they value that. . . .

"Sue thinks that she sees this work functioning in culture, not just in documenting what is happening, but actually educating and helping to change things. And so it helped me . . . really try to direct [my work] back at the public. And Sue is the one for me who used the words that I am a cultural worker, that I'm working just like a day laborer works, that . . . even though it is a great pleasure for me to make my work, that it is labor and that I need pay for that and not give it away to people. She has helped me understand that. My class background is upper-middle-class . . . a bit higher in my father's family, [and so] my values [had] come out of an understanding of artwork that is much more decorative and something that you accumulate, that shows you have wealth, more than [the artwork] actually functioning" (interview by author, 2 December 1997).

Better to face the sharks of the sea than the jaws of Duvalier

The other important large print addressing the issue of refugees is the multicolored *U.S.A. Dishonor and Disrespect (Haitian Interdiction, 1981–1994)*. It is a tour de force reworking of one of America's most famous ideological paintings, J. S. Copley's *Watson and the Shark* (1778), also using two other famous European source images, Rembrandt's *The Storm on the Sea of Galilee* (1633) and Théodore Géricault's *Raft of the Medusa* (1818–1819). Watson, a Tory merchant, commissioned Copley to paint the scene of his rescue by an African American seaman after Watson had fallen into the Havana waters and lost a leg to a shark. He instructed Copley that the seaman be placed in the central position for having saved his life by throwing him a line. Although often claimed to be the first celebratory portrait of an African American in U.S. art, the painting was meant on the contrary to be a political allegory, a Tory warning that American independence might lead to the emancipation of slaves and the overturning of the social order.

Eric inverts Copley's politics. His print is in protest against the racist discrimination of the Reagan policies. Avery names the boat *Honore Respet*, the greeting of solidarity in Haiti under Duvalier. "In the detention center in Laredo . . . these Haitians were being detained. They spoke Creole and French. Laredo was Spanish-speaking. Nobody could talk to them. These Haitians had a saying, 'Better to face the sharks of the sea than the jaws of Duvalier.' People would actually threaten to throw their children off into the water so that they wouldn't have to be sent back to Haiti. I packed that understanding that I had of what was happening with the Haitians [into this print].

"The interdiction program was really set up after a bunch of bodies washed up in front of one of the hotels in Miami Beach which is the background scene for this print. And they had three blimps watching for small planes smuggling drugs across the border. There is a blimp in the print [that] comes from a photograph of what was happening around that time" (interview by author, 1 December 1997). Jane Petro recalls, "The U.S. government was denying that they were removing people from the U.S. waters and returning them to Haiti without appropriate hearings. My secretary's father

19. *U.S.A. Dishonor and Disrespect (Haitian Interdiction, 1981–1994)*, 1991. Linoleum block printed on seven-color lithograph by Mark Atwood, at Tamarind Institute, Albuquerque, New Mexico. Photograph by UTMB Biocommunications.

was sitting on the beach in Miami in 1991, and a boat came onto the beach; the police . . . put the people back into the boat, and the Coast Guard came and towed the boat off the beach while all these tourists were sitting there" (interview by author, 1 December 1997). Eric's print shows a Haitian boat being towed away from the Miami beach by a Coast Guard boat, passengers falling overboard, an interdiction helicopter and surveillance blimp above.

After receiving 35,000 to 45,000 Haitians by boat between 1971 and 1981, after the Mariel boat lift of 120,000 Cuban asylum seekers in 1980, and after a flood of Haitians sought to follow suit, President Ronald Reagan issued an executive order in 1981 to intercept at sea, with the possibility of interviewing at sea on Coast Guard boats. Of 21,361 Haitians interviewed at sea between 1981 and 1990, only eight were granted admission to the United States. In January 1990, a thirty-foot wooden sailboat carrying forty-eight Haitians sank in rough seas off the coast of Miami as the occupants were being transferred to the U.S. Coast Guard cutter *Thetis* to be returned to Haiti. INS officer Mike Rodriguez determined that they were economic, not political, refugees. (Two more persons, according to the passengers, may have drowned.) A few months later, in July 1990, thirty-nine persons drowned when a Bahamian Defense Force boat intercepted and towed a Haitian boat, raising cries of protest from the U.S. Committee for Refugees and allegations of U.S. violation of the United Nations charter's right of individuals to seek asylum and failure to treat Haitians with dignity and respect. Early in 1984, a boat carrying some seventy to ninety persons sank when it was boarded by the U.S. Coast Guard: six bodies were recovered, and sixty-three persons survived.

I found the image torn out of a book in Mexico City in a market.

Avery made two more prints while working for Amnesty International, one against the Bush administration's Gulf War, the other a satirical comment on the quincentenary celebrations of Columbus's discovery of America, both using source images found in Mexico.

As President Bush geared up for the Gulf War, Eric made a three-by-six-foot silk screen with a linocut overprint on paper. "They were calling it the 'Mother of All Battles,' so I made a print called *Our Father of War*, which is a chimera. The chimera was a multiheaded monster . . . and so I've got [as three of its heads] Bush's face, [General Norman] Schwarzkopf's face, and [Secretary of State James] Baker's face" (interview by author, 15 May 1998). The source image is Jean Louis Desprez's eighteenth-century etching of the chimera, born in the "burning sands of the Sahara" and said to live in the

20. *America Discovers Columbus, 1492–1992.* Inked wooden bowl before printing. Photograph by UTMB Biocommunications.

ruins of the palace of Masinissa (c. 240–148 B.C.E.), whence it sallies forth to feed on animals and unwary travelers. "I didn't know any of this stuff when I found the image torn out of a book in Mexico City in a market. I just saved it, and when I was thinking of making an image about the Iran-Iraq war, I thought of this image. I was in Austin at the University of Texas, where I did the silk screen as a visiting artist. The print curator said, 'Oh, that's Desprez's *Chimera*' and gave me information [about it]. . . . I took off its breasts and put on testicles [and a missile-like phallus and put the American colors on its back]. . . . The Fogg owns this print. It is how Jerri Cohen found me: she saw the postcard [of the print]" (interview by author, 15 May 1998).

For the quincentennial, Eric made a twenty-four-by-thirty-inch commemorative cast paper wood-cut bowl, *America Discovers Columbus, 1492–1992* (1992). Drawing on Diego Rivera murals in Mexico City, and fitting in with the countercelebratory mood of many Mexican and Mexican American artists, the woodcut shows a prostrate Columbus being stabbed in the heart by a jaguar-costumed man. The image was carved into a large shallow wood bowl that Eric bought in Nuevo Laredo, Mexico. The sale of both the wood bowl and the commemorative paper bowl print (which were on display in the 1992 Boston Museum of Fine Arts show *Outspoken and Handcrafted*) to Eric's friend and supporter Jane Petro enabled him to move back to Galveston.

Clinton got elected, things changed on the border. . . . The art world
collapsed. . . . I was broke and wondered if I could return to . . .
medicine, perhaps to work with AIDS.

"I did this [work for Amnesty International] for eight years . . . I burned out.
. . . At the end, I got to go to the International Council Meeting in Yokohama,
where 'sexual orientation' was introduced as a new category of prisoner of
conscience, and then traveled on to Pakistan with the chairwoman of the
board of directors of Amnesty International U.S.A. . . . Then Clinton got
elected, things changed on the border, there was no pro bono Refugee Assistance Council in Laredo. The art world collapsed. . . . I was broke and
wondered if I could return to the practice of medicine, perhaps to work with
AIDS. I was doing continuing medical education in Laredo. One day Mike
Fuller, a consult-liaison psychiatrist from Galveston, rode up on a motor-
cycle and gave a brilliant talk on HIV. I went up and talked with him, saying
I once was a doctor but had not practiced for a while, and was doing art, and
wanted to return to the practice of medicine. He said he loved my artwork
and that I should come and work with them in Galveston. I got a fellowship to retrain for a year and a half in Galveston. The first six months was an
ordeal: anxiety [once again overwhelmed], I felt I didn't know what I was
doing" (interview by author, 1 December 1997).

The image was so frightening . . . if I actually cut the woodcut,
I might get AIDS.

"It was when I first started working and was massaging the feet of one of my
patients who had Kaposi's sarcoma. I was afraid that I was going to get it.
I think a lot of us who work with HIV have this fear of contagion. It really
does affect our lives, our personal lives. I've done a series of blue prints. The
Whitney bought a set of these prints. When they took one of them into their
acquisition meeting, they said, 'This is a smallpox [image],' and they said,
'It's a print of hope.' So the title is *Blue Smallpox, the Print of Hope* (1994),
which for me is the viral scourge [around which] people organized and were
able to remove it" (interview by author, 1 December 1997). The source image
of the print is the life-size plague-Christ in the Issenheim altarpiece, Col-
mar, France (carved in 1512–1516). Another print using an image from the
Black Death is a skull and crossbones used to indicate a house where plague
had been present. Eric's version is a stark black-and-white woodcut printed
on Mexican wrapping paper patterned with a field of flowers, producing a
double powerful effect. "I drew it out on a piece of wood in the eighties, and

21. *Not the Feet of the One and Only*, 1994. Linoleum block print. Photograph by UTMB Biocommunications.

underneath it wrote 'AIDS,' and that image was so frightening to me that I thought if I actually cut the woodcut I might get AIDS, and so I couldn't, I didn't cut this image for years, just kept it turned to the wall, it was so frightening to me. Of course, this whole risk of being exposed and all that. I'm HIV negative. I've certainly been in places where I could have been exposed except I didn't do the right things to get it. I'm a failed homosexual in that way. So I was really always afraid that I might end up getting HIV. . . . I called it *1984* after George Orwell's *1984*. I drew it in 1984, and carved it later in 1992" (interview by author, 2 November 1997).

The other effect was of ephemeralness. "It is a sort of memento mori . . . David Becker, a collector and former curator of the Fogg print room, bought this print on wrapping paper at the Mary Ryan Gallery [in New York]. I was present when he was buying it, and I said, 'Don't buy that one, David, because it is going to fade. You put it in the sun, it's going to disappear.' He then bought it . . . and when he gave it to Bowdoin College, where he is depositing his collection, he wrote in the text that he bought it because it would fade, [that] it seemed to be a metaphor for the whole HIV and life and death during the fading. So he bought it because of the defect in how it was made" (interview by author, 2 November 1997).

Ephemeral art can be technically self-consuming. It can be metaphorically of the order of still life that marks the passage of time, of decay, of the fragility and temporality of life. It can also be of the ritual order of sacred sand paintings: of the Hopi, of the Australian Aborigines, of Jain colored-sand mandalas and devotional murals, but also of the happening, the art installation, and what Eric would come to call "clinical art space." As Jane Petro pointed out, what Somalia (and the disgust with journalist photographers' handling of the suffering of refugee children) did to Eric's work was that he "gave up any sense of permanency. Most of what you made in Somalia you printed on tents that would disappear in the wind, and on really fragile paper. And you sent me some things which I had framed, and you were angry that I had framed them, because they were supposed to be transient" (interview by author, 1 December 1997). Art actions and installations, too, are ephemeral or made partly permanent only through photographs and video recordings. As institutional therapy, they are educational and political, requiring timing and tact, and are no less anxiety inducing.

Gay people buy the Warren Hadler retablo with the words "We are with you," . . . AIDS workers buy the Summer Boogie Woogie retablo.

From European altars, Eric turned to Mexican ones and to the *retablo* for a suite of stunning multicolored lithographs overprinted with woodcuts. The first was patterned after a retablo Eric bought in San Luis Potosi, Mexico, and was done as an homage to Warren Hadler, a well-known gallery owner in Houston, who was also Michael Tracey's dealer. "He died of AIDS real early, and I made this and gave it to him before he died. He had it with him in his house. The image [depicts] his gallery [with Hadler on a couch]: two Michael Traceys are on the wall; Cézanne's *Great Bather* (1897); a piece by the sculptor David Smith; this would be my mother, with little [HIV-infected] lymphocytes on her dress, praying for healing; and a Miró. . . . the blue [is] a connection to the blue in [*Blue Smallpox* and] in the other prints [in this suite]" (interview by author, 15 May 1998). Eric calls it *Healing before Art*, and it became the first in a series following the seasons.

A print after Albrecht Dürer's *Bath House* (1496) shows the site of play and infection. It is both a commentary on the gay bathhouses of the 1980s and also an invocation of a gay reading of Dürer's original image. Dürer's image "has been interpreted as a homosexual spoof print. In it Dürer has a self-portrait: he is leaning on a water post with a spigot coming out, and there are all these phallic references. They are all men in this bathhouse: there's Bacchus drinking, and these are all identified friends of Dürer. . . .

It would be real shocking . . . and funny. So I took that image and adapted it" (interview by author, 15 May 1998). Eric has placed himself and a lover in the left corner; tiles from the Sanborn House in Mexico City are also on the left; a horned older man wraps himself around a younger man holding a corkscrew; a tree looks like a body; Dürer's Bacchus on the right remains, as does the post with the spigot in the center left, spilling out blue into the pool. The spilling blue has several references, a primal one being an image of contagion, like the mist in the film *The Ten Commandments*, flowing through the streets, killing everyone except those who have smeared lamb's blood on their doorposts. *Blue Bath* is the spring of playful, transgressive joy before the epidemic.

Spring is followed by *Summer Boogie Woogie*, a homage to the physician Robert Campbell as he lay dying of AIDS. Based on the Austrian expressionist Ferdinand Holder's *The Night*, Avery's print depicts a man under a sheet with something else. Here the scene is reworked for south Texas: hot sun comes in through the window, the unwanted visitor, Death, is under a Mexican blanket, a Coors beer bottle holds the window open, and Eric's head in the doorway watches over his friend.

Max Beckmann's *Morgue* (1915 and 1922) provides the source image for grief spilling over in the fall (*As It Is*). Death appears in many guises. The stroke victim cadaver, source of Eric's *Death's Head*, lies on a morgue table. On another is a cancer victim, and to the left is Eric's *Gag Reflex* (1990) (recycled in *Portrait of George Bush's Mouth, Read My Throat* [1991]), from the Amnesty period. To the right is a heart attack victim, and above, images of dead babies from Africa. While doctors and technicians in green scrubs stand around, a bucket in the foreground spills over with grief. "Part of the idea is [from] the Shanti project in San Francisco, the idea that all grief goes in one bucket and that in order to process it, you have to process your past grief in order for more grief to go in. If your bucket is full and somebody else dies, then it all slops out, whatever is unprocessed. Anything can flop out when you are grieving. It is all the same grief, just one big process" (interview by author, 15 May 1998).

"Because it is hopeless to end with death," the final piece, a black-and-white woodcut, is more hopeful. "I needed to do something that didn't just end on death. . . . I read about a hospice in New York, a story of a nun who as the patient was dying would whisper in his ear, 'We are with you.' So, as the Warren Hadler figures lies dying, a healer puts his head to the ear of the dying man and says, 'We are with you.' . . . So that is the suite. It is called *Damn It!* as in 'Get thee behind me, Satan' . . . *Healing before Art* is the one that sold. . . . I think it is something people can relate to, . . . some-

22. *As It Is*, 1987. Five-color lithograph with woodcut overprint. Photograph by UTMB Biocommunications.

23. *Healing before Art*, 1986. Five-color lithograph with woodcut overprint. Photograph by UTMB Biocommunications.

thing people can feel warmly about. Gay people buy the Warren Hadler one with the words 'We are with you,' ... and AIDS workers buy the death piece' (interview by author, 15 May 1998).

To get clinical art events into these institutional settings, you have to work through resistances, like with a patient, resistances that are projections of their fears, anxieties, and their own stuff, so they often don't recognize this.

"I sort of flip things. It is partly being a printmaker. Printmakers always work in reverse. . . . I do it a lot when I'm working with patients, because they are telling me one thing and I'm thinking the opposite. . . . Now I was in a medical institution, and now it was the art people who didn't acknowledge me. So I turned around and started working toward them. In order to get these events into these institutional settings, you have to work through resistances, like with a patient. The resistances are projections of their fears, anxieties, and their own stuff, and so they often don't recognize this. . . . [You] work through it as best you can, and in that process you might not be successful in getting what you would like to have happen.

"Like my wallpaper *How to Use a Male and Female Condom, Toilet Paper Motif* [1996]. It was commissioned for the 1996 Houston Contemporary Arts Museum (CAM) exhibit *Wallpaper Works*. It was installed in Houston nightclub and coffeehouse bathrooms, but when I asked to install it in one of the museum bathrooms, the museum refused. It was art which could educate and save lives. I pointed out to them that they had hung upstairs at the same time an Andre Serrano show . . . which is the artwork with blood, semen, urine, and had . . . photographs of dead people, big four-by-eight-foot photographs of bodies from a morgue. . . . They did agree to let me hang a strip of the wallpaper in the large exhibition space because no one would be forced to enter the exhibit area. The bathroom, on the other hand, was off-limits because anyone who entered would be forced to look at the condom wallpaper. I said that was the point. The museum director refused. Here the culture had processed Andre Serrano, and [Robert] Mapplethorpe and the whole [debate over the National Endowment for the Arts subsidizing such work]. The cultural work that had to be done to make these people acceptable in the CAM was done not in Houston, but it had been done in other places. The CAM was all geared up to deal with all the complaints about those pieces because they knew the rap to give back to people. But in terms of doing something original with their own institution, they wouldn't do it. . . . I did not make friends with the director of that museum, and she will never have anything to do with me again because of it, but I did make some friends with junior people who will move on to other places, who saw the paradox and thought it wrong" (interview by author, 2 December 1997).

"Resistance" also happened at the Brazil coffeehouse: "It got busted by the vice police . . . because a twelve-year-old girl went in to use the rest room, and she brought her mother in to ask what was going on in the picture. Her mother complained to the owner, who said he would put up a sign so everybody would know there was sexually explicit stuff. The mother went and called the vice police. The owner got busted. He got cited for displaying harmful material to minors, and it actually was the female condom insert that is available in a drugstore that any twelve-year-old girl could go in and buy. It got press. It got written up. . . . People wrote letters back, saying, you know, that they worked in health departments and were seeing children that had HIV. So it was a way of getting the condom message out" (interview by author, 2 December 1997).

In 1993, the CAM had allowed Eric to put up large prints of his peripheral blood smear on a very large space over the gallery entrance, to hang round woodcuts of the HIV virus, and even to do public demonstration HIV testing in his white coat. Those who were tested spoke for news cameras about why they took part, often witnessing in the name of someone who had died of AIDS. The large repeated peripheral blood smear wallpaper (The Stuff of Life) — magnified macrophages and lymphocyte cells — was an Andy Warhol strategy, but "I think I made the first round woodcut in the history of art. . . . call it an HIV condom-filled piñata, which I sell" (interview by author, 2 December 1997). Similar installations of the peripheral blood smear wall paper, "piñata" woodcuts, and public testing were done in 1994 in New York at the Mary Ryan Gallery, and at the University of New Mexico. In the New York show, a member of ACT UP agreed to be a subject to demonstrate in public how risk factor assessment and counseling works, and other participants explained why they were being tested publicly, and the event was videotaped.

The 1997 version of the installation at the University of Wisconsin-Madison introduced the miniature temple-clinic (which would be more elaborate in the Fogg show) and in it Dr. Jane Petro did consultations on plastic surgery and general medicine with visitors to the installation. On the surrounding walls were some of Eric's works. Eric in his white coat engaged visitors, showing them on a little 3-D viewing device the stereoscopic Death's Head photograph. In the hallway, "we had a managed care representative," in the form of performance artist Karen Feinberg (Lily Pink), in black tails and bowler hat, "hawking snake oil . . . liposuction, surgical sex reassignment,"

24. Managed care representative Lily Pink. Performance photograph during Eric Avery's *Art, Medicine, Action: The Lost Art of Healing*. Sponsored by the Center for Twentieth-Century Studies at the University of Wisconsin–Milwaukee, April 1997. Photograph by Alan Magayne-Roshak, 1997.

"recycling the lipo into breast augmentation and all sorts of things" (interview by author, 1–2 December 1997). The focus here was on "doctor-patient interaction: listening, touching."

"Cracking open the museum" was one direction; equally challenging was to crack open the Institute for Medical Humanities. Eric has a unique job. He is on a medical school faculty, so he teaches medical students and house staff; as director of HIV Psychiatry Services, he works as the "AIDS psychiatrist in a 1,500-patient clinic, largely indigent, who come from thirty-seven counties. . . . And then I'm the psychiatrist on the inpatient HIV/AIDS ward, a fifteen-bed ward with really sick people. Also one half-day a week, I work in the women's prison . . . two hundred women, one hundred of them have HIV. . . . The University of Texas Medical Branch at Galveston (UTMB) has a managed care contract for 80 percent of the Texas prison system, which is the second largest prison system in the world: 120,000 inmates." But he is also "an associate member in the Institute for Medical Humanities, where they pay me one day a week to make art in my studio and reflect on my art as a physician" (interview by author, 2 December 1997).

"People in the medical humanities don't have any training in the visual humanities, by and large, so they don't know how to apply the same techniques of analysis [as they might for literature]. . . . If there were three of me working like this in the medical humanities, [visuality] would be a phenomenon that people [could recognize], whereas if only one person does it, he seems eccentric, or there is something special about you [being] able to do this. It gets personalized, and I'm seen as the phenomenon instead of, what I would much rather, being seen as a connection with the visual realm. . . . connected with MRI [magnetic resonance imaging] experiences or with the visualization that's happening in other medical technologies . . . how visual processing of images is the basis of what is happening in computer work. . . . [The art historian Mary Winkler] and I . . . did a graduate seminar together called 'Ways of Seeing.' . . . Students took their cameras out on the campus and brought back primarily visual material. . . . It was really interesting. . . . We did a presentation at a national meeting, and then it died. There was no support for doing this kind of work. Another problem in the institute is that a number of members do not have an integrated presence in the medical experience. . . . They need to come on ethics rounds . . . into the clinical setting . . . to deal with bodies" (interview by author, 15 May 1998).

All these issues — institutional rigidity, lack of visual skills, of seeing things otherwise — are intensified in the transgender clinic. The battles in psychiatry between psychopharmacology and talk therapy over the past decade have increasingly driven the talk therapy people out of medical institutions. If you believe, as Eric does from his clinical experience, that placing oneself at risk to AIDS infection is psychodynamically driven, this shift toward treating everything only psychopharmacologically means that doctors increasingly do not understand their patients' behavioral patterns. "It is rare of a psychiatrist where I work to ask about HIV risk in their work with patients. The psychiatric vector of infectious disease is not part of the general training of the residents I work with." If working with prison patients and HIV patients is intense enough under conditions where many care providers do not have a clue about the psychodynamics involved, working with transsexuals intensifies the challenges even more. Not only are transsexuals stigmatized, but the doctors who do research on issues affecting transsexuals are also stigmatized.

"My other research area was in the safety of prescribing estrogens to transsexuals who have HIV and hepatitis C. So in the process of working on this group of patients, I have become an expert in working with transgenders who have HIV and hepatitis. It is one of those areas in medicine that is so stigmatized. . . . these very exotic liminal creatures . . . The HIV team has these research seminars, and they ask me to present my research interest, and I told them I couldn't expose myself to this group, because they would just laugh me out of the room for working with these people in the first place. There is a very small group that really specializes in working with these people . . . A social worker came to me in the HIV clinic and said that if I wanted to change one thing, change the way these people are treated in this clinic" (interview by author, 2 December 1997).

Eric has some wonderful, hilarious, and sad stories of his own confusions in dealing with transsexuals initially, and photos of a few of those who became friends as well as patients. "Spansexuality . . . these are names that people call themselves . . . I just keep collecting names: gender dysphoria, transvestite, drag queen, cross-dresser, transvestite fetishism, 24/7/365, transie, he/she, blended gender, unstable extrovert. . . . Anyway, there is a lot going on . . . taking apart the ability of surgeons to decide who is what. This funnel that drives people towards the surgeon, people are saying they want to stop at different places. . . . As the concept of spansexuality names people in this expanding liminal zone of transgender, deconstructing gender, I'm sort of on target."

"HIV is another example [of liminal space]: when you push 'infected' until whatever happens . . . there is a point where you are no longer HIV negative, and another point when whatever is going to happen . . . You are in a space where you don't know what will happen. Part of my job is to help people rethink their lives and reset their goals. And now when multiple medications are available, you might even come back out of this zone of not knowing. Everyone infected was expected to die, and now they are not going to die. So now I have to get my credit back, now I am going to have to work, I am going to have to get disability, how long is this treatment going to work, I cannot get my disability back, and what if I get sick again? So again we generate the not knowing, the in-between space even when we get patients better" (interview by author, 1 December 1997).

Conclusion: Catacoustis

"Goya . . . lived in a very violent time in Spain. A lot of his work is disasters of wars, caprices, obtuse suites of etchings that deal with violence and death. . . . I think I am living through a very violent time . . . be it working with people dying all around you in Somalia, or just being a physician, where your enemy that you fight with all the time is not a bacteria, not age, not a tumor. The enemy that you fight with all the time is the end of these processes if they are left uninterrupted" (Avery 1982b: 8–9).

Four of Walter Benjamin's ideas about the work of art seem useful in thinking about Eric Avery's artworks: (1) "Geschichte zerfallt in Bilder, nicht in Geschichten" [history resolves into images, not narratives]; (2) the most powerful of these images are dialectical, or doubled indexes, pointing both to the time of their composition and to the time of their recognition or legibility (like Freud's *Nachträglichkeit*); (3) their mechanical or technical reproducibility is central to their functioning in cultural politics; (4) psychodynamic displacements, secondary revisions, defenses against anxiety and trauma, can be basic to their production and effectivity *(Shockabwehr)*, as also can the material kinetics of mechanical communication in innervating the body, body-image space, and thinking with images *(Bilddenken)*. (On this tension between psychic processing and the nonpsychic material physical effects of new communication media on both individual bodies and collective ones, see chapter 9).

Just as Benjamin was fascinated with photography and film as loci where the distinction between production and reproduction begins to break down, so Eric Avery is fascinated with photography and printmaking as loci where the velocity of film (and digital media) can be put into slower motion, where the bodily sensorium and psychic apparatus can be foregrounded. Printmaking is both a form of mechanical reproduction and also a craft skill. Sue Coe's strategy of using this form of reproduction to work around the commodified auratic manipulations of the high-art market and traditional museum is a device for exploring the possibilities of the work of art to function other than as mere commodity. Printmaking, Eric emphasizes, is a way of bodily working through anxiety and stress, and also a way of transmuting engagement with the trauma of others that seems less invasive and exploitative of others' pain and suffering than journalistic photography. It is, of course, in the personal, dialogic, even therapeutic relations with people that feelings of exploitation or affirmation of dignity occur. The attention to this dialogic, therapeutic, educational, and perhaps even ethical tact of the performative dimension of Eric's art actions (as in Benjamin's attention to the political effects of his art, such as his children's radio shows) make his art transgressions both challenging and gentle. The reworking of images performs in a fairly direct way Benjamin's dialectical notion of images. The Haitian boat print, *U.S.A. Dishonor and Disrespect*—playing on the "Honore et respet" of the Haitian salutation—is paradigmatic. It is this reworking that makes the psychodynamic thread of Eric's own family romance within his work only one string in a more powerful social and cultural chordlike resonance. Where Benjamin speaks of the shock of modernity shattering tradition and the traditional sensorium into new dialectical fragments, Eric speaks of trauma and retraumatization—of himself, but more fundamen-

25a, 25b, 25c. *The Arrivederci Face Project*, 1997. Woodcut block print. Photograph by UTMB Biocommunications.

tally of the social traumas of the twentieth century in whose aftereffects we all continue to participate.

Perhaps most striking are his observations about what it is like to work in a medical humanities institute. Medical schools across the country have instituted such humanistic programs in various ways, and Eric's career is a testament to them from Hershey to Galveston. And yet, Eric asserts, both physicians and most humanists working in such institutes are visually illiterate. Insofar as they support work such as Eric's, many do so out of a deference to traditional humanistic high culture; many of them might do hobbyist art on the side. But in an age of MRI development and other techniques of medical visualization, it is remarkable, says Eric, how little thinking is given to how the visual might operate as a critical psychic and sensory faculty for processing the traumas that surround us and, as he puts it, "where your enemy that you fight with all the time is not a bacteria, not age, not a tumor. The enemy that you fight with all the time is the end of these processes if they are left uninterrupted in that step."

Many of these processes are social and historically resonating, as well as medical or individually psychodynamic. After Eric's visit to the Fogg Museum, the Science Technology and Society Program at MIT, and the Health Science and Technology class at the Harvard Medical School, we attended (along with many of our medical and STS students) a rally at Faneuil Hall of the Ad Hoc Committee of Doctors and Nurses against Managed Care, presided over by Dr. Bernard Lown, the author of *The Lost Art of Healing*. (Earlier in the day, activists for doctors and nurses had staged a second Boston Tea Party.) Later Eric would lead a discussion with Harvard undergradu-

26. Eric Avery's sketch of rally at Faneuil Hall by the Ad Hoc Committee of Doctors and Nurses against Managed Care, presided over by Dr. Bernard Lown, Boston, 1 December 1997. Photograph by UTMB Biocommunications.

ate peer counselors dealing with drugs, sexuality, and HIV. At the rally, Eric sat in the balcony with his little black sketchbook, drawing the stage and the audience. Cameras were set in the balcony across from the dais. Above them was the American eagle, wings half raised in preparation for flight, head out, like a zoom lens. Eric carries a small sketchbook everywhere. From it grow ideas for artworks. A series of sketches from his rounds are now being made into black-and-white wood-cut portraits; the frames contain icons of the traumatizations of their life course from childhood molestation to drugs, AIDS, and PTSD. It occurred to him to talk to his therapist about needing to ask permission of patients to turn them into art, a question arising not as a legal issue but as a personal ethical one.

"I'm working on a set of portraits of some of my AIDS patients. They are really strong and very graphic and communicate some of the horror of this terrible illness. I'm making frames in paper to go around some of the portraits that tell the HIV risk stories I hear again and again. The best part is the physical cutting of the woodcut and the enormous pressure used in printing them. I think they will be hung this fall at the Galveston Art Center. In front of them, I'm trying to imagine how I can get some of my patients to give voices to the portraits in some kind of performance. Not sad, but strong and about life" (e-mail to author, 31 July 1998).

5

Ethnographic Critique and Technoscientific
Narratives: The Old Mole, Ethical Plateaus, and
the Governance of Emergent Biosocial Polities

At a time when Vienna is making itself heard once again through the voice of its Opera
... the eternal city of Freud's discovery, if it can be said that as a result ... the very cen-
tre of the human being was no longer to be found at the place assigned to it by a whole
humanistic tradition. — Jacques Lacan, *The Freudian Thing*

Memory has value only as foresight. — Balzac

Both opera and novels theatricalize society and culture, dramatizing the
conflicts, uncertainties, dilemmas, misrecognitions, differences, fantasies,
wills, psychodynamics, obsessive repetitions, labilities of desire, and power
differentials that individuals and institutions negotiate. So does much good
ethnography, in the sense of showing how people appropriate and use cultural forms in multiple ways, and showing the unfolding of social action
over historical time and across social structures. In his 1955 lecture at the
Neuro-psychiatric Clinic in Vienna, Jacques Lacan recalled Sigmund Freud's
observation that there are three impossibilities: to educate, to govern, and to
psychoanalyze.[1] In each endeavor, what escapes is also formative. As Walter
Benjamin, Lacan, and Slavoj Žižek all elaborate, phantasmagorias ground
and structure the terrain in which reason, will, and language operate. To
understand our experiences and place in the world requires a study of language and institutions and of the resonances of history, memory, literature,
and the arts.

Cautionary Tales:
The Phantasmagoria/Real of Biotechnology

Among the quasi-mapping functions that technoscientifically literate novels help put on the table are the ways in which technologies interact and help define historical horizons, social landscapes, and what I will dub "ethical plateaus" (horizons of ethical issues posed by the intersection of several technologies, their institutional formattings, and their deployments through markets and other mechanisms). Novels also often describe changing and temporary ethical boundaries, ways of handling the phantasmagoria of technoscientific possibilities, and modes of narrating or thinking about those elements. What does fiction leave out that ethnography supplies? Two first approximation hypotheses: First, ethnography provides better socio-logical imagination about how social institutions work and might integrate and regulate new technologies (for some reason, thinking about institu-tional development is not a task that most novelists have taken on, although some of the aggressive competition, blocking of information flow, and work-ing around the rules is described realistically). Second, ethnography is a better "reality"[2] check about what is actually the case, against the hype of promoters of the new technology (hype is often a necessary part of the de-velopment of these technologies, and thus, in ethnographic terms, itself a discourse needing documentation and putting in its place or mapping of its contours, limits, contradictions, and departures from reality), and also against the cautionary tales, as well as fantasies of hope, in which novels excel. In a sense, then, novels can often be tools for exploring the ideologi-cal cultural armatures of technoscientific developments, while ethnography can play the complementary role of exploring the institutional or sociologi-cal placement of these armatures, constituting a form of cultural critique by staging such armatures vis-à-vis other perspectives or cultural formations.[3]

A wonderfully satirical puzzle novel, *Vienna Blood*, by Adrian Mathews, an author of English and Czech background who lives in Paris, may serve as an initial nexus of emergent ethical, regulatory, policing, civil society ver-sus expertise-run oversight issues in the space of overlap between new mo-lecular biology, computer and informatics technologies, and environmental challenges.

Vienna Blood is one of a number of novels (and bioartist performance pieces)[4] I would use as novelistic probes into the contemporary landscape of dilemmas — ethical, social, and conceptual — posed by the new technologies. Among the others are *Mendel's Dwarf*, by Simon Mawer, on achondropla-sia dwarfism and the transformations from biological gardens to molecular biology laboratories; Günter Grass's novels and essays on the destruction of that cultural icon of German Romanticism, the forest; Greg Bear's two science fiction novels about biotechnology entrepreneurship, *Blood Music*, on molecule production that gets out of hand, and *Darwin's Radio*, on stresses that activate distributed retroviruses lodged in our hereditary genome; Amitav Ghosh's *Calcutta Chromosome*, on computer data banks and the displacement of Third World contributions to malaria (read biological) research; Rohini Nilekani's *Stillborn*, about the transnational entrepreneurial terrain in which poor Third World women are used as test beds for clinical trials and the expansion of new medical technologies; and Richard Powers's novels on molecular biology (*The Gold Bug Variations*), artificial intelligence (*Galatea 2.2.*), and the uncertainties of cancer etiologies in industrial production (*Gain*).

Vienna Blood is about precautionary germ plasm modification and chemical camouflage justified for the purpose of protecting against ethnically targeted biological warfare. These are technological possibilities that are in fact under current investigation, if of somewhat dubious potential. If, however, one understands ethnicity, as the Human Genome Diversity Project encouraged us to do, in terms of the eight thousand or so genetic population clusters defined by HLA markers, rather than as biologically meaningless race categories or merely culturally defined ethnicities, the idea of ethnically targeted biological warfare is not quite as fanciful as it may at first seem. In any case, the attendant questions of new reproductive technologies, genetic engineering, eugenics, biotechnology entrepreneurship, ethical review boards (and their circumvention), privacy (and its violation), electronic databases, cryptographic defenses and attacks, electromagnetic monitoring devices, virtual reality devices, networked communication devices, including customized personal agents, pagers, and remotely operated cyborgian enhancements for the disciplining of the body—these are already very real contemporary technologies and issues.

In this chapter, I explore new roles and challenges for anthropology in terms of three frames: the cautionary tales of novels; the ethnographic cultural critique of challenging the constitutive hype of new technologies, including the constructions of "risk," "cost-benefit," and "bioethics"; and the delineation of new social theory and new ethical landscapes not reducible to the dyadic choices, rational-man calculus, binary trade-offs of pro and con and split-the-difference adjudication television-style debate, or the "for the moment" pragmatics of political decision making that go into the "policy" industry. The next section's novelistic figuration and literary critical reading is followed by ethnographic sketches of ethical discourses and new arenas of ethical challenges; the novelistic and ethnographic sections are intended to comment on and complement each other, each skeptically quizzing the other, and together composing a (set of) ethical terrain(s).

The continued viability of critique by the individual moral voice (novelist, ethnographer) is also at issue in this post "death of the author" age. Novels and other story forms constructed by individuals remain invaluable modes of access to social worlds, to scenarios of how the *conscience collective*, collective representations, and symbol systems of society are deployed and work their effects. Ethnography, like literature, can function as a check on the mechanisms of abstraction and universalization that frequently bedevil the nonanthropological, non-cross-culturally or cross-temporally comparative social sciences. Though a fuller exploration of the semisocialized individual authorial voice, or hand, cannot be pursued here, it is worth noting that narrative theory in the new highly technologized arenas of computer-mediated communication and the neurosciences is supplementing the traditional humanistic approaches to narrative by considering the ways in which, for instance, micronarratives might be temporal units of mapping, rhythm, and memory physiologically in the brain (see, e.g., the MENO workshop),[5] and in any case by showing that the history of technology can be made much more powerful by asking "who" did it, a feature that is replicated in the obsessive attempts among software innovators to give credit to one another. Consider also the degree to which the understandings of social theorists (Marx, Weber, et al.) are rarely separable from their biographies, historical horizons, and literary technologies. This is not so much a matter of the individual escaping social generalization or the impossibility of modeling social processes. Rather, it is a matter of precipitating loci where historical and cultural social processes intersect, allowing detailed accounting of particularities and strengths and blinders of perspective. Whether or not anthropologists of the present can ever again have the public voice that once accrued to Margaret Mead, Bronislaw Malinowski, Franz Boas, Robert Redfield, Claude Lévi-Strauss, and perhaps Clifford Geertz—and whether or not anthropologists can ever have the kind of functional moral voice that Mary-Jo DelVecchio Good notes accrues to some senior physicians through the accumulation of experience, credit, and grappling with public medical issues—they can continue to play various "reality check" roles. "Reality check" here can be taken in its ordinary language usage, but also in its more quasi-Freudian, Benjaminian, Lacanian, or Žižekian resonance of going through the city of phantasmagoria out of which humans spin their worlds of anxiety and meaning, walking with a lantern, not to shine the light of truth (an impossible locution) but rather to shed some light on the technologies of displacement, symbiosis, production, testing, and marketing on which the technosciences depend.

At issue thus are three methodological questions: (1) the relation between the literary and the ethnographic, that is, the roles of cultural resonances in shaping and understanding the technosciences, along with the roles of the social peopling of technologies in their nonperfectionist implementations, real-world operations, and entropies; thus conversely the ways in which ethnographic projects might be entered from the literary to complement and contest literary insight and blindnesses; (2) the role of critique more broadly, both in its more systematic "reality checking" modalities (cultural, historical, and discursive juxtapositions; mapping differential demographic, sociological, and institutional terrains; probing meaning structures at the individual, structural, and cultural levels) and in its more individualized craftlike signatures; and (3) the probing of whether the field of politics is undergoing structural shifts such that traditional terms of politics misrecognize more fundamental changes, or whether (à la Ned Lukacher's mid-nineteenth-century Karl Marx, and Antonio Negri's twenty-first-century Empire) politics for the moment is impossible as a "viable alternative," that we are in a transitional period waiting until a different politics may again be possible, the period of the old mole being driven underground by the imperial eagle.[6] Can the figure of the "old mole" of critique—the artisanal voice or textual hand of situated experience, of historical and cross-cultural juxtaposition—continue to play the role of outsider, of letter carrier from earlier or culturally other temporal horizons, and of witness to human singularities?

Two modifications or mutations of the old mole make it appropriate for contemporary biotechnological settings. First, the authorial/ethnographic voice/hand is often best pursued in a hybrid/collaborative insider/outsider tension with the scientist-technologists of new technoscientific worlds, either to elicit their informing worlds of meaning (with the attendant seductions of playing into the public relations advertising/advocacy that shapes the futures of the scientist-technologists) or to help in the evaluation and advocacy that attempts to place some civil society oversight on technoscience and correct for adverse by-products of industrial accidents, toxic wastes, and the like. In a wonderful science fictional re-creation of Freud as a psychologist taken along cryogenically on a space voyage, unfrozen whenever there is a human crisis, author Barry Malzberg (1985) humorously shows Freud as failing each time to be of much pragmatic help, and yet the fantasy of his presence and mode of inquiry helps to humanize the technoscientific project, to serve as passageways between historical periods, and to remind the reader of the human composition of technoscientific projects. A similar but ethnographic "peopling of technology" is Rayna Rapp's study of how different communities of families react quite differently to amniocentesis detections of Down's syndrome, some using it to trigger abortion, others to mobilize familial resources for care and support, invoking different religious and moral imperatives.

The second genetic modification or mutation of the old mole, like the antibody or enzyme productions of its oncomouse relative, is the production of new social theory to provide at least partial metanarratives for creative thinking about the structuring of these new worlds (social movements, risk society and reflexive or second-order modernization, deliberative politics, mediated civil society). As the new technosciences and their media make our social worlds more complicated (often more locally demanding/disciplining of individualistic choice/responsibility while increasingly more dependent on global economies of scale, changing temporalities of social calculation and spatialities of accountability; and shifting the parameters of life and health into data sets that are not directly perceptible to the individual's senses but require scientific instrumentation, processing, and testing for visibility, themselves subject to various sorts of manipulation and interpretation), consequent to these processes have a New Man/Woman,[7] new biosocialities, and new governances emerged? Are the technosciences creating not only new subjects (cyborgian bio-machine hybrids, genetically engineered new life-forms, self-disciplining objects of testing regimes, bureaucratically recognized/excluded citizens, etc.) but also new political stakes and processes that escape traditional institutions and categories of politics and regulation?

Wiener Blut

Is not all this dream interpreting and newly emergent psychoanalysis, which expressly and polemically dissociates itself from hypnotism . . . itself part of Art Nouveau, with which it indeed corresponds in time? Art Nouveau replaced interiority with sexuality. . . . it was only in sex that private individuals could encounter themselves as corporeal rather than as inward. — Theodor Adorno and Gretel Karplus to Walter Benjamin, 2–4 August 1935

Vienna Blood is dense with Viennese localities and cultural references, doing for early-twenty-first-century Vienna, if more sketchily, what James Joyce did for early-twentieth-century Dublin (or if much more briefly, what Robert Musil did for an earlier Vienna), but also lightly and ironically gesturing at Viennese and Hapsburgian literary themes of the uncanny, vampiric, masqued, and faux facade. The historical layering provides a way of referencing the generational changes in popular usages, confusions, and correct understandings of eugenics, racism, antiforeigner feeling, anti-Semitism, and new postgenomic eugenics. Right-wing attacks by groups called Fortress Europe (Festung Europa [FPÖ])[8] or Neues Östmark (New Austria, Österreich) against immigrant workers' hostels, thus, are part of the plot, together with the disconcerting youth culture of Nazi-like symbolism, without asserting any sincere historical connection, yet grounded in resentments of aliens being given jobs or welfare benefits.[9] More arresting is the explanation by some of these youths that violence is no longer necessary as in earlier right-wing politics, because they say aliens will not survive long in the local environment. What makes this archaic and recirculated reasoning arresting in the contemporary setting is that a scenario is constructed whereby environmentally disseminated biological toxins affect population groups differently: in this case, the affected population is not Turkish but Slovak.

The novel is plotted as a peculiar kind of murder mystery, displacing the genre, not quite turning it inside out as did Kafka's *The Trial*, where at issue is not who did it or why but rather what, if any, was the crime, and what, if any, was the justice of the process. *Vienna Blood* instead involves a displacement of the opening murder and so mirrors the ethical substitutions that biotechnology effects through changing what counts as the basic terms of life, kinship, bodily integrity, genetic makeup, ethnicity, national identity, sovereignty, and international accountability. Germ plasm genetic engineering is currently one of those unstable ethical boundaries: there are many who say that somatic gene therapy is fine (to correct diseases), but germ line genetic engineering is taboo because it turns future generations into commodities, and worse (for some), it is the slippery slope toward changing the fundamental nature of the species, and along the way probably instituting a caste society of the gene rich (or genetically enhanced) who might in time not even be able to interbreed with those who have not been genetically enriched. Put into question, then, could be many of the major categories by which we understand life, kinship, and other such categories. The person we assume to have been murdered at the opening of the novel turns out to be other than what we think (physically, genetically), involving a kind of Möbius-like reconstruction of various assumptions the reader (and the characters) initially makes. And indeed the genre is itself, in fact, not so much a peculiar kind of murder mystery as an updated play on the story of Gawain and the Green Knight,[10] crossed with bits of Disney ("Where da wabbit go?" and "What's up, Doc"? are chapter section titles), and an homage to Graham

Greene's *The Third Man*, with its themes of a penicillin racket, disappearance, and Oedipal rivalries.[11] Like a murder mystery puzzle, however, the path through a maze of clues to a predetermined end both raises questions about the hiring of bioethicists by corporations (in the novel, a figure of this type plays a role in laying down the clues) and raises the ethnographic question of how we are to narrate to ourselves the changing ethical plateaus in which we live (new technical possibilities that initially seem like warning flags rapidly become absorbed into routine markers of a changed common sense).

The novel is set a quarter of a century into the future, so that it can revolve around two generations of characters: young adults born with the aid of reproductive technologies of the 1990s, and the adults today who are creating those reproductive technologies, who will then be in their sixties and seventies. The science in *Vienna Blood*, with some minor extrapolations, is that of contemporary biology. Passages of explanation sound exactly like what one gets from 1990s molecular biologists and entrepreneurs of the Human Genome Project. It is as if the literary form has been dipped into the circulation of today's scientists' explanations, with the effect of (slightly, but only slightly) widening the speculative horizons that scientists allow themselves in thinking through the ethical, legal, and social implications (ELSI) of what they do. The head of the Whitehead Institute's Human Genome Project at MIT, in his public and pedagogic presentations in 1999 and 2000, would, at moments of reflection, say that he is personally opposed to any tampering with the human germ line but cannot find any firm philosophical or principled groundings for that opposition, because he is also opposed to any regulation or constraint on scientific investigation. It is just a deep personal unease and ethical dilemma for him about the shifty line between therapies for disease and unacceptable commodification of human beings.[12] (In fact, the same "slippage" or "contradiction" or conflict between principles can be found in the 1997 UNESCO Universal Declaration on the Human Genome and Human Rights.) In the meantime, he is engaged in a high-speed, highly capitalized race to pursue the science, the creation of a new biological "periodic table" that will form the basis of new practical tools. This race, of course, allows relatively restricted space for ethical discussion or redirection.[13] Or again, if one thinks about the debates concerning cloning (a technology that makes a cameo appearance in *Vienna Blood* as older and less acceptable legally and biologically than the lead technologies of the book), genetically modified food crops (at the center of 1990s trade wars and struggles over the World Trade Organization's intellectual property, labor, and welfare rules), or Iceland's model of genetic information mining through Kari Stefansson's company deCode, which by Icelandic parliamentary agreement in the 1990s has monopoly control over creating a triple-linked database from the Icelandic genome, Icelandic genealogies, and Icelandic health data (with an exclusive license with the Swiss multinational Hoffman-LaRoche to develop therapeutic drugs, and various agreements with other research groups), one sees again and again the temporary boundaries of (un)acceptability placed under economic, scientific, and legal pressure. We are *always*, says Harvard ethicist and pulmonary heart-lung transplant surgeon Dr. Walter Robinson, on the slippery slope.

I will provide a reading of the novel in three parts: a preliminary setup; a listing of interlocking new technologies explored or referenced; and, most important, an account of the key molecular biology technologies and the series of ethical plateaus worked through from older traditional dilemmas to newly emergent ones.

A Reading of Vienna Blood: The Setup

The title *Vienna Blood* is worked to signal the ethical thematic of the ways in which rules and regulations about genetic engineering, clinical trials, privacy, and so on can be subverted. *Vienna Blood* is a pun referring to Strauss waltzes as well as to blood and its fractionable products. An opening epigraph from Otto Weininger depreciates the waltz as circular, thus suppressing liberty, thus immoral; and the Viennese as fatalists ("leave things be, there's nothing we can do"). The ostensible initial murder victim is described characterologically as "waltzing from the waist down." "It's what they say about the Viennese, isn't it? . . . Stiff as a ramrod from the waist up, a picture of honesty and rectitude. Then down below, all the fancy footwork" (Mathews 1999: 45). This is not so much a serious commentary on the Viennese (even though these characterological aspersions are part of old Viennese self-deprecations) as it is a signal of the ethical problematics staged by the novel.

Narrated by a journalist, Oskar "Sharkey" Gewinnler, the story opens with the obituary of Leo Detmers and a phone call from the pregnant widow, Petra, who asks Sharkey for help because Leo told her he was a friend. Although Leo's death was reported as a hit-and-run accident at the Prater, Vienna's famous amusement park, Petra thinks Leo knew he was targeted to die. Sharkey and Leo had met going to a conference in Hamburg on Securicom (secure communications); Sharkey thought him a boor, but Petra hints at a deeper connection. The opening chapter is littered with allusions and markers, operating both as clues in the murder mystery story and as technoscientific, political, and cultural pointers or resonators.

Environment: for the first time in seven years, it is snowing in Vienna (global warming, "perverse decaying laws of the physical universe"). *Genetics*: Leo Detmers may have been a boor, but there is something disarmingly familiar about him, "a common Austrian phenotype," "like generic supermarket packaging," and Sharkey finds himself mentally "proof-reading the human galleys" of Leo's quirks. Sharkey also eerily feels an echo of Leo in Petra's movements, which turns out to be more than just the long-term behavioral mirroring of spouses who met in kindergarten and married at eighteen (in the same church where they also held Leo's funeral). *Computer technologies*: Leo was a hacker, who worked at home — ostensibly as a commodities and precious metals trader — on an "early green fluorescent protein computer, the kind where the silicon's replaced by jelly fish molecules." Leo was the kind of hacker who would walk his dog "by putting an old fashioned electronic pager on its collar and when it was time, ring up the pager on his Networker." *Genealogies*: among the clues Leo has left are serial numbers on Post-its "in frantic blue felt tip," stacks of Mormon publications, and a GeneDraw software handbook. *Forensics*: his dog, Argos, is named after Odysseus's dog, the only sentient being to recognize Odysseus when he returns to Ithaca, and Argos plays an analogous role in the forensics of the novel by way of the night traffic camera at the Prater that records one angle on the hit-and-run crime scene. *Names*: One wonders if some of the other names are not similarly significant. For instance, is "Oscar" a nod to Günter Grass's *Tin Drum*, especially given that it also becomes the name of Petra's child, born into what may become a genomic brave new world of the twenty-first century?[14] Petra is perhaps more literally descriptive: Sharkey tells us she has presence, she is "class but high maintenance," and that "life arranges itself obediently around women of her sort, like iron filings around a magnet." She is also an homage to the filmmaker Fassbinder.[15] *Experimental systems*: there is a play between down-to-earth gravitas and biologial life versus virtual reality environments and wall screens, the Marriott Hotel orbiting in space above Vienna where one can go to experience sex in zero gravity, and behind-the-scenes genomic manipulations that may or may not be evident to the phenotypic, sentient carriers. *Transnational science*: then there is Hannah Delbrück, whose name could be a nod to Max Delbrück, the physicist who emigrated from Germany to America and from physics to biology, a key figure in the early history of molecular biology.[16] *Politics and history*: The political landscape in which this all occurs is sketched deftly: Sharkey[17] lives in the Karl Marx Hof ("Stalinian Red Vienna home to two thousand proles," but in fact solidly middle- and working-class since the 1930s); Leo and Petra live across town in the 1980s Hundertwasser Haus apartment block ("a touch of the Grimms, a dash of Arabian Nights, more than a hint of Klee and Mondrian"). *Contemporary politics*: As Petra and Leo start to light a Cannoboid, a detonation goes off in the distance, which Sharkey analyzes as probably being a firebomb against guest workers from the Balkans or Turkey by one of the right-wing groups, Festung Europa or Neues Östmark.

Interlocked Technologies
The inventory and interconnections of contemporary technologies under development invoked in the novel function both (1) as a repeated crossings between fantasy and reality, between the promises that scientists and technologists make to get funding and political support for their projects and the more mundane workings of these projects; and (2) as the confluence of two temporalities or loci in two ethical plateaus, the one—pasts present—operative as legacies of the past in the present, the other—futures present—operative already or potentially operative as the result of promised technological futures.

Forensics stories, and stories about policing and computing-hacking of databases, involve issues of surveillance versus privacy, conspiracy and proprietary information versus openness of information, civil rights and policing, but also the ability of multinational, transnational, and even primarily national corporate organizations to operate around state and international regulatory and governance organizations. The forensics technologies (investigating Leo's death, and the later explosion in Petra's apartment which kills Argos) include both current technologies and some that might soon be developed: night camera traffic monitors (for low-security areas taking only a photo every two seconds and using fractals to fill in between); virtual reality animation reconstructions that can be programmed for different velocities of impact; blimps with thermal imaging and surveillance equipment with computerized face recognition that can scan crowds at twenty faces per second and match against a database of millions of photos; voice recognition machines to take depositions that print the transcripts and use biometric signatures for verification; chromatographs, chemical analyses, and spectrometers to distinguish Semtex plastic explosives from other kinds (211).

The hacking stories are basic to individual and journalistic efforts to fight corporate secrecy and include not only computer skills but "hacks" of wit, including verbal, nontechnological gambits. Leo had been hacking into databases of financial and medical records in search of his own past. The trail of his efforts provides clues for Sharkey. In a classic hack of wit or gaming, Sharkey breaks into the first levels of a secure database (a closed architecture not connected to the Net, protected by multiple levels of symmetric and asymmetric or public key style encryption algorithms, dynamic pass-words with voice and biometric authentication, and information segregated into different levels of access) by simply putting on a uniform that looks like that of a telecom repairman, calling the proprietary organization on a videophone, and asking if they've been having computer problems ("Who doesn't?"), thereby getting the dial-up number. In a satiric aside, we are told that bits of partial, distributed information held in the highest level of security in this elaborately protected database are not in fact secured electronically but known only orally to the people with the highest authorization.

The medical technologies are all contemporary ones, tweaked by a few slight extrapolations, and likewise their ethical problematics are that they are mediated by markets, both white and black, as well as by various forms of health maintenance organizations. Thus while in real life we already have organ donor cards, in the novel these are slightly extrapolated into harvest contract cards that allow major organs from a fresh cadaver to be auctioned on the Net (liver, kidneys, heart, and lungs), that distribute corneas, inner ears, jawbones, heart pericardia, pancreases, stomachs, bones, hip joints, ligaments, cartilage, bone marrow, over two square meters of skin for burn victims, a hundred thousand kilometers of blood vessels ("they reckon one card-carrier can end up in over fifty people"), and that in Leo's case allow special uses for his high concentration of antibodies for hepatitis B ("take the plasma, . . . fractionate . . . a little cloning and you've got vaccines and diagnostics" [26]). Similarly, fermentation biotechnologies are market driven, with both salutary economy-of-scale outcomes ("installing the basic technologies as they came along: recombinant DNA, biochemical reactors, mass cell-cultures") for producing marketable diagnostics, reagents, growth hormones, and human insulin; but also (as is the case) ethically problematic results in companies trying to avoid orphan drugs (potentially useful, but for illnesses that afflict relatively few people, thus not yielding the profits obtainable from mass markets [98]). Among the latest of technologies registered in the novel are genome mapping by machine-gun sequencing and flow cytogenetic analysis (163); efforts to understand pleiotropic genes that affect more than one characteristic; and testing the switching on and off of genes at particular times.

More sardonic are the new uses for human growth hormone, such as boosting athletic performances in ways not detectable by drug tests, an application said to be popular with cyclists, despite killing a few by putting too much strain on their hearts. More controversial today is fetal tissue research, initially for use experimentally to treat Parkinson's disease, but then to accelerate wound healing and athletic performance. The downside temptations, much debated today, are of encouraging abortions, or taking embryos without permission (219). Again a bit satirically, but raising a central issue about who might be in control of decision making, is this comment on new reproductive technologies: "There are sixteen ways of doing [sex] now . . . gamete intrafallopian transfer . . . zygote interfallopian transfer, . . . tubal embryo transfer, partial zona d-dissection, microsurgical epididymal sperm aspiration . . . You do it one way, right? But *they* can do it any way they like!" (39).

More marginal to the story line of the novel, but suggestively linked to some of the more central technologies, are genetically engineered crops (the genetically engineered Virginia creeper that grows on the Karl Marx Hof walls and produces strawberries and beans); virtual reality devices (the data headset worn by police inspector Uscinski; Plasmavision wall screens for news, entertainment, communication); and remotely networked haptic feedback devices (the finger sheaths that allow distance-learning-style piano practice with a master teacher controlling the fingers from afar, also able to make one's own hand slap oneself if one is not paying attention or following instructions).

As important as the genetic technologies are the ecological ones. Ecological understanding involves recognizing how activities might be interconnected and is a cognitive terrain for puzzling out what is technological intention and what is unintended consequence. Differential ecological die-offs of fish, and flu affecting different human populations, are clues to biological warfare testing. Biological warfare involves national (or ethnic) security arguments, justifications for secrecy, and avoidance of normal civil society oversight. On a more global scale, reference is made to pollution and other factors beginning to affect fertility rates, the rise in multiple chemical sensitivity (the comic agoraphobic, allergy-ridden, MCS [multiple chemical sensitivity] -affected officer who operates the computer data bank for police intelligence, named Walter Reik [Wilhelm Reich in an inverse orgone box?]), and the comic series of posters on the outpatient clinic of the Allgemeines Krankenhaus (General Hospital): " 'Did you possess one of the following cellphones between 1998 and 2013? If so, you were exposed to unsheathed e-m radiation. Make an appointment for a brain-scan now.' There are posters for Creutzfeldt-Jakob clinics, posters featuring syringe-crucified heroin addicts, posters on all the latest T-cell lymphocytotropic viruses . . . I look around for a poster warning against posters. The place is an angst-factory, scrupulously designed to induce mortal terror."

Ladder of Ethical Plateaus and New Social Theory

Kafka's novels . . . represent rather the last and disappearing connecting texts of the silent film (and it is no accident that the latter disappeared at almost exactly the same time as Kafka's death. — Teddie Wiesengrund [Adorno] to Walter Benjamin, 17 December 1934

The linkages of interconnections among technologies, and how they are part of the ladder of ethical plateaus, whereby one works from easy and historically older issues to more complex ethical landscapes, might provide a way to think about how traditional critical social theories are being challenged to evolve in new directions. Thus Ulrich Beck's account of "risk society" and pressures toward reflexive modernization begins from the generation of toxins that cannot be perceived by the ordinary senses and need to be registered by scientific instrumentation and interpretation not available to the person on the street, hence demanding social tools to force companies and governments to disclose what they know. Among the sources of such demands are industrial accidents and the demands that "polluters pay." While companies and governments tend initially to respond to cancer clusters and other indications of trouble by denial (in laboratory handling of our chemicals, such outcomes do not occur), they can often be forced to acknowledge that, for instance, the handling of chemicals on the shop floor differs from conditions in the laboratory, and that they would be better off with a system of information inputs from many actors within a complex system, rather than relying on design diagrams from the top down that can be like fantasies of perfect control. But actually pinning blame on particular sources can also turn out to be complicated and elusive where multiple causes may be involved, accumulated effects over time may work differently than single direct causation, and society needs to share risk rather than shut down economically vital industries. These pressures and contradictions can be formulated into a new social formation struggling to emerge from first-stage capitalist modernization, much as Marx described the emergence of capitalism out of the contradictions of feudalism. Among the actors forcing this emergence are new units of politics that have been dubbed "new social movements," originally focused less on traditional electoral politics than on the insistence that everyday life needed tending. While organizing and lobbying tactics can be drawn from traditional politics, there are also new modalities that have powered the environmental, women's, and patient-support movements. The Internet has become an important tool of access to information, sharing of knowledge, and reconfiguring power relations based on access to knowledge (among doctors and patients, or insurance payers and patients, or the data banks of industry scientists or bureaucracies and local communities). And in turn the Internet has generated a sophistication in the use of the media generally, including the countering of grassroots organizing by corporations attempting to undo the force of new social movements. These forms of local activism in alliance across communities have also directed attention — given the widespread despair about the deadlock of, or capture by market forces, of conventional politics — to new formats for "deliberative politics." The ways in which patients and others are able to insert themselves in bureaucracies as empowered citizen-actors often take the form of new biosocialities constructed by new modes of accounting for life, illness, and degrees of access to citizenship. These components of new social theories — second-order modernization through distributed, participatory decision making; social movements; critical deployment of media; deliberative politics experimentation; shifting biosocialities — are not well represented in novels like *Vienna Blood*. Instead the novel presents scenarios of why such initiatives might be necessary and does so in at least a two-step appreciation of older biosocial understandings and newer ones.

At a first low level on the ladder, there is the logic of old-style eugenics, and its legacies in the neo-Nazi right-wing parties fueled by ressentiments against ethnic immigrants, and sometimes acted out through firebombings of guest worker hostels. These are guarded against by policing and surveillance balanced by protection of civil liberties ("That's life. People get killed, kids get orphaned. It happens everyday . . . The only preventive medicine is good information. Good information in the right hands." With a certain German irony, Uscinski continues: "Ruhe und Ordnung. Remember that, my friend" [142]). This ethical landscape operates on a macrolevel of the Cold War overtly, but also secretly and subterraneanly: there are rumors of weapons and money caches buried by the American forces after World War II in preparation for use against Communist incursions. These weapons were perhaps funneled to the Resistance in Czechoslovakia in 1956. The money may have flowed into right-wing anticommunist politics, unintentionally flowering in the various 1990s anti-immigrant and neofascist parties across Europe.

The next ethical plateau is a kind of second-order deployment of that older first-order politics. Suppose one were not just deploying money to influence the balance of politics in a backstage, but fairly ideologically obvious, manner. Suppose one were using the tactics of small-scale shifts in the balance of power within national governments to block too much open attention to the rules of ethics about bioengineering and experimentation, justified in the name of national security defense against biological warfare. Here the resources of the old eugenics serve as a serendipitous clue for Sharkey: the neo-Nazis continue to circulate old Aristotelian, Galenic, and romantic notions of organisms adapted to place, and foreign organisms inevitably becoming diseased. The neo-Nazis use this to claim that they will not have to resort to violence, but their claim triggers in Sharkey some worries about why certain kinds of fish in the Neusiedler See have died but not others, and why Slovaks, but not Austrians, came down with the flu at meetings of the Slovak-Austrian Friendship Society. Might there be a way to target particular ethnic groups within a multiethnic society? Might first trials be with delivery systems like aerosol sprays in air-conditioning ducts, or through water systems and subways, using nonbanned substances like flu or pneumonia viruses ("Flu viruses, for example, are not outlawed particles. . . . Nor is it a criminal offense to pass flu on to another person." Sharkey: "But spraying it into ventilation ducts with patent periodic aerosol deodorisers may well be" [296–97]).

The history of biological warfare is not new, but molecular biology can refine the targeting. The novel invokes the genealogy of such warfare from Tartars catapulting the bodies of plague victims over the walls of Kaffa, to the British giving blankets infested with smallpox to Indian allies of the French in the French and Indian War, Japan aerially dropping flea-infested material into China to cause bubonic plague, suspicions about what the United States might have used in Indochina or the Soviet Union in Afghanistan, or even the legacies of defensive testing of anthrax on the island of Gruinard off Scotland. The fear of biological weapons has long been a strategic concern (294). Despite the 1972 Biological and Toxic Weapons Convention, the Gulf War again put the issue on the public agenda, as did the outbreak of anthrax from a Russian biological weapons facility, and the Aum Shinrikyo's sarin nerve gas attack in the Tokyo subway.[18] Suppose you could "engineer your agent to search the HLA system and VNRRs for sequences specific to certain population groups . . . Those are the mantras of modern warfare. . . . In attacks on multiethnic communities you avoid, for example, killing members of your own population group who happen to be in situ" (295).

How would you protect your population against such targeted attacks? Suppose, the novel speculates, you took frozen embryos, all from one egg donor and fertilized by one sperm donor, and genetically engineered them at the two to four cell or morula stage, screening them for any life-threatening abnormalities (e.g., spina bifida, Down's syndrome, hemophilia, cystic fibrosis, Huntington's chorea), and then chemically masked these "Safe" individuals using population-specific sequences in HLA (human leukocytes antigens), VNTR (variable numbers of tandem repeats), and non-coding stretches of "junk" genes. (Such masked sequences would function normally but would not show up on an ACGT readout or would be scrambled, and so would seem to be ethnically neutral. While population groups are not closed systems, and there are not races in the nineteenth-century sense, there are some four to eight thousand relatively distinct population groups that carry thirty different systems in the blood that can be analyzed and used to map population migration patterns.) And suppose then you substituted these "Safe" embryos for IVF-harvested or -donated gametes in couples seeking infertility treatments (255–56). You would thus create a "eugenically cleansed population" safe from biowarfare targeted for your population, a technology that, like all technologies, could be used for good or ill ("It is new science and therefore ethically controversial. The code of silence, therefore, had the dual benefit of being good eugenic practice and sparing new parents [suffering all the stresses and strains of IVF] from becoming embroiled in a moral dilemma which, given the complexity of the issues involved, lay beyond the scope of simplistic or rapid clarification" [257]).

Two implicated issues arise in this scenario: (1) what escapes the various ethical review boards and conventions; that is, what is the status of contemporary institutions for ethical review; and (2) how does one protect patent, proprietary, and other secrecy demands of developing new science while at the same time protecting the right to know by individuals and populations affected; that is, how do the technologies of the law, cryptography, data banking, and data mining intersect with science?

The corporate history of the novel's biotechnology firm provides a review of the second of these, placing it, like Zelig, within the actual history that we have experienced since the 1980 Chakrabarty decision that allowed the patenting of a bacterium that could eat oil slicks. Plant materials had been open to earlier patents, but this decision opened the U.S. patent system to a flood of patent applications for manufactured living materials and dramatically changed the relationships of biology among the academy, private industry, venture capital, and government regulation. Chakrabarty was followed in 1988 with the transgenic mouse, and in 1991 a patent for a bone marrow immortal cell line taken from a cancer patient. By the late 1990s, not only were there popular films like GATTACA about designer babies and the possible fascist genetic caste system of controls such technologies might encourage, but Iceland was the first nation to give a corporation monopoly control over a population's genetic database.

In *Vienna Blood*, the character Hannah Delbrück is a genetic engineer turned patent lawyer who first lobbied in the United States against the patenting of animals and then became a watchdog on ethics review boards in the United States and Europe against corrupt practices in the biotechnology field: inducing abortion for the purpose of harvesting fetal tissue, taking embryos without permission, as well as blood and body parts that came in through the back door (all practices that have occurred in reality). Biomass, as the novel's biotechnology company was originally called, was challenged at various times by biomedical ethics review boards, and so its CEO moved to Austria, where, in the world of the novel, there is more latitude, Europe not having a unified system of constraints on research.[19] Biomass continued in the United States, working on less controversial genetically engineered crops: pest-resistant plants, less stringy celery, decaffeinated coffee beans, plants with genes from flounders to prevent damage from freezing, fluorescent genes from fireflies in tobacco. The more controversial pharmaceutical, health care, and reproductive technologies research moved to Europe. There were three interlocking companies: Biowares, the pharmaceutical and pesticides firm that also distributed Biomass U.S.A. products; Primogen, a consortium of maternity and IVF clinics, general clinics, and genetic engineering labs; and Reprotech, an umbrella organization that did specialty research but also provided the lawyers, licensing services, and financial staff. (The ability to avoid the Austrian and European review boards revolves around the device of an assumed identity of a key board member who is part of the Primogen/Reprotech conspiracy to create a "Safe" Austrian population.)

Primogen's computers are the target of Leo Detmers's hacking efforts. After he succeeds, with the help of an insider, in hacking partway into Primogen's system, the company hires Nathan Buczak as a cryptographic architect to add layers of protection. He changes their multilayer kernel-proxy architecture into a totally closed cellular system, with no remote access to core information, and internally using very large integer public key algorithms that are difficult to factor. Session keys are random numbers generated by the ambient noise of Lake Neusiedl. Leo could hack in because Buczak signed him in as a technical assistant on a three-day pass, and they rigged a debug port or back door by placing a microphone on the outside of the building camouflaged by an overflow pipe, to which they tied Argos, and when Leo bipped Argos on the pager on his collar, the generator used the bip sequence to deliver a decryption key. They recorded the whole encrypt-decrypt sequence on Leo's Networker. Buczak transfers this protocol onto Sharkey's Networker, and he is able to use it to get past the first level of security; to get further, he uses a clue left by Sharkey, a date of a car crash in California, which is also an amount that Leo debited on a credit card belonging to Sharkey. While the defense-attack-defense-attack of cryptography becomes quite fanciful here, the point is the way in which defenses around scientific data banks are now being constructed. Indeed, this is one of the touted innovations of Kari Stefansson's deCode company in Iceland in real life. Amusingly enough, the most secret information of all is not kept electronically and is only available to the top officials of Primogen.

Primogen, of course, is not totally secure. One of the reasons for security is that children born of their scheme need to be given lifelong care in their clinics: otherwise genetic tests might reveal the lack of biological match between the children and their social parents. But this provision of care has to be ensured with noncoercive inducements to stay with the Primogen system. Indeed, as the elaborate stratagems of Primogen are gradually unraveled to Sharkey, a non-life-threatening genetic abnormality that has been neither masked nor removed comes into play: G6PD deficiency, which is on a gene next to that for red-green color blindness and becomes a marker to verify siblingship among the Safe population raised in the Primogen trials. G6PD, of course, is associated with malarial areas, has been used as a marker in migration studies, and is connected in the novel with both African Americans, who are not particularly relevant, and Jews of Mediterranean backgrounds. Jewishness is a subterranean theme, and also — as in Romain Gary's comic novels about a post-Vichy France where everyone including Charles de Gaulle turns out to have Jewish ancestors (Gary 1967/1968) — who might have Jewish genetics (the Biomass geneticists' fathers were Nazis in the 1930s, were recruited to the United States before the war, and yet . . .) or Jewish upbringing (the police inspector of "Ordnung und Ruhe" and Sharkey both went to a largely Jewish populated gymnasium and were taught by the same Jewish physicist).

This is the iconicity of Jewishness of which Homi Bhabha writes as the experience of a "lethal modernity," a danse macabre, but also a space of "passage-ways . . . open for a range of border crossings and cross-border identifications" among those who have suffered colonialism, racism, and discrimination, that can provide the grounds for self-critical communities, able to reflect on and puzzle out the new ethical dilemmas of our emergent technologies and the forms of life and life-forms they are creating (Bhabha 1998).

As a novel, however, and one written as a variant of a murder mystery, it is better as a cautionary tale, exploring the cultural armatures and fantasies of new technologies and the dark sides of institutions (driven by parental rescue fantasies, technocratic fantasies of knowing what is best for whole populations, as much as by drives for money or power in themselves), than at imagining how to build a stronger civil society oversight of technoscientific development, or how to build new forms of continuously renewed, open, distributed governmentality and legitimacy. For that, we need to turn to what I will dub the ethnography of ethical discourses and their place in the development of new social theory around risk society, new social movements, media and public relations contestation, contemporary capitalisms and biosocialities, deliberative democracy, and other modalities of public consultation.

The Ethnography of Ethical Discourses:
Biotechnological and Advertising Embraces

In an elegant essay on organ transplantation in India, the anthropologist Lawrence Cohen asks whether ethnography — the thick description of actual social relations, cultural perceptions, and experiences on the ground — can challenge both ethics publicity and scandal publicity (L. Cohen 1998). Both are fantasy formations. By ethics publicity he means the professionalized bioethics and philosopher's view of ethics that reduces all choice to "rational actor" dyadic exchanges eliding contextual conditions; and by scandal publicity he means the conflation of imaginary and real bits of information into an often powerful rumor/propaganda mill, as in the periodic allegations in Central and South America that people from the United States come to abduct children in order to sell their organs. As the spread of new technologies and their associated market redistributions of risks and benefits proceeds, it seems that we are in fact charting new political and ethical terrains, which may well require new forms of commentary by fields such as science and technology studies, new forms of public consultation around the legitimacy of technoscientific research and innovations, and new forms of media contestation in the public sphere. In Lawrence Cohen's case of south India, cyclosporine, the drug that helps prevent organ rejection, also offers new biosocial strategies for the cultural elaboration of debt markets in new cultural forms. Kidney commodity zones emerge through the interaction of entrepreneurial surgeons, persons in great debt, and medical brokers. Sales of organs are now (since 1994) illegal, but donation by fictive kin is often an easy bureaucratic dodge, and the question of "where does it hurt" reveals much about gender dynamics and other hierarchies (on Turkey, see Sanal 2003). An unintended consequence of criminalizing the sale of organs for transplantation has been the demise of at least one clinic that actually paid attention to donors and their after donation care.[20] There is perhaps a certain irony in the fact that the doctors involved are often trained in the First World, returning to India with the intention of bringing the best of world-standard care to India, working in the most modern hospitals and clinics, subverted by the economics of this desire (on their part and that of their patients) to need more and more donors. There are, no doubt, both relatively more honest and more deceitful entrepreneurs among them; there is also a structure of opportunities; and there is a policy debate about whether a regulated open market in organs might not be a more rational and more ethical system of governance than making sales of organs illegal and thereby encouraging a gray or black market.[21] (A partially parallel novelistic account of these tensions, also set in the same region of India, is *Stillborn*, by Rohini Nilekani [1998]. It is not about the trade in organ transplants but about the transnational networks of research, and the drive of scientist-doctors who have returned to India from the United States to pursue research and clinical trials, and how these too may become ethically subverted. Neither this novel nor the project on the trade in organs should be read in any way as casting aspersions on researchers or clinicians in India in general: rather, they are ways of raising the ethical issues that need to be faced in the search for systems of oversight, transparency, and accountability.)

If Lawrence Cohen suggests a partial typology of two kinds of ethics discourse, other kinds of ethics discourse are worth elaborating, including those that emerge within doctor-patient relations, and those that emerge in the use of the market and intellectual property rights to promote biomedical research.

Narratives of Hope and Biotechnical Embrace
Mary-Jo DelVecchio Good has been exploring what in the nuclear world is called the seduction of "technical sweetness,"[22] and what, for the medical world, she calls the "biotechnical embrace": the powerful moral, not just technical, forces that cause physicians to buy into the hype of doing for their patients whatever medical technologies might be able to do, whether or not it is really in the best interests, or ultimately the desire, of the patient (M. Good 1994, 1996, 1998, 1999). In part this is a consequence of an interpretation of the Hippocratic oath ethos of always trying to preserve life, of being a healer, not someone who colludes with death. This is often at the expense of an equally venerable ethos that would be concerned with the good death, with not only paying attention to comfort but doing the work of psychological, familial, community, or spiritual closure or passage—a kind of work that in older societies was often ritually facilitated at length, continuing after the death of the individual, and that in America is facilitated before death by the hospice movement. But in part it is also a critical component of attempting to manage what Good calls the "narratives of hope"

which are important components of both the patient's will to live, and the doctor's ability to cope with losing patients who have terminal illnesses. In detailed, longitudinal interviews and following of treatment protocols with breast cancer patients, Good lays out the conflicting pressures on patients and doctors in how to convey and interpret statistical information and the uncertainties and trade-offs of any course of treatment.

The notions of the biotechnical embrace and narratives of hope (including the shaping of time) can be applied in a number of medical settings, ranging from end-of-life dilemmas to difficult choices about lung transplants for children with cystic fibrosis. In all these cases, among the ethnographic data points is the shift during the past three decades from paternalistic care (with limited information given to patients) to an ethos of patient autonomy (and disclosure of whatever information the patient can handle) to realization that the complexity of issues, as well as psychological pressures, can make pure patient autonomy untenable or at best an unattainable ideal. The role of physicians in subtly influencing or negotiating how patients receive information is an important way that these issues are resolved. Moreover, the shifting power relations between patient groups and physicians (and provider groups), due increasingly to the use of patient support groups mobilized through the Internet, open up the evaluation of information and treatment options to a wider set of inputs than just doctors and their patients, or doctors, payers, and patients. There is an important interplay between the political economy of health care in the American system (with cost-cutting efforts by managed care administrators) and the need for patient support groups to sometimes act as pressure groups to get procedures and options to be offered.

The Advertising Embrace: Constitutive Prolepsis
In a study under way, Kaushik Sunder Rajan is exploring the ways in which genomic research provides a window into contemporary capitalism. One strand of the research focuses on how biology has become caught in a parallel "advertising embrace," buzz, or hype, as the computer software and dot.com industries (Sunder Rajan 2002). Building on the work of Emily Martin (1994) and Joe Dumit (1995) on the circulation and remaking of scientific information among different user groups in society, and of Paul Rabinow (1995) on the dynamics of biotech companies, as well as on the dissertation of Chris Kelty (1999) on the constitutive role of hype or buzz in the computer start-up worlds, Sunder Rajan explores how information is turned into value (use value, exchange value, symbolic value) in a directional "flow" from upstream patent claims to downstream uses, and how the play

for market position requires both speed and high-throughput techniques and machines, which in turn set up a series of contradictions or tensions that are constantly being fought out over what counts as part of the market (as opposed to public domain). Thus, for instance, the highly publicized competition over the mapping of the human genome between the NIH and the Celera Corporation turned on the latter's deploying of new Perkin-Elkins machines which could speed up the mapping process, albeit at lower resolution, and deploying a tactic of cutting up the genome for sequencing and then reassembling it later. The effect was to force NIH-funded genome centers to buy the faster machines, and to adjust their goals and timetables to a new goal. In the process, Celera is hoping to make money off access to the highest level of information, and to patent what it can, while NIH is hoping to preserve as much of a public domain registry of mapping as possible. A new game is now reshaping the next phase of genomics research: the mapping of single nucleotide polymorphisms in the race to produce maps of variable characteristics that can lead to individualized therapies. In order to again contest the shaping of the market, of what can be patented and what not, two consortia are attempting to capture the information first, the one a consortium of private companies, the other a consortium of NIH and its genome centers along with some of the pharmaceutical majors, promising that the mapping itself will become public, because after all it is the more valuable downstream applications which are really worth owning, and access to these rights can be complicated by too many upstream licensing and royalty agreements.

Among the most interesting of the contradictions in these races, for my present purposes, is that between speed and what Sunder Rajan dubs "speed bumps," institutional mechanisms that slow things down. For my purposes, I would include among the important speed bumps the institutional need to slow down the pace to allow society to assimilate change. Associate justice of the U.S. Supreme Court Stephen Breyer, in an address at the Whitehead/MIT Conference on Genetics and Society in May 2000, argued that in many of the new disputes raised by new technologies, it is premature for the courts to deliver definitive decisions. The appellate and supreme courts do best when the ground has been prepared by numerous lower-level and community contests, and the submission eventually to the courts of briefs from the many parties and interests, so that what the courts can adjudicate is not the science but the social consequences.

It turns out to be an older ethical plateau to believe the challenges here to be an open field of public consultation, without detailed considerations of media strategies deployed, and hence again "caught in the advertising embrace." Numerous studies are now pointing out that when flows of capital are involved, public relations efforts to manage the information and impression flow are becoming more and more central. Corporations are learning how to organize "grassroots" campaigns to offset citizen action groups, as well as to carefully stage-manage what gets reported in the media. The long struggle against the American tobacco companies, which managed to hide the "smoking gun" scientific studies that demonstrated unequivocal nicotine addiction, as well as their strategies to increase nicotine levels and target market niches, is but the most public and currently obvious of these tactics (Greife and Linsky 1995; Stauber and Rampton 1995; Rampton and Stauber 2001; Allen 1999). Counterforces of concerned independent scientists and citizen action groups, sometimes with government support, are using the Internet as a new tool to help build alliances. One wonders to what degree the public sphere is being forced to move in the direction of a play of advocacy positions (K. Fortun 2001).

If information flows are managed, what role for the anthropologist? These are not new questions, but it is often the case that if anthropologists can provide something back to the people being worked with, access is easier. In the case of Mary-Jo DelVecchio Good, she began by providing feedback to residents and young doctors on how they were taking medical histories, and how they listen and give information to patients. In the breast cancer study, one of the goals was to continue to provide feedback to doctors about how patients were hearing them, and to provide additional channels of information for new patients (an information booklet was one outcome, including information about the way many women experienced different phases of treatment protocols). In the case of Paul Rabinow's three studies with biotechnology projects (1995, 1998, 1999), and most especially with the still new and emerging relationship with Kari Stefansson, CEO of Iceland's deCode corporation, the question has been put on the table whether Dr. Stefansson says anything different in private, as it were, with the anthropologist, or whether this is a stepping into the same public relations role that has become Stefansson's persona (see also Sigurdsson 1999, M. Fortun 2000). In the cases of start-up companies (and even larger ones) in the dot.com world, and the biotechnology world, hype about the promise of future products is required first for venture capital to flow, and if there is a product, for larger firms to buy either the development rights or the company itself. The hype is constitutive. The point is that in all of these cases, the mediated and performative nature of ethical discourses needs to be taken into account in ever more careful ways, not simply to dismiss false claims but to understand the different kinds of functionalities that claims help constitute.

The next instrumental question then becomes: can one create an informed public in the context of complicated technologies, with uncertain outcomes, packaged in semisecret, proprietary, and veiled or performatively shaped media of information distribution? But perhaps more important is the question about whether the very notion of an informed public is not itself a fantasy that can only be asked in relation not merely to what came before (a fantasized less-informed public) but also to what is excluded from "knowing," "accounting," or "recognition." As has been outlined in the cases of the victims of the Bhopal disaster (K. Fortun 2001), the shaping of the statistics and self-monitoring of AIDS in Brazil (Biehl 1999), and the assertion of rights and access to attention by radiation sufferers from the Chernobyl disaster (Petryna 2002), the biosocial structure of truth, health and illness, life and death, changes with accounting procedures, and so the lantern of critique is sent back to shed light on these feedback loops, rather than being able to simply illuminate and clarify a reality that is uncontested or unproblematic.

New Ethical Challenges: Xenotransplantation

Perhaps one of the most interesting of the complicated new sets of ethical challenges presented by new biomedical technologies is the case of xeno-transplantation, the potential for supplying whole organs to humans from pigs in particular, either knockout pigs or transgenic ones. Among the reasons this is an interesting case is that in addition to many of the ethical problems that attend other difficult biomedical issues of informed consent (as at the end of life), of choice among unpalatable therapies (as in pediatric cystic fibrosis cases), and of evaluating uncertainty and the play of powerful ideological forces such as the biomedical embrace, xenotransplantation presents two other features. First of all, the risk of xenosis (infection across species) is to populations at large. That is, the threat is of unleashing pandemics like the current HIV one. So both risk and decision making cannot be left alone to the doctor-patient relationship, or the doctor-provider-hospital-patient institutions. Moreover, this is a risk that affects populations transnationally, and if a public health risk is to be contained, it cannot be decided (or managed and regulated) within national sovereignties alone. Secondly, despite the urgency of recipients waiting for organs, of the pressures of surgeons vying to claim the credit for innovative procedures, and of the monetary profits that might be reaped, the severity of scientific problems still bedeviling chances for success, if taken seriously, may help militate toward time for some of these issues to unfold and be widely discussed.

Indeed, I draw on this example precisely because an effort to guide such a broad public consultation is being mounted by one of the leading xenotransplant and basic vascular biology pioneers, Dr. Fritz Bach, the Lewis Thomas Professor of Medicine at the Harvard Medical School, with the aid of former dean of the Harvard Medical School Harvey Fineberg, bioethics philosopher Normal Daniels, and other colleagues, and more recently Dr. Elizabeth McGregor, a veterinarian and staff member of the Canadian Privy Council. Following the 1997 UNESCO Universal Declaration on the Human Genome and Human Rights, Dr. Bach and his colleagues published an article in *Nature Medicine* in 1998 and testified before the U.S. Congress for a moratorium on xenotransplantation experiments at least until the public could be consulted. In 1999 Dr. McGregor and Dr. Bach convened an international working group on xenotransplantation to draw up a series of white papers, create and test teaching modules for high schools and public discussion forums, and initiate preliminary experiments in Web-based Internet outreach.

Dr. Bach has called for a moratorium on xenotransplant experiments at least until "society" is able to make the decision whether or not, and under what conditions, to shoulder the risk, rather than allowing the experts (i.e., those with interests at stake) to make the decision all by themselves (Bach et al. 1998). What could such "public consultation" look like institutionally? The closest immediate analogy to the moratorium called for by Dr. Bach is the moratorium in the 1970s on recombinant DNA research called for by that technology's pioneers when they perceived a rising public fear and faced their own sense of uncertainty about whether they might be on the verge of inadvertently releasing new organisms into the environment with unclear consequences. In that case, through the calling of the Asilomar Conference to discuss standards for containment, and step-by-step rules for experimentation, the scientific community was able to self-police. The rules were turned into NIH guidelines, and gradually, as experience was gained, the rules were relaxed (Weiner 1999). In the present case, the risks may be greater because of the complexity of the organisms, and the incalculability of potential long-term latencies of retroviruses like HIV.

A second, negative comparative example is the growing debate about genetically engineered crops, where the effort of for-profit corporations to assure the public of the safety of transgenic crops has turned into something of a public relations fiasco. In this case there was, and continues to be, little public consultation, but rather a classic confrontational politics between some consumers and producers, and between national sensibilities and regulatory systems (mainly in Europe against the United States and Argentina). In any case, the efforts of Bach's group to stimulate broad discussion may provide some fascinating materials with which to think about decision making in the public interest.

Without going into the science at any length, among the ethical conundrums is that organ transplantation has been a quest since the nineteenth century, and an active research arena for at least forty years. In the beginning, "sledgehammer" immunosuppression was used to try to prevent rejection of organs before one even knew about T-cells or lymphocytes, or endothelial cell activation. A great deal was learned about vascular biology in the process, and eventually allotransplantation techniques became successful for hearts, lungs, and kidneys, especially if they came from identical twins, but increasingly from others as well. Xenotransplants, however, present daunting problems. Most work at the moment is directed toward preventing hyperacute rejection (HAR) in the immediate short term of minutes and hours. The immunosuppressant drugs that work with allotransplants do not seem to work across species. And so the techniques of genetic engineering are being tried to create pig organs that will be tolerated by human hosts. These are either knockout techniques (i.e., removing genes that code for antigens on the surface of porcine cells that are recognized by human hosts as foreign) or transgenic techniques (i.e., inserting a human gene into pig cells that block the action of human complements that attack foreign cells). But even if the HAR problem can be solved, at the moment we have no means of dealing with either medium-term rejection, or so-called delayed xenograft rejection (DXR), or long-term chronic rejection (Bach 1996).

The short-term benefits of these paths of research are to the increase of basic biological knowledge rather than to therapy for organ recipients, although the longer-term hope is for ways to make such techniques therapeutic and to save hundreds of thousands of lives. Ethical questions already loom here about whether desperately ill patients and their families can give truly informed consent under these pressures of the biomedical embrace, particularly when the protocols for observation and monitoring will probably be lifetime, and perhaps (as rules in Holland already envision) complete quarantine. Normal rules for volunteers in medical research protocols allow withdrawal at will, but this would perhaps not be possible, and yet it is unclear how one could enforce compliance. Moreover, if one is worried about pathogens whose latency may not appear for years or even generations, or unknown pathogens for which there are no diagnostic assays, the complications multiply, though rules have been formulated for the registry of all such experimentation, and standards will be developed.

Whether there are other paths of research that can deliver the same biological knowledge, for example, the efforts to grow organs from pluripotent stem cells, remains to be seen. From the general questions about ethics and the evolution of technoscience, there are also the series of issues surrounding the use of animals in research. Bach and McGregor have included an animal rights lawyer, Steve Wise, in their discussions (see Wise 1999), but more interesting than animal rights issues per se are the questions of whether the more we learn about the complex species-specific features of immunology, the less useful many of the animal experiments may be. It has been argued that monkey clinical trials in the past have seriously misled researchers developing the polio vaccine and treatments for AIDS; that most new therapeutic drugs are discovered through in vitro cell and tissue culture, biochemical, and computer simulation methods; and that patient groups such as the AIDS community are increasingly putting pressure to shorten animal trials, bypass them, or do them retrospectively (Greek and Greek 2000; see also Das 2000 on issues of political representation in clinical trials).

Efforts to stimulate discussion began with the guidelines laid down by the 1997 UNESCO Universal Declaration on the Human Genome and Human Rights, and involved an initial working group of representatives from the Third World as well as the First World convened by Bach and McGregor at Meech Lake in Canada. Many of these participants were ministers or deputy ministers in their respective governments and undertook to begin forming national committees in their home countries to stimulate discussion. In the meantime Bach and McGregor commissioned a series of white papers on the scientific, legal, ethical, regulatory, and economic issues and began to develop discussion kits for use in high schools, colleges, and churches. Initiatives continue on both high diplomatic levels and grassroots educational ones. The high school kit developed during the summer of 2000 presents an interesting model of having students spend a week being informed about the science, who the stakeholders are, and what the risks and benefits are, exploring the topics of the white papers. A second week is then spent role-playing stakeholders' positions on both pro and con sides of the debate as to whether the risks are worth proceeding with the research protocols, with an effort to work toward an ideal "consensus" or at least the kind of decisions that a minister of health might face. In the third and final week, various models of becoming agents of change are explored according to a matrix of using the judiciary, government executive agencies, elected officials, NGOs, and the media, at both the national and international levels. Students work through the ways in which, for instance, court cases involving the Harvard oncomouse were contested in Canada, or the ways in which the moral suasion of the World Court could be invoked, or the role of House Committees of Parliament, or royal commissions, trying in each case to compare historical actual cases to their utility in the issues surrounding xenotransplantation. In both these high school kits and in college workshops, students compare various models for initiating discussion and action: the World Court, international agencies such as WHO or UNESCO, the Asilomar example, national research ethics boards, and so on. Other models include the Danish consensus conferences, in which a group of lay citizens is informed and delivers opinions, which are then disseminated in the news media, prior to electoral or parliamentary decisions.

The general model here is, as Justice Breyer argued, that for broad social decisions to be made, many different groups must be able to argue the issues, take positions, and present their interests and differences. The ideal is an informed public, one that can modulate the dilemmas of expertise versus lay understanding.

What is potentially revealing here, thinking of this as a model for other issues, is seeing to what degree the process can remain open, against the spheres of discussion being colonized either by the power play of experts seeking to rationalize risks into controllable quantifications that can be discounted in various ways, or by the power play of the interested use of the mass media of veiled advocacy advertising. Particularly important here, one suspects, is the ability to be able to identify "speakers" and their interests. When the chief medical officer of Genzyme Corporation talks about the difficulties of multiple review boards and informed consent ("22 pages long"), he is being neither disingenuous (the problems are real) nor disinterested (he's also concerned about time, expense, and barriers to market). Likewise, when the COO of Imutran, one of the lead contenders to do the first xenotransplants, reviews all the known cases of porcine transplants to primates, and human patients perfused through porcine spleen and livers, and finds plenty of porcine cells, but no evidence of infection, or anti-PERV antibodies, is this to be taken as lack of evidence of harm (yes, as far as it goes) or a citing mainly of evidence in support of the business plan?

The case of Imutran is of interest also as one about the dilemmas of secrecy in science and allegations of potential circumvention of regulatory efforts. In addition, the whole xenotransplantation debate is part of the larger debate about the trade in organs, including where (as in the United States and Europe) there are national organ-sharing mechanisms and efforts to distribute organs by public and equitable criteria. The trade in kidneys provides a window on many of the dilemmas, beginning with the disconcerting shift from early cases where providing an organ was honored as altruism, to an increasing trade that exploits poor donors to yield up organs for rich recipients.

Some transplant surgeons have argued for years that the only solution (both to inequities in the organ bazaar and to the risks of xenotransplantation) is to increase the voluntary donation of organs through public education campaigns, that money in this trade is absolutely corrupting. Some countries have now passed presumptive donation laws, meaning that unless one stipulates that one's body not be harvested, if there is a need and match, organs may be taken. Controversial in Italy (where such a law passed against much opposition in 1999), such laws in countries such as Brazil are seen by many as further disempowering the poor. Other proposals for avoiding monetary sale are futures markets organized so that only if one agrees to be a donor would one be eligible oneself to be a recipient. Other proposals include schemes for "compensated gifting," rather than monetary sale, that is, provision of contributions to scholarships or funeral funds. Efforts, as in India in 1994, to outlaw the sale of organs can have the unintended effect of stimulating a black market. And so other transplant surgeons say that black markets are so pervasive that it would be better to legalize organ markets and regulate them.

Disempowerment of the poor or of political dissidents is intensified by those countries (China today, Argentina and Taiwan in the recent past) that use executed prisoners as sources of organs, and where increase in number of executions can be correlated with demand for organs (Scheper-Hughes 2000, Ikels 1997). The historical genealogy of such appropriation by the state or by society goes back not only to medieval use of corpses of hanged criminals for medical dissection but also to the 1883 Anatomy Act in England, which made workhouses and public hospitals "lawfully in possession" of the dead whose families did not claim the body or who could not afford funeral costs (Das 2000). Morgues and end-of-life clinics can also provide organs in ways that are suspect (Scheper-Hughes 2000).

These considerations lead to three difficult moral issues. There is first what Veena Das, quoting Margaret Lock, calls the "Shiva-like character" of many new biotechnologies, which are "potential creators of happiness" while simultaneously "destroyers of society as we know it"; the microsocial relations in different parts of the "technoscape" are put under pressure and slowly transformed: between doctor and patient, family members who might be donors for one another, definitions of citizen and social waste, of entitled and nonentitled. There is a sense, Das continues, now quoting Bruno Latour, that the creation of a free political subject is simultaneously the creation of the nonhuman, including those persons dealt with as if they were human social waste (Das 2000; Biehl 1999), bodies appropriable by the state or society through direct means (executions, workhouses) or indirect ones (markets, regulatory rules, access to clinics), including perhaps the definition of death as brain stem death in order that organs and tissues can be harvested before they are deemed dead by other criteria.[23] Second, there is the ongoing tension between outcomes that are contributions to scientific knowledge, but not therapeutic successes, though they are sold (to doctor and patient alike) as contributing eventually to the latter. Third, there is the challenge that Das poses against even the most pragmatic of justifications for heavily regulated markets in human organs: that she can think of no principles that allow us to think of this as fair exchange. She invokes the legal recognition of background assumptions or counterprinciples in contract law that prevent contract law from imperializing all areas of life: contracts are arguably invalid if they imprint permanent character on things (workers are entitled to compensation for industrial hazards; the employer/capitalist is not free to invoke the idea of consent); the law refuses to see contracting parties as high-risk gamblers (where value is only what the parties place on things).

In the end, from the point of view of critical theory, the issue is not the pragmatics of decision making but rather the ways in which the ethical dilemmas and trade-offs reproduce themselves in a variety of other settings, with changing boundaries of what is felt to be taboo and permissible, the fantasies of solution and the ways these fantasies are displaced elsewhere. From such questions, the contours of social differences and change remain visible in ways they cannot from inside pragmatic decision-making "solutions."

New Social Theory for Emergent Ethical Issues
The ethical dilemmas, discourses, and scenarios invoked in this chapter are among the kinds of challenges that have led to the formulation of a series of new social theories, including the bodies of work on risk society, social movements, biosociality, deliberative politics, and the uses of the new media from advertising to the Internet.

All of these increasingly operate on globalizing as well as localizing levels, giving increasing choice and responsibility to individuals while at the same time forcing these choices to be made in globally extended networks and terrains. New forms of transnationally extended, but not necessarily uniform, governmentalities are thereby being elaborated.

Composing ethnographically rich texts on emergent governmentalities, biosocialities, and forms of life generated under late and post modernities and capitalisms that can explore connections between changing subjectivities, social organization, modes of production, and symbolic or cultural forms is a challenge that the anthropological archive is increasingly addressing. This challenge requires being able to work in technoscientific imaginaries and infrastructures through multiple temporalities, cycles of political economy, and reconstructions of social arrangements across local and global expanses, as well as deploying and critiquing new, lively, metaphor-rich languages and semiotic skeins that arise from and articulate new cultural expressions, understandings, and forms of mediation. Such ethnographic work can help clarify emergent forms of life for which conventional ethical guideposts from the past are not always sufficient, and while we have run out of "giving grounds" (Wittgenstein 1969: 17e), we can nonetheless watch ourselves perform ungrounded ways of acting that have both social and ethical weight and consequences. It is perhaps in this insider-outsider ethnographic effort at knowing ourselves that we can formulate answers about the shaping of new subjectivities and subjects of science and technology. As to the question when it could be possible to have an alternative politics to the dominance of the globalizing market forces today, it is likely that the "old mole" must remain underground yet awhile longer, attentive and awaiting opportunities.

SUBJECTIVITIES IN AN AGE

OF GLOBAL CONNECTIVITY

6

Autobiographical Voices (1, 2, 3) and

Mosaic Memory: Ethnicity, Religion, Science

(An Inquiry into the Nature of Autobiographical

Genres and Their Uses in Extending Social Theory)

The word's power does not consist in its explicit content — if generally speaking, there is such a thing — but in the diversion that is involved in it. — Chaim Nachman Bialik

Autobiographical voices: avoiding having to define autobiography as a neatly typified genre, "autobiographical voices" call attention to subject positioning in autobiographies, in memoirs, but also in life histories, in certain kinds of autobiographically figured fiction, in the tracings of authorial perspective in the writing of biographies, and in the human screenings of writing about scientific discovery. One, two, three voices, or compositions of identity, dialogic relations with alterities, and triangulations of post(modern) sensibilities: autobiographical voices are often thought of as deeply singular attempts to inscribe individual "identity" (one voice); however, they not only are mosaic compositions but often may be structured through processes of mirroring and dialogic relations with cross-historical and cross-cultural others and thus may resonate with various sorts of double voicings (two voices); in modern times, increasingly important is mediation by collective (three voices) rational and rationalizing endeavors such as the sciences, which themselves depend on explicit triangulations among multiple perspectival positionings and understandings. "Sondage" is the archaeologist's Francophone term for soundings, for the search techniques of an exploratory dig. The "experimental sondages" here are efforts to listen to the many kinds of voicings in autobiographical forms that might on the one hand expand the ways genres of autobiography are recognized (beyond, for instance, the fairly narrow master narrative of Western individualism, or universalizing theories of individuation-maturation, that studies of autobiography are so often used to celebrate, innocent of any effort at serious cross-cultural validation) and on the other hand provide clues for keeping social and cultural theory abreast of a rapidly changing, pluralizing, world.

Mosaic memory: memory is layered in differently structured strata, fragmented and collaged together like mosaics in consciousness and in unconscious maneuverings, all of which takes hermeneutical skills to hear and unpack, which in another sense might also be called Mosaic, as a figure of the hermeneutical traditions created in the interface between orality (face-to-face, relational, immediately monitored and adjustable communication) and literacy (distanced, ambiguously playing on the graphics of absence). These hermeneutical traditions are located in old scriptural-moral discourses (Judaism, Islam, Christianity, Buddhism, Jainism, Hinduism, Confucianism, etc.), but they are also the less acknowledged taproots of contemporary literary and philosophical hermeneutical explorations (Freud, Joyce, Gadamer, Levinas, Jabès, Derrida). The story is that the Tablets of Moses had to be broken so that they could become humanly usable. The Islamic version is that there are two sets of revelation: the sequence of the Qur'anic text, ordered by metrical length with the longest chapters first (this is the order of the primordial Qur'an in the seventh heaven); and the historical sequence of revelation in fragments over the twenty-three-year period of the Prophet's autobiographical prophetic career. In other words, deconstruction is nothing new. As Joyce puts it: "In the bugining was the woid, in the muddle was the sounddance, and thereinafter you are in the unbewised again."

Autobiography, Anthropology, and the (Post)modern Condition

And if you want [auto]biographies, do not look for those with the legend "Mr. So-and-so and his times," but for one whose title page might be inscribed, "a fighter against his time." — Friedrich Nietzsche, *The Use and Abuse of History*

For the anthropologist, autobiography is a challenging threefold force field of desire:

1. Standing between the individual and the social, autobiography is a site of interplay between the modernist vision of autonomous bounded egos and postmodernist decentered selves. On the one hand, autobiography can provide access to the "native point of view," claiming a subjectivity grounded in cultural specificity that is both empirical and accessible otherwise only through in-depth interviewing. On the other hand, anthropology as a social

science is committed to the elucidation of how individual experience is socially and culturally constructed. In that frame, autobiographical accounts are fallible data that need to be interrogated for their cultural structures, and for their culturally formed blindnesses and unconscious programming.

2. The second deep attraction for anthropology is the possibility that autobiographies can help sketch out cultural and social terrain where traditional social theory is blind or archaic. Nowhere is this more evident than in the rapidly changing environments of what is often referred to by the much disputed term "postmodern."

"Postmodern" for me is a simple cover term for three interrelated ideas. First, it is a marker for the late twentieth century, for what is sociologically different about the late twentieth century from the nineteenth and early twentieth centuries, when almost all the social theory still being used by professional social scientists was formulated. Bentham, Malthus, Mill, Marx, Freud, Durkheim, Weber, Nietzsche—these are theorists who formed their ideas out of the experience of the nineteenth century and the early twentieth. Whatever it is about the late twentieth century—the increased speed of transportation and communication, the electronic media and information society, the industrialization of science and technology, the globalized movements of mass populations—there is a widespread feeling that social relations, culture, and psychology are being structured in significantly new ways, and we need to reconstruct social theory to match our contemporary experience and prepare for future changes. Second, "postmodern" does not mean "after" modernism or modernity but rather refers to the cycles of renewal and decay of modernisms or modernities. "Postmodern" refers to those modernities and modernisms which set themselves in distinction to previous modernities and modernisms. The postmodern involves a historical consciousness about modernity. Hence the typographic "(post)modern," to accommodate both those who prefer to still speak of the late twentieth century as modern and those who differentiate modernisms and modernities. Third, substantively, one of the things the postmodern is about is the juxtaposition of things, events, and experiences that once were separated by time and space. Global integration is increasing in pace and penetration. It is not uniform: there is a new global stratification. It is not only jet set elites who move across the world; there are also mass movements of guest workers and displaced persons from war or from destruction of previous agrarian and industrial production, who form new proletarianized cross-national strata: Koreans, Indians, and Filipinos working in the Persian Gulf, Turkish and Moroccan guest workers and new citizens in Europe, Mexicans and Central Americans in the United States. If jet set elites are increasingly subject to the weightlessness, commodification, and volitional lifestyle that have been the subject of high culture complaint since at least Nietzsche and Dostoyevsky, and if the proletarianized masses are subject to the belatedness and anxieties of political-economic inequality, still in both cases there is a cross-cultural awareness and constant comparison that is of an intensity and pervasiveness that is new and defining of the contemporary era.

This postmodern condition allows for a degree of serious cross-cultural critique that was utopian only fifty years ago. Compare the impact of the style of cross-cultural critique practiced by Bronislaw Malinowski or Margaret Mead, in which an exotic pattern of child rearing could be held up as a foil to our own patterns of child rearing to show that they were not "natural" but alterable cultural conventions. Contrast the degree of intellectual control that is necessary under contemporary conditions of multiple readerships, where what one writes is read by those one writes about as well as by one's colleagues or cultural fellows.

Moreover, in the contemporary world, people increasingly construct their sense of self out of pieces that come from many different cultural environments. Maxine Hong Kingston encapsulates the point when she says, "To be Chinese American is not the same as to be Chinese in America," and to be Chinese American has no role model. It is a new construction. Life histories of various forms have been used in the past for a variety of purposes, often in the social sciences as organizing devices for typical life cycle stages in relatively stable cultural environments. But perhaps the most important use of life histories, and increasingly so in the contemporary world, is the strategic use of a life frame that straddles major social and cultural transformations. This is, for instance, one of the richest veins of contemporary writing in English, drawing on interlinguistic and intercultural differences to remake culturally fuller individuals and social actors. James Joyce was a pioneer of such writing, followed in the contemporary period by writers such as Salman Rushdie, Michelle Cliff, and many others who are gifting to English linguistic and cultural resources from South Asia, the Caribbean, Africa, the Middle East, Latin America, and elsewhere.

3. There is the epistemological attraction of autobiography as a privileged genre where the reflexivity of human storytelling is foregrounded. Autobiography is not only a good place to observe how art follows life, and life art; it is also a vehicle to reflect on the discovery and construction processes of anthropology itself, and of science and knowledge in general, including the human sciences and the cultural products studied under the rubric of the humanities.

In the following pages, I want to sketch out more fully these three areas where autobiography seems particularly useful as a vehicle of access for anthropological investigation (and perhaps at the same time expand the somewhat parochial traces into which the study of autobiographical genres has fallen, particularly by insisting on the cross-cultural as a tool for checking the validity of generalizations and readings that claim to be contributions to theory): (1) identity processes in the late twentieth century that are coded under labels such as ethnicity (both domestic and international), feminism, and regionalism or localism—in this essay, I will primarily consider, and in abbreviated form, ethnicity, drawing on a longer essay published previously (M. Fischer 1986); (2) cross-cultural comparison and critique: alternative frames for articulating emotion, self, and agency, focusing particularly on the way these articulations work in alternative moral traditions, and their critical apparatuses, as they are being reinvented for the (post)modern world; and (3) science as a collective human and cultural social endeavor, which constitutes a major component of contemporary epistemology, worldview, and basis for moral judgment.

Autobiographical Voice (1): Identity Processes

The story of the *bi-langue* and the *pluri-langue* exorcised his obsessions. He also needed the other language—your language, foreign in me—to tell himself the tale of how unadapted he was to the world and tell it with the joyful enchantment of a living man who sees his life before him, a life which sees itself enter into him, marry him, and of a dying man who glimpses death over his shoulder, behind him.... when questioned, he hid himself in his fictions: the soul of a pidgin screenwriter.—Abdelkebir Khatibi, *Love in Two Languages*

Identity processes are complex compositions, as often using noncognitive as cognitive modes. Recent autobiographies by talented and ethnically musical authors provide one tool for gathering clues about these processes that might be used for further exploration both of identity processes and of sociocultural reorganization in the late twentieth century among certain strata or segments of society.

My attention was drawn to autobiography as a methodological tool in reconstructing theories of contemporary ethnicity in the context of a course on American culture, when I became aware of a rich vein of autobiography and autobiographical fiction that takes ethnicity as a focal puzzle but seemed poorly accommodated by the sociological literature on ethnicity. Maxine Hong Kingston's *Woman Warrior*, Michael Arlen's *Passage to Ara-*

rat, and Marita Golden's *Migrations of the Heart* were not well encompassed by sociological categories such as group support (mobility, political mobilization), transition (assimilation), or transmission from generation to generation (socialization). There is a literature that does fit these sociological categories: older immigrant novels centered on themes of rebellion against the family or intermarriage. In a paper on the newer autobiographical literature (M. Fischer 1986), I attempted to compare five ethnicities in the United States — Armenian Americans, Mexican Americans, Chinese Americans, African Americans, and Native Americans, plus in the margins of the introduction and conclusion I also brought into view my own ethnicity — giving attention in each case to both female and male writers. Methodologically I stressed the need in comparative work to use a minimum of three cases, to avoid the better-worse false moralisms that dualistic comparison tends to fall into.

What these newer works communicate forcefully is the sense that ethnicity (and similar identity processes) is (1) reinvented in each generation by each individual; (2) what is invented is something new (Kingston's observation that there is no role model for being Chinese American); (3) that this something new is achieved by an inner listening to different components of the self, finding a voice or style that does not violate those multiple components; and (4) that ethnicity is often something puzzling to the individual, something over which he or she does not feel in control, something transmitted often through processes more like dream-translation from visual into linear verbalization or more like transference than like cognitive language and learning. Five strategies or modes of articulation (both of identity and of texts) were explored: transference, dream-work, alternative selves and bifocality, bilingual interference/interreference, and ironic humor.

Two quick illustrations. Kingston's talk stories illustrate the dream-translation analogy. Her talk stories are fragments of stories, customs, and events, told by parents but not explained. "No Name Woman," for instance, is a story of a father's sister who had an illegitimate child and was forced by the shame to commit suicide. It is a story told to young girls as a warning ("Now that you've started to menstruate") at a particular point in their life cycle. It is also told to test American-born children's ability to establish realities: to distinguish what is peculiar to one's family, to poverty, or to Chineseness. The story gains force as Kingston considers alternative interpretations — was this father's sister coerced (is she a figure of female submissiveness), or was she an active temptress? — and uses these alternatives as allegories for adolescent struggles. She wants to be attractive, but selectively (how to make a Chinese fall in love with me, but not a Caucasian). If Kingston's text illustrates dream-translation-like processes in which fragmentary images must be turned into coherent narratives, Michael Arlen's text illustrates transference-like processes (Arlen 1975). Arlen suffers an anxiety generated by the silence of a father who wishes to spare his son the pain of the past (the massacres of the Armenians in Ottoman Turkey), but instead his silence about the past creates a void, an obsessive need to explore, to fill in. Arlen goes to Soviet Armenia, where he does not so much find missing information or narratives but rather begins to recognize that he himself acts out behavior patterns that he recognizes in his father (and his text enacts this pattern, as well).

To explore such subtle patterns as transference or dream-translation (and other complex modalities of negotiating ethnicity), one needs good informants/autobiographies. I found this recent set of ethnically accented autobiographical texts particularly facilitating in thinking through the move anthropology (and the social sciences and humanities generally) is making from behaviorist and symbolist models of communication to structuralist and poststructuralist ones. Behaviorist models take words and symbols to be unproblematic tokens, combined and rearranged in meaningful chains of sentences or utterances, done in turn-taking, stimulus-response sequences. Analysts can thus build up models of culture based on sets of belief statements made by actors. Symbolist models recognize that symbols are not univocal simple tokens but have fans of meanings, and that more is exchanged in any speech act than either speaker or receiver comprehends. Nonetheless, in symbolist models, symbols are still but more complex sign tokens — like overly full bouquets or pockets of fertile sediment — richly polysemic yet discrete. Indeed, the richest symbols are like black holes: the entire culture is said to be condensed there. Symbolist analysts organize their models of culture around key symbols, symbol clusters, and nodes of semantic networks, somewhat like a crystal structure. There is a reassuring sense of relative stasis or stability of the symbolic system. Structuralist, and particularly poststructuralist, models decompose symbols and metaphors into chains of metonyms or associations that play out into disseminating, ramifying, transmuting dynamics, attempting to model, in the structuralist case, the semantic-symbolic parameters of variation and transformation, and in the poststructuralist case, the transmuting ambivalences of meaning that keep texts and communication labile (unless forcibly controlled, in which case poststructuralist deconstructive sensibilities highlight the tensions and pressures of alternative meanings subversive to those intended and authorized by the controls). Thus, for instance, we find the multiple alternatives that Kingston explores in the "No Name Woman" fragment of her mother's narrative, or the quite unexpected behavioral and psychological understandings Arlen finds in his interactions in Armenia.

To recapitulate, these ethnic autobiographies are useful in three ways.

1. Substantively they show places where reduction to sociological function is inadequate, and they thereby highlight the cultural. My tag for this is cultural *interférence*, a pun taken from Michel Serres, meaning both cultural interference and cultural interreference of two or more traditions: this is one of the key tasks that ethnicity performs. Parallel social and cultural processes work across ethnic groups in America, but they produce only families of resemblance, because ethnicity is a construction out of two or more particular, historical, cultural traditions. Consider Abelardo Delgado's poem "Stupid America," which exposes the inability of Anglo-America to recognize in Chicanos their rich antiquity, creative modernity, and synthetic fertility. Chicano knives can be put to use in creative sculpture, as in the past santeros carved religious figures; Hispanic modernity in painting (Picasso) outpaced Anglo, and barrio graffiti could be much more, given the chance; literature, too, can be powerfully synthesized out of a bicultural situation: witness this poem:

> stupid america, see that chicano
> with the big knife
> in his steady hand
> he doesn't want to knife you
> he wants to sit on a bench
> and carve christfigures
> but you won't let him . . .
> he is the picasso
> of your western states
> but he will die
> with one thousand masterpieces
> hanging only from his mind

2. Methodologically, to explore these cultural "intereférences," poststructuralist notions of nomadic meaning are helpful, because cultural "intereférences" are embedded historically through fragments of language, sedimented metaphors, and linguistic disseminations. For example, Diana der Havanessian's poem "Learning an Ancestral Language":

> My ancestors talk
> to me in dangling
> myths.

On sunny days
I bury
words.
Each word a riddle
each dream
heirless
They put out roots
and coil around
forgotten syntax.

Next spring a full
blown anecdote
will sprout.

Once verbalized, articulated, worked out, these sedimented and embedded linguistic roots open into cross-readings of different cultural traditions with historical depth. This is the work that the often uncomfortable position of being ethnic generates, often expressed most powerfully in
ironic humor. Thus Gerald Vizenor's down-and-out Amerindian character
Bart IV, "who fails as a trickster and settled for the role of a fool. Evil was too
much for him to balance. As a fool he was a brilliant success, talking hilarious nonsense to get his case dismissed in court," or to weasel money out of
his social worker. He's not really a trickster in the mythic sense of one who
can play the cosmic forces of evil and good against each other, overturning
one with the other to show how they work; but in his role as ordinary human
fool, he is able to play on cultural expectations, stereotypes, and condescen-
sions of white folks toward Indians in order to get things he wants, and to
show the reader not only the falsity of assumptions on which social relations
are so often built but also the microcultural cues that are powerful structuring features of knowledge and power for both underdog and mainstream,
majority and minority, actors.

3. The figure of the ethnic (often called marginal, stranger, or insider-
outsider) thus becomes not a figure of partial assimilation (child-learner)
but a figure of learning, of access to further realms of meaning (teacher).
This is a key to questions of depth/weightlessness in modern culture, and
of ethical individualism.

Since Nietzsche, at least, modernity has been called weightless (see T. J.
Jackson Lears's *No Place of Grace* for a vivid account of this mood in 1890s
America), and things have only gotten worse as the pace of life, travel, and
communication has increased. The grounds of moral certainty, and thus the

sense of human actions and beliefs having true gravity, have become more ambiguous as life has shifted from small communities to globally interacting cosmopolitan urban societies, as, for instance, the numinous power of ritual has been undercut by other people's different rites, values, interests, and perspectives, as alternative lifestyles can be simply chosen, and as civic rituals have become ironic, entrepreneurial, and performed with a sense of playacting. To many over the past century, all meaning has seemed to come unrooted: all seems increasingly like semiotic play, with a purely hedonistic ability to chose alternative lifestyles (generating resentment by those who feel locked into traditional lifestyles), and with civic rituals no longer secure in a sense of purpose (generating resentment by those who feel traditional patriotism is being undercut by hedonistic others).

One of the contributions of anthropology to an overcoming of this sense of unease about the modern world is a wider comparative understanding of cultural, social, moral, and psychological processes, and of multiple identities held simultaneously by individuals and groups. The search into forgotten languages, histories, and traditions is one way that depth — and gravitas, a sense of rootedness without implying single or exclusive roots — may be sought, not for simple appropriation, but for the strength that comes from comparative perspective, and from thinking through the ethical implications of one choice versus another. Exhortations to Progress, History, or Reason, for instance, are often slogans of the powerful, who feel themselves in charge of a linear history or in a vanguard legitimized by the direction of "progress"; these words and their sloganeering power do not look the same to the small nations, to subaltern groups, or to ethnics, for whom such slogans often mean destruction of their ways, their interests, their values (see, for instance, the writings of Milan Kundera for the notion of small societies of Central Europe for whom "Progress, Reason, History" meant the victory of other groups over them; or the writings of the Subaltern Group of historians for a somewhat similar perspective on the part of the colonized in India; or Gilles Deleuze and Félix Guattari's elaboration of "minor[ity] literatures"; and many others, e.g., Karl Marx, W. E. B. Du Bois, Walter Benjamin, C. L. R. James, Mikhail Bakhtin, Gershom Scholem, and Antonio Gramsci's notions of hegemonic and counterhegemonic discourses).

Ethnicity can thus be a crucible for pluralism, for the coordination of diversity, for a new grounding and gravitas in multiple cultural resources, for understanding the arenas in which the creation of (post)modern society and psyches must be negotiated. Internationally, two recent autobiographical texts illustrate some of these processes, as well as the new (postmodern) media through which modern ethnicities are disseminated and may be ethnographically presented. Edward Said's *After the Last Sky*, done in collaboration with the photographer Jean Mohr, attempts to be a postmodern text materially as well as conceptually. Materially the effort is to use photographs and texts not to caption or illustrate each other but as two voices mutually calling attention to the limitations of the other, and thereby keeping the reader's critical skills awake. Indeed, the pictures often show up the contradictions in the assertions of the text. The text constantly invents stories to con-text the pictures, stories about loss and expropriations, saying, for instance:

> Sometimes the poignancy of resettlement stands out . . . the fit between new body and setting is not good. The angles are wrong. Lines supposed to decorate a wall instead form an imperfectly assembled box in which we have been put. . . . Exile is a series of portraits without names, without contexts. Images that are largely unexplained, nameless, mute. I look at them without precise anecdotal knowledge, but their realistic exactness nevertheless makes a deeper impression than mere information. (Said 1986: 12)

But of course these portraits are posed by Jean Mohr, who chose the angles, and the walls against which to take the photographs. Edward Said could ask Mohr the names, the contexts, the precise anecdotal knowledge. To choose to ignore the easily obtainable "mere information" in favor of invention is to engage in explicit artifice, which at times works with wonderful poetic insight, as in the commentary on the photos of young men body building: "The cult of physical strength, of fascination with body-building, karate, and boxing which has been a striking fact of life among Palestinean youth for quite a while, is obviously the response of the weak to a strong, visibly dominating other. But it is also an eye-catching, almost decorative pattern . . . an assertion of self, an insistence on details beyond any rational purpose" (54).

But at other times—as in the attempts to invest the photographer's choice of pose with laments of loss that we are invited to see in the posed subjects— the artifice draws attention to itself, undermining its seduction; advocacy and persuasion turn to simple propaganda; and the photograph mocks the text. In another example, the lament imposed on a little girl looking at the camera with attentive curiosity waxes so romantic that it moves the Garden of Eden (Paradise) from its traditional locus in Mesopotamia to what is now proclaimed its *locus classicus*: Palestine (36). Despite these problems, conceptually the book attempts to counter the negative imagery of Palestinians in the mass media, both with counterimages and with a text that chronicles the creation of a new identity, Palestinian, out of both the fragmentation of old small cultural worlds and a dialogue (often violent and agonistic) with, and modeling of self after, contemporary cultural others, particularly Jews and Israelis. Although the text tends not to be as helpful in dissecting the artifice of the photographs as the photographs are in undermining the pretensions of the text, still the possibility of this mutually critical double voicing is suggested as a valuable tool in cross-cultural texts. Above all — and in this lies the true charm of the text, and the book as a whole — the text is personal, autobiographical, and disarmingly open about the difficulties of creating a modern identity:

> We have no dominant theory of Palestine culture, history, society; we cannot rely on one central image (exodus, holocaust, long march); there is no completely coherent discourse adequate to us. (129)

> ... you can easily construct the plot of a logically unfolding conspiracy against us. Like all paranoid constructions. . . . Perhaps I am only describing my inability to order things. (130)

> All across the Arab world there is a mixture of cultural styles. . . . The commonest symbol of this process is to be found in the typical photographs of an old city across which is laid a grid of radio and television antennae. (147)

> Plane travel and phone conversation nourish and connect the fortunate; the symbols of a universal pop culture enshroud the vulnerable. (23)

Despite the rhetoric of a specific expropriation, there is also a recognition of a multiplicity of forces and contradictions that go into making modern identities.

Salman Rushdie's *Satanic Verses* is an even more controversial text that describes the interiority of a certain kind of urban Muslim immigrant in London constructed out of a struggle between film and traditional religion. Rushdie's entire corpus has been centrally concerned not only with the hybridizing processes of modern history and migration (partition of the Indian Subcontinent with its population transfers; emigration to Britain) but also with the role of the modern media and their interaction with traditional genres, media, and forms of storytelling and identity construction (see M. Fischer 1990). These processes are also being described and enacted by a series of other talented South Asian writers such as Amitav Ghosh, Bharati Mukherjee, Rustam Mistry, Hanif Kureishi, Farokh Dundy, Sara Suleri, Bapsy Sidwa, and Adam Zameenzad.

Other identity processes in the (post)modern world work analogously— albeit perhaps each with some distinctive differences—to the new ethnic processes. Among the elements of this newness is the stress on diversity and multiplicity by important, if by no means all, social fractions of those involved in defining new identities. Feminism, for instance, is perhaps the most potent contemporary reference point in academia both for thinking through issues of identity and personhood and for many other areas of reconstructing social theory. Mary Dearborn's *Pocahontas's Daughters* explicitly uses an ethnicity model for analyzing women's writing tactics, and to some degree the parallel is a useful one. More powerful is Alicia Ostriker's *Stealing the Language*, a reading of women poets over the last twenty-five years, for example, H.D.'s reworking of the Helen of Troy story, Anne Sexton's reworking of the Brothers Grimm. These are strong poets, in Harold Bloom's sense: once they have retold these old stories, one can never think of them again in their unaltered form. They call attention to biases in older tellings, highlight possible readings and interpretations subversive to traditional understandings, and release new models and justifications for action. The tactic of telling strong alternative stories is a potent device, a far more powerful one than mere complaints against injustice or orthodoxy. (It is a tactic only partially recognized by the Said text. It is used more fully by Rushdie, generating strong counterreactions from those who would define modern identities in less pluralistic ways.) Feminist identity searches and ethnic ones have both similarities and differences. Among the differences, one advantage feminism has is that there is no tendency toward nostalgia, no illusion of a golden age in the past (a constant romanticizing danger in ethnicity searches). But as with ethnicity, what starts as individual quests becomes first discoveries of (partially) shared experiences and traditions (allowing common cause), and then recognitions of multiple perspectives. An alliance of multiple interests and perspectives is often a stronger political and social force than attempts to enforce a unitary movement.

So far, then, autobiographical voice (1) addresses identity processes. I've attempted to suggest ways in which the interrogation of autobiographical texts is useful in analyzing processes of identity formation in the (post)modern world. I've suggested, albeit all too briefly, some of the ways in which identity processes seem to be new in the late twentieth century; but the point is less the adequacy or inadequacy of these formulations than the methodological promise or suggestion: that since there is a widespread feeling that social changes in the late twentieth century are outrunning the adequacy of social theories largely formulated at the beginning of the twentieth century, autobiographies, carefully interrogated, can provide *one* important database for reconstructing social theory "from the bottom up," because they provide fine-grained experiential loci of the interaction of changing social forces. Reading a few autobiographies is not a systematic source for verifying new theory, but it is an invaluable source for generating ideas on which to base new formulations: sites for seeing new connections, new articulations of how cultural, social, and psychological forces are interacting in the consciousness of writers situated in various strategic social and cultural loci. Identity quests do not all fit liberal ideals of cosmopolitan celebration of diversity and multiple identity; some new identities of the modern world are reductionistic and "fundamentalist," yet nonetheless redefining of moral personae from what existed in previous generations: for instance, neither Muslim Brothers in Egypt nor those who burned Rushdie's novel in Bradford, England, are the kinds of Muslims that their grandparents in the villages and provincial towns of Egypt or Kashmir were. "Fundamentalist" here, despite the rhetoric against the materialism and moral anarchism of "the West," often, for instance, does not include a rejection of modern technology or science: on the contrary.

Identity quests are focal points for the cultural creation of a new ethos for the postmodern world. The individual is one locus for the intersection of wider historical processes. The frame of a life history or an autobiography is one experiential field for identifying the ways these intersections articulate. The mosaic composition of an autobiographical voice is one access and needs to be read for the indirections and complexity that the mosaic texture provides.

Alter Egos and (Auto)biographical Voices (2): Reinventing Moral Traditions

When she listened to me speaking Arabic, she felt left out, rejected from any absolute understanding. . . . It was a kind of linguistic frigidity, clothed in a scene of permanent seduction. I liked the fact that she maintained this distance, that she always spoke to me formally. When she used *vous*, she did so with a sovereign charm. However, the day she spoke Arabic in a familiar manner to a maid, it sounded so fierce that I felt my dialect had been humbled. She was face to face with that which had so humiliated me when I was a child. . . . that which I desired in her was reversed in me: love's mirror, so they say.

Something had shattered there. I try to reassemble the fragments. — Abdelkebir Khatibi,
Love in Two Languages

Autobiography is often pursued through dual-tracking processes I will call
"mirroring," "dialogic storytelling," and "cross-cultural critique." Some of
these have already been implicated in the ethnic autobiographies discussed
earlier through the strategies/modes I called "cultural intereférence," "bifocality," and "alternative selves." A second set of texts elaborates these processes even more centrally and perhaps throws light on the ways in which
religious and moral traditions are being reconstructed in the (post)modern
world. Although ostensibly biographies, this second set of texts centrally relies on a dual tracking between the life of the author (autobiography) and
that of his or her ostensible subject (biography).

Just as I was struck by the recent efflorescence of autobiographies that
seem to explore ethnicity in a way helpful for thinking about identity processes in the late twentieth century, so too there suddenly seems to be—
providing a second ethnographic data set of the late twentieth century—a
stream of superb biographies of religious leaders, which are quite different
from traditional biographies and take a large part of their meaning from
a mirroring relation between the author and the subject of the biography.
In other words, to use the rough conceit of this chapter's title (which I will
want to push one step further later in the chapter, with reference to autobiographies of scientists), if the ethnic autobiographies, at least superficially,
are written with the appearance of a single voice, these texts are written in
two dominant voices. Two voices, two lives, are involved in the construction of coherence. If in the ethnic autobiographies there was a listening to an
inner voice, a finding of a style that synthesized different facets of oneself,
and the creation out of cultural *interférences* a bi- or multifocal comparative
perspective, in these texts there is an even more explicit dual tracking.

Insofar as the late twentieth century is seeing a pluralization of cultures on
a global scale, the juxtaposition of life histories (autobiography, biography,
life histories of various literary formats) taken from different traditions can
serve as a tool of cross-cultural comparison and critique. Anthropology is
uniquely charged with testing our own taken-for-granted assumptions and
categories of thought against those of other cultures, including such categories as the individual, or autobiography. One of the ways in which anthropology has pursued this task is to explore alternative cultural frames for
expressing emotion, psychology, personhood, and agency, and, at a more
aggregated level, alternative moral traditions that work through their own

"critical apparatuses," that is, have their own hermeneutical, epistemological, and philosophical tools.

I will not take the time here to say much about alternative cultural frames for expressing emotion, psychology, personhood, and agency, since I have written about them at some length in *Anthropology as Cultural Critique* (co-authored with George Marcus), except to illustrate the issue with two brief recent examples. Lila Abu-Lughod's *Veiled Sentiments* describes the way in which emotion is expressed in slight alterations of a word or an intonation of otherwise stereotyped couplets of poetry among the Awlad Ali bedouin of Egypt's Western Desert. Ordinary public language, for women as well as for men, is an arena in which vulnerability is not expressed; one must always put on a front of stoicism, autonomy, and invulnerability. In the 1950s Arab researchers from the American University of Beirut attempted to use survey questionnaires to learn about Arab psychology. Given the linguistic usages described by Abu-Lughod, one can understand why so much of what these researchers collected was trivial, wrong, and silly. (What would an autobiographical or life history text of such a woman look like were it to be constructed with explicit attention to the ways in which interiority is in fact expressed in such a society?) A second example also from the Middle East: Miriam Cooke, in *War's Other Voices*, describes how the poetry written by women in Beirut during the long civil war is quite different from the writings, both prose and poetry, of men, how instead of becoming enmeshed in the clichés of ideological-political discourse, these "Decentrist" poets encode in everyday events a richness of emotional and moral complexity that provides a unique access to the experience of women and probably also of men. The experiential, the emotional, the cognitive all take on a different gestalt when explored in this way. These two examples may be sufficient to illustrate that cross-cultural comparison can be epistemologically extremely rewarding but requires serious attention to local modes of thought, communication, and expression.

Among such "modes," I want to highlight alternative moral traditions and their critical apparatuses by mentioning two projects that attempt to deal with autobiographical tools, that attempt to do cultural critique by juxtaposing moral traditions in elaborated or extensive ways, and that explore how these "traditions" are being reinvented for the late twentieth century. In contrast again to the simple collection of an exotic way of doing something to use as a foil for our own ways of doing things, the challenge here is to explore moral traditions that have hermeneutical, epistemological, and philosophical tools of their own, and that moreover are aware (to varying sophisticated degrees) of alternatives to their own methods.

The first of these projects is a comparative essay on religious biographies, tentatively entitled "Torn Religions: From Gandhi to Rajneesh, al-Hallaj to Khomeini, Shabbatai Zvi to R. Nahman and After." There is something about the contemporary world that militates against good biographies being written, as traditional ones were, as didactic models for emulation. All these biographies are deeply problematic texts, problematic in the relationship between author and subject, in the relation between biographical figure and social and psychological forces, and (most importantly) in the shifting moral grounds from small-scale communities to international networks of migrants and social strata. I am working with three moral traditions: Jainism, Islam, and Judaism. The texts include the following: for Islam, the magisterial four-volume reconstruction of the life of Mansur al-Hallaj by Louis Massignon (a case where Massignon, as a mystically oriented Catholic, finds a more enriching home in mystical Islam than in a Catholic world grown alienating to him), the account of Musa Sadr by Fuad Ajami (a case of a rediscovery of Shiite roots by a secular author, in which the personal exploration leads to a rich account of sociological and political currents of Lebanon that allowed the charisma of Musa Sadr to flourish), the account of Khomeini by Amir Taheri (in which the author enacts the ignorance of elite Iranians about the Shiism of the madrassas and bazaars that was itself one of the most dramatic features of the revolution), and the account of a moderate mullah, now teaching in the United States, by Roy Mottahedeh (which enacts the nostalgia of so many Iranians for a past glory of culture that cannot explain the present). For Judaism: the extraordinary account of Rabbi Nahman of Bratislav by Arthur Green (which reconstructs the powerful manic-depressive personality of the rabbi, who tried at the end of his life to engage secularized Jews in a way many of his followers did not understand), written by the leader of a group of modern young Jews who attempted to invent an orthodox but fully modern Judaism first in Somerville, Massachusetts, later in New York, and recently at Brandeis University; and the account of Shabbatai Zvi by Gershom Scholem, which did so much to reconstruct the whole course of modern Jewish historiography. For Jainism: a tour de force memoir of the Gandhian Jain Stanakvasi monk Santabalji, by the Gandhian social worker and former Gujurat state minister for education Navalbhai Shah, in which the life of the latter mirrors in uncanny ways the life of his mentor, for whom he worked and with whom he broke over political differences, just as Santabalji earlier had broken with his own mentor; and a set of ethnographic accounts of the ways in which the lives of those who take the vows of monkhood or nunhood both mirror their prior lives and alter the lives of their former families. One of these, for instance, is about a young woman with a college education, from a family that had lived in East Africa, a girl who herself had been "a fancy girl," tooling about on her scooter in designer jeans, whose decision to become a nun caused her father to reevaluate his own life and adopt an increasingly ascetic lifestyle himself.

All of these texts have four critical features: (1) they are narratives that in modernist fashion bring together several interlaced plots from different but mutually determined perspectives and locate their composite coherence in the biography of individuals because the larger myths of sacred history are no longer easily sustained in a pluralist world; (2) they can be situated as indices of larger cultural transitions, as these are all figures who crystallize generational or epochal shifts of cultural perspective, and it is this quality that makes them of interest beyond their own communities (e.g., Green describes Nahman as a first-generation modern man, displaying in elaborate form the anxieties and conflicts of that transition); (3) they develop at least one side of what Steven Toulmin calls the two radical sources of cosmological speculation, the heavens (physics, astronomy, natural science) and ethics (moral life, but especially the social psychology of changes in the moral life); (4) they all display rich psychic struggles and draw attention to global interconnections of worlds once more separate, foregrounding the differences between religion as the focus of modernist anxiety versus religion as exploration of paradoxes and aporia at the limits of reason in a pluralist world: between a Gandhi and a Rajneesh, between a Khomeini and individualist Sufis, between affluent Jain or Hassidic diamond merchants who invest in elaborated religious forms and their liberal, ecumenical cousins, between new nativisms and nationalisms (Hindu revivalism, Islamic fundamentalism) and communal mutual support (social welfare of mosque and temple networks in immigrant America, as well as in countries where state infrastructures have been failing).

Again the juxtaposing of these three traditions uses the methodological injunction that comparison must involve at least three. But it is also an opportunity to read social theory through alternative cultural eyes, to read, for instance, Weberian theories of the "Protestant ethic" through the entrepreneurial Jains, and indeed to explore the interesting fact that at the same time as the rise of Freudian theory in the West, there was also an interest among Westerners to explore alternative imagistic and practice modes for dealing with the psyche that were part of Eastern traditions. Meditation and experimental techniques for gaining control over the bodily processes are not the only elements in, say, Jain and Buddhist traditions: confession is also a major technique, one that is manipulated to exacerbate, vent, and thereby relieve anxieties, obsessions, pride, and other inhibitions to spiritual and social development. (What would autobiographical texts constructed through these alternative symbologies, practices, hermeneutics, and projections look like? For some hints, see the efforts of Obeysekere (1981, 1985), Goonasekere (1986), and Roland (1988) to present detailed "case histories" from South Asia.)

In these "dual-voiced" biographies, I am fascinated by both the mirroring relationships between the life history of the author and the life history of the subject (mirrors can be set at varying angles: the reflections are not simple repetitions), the ways in which the life histories of sometimes long dead individuals provoke reflections on clarification and self-reconstruction in contemporary lives and reinterpretations of moral traditions. But I am also interested in the fluidity of the line between autobiography and biography or life history as narrative procedures.

Debating Muslims: Cultural Dialogues in Postmodernity and Tradition (written together with Mehdi Abedi) explores this fluidity a bit further and is partly structured around seven life histories of people standing in different relations to the Islamic revolution in Iran, a revolution that claims to draw on the deep hermeneutical and moral traditions of a world religion to which one-fifth of the world's population at least nominally belongs. The longest of these life histories is an autobiography that we (2) constructed out of stories from Mehdi Abedi's life. Shorter life histories of two provincial religious leaders are constructed similarly out of stories from participants in their lives; life histories of two national religious leaders are constructed out of stories, written materials about them, and their writings. Stories, oral narrative forms, are also the stuff out of which the Qur'an is composed and with which (hadith) the Qur'an is interpreted. The stories we select in the life histories are often attuned to the theological and hermeneutical issues of the Islamic tradition, resonating with the chapter on how Muslims read, interpret, and evaluate (what is symbolic, what is historical, what is allegorical, what is plain sense in) the Qur'an, which in turn should reflect on the rhythm of attribution and evaluation of information characteristic of oral cultures, and the stories out of which the local life histories are composed. A key feature of storytelling (and of learning) in this tradition is oral dialogue, both in the sense of being composed by an exchange between two persons and in the sense of arguments clarified by a play across counterarguments (dia-logue).

The use of multiple life histories and autobiographical accounts is intended as a technique of juxtaposition or dialogue similar to the juxtaposition of five ethnicities I have described. Juxtaposition is a technique of triangulation, using a number of different (sociologically contextualized) perspectival positions to explore the social changes of Iran and Shiism over the past several decades. The interpretive resources of Shiite Islam are juxtaposed further with, in dialogue with, those of Judaism, Christianity, and post-theological Western philosophy (Joyce, Derrida, Jabes). The effort is to use autobiography and life histories as an access to hermeneutical and moral traditions, and in turn to interrogate those traditions to show their possibilities and their historical "arrests" in frozen limitations. One wants not only to break up Western classificatory and monological stereotypes about legalistic or arbitrary *qadi* justice alleged to be definitive of Islam, and not only to block fundamentalist (equally monological) claims to speak exclusively for Islam, but also to show how contemporary hermeneutics has historical roots and is not just a passing fad from Paris, thereby to invite Muslims as interlocutors in contemporary debates rather than marginalizing them as "archaic," and thus to expand the resources for contemporary hermeneutics as well as create an arena for cross-cultural negotiation and dialogue. Muslims are now increasingly members of European and American societies, and the cultural resources they bring can be valuable, including the experiences of immigration itself and the hybridization it encourages, but also reflections on pluralisms of old empires, different from the pluralism rapidly being created in the postmodern world, but which may yet have some things to teach us.

(Dual) autobiographical voices (2): cross-cultural and cross-historical self-reconstruction. Studies of autobiography are still too often romantically focused on self and individual within an uncritical celebratory master narrative of the rise of individualism in the West. The point of this second voicing section is to draw attention to the ways in which individuals construct themselves through mirrorings with others and are constructed through systematic traditions of narration and dialogue that draw on culturally different principles, and that need to be unpacked at various levels from alternative cultural frames for expressing emotion, psychology, personhood, and agency, to more aggregated levels of narrative, dialogic, and moral traditions that have their own hermeneutical, epistemological, and philosophical tools. Not only are cross-cultural and cross-historical comparisons becoming part of everyday consciousness in the (post)modern world, but only through serious cross-cultural and cross-historical comparison can purchase be gained on the validity of commentaries and analyses of autobiography as a genre or set of genre forms.

Autobiographical Screenings of Science and the Triangulating (3+) Voices of Rationality

What are we to think of such a civilization which has not been able to talk of the prospect of killing everyone except in prudential game theoretic terms. — Robert Oppenheimer

Visvanathan argues that the life histories of the major nuclear physicists in this century have been a movement from innocence, freedom and conviviality — from play, discovery and communitas — to the tyranny of secrecy, control and in some cases, elatory nihilism. The biographies reflect . . . the prototypical relationships between nuclear science and the scientists' self-defined social responsibility, which in turn reflects the culturally defined relationship between knowledge and power in the modern west.

[India] because it straddles two cultures has the capacity to reverse the usual one-way procedure of enriching modern science by integrating within it significant elements from all other sciences — premodern, modern and postmodern — as a further proof of the universality and syncretism of modern science. Instead of using an edited version of modern science for Indian purposes, India can use an edited version of its traditional sciences for contemporary purposes. — Ashis Nandy, "Science as a Reason of State"

Let me complete the conceit of number of voices, a conceit like Wittgenstein's ladder, which once it has served its purpose should be thrown away: if autobiographies have the (false) appearance of being dominated by one voice, and the biographical texts just described by two voices, then autobiographies of scientists ought to foreground the third (or multiple), since science is a collective product composed of cumulative empirical and theoretical contributions. Again we are interested here in autobiographical texts both to provide access to a substantive cultural field (the anthropology of science) and at the same time to interrogate the uses and constitutive forms of autobiographical writing.

Science is a collective social and cultural system we all share: we all have tacit faith in science; we certainly all depend on the goods produced through its use; and we also share the risks and dangers from its misuse. Scientists' autobiographies, then, might be a set of texts in which the construction of an autonomous heroic ego, the "genius," can be placed in tension with the collective expansion of the aesthetics of rationality, which is often the outcome of fallible cooperation and competition, playing games, including at times deceit, as well as often becoming captive of state-, market-, or corporation-driven rationales that impersonally institutionalize violence. James Watson's *Double Helix* was one of the first autobiographical accounts of science that helped demystify the actual process of scientific discovery in the popular imagination. Rita Levi-Montalcini — Nobel laureate in medicine for 1986 for the discovery with Stanley Cohen of nerve growth factor — more recently entitles her autobiography *In Praise of Imperfection*, in the quite serious belief that imperfection and making educative mistakes (rather than perfection and immaculate knowledge) lead to evolutionary progress. Putting it this way immediately problematizes, for instance, the genius trope, heroic mastery of the universe, that structures and mystifies so much popular writing about science. It is interesting to ask if there is patterning in the use of such tropes by country, ethnicity, class, generation, gender, or in-group student-teacher lineages. Do European women scientists write about their careers differently than do Americans?[1] Do upper-class women scientists have different experiences than women scientists from lower-class backgrounds?[2] (Why the insistence, for example, by young American feminists that pioneer European women scientists rewrite their experiences to stress the slights and injuries that the former, but not the latter, feel?)[3] Do certain fields of science encourage myths of individualism more than other fields? Are there patterns of social recruitment to particular fields? Sharon Traweek has been exploring some of these issues with respect to physicists and women scientists in Japan and the United States (1988, 1992, 1995, 1996).

The troublesome issue of the relation between science and "reasons of state" that legitimate various forms of institutionalized violence has been the subject of a series of studies, such as the provocative volume from the Center for the Study of Developing Societies in New Delhi and the United Nations University's Program on Peace and Global Transformation, *Science, Hegemony, and Violence*, edited by Ashis Nandy (1988). In one of the liveliest essays of this volume, Shiv Visvanathan uses an analysis of the lives of different scientists to construct a matrix of competing positions on the relation between political democracy and big science, with Visvanathan in turn relying on the Viennese science writer Robert Jungk: "Jungk is a master of what anthropologists call thick description. The multitude of anecdotes he provides coalesce into a choreography of positions available to science in relation to the violence of the atom bomb as a social fact. Within such a perspective, scientists like Einstein, Szilard, Teller, Bohr, and Oppenheimer appear not as idiosyncratic figures but as permutations within a scientific code. Names become role tags listing various possibilities as the table shows" (Visvanathan 1988a: 116).

Thus Enrico Fermi stands for an "apartheid science — aloof from politics" ("Don't bother me about your conscientious scruples. After all, the thing is beautiful physics"); Niels Bohr stands for "the social organization of science itself as a model of communitas" ("Pure science had managed to avoid the violence of war by sublimating it into agonal play. The scientific paper was a precious gift, and it circulated in joyous exchanges. . . . Every conference was a kind of potlatch, each scientist showering the others with knowledge in exchange for eponymous recognition. The internationalization of science withstood the pressures of war"); Edward Teller "embodies the scientist as a political lobbyist playing on military and political fears to obtain larger financial sanctions for research"; Szilard and Franck in contrast "urged greater public understanding and control of science" (116–18). The most compelling and disturbing portraits are the contradictory lives of men such as Karl Fuchs, who like Prometheus stole the gifts of nuclear fire and gave them to the Russians that a monopoly of terror be broken; Hans Bethe, who opposed armaments research after Hiroshima yet by 1951 was seduced back into H-bomb research; and "the most fascinating figure in this danse macabre," Robert Oppenheimer, "a humanist Hamlet struggling against a scientific Prometheus." Sociologically, Jungk and Visvanathan argue, all these different lives were caught in a threefold shift in the nature of science: "the degeneration of science as a play form; the shift within science from epistemic uncertainty to vivisectionist hegemony; and the displacement of science from the university to the company town." All three, Visvanathan continues,

> are symptomatic of the transformation of western liberalism into occidental despotism, heralding the coming of the atom staat. . . . For liberalism, the private was sacred and the public was open and accessible. In a bizarre inversion, vivisectionist science has opened up the privacy of body and soul to the public scrutiny of the clinical gaze, while science as public knowledge has become increasingly secret and forced into the most monstrous of total institutions — the research cities of the twentieth century. . . . As a mode of production, [the nuclear energy regime] demands a fail-safe system of security . . . and superhuman precision. . . . However, the human body is a reluctant machine. (130, 146, 148)

What is important about Visvanathan and his colleagues in New Delhi is that they are not antiscience Luddites: science is not evil, but it must be controlled, redeemed through spiritually, ecologically, and democratically sound values.

One of the ways suggested, if not explored fully, in their contributions is the idea of alternative sciences, updated traditional sciences, and bicultural perspectives. Ashis Nandy:

> Contemporary India, by virtue of its bicultural experience, manages to epitomize the global problem of knowledge and power in our times. There is a continuity between the Indian experience of an increasingly

violent modern science, encroaching upon other traditions of knowledge and social life [e.g., the rising debate over large-scale dams that displace thousands, can erode the landscape and cause long-term ecological damage, and transform the nature of agrarian relations], and the western experience with modern science as the dominant cultural principle resisting the emergence of new cultures of knowledge [e.g., the resistance to investing in exploration and production of alternative forms of energy]. (Nandy 1988: 11)

As Visvanathan illustrates, the use of lives containing the principled contradictions in the transformations of modern science can be a valuable tool of explorations of the institutions and social organizations of science, and also of the narrative devices by which scientists make sense of their own activities.

Again, as with ethnic autobiographies and modernist religious biographies, there are criteria that distinguish more useful from less useful texts. There are a series of things autobiographies of scientists could help us explore: the sociology of science, the sensibilities of the scientific mind-set, the aesthetics of science, the human history of the creation of the material conditions of modern life, the contradictions and bridges between pure and applied science and the facilitators and blocks to hybrid modern organizational forms such as research institutes in the First World and the Third World, and even perhaps the heuristics of discovery procedures in science. For instance, feminist research on gender and science, using biographical information, has become a growth field (Keller 1983, but see Comfort 2001; Haraway 1989). Among its payoffs is a working sense of patterns of sociability, exclusion, ethnic and gender patterning, and ways of foreclosing some lines of inquiry and speeding others.

The aesthetics of science is another area that is slowly being explored, both in texts that attempt to popularize science and more impressively in books such as Thomas Pynchon's *Gravity's Rainbow*, and Friedman and Donley's *Einstein: Man and Myth*—written by a physicist and a literary critic—which explores the ways in which science has been seriously taken up and explored in contemporary fiction, as a way of talking about the changes in modern consciousness as well as the continuing misunderstandings of nonscientists about what scientists say. But little yet has been done in reverse fashion to use well-crafted autobiographies (and perhaps other literary genres used seriously by scientists to explain their sciences) to explore aesthetics. A more technical potential of good autobiographies in science possibly is a contribution to the heuristics of science. Philosophers of science such as Karl Popper have long argued that while confirmation and falsification procedures can be formalized, discovery processes are serendipitous. But recently there has been a countering line of thought, primarily by European historians and philosophers of science, that the historical circumstances of discovery can in fact be plotted and mapped, and perhaps thereby some insight may be gained into reasoning processes and heuristics. Perhaps the most intriguing of these efforts is by the inconstant student of Popper, Imre Lakatos, who in the footnotes to the dissertation submitted to Popper, developed a counterargument about the historical dialectics of the evolution of mathematical ideas (Kadvany 2001). It reminds one of the dialectical ideas of two of the well-known students and colleagues of the Japanese Nobel laureate for physics Hideki Yukawa, summarized briefly in the introduction to his autobiography.

In the following pages, I want to look at several science autobiographies and in a very preliminary fashion probe some of the ways they are structured, and suggest that some of the reasons for their structuring have to do with the science fields in which their authors participate: that their form as well as their content may have something to tell us. But further, I want to see if these autobiographies can tell us anything about the nature of the wider (post)modern world in which we live. I'll do this first by looking at autobiographical openings, and then at a couple of middle passages.

One way to get a feel for ranges of autobiographical style is to read the openings of a range of texts. Beginnings are wonderful places to examine notions of coherence, the degree to which autobiographers feel themselves to have coherent selves or narratives; the ways in which other autobiographers who acknowledge decentered, conflicted, contradictory, fallible selves position their multiple parts vis-à-vis linguistic, libidinal, social, historical, familial, generational, ethnic, gendered, technological, intercultural, or other processes; the ways in which attention is given to the media or vehicles of memory and forgetting, desire and information, documentation and impression. Some autobiographies enact, are performatives, in ways their authors perhaps do not realize, and that too is interesting and is often signaled in beginnings.

For instance, let us take a quick, unsystematic sample of the openings of six autobiographies (of five scientists and one philosopher of science): Hideki Yukawa, Philip Morse, Irene Fischer, Karl Popper, Norbert Wiener, and S. E. Luria. Two of these begin with visual tableaux or set-piece dramatic scenes that work as emblems of the text to come; two begin with meditations on the cliché that only when a life is nearly over can one hope to find a pattern because human life stories are recursive, hermeneutic, ever changing; and two begin with meditations on the problems and problematics of writing autobiographies of lives rooted in scientific careers for nonscientific audiences. Of these, two come across as self-centered in inappropriate ways, cautioning the reader that the narrator is not to be fully trusted, although enacting the grounds on which trust and distrust might be evaluated. Sir Karl Popper is one of those wonderful characters whose philosophy is perfectly rational and democratic in ways that he himself fails to live up to: one is amused by his posturing, offended at times by his authoritarianism and eccentricities, and yet reassured by the explicitness of the arguments he makes. Norbert Wiener, on the other hand, while also arrogant, is more self-aware of the fact, calling constant attention to it himself. Wiener is one of the two who uses the meditation on the difficulties of writing a scientist's autobiography: the difficulty for him centers on the difficulty of writing science nontechnically, and there are repeated explicit put-downs of laymen, and unconscious insistence that only males are scientists. By contrast, Luria's meditation on the difficulties of writing a scientist's autobiography focuses on the challenges of presenting personalities from multiple perspectives. Pasteur's religious faith, Darwin's neurasthenia, and Newton's mental illness are keys to understanding these powerful personalities at work; "to examine Pasteur without his roots in French provincial bourgeois life, or Einstein without his relation to Judaism, is to diminish them"; "personality should emerge as a landscape composed of many vistas like . . . a Breughel panorama of peasant life." Luria has formulated here, of course, a neat criterion that distinguishes uninteresting autobiographies from those that are in fact illuminating about the processes of life that go into the making of science. (Compare his compatriot Rita Levi-Montalcini's autobiography, discussed hereafter.)

Thus one can also distinguish between the two examples using opening tableaux or dramatic scenes as emblems: Karl Popper's is the story of how he apprenticed himself to a carpenter, and how this craftsman taught him everything; it is a nose-thumbing gesture to be repeated in the autobiography itself, where one of the main themes is to insist that he is very, very different from the logical positivists of the Vienna Circle, when in fact much of what he claims as his personal discovery was also their perspective. Irene Fischer's tableau, on the other hand, is of her retirement party, of the flood of memories that came to her at that moment, of the stories she began to share with the many people who had been her longtime colleagues, which were commented on in the following days and weeks and in turn stimulated the writing of her scientific memoirs. Here there is an interesting generative process: storytelling and shared experience are the markers of traditional solidarity, and yet this scientist, almost uniquely in these autobiographies, grounds the string of stories by faithful consultation with diaries, work logs, correspondence files, and published papers. Reference to these records punctuate the text, with a rhythm of collegiality, at once narrative and documentary.

Of the two scientific biographies that begin with meditations on looking back at a life as it comes to some sort of point of retrospective, Morse explicitly alludes to a theme that arises less explicitly in several of the others: that is, a key motive for writing and understanding the lives of scientists is that it is increasingly imperative for governments, industrialists, and citizens to understand the workings of science in a world where the links coupling basic research and final application are becoming closer, and the conditions of everyday life are becoming more dependent on those linkages, including the possibilities of gross disaster if the linkages are misused.

Hideki Yukawa is the other meditator on the retrospective point of life, but his is a much more hermeneutic, scientific account of multiple perspectives. And it is that, too, which I find fascinating: the demonstration that the distance between scientific perspectives and humanistic ones is not as great as is so commonly assumed. Yukawa's is an exquisite text with multiple openings, each containing multiple frames, seeming to parallel the multiple alternative explanations and perspectival, partial models in physics. There are four openings: the foreword, the chronology, the translator's introduction, and the opening chapter.

The foreword, only two pages, is an extraordinary collage of shifting perspectives, *Rashomon* done in cubist style, not just four points of view. Yukawa begins by saying that now that he is fifty years old, he can review half a century. The expectation of a coherent narrative thereby set up is disrupted in the next sentences, which meditate on his two lives which are one—the easy middle-class life of the son of a geology professor, easy enough, that is, to narrate; and the academic life, which is not so easy to analyze; yet both these lives and paths are one. The life of physics is further refracted in two: on the one hand, one could describe it easily enough as a life that was just carried along on the tide of a science that was rapidly changing in this century (a sweetly modest metaphor, for someone who later does admit that he helped shape the course of that science); but on the other hand, the neat metaphor is dispelled in the observation that holds both for physics and for narrating a life: "today's truths may tomorrow be disproved, and that is why, from time to time, we must look backwards in order to find the path we must take tomorrow." Note this recursiveness is like the stream into which one can never step twice; one looks backward not to achieve closure but to track a course into the future; it is like the hermeneutical circle that never achieves closure, since each new reading generates awareness of further horizons.

The pace of the text does not pause: again softly it notes that this particular life has already had multiple accounts of it written, both by Yukawa himself and in the form of biographies by others. Gently the author suggests that the public has an image, and he wants to offer more information so that that image can be judged. Note again the imagery being used: this is not the normal public-mask, private-interior dichotomy, nor the correcting of a false public impression (the binary logic of public/private, right/wrong); instead it is a modern scientific sensibility of triangulation amid more and more kinds of data, an image of increasing approximation, increasing comprehension of complexity.

Next the interior/public, subjectivity/objectivity trope is muddied. The Nobel laureate claims to have trouble expressing himself, to tend to view matters subjectively, and to know that if he tries to view things "objectively," he may "betray" himself. Objectivity and subjectivity here, of course, are not the popular body/mind, reality/emotion, hard/soft binarisms but rather something more like simplistic reification versus perspectival truth. "In any case," the text hastens on, "not even I can perceive clearly what is about to take shape": indeterminacy, and note: here he is talking not of the future but of the nature of the text that the reader is about to commence.

The falsity of proper names is next. Names are not what they seem, especially in Japan: we learn that Hideki Yukawa is Hideki Ogawa. Ogawa is his father's family name; when he married, he took his wife's family name, Yukawa. Moreover, we eventually learn that his father had done the same, and that name in turn was also such a name. A lovely regression of ever-receding uxorilineal nominations.

Finally, the foreword ends with a lyrical sentence that brings temporary closure to the opening sentence: Hideki Ogawa was born in 1907 at old Tokyo's Ichibei-cho Azabu. The house smelled of plum blossoms each spring. But later in chapter 1, we learn that this is but a reported description, elicited from his mother, about a birth house of which he had no memory, certainly no olfactory one, a birth house moreover that no longer existed, having been burned in World War II (traces of the ineffable).

I won't go on with the description of the text, except to say that it continues in this fashion, insisting on the multiplicity of truth, perspective, and modeling. And I will suggest that this is not a function of writing style, or of simple Derridean poststructuralist reading on my part, but that it reflects a fundamental modern scientific perspective on reality. And finally I will suggest that the result of multiplicity is not (as Alan Bloom fears) the undermining of knowledge but the increase of purchase on truth and knowledge, by identifying the sources of uncertainty, the limits of particular angles of vision, and by triangulating them together.

Sciences are diverse in their procedures, methods, aesthetics, and organizational structures. Let us look at some middle passages of two scientists' autobiographies, one from the science of geodesy, which is closer to the applied mathematics end of the continuum, and one from neurobiology, which is closer to the life and human sciences end. Such a juxtaposition of different sciences may help pose questions about the varieties of models and practices of knowledge production we call science. Geodesy is a particularly clear example of procedures of modeling, mapping, indirect measurement, and increasing degrees of approximation or accuracy. Neurobiology is closer to that other image of science as almost anarchically experimental, trial-and-error, inductive empiricism, leavened, in this case, with analytical biochemical detection of molecular weight and other physiochemical properties. The notions of multiplicity and triangulation invoked by Hideki Yukawa apply also in these two sciences in interesting variants: triangulation is a literal mapping procedure in geodesy, while the complementarity of neurobiological experiments and biochemical analysis was the sine qua non for isolating and beginning to explore the still-mysterious hormonal mechanisms of the nerve growth factor for which Rita Levi-Montalcini and Stanley Cohen received the 1986 Nobel Prize in medicine.

These two autobiographies (of Rita Levi-Montalcini, the neurobiologist, and of Irene Fischer, the geodesist) might also be usefully juxtaposed to accounts in the emerging fields of studies of science and technology, not only to have other frames of reference with which to critically interrogate the autobiographies, but also to provide a reality check to the theorizing by nonscientists (albeit, importantly, often science-trained persons who either chose or were forced to leave the science career fast track) about what drives scientists to discovery and accomplishment. (No serious anthropology or even journalism takes native accounts at face value, yet no anthropological or journalistic account can be credible without building on native perspectives.) A useful preliminary foil, for instance, is provided by Donna Haraway's survey of the four temptations in studies of science, four tempting perspectives on science, each valid up to a point, but dangerous if allowed to silence the other perspectives.

The first temptation — useful to read against Rita Levi-Montalcini's quite different perspective — is the social constructivist view of science that inquires into the power relations that affect the progress of particular lines of inquiry, particular careers, and, in its strongest form, the ways in which scientific knowledge polices its own boundaries against new ideas or new information that it cannot easily incorporate. In its strongest versions, such as that elaborated by Bruno Latour and Steven Woolgar in *Laboratory Life*, the social constructivist view rejects ordinary notions of realism, ordinary separations of what is technical from what is social, and regards the criteria of pragmatic feedback from success in the world to scientific models as fundamentally underestimating the ways in which science can protect itself from falsification. Latour and Woolgar see science as a tactic of reducing conflicting interpretations of messy reality into unambiguous facts through various methods of transcription, translating into equations, and machine outputs. Or to take a clearer example from Sharon Traweek's study of high-energy physicists, what gets defined as elementary particles and the equations of their relationships, after all, are observed only through the construction of machines, accelerators, devices for turning the imperceptible into traces that can be recorded, inscribed, calculated, and modeled. Over time, say Latour and Woolgar, what begin as probabilities, tentative generalizations, or approximations are incorporated into later stages of model building as undisputed facts. In the competition for success, scientists become invested in power struggles, defined in part as simply raising the cost to competitors of destabilizing reigning accounts so high as to be unworthwhile pursuing. Haraway rightly calls such a description of science both attractive and dangerous: drawing attention to the constructedness and contingent nature of reigning scientific ideas, but wildly overstated if treated as a complete account.

I will come back to put Rita Levi-Montalcini's observations in fuller context, but I want to simply observe here that she—like many scientists— foregrounds and revels in the contingency of scientific knowledge. Latour and Woolgar's "demystifying" account is demystifying only to popular accounts of genius and absolute truth, not to working scientists. But Levi-Montalcini places a different set of implications on this contingency: it is part of a larger picture of both science and life as an evolutionary process created through a capricious game of mutations and selection. She notes both in life and in science the necessity oftentimes of repressing knowledge that cannot be incorporated and that can be self-destructive: thus immersing herself in her experiments while the Nazis raged around her was one form of healthy repression, but she also cites Russian neuropsychologist Alexander Luria's "law of disregard of negative information" in being able to repress negative experimental results that she would not be able to explain until years later, and that had she focused on might have derailed her work. Furthermore, retrospective histories of science often include, as Levi-Montalcini's does, explanations of powerful ideas that provided false confirmation for what were thought at particular points in time to be scientific results: thus she cites the sway of gestalt theories as providing support to Karl Lashley's experiments that seemed to suggest that the capacity to learn and memorize was not localizable in particular parts of the cortex. From a scientist's point of view, then, the social constructivist account is largely true but trivial, not very interesting (not adding systematic new information).

If social constructivism is Haraway's first temptation, her second temptation is a political mediationist view of science that inquires into the ways in which language, laboratory hierarchies, industrial or governmental patronage, et cetera, structure the perspectives through which truth is recognized. This could be taken as a variant of the social constructivist inquiries and differs primarily in its concern with exposing the systematic political, state- and money-generated patternings of what might otherwise seem to be more individualistic, contingent outcomes of strong personalities and organizations, or effects of measuring and inscribing devices. Haraway derives her version of the political mediationist questions from Marxist, feminist, and minority observations that the conflictual and inegalitarian relations of society are often opaque to those in positions of systematic domination and power; what seems to be true from one perspective may conceal problems that are visible from other positions. Weak and relatively trivial versions of the mediationist accounts of science are descriptions, for instance, of how popularizing accounts of science draw on sexist imagery. Emily Martin's work on medical textbooks' metaphors for the biology of human reproduction is an example that foregrounds important ways in which the laity and the poor may be disempowered in their own thinking about reproduction or in their interactions with physicians, social workers, and others by the circulation of such metaphors; but this points up more about the poverty of scientific literacy in America, or of translation languages, than about the trajectory of scientific models. Haraway herself has a field day with the metaphors that have structured research programs in primatology from the days of "Man the Hunter" (of Science) — individualistic tests of manhood by science explorers such as Carl Akeley, who went into the wilds to shoot great apes with gun and camera (with gun for specimens, with camera to preserve without destroying nature) — to the 1970s, when *National Geographic* popularized Jane Goodall, Shirley Strum, Birute Galdikas, and Diane Fossey as "Woman the Nurturer" (of Science), for example, of orphaned apes, females being "closer to nature" and thus being able to provide the conditions for animals to approach human beings, and for human beings to reapproach the secret garden of nature. (Meanwhile, says Haraway, the cameras record-ing/"shooting" these women and apes were held by their male husbands and consorts in good traditional gender-divided roles.)

A more serious part of Haraway's *Primate Visions* is the correlation of research paradigms in primatology with more general cultural anxieties: the concern between 1890 and 1930 with the fear of decadence, stress-ing preservation and conservation of pure nature (including eugenics and racial purity); the concern in the 1940s instead with obsolescence and stress in an increasingly technologized age, stressing molecular biology, sys-tems engineering, the recognition that human beings are parts of human-nonhuman "cyborg" systems, and management systems of social control (focusing on food, sex, dominance-subordination, hormones) involving a movement from laboratory experimental settings with chimpanzees (condi-tioning, learning, behavior modification) to watching free-ranging animals in created colonies, in nature, and in "nature preserves"; the concern in the post–World War II period with antiracism and decolonization, and a bio-logical anthropology that supported the unity and equality of all human beings, centering itself on population biology and adaptive complexes of functional anatomy and culture (upright bipedalism and tool using); and finally in the 1970s and 1980s a sociobiology (genetic calculus, strategic rationality) that paralleled the rise of yuppie stress on competitive individu-alism.

But most importantly, Haraway acknowledges that in the course of the development of primatology, biological anthropology, genetics, and related fields, there has been a real positivist increase in knowledge base and sophis-tication that is not contained by either the popularizing metaphors or the correlations with encompassing cultural anxieties of the age. Hence again her recognition that while political-mediationalist accounts of science have a degree of validity (especially in a field that is so prone to be a projec-tive screen for thinking about human culture, psychology, physiology, and sociability — and hence her critical focus in the last third of the book on four women primatologists who have helped reorient the field and its generaliz-ing implications), they are dangerous if allowed to silence other accounts of science.

Again, it is perhaps interesting to juxtapose Rita Levi-Montalcini's ac-count, both to point out that even when scientists write popular accounts, they often eschew the kinds of metaphors Martin and Haraway foreground, insisting on simplified yet technically precise language, and also more im-portantly to note the enactment of the separation between ordinary life, full of metaphors, emotions, and chaotic forces, and a sphere of inquiry where inferences and implications are more narrowly interrogated and controlled. Indeed, Levi-Montalcini goes so far as to concentrate her account of her scientific career in the third part of her autobiography, with only occasional references to the scientific developments themselves in other more familial, organizational, or historical sections. Irene Fischer's account does not engage in this sort of segregation but does similarly insist on simplified yet technically precise language, pointing out the ways in which metaphors introduced for popularizing fun (as in the case of the "pear-shaped earth") are analogically apt or not. Haraway's field of observation, primatology, is, as noted, one particularly subject to popularizing projections, and the recent subfield of sociobiology has had a spate of practitioners who have been particularly promiscuous and deliberately provocative in their use of popularizations that shift ambiguously between technical and inappropriate connotative meanings (e.g., in the use of the word "altruism").

More strictly political economy inquiries might also pursue Chandra Mukerjee's suggestion that scientists at work on big science projects (oceanography, the supercollider, the genome project) are a reserve labor force of experts available to government, which can by selective funding both ensure access to the expertise it needs and reduce the threat from expertise that might undermine its own policies. Scientists can remain autonomous in the details of their work while being simultaneously dependent in the major guidelines of their work; science in this sense is politics writ in a larger sense than the politics of labs and individuals fighting for the prizes of recognition, or in the various strategies that individual scientists use to extract resources for their own projects in the interstices of large science and bureaucracy (again, see Levi-Montalcini on the loss of interest in Italy in neurobiology, yet its continuation, and also her comments on the differences in individualism — greater in Italy than in the United States — and publishing demands in Italy that affect the course of risks and innovations scientists attempt).

The third of Haraway's four temptations is the accounts of science by scientists themselves, which Haraway describes as usually realist and positivist. These accounts claim for science a degree of autonomy from the realities of their institutional and political settings which are freely acknowledged to affect the progress of science. These accounts also frequently remind us that the metaphors of popular science are only very rough approximations of relationships that can often only be accurately rendered in the technical language of mathematical functions, that the two kinds of language do not translate very well, and that therefore to critique science by critiquing only the popular metaphors by which it is approximated is not tenable. Scientists distinguish between discovery (which may be serendipitous) and confirmation/falsification, between the sociology of science and the content of science, between theoretical models that are simplified approximations of reality and reality itself, between levels of precision and pragmatic feedback provided by the ability to predict or control outcomes, between probabilistic truth and particularistic knowledge, and so on. Science is heuristic, pragmatic, partial, approximate, evidence-relational, and modeling; all of which may involve reductionism, deterministic causality, mechanical as well as statistical models, but less as totalizing accounts than as components within larger modeling intentions. Internal scientists' accounts are "temptations" (insufficient by themselves) insofar as they ignore or downplay the sociological and political environments that enable them, or insofar as they tell the story of science discovery self-servingly from a particular individual's or group's point of view.

Finally, the fourth of the temptations is to consider science as a species of storytelling, which immediately opens the possibility that the same science may be narrated in multiple ways. The attraction of trying to tell multiple narratives of science is that it provides a sense of how coherence is created, while drawing attention to perspectival and approximative tactics, or, as Haraway puts it, individually having no power to claim unique or closed readings. To problematize and describe science in terms of the various stories (such as the four temptations) that can be told about the histories of discovery, the relation between science and nonscience parts of cultural understanding, the uses and abuses of scientific knowledge, unintended consequences and implications, and so on, is a relativizing move quite popular for cultural critique. To cast the first and second temptations as stories is in part to relieve them of their arrogance or sense of claiming to be the whole truth, rather than important aspects of the truth. But the temptation of turning all accounts of science into the status of mere storytelling must be resisted: the chemical effects of drugs, or the geometry of the earth, or the physics of atmosphere are not just stories.

One of the compelling characteristics of good science autobiographies is that they are not dry accounts in terms of the third temptation but involve several, if not all, of the four temptations or perspectives or stories, as well as others such as the historical and personal resonances between scientific activities and other parts of scientists' lives, including well-crafted allegories of methodology and meaning such as those of Hideki Yukawa. Resonances between scientific activities and other parts of scientists' lives are part of the social and cultural constructedness of science that is often screened out by "social science" accounts such as the Latour and Woolgar study but can contribute to an understanding not only of the psychology or motivation of scientists but also of the larger aesthetics that inform and encompass their work. Let me turn briefly to the autobiographies of Rita Levi-Montalcini and Irene Fischer. Both are written by women with European backgrounds, features that might be read against monochromatic feminist critiques of the science establishments that emphasize the difficulties for women in pursuing scientific careers: not to dismiss those difficulties but rather to emphasize Levi-Montalcini's philosophical observation that more important to success in scientific research than either special intelligence or ability to be precise or thorough are the qualities of dedication and optimistic underestimation of difficulties.

The beginning of Levi-Montalcini's autobiography is, like other openings already cited, emblematic of the account to follow. It is a threefold meditation on the object of her science (nerve cells and nerve growth factors), on science and technology, and on the relation between rationality and life — each of these three an analogue of the other two, all fitting a model of "capricious games" of mutations and selection, an evolutionary process in which advantages are built on so that retrospectively there is a line of irreversible progress. This is a facilitating frame for an account of the development of neurobiology involving the interplay between the availability of techniques (chrome-silver impregnation so that nerve cells stand out), technology (the electron microscope, which allowed one to see synapses, cathode-ray oscilloscope and camera), the complementarity between biochemistry (to analyze the nature of snake venom and mouse salivary gland serum, and to purify fractions of these, which were important steps in identifying nerve growth factor) and neurobiology (to explore experimentally the spectrum of action of these protein molecules by injecting them in developing organisms and in differentiated organisms), including a number of false leads. There is place here both for the expansion of knowledge and rationality, a sense of historical horizons (what was possible or conceivable at different points in time), and for the chaos of reality. She sees progress as stemming from imperfection — in technology, she contrasts the efficiency of the bicycle, which has not evolved much since its introduction, against propulsion mechanisms that have evolved in speed and efficiency; in science, she says of herself that she lacks strong powers of logical thought, lacked aptitude for math and physics, and so on, but nonetheless, thanks to characteristics such as determination and underestimating difficulties, was able to make major contributions. Indeed, her account in the third part of the book, where she chronicles both her own career and the advances in neurobiology that led to the explorations of nerve growth factor, is one of trial and error, of complementarity of competencies between investigators, of putting aside intractable problems and results that could not be solved until further advances had been made. And in an unintentional feature of the book, she enacts dialectics of fallibilities and contradiction as well, first denying emotional complexes and proceeding immediately to enumerate childhood anxieties (tendencies to solitude, neurotic fears of windup toys and mustaches) and complex emotional relations with parents, siblings, and mentors; or more importantly in the present context, arguing against diaries and journals (and life histories?) as vanities, yet at the same time thankful for the return of letters that both allowed her to relive intense periods of her life and allowed her to construct key portions of the present text.

> I never developed the habit—nor do I regret not having done so—of keeping any kind of record, still less a diary, because I believe that, if memory has not taken the indelible imprint of a given event, then it could not and should not be brought back to life by mere written witness. I believe, in fact, that the very act of recording an event causes, if only unconsciously, a distortion resulting from the blatant desire of the diarist to make use of it as an account to be exhibited to third parties, as a way of reliving in old age a particular moment, and of making one's descendants partake in it or even, if one is especially vain, for its value to posterity. (Levi-Montalcini 1988: 170)

> Having never kept a diary, I was very pleased when, in June 1980, Viktor Hamburger sent me a large envelope containing all the letters—carefully preserved for so many years—that he had received from me during the period I spent in Rio, from September 1952 to the end of January 1953. . . . In reading them, I have relived one of the most intense periods of my life in which moments of enthusiasm and despair alternated with the regularity of a biological cycle. (154)

The picture of knowledge and science here is one of chaos, and often adversity (lack of funds, bureaucratic opposition, war, etc.), against which the drive to creativity leads to lasting results. She ends with a tribute to Primo Levi, and his citation, in the midst of concentration camp adversity, of Dante's Ulysses, "You were not born to live as brutes," a motto that holds as well for the promise that neurobiology and the nerve growth factor studies may eventually bring cures for nervous system disorders. There is, to be sure, a certain kind of heroic trope here, but it is a markedly humble one, neither the macho version critiqued by Haraway nor one that sees the scientist as a lone genius. The scientists described are all fallible creatures creating a collective understanding that itself is historically situated and contingent, if no less remarkable and promising for all that.

Levi-Montalcini's book is one in a series sponsored by the Alfred P. Sloan Foundation, which are largely popular accounts rather than attempting systematic inquiries into the sciences themselves or their histories, though one does get capsule histories as in Levi-Montalcini. Irene Fischer's *Geodesy? What's That? My Personal Involvement in the Age-Old Quest for the Size and Shape of the Earth, with a Running Commentary on Life in a Government Research Office* is a more concentrated and sustained account of the development of a scientific field and career over a twenty-five-year period. Unlike Levi-Montalcini's book, which tends to segregate the account of the science in one section, Fischer's text is characterized by an interlacing rhythm of personal life, technical scientific problems, collegial relations (both complementary and competitive), publications, bureaucratic difficulties, accomplishments, and rewards. Although at first sight the text may seem a forest of names of people, articles, and groups, as one reads, it takes on an almost mimetic rhythm of the social networks and step-by-step solution of the large puzzles posed by measuring the earth, aided by hints in the literature, personal interactions, technological breakthroughs, patient data accumulation, recalculations and reconceptualizations as new thresholds of descriptive competence are achieved.

Unlike Levi-Montalcini's ambivalence toward diaries, Fischer's text is built on rich documentation of diaries, correspondence, and publications, allowing a textured interlacing of stories like Haraway's "temptations" (particularly the first and third), as well as personal and world-historical stories. Each chapter is constructed around an advance in terms of the scientific puzzle of being able to measure and model the earth's size and shape: the advance of surveys along the earth's surface, the different results that one obtains from different astrogeodetic, gravimetric, and oceanographic measuring techniques, the efforts to find a best-fitting ellipsoid to the irregularities measured on the actual earth, the efforts to piece together geoid maps for different parts of the earth into a unified world datum (of which the Fischer North American Geoid Chart was the first to cover the North American continent, the Mercury Datum or Fischer 1960 Ellipsoid became the official NASA and DOD world datum, and the Fischer South American Datum was the first to bring the various efforts of Latin American countries together), and the revolution introduced by satellite technology. This strand of the account works from chapter to chapter as an incremental series of historical snapshots or a processual history of the creation of more complete, more secure, and reconceptualized knowledge.

Each chapter interlaces such scientific advances with accounts of the competitions and cooperation among different government agencies, scientists and support staff, different countries, and individuals (the "third voice," the sociological and social constructivist narrations). There is a trajectory to this narration from the esprit de corps of a tiny pioneering group within a larger social setting of gender, race, and nationality consciousness to, toward the end of the autobiography, assessments of the effects of changing government management policies on the conduct of science. Each chapter as well plays off the family and immigrant consciousness not only of the author but of a scientific world in the United States after World War II, invigorated by the inflow of European scientists and of closer international cooperation and competition. (Levi-Montalcini's book also contributes to this story—her medical school classes included Salvador Luria, Renato Dulbecco, and Rudolfo Amprino, and her own career benefited from cooperation between St. Louis, Rio, and Rome—but she focuses reflectively on this, primarily regarding the reestablishment of science in Italy after the war, not in the sea change transformation of American science and academia.)

These were still the days when the author could be told by a fellow female employee not to work so hard because women would never advance beyond a given level, when a Military Air Transport steward refused to believe that the GS-12 Fischer listed on his flight roster to be boarded first could be a woman, when her 1957 Meritorious Civilian Award pin was designed to be worn only in a male jacket lapel buttonhole (subsequent awards corrected this oversight). These are remembered as only amusing markers of breaking through barriers. Somewhat more serious were the time a paper had her name as author removed because the bureaucrats thought it unseemly or unlikely that a woman should be the author (much to the embarrassment of her superiors) and the earlier loss of a job at Harvard as an assistant to Vassily Leontieff when students found out and protested that a woman was grading their papers. (MIT students of Norbert Wiener did not similarly object when she graded for him. Working for John Rule at MIT developing stereoscopic slides, she excitedly tried to show them to Norbert Wiener, only to learn that he had only one functioning eye and so without depth perception could not appreciate these three-dimensional figures.) More poignant still are memories of trying to break segregation patterns—women ate lunch together to celebrate promotions, but African Americans were usually not invited; this was morally unacceptable to a Jewish refugee from racist persecution, and so on her first promotion she invited all her coworkers to a party at her home, only to have one black woman not show after offering a particularly flimsy excuse.

The immigrant sensibility provides a useful bifocal vision, a constant sense of alternative perspectives, a reality check and stabilizing force. A charismatic mentor, Dr. John O'Keefe, initiated and taught Fischer what she needed to know of geodesy and surveying, but in an environment of the esprit of a small elite group where she proved herself by deriving formulas during a placement quiz, and by passing a series of covert informal tests of knowledge. The group of five or so included a German-speaker who knew of the Vienna Circle, of which she had been a junior follower, which made her feel at home. The group also included another refugee, the former head of a geodesy organization in Yugoslavia, saved from a dead-end bureaucratic job by O'Keefe. That she could read the basic Jordan-Eggert geodesy text in the original German helped (there was only a partial in-house translation in English available at the time, done by another German refugee), and her Viennese training proved superior in many ways. The philosophy of Austrian physicist Ludwig Bolzman also stood her in good stead both against show-off methodology for methodology's sake that got others into unnecessary trouble and against lack of interest in issues that she felt important, and that she was willing to doggedly pursue until others realized the relevance (e.g., surveyors never thought the curvature of the earth important enough to be calculated for their purposes, and this simplification was carried over into early geodetic models as well, an absurdity that Fischer refused to let lie; and eventually as the field progressed, the fact became important and required explicit incorporation [contrast the foreshortened time frame and unduly pessimistic thoughts of Latour and Woolgar about the freezing of "facts," and compare Levi-Montalcini's similar perspective to Fischer's]): "Bring vor was wahr ist. Schreib so dass es klar ist. Und verficht's bis es mit dir gar ist" [Propose what is true. Write so that it is clear, and fight for it to the death].

Amused by a colleague whose fancy math allowed him to set up 199 simultaneous equations with just as many unknowns, in contrast to her own step-by-step compilation for the same task of 300 equations but with only three, four, or five unknowns that could be solved with a simple desk calculator, she allowed herself the comment "An American scientist would rather bite off his own tongue before he permits his technical work to appear in easy detailed steps." Their results disagreed, and it took him months to find his error. Another friendly saying in German, by Einstein, also helped her keep her equanimity between conflicting geodetic and astronomic methods based on unexamined different a priori assumptions: "Der Herrgott ist mutwillig, aber nicht boeswillig" [the Almighty God is mischievous, but not malicious].

Scientific life, in this account, in other words, was not just a wonderful puzzle-solving delight but a network of intellectual lineages, historically created assumptions that could not be taken for granted, personalities, protocols, and bureaucracies, ranging from the genial brigadier Guy Bomford, who used his outsized belly to teach students about the equatorial bulge, to the indirection needed to get answers from the Russians. In one case, she asked which of two methods the Russians had used in a 1939 paper: the Russian geodesists at the international meetings claimed not to know, so she presented calculations based on two possibilities. A few months later, she read their report on the meetings, in which they gave only one of her calculations: the one based on the correct method.

Indirection and competition, of course, occurred not only across international and Cold War lines: there was the case of the computation division within her own agency, which under much pressure finally agreed to teach the researchers how to program the new UNIVAC computer, only to discover when they tried to run some real computations that the computer people, jealous to protect their expertise, had taught them a no longer operational program; and there was the case of the rival agency in the U.S. government that squelched them by having their work classified so that it could not circulate, and another agency that plagiarized their work. More amusing is the case of Charlie Brown: in 1958 the Vanguard satellite went up, and O'Keefe explained at a news conference that the new calculations of the shape of the earth showed it to be more pear-shaped than round. This showed up in a Charles Schultz cartoon of Charlie Brown happy with a new globe until Linus told him the earth was not round but pear-shaped. Later when Fischer wanted to use this cartoon in a publication, Schultz's syndicator refused permission, claiming it as his/their own intellectual property. This, of course, did not prevent Fischer from using a series of vegetable metaphors in training manuals and in speeches, such as the one to the American Philosophical Society delivered at the Cosmos Club, where women were at the time not officially allowed. On the more cooperative side, Fischer was able to locate and return materials from the famous 1927–1935 Sven Hedin expedition that were secreted away in Washington to Erik Norin of Sweden, who was putting the final touches decades later on a book to accompany the Hedin atlas. And in 1965 she won a vote of applause of the Organization of American States by managing to break the competitive logjam since 1944 on cooperating with data, by showing how a unified South American Datum could be constructed and thereby generating the enthusiasm for all to contribute their information. Even more impressive, perhaps, given nationalist sensitivities, was her skill in getting Argentinean cooperation: acknowledging their wariness of allowing their work simply to be appropriated by others, she invited the Argentineans to come to Washington to train and to use computer facilities, and they in turn were willing to share their data, not with Fischer's agency (a part of the Department of Defense) but with "me personally for the scientific purposes of the Figure of the Earth and the South American Datum."

Again, only this initial taste of the text will have to suffice here, enough to indicate the historical richness of the presentation of the evolution of a basic field of research needed among other things for all satellite and space technology; the analogical utility of this model of science both in constructing this text and as one of several models of science involving mapping, degrees of approximation, modeling, triangulation, collation of multiple perspectives, indirect measurement, and constructivist-pragmatic approaches to knowledge; the human dramas, comic and serious, fallible yet cumulative result producing, historically situated in world-historical terms as well as sociologically and culturally, dependent on individualistic persons but in a collective enterprise; and the joyful optimism of so much scientific endeavor, which all too often contrasts with the dour, suspicious, even angry, affect of much social science critique of science. The capsule accounts of changing methods and problems, from actual measurements on land, in the sea, and from space, to creating models and measuring irregular reality as deviations from theoretical surfaces, be they geoidal equipotential surfaces, or oceanographic theoretical levels, to collation and compromise temporary solutions among competing methods—for example, the early heroic achievement by surveyors of long triangulation arcs from Scandinavia to Cape Town, from Europe to Japan, from Canada to Tierra del Fuego; the calculation of deflections of the vertical (variations in gravity forces of the earth from place to place, which can affect rocket or missile trajectories) either by dense gravity surveys or by calculating the difference between astronomic and geodetic positions; the introduction of marine geodesy (stationing three transponders in an equilateral triangle on the ocean's bottom, with a ship above sending acoustical signals, as a basic unit of triangulation; utilization of bathymetry to help estimate differences of deflection of the vertical from terrestrial measurements); the introduction of satellite geodesy (geometric satellite techniques, analogous to terrestrial triangulation, photographing a moving satellite against a star background from two stations, one of known position and one to be determined; dynamic satellite techniques, analogous to terrestrial gravimetry, measuring distances, not angles, by electronic, not optical, means), the disputes between oceanographers and geodesists about calculating equipotential surfaces of the earth and over the slope of mean sea level, the measuring of the irregularities of the earth against locally best-fitting ellipsoids and finding a global datum, bureaucratic solutions of taking discrepant scientific results by differing methods and dividing the difference to produce a compromise datum for widespread use—provide a fascinating conceptual education as well as a history. Along the way are wonderful side studies into historical issues illuminated by new scientific understandings: application of the world datum to the ice age, reevaluating the classic lunar parallax determinations, refiguring calculations by Eratosthenes and Posidonius of the circumference of the earth and showing how errors have crept into the literature about those calculations, and more generally application of Vienna Circle pragmatic language philosophy to a retranslation of a famous but often misunderstood dictum of Rabbi Akiba about free will. Also along the way are astute analyses of attempts at management of science in the government—not jeremiads but observations on how a new commanding officer was able to rekindle morale among researchers by separating status- and control-seeking administrators from scientists, by dismantling stovepipe organization, as well as observations on the triviality, inappropriateness, and self-defeating philosophies of management courses, and an analysis of civil service reforms. And there are anecdotes rich in psychological, historical, and cultural resonance.

These historical soundings might bring us back to the voices and mosaic of this chapter's title, the layerings of memory that are powerful anchors for the present. These are personal, as in the inner voice of Fischer's father, who gives her support at various moments of significance, or in the banter of O'Keefe and Fischer over fear of flying in her first overseas flight in 1955: Catholics have it easier, joked O'Keefe, they know there's an upstairs, causing Fischer to reflect on Shaw's vision of the boring hymn singing upstairs, and also the Jewish version of sages debating, "But I did not think they admitted women there, and even if they did, I was not interested," followed by a lyrical description of the world seen from the air, resonating with psalm, Beethoven, and Isaiah, and a traditional blessing on touching down safely—culture and religion. They are also historical, as in the connections and hesitancies of the last half century, as when she returned to a symposium in Vienna—the first return in over thirty-five years—and the convener addressed her in an inimitable Viennese idiom mixing polite and colloquial language, "Gnädiger Frau, ich habe ein Hünchen mit Ihnen zu rupfen" [Dear lady, I have a bone to pick with you], admonishing her for forcing him to speak in English for decades not realizing she spoke German; but she poignantly remarked about her childhood city: "There seemed to be two towns on the same spot: the lively town of the symposium, a beautiful town strangely suggesting we may have visited here before; and another personal town that was crying with silence, a ghost town."

And she found sometime later, in the course of giving thanks for an honor, that it was easy enough to speak the thanks in German, but as she tried to turn to geodesy, she had to ask permission to speak in English. The third level of such mosaic memory is the soundings in much deeper histories, to Eratosthenes, for instance, and the ice age, but also Petronius Arbiter (66 A.D.) on management: "We trained hard — but it seemed that every time we were beginning to form up into teams, we would be reorganized. I was to learn that later in life we tend to meet any new situation by reorganizing, and the wonderful method it can be for creating the illusion of progress while producing confusion, inefficiency, and demoralization."

This she posted on her file cabinet to provide a "long view [which] had a soothing philosophical effect," together with a pinup of Galileo Galilei: "He had a pensive look into the far distance. . . . His presence reinforced awareness of a clear distinction between real work and busy work in a researcher's value system, and helped allocate precious time and energies accordingly." She had to fight repeatedly to protect his freedom on the wall against the government's inspectorate, and she hid away in her desk drawer Lord Acton's "Power corrupts, and absolute power corrupts absolutely," also as a reminder to herself as an administrator.

These "mosaic" features are not just ornaments but repositories of philosophical perspective, of will, of motivation, of sense of proportion, things that help foster the determination and discounting of obstacles that Levi-Montalcini also spoke of.

Autobiographical triangulations (three plus voices). Two features of these scientists' autobiographical texts are most important in the present context: the utility of autobiographical forms as exploratory access into the systematic features of science as a human endeavor, and the well-craftedness of the best of these scientific autobiographies, well-crafted not only in the sense of being a pleasure to read but also in the sense of using their literary forms themselves to provide access: the suggestions I have made with regard to the three texts of Yukawa, Levi-Montalcini, and Fischer that the form of their life history narrative and the form of their scientific endeavor are formal analogues of each other, consciously, deliberately so, and provide in their variety access to the diversity of science, its procedures, methods, and models. One of the interesting effects is the demonstration that the distance between scientific perspectives and humanistic ones is not as great as is so commonly assumed, and that the multiplicity that some people fear as destructive of traditional pieties is not a pandering to irrationalities of postmodern irresponsibility but on the contrary ever more a feature of the contemporary condition, of rationality, and of grounded positions of critique that allow understanding (and perhaps social reconstruction) to advance.

Soundings and Si(gh)tings: Triangulations in (Post)modern Sensings/Sensibilities

Who will reassemble these pieces, continued Plato, and restore to us the robe of Socrates? — Denis Diderot, *Les bijoux indiscrets*

At the beginnings of modern times, Denis Diderot satirized the new empirical sciences in a ribald allegorical tale about an inquisitive Sultan Mangogul, whose dreams and hundred diverse forms of experiment seemed only to deconstruct the foundations of deductive, rationalist philosophy. On the basis of empirical science, no new eternal synthesis was possible to replace systematic philosophy, only tentative, provisional constructions requiring constant further testing and securing in the physical properties of nature. The constant further testing was allegorized as a continuation of *The Thousand and One Nights*, Scheherazade's multiple substitutions and diversions that keep her tale and life viable and responsive to the changeable world. The structure of perception is voyeuristic, panoptic, third-person listening, caught in the paradox; as James Creech puts it, "No conclusion is possible then until the whole is metaphorically repossessed. But all metaphor for the whole is undermined by the synecdochal (metonymic) concatenation of the private parts that propel the sultan's quest" (cited in Pucci 1990: 161). It is an obsessive quest of desire, which Diderot literalizes through a tale of a magic ring that allows the sultan to stage and hear the desires of his harem women, ambiguously playing on whether his presence otherwise would or would not be any more distorting than this magical instrument of inquiry: sexual desire and *libido sciendi* (the desire to know), as Suzanne Pucci puts it (1990: 157), are allegorizations of one another. The sultan (the subject, the knower, the wielder of the instruments of power and surveillance, the self) in these tales (both Diderot's and *The Thousand and One Nights*), Pucci points out, is "a perceptual subject [who] is reacted upon by the properties of the physical world and in conjunction with his own physiological processes" (his dreams) (159); he is, in relation to his experiments, a third party (Scheherazade's tales are told to her sister Dinarzade while the sultan Shahriyar listens) who explores worlds, unknowable directly, through sounding and projecting instruments:

To the aged philosophers described as garbed in the tattered pieces of Socrates' sacred mantle Mangogul's dream juxtaposes an allegorical figure, an unintimidating infant who nevertheless as he approaches the temple of philosophy grows to giant proportions, becoming the colossus of "Experiment/Experience." "In the progress of his subsequent growth, he appeared to me in a hundred different forms; I saw him direct a long telescope toward the sky, estimate with the aid of a pendulum the fall of bodies, ascertain by a tube filled with mercury the weight of air; and with a prism in his hand, decompose light." (Diderot, *Les bijoux indiscrets*; cited in Pucci 1990: 158)

If there is a parallel between the eighteenth-century sensibilities — a feeling of transition from stable knowledge that however is no longer viable as a worldly guide into an insecure world knowable only through multiple probes and perspectives — and those of the twentieth century, it does not help to collapse the differences, to succumb to the mechanical Orientalist industry of Edward Said imitator-manqués of imposing us/them, self/other, omnipotent/subaltern essentialisms. As Pucci nicely asks (albeit then herself succumbing partly to the masculine-feminine, voyeur-puppet industry):

From whence comes the necessity at the present moment of relegating the varied cultures of the East to the non-specific, monolithic term of exteriority, of an "outside" ("exo[tic]")? At the time of a newly emerging economic, political and even cultural context, in which the exigencies of global interdependence appear to be, at the least, challenging Western hegemony, what critical value obtains in analyzing, perhaps even in fetishising the discourse of the exotic? . . . The eighteenth century fascination with foreign lands and in particular with the Orient remains closely tied to the discrete entities that constitute a perspective still formally and textually separable into self and other, as yet unblurred by the notion of an otherness within, characteristic of the Romantic period. In effect, "exoticism" is defined *(Larousse Encyclopédique)* with respect to nineteenth century interest in the new world of America in contradistinction to modes of the exotic linked to the Orient and to the rare object of the collector. (145, 146–47)

The late twentieth century is different from the eighteenth century, the romantic period, and the nineteenth century, in part, through the actual cultural interreferences and pluralized perspectives that are no longer one-sided fantasies or projections but internal realities on increasingly large demographic scales, with effects that play themselves out not only in refined cosmopolitanisms of liberal desire but also in devastating conflicts generated by political reorganizations, disruption through development schemes and wars, and economic competition.

One way to probe these changes of the contemporary world is to use autobiographical and life history frames to examine the ways the social processes of identity, moral understanding, and scientific worldview are being reproduced and transformed. Autobiographical frames themselves are not given genres: if we wish to use them to extend social theory, to understand the changes of the contemporary world (rather than reaffirming the pieties of the past), we need to be attentive to the variant, culturally diverse formats they may inhabit.

I have raised many more questions than I can answer, from "what is an autobiography?" to "what do they signify?" As an anthropologist, I have been trying to ask the beyond-the-text questions: how do real selves in the world assemble themselves, and can autobiographies help analogize or investigate this? How do genres of self-portraiture change under different social conditions? Is it true that autobiography is a relatively new form? What does that mean? How different is Augustine's *Confessions* from Jain monkishones (M. Fischer 1990), or those of the hunter-gatherer Okiek people of west central Kenya (Kratz 1990)? And what are we doing when repeatedly and repeatedly, over and over again, we analyze only the first? How do social enterprises such as science refract themselves through the lives of their practitioners, and can individual-focused accounts provide larger-than-individual-limited knowledge? Beyond the text, beyond the single self, beyond the ego.

I have been making a plea for the cross-cultural, the comparative, the critique of the categories we use, and for cross-disciplinary conversation on uses of life histories to rebuild social theory, to rebuild the technological polity, to rebuild theories of psychology, and to refashion the world we live in. That seems to me to be a not unambitious project for the study of autobiography to undertake.

7

Post-Avant-Garde Tasks of Polish Film:
Ethnographic *Odkłamane*

Geschichte zerfallt in Bilder, nicht in Geschichten [History resolves into images, not narratives]. — Walter Benjamin

Two ideas generated intense discussion in 1990s Polish film circles: that there is something called *the ethnographic* that might provide a compelling direction for Polish film in the postcommunist period, and that the kind of cultural critique expressed by the Polish word *odkłamane* (undoing lies, propaganda, myths, conventionalized understandings) could provide the form and content of this ethnographic move. *Odkłamane* (past perfect), or *odkłamywavie* (gerund), means the countering and undoing of the lies and myths of conventional understanding, not to be replaced by a simplistic faith in new truths but rather to foreground and recognize the complicities and complexities of reality. Ethnography and the ghosts of the past are important components of this project not for their own sake but as pieces of a mosaic out of which an emergent future can be constructed, one neither in thrall to romanticisms of the past nor naively believing in a transformed future with no connection to the past.[1] The signature modality of this project for the transition from the 1980s to the 1990s was rock music, the carrier of a locally inflected global consciousness that undid the pieties of both the communist past and the romantic tropes with which resistance to the communist state was composed. Eruptions of the past, the ghosts, led to a kind of double vision, not unlike Walter Benjamin's dialectical images.

Film and the Reinvention of Ethnographic Techniques

Anthropological accounts similarly step into an ongoing stream of representations. Anthropology is no longer the "discovery" of *terra nova* or undescribed cultures but rather a method of informed critique, pursued often

by placing into strategic and disjunctive juxtaposition different representations or perspectives so as to throw light on the social context of their
production and meaning, and to draw out their implications for the future.
Anthropology, in its ethnographic technique, is as much up for reinvention
in the contemporary era as is Polish film. The parallel has at least one common historical taproot. Poland is the land of Bronislaw Malinowski, a key
founder of twentieth-century British social anthropology, a land for which
his modernist literary and folklore colleagues arguably did the service there
that Malinowski did only elsewhere.[2] It was an era of folklore recollections:
the Grimms in Germany, Yangit Kunio in Japan, Sadeq Hedayat in Iran, Itzik
Manger for Yiddish Poland, each influenced in his own way by modernist
movements.

Maria Zmarz Koczanowicz's films, set in Wroclaw, Warsaw, and
Rymanov-Iwonicz, provide an access to this moment of Polish cultural politics in the 1990s, and to the parallel challenges facing film and ethnography in a media-saturated world. In a series of peripatetic conversations
with her and her philosopher husband, Leszek Koczanowicz, we used her
films and their physical sites as refracting cultural prisms. The conversations
operated less as formal interviews (though tape recorder and notepad were
always present) than as tympana—those convoluted passages of the inner
ear that complicate the distinction between inner and outer ear but function
as resonator and amplifier[3]—that is, partly self-reflexive readings, elaborations, and commentaries on contradictions or puzzles in one's own cultural
texts, and partly translations-amplifications of associations and contexts for
English-speaking foreigners. There are constant eruptions of uncanny and
unsettling pasts, of ghosts, or specific locations and their associations—these
are part of Maria's films as well.

In our two weeks of travel (8–20 August 1993) across Poland from Maria
and Leszek's home in Wroclaw, we encountered a number of other contributors to our conversations, including especially the film critic and editor of
the journal *Kino*, Tadeusz Sobolewski, and his wife, the literary scholar Anna
Sobolewski, as well as a local producer, Felix Pastursiak, who worked with
Steven Spielberg in Cracow on the filming of *Schindler's List*. The travel itin-
erary began in Wroclaw, the German Breslau, and a visit to the still intact
German-Jewish cemetery full of famous names even for today's America.[4]
Wroclaw is now home to a Slavic population displaced after World War II
from Lvov, complete with a grand Ukrainian Orthodox church and Lvov's
monumental nineteenth-century patriotic panorama of the defeat in 1794 of
the Russians at Raclawice by a peasant army under Tadeusz Kosciuszko.[5] We
drove through the grimy coal and steel regions of Silesia to Cracow and south

to the Carpathians and Gorce, the spa villages of Rymanov and Iwonicz, and the farming village of Lubomierz.

Maria's films catch Poland in transition from the Soviet command economy and political domination to parliamentary democracy and induction into the global economy. The films experiment with visual techniques, both with ways visual icons evoke historical specificity (*The Edge of the World; The Wedding*) and with ways they are made generic, erasing specificity, as in the journalistic use of photo archives of war, famine, and disaster, where it is hard to tell if an image is actually from the Balkans today or World War II (*Traces*). Still, such archives can serve to deparochialize and provide a comparative perspective, as in images of vigorous and indecorous parliamentary debates from Britain, Israel, Taiwan, India, and elsewhere, that function to demystify them and, more importantly, to hold to account Polish members of parliament, undoing the sense that to publicly disagree demeans the dignity of parliamentary debate (*Democracy*). Carnivalesque happenings (*Major, or The Revolution of the Elves*) and street theater (*Don't Trust the Politicians*) were important to the 1990s, to the implosion of the Soviet Bloc, and to the recall and response of a world that is always already mediated.

Walter Benjamin wrote of film as the technology through which one learned to deal with the shocks of modernity almost through a Freudian *fort-da* mechanism of dealing with speed (the Lumière Brothers' famous film of a railway engine coming toward the viewers made the first audiences flee their seats in panic, only to return and demand a replay), with the fragmentary inputs of kaleidoscopic and sonic channels of communication (images, words, sound track, music) that require a "distracted" mode of attention and a social reality checking of reactions by others (the theater as a gymnasium for training the senses in new modes of apperception). His speculations about images and their relation to a noncontinuous memory that could be used to construct a new form of history provide an interesting counterpoint to Hegel's continuous history constructed out of similar figurations.[6] Benjamin was also optimistic about the potential of the new technology to foster more democratic modes of communication, turning the tactics of the avant-garde to the needs of popular critical consciousness. But Benjamin wrote of a generation that came of age, politically and otherwise, between the two European world wars. Much has changed since then.

Gilles Deleuze, among others, suggests that after the appropriations of modernist forms by fascism, communism, and mass consumerism, the shock of cinema can no longer be that of Eisenstein's montage. Instead he suggests a new set of time-space images have emerged, beginning with Italian neorealism and the French New Wave, that are virtual rather than spatial, by which he means a multiplication of the sign systems available for fore-grounding. Not only can optical and sound elements take on autonomous existences, but there is an opening to a variety of chronosigns, lectosigns (modes of inscription), noosigns (interior mental associations), and other dimensions of signification. At issue is both an epistemological and a po-litical shift. Epistemologically there is increased precision, and less facile "realism"; politically there is attention to the powers of the false, toward in-dicating what is out of frame, toward illustrating how much our conscious recognitions are but partial understandings (Abbas 1992). In other words: odkłamane.

Hieroglyphics: What Cinema Are We Waiting For?

Zmarz Koczanowicz does not like tragedy and so she ironizes. She shows the moment of the breakdown of the myth of Solidarity very coolly. In the very first shot we see a cockroach, and so we see everyone in the film coolly the way an entomologist sees a cock-roach. —Tadeusz Sobolewski, "What Cinema Are We Waiting For?"

Zmarz Koczanowicz's first feature film, *The Edge of the World*, premiered at the 1993 Gdansk film festival. A kind of calligraphic or hieroglyphic film, it is composed of resonant images enchained in a narrative sequence. It trans-mutes into film the feuilleton style of characterizing life in Poland of the writer and the film's scriptwriter Janusz Anderman. Anderman's vignettes, including the collection *The Edge of the World* (1988), are among the most incisive accounts of life under the communists, under martial law, and the postcommunist period. For the cognoscenti there are references to real-life events, but Maria chose not to turn to a cabaret style in which these refer-ences would be stressed. Instead she chooses a kind of abstraction, a callig-raphy of images, a narrative enchaining of hieroglyphs.

The film begins, as many films do, with a preview of images that will con-stitute the "characters" or hieroglyphs of the filmic writing (image-narra-tive). The images are ones of emergency, transformation, and hope, framed in the ironic, self-deprecatory black humor of Eastern European neosurreal-ism. They are images of emergence from surveillance into freedom; from ple-biscitary referenda to genuine democratic elections; from Christian vision-ary hopes for miracle and divine aid to international travel and trade to transform the economy; from passive breadlines into empowering linked chains of solidarity. The images include a bank of television monitors, a cockroach, and a jail. Also: a man with a microphone by the Palace of Cul-ture in Warsaw organizing people into a "chain of hearts" to "stand united";

two writer-commentators à la Samuel Beckett's Estragon-Vladimir in *Waiting for Godot*; a policewoman watching via the monitors a knot of excited women staring at a tree where the holy one was seen; a passport line and talk of trade and bargains in Bulgaria and Yugoslavia. As a tree waves in the wind and a radio announcer talks about elections, the two drunk writers, covered in white flowers of spring (renewal, hope, transformation), talk about the aporia of whether anything in fact has changed since the collapse of communism. It is the day before the elections of 1989.

The sequence moves from confused hopes to skepticism to attack on false hope. A woman in the passport line talks about her Kafkaesque problem: she's been denied a passport on the absurd grounds that her identity card has a secret code that identifies her as a male priest. Another person in line worries, "What is it we must sell in Bulgaria?" A person in the Chain of Hearts is asked what the line is for and says he doesn't know. Another poses for a Japanese tourist with a video camera, shouting, "We will not give up!" while a third gives the Japanese man the finger, shouting, "Sell this!" and others cheer, "Good man! Freedom!" as if the Japanese represents the bewildering tyranny of consumer capitalism, newly invasive and disciplining. In a parody of a real-life policeman who ran for office, a horse-drawn cart passes with a man in police uniform campaigning, "Vote for me! I'll give you dollars with my picture on them." (It is also a reference to the satirical campaigns chronicled in Maria's earlier documentary *The Orange Alternative: Major, or The Revolution of the Elves*, described hereafter.) Meanwhile a woman with a banjo sings a well-known political lament about martial law, the failed promises of independence since World War I, and worries about the promises of Lech Wałęsa and Solidarity.

The imagery turns more skeptical: In the Chain of Hearts, a man wears a folded newspaper hat reporting a story about animals in the Moscow zoo, not merely a generic metaphor about Poland but also a reference to earlier election jokes.[7] Through the television monitors, the policewoman spies a poster of Jacek Kuron defaced with the misspelled word "Jew!" "There's a mistake!" Then in the double take of absurdist humor, "I didn't know he was a Jew," followed by "He's a Jew, but the word is misspelled." A woman at the tree where the miracle is rumored to have occurred asks where she can lay on hands to cure her alcoholic husband, and a man retorts by citing previous "miraculous" visions seen in Poland in the 1930s and 1940s.

To attack these false hopes, a man with a saw cuts down the miracle tree as rock music wells up with images from the carnivalesque demonstrations of the Orange Alternative; the statue of Felix Dherjinski, the Polish founder of the KGB, is pulled down (intercut with documentary footage of the real pulling down of the statue), and as the crowd cheers, the policewoman re-moves the official portrait from her office wall. But one of the drunk writer-commentators asks, "How long will we write about this?" (clearing away ide-ology, superstition, and false hopes). The other replies, "It will always only be short stories." Indeed, the policewoman tries to touch the miracle tree through the television monitor. The Chain of Hearts line stretches across a bridge with umbrellas unfurled against the rain. The two writer-commen-tators drunkenly wave their bottle of vodka as the Dherjinski statue falls: "You like it? Now we are at the beginning!" A man in a white coat pulls a cart with mineral water, and the crowd finally finds something to follow. A politician, the libertarian mathematician Janusz Korwin-Mikke, makes one of his signature speeches figuring politics as a play of paradoxes. An orches-tra leader asks, "Do we need to play the Polish national anthem, *Is it still Poland? / No, not yet!*"

Ethnography and Odkłamywawie as a Future for Polish Films: The Lubomierz Seminars

Maybe in fact it was easier to talk to the man in the street under communism when every-one had to stand in lines to buy anything. Now the lines are gone, and the only opportunity the intellectuals have to rub shoulders with ordinary people is on vacation when they stay in peasant homes. They come here during the summer vacation, talk to a few peasants, then write an essay claiming that "I have talked to the common folk, and what they think is . . ." — Leszek Koczanowicz

Lubomierz is a village in the Gorce foothills along the Czech border, just past Peim, one of those towns afflicted by being used in popular idiom as symbolic of the quintessential small-town mentality. Lubomierz is agrarian country, where urban folk spend their summer vacations, the perfect site for a seminar of intellectuals on holiday. Over the hill is a national forest, and there are fears that Germans or other moneyed Westerners might come and set up a hotel and ski lodge, not only destroying the character of the landscape but also raising land prices above the means of Polish intellectu-als hoping to buy a bit of land for a summer cottage. The farmhouse where we lodged had been built with help from money earned in America, but it is a full working farm, the lady of the house feeding a crew of twenty each day. A son and daughter live in Chicago. Here we met Tadeusz Sobolewski, the editor of the film journal *Kino*, his wife, the literary scholar Anna, their young daughter, and Felix Pastusiak, one of the local Polish producers for Steven Spielberg's film *Schindler's List*.

Tadeusz Sobolewski had written a review of *The Edge of the World* titled "Feliks Edmundowicz [Dherjinski] in Styrofoam," in which he wrote that it parodied "what has been since the time of Partition the most sacred in our country, the desire for unity, mystical unity, endless expectation of the miraculous. . . . I think there will be great trouble with this film: is it a satire on communism or on Solidarity? . . . In Anderman's screenplay there is a bitterness à la Zeromski [who died in the 1920s, famed for his expression 'It is necessary to tear apart the national wounds, because they can cover up like a membrane underlying meanness and baseness'] . . . a kind of intellectual's pessimistic anxiety about the future of Poland. . . . But Maria Zmarz-Koczanowicz tells the story in a different way. As she did in her documentary on *The Orange Alternative*. The same actions as this Chain of Hearts were performed then by Major in Wroclaw and as Maria filmed them in *The Revolution of the Elves*. She uses the experience from this documentary. She laughs at the form in which we express our desires for unity. She tries to trickster us into a national drama by referring to *The Wedding* [of Stanislaw Wyspianski, 1901] through the use of the *chocholi*, the straw covering of roses protecting them through the winter, a symbol of hope and of the spring renewal of the roses." (In *The Wedding* the straw covering comes to the wedding and plays the fiddle. People dance hypnotically. The chocholi dance is a symbol of the perennial inability of the Polish society to unify, to be set free.) Sobolewski continues, "Is this a chocholi dance? No, not yet. It is not possible yet to play with such holy things, especially things which are not holy, but taboo. Is it possible to play with taboos, taboos whose power has now evaporated?"

Sobolewski recounts watching the filming of the pulling down of the statue of Dherjinksi. He describes a surreal scene of onlookers not sure what to make of the reappearance of the statue of this hated figure. He eavesdrops on the street chatter: "They are making a film." "They put him a bit higher than he used to be." "Was it really that big?" "You know it is still not funny to me: O Felush [diminutive of Felix]! Stay, old steed, and see how they destroy it." And there is the old man who cries in fear that "Lenin" is returning. Not Lenin, people reassure him, it is Dherjinski. But the fear is real: many people, in fact, are calling for the return of communism. Is that related to the resurrected statue? Sobolewski teases: maybe the statue should be put up every second day and torn down in between as the only way to unify all the conflicting parties. A further twist, Sobolewski teases or fantasizes: a man next to him with a black suitcase says, "The statue should remain here in its place," and Sobolewski wonders if the man is a provocateur sent by the author, Anderman. Fancy cars arrive, flowers are put at the statue, as in the old days: a Soviet-style anthem is played, and a black man from Cuba gets out: it is one of Anderman's vignettes about the son of a foreign black student in Poland and a Polish girl, who had gone to America and returned, not finding a place in either society.

In another review discussing Maria's film, fellow filmmaker Janusz Kijowski, in the 14 August 1993 issue of *Polityka*, articulates the key notions of a new kind of "ethnographic film for Poland and a task of cultural critique" (odkłamane). This article, called "The Dirty, the Cruel, and the Bad: Why Should People Want to See Our Films about Heroism and Suffering?" begins by expressing dissatisfaction with the film festival prizes at Gdansk. *Dogs*— or, in American idiom, "Pigs," the pejorative for police—the current box office leader, had won only a second prize. True, it was not a particularly good film. It is about two friends who go through the process of vetting their communist backgrounds: one passes and becomes a policeman, the other, who is not cleared, becomes part of the Mafia. Clichéd and banal, the film tells us little about Poland today, yet it draws audiences due to a hunger for films about real-life issues in Poland. The top prizes at Gdansk were given to films about heroism and suffering that no audience would want to see. In what direction, then, should Polish film go?

There are three possible directions, Kijowski suggests. Least satisfactory would be to try to follow the examples of Hollywood action or French love films; audiences would go to the real thing rather than the imitation. A second possibility has more potential: the ethnographic of "closely watched" local particularities. *The Edge of the World* is such a film, depicting "the Polish aquarium" (Moscow zoo) faithfully, impressing on the viewer in an almost physical, sensual way all of Poland's "bitterness, bad smells, stupidities, and disappointments." It reminded him, in fact—high praise— of *Rejs* ("Trip," or "Sailing"), the cult film of the late 1960s, directed by Marek Piwowski in quasi-documentary style and vernacular idiom, structured loosely as a set of "happenings" or improvisations by actors and ordinary people on board a ship sailing down the Vistula. At the time, *Rejs* had seemed to its fans to be a condensation of what life in Poland under communism was like. Maria Zmarz-Koczanowicz's film, he says, is so much sharper and more cutting that it makes *Rejs* seem naive. Sailing through Poland in 1993 must be stripped, he says, of easy irony or humor that easily purges the viewer; instead the voyage becomes gloomy, a chocholi dance, full of evil spirits, a museum of prejudices and stupidities.

Kijowski fears that the distanced techniques of ethnographic observation make the present seem distant in space and time, and so it may be easier for foreigners to see what is depicted, harder for the film to function domestically as cultural critique. People will displace the depictions from themselves onto others, onto Pomeranian and Mazovian tribes (two regions of Poland). The film is likely to be acclaimed more abroad than in Poland.

A third option would meld together the best parts of these first two options—narrative and ethnography—with odkłamane (od = negative particle + klamane = lies), the tactic of countering lies, myths, and unexamined assumptions; not necessarily telling the truth, but undoing the falsehoods, not just political untruths but also Polish mythologies and mentalities. As an example, he provides possible screenplay scenarios. Take a standard melodrama of boy gets girl pregnant, she has a botched abortion and dies. Polish context: abortion has just been made illegal; the boy's father has lost his job (under privatization of the state economy), begins to drink and beat the boy's mother; the boy's teachers go on strike before final exams, so that he will lose a year; skinheads destroy his prized drum set. Action conflict: when this nineteen-year-old boy goes out into the streets and sees the election posters, should he (1) believe in hard work and self-reliance and start a small business (the film could get funding from private industry); (2) become a believer that only the church can give happiness and freedom from sin (this film could get state subsidies); (3) seek revenge at the grave against the doctor (such a film would be a Clint Eastwood–style audience pleaser); or (4) become self-destructive, making the mistakes of someone stressed to the extreme (the most realistic and productive of creative thinking about real social issues, but where would funding come from?)?

Tadeusz Sobolewski is kinder to the second, ethnographic option, citing in addition to *The Edge of the World* a half-dozen other films of the 1990s, including Marcel Lozinski's *Seven Jews from My Class* (about the post-1968 emigration of Jews); Pawel Lozinski's *Birthplace* (about the poet Henryk Grynberg, who returned to his birthplace where his father, having survived the Germans by hiding in the forests with the help of Poles, went to buy milk for baby Henryk and was killed by a Polish peasant; when Henryk returns as an adult to find the grave, the body is exhumed, the milk bottle still by its side); Marcel Lozinksi's *Eighty-nine Millimeters to Europe* (89 millimeters is the difference between wide and narrow railroad gauge, between Soviet and Western railroads); and Maciel Drygasa's *Listen to My Cry*, about a suicide. Sobolewksi argues that cultural critique must include something redemptive, something to believe in.

I asked Sobolewski if he had seen any of the remarkable Iranian films by Abbas Kiarostami, Mohsen Makhmalbaf, and Bahram Beza'i, and if so, if he would recognize them as "ethnographic" in Kijowski's or his own sense. Sobolewski had seen one of Kiarostami's films—*Life and Nothing Else* (*Zendegi va Digar Hici*)—and after puzzling at the possibility of comparing Polish and Iranian films ("It is different because Iran is still discovering reality, while Poland has already discovered reality so many times"), he acknowledged the possibility. He invoked the Fifth Generation Chinese films as melodramatic but providing a structure on which not merely ethnographic footage but also ethnographic interrogation in the present sense could be framed.[8] He had seen Chen Kaige's *Farewell, My Concubine* and had been impressed by the mirroring of the filmmaking with its diegetic story. The Chinese, he said, use melodrama and romantic image well; we need something like this. "We've gone through three years of chaos," he said, "and maybe only now are filmmakers able to begin to think about a 'new turn.'"

Steven Spielberg's *Schindler's List* and Andrei Tarkovsky provided more contrasts. Felix, who worked on the local production team for the filming of *Schindler's List* in Cracow, pointed out that 4 June 1989 (the date of the first elections of the new Poland, and the day being awaited in *The Edge of the World*) was also the day of the crushing of the demonstrations in Tiananmen Square. He had watched the European Broadcasting Union move their coverage from Warsaw to Beijing, to the bigger story. The point was that international circuits of information and cultural flows, as with the political economy of emigration and peasant life of the house in which we were sitting, are always already infrastructural, never incidental or accidental to such discussions.

Although Spielberg could film in Kazimierz, the Jewish quarter of Cracow, and in the Plaszow work camp in a quarry (both remain somewhat as they were), providing a kind of realism to the film, Maria Zmarz-Koczanowicz dislikes such realism and its associated psychological melodrama. She also has reservations about her onetime teacher Krzystof Kieslowski's films: they are too scripted, and therefore he gets relatively shallow results, not the richly layered resonances that she tries for in her films. Tarkovsky, on the other hand, is a constant inspiration: his images are dynamic, full of allusions and references, so that one sees something new in each viewing. He rejected Eisenstein's notion of montage as too literary, too dictating of meanings through juxtapositions, too little open to the elusiveness of art.

Tadeusz Konwicki, an avant-garde writer who also experimented with filmmaking, she finds quite similar to Tarkovsky. Even if he never produced a polished film, many of his scenes are extremely interesting. His film *Lava* takes up Adam Mickiewicz's poem *The Forefathers*. It is set in a graveyard, using footage from the Warsaw uprising, Auschwitz and Katyn. The graveyard is a space in which different time periods intersect, and conversations are held with ghosts of the past. Time is eternal, and the film's own temporality plays with the arrow of time by having part 4 come first, followed by part 2, and then part 3; there is no part 1. Priests exorcise the messianism of the poet, while the poet accuses God. Konwicki is thematically interesting to Maria: Jews, Lithuanians, Ukrainians, ghosts, weddings, and funerals are uncannily always already present. As Maria puts it, both in his films and in Polish life generally, "Jewish motifs keep appearing."

The techniques that fascinate Maria have a layering that is often registered in ways that are otherwise denied, and reflexively do not displace evil onto others, but find the reverberations of evil in ourselves and in the relations within which we perforce must live. In Pawel Lozinski's film about Henryk Greenberg, the question is posed: how to be a witness to a murder? The technique is that used also by Claude Lanzmann in *Shoah*: the camera registers things on the faces of people that they are verbally denying. So, too, in a second scenario for a new kind of cinema, Janusz Kijowski proposes a film about a pogrom in which the "resolution" is not to suggest a sociological answer as to who caused it (secret police, Russian provocateurs, the resentful anti-Semitic poor) but rather to use the documentary footage and the living witnesses to explore the evil that lies just below the civilized surface of us all.

Maria's editing technique, thus, is composing with fragments. She works with short, Anderman-like anecdotal structures. In the shooting, she gives her cameraman only general instructions; her art then shapes what the cameraman provides as if it were a kind of clay to shape, cut, and rearrange. Sobolewski suggests that her work with multifaceted fragments contrasts with Andrzej Wajda's search for romantic holistic symbols. Both tap into a sensibility of change but at different defining moments of the transition from communism. Wajda's films proved prophetic, presaging Solidarity. But, suggests Sobolewski, Wajda's symbols have a vampiric quality toward their successors. And this is also reflected in the lack of full recognition and use of the generational experience of his scriptwriter, Agnieszka Holland. Her circle of young people were part of what would become Solidarity. As Solidarity's promise faded, she would find her own career in Paris rather than in Warsaw. She provided the model for the actress in Wajda's *Man of Marble* and wrote the screenplay for Wajda's *Korczak* (the Jewish physician and educator who accompanied two hundred children in his orphanage to Treblinka, although he had offers to secure his personal safety). Agnieszka Holland's own films, as well as her life, are very much bound up with the Polish-Jewish symbiosis.[9]

Maria's work with Wyspianski's play *The Wedding*, by contrast to Wadja, and further into the transition midwifed by Solidarity, is open-ended. It ends with a scene of "going to Poland" when Poland did not exist (was divided between Russia, Germany, and Austria), and so "going to Poland" is signified by a boy at play donning a Polish hat. It is such fragmentary elements, Sobolewski seemed to suggest, that Maria uses in an alchemy of resonances among pasts and utopian hopes, which do not fuse into single key symbols but keep open irony and critique against the various claims for symbolic and historical closure.

Revisiting *The Wedding*

A group of eminent artists, all natives of Cracow, including Wyspianski, the greatest poet and playwright of Polish modernism, set out to enhance their appreciation of folk culture by sealing it with marriage. So three of them, Wyspianski, W. Termajer, and Rydel married village girls from the small village just outside the city, and vowed to lead a genuine peasant life. The marriages did not contribute in any significant way to better understanding between peasants and the intelligentsia, let alone integrating the two classes. The whole affair had the air of real farce and was seen as such by society . . . it provided an inspiration for the playwright Wyspianski, who based the plot of his play *The Wedding* on the authentic events in which he personally participated. This may also have contributed in a way to the methods of field research used by Malinowski. — Jan Jerschina, "Polish Modernism and Malinowski"

Stanislaw Wyspianski's play *The Wedding* opened in Cracow in 1901 and was, notes Czeslaw Milosz, a revolutionary event that informs the entire modern Polish theater, breaking with realistic imitation of life, and conceiving of theater instead as a "unit of color, movement, and sound" in which "fantastic symbolic creatures appear on stage on an equal footing with lifelike characters" (Milosz 1977: 33). For Maria, the play is about marriage between aristocrat and peasant, that is, about whether there can be unity in Poland; at the wedding a Jewish girl complicates matters by inviting the ghosts of the past. Set at the time of a gentry-planned revolt against the Austro-Hungarian Empire, the clever Austrian bureaucrats are able to turn the peasants against the gentry, and so to suppress them. At the wedding, talk of insurrection turns into a drunken chocholi dance, symbolic of the rebels' impotence and inability to unify classes, ethnicities, and religions.

Imagine now in 1993 — after a century of turmoil, Poland attempting to integrate into a new Europe — another wedding set again in Galicia, this time a gentry family returning from abroad to celebrate a wedding with various sorts of "intermarriage." Maria sees it again as a wedding with ghosts (including memories of the past that brought the bride back). The bride — daughter to a landowner who fled when he was eleven — raised in England and Scotland, residing now in Switzerland, is engaged to a Swiss Protestant.

She decides to have the wedding in her father's ancestral village, bringing together family and friends from all over Europe together with the local villagers and townsfolk. Symbolism and ironies inevitably inhabit any such ritual of kinship (re)creation. Given permission to film, Maria asked the guests to engage in a theatrical exercise: look into a mirror for five minutes and think of what spirits you would invite to the wedding. Poles, she reports, invited ghosts of the past, while the Swiss invited spirits of the future. Swiss and English guests did not mix easily. A French-speaking officiating priest was imported from Cracow so that the groom could follow. The Swiss complained, in their Protestant fashion, that the Catholic wedding was too showy; the Polish newspapers clucked that the groom had not taken communion.

Does the documentary/ethnographic filmmaker edit out (or use?) the bits when people did not know what to do or when things went wrong, as when the horse cart to take the bride to the church failed to arrive and a car was substituted, or the discussions about who should enter the church first? The ironies of chatter speak volumes about class and exile: "It's so wonderful to be among the common folk"; "Did you know that X was dead?" "No." "Oh yes, in 1978." A macrobiotic meal is organized for the wedding, and a woman talks about the macrobiotic ideology. Someone says something about our grandmothers knowing all about the ingredients of cooking, to which someone retorts, "Our grandmothers never did any cooking" (they had servants).

Interview the bride. Add a touch of sepia, a few old photos from before World War II. Add some shots of scenery, like the lovely ruin of the old Ukrainian church and cemetery. Juxtapose shots of the slim, tall serving girl from the village with the interview of the old woman servant who worked in the manor house before the war. Juxtapose shots of the half-Polish, half-Mexican opera singer with old photos of her mother dancing; flip the old photographs to create the effect of a moving picture. Ghosts and spirits come alive, and possibilities rapidly move beyond documentary toward feature film. Seventeen hours of footage provide plenty to edit into odkłamywavie.

The wedding itself is filmed mainly in two manor houses belonging to branches of the family: The one in Ladzin, near Rymanov, is where a distant cousin, recently returned from many years of being a ski instructor in France, runs an exquisite bed and breakfast (where we stayed during this revisit). The other, in Iwonicz, was used in the past decades as an agricultural extension center. At Iwonicz Zdroj (the spa, founded in 1578) on the hillside above, the bride's husband offered to buy the decaying two-story wood house without running water that the bride's father had grown up in and to restore it. The spa is to be privatized, but the rules for this process have not been worked out; at today's prices the building could be renovated, but in a year the bride fears it will be too expensive, and there is no guarantee that she can get it in open-market bidding. Interview the father as he walks through his childhood house, bringing back memories.

In the rolling countryside behind Rymanov, we come to the ruins of the Ukrainian church and cemetery, its rust-red roof and brown walls richly alive in the sparkling afternoon sun. Inside the empty church, Polish graffiti says, "Forgive them, for they did not recognize that it was Your temple." I ask what happens in the film here. A little boy goes into the church with a horse; there is a shot of the graffiti and of the cemetery, where there is a tree wrapped around an old metal cross; three trees stand in a row across the way and were shot against the moon to make the scene look dangerous, a place of magic, perhaps.

The Wedding as Odkłamywavie

A girl (Maria?) in a nineteenth-century long dress walks through the trees and grassy hills of Rymanov reading about Iwonicz from a nineteenth-century guidebook. She sits by a stream and reads about the waters of the spa. The actress is from the Zaluska family. Her mother, daughter of the gentry, married a local butcher. The girl looks into a mirror, and we see wedding guests chatting on the porch of the Iwonicz manor house. As appetizers are served and a string quartet plays, the octogenarian lawyer Stanislaw Bielecki and his wife arrive. He has figured as a guide also beyond the film in providing access to Rymanov's Jewish and Austro-Hungarian past.

A cousin of the bride looks into the mirror, saying he wishes to see their grandmother Mary Didur, the half-Mexican opera singer who married into the Zaluski family. Old pictures of her intercut the 1990s wedding in the church, and Bielecki comments that her talent had not sufficed to bridge the class differences. She just was not of the same "niveau"; she should have been at least six sticks gentry (having a coat of arms), seven sticks (a graf), nine sticks (a baroness), or ideally a miter cap (a countess). An old servant woman recalls the dancer's unconventionality, singing from the balcony in the early morning so all in town could hear, bathing in the pond, and not knowing how to drive, driving the car into the pond. Antek wants to see through the looking glass his ancestor the slightly mad scientist-inventor Ostaszewski, who argued that the sun was inside the earth and what we see above us is only an illusory projection. Ostaszewski, says Antek proudly, built and flew an early airplane. Bielecki sardonically says it was only a kite, and he couldn't get it to fly. On the piano Ivo plays Klemens Oginski's famous "Farewell My

Homeland." It is treated by Poles as a patriotic song, although it was written as Klemens abandoned Poland for France. Ivo wants to look into the mirror to see an earlier generation's Ivo, a black sheep of the family, whose name he was given in an effort to obscure the memory of the earlier Ivo. The bride wants to use the looking glass to meet the founder of the spa. A villager tries in Polish to tell a Scotsman about his brother's meeting with the pope to obviously total incomprehension.

Andrej looks into the mirror and recalls the first of September 1939, when the Germans bombed Krosno and the war began for the Zaluski family. A Strauss waltz, sunset, guests in slow motion, Ivo at the piano, and the moon against the Ukrainian church. The structure of recall and eulogy extends to the absent Ukrainians and Jews. We view the ruined church and synagogue. We listen to old servants recalling these now long gone communities.

Rymanov-Iwonicz: The Ghosts

The great stone synagogue of Rymanov still stands in ruins with stately elegance on the hillside overlooking the agricultural plain. It is just below the main square, where the Jewish houses now have other inhabitants, and just below where in the 1990s there was a makeshift bazaar where Russians and Ukrainians sold odds and ends. Further above on the hill overlooking the town, higher even than the Christian cemetery, is the Jewish cemetery with its carved gravestones, overgrown but eloquent in its silence. (A small Catholic shrine was placed even higher, and in any case, the town church is above the synagogue.) The only remains of the surrounding Ukrainian-Ruthenian villages, wooden buildings that were burned leaving no trace, are the fruit trees and the picturesque ruins of the church that has a role in Maria's film.[10]

The famous Hasidic zaddiks Menachim Mendel (1745–1815) and his disciple Zvi Mesharat (1778–1847) had their seats here. This is the land of Hasidism, the stereotypical land of American Yiddishkeit nostalgia. In Yiddish, American Jews give this town the lilting tonalities of *Rymanov*; in Polish it is *Rymanov*. Galicia was a territory of the Austro-Hungarian Empire. Some trace the name to the Galicia of Spain, a trace perhaps of the knights from Spain who were given lands here, and also of the expulsion of Spanish Jews, some of whom migrated to this area.

one of those great aristocratic families in Poland, and her story is one of those in which Poland and Eastern Europe specialize—of a life so tested and wrenched and molded by stormy events that it seems to have the design of an all too unlikely or all too stereotypical historical melodrama.—Eva Hoffmann, *Exit into History*

For me, however, the memory of the non-Hasids is even more impressive. Isidor Isaac Rabi, the 1944 Nobel Prize winner in physics, was born here in 1898, and a photograph of the town's Jewish elite reminds one of the high bourgeois culture of Paris, Berlin, or Vienna. Nathan Altgold, who now has the Hilton Hotel franchise in Brussels, was born here. Adam Michnik's grandfather was from Rymanov. It was a spa town, the upstart spa, rival to the nearby older spa of Iwonoicz Zdroj. Lemburg/Lvov bourgeois folk and others came for the waters. A 1903 *Kurhaus* (sanitorium) guest register lists families from many places with their servants and tutors.

Rymanov was founded in 1376 as a grant of forest land to a German knight, one Raimond from the Rheinland. Over time, land ownership devolved to four families: the Sienienskis, Ossolinkis, Skorskis, and Potockis. Like the Jews, these gentry families also have checkered histories: Ignacy Potocki survived the Nazis disguised as a Polish laborer in the forest by the name of Jan Zabrzenski; the Sienienski family in much earlier times had been patrons of the Arian church, and the church on the main square had itself been an Arian church. They were part of the same gentry stratum as the Zaluski and Bojanowski families that figure in Maria's film of *The Wedding*.

Maria's own family's summer house is located just up the road from the Rymanov spa. The house was bought in 1911 from Kalman Bezea, the Hungarian Jewish carpenter who had built it. Maria's great-grandfather bought it and named it Zaosie after the Lithuanian village of the national poet Adam Mickiewicz, whose mother is widely thought to have been Jewish or from Frankish converts from Judaism.

I stayed up late one night immersed in the vivid descriptions of life in Rymanov provided in the Rymanov Commemorative Book compiled by Rymanov's Jews scattered abroad. Four hundred of Rymanov's fourteen hundred Jews survived World War II, eighteen in concentration camps, four saved by getting Gentile papers. The streets came alive with names and actions and addresses of individuals of an incredible variety in a town of some three thousand in the interwar period. The events of September 1939 to August 1942

The story of Maria's family and the gothic tales of the house are themselves as richly complex as those of the gentry families she chronicles in *The Wedding*. Her paternal grandfather was an educated son of a peasant family from Lvov that probably summered in Rymanov. Some accounts claim the bloodline was from Swedish troops who fought and settled Poland. German nationalists claim these were German mercenaries because of the short ("un-Polish") names such as Zmarz. Others say such names are evidence of peasant ori-

are recorded in personal detail, including the movements of the carpenter brothers Yakov and Nahum Weinberger back and forth across the borderlands between Nazi- and Russian-held territories, and the more tragic story of the thirty-three-year-old R. Alter Moshe Eliezar Horowitz Rymanov, who escaped from Auschwitz, was captured in Budapest and returned to Auschwitz, escaped again, and again was recaptured and returned to Auschwitz, where he was shot to death in 1944.

The spry octogenarian lawyer Stanislaw Bielecki, who had lent me this book, also had photographs. The last town council before the war included seven Jews as well as his father, a physician who delivered many Jewish babies, including Nathan Altgeld. Jews and non-Jews ran on the same lists for town council. The Bieleckis had Jewish renters (who escaped when the Nazis came but did not survive the war). Stanislaw Bielecki has turned part of the family house, built in 1885, into a museum of Judaica from Rymanov—Torah fragments, menorahs, mezuzot—and of Austro-Hungarian documents and memorabilia, including his father's medical instruments.[11] The father, Iznatz, had been an officer in the Austro-Hungarian army and was treated with respect by the Germans who commandeered his house but allowed the family to also live there. (The Russians had a worse reputation for shooting Polish and Jewish officers, while the Germans treated even some Jewish officers as prisoners of war. Consequently, when the Russians came to commandeer the house, Ignatz refused to allow the officer to sit.)

gins. The grandfather identified with German culture through his education but could not come to terms with the Germany of the Nazis and apparently became unhinged. At the time of the population transfer from Lvov, he went with the first train of teachers to start schools in western Poland but disappeared and was never heard of again.

When Maria's father was in his teens, a young woman was murdered in the house for having affairs with soldiers from all the various invading armies. Her blood dripped down into his room. Another room is dubbed the mortuary because it housed one of the elderly persons expelled from Cracow by the Nazis and billeted with the villagers.

Today the house is divided into rooms for nuclear units of the extended family, all now doctors and professionals.

Other photographs showed twenty of the lawyers and judges of Rymanov, including the Jews Hill, Wiener, Schiff, and Hirscheld. Another was of five women and nine men of the intellectual elite. There was also a photo of

Rebbe Hirsch Horowitz in fur hat with his Hasidic court. Hasidic life was vigorous with the followers of the Sadigora Rebbe and followers of the Sanzer Rebbe. In the 1930s there were, remembers Stanislaw Bielecki, besides the great synagogue, four other houses of prayer, including a reform one.

Bielecki opened a door to the past, but it was the memories and tales in the pages of the Rymanov Commemorative Book that fixed the voices and places of those days in my head. At 3 Sanocka Street, at the beginning of the descent from the square, was, for instance, the Selenfreund-Chili house. Shlomo Selenfreund for thirty years was the chairman of the Jewish community *(kehilla)*, and the house was an open meeting place for Jews and Gentiles alike, as well as where kehilla officials would gather to deliberate all problems before official meetings. Here was the only private phone in Rymanov during the immediate post–World War I years. From here the community leaders phoned the district government to request typhoid pills in the annual fall typhus seasons. It was a large house with a basement that once housed a liquor factory, later Moshe Friedrich's winery and a courtyard with fruit trees and a vegetable patch. Next door on one side was a pharmacy, on the other side the Zeliczokova Kasa. All three buildings had been built by Shumel Chil, an ancestor. Shlomo Selenfreund's son-in-law, also named Shmuel Chil, had a grocery, and his brother Herman had a tavern, both in a building on the square, also owned by the family. On Simhat Torah, townsfolk would gather at the big house at 3 Sanocka Street to read from the Torah with celebratory wine, and at the end of the day kehilla leaders would convene to elect officials for the great synagogue, the study hall, and the burial society. Shlomo Selenfreund was a delegate to the sixth and seventh Zionist congresses in Basel, and a confidant of founders of the Mizrahi movement. His widow, Bracha, would hold gatherings on Sabbath afternoons with tea and cookies for the women to discuss the week that was. On Sunday mornings, men would gather in Herman Chil's tavern to swap stories of suffering and survival in the days before World War I. (Before World War I, Rymanov was built of wood except for the stone synagogue and the church. During World War I the town was badly destroyed and rebuilding had not been completed by the beginning of World War II.) Monday was market day. The farmers would park their wagons in the Selenfreud-Chil yard while they went to sell and buy in the shops, mainly Jewish owned. Shmuel Chil and a cousin, Shmuel Stoff, were town council members.

In 1937 things had already become tense, with the Polish government orchestrating anti-Semitic propaganda. The district governor *(starosta)* asked the Jewish town leaders to come to his office in Sanok to discuss the tensions. His suggestion was that to appease the anti-Semitic feelings, they settle for four seats on the town council instead of the six held by Jews. The Jewish leaders refused, and in the elections that year, they increased their seats to seven. Joseph Halpern, the director of a savings and loan company, was the leading vote getter in seven elections from 1920 to 1939, outpolling even the local priest.

Off the entrance corridor of the great synagogue, remembers Freda Vogel-Stari, was the *heder* (school) run by R. Shimon Nosla, which also served as the place for self-led services by "bakers, tailors, metalworkers, wagoneers, porters, those not rich enough to have fixed places in the great synagogue." There was a mutual aid society (Yad Harutzim) for the working people: if a metalworker bought raw materials with uncovered notes, the wholesaler could redeem the notes from the Yad Harutzim, and the metalworker would reimburse the communal fund after the next market day. If one needed to take up a collection for a dowry, or if a wagoneer's horse fell ill and he needed a replacement, one could turn to the Yad Harutzim. Meir Lankar even donated a horse to the communal assets. There are stories of Reb Hirsch Mesharat's Purim feasts, and the jokes and tales he told; of the Jewish pressure to improve the public schools, resulting eventually in a new building with classes of thirty-six in which only five or six were Jewish children.

On the first Friday of September 1939, German planes flew overhead, and the bombing of the Krosno airport could be heard. "We debated," remembers Moshek Selenfreund, "should we flee or should we stay; we stayed." On the following Sabbath eve, 8–9 September, two days before Sukkot of the new Jewish year 5700, the Germans attacked Rymanov. There are a series of vivid accounts of that Sabbath. A few Polish soldiers took shelter in the Christian cemetery above the town; they fired on German patrols trying to enter the town and killed one German officer, remembers carpenter and youth organizer Nachum Weinberger. "We [took cover] in the cellar," remembers Moshek. On 9 September the Germans shelled the town, then stormed it. At 2 P.M. they lined up all the men of the town, separating Jews and non-Jews, ordering them to stand for several hours, hands raised, in the central square facing trucks with machine guns. Then ten hostages were taken—five Jews and five non-Jews—including Moshek's father, Lazar Selenfreund. (The hostages were released a month later, when Rymanov came temporarily under Slovak rule.) Women and children were released from the square. Three hours later the men, with the warning "This time you are lucky," were sent to put out the fires that had sprung up from the shelling. The Germans photographed the entire four-hour ordeal. In the following day, the eve of Sukkot, notices were put up that all Jews, on pain of being shot, had to be out of town by 8 A.M., with the exception of the eighteen wealthiest families. They should go east to Sanok, across the River San (the border with Russian-held territory, according to the Ribbentrop-Molotov agreement). Most obeyed, going on foot or in hired carts. Some later drifted back, and Jewish refugees from elsewhere began to appear.

The Weinberger brothers—Nahum, Zvi, and Yakov—illustrate the unsettled nature of the border. Yakov and Nahum came to Rymanov in 1931 as young freelance carpenters from Lask and brought their families in 1938 to what seemed like a relatively prosperous place, thanks to the spa. It was also a place where the various Jewish youth groups were allowed to organize. When the war broke out, men began to be drafted, and some—Jews and non-Jews alike—fled eastward. Yakov went into the army. After the 1939 expulsion from Rymanov, Zvi and Nahum went back to lask, where they helped organize refugee kitchens and other support. In 1940 they moved to Drohboycz, working in a carpenter's cooperative until the Germans arrived.

For a while, under deteriorating circumstances, they did work for the Germans. Then they returned to Rymanov, where a Christian carpenter gave Nahum work and food. In 1942 Yakov also smuggled himself back into Rymanov, in a truck that crossed checkpoints without being searched because it had Deutsche Wehrmacht markings.

Rymanov remained a somewhat fluid borderland. It was under German rule, but no Gestapo were stationed there. The Germans were based in Krosno and made periodic appearances, but the town was overseen by Polish police and a Polish mayor. The police chief, sickened by the Germans, helped the Jews when he could, says Nahum Weinberger. Rymanov was on the road to Slovakia, and there was cross-border trade, some of which was done by Jews through Poles. Slovakian Jews had also been expelled into concentration camps,

In the corner of the Plac Zgody (Peace Square) [in Cracow] stood an Apotheke run by Tadeusz Pankiewicz ... He was the only Pole permitted to remain within the ghetto walls. . . . The Polish impressionist Abraham Neumann, the composer Mordche Gebirtig, philosophical [*sic*] Leon Steinberg, and the scientist and philosopher Dr. Rappaport were all regular visitors at Pankiewicz'. The house was also a link, a mail drop for information and messages running between the Jewish Combat Organization (zob) and the partisans of the Polish People's Army . . . furious and unequivocal resistance.—scene left out of the film version of *Schindler's List* (Keneally 1982: 130–31)

the young Zionists of the Halutz Youth and zob . . . acquired uniforms of the Waffen ss and, with them, the entitlement to visit the ss-reserved Cyganeria Restaurant. . . . they left a bomb which blew the tables through the roof, tore seven ss men to fragments, and injured

and Jews in the border areas were brought to Rymanov. A Judenrat was formed to help the Germans extract funds and forced labor. Sixty men a day (more later) were conscripted to build roads and prisoner-of-war camps. Nahum Weinberger was elected head of the artisan's association but refused to serve on the Judenrat. He helped build the prisoner-of-war camp for Soviet soldiers outside town and witnessed the terrible conditions of the twelve thousand prisoners of war, who were being starved to death and then buried in mass graves. He also reports on the execution of the Jews Getzler, an American, and Weinnig, caught for trading in foreign currency. Weinig, asked from whom he had received the money, named a dead man and was beaten to death. Getzler was shot by two Gestapo troops.

Nahum describes the expulsion of the Jews on 1–3 August 1942 to the concentration camp in Plaszow (where Schindler's factory was) and then ten days later to the camp at Belzec. He described Plaszow as containing thousands of people who looked like skeletons in rags, with posters on the walls threatening death for any offense. Skilled metalworkers and carpenters such as Nahum were separated and given permits to work outside the camp. After thirteen months in Plaszow (September 1943), warned by a Jewish woman living in Polish disguise

some forty more. . . . They bombed the ss only Bagatella Cinema in Karmelicka Street. . . . The zob would in a few months sink patrol boats on the Vistula, fire-bomb sundry military garages throughout the city, arrange Passierscheins for people who were not supposed to have them, smuggle passport photographs out to centers where they could be used in the forging of Aryan papers, derail the elegant Aryan only train that ran between Cracow and Bochnia, and get their underground newspaper in to circulation. They would also arrange for two of od Chief Spira's lieutenants, Spitz and Forster, who had drawn up lists for the imprisonment of thousands, to walk into a Gestapo ambush. — scene left out of the film of *Schindler's List* (Keneally 1982: 143)

a courier for a Zionist rescue organization in Budapest . . . a bureau in Istanbul to gather hard information . . . would you come to Budapest and pass on what you just told me . . . I'll come, said Oskar Schindler. — scene left out of the film of *Schindler's List* (Keneally 1982: 145, 149)

Julius Madritsch, owner of the Madritsch uniform factory inside this camp of Plaszow . . . kept nearly four thousand prisoners employed and therefore safe from the death mills. — scene left out of the film of *Schindler's List* (Keneally 1982: 18)

shrewd Zionist prisoners inside Plaszow put pressure on convinced outsiders, people like Oskar and Madritsch, who could in turn put pressure on the Arma-

that the camp was to be sealed, Nahum and his brothers escaped, walking to Piaski and Wialkia.

The Mizrahi underground in Cracow led them through the forests to Budapest. With the aid of a Swiss organization, they were smuggled to Palestine in June 1944 and fought in the Israeli war of independence.

ments Inspectorate. On the ground that hunger and sporadic murders of Plaszow were still to be preferred to the assured annihilations of Auschwitz and Belzec. (Keneally 1982: 223)[12]

All these ghosts, recollections, and remains of Rymanov—Jewish, aristocratic, bourgeois, peasant, skilled labor, Arian, Ruthenian—as the Lubomierz discussions pointed out, call for a different kind of film than Spielberg's *Schindler's List* (which Sobolewski calls "an American rescue fantasy"), one that engages odkłamane.

Against Metaphor: Weddings and Funerals as Filmic Tropes

Anderman and Maria's collaboration began with a dialogue of friendly disagreements. She suggested a screenplay about filmmakers doing a documentary on voting as a device for connecting the scenes of his vignettes in *The Edge of the World*. He found this insufficiently original and came up with the device of a policewoman in a room with television monitors that would allow changing narrative and situation. This allowed him to begin dictating dialogue. He then wrote a screenplay for Maria about AIDS, which she refused as too difficult. She suggested a film about this wedding. He objected and suggested a funeral instead. There are too many Polish variants on *The Wedding*, he said, but funerals to rebury people from the past had recently become very popular.

Reburials could be quite surreal: Paderevsky was brought back from the United States, but no one in Poland cared; it had no political meaning, and it was difficult to find anyone to welcome the casket. On the other hand, General Sikorski, the head of the Polish army during World War II, and a former prime minister, was to be reburied at Wawel Castle in Cracow, two days before the general elections, in a ceremony organized by Lech Wałęsa. Maria didn't like the idea: she feared what Anderman's humor might do with such funerals. For instance, she noted, Stanislaw Witkiewicz was buried in the Soviet Union (Ukraine). In Poland, people insisted that this great avant-garde literary figure must be reburied next to his mother. In the Soviet Union, however, no one knew where he was buried, only that he did not have any teeth. The body they selected had wonderful teeth. Now this corpse of perhaps a Soviet hunter lies in the grave of Witkiewicz's mother, and everyone knows. Meanwhile Witkiewicz is still in his grave in the Soviet Union. Complications did not rest here: Witkiewicz had committed suicide when the Soviets invaded Poland on 17 September 1939, and his funeral was like something out of his plays. A suicide could not be buried by a priest, so they got Father Jozef Tischner, a Catholic philosopher, who gave a eulogy saying that Witkiewicz had died resisting the Russians, that his death was not really a suicide but more like that of a valiant soldier defending the nation.

Maria worried about the topos of a funeral, given Anderman's bleak view of Poland as a country of antiquated and handicapped people, left behind by history. In a 1993 vignette he depicted Poles in an apartment building all watching cable TV with the sound turned off because they do not understand the German and English of the broadcasts. One of the characters says he fears leaving the sound on, since in the past he would watch with sound and end up beginning to pray in strange languages that he did not understand. Another Anderman story is about an order to destroy millions of books because storage space has become scarce and costly. Two soldiers guard a warehouse of books, and one sees a woman trying to steal some of them. He begins to accost her but is stopped by the other, who says, I know the woman, she used to be my teacher, books were important to her. In the final sentences, Anderman wryly tells us that she uses the books to heat her apartment, an image of the desperate circumstances of the elderly and the poor.

Aside from Wyspianski's play *The Wedding*, Maria was attracted by the short story "Wedding in the Countryside," by Maria Dombroska, written in the 1950s in the aftermath of Stalinism, one of the first expressions of the changes afoot. People meet at a wedding and complain.[13]

Weddings lend themselves better to Tadeusz Sobolewski's plea that there must be something in our witnessing of the Holocaust and other cruelties of the twentieth century, something that gives hope that we do not just stand condemned, that there is humanity even in history's handicapped.

Evolving Documentary Rhetorics

Politics would give Polish punk a role and an audience like no other in the history of Polish rock. . . . The imposition of martial law in Poland on 13 December 1991 gave punk a new lease on life. . . . The punk festival at Jarocin . . . grew into an annual ritual of the Polish punk nation. By summer 1984 the Baltic town was bringing in 15,000 to 20,000 punk rockers. . . . In 1981, the Jarocin festival's founder, Grzegorz Brzozowicz, initiated what he called the Rock Front at Warsaw's Remont Club, which brought in punk bands from all across Poland. The house band ss-20 took its name in honor of the new generation of Soviet nuclear missiles. . . . ss-20 gave antimilitary rock to a generation living under martial law. — Alex Kan and Nick Hayes, "Big Beat in Poland"

Before making *The Edge of the World* and *The Wedding,* Maria had made a series of short documentaries about life under and just after martial law: *Everyone Knows Who Stands behind Whom* (1989), *The Repossessors* (1989), *I Am a Male of a Man* (1989), *Major, or The Revolution of the Elves* (1989), *Don't Trust the Politicians* (1990). They are inventive experiments in documentary technique, in using punk rock music and the carnivalesque theatricality that became hallmarks of the revolutions of 1989.

Everyone Knows Who Stands behind Whom is an exquisite six-minute short that functions like an Anderman feuilleton or newspaper vignette. It traces one of those ubiquitous lines in which one stood under communism without necessarily knowing what the shop might have for sale, and which, like the children's telephone game, often provided distorted information to the newest members passed down from the head of the line about the imagined objects for sale and rules of the line. The film begins with the screeching of an unoiled door, and faces in the line, hands and feet. For much of the film there is no dialogue. There is a snatch of a dispute over whether once in line, one needs to stay in line, or whether one's place can be held, resolved by the "captain" of the line, who negotiates the rules. The most significant bit of conversation is the title, which takes on a parabolic meaning about the nature of surveillance in a communist state, as well as being a simple observation about one's place in line. The collage of conversation bits is incoherent, and yet it provides an instantly recognizable portrait:

> Why aren't you at work? He was here before, it is all right. What's your problem, mister? You come at seven and you ask what is this line for? . . . Some people have been here since August. Don't give me that kind of crap. Keep your hands to yourself, behave yourself. See, people are standing in line, who do you think you are? Go ahead, step in, you aren't buying anything anyway. We wait honestly, and that's why somebody is first. Everybody knows who's standing behind whom. I've been standing here six nights now, and I reckon I'll be here five or six more. . . . I'm kind of second, but it's been a whole week that I've been second. If I'm strong, if I'm the first, who will kick me out of this line? Why do we stand, because if the line . . . Although the line . . . our line . . . People of this line . . . and this is exactly the result of all these lines . . . obviously they'd prefer to avoid standing by using numbers. Some eleven years people stand. Day

by day to have to run like this. The line according to the list is the proper order. We form a line on a side, everybody who is not in line, please step out.

The shop door opens and screeches as legs push into and out of the shop. We never see the shop itself or what might be inside. We see only the weathered faces of the elderly characters in the line. A final signature shot pans slowly along the heads like a line of calligraphy or notes written on a musical staff of brickwork.

In the next film, *The Repossessors*, the tactic is the inverse: instead of visuals with minimalist dialogue, the film consists of detailed interview tapes but restaged sketchy visuals. The interest is in the talk, the strategies of persuasion, used by repossessors to worm their way into people's apartments to seize appliances. The tricks of the trade are revealed by willing repossessors, but they cannot afford to be visually identified. Against the visuals of dreary apartment blocks and grubby offices, the situations described are full of absurdist, melancholy humor. A third film, *I Am a Male of a Man*, uses a mock newsreel format to satirize the communist rites of community: a pretentious local male official holds every available position, including the presidency of the women's league. The satire works simply by playing back the words of the official to comic effect against visuals of one of those absurdist folklorized pageants in which "uncultured" citizens in peasant dress accompanied by polka music were made to perform like children.

With *Major, or The Revolution of the Elves* (aka *The Orange Alternative*) and *Don't Trust the Politicians*, real-life political demonstrations are recorded, replayed, and redeployed. These showcase the music and satire at work in the society of the 1980s that helped implode Poland and the Soviet empire (on Armenia, see Fischer and Gregorian 1993). In Wroclaw, a politics of laughter was disseminated by an arts student calling himself "Major" (Waldemar Frydrych). Born in Torun—the center of punk rock in Poland in the late 1970s, also the birthplace of Copernicus—he became well known in the 1980s, discomfiting not only the Communist Party and police but equally the Solidarity movement and industrial strikers, who felt that their serious politics were being made fun of. A secret police memo is said to admit they did not know how to react to politics of laughter and carnival. Frydrych wrote a "socialist surrealist" manifesto about his staging of carnivalesque "happenings" as a master's thesis at the University of Wroclaw but was refused permission to turn it into a doctoral dissertation.

Originally Maria planned to film Major in juxtaposition with the then minister of culture, who while still championing "socialist realism" by the

1980s had become an aging playboy known for his erotic exploits. Both agreed, but she could not obtain funding, and so she concentrated on a collage of Major's exploits, beginning with his early wall graffiti. Instead of slogans painted on walls by activists, Major painted little elves. There were elves in upside-down cars, penises emerging from televisions. The elves drew a lot of attention. Neither the police nor political activists knew how to react. Next Major began to stage happenings, often as inversions of state rituals. There was a Secret Agents' Day, in which he had his friends march in trench coats and shades, demanding an eight-hour day for the police. Taken in, some police actually joined the demonstration. When there was a shortage of toilet paper, Major handed out free rolls in the main square *(rynek)* of Wroclaw and surreptitiously filmed the results. The camera caught one woman taking a roll, hiding it, and returning to get another. The crowd, not knowing how to react, not knowing if this was something official or merely a street fair act, turned angry. The police did not know what to do: there was nothing illegal about handing out free toilet paper.

On International Women's Day, 8 March, Major handed out free tampons. This time he was sent to prison for two days—to the prison that had once held Rosa Luxemburg. At carnival time, he staged a parade with papier-mâché effigies of General Jaruzelski, Lenin, and Marx with slogans like "Carnival in Socialism, Socialism in Carnival," "Exhume Stalin," "How to Laugh at the Soviet Union," and posters of himself as John Lennon, Jesus, and a cowboy. On the twentieth anniversary of the Prague Spring, he issued a call to arms to help the communists. He had people dress up in military uniforms, including samurai outfits, and march to the Czech border, where Czech colleagues were to join in, but a heavy Czech police force blocked the way. And, of course, he waged a political campaign to be elected: "Vote for Major, a new kind of politician"; "A carport for everyone, and let's make love in them."

After the fall of the communist regime, Major's politics of laughter needed adjustments that he could not find: he tried to run for parliament but lost and was accused of betraying Solidarity. Andrzej Wajda tried to help Major, giving him a video camera to use. But people began to turn suspicious, for example, when he was given one thousand dollars and tried to stage a free distribution of this money as a happening against the worship of money. When the money ran out, people, instead of just turning angry as in the toilet paper incident, began to suggest that he had hidden more money for himself. Discouraged, Major withdrew to Paris to set up a "government in exile."

Meanwhile, in Warsaw, street theater had a different kind of gravitas. In

Don't Trust the Politicians, Maria surveys youth demonstrators of the 1990s, from anarchist-punks on the Left, to the skinheads on the Right, and mystical New Agers in between. The music is political punk rock. As footage shows water cannons and tear gas used by the state as crowd control in the great parade square of Warsaw, a pounding electric guitar accompanies the lyrics "Fear stopped us from speaking aloud / Fear stopped us loving and smiling / Fear made us lower our eyes / Fear held us in its grip. . . . We get poisoned / Do you remember paradise on earth? / No! Nobody does / My heart is weeping, my body is crying / What's happened to all this?" A boy recalls, "I was six then and not really interested. What I remember is Jaruzelski's speech. . . . I was close to punk culture, and I know that if I really want to be a human being, I have to be a nobody in this society." An anarchist demonstration with black flags marches through the great square as speakers berate the communists and Lech Wałęsa for selling out at the roundtable negotiations. Wałęsa's team, they shout into the microphones, in a premonition of charges that would be made in 1993 in a very different electoral context, has gained control of the mass media in as undemocratic a fashion as the communists. "They talk of a return to Europe, but in Europe there is pluralism. . . . We have no independent trade unions; we have only a single-party system; the government is not ours." They march on Parliament shouting, "[Leszek] Balcerowicz must go!" (Balcerowicz was the economist who was to design the privatization and transfer to a free-market economy in the first Solidarity governments.)

But this is still a moment of street theater. When a militia officer admonishes, "Don't throw stones if you want Parliament to do something," the young demonstrators retort, "If the militia is quiet, we won't use force. This time we can let you go." A young militiaman shares the microphone with the young anarchist: "If it is a peaceful demonstration, if you don't use force, we won't either, but if you attack, we will defend ourselves: we've got our ways." The anarchist takes the microphone back and mockingly echoes, "Yes, we've always got our ways." The demonstration marches on the Intercontinental Hotel, chanting, "Kuron into soup, soup for Kuron, down with the bourgeoisie." Angry motorists blocked by the demonstration shout, "Go get a job!"

Yippie style, they march into the hotel, staging a holdup with their fingers as guns, and drinking "bourgeois wine" in celebration. The young anarchist explains: "In this decade there can be a French-style 1968 here in Poland, except we are going to win." Things do escalate to stones and setting some fires, and brave sentiments: "Our anthem is, if they lock us up, Bader Meinhoff will help us out; if we are down, the Red Brigades will come to our aid; and to the rear there is the sabotage of Karol Wojtyta. . . . Rise up, wretched of the earth, for when the earth glistens back, a black banner of wrath is carried in the wind by an anarchist hand."

Before turning to the right-wing club of the Confederation for an Independent Poland (which still idolizes Marshal Pilsudski), a pacifist graffiti stencilist touts the mystical energy of Tibetan letters, effective even if you cannot read Tibetan, magical and unverbalizable. Politics, he says, is the devil's work: one must be corrupt to be a politician, the political elite are separated from the people and have no idea of what is going on, culture is pap, and even the Catholic Church only provides a reactionary counterposition. Instead he fills the visual space with power of Tibetan letters.

The electric guitar wells up again as the film returns to the more disruptive skinheads. In a courtroom, they show no remorse for disrupting and beating African students on 23 February 1993, demonstrating in support of Nelson Mandela. Their discourse is defiant: "Because Mandela is a communist," "White power!" "We are also against Russians and Germans," "Hatred of Jews is second nature," "Apartheid!" "Poland for Poles." As the electric guitar wails, "We are surrounded by wild beasts, we are surrounded by people of evil, there is nowhere to go," a skinhead teaches us the dress code involving an American imaginary: "A skin's outfit consists of boots, high, laced, fourteen eyelets, jeans, Levis would be best, jackets of traditional cut or American aviator jackets, suspenders are important, as narrow as possible, hair should be very short."

Transformation of the Public Sphere

If any group was to Polish punk what the Sex Pistols were to the West, then that group was Perfect. . . . the song "We Want to Be Ourselves," with a slight alteration of accent the song's refrain . . . came off as indistinguishable in Polish from "We want to beat up the zomos [riot police]."— Alex Kan and Nick Hayes, "Big Beat in Poland"

Maria's 1993 documentaries — *Camera*; *Sexshops*; *The Vocabulary of Democracy*—thematize, and in their own production illustrate, the changing political economy of film and television production in Poland. Under the communists, no one had kept tabs on expenses, and so there were film studios in Wroclaw that would fly in actors from Warsaw as needed. Now those studios were closed. On the other hand, a law was in effect that 30 percent of television airtime must show Polish productions, so there was funding for, and airing of, documentaries. Efforts to privatize quickly ran into the problem of an Italian entrepreneur buying up stations and demanding they show cheap videos he supplied. Commercials began to become sources of funding, and

Poland became a production center for commercials on Russian television. In January 1994 a scandal erupted over the award of a license to Polsat, a regional satellite broadcaster, owned two-thirds by thirty-seven-year-old entrepreneur Zygmund Solorz. It was alleged that he used three aliases and maybe four passports, and Lech Wałęsa alleged that Solorz had been connected to the secret police. Pundits also suggested that Wałęsa, whose popularity was plummeting, was trying to gain control over private television to position himself for the next elections.

Camera, like *Everyone Knows Who Stands behind Whom*, is a brief vérité parable. Using archival footage, Maria follows a camera that was given to Solidarity by the International Trade Unions. The camera was seized by the communists and was used by them to film their final party congress. When Solidarity came to power, the camera broke. The parable is economic, incisive, and humorous.

Sexshops, done by Maria with Piotr Marawski, like *Repossessors*, explores (with a sense of humor that comes to the fore in a staged Major-like happening toward the end of the film) the shadows of economics, desire, and commodification. In a not entirely successful ironic look at sexshops as small businesses, rueful entrepreneurs, both female and male, complain that Polish-made products cannot compete with Western ones. A woman wholesaler talks with a straight face about one of her better sellers, a penis that squeaks, bought by ladies as a toy for their dogs; and about a Polish vibrator that was returned because people thought it would contain drugs but found it only contained Poznan flour. A retailer says he's going to switch to church items because the competition is less. The music is a lighthearted melancholic tango, "La Comparsita." For Maria, as she explains in a television roundtable with Tadeusz Sobolewski and a woman interviewer, the most interesting part of doing the film was interviewing the topless dancers about their sense of self and relations of power. Several dancers talked about starting because of money and being curious, but some also talked about learning to have a power, of feeling like real women, and of learning to return the stare of men. The most amusing part of the film is a happening staged by the filmmakers with a hidden camera. They had a male and a female student set up a table in a public passageway with a sign saying "Give money, help the poor have a comfortable place for sex." People stop. A man harangues them: "Sex is a sin outside marriage, you lose your soul; in Poland ninety percent of people go to hell because of sex." Others give enough money so the filmmakers can go have a few beers.

While *Sexshops* suffers from one of the same dangers of capitalism as does its subjects—the filmmakers never get paid because the private company that promised funding goes bankrupt — *The Vocabulary of Democracy* is a much more polished affair, as befits its "relations of production."

Commissioned for television to be aired just before the fall 1993 elections, in part to help bolster the chances of the Democratic Union, *The Vocabulary of Democracy* is an explicit effort to use the filmic media to help reconstruct the public sphere. It introduces fast-paced jump cuts and rock music with a message that works by juxtaposing Polish issues with comparative analogues. There are six ten-minute segments: "Law," "Power," "Democracy," "Freedom," "Election," and "State." Each is composed of footage, discussions with youth, man-on-the-street interviews, discussions in a family, rock music, and a narrator. The man-on-the-street interviews were often disconcerting: people said they did not want democracy or freedom, but only money and security.

One of the funniest, and most important, scenes (in the "Democracy" segment) is a sequence of fights in parliaments around the world, ending with Jacek Kuron asleep in the Polish Parliament. The sequence was a response to those who say it is unseemly to have public disputes in Parliament. In rapid sequence, one sees a debate over corruption in the Italian Parliament with shouting and one MP shaking a rope noose at another; Margaret Thatcher being shouted down; a shouting match in the Israeli Knesset; a brawl in the Taiwanese Parliament; and delegates pounding on their desks in the Indian Parliament. The contrast with Kuron asleep is hilarious: the woman next to him nudges him for a vote; he pushes the button and goes back to sleep. The big editing challenge was to get the music timing right. The theme song is Perfect's "We Want to Be Ourselves" (Chcemy byc soba), which can be heard or slurred as "We want to beat up the zomos" (Chcemy bic zomo). As the theme song, it is meant to suggest that "we can only be ourselves through democracy." Maria joked she had no need to make "we want to be ourselves" the tag for sleeping on the job ("I don't have anything against Kuron"), though perhaps it could equally be read as Kuron dreaming about democracy. It was, however, a truly delicate moment: there had been a scandal about MPs who pushed the voting buttons for absent members, some of which had been caught on camera. From then on, Parliament began to control television access.

Repetitions and Archives: Film and Ethnographic Recall and Response

"Carnival, Caricature, Catastrophe, Coalitions, Conflict, Constitutions, Controls, Cosmos . . . Abortion, Administration, Affairs, Alcohol, Balls, Banks, Bazaars . . . Demonstrations, Denomination, Depots, Diplomacy . . . Economics, Electrical Plants, Electro-magnetism, Eroticism."

"Who'd remember? Nobody can remember. Halina calls me and said, 'Maneuvers,' but I can't remember if they were in the Pacific or the Barents Sea."

"People being rounded up, you don't want that." . . . "the part with the exhumations, I want that, a dead child, meals being handed out. Is that a Jewish child?" "Yes, and here you have the streets of the ghetto, pictures from a roundup, notices of executions. . . ."

"Good morning, this is the news for Saturday, June 25 . . . Tomorrow will be sunny and even warmer." — from *Traces*

In the final two, disturbing films of 1994, with which this essay will end, Maria deals with ghosts of two different kinds, both reverberating with un-settling repetitions in the present. *The Last Gypsy in Osweicm* (Auschwitz) stylistically is a documentary interview with a Gypsy, who tells how his family was forcibly sedentarized after World War II in Osweicm, how they were still segregated, but he managed to go to school with Polish children. He married a Polish woman who spoke the Gypsy language. The response of the authorities to a riot against Gypsies was to drive them out of town and to encourage them to emigrate. The last Gypsy went to Sweden, not realiz-ing his passport was only a one-way exit permit, but he struggled to return and was eventually allowed to do so. What is most stunning in the film is the repetition: that *this* form of riot could have happened in *this* place with *this* response on the part of the state.

Traces deals with equally troubling subjects, but in a quite different style, and with quite different dilemmas posed for filmmaking and ethnography. Done in hieroglyphics, it begins with five images or icons of invading com-mercialism, the breaking of a closed world, the evanescence of the moment: Green leaves. A red Coca-Cola paper cup against the green leaves of a weed. A metal chain with an open link, followed by the solid white line and then a broken white line (passing allowed) of a road. A leaf on the pavement in the dappled shadow of a tree.

The title is followed by three more establishing shots: of a television news-room; of two cameras, one pointed outside a window, and one to the in-side at the newsroom; files of videos, film reels, and clippings. (Compare the parallel scene in Milcho Manchevski's *Before the Rain*, also done in 1994, a Macedonian film about a war photographer in the Balkans whose English girlfriend works in a London photo archive, where photos of the former Yugoslavia look like images of World War II concentration camps, and where the radio similarly blares out banal pop music and weather re-ports as she selects, marks, categorizes, and files images.) The images are at first disorienting: a woman's eye, a red fingernail of a hand typing at a computer, photo archives, alphabetized folders, computerized indexes, video clips downloaded from the Internet for rebroadcast. A ballot box in Moscow is dumped out, scissors cut off corners of the ballots, a cat watches the corners flutter to the floor. A male voice asks for a transmission from Rwanda, and we see images of the Rwandan carnage. A query about Bucharest follows; an image of a machine gun firing from and on cars in Bosnia. Red-lipsticked lips read an alphabetized list, which is later shown to be folders in the archives and lists on the computer screen. Gradually there is a search for particular images, for an incident in Bydgoszca. ("If it wasn't in Bydgoszca, we'll have to check under children. I've got it: three children killed . . . in Rucewka near Bydgoszca.")

As the camera pans across several monitors, women mutter about the difficulties of finding images: "Who'd remember? Nobody can remember. Halina calls me and says, 'Maneuvers,' but I cannot remember if they were in the Pacific or. . . ." A computer screen with an alphabetized index. A female television anchor announces a B-52 has crashed; it is shown bursting into flames, caught by an onlooker's video camera. The red lips read: "Carnival, Caricature, Catastrophe. . . ." There are also sound files: orchestra music, slogan chanting, women chanting "Put compassion into fashion, don't wear fur!" Another drawer opens with folders in the Z part of the alphabet. A library of tapes: "Marine, Media, Medicine, Militias, Minorities." A woman is being lifted to safety by a helicopter, the wind whipping her dress above her head; Glitter Gulch Girls wear see-through tops and fantastic hairdos; helicopters and blimps fall out of the sky. A female weather announcer gives an ambiguously banal, parabolic report ("The night was very cold . . . Poland is a sunny high-pressure area . . . Tomorrow will be sunny and even warmer"). The female news anchor concludes, "That's all the morning news." She takes off her mike and gets up; the camera pans to the camera shooting out the window and shows an ad for Sprite. Image of the Coca-Cola cup from the film's opening.

News and entertainment, gravitas and silliness, are mediated in fragments. We recognize the horror of war and catastrophe instantly, but the speed of the fragmentation does not allow immersion in traditional sentiments. Ethical responses require acknowledging that we have seen this all before, and that other worlds — of Las Vegas showgirls, animal rights demonstrators, staged film stunts with falling helicopters and falling buildings — continue in parallel time, and that the images themselves can be ambiguous as entertainment or tragedy.

In a world that pastiches reality's sounds and sights by taking snippets off the air and out of archival drawers, the immediacy of what is seen or heard is not the whole story, and montage does not itself provide meaning. We need to know what is beyond the frame, how the pictures of the world are constructed, the nature of the archives, the substitutions and variations that make up the grammar (and grammatology) that structures our subjectivities, epistemologies, and apperceptions of what is really going on. In an increasingly mediated world, more and more of the world is immediately available to the eye, and also in danger of being drowned in indexical horror houses of mirrors. "Carnival, Caricature, Catastrophe, Coalitions, Conflict, Constitutions, Controls, Cosmos. . . ."

So too for anthropology, as for film in Poland after the fall of communism, the lessons and discussions of the Lubomierz seminars apply. Anthropology too needs to contend with the layered streams of representations into which it ventures. For Polish film, the old strategies of allegory and indirection no longer made as much sense, or had as much bite, when the burdens of censorship and heavy state ideology lifted. Likewise for anthropology, the rationales of nation-building ideologies, as Ernest Gellner pointed out in his reflections on the ahistoricism of Bronislaw Malinowski despite or because he came from a world of collecting and redeploying folklore, are no longer as manipulable as once thought. History matters, trauma matters, ghosts matter, and the circulation of images matters in the ways they can be either genericized (get me a massacre) or turned into resonators and tympana of local forms of cultural critique that have bite and traction for the reconstruction of society in ways more democratic, pluralistic, and interrogative of the various utopian promises urged upon, or from within, us.

NEW PEDAGOGIES AND ETHICS

8

Worlding Cyberspace: Toward a Critical
Ethnography in Space, Time, and Theory

The growing realization of the inherent dangers of technology as such — not of its sudden
but of its slow perils, not of its malevolent abuses which, with some watchfulness, one can
hope to control, but of its most benevolent and legitimate uses . . .

    . . . our actions have opened up a whole new dimension of ethical relevance for which
there is no precedent in the standards and canons of traditional ethics. — Hans Jonas

For philosophical or political reasons, this problem of communicating and receivability,
in its new techno-economic givens is more serious than ever for everyone; one can live it
only with malaise, contradiction, and compromise. — Jacques Derrida

Cyberspace is (check one): [if reading this on the Web, click on one of
the links]: (1) a game of finance and corporate maneuver; (2) an undoing
of the legal system of intellectual and economic property rights, patents
and copyright, secrecy and military export laws, and community standards for moral codes, as well as an undoing of several other traditional
intellectual arenas of distinctions such as the economics of (free) speech
versus (commodifiable) texts, and materialities of (patentable) machine
versus (copyrightable) text (software); (3) a hardware technology of jury-
rigging together computers, satellites, copper and fiber-optic cables, and
perhaps soon silicon to neural tissues, with uneven coverage into the Third
World, and also in the First World, but with potentials for providing access around traditional deadened schools, local censorship, and bureaucratic stonewalling; (4) a conceptual space of connectivity, information, as-
sorted desires for escaping or enhancing the body or material world, new
paralogical language games for creating selves and socialities; (5) a research
space of postliterate, graphic, self-organizing, and experimental models,
simulations, and constructions; (6) a cultural-ideological, even ritual, space
of (con)fusion, at least in the United States, between a "cowboy-hacker-

individualist-anarchist-libertarian" ethic and a series of market and political mechanisms for restructuring labor in new forms of manufacturing
and services; (7) an object world with which to think about the changes of
the late twentieth century that go under the name of the postmodern, poststructuralist, or second-order cybernetic; and an arena productive of humorous, fertile, and mind-shaping metaphors for dealing with (8) all of
the above.

Ethnographies provide fieldwork tools of investigation, but ones that are
themselves challenged by cyberspace not to become absorbed, to maintain
insider-outsider critical and comparative perspectives, and to adapt writing
strategies that can map voicings and tonalities, locate people and their social
structures, and thereby articulate critical sites of constraints and openness.
There is a pervasive feeling in many fields touched by cyberspace that things
are beyond traditional control, that realities have outrun our usual conceptual categories. The very rhetorics of cyberspace make a claim for the new:
both that there are new realities and that cyberspace provides tools for handling interactive complex realities beyond traditional disciplinary vocabu-
laries or methods. Cyberspace is chronically "under construction," rapidly
changing, expanding and mutating among technologies and populations.
Ethnographies, to keep up, must themselves become more open textualities,
with "ports" to many dimensions and connections, without succumbing to
incoherent fragmentation. Ethnographies must attempt simultaneously to
unveil the underlying "constricted potential of a combinatory grid that is
both exhausting and indefatigable,"[1] and to publicly screen emergent social
and cultural configurations.

Ethnographies of cyberspace need to deal in theory, time, place, languages (and cultures), institutions (legal, economic, psychological, science),
and reconfiguring the knowledge-power nexuses involved in all these arenas.
They are challenged to do so both substantively and in their own forms
and force of writing. Even more than a multisited ethnography, cyberspace
presents a topological challenge for a multidimensional ethnography that is
able to bring into sharp juxtaposition the contradictory elements of cyberspace's political economy, cultural elaborations, liberatory and subjugating
potentials, new information-based sciences, alternative engineering designs,
and their social implications.

Ethnographies, in their traditional forms of *writing*, may increasingly
seem now under pressure of a growing cyberspace pedagogical regime to
operate under the *anxiety* of being endangered, the anxiety of being already conceptually and pedagogically *archaic* [click for links to psychody-

namic and philosophical, techne or logos-en*gender*ed, doppelgänger track-ings of this *discourse*]. But, more realistically, while it is not the case that there is no more place for traditional writing, it is from the perspective of "twenty minutes into the future," as science fiction often likes to posit, that we can gain a sense of possibility, enrichment, as well as difficulty and dan-ger, amidst which we might strive with our future-looking but present capa-bilities, making ourselves open to the ear and desire and positioning of the other, facilitating of social institutions that are flexible and reflexively mod-ern, rather than brittlely hierarchical, dogmatic, and univocally normative.

In Theory, In Time, In Place, In Language—all these categories or dimen-sions for ethnographies of cyberspace foreground linguistic and conceptual double-voiced articulations of the potential/actual, the located/unfolding, the rooted/differentially dispersed. Temporalities as well as topologies fold themselves into interesting configurations. The ethnographic task of world-ing cyberspace "In Theory" is to situate preliminary frames for thinking about the emergent computer-mediated worlds in which we are all inserted or enframed, if not always with equal access or capacity. These theories them-selves need placement in historical horizons, the task of worlding cyberspace "In Time": while the 1970s were fueled by certain texts of theory in general, although they were intended as models of and models for, as proleptic of and pedagogy for, an emergent common sense, the 1990s more concretely finds practical institutions—law ("In Brief"), economics ("In Exchange"), psy-chology ("In Consciousness"), science ("In"-formation Sciences")—under pressure in their very conceptual formulations thanks to the technologies of computers and computer-mediated communication. The uneven distribu-tion of these technologies and their attendant thought styles indexes both new, and intensifications of old, horizons of power and inequalities and con-stitutes a task of worlding cyberspace in geographic and social space. Many of these challenges are registered "In Language" and new forms of writing, electronic, multimedia, cross-generic, crypto-figural, paralogical, paradoxi-cal, and otherwise. The literature of cyberspace, like that of ethnography, "re-establishes contact between the corpora and the ceremonies of several dialects" and so runs the risk of eliciting anger and charges of unreadability, frivolity, and transgression (Derrida 1992/1995: 116). As Derrida wryly notes, "No one gets angry at a mathematician or a physicist whom he or she doesn't understand . . . but rather with someone who tampers with your own lan-guage, with this 'relation,' precisely, which is yours" (115). It is a cultural poli-tics that works its magic as powerfully in popular culture idioms (tech talk, science fiction, advertising) as in academic theory, and that is in play against a concentration of media power which "tends to put technical modernity to work in the service of worn out things" (124).

In Theory

The computing capacity of even bacterial DNA was enormous compared to man-made electronics. All Virgil had to do was take advantage of what was already there—just give it a nudge, as it were. — Greg Bear, *Blood Music*

In theory—and unevenly in time and space—many of our communicative and perceptual structures are being changed by computers and simulation technologies from a world of direct experience to one more accurately knowable through indirect play with structural coordinates and physical worlds available to the human consciousness only through technological prostheses.[2] (Examples abound in medical technologies—such as imaging diagnostics or being able to perform more delicate surgery with virtual reality technology—in architecture and planning, in aeronautical and space engineering, in sciences such as molecular biology or nanotechnology, in financial planning models, as well as more vulgately through the entertainment and communications media.) In a sense this is merely a catching up by everyday experience and common sense to the movement of the sciences since the late nineteenth century where direct experience has long been understood to be either misleading or at best a partial and supplementary access to the complexities of reality. But the world mediated by computers and simulation has taken us a step further yet, one that requires at least two kinds of knowledge simultaneously, that of the indirect structural precision of the sciences, supplemented by that of the experiential, relational world of social relations and cultural mapping.[3]

In theory (to condense and summarize the arguments about the contemporary era as systemically different from the earlier modernities of the twentieth century), we now live in a poststructuralist world insofar as the world constructed in the 1940s by cybernetic control systems has continued to evolve to the point where decentralized systems (such as the Internet) are necessary lest there be systemic breakdown. The Internet is an important icon of "reflexive modernity,"[4] of the gradual move toward a more pluralistic world of decision making that can restructure the now increasingly ineffective and dysfunctional division of labor between weakening parliamentary politics and increasingly more powerful but nonpublic decision making by the market or by military-subsidized research and development.[5] The phantasmic, speculative, indeterminate threats of ecological decay and catastrophe are among the fields of pressure in public consciousness toward new institutions of reflexive modernization, which depend on contemporary sciences and their computerized information modeling, processing, and institutional coordination.[6] As Ulrich Beck argues, ecological consciousness in the 1990s has moved beyond nostalgias of attempting to "preserve" or "conserve" nature conceived as primordial and is premised on the dynamics of consumerism. Consumerism is a cause of ecological damage, but it also provides the market and political demand for rights to clean air, water, and products that are not toxic. Ecological or Green consciousness depends both on scientific mediation, since much of the pollution and toxicity of environmental damage is only visible and monitorable through measurement, rather than to ordinary perception, and on the experiential and differential knowledges that people in different positions in the production and consumption chain can provide. Even traditional bureaucratic institutions such as federal law enforcement agencies can now be put under pressure: computerized records of prosecutors' selection of cases and severity of punishments can be tracked and compared by investigative journalists, thereby exposing to the public tacit and behind-the-scenes patronage networks that have structured Justice Department allocations of resources, personnel, and interests (Burnham 1996; Transactional Records Access Clearinghouse [TRAC]: http//:trac.syr.edu).

"In theory" plays constitutive, proleptic roles as well as provides models from which realities deviate, ever generating need for new theory. The illusions or projections of recent French theorists remind us through their proleptic missteps of the differences between theory and world (for instance, Lyotard's 1979 "report on knowledge," *The Postmodern Condition*; see "In Time," hereafter) yet are themselves productive, constitutive, ethico-aesthetic, or symptomatic of new subjectivities made possible by new machinic assemblages (Guattari 1992/1995). Among these "effective dreams"[7] of theory are the ways in which technologies change temporal and power relationships (Virilio 1977, 1993/1995; Latour 1988); provide sensory prostheses, object relations for libidinal investment, evocative objects for self-definition and social engagement (Guattari 1992/1995; Ronell 1989; Stone 1995; Turkle 1995); operate through language games of paralogy, mutation, modification, rhizomatic generativity, play and dissemination (Lyotard 1979/1984; Serres 1980/1982; Deleuze and Guattari 1980/1987; Derrida 1972/1981, 1992/1995; Bukatman 1993; McHale 1992); and illuminate the tensions between intensification of old political economic mechanisms of restructuring and potentially new economic logics and flexible capital accumulation at the expense of atomized professionals as well as manufacturing labor (Aronowitz 1994; Barlow 1994; Gilder 1989; Hayes 1989; Lanier 1994; Samuelson et al. 1995).

In Time

email: (i) electronic mail (ii) c. 1480: embossed or arranged in a network, from Fr. *emmaileure* (network) — *OED* — *The Hacker's Dictionary*

Just as "In Theory" two kinds of knowledge, two kinds of science — explanatory structures that are breaks with normal experience, that can only be arrived at through the prostheses of instruments, experiments, models, and simulations; and experiential, embodied, sensorial knowledge that acts as situated feedback — can no longer do without each other, so too two charter mythologies of temporality vie in our understanding of cyberspace: skeins of genealogical origin stories that shape hopes and fears about technological innovation; and cycles of political economy liberatory hopes repeatedly disciplined by market processes of capital accumulation facilitated or redirected by law and politics (legislation, regulation). One thinks in the latter case of the democratizing and decentralizing hopes for a "people's" minicomputer in the early 1980s (Brand 1989; Rheingold 1991; Wooley 1992) as undoing the oligopolistic industrial structure of mainframe suppliers, and the disappointment that was later to set in; and how that cycle is (in danger of) being repeated with the Internet. The danger fuels the politics of cypherpunks, cryptoanarchists, and others dedicated to keeping the Internet democratically or anarchistically open.

In time: technological origins and futures are shifting complicities. Insofar as origins in technological matters are ordinarily belated — they exist in concept, desire, imagination, and linguistic metaphor before they are installed — the gap between expectation or fantasy and implementation can resonate with, and be used to provide openings to, alternative worlds through multiple precursor genealogies;[8] utopian hopes foreclosed;[9] designers' inabilities to foresee users' appropriations (Feenberg 1995); alternative styles of using a technology (Turkle 1995);[10] desires, family romances, and spirit worlds that provide the obsessive urgency and dedication for the tedium of experimenting until invention is achieved (Ronell 1989); machinic assemblages that facilitate/enforce new subjectivities (Guattari 1992/1995), that speed up the flow of mutation (Virilio 1993/1995) and leverage displaced relations of power (Latour 1988; Koch 1995), that encourage a shift in thinking about technology as task-specific tools to technology as instruments of play and experimentation in social learning (Stone 1995; Turkle 1995).

Prefigurations of technology are often simultaneously wrong and prescient, particularly for our ambivalent and ambiguous computer technologies which, on the one hand, threaten to create totalizing cybernetic control in more powerful shadow worlds than that of RL ("real life") such as the data banks in which our juridical, fiduciary, medical, and other "doppelgänger" personae are created, monitored, and manipulated often beyond our knowledge and control (Branscombe 1994; Burnham 1983). Yet, on the other hand, these technologies could create decentralized worlds that play out Enlightenment or modernist fantasies/nightmares of out-of-control dangerously exciting worlds (à la *The Cryptoanarchists' Manifesto* predicting the emergence of numerous nefarious as well as beneficial black markets once strong cryptography becomes widespread [May 1994]); playful, sensuous, multiple worlds of continuously recontracted identities (Stone 1995), and recontracted freedoms and ethics of answerability (Derrida 1987/1989, 1992/ 1995; Ronell 1989); or through decentralization able to create more diffusely stable worlds than centralization could dream (Foucault 1975/1977, 1978, 1980).

In time: two dates or two decades conventionally serve as markers of these ambivalent transitions: 1979 or the early 1980s, and the early 1990s. These are not origins of either the computer or the Internet, the one that extends back to the early post–World War II period, the other to the late 1960s, the one an outgrowth of World War II command-and-control, trajectory-and-firing, feedback-calculation needs (Norbert Wiener's cybernetics), of general calculators and decryption (Alan Turing, John von Neumann), as well as of telephone information technology needs (Claude Shannon's information theory); the other an outgrowth of the need for a communication system that could withstand nuclear attack and not be knocked out by hitting a centralized switch. Rather, they are transitions in theory, in outlook, in historical horizon.

Nineteen seventy-nine was the date of Jean-François Lyotard's *The Postmodern Condition: A Report on Knowledge*, produced for the Quebec government's council on universities, a book that became a touchstone for electric (hysterical?) debates about theory (the "postmodern"). Praised for its enigmatic acknowledgment of the computer as a medium for social changes of the late twentieth century, the book depended, as Andrew Feenberg points out (1995), on a slightly misguided vision of the computer. This was the era just before the introduction in France of Minitel, and in the United

States of minicomputers (IBM's personal computer was introduced in 1981, Apple's Macintosh in 1984). The French Minitel was part of a state-directed modernization program to upgrade the French infrastructure and to carve out a niche in the global trade system. Six million terminals, networked to X.25 time-sharing hosts, were given away to households in a bid to acculturate the French to the new medium, to provide access to information as part of the state telecom utility, and to provide a protected market for terminals which could subsequently be the basis for a global export industry. But designed not to tax users with skills beyond their telephonic habits, the primitive terminals and keyboards were unable to expand into the international market, and Lyotard's vision of increasingly decentralized self-government through free access to data banks was more a vision of a technocratic information society than the many-to-many computer-mediated-communication society that was to emerge.

Still, Lyotard was prescient about many of the forms that such computer-mediated communication would take, including anonymous pseudonyms (institutionalized by Minitel services requiring pseudonyms) that called forth new language games, where identity is assumed-constructed rather than assumed-presupposed, where "cognitive regimes of phrases" can lead to incommensurable "differends" or multiple worlds based on different social contracts, where social and cultural forms are generated paralogically (through modification, mutation, and innovation) rather than through centrally planned rational, transparent design. When Minitel's Videotext system was first tested in 1981, a means for feedback to the designers was included, but the popularity of such messaging from users was not recognized as a precursor to mass demands for interactivity. In 1982 hackers turned Gretel, a host machine where users could send messages to system operators or post advertising, into a decentralized messaging system, and other services quickly followed, with names such as Desiropolis, SM, and Sextel. Paris walls were filled with graffiti about the new "pink" entertainment form; telephonic habits colonized the Minitel in the desire of users to communicate, not just access information; and by 1985 the system crashed because the volume of messages had exceeded capacity.

Feenberg points out that it was not only the French state and its intellectuals, such as Lyotard, Derrida, Deleuze, and Guattari, who were thinking about the implications of computers; science fiction writers such as Ursula K. Le Guin, Philip Dick, and Stanislaw Lem were also making a break in conventions and obsessions toward interactivity, the fragility of reality, and the multiplicity of selves. The first minicomputers in the 1980s, especially the hopes surrounding the introduction of Apple's Macintosh and a number of IBM-compatible models by other companies, were widely discussed as a powerful democratizing potential against monopoly mainframe industrial machines, hierarchical corporations, and oligopolistic markets. Sherry Turkle (1995) and Susan Leigh Star (1995), writing about computer cultures in the United States, talk about this period as one gradually shifting from computational styles of using computers, formalist pedagogies (the "right way" of programming was by linear, logical, rule-based thinking), reductionist epistemologies (one learns how things work by breaking them down into simpler parts), and anxieties about whether computers could think (the Turing test), toward an "aesthetic of simulation," evocative metaphors for programming and user interfaces (the desktop as dialogue partner), and a joyful sense of complexity or epistemologies of emergence from simultaneous interaction of many parts, and a looking to connectivity (rather than single user-machine relationships) and to computers for emotional and social feedback and effects. No one, Turkle says, in the 1990s confuses computers with sentient beings (the anxiety of the 1970s posed in the fear of replicant humanoids in the film *Blade Runner*, the fascination with what computers and automation could and could not do, with Turing tests, with fears of surveillance, Taylorism, and job loss), but people instead take pleasure in treating computers as quasi-sentient and exploring the enriching potentials of simulations, virtual reality prostheses, interactivity facilitating new social arrangements and psychological spaces. "Design" and "configuration" are slogans, foregrounding claims for the expansion of human relations and capacities.

The early 1990s are often spoken of by the computer science community as a second major turning point, with the reorganization of the Internet, changes in the global competitive structure of the semiconductor and information technology industries, introduction of new user-oriented tools, and the huge influx of general users to the Internet, previously inhabited by relatively small, technically knowledgeable communities of hackers, students, researchers, engineers, and programmers. Rather than "theory" in general being at issue, now one practical and institutional arena after another — law, economics, sciences, psychology — find their traditional terminologies, premises, and models under profound pressure.

In time: just to cite a few dates, in 1990 coordination of the Internet backbone shifted from the Defense Department's Advanced Research Projects Agency to the National Science Foundation as part of a continuing and broad-based shift from a government- and university-dominated research community to privatization and impending commercialization. 1992 marked a sea change in competitive dynamics requiring internationalization and modularization, and it became clear that information technology industries could not survive in domestic markets alone or build self-contained machines. They had to become transnational, dedicated to "open systems architectures" (rather than self-contained machines), compete over flexible features, pursue alliances and cross-licensing among firms, and develop networking (connecting computers to one another) and value-added services (moving data and images across the networks) (Yoffie 1994). In 1993 the introduction of Mosaic, the World Wide Web, and (two years later) Netscape interfaces and indexing robots ("search engines," "spiders," "crawlers") made the Internet easy for a broad range of users. Commercial providers (America Online, CompuServe, Prodigy) began opening gateways to the Internet. Businesses began to advertise and sell via the Internet, and encryption and problems of privacy, authentication, and digital money became foci of attention.

How does one access ethnographically the tension between market cycles and the kinds of cultural mutation that Lyotard's text, among others, focused the energies of cultural imagination on? Two strategies are to focus on its geographies (its uneven construction, costs, usages in different places, resistances to it on the part of bureaucracies and employees) and on its body politics (the Third World women who manufacture the chips, toxicities of clean-room production, surveillance and invasiveness of its "availability" imposed on professionals and service providers, the global division of labor, the dispersive, cottage-industrialization of the virtual office).

In Place (or Sites under Construction)

Cyberspace remains a frontier region, across which roam the few aboriginal technologists and cyberpunks who can tolerate the austerity of its savage computer interfaces, incompatible communications protocols, proprietary barricades, cultural and legal ambiguities, and general lack of useful maps or metaphors. — John Perry Barlow, "Coming into the Country"

Is your routing protocol complex? You've raised the cost of entry. Do you have an acceptable use policy? You've limited your population. Have you invented an anonymous FTP mechanism and an RFC series? You've encouraged the spread of the network. . . . Infrastructure . . . reflects how we apply . . . fundamental human values. Privacy, for example, can be protected or destroyed by a network. — Carl Malamud, *Exploring the Internet*

Carl Malamud (1993) provides a preliminary pilot survey for a global geographic and ethnographic history, stylized as a ribald hacker's (and gourmet's) traveling account, with himself as one of the free-spirited aboriginal technologists on the new frontier. He begins in good ethnographic fashion with an emblematic scene, a celebratory, almost ritual space: a 1991 trade show that serves as a microcosmic workshop for assembling the global Internet. Some thirty-five miles of cable were hung from the ceiling of the San Jose Convention Center using five cherry pickers. These supported two different backbones (FDDI, Ethernet), fifty subnets, microwave links, and T1 lines, connecting to the NSFNET (and video-link laid by Sprint from Geneva via Atlanta and Kansas City), so that three hundred vendors could demonstrate interoperability of their wares, and engineers could pinpoint ambiguities in standards. Enough components to wire a twenty-story high-tech skyscraper such as are being built in Singapore and other leading-edge high-tech sites.

Imagine expanding this globally. Malamud provides a humorous twenty-country field guide to the heterogeneous sites around the world that in 1991 were gradually linking themselves into a global Internet. The account provides a sardonic counterpoint to the usual histories of the Internet that celebrate a seemly, smooth development from the U.S. Defense Department's ARPA project to a civilian NSF-supervised backbone to a privatized Internet and a spreading international network. Malamud traverses Europe from Geneva to Prague to Dublin, the Pacific from Hawaii to Tokyo to Singapore to Canberra, Bombay, Bangkok, Kuala Lumpur, and various other places with different problems, situations, and goals. His account gets beneath the glib hype of magical connectivity and indicates the heterogeneity of the actual hardware, wiring, design, and organization of the various segments of the Internet; provides a historical account of the efforts to create, the resistances to, and efforts to limit or control, connectivity; and in the end also provides a bridge to a recognition that universal connectivity may not quite be the metaphor for the future, as design must cope with a flood of users who might better be served by a congeries of subnetworks, a field of diversity.

In Geneva, for instance, headquarters of the International Telecommunications Union, Malamud finds a bureaucracy at odds with its electronic communications environment, providing in concrete microcosm the historical picture of decaying bureaucratic control and emergent electronic connectivity that theorists such as Marshall McLuhan, Michel Foucault, Jean-François Lyotard, and Jacques Derrida have also been describing, albeit in more philosophical, less concrete registers. In 1991 the ITU headquarters (despite rights to free telecommunications throughout the world) had a telephone system with an old Siemens PBX that did not allow a secretary to transfer calls; there was only one fax machine for nine hundred employees (deliberately, to control communications with the outside), and officials were ambivalent about putting ITU recommendations for standards the ITU wished adopted on the Internet because they made money on selling the recommendations in book form (although dissemination on the Internet was one or two orders of magnitude beyond what they would ever reach through book sales). Things were so bad that high-powered officials brought their own AT&T phones to work so that they could have a few stored numbers, and got themselves guest accounts at CERN, the European high-energy physics lab, a key node of the Internet.

By contrast, Prague had been dependent until 1989 on reverse engineering IBM mainframes and attempting to fit these together with Bulgarian front-end processors and local operating systems. At the end of the Cold War, Prague was able to put in (still expensive) 9,600 bps leased lines to Western Europe and, with the aid of several IBM-donated 3090 mainframes, was beginning to establish networking capabilities. "As fast as the [Eastern Bloc] countries could persuade the United States to process the paperwork for Cisco routers [as a legacy of the Cold War, all these countries were on the U.S. export restrictions list; it had taken the Poles, for instance, a year to get a Cisco router], countries were plopping in TCP/IP nodes, enhancing EARN connections, and using UUCP and EUnet to spread connectivity into new places" (Malamud 1993: 271).

Malamud contrasts sites around the world and visits key individuals who made the initial connections in various sites happen: Torben Nielsen in Hawaii, who linked four university buildings with rented power tools, digging ditches and using salvaged materials from military aircraft to create a local area network (LAN) for $1,500; Jan Murai in Japan, who tied networks together into JUNET and, when Nippon Telegraph and Telephone deregulated, used two modems and a university-provided phone line to establish links to Amsterdam, Washington, and Hawaii; Dennis Jennings in Dublin, who in 1979 networked two Dublin universities, in 1983 became president of the BITNET that was being introduced by IBM to Europe as EARN (European Academic Research Network), in 1985 became U.S. National Science Foundation Program director when NSF was only beginning to think about networking its four supercomputer centers and nudged them into bringing about the NSFNET backbone, and in 1991 helped create EBONE, the European backbone.

Malamud's account provides a preliminary matrix to which can be added other accounts of struggles and competitions to establish networks (see the 1996 "hacker tourist" account of laying a third-generation fiber-optic cable from England to Japan [Stephenson 1996]). In Iran, for instance, the Institute for Studies in Theoretical Physics and Mathematics in Tehran has had an Internet site since 1992; in 1994 it upgraded its 9.6 kilobyte connection with a 64 kilobyte satellite telephone line leased from the American Hughes Corporation (Jahanshah 1995). In 1994 the institute leased part of its network to a private company that provided access to individuals, some two hundred. The government telecommunications company began showing interest in the Internet and tried to run the private company out of business, even using tactics such as cutting off its phone lines. The private company went to court with the support of customers such as the Tehran Municipality. Qum, the theological center of Iran, as always, showed interest in the newest technological means for spreading its messages. Meanwhile the American NSF briefly ordered the connection between Tehran and the University of Vienna closed, on the grounds that Iran should not benefit from federally funded infrastructures, but on review this position was reversed. Such competitions are not unusual. (By 2002 there were some 1.75 million users of the Internet in Iran.)

In India parts of the bureaucracy are dedicated to the expansion of networks, but other parts (including segments of the banking system) are attempting to protect jobs and self-reliance of production and to restrict access to computerization and the Internet. Meanwhile businesses are establishing their own links, and the software industry and chip design are beginning to take off, both as offshore support for American and multinational companies but also in producing products on their own account. Such competitions are sites where the strains and differential needs within a society may be exposed to view, and are indices of sociocultural change.[11]

Compared to Finland, a country with more than ten thousand hosts (10 percent of the European hosts on the Internet), the United States seems a bit archaic: in Finland utilities and all sorts of services are normally ordered and paid through the computerized network, eliminating separate checking, paperwork, or standing in line. Experiments with municipal networking exist in many parts of Scandinavia, and the Sophia-Antipolis "Silicon Valley" of France (near Nice), which is a nine-town joint venture with the regional government and the Nice Chamber of Commerce, but rarely in the United States except for the much touted Blacksburg, Virginia, experiment.

In Language (Tech Talk, Hackish, Fiction)

It's in words that the magic is — Abracadabra, Open Sesame, and the rest — but the magic words in one story aren't magical in the next. The real magic is to understand which words work, and when, and for what; the trick is to learn the trick. — John Barth, *Chimera*; used as epigraph to chap. 4 of Abelson and Sussman, *Structure and Interpretation of Computer Programs*

Either Elvis Presley is dead, or he isn't!—complaint attributed to Eric Hobsbawm

Isn't this an "interface" here, a meeting surface for two worlds . . . sure, but *which two?*— Thomas Pynchon, *Gravity's Rainbow*

Tech talk, hackish, infinite loops, future Bostons—the lively languages of the denizens of the several subcultures on the electronic frontier provide rich arenas for exploring emergent cognitive styles and new worlds of interaction. The languages that hackers and techies use and that leak into general discourse (how do they sound and reconfigure thought in Japanese, Portuguese, Hindi,[12] Malay, Russian?), the literary languages of science fiction (especially cyberpunk) and science-incorporating novels (e.g., Richard Powers's *Galatea 2.2.*), the advertising language used to sell new technologies in medical and science journals (see also Haraway 1997), and the figurations and metanarratives that lie behind the ways scientists and engineers explain what they are up to, and how they conceive their discoveries as contrasting with the recent pasts of their fields—all provide rich entries into new ethnographic worlds both of the present and of the near future. Nanotechnology, chemistry and materials sciences, molecular biology, genetics, evolutionary and theoretical biology, remote sensing and environmental monitoring, PET scans and medical imaging are among the many arenas that are mediated by the lively new languages of the information and computer technologies that form a skein of threads in this new fabric of understanding.

Imbricated in the use of these languages is also a pragmatics of engineering interaction premised on partial knowledge and constant need for translation, interfacing, sharing, and updating, as well as a willingness to deal with real-world complexities that cannot be completely controlled (hardware always goes wrong; software can never be completely debugged). This pragmatics cannot be separated from the hardware material worlds of the new information highway, the market pressures that are gradually sharing dominance with earlier state funding for shaping the evolution of cyberspace, and the legal structures that are lagging behind the technological changes but can powerfully affect their development.

The worlds being constructed and mediated by the new biological, material sciences, and information technologies, moreover, are not merely cognitive ones but also profoundly, if also playfully, sensual ones. The debates about virtual reality systems are many, but as yet quite underdeveloped, often split between those who can see only testosterone-driven entertainment examples (Kramarae 1995), and not, for instance, the medical surgical systems for allowing finer kinesthetic control than ordinary human haptic sensation or seeing into the body in ways not otherwise available. Feminist literary criticism of both science fiction proper and computer scientist fantasies such as Hans Moravec's *Mind Children* (1988) (downloading wetware brains into silicon form so as to escape the body) has focused attention on the embodiments of cyberspace prostheses (N. Hayles 1993, 1996; Stone 1995).

There is something special about the lively languages of tech talk, hackish, and the science fictions that engineers and scientists enjoy. For the ethnographer, even if the distinction eventually breaks down, one needs to pay attention to these as native languages, as pragmatics deployed situationally by computer scientists and other information scientists, before lumping them with general popular culture variants. Thus, for instance, Scott Bukatman (1993) is onto something when he suggests that science fiction writing often exploits a distinctive writerly and playfully paradoxical style that requires active inferential work by readers, and that it is on this formal level — Joycean semantic fusions, syntactical revisioning, presuppositional implications — that the genre provides some of the most sustained attempts to identify and narrate the ambiguities of contemporary culture.[13] But the traditions to which he links this style are the neologistic play of William Burroughs and the literary theories of Roland Barthes. One wonders if more important might not be a different set of traditions that await excavation: the lively, playful, polysemic, working languages of engineering and software techies, such as are cataloged in *The New Hacker's Dictionary* (Raymond 1993). These are, of course, not entirely separated traditions, as the epigraph to this section from one of the leading textbooks for computer science students indicates (and as Raymond protests, "Hackers often have a reading range that astonishes liberal arts people" [484]). Still, there is an ethnography waiting to be done on the nuances (and pragmatics) of, for instance, why William Gibson's *Neuromancer* is initially dismissed by techies when cited by humanists as a foundational cyberspace or cyberpunk text. Not that techies and hackers have not read it — Pengo, one of the (in)famous German hackers who broke into the Lawrence Livermore Laboratories computers, said his image of himself as a hacker was modeled on Case in *Neuromancer* (Hafner and Markof 1991: 15) — but its valuation or intertextual location is marked differently. It is not that techies and hackers have not read Gibson, but that in their view, liberal arts people have read little else, little of actual substance that pertains to, or is generative of, this emergent arena of communicative connectivity; and of course that Gibson famously describes himself as not being computer knowledgeable when he wrote the book.[14] Such relative marking is itself a field of pragmatics, constitutive of difference in the ways that different communities relate to, and interact through, computers, informational technologies, cyberspace, or the information highway.

Literary critics such as Brian McHale (1992) and cultural historians of science such as Paul Edwards (1996) are similarly also onto something when they try to chart the shifts in plot structures and metanarratives that science fiction literature and films have gone through in the last few decades, and in Edwards's case, the correlations of such shifts with thinking among planners and funders in the military-industrial-university complex are usefully at issue. McHale distinguishes cyberpunk from older science fiction through the way that microworlds, cyberspace, cybernetic or bioengineered prostheses, artificial intelligences, and mediated deaths are deployed. No longer are the orbiting space colonies or subterranean cities so often showcases of technology and egalitarian liberal governance; there are decaying slums, enclaves of privilege, ghettos of crime and commerce, multicultural juxtapositions and interspecies heterotopias. No longer are there humanoid robots; now there are more often AIs, bioengineered improvements, alter egos, and prostheses of all sorts, renegade cybernetic systems attempting to absorb humans, and hybrid human-machine interfaces that allow the biological metabolism to shut down (die) and reboot for varying periods. More skeptical is Paul Edwards's survey of science fiction films and novels over the post–World War II period, looking for alternatives to closed worlds of cybernetic command and control fantasy, some alternative structures that would lead to more open and green worlds.

And yet there is a striking difference in "structure of feeling" in how writers immersed in the new technologies and sciences pose these issues— one, I think, that is not explained by their being Panglossian enthusiasts. Kevin Kelly (1994) and Claus Emmeche (1994), for instance, find precisely these alternatives to the post–World War II closed-world modernisms in the language of "out of control," self-organizing, evolving learning systems and parallel processing. One needs to read these with critical care, attuned to the metanarrative utopias, teleological aspirations, or simple idealizing hopes that are structured into speculative models (Egger 1993), and look for the alternative accounts that can be given of the same technologies and scientific developments (Porush 1993). But we need to read for the connectivities and emergences as well that are growing through our everyday practices of using these technologies, and not dismiss them through an equally metanarrative, but cynically dismissive, application of past (Luddite, Marxist, or romantic) frames to new forms.

Might the language and creative writing of techies and hackers be a guide to the worlds that many of us are now entering with our laptops, desktops, and workstations, networked into a global information network? Consider the "handles" or "aliases" used by hackers—Phiber Optik, Knight Lightning, frogrot, Koda.Krome, Notjeff—both the worlds to which they allude and also the metaphorical play they put into motion, part of the larger universe of puns, contractions, acronyms, verbal forms, and other linguistic humor that makes up hacker reference and repartee, and the degree to which these reflect a technical concern with substitutability, abstraction, alternative coding, and signal-to-noise ways of regarding communication. These play on and extend the recombinant material forms that computer-mediated sciences invoke, and science fiction written by programmers reflect on: bots of various forms (robots, nanobots, mobots, fleabots), simulated intelligence forms (stims, microsofts, personality chips aka perks), biological computers and transgenetic animals, prostheses and cybernetic machine-biological cyborgs, objects made of new materials, new languages, and trans-species multicultural social formations, new illnesses of multiple chemical sensitive and virally transported transgenetic modalities. These are the worlds we are entering, and they are not accessible through the old languages of nature-versus-culture dichotomies. We turn first to hackish, then to creative writing by computer professionals.

Hackish

hack: (i) an appropriate application of ingenuity; (ii) creative practical joke.

banana problem: [from the story of the little girl who said, "I know how to spell banana, but I don't know when to stop"].—*The Hacker's Dictionary*

To what degree does "hackish" not merely reflect a love of language play but provide a "particularly effective window into the surrounding culture" (Raymond 1993: 20)?[15]—into how its inventions grow out of the way in which computers are configured and software language is designed, showing if there is in fact a new style of technically grounded cultural logic, in which "flavorful," elegant puns bend phrases to include a second jargon word as a function of a kind of condensation that increases awareness of linguistic form, logic, multiple allusions or references, precision, and yet maintains transparency, efficiencies of communication, and relatively easy accessibility. As a friendly visiting anthropologist to hacking culture—and as a slow but determined learner-user of computer literacy, e-mail, and World Wide Web connections—I am constantly amazed by the openness of these subcultures, and of the degree to which everyone is dependent on others for help in keeping knowledge current, growing, and adaptable to a state of constant and rapid change. I am also impressed by the degree to which speed of communication is mimicked by the density of punning allusions to multiple referents, and the pressure that the speed and volume of information places on my old-fashioned tendency to take notes, an increasingly out-of-phase slowness for pacing the "fire hose" flow of electronic connectivity (part of what was called, in this chapter's opening section, the anxiety of operating under a growing cyberspace pedagogical regime, and the need to develop new reading and processing tactics).

There are many ways in which a "technically grounded new cultural logic" might be sifted. For instance, "much to the dismay of American editors," hackers "tend to use quotes as balanced delimiters, placing punctuation outside the quotation marks: 'Jim is going', 'Bill runs', and 'Spock groks'." For programmers, putting the commas and periods inside the quotes violates the integrity of literal strings with characters that don't belong, and would, if it were a piece of code, issue false instructions: a tutorial that tells you to delete a line by typing "dd" is quite different from one that tells you to type "dd.". *Hart's Rules* and the *Oxford Dictionary for Writers and Editors* accept the hacker sensibility and call that convention "new" or "logical" quoting.

This is a more technological grounding of cultural logic than simple terminological coinages. However, insofar as coinages have extended hermeneutical relations and histories, they can begin to tell us a good deal about the cultures in which they are shaped. A few examples, like the spoken hackish "bang" referring to the grapheme!, aka "excl" (pronounced /eks'kl/) or "shriek," begin to resonate with Jacques Derrida's sub-version that writing is prior to speech, and provide a grounding for the interpretation of Derrida that Greg Ulmer (1994) advances: seeing grammatology being mediated through the new electronic media and cultural writing becoming increasingly an experimental "heuretics." But one wants to immerse oneself in this concrete world of sounds and silent electron traces before jumping into the Derridean sea, or into the Deleuzian complementary intuition (in the interpretation put forth by the Critical Art Ensemble [1994]) that the new electronic media allow a new literal "logic of sense" (where the sensorium is not separated from the intellect as an other; indeed, a fascination for many people of digitized multimedia virtual reality is the ability to place oneself in altered states). Another Derridean trace: There is also an accepted convention for 'writing under erasure'; the text, 'Be nice to this fool ^H^H^H^H^H gentleman, he's in from corporate HQ.' would be read as 'Be nice to this fool, I mean this gentleman . . . ,' the diagraph ^H being a print representation for a backspace. Quelle différence!

Form-versus-content jokes seem to follow easily: "This sentence no verb"; "too repetetive"; "bad speling"; "incorrectspa cing"; "excuse me I'm cixel-syd [dyslexic] today." As does patterned play with verbing ("I'll clipboard it over"; "I'll mouse it up"), pluralizing with inflection particles from imported languages or archaic strata (Yiddish *frobbotzim* as a plural of *frobnitz*, little things you can tweak, manipulate, adjust; VAXen using the Anglo-Saxon plural *-en*), and anthropomorphizing. (This last apparently gives great difficulties to some philosophers and certain anthropologists whose theories of metaphor refuse to acknowledge the uses of humor. As Raymond patiently admonishes: "This isn't done in a naive way; hackers don't personalize their stuff in the sense of feeling empathy with it, nor do they mystically believe that the things they work on every day are 'alive' " [13].) You may hear "The protocol handler got confused," and explanations like "And its poor little brain couldn't understand X, and it died" (13). Which leads to the quite important observation, not unlike the old cliché about the many words Eskimos are supposed to have for snow, that "hackers have even more words for equipment failures than Yiddish has for obnoxious people" (14). Important, because it points to the material grounding of the cultural logics, but also because it points to the continual adjustments, patching, flexibility, rerouting, reconfiguring, sharing, negotiating, translating, interacting, communicating, clarifying, that working with this technology requires and that is accepted as reality by its resident hackers, viz.:

> *creationism* (the false belief that large innovative software designs can be completely specified in advance and then painlessly magicked out of the void by the normal efforts of a team of normally talented programmers. In fact, experience has shown repeatedly that good designs arise only from evolutionary interaction between one [or at most a small handful of] exceptionally able designer(s) and an active user population . . .)
>
> *heisenbug* (a bug that disappears or alters its behavior when one attempts to probe or isolate it: not even particularly fanciful since use of a debugger can alter a program's operating environment)
>
> *mandelbug* ([From the Mandelbrot set], a bug whose underlying causes are so complex and obscure as to make its behavior appear chaotic or even non-deterministic; the term implies the speaker thinks it is a Bohr bug rather than a heisenbug)
>
> *Bohr bug* ([From quantum physics], a repeatable bug that manifests

reliably under possibly unknown but well-defined conditions; antonym of heisenbug)

schroedinbug ([MIT: from Schroedinger's cat thought experiment], a design or implementation bug in a program that doesn't manifest until someone reading source or using the program in an unusual way notices that it never should have worked, at which point the program promptly stops working for everybody until fixed. Though (like bit rot) this sounds improbable, it happens . . .[16]

If an engineering pragmatics of sharing, patching, and kluges (from German "clever," i.e., a patch) is basic to the technological mode, contradictory principles are nonetheless also basic to the landscape, including various ways of limiting freedom of action, ranging from "bondage and discipline languages" (e.g., BASIC, PASCAL, early versions of the Athena Project at MIT) to marketplace proprietary rules and competitive blocking of opponents' freedom of action. This provides the grounds for the elaboration of the hacker ethic in favor of open systems, but also the grounds for the intense debate over the evolving direction of law and ethics on the electronic frontier (see "In Brief").[17] Again a few simple terms can help index the nature of the terrain. BASIC (Beginner's All-Purpose Symbolic Instruction Code), originally designed for Dartmouth's experimental time-sharing system in the early 1960s, like Pascal, another instructional "toy" designed in the late 1960s, according to Raymond, although allowing some simple programming, not only becomes difficult to use for longer and more complicated tasks but is counterproductive because it instills habits that impede learning more powerful languages (54). A more general version of this type of relatively benign dilemma is "candygrammar" using mostly "syntactic sugar," that is, the effort to design English-like languages (COBOL, Apple's Hypertalk, many "4GL" database languages) to help unskilled people program. Hacker aesthetics hold that since it is not really the syntax that makes programming hard, candygrammar languages are often just as difficult to program as more elegant, terser ones and end up simply creating more pain for experienced hackers who have to help out inexperienced users.

More serious are real situations of "fear and loathing": "[from Hunter Thompson] . . . a state inspired by the prospect of dealing with certain real-world systems and standards that are totally brain-damaged but ubiquitous — Intel 8086s, or COBOL, or EBCDIC, or any IBM machine except the Rios (a.k.a. the RS/6000)." EBCDIC, for instance, is an "alleged character set" that exists in a number of incompatible versions and lacks several ASCII punctuation characters important in modern computer languages. Hackers suspect that IBM made people use this as a customer control tactic, a form of "connector conspiracy" (designing products that do not fit with competitors' products), since the ASCII standard was already well established at the time. Moreover, as Raymond notes, although "today, IBM claims to be an open-systems company, IBM's own description of the EBCDIC variants and how to convert between them is still internally classified top-secret, burn-before reading" (159). IBM is the target of much hacker hostile humor, the company acronym itself being said to stand for "Inferior But Marketable," and many other such witticisms.[18] (The barbed humor parallels similar, more recent witticisms against Microsoft, for similar reasons, as Microsoft dominates the operating system and Internet markets.)

"What galls hackers about most IBM machines above the PC," explains Raymond, "isn't so much that they are underpowered and overpriced . . . but that the designs are incredibly archaic, crusty and elephantine . . . and you can't fix them—source code is locked up tight, and programming tools are expensive, hard to find, and bletcherous to use once you've found them" (235). FUD and FUD wars are a result. FUD (fear, uncertainty, and doubt that IBM sales personnel instill in the mind of customers thinking about buying from competitors) was coined by Gene Amdahl after leaving IBM to found his own company. FUD wars thus are the posturing of vendors ostensibly committed to standardization but actually attempting to fragment the market to protect their share of the market. (See also the 1979 Charles Andres comic allegory about "brainwashed androids of IPM [Impossible to Program Machines] to conquer and destroy the peaceful denizens of HEC [Human Engineered Computers]," containing, aside from many references to the prototypical computer game Adventure, also the immortal line "Eat flaming death, minicomputer mongrels!" [uttered, of course, by an IPM storm-trooper].) Tactics in this economic war of position are varied (and a large subject for business school case studies [Yoffie 1994]) ranging from minor and ineffective forms such as "crippleware" (software that has some important functionality deliberately removed to entice you to pay for a working version; compare "guiltware" for shareware pleas to send money if you are using their product, also "nagware") to the attempts to utilize increasingly archaic and ill-adaptive intellectual property law protections and lawsuits.

The hacker ethic, by contrast, located naturally enough in universities like MIT, insists that information sharing is a "powerful positive good, and that it is an ethical duty of hackers to share their expertise by writing free software and facilitate access to information and to computing resources wherever possible," including the more controversial "belief that system-cracking for fun and exploration is ethically OK as long as the cracker commits no theft, vandalism, or breach of confidentiality." This puts hackers often, and in principled active ways, at odds with industry, the archaic legal structure, and government attempts at regulation, national-security-justified controls (the export control act), and computer crime surveillance (FBI and Secret Service).

Underneath the pragmatics of computer subcultures and their differences, underneath the competitions for control of various forms (market share, security, privacy, freedom), is a material substratum of historically changing hardware and institutional legacies and possibilities. The hacker subculture, for instance, whose jargon is collectively compiled in *The New Hacker's Dictionary* (and its 1983 predecessor), has a history traceable to the early 1960s PDP-1 machines at the AI Labs at Stanford (where the Jargon File was started in 1975) and MIT (where a duplicate copy of the Jargon File was maintained from 1976), Carnegie Mellon, Worcester Polytechnic, and similar sites. The first *Hacker's Dictionary* (Steele 1983) was thought at the time to be a monument to a subculture dealt a death blow by funding cuts, the introduction of personal computers (fear of atomizing the social relations fostered by time-sharing machines), and the seduction of the best and brightest into industry. There is a machine-specific set of implications surrounding the 1983 cancellation of Digital's Jupiter Project (meaning the death of PDP-10 centered cultures that nourished the Jargon File), the shift from "home-brew" hardware engineering to vendor-supported hardware, the shift of MIT to dedicated LISP machines, and the shift at the AI Lab from the beloved ITS to TWENEX.[19] It is significant, for instance, that GNU ([acronym: "GNU's Not UNIX!"], a UNIX-emulating set of developments, including the popular GNU EMACS and GNU C compiler) is part of Richard Stallman's and the Free Software Foundation's efforts to agitate for the position that information is community property and all software source should be shared. In this context, the history of networking developments from Multics to UNIX takes on more than a technical significance, opening onto ethical, political, and economic issues as well.[20]

While hacker culture grew up around certain kinds of machines and artificial intelligence labs, it is only one of several distinctive and overlapping subcultures, including techspeak and SF fandom, in which many hackers participate. There is a danger among humanists to make SF fandom stand in for these other cultures rather than recognizing them as interactive subcultures. My interest here is attempting to move ethnographers toward a mapping of the overlap with various techspeak and science subcultures, rather than continuing to replant in the much-used garden of popular culture/science fiction versions of the scientific and technological imaginary. I am interested both in the ways those (real-world) scientific and technological imaginaries grow and in the social worlds they inhabit, grow from, and shape.

Raymond claims that the network constitutes a geographically dispersed think tank, pointing to the fact that during the 1988 cold fusion controversy, many papers were disseminated on the Net before making their way into print. There has in fact been a good deal of experimentation with various forms of communication on the Net, and considerable dubiousness about the degree to which serious discussion can be pursued and protection from troublemakers of all sorts can be prevented, problems of netiquette and of governance. Initially, many BBS (electronic bulletin board systems) appear to be poor forums for serious discussions (see Stone's 1995 account of the history of CommuniTree; Lotfalian 1996) despite their democratic promise of open access in contrast to hierarchical and/or heavily screened, gate-guarded arenas such as the classroom, journals, television, and radio. They initially appear to be poor forums because they are heavily spur-of-the-moment opinion driven, rather than carefully analytic or documented; also because their space seems to be markedly male voiced, often increasingly so (with time, female voices fall silent). Things need not be this way. The World Wide Web, with interface programs like Mosaic and Netscape with (hypertext) links to databases of all sorts, can transform the opinion-driven nature of initial BBS; discussion groups can be self-disciplined arenas (various forms of governance mechanisms have been experimented with); and genuine interest-driven discussion lists—like the breast cancer or other disease-focused support groups—can contain an inherent process of warning and skepticism toward poorly supported assertions or advice and can provide an important counter to the self-protecting authority systems of institutional medicine. Gender and other identity play in the place of user IDs can change the communicational dynamics (for good or ill). One old gentleman, it is said, who plays bridge on-line, signs on as a woman because he has found he is invited to join games much more quickly than if he is a man.

Our class discussion list at MIT in 1994 with PGP-encrypted signatures and pseudonyms for interaction showed a quite interesting gender distribution: eighteen of the twenty-six registered names were gender neutral: bitdiddle, nexus, axis, quickster, swizzle.shtick, cactus, the hacker, gyphon, Kipple, shalako, jello44, koda.krome, lizard, notjeff, bagel, frobgrot, elephant, the Keeper).[21] In time some of the posters felt signature pressure, so The Hacker began to sign Alyssa or Alyssa P. Hacker; bitdiddle soon gendered himself as ben bitdiddle. There were then perhaps a half-dozen male names (ben bitdiddle, sean, Prof Charles, joebloggs, Ishmael Gabanzai, notjeff, gilligan) and two or three female ones (Morrighan; 3 Jane or Lady 3 Jane Tessier-Ashpool, a character from William Gibson's *Neuromancer*). Only four were vaguely ethnic (Morrighan, shalako, Ishmael Garbanzai, Prof. Charles). Some draw on specific hacker jargon (joebloggs is a reference to the imaginary family, Fred and Mary Bloggs and their children, used as a standard example in knowledge representation to show the difference between extensional and intensional objects [Raymond 1993: 72]; frob is a productive particle [frobnitz, frobinicate, frobnosticate, etc.] referring to a small thing that can be tweaked or frobnicated, from a command on some MUDS to change a player's experience level, and to make wizards or request wizard privileges [193]), or stylistic linguistic play (koda.krome; notjeff>notwork as network not working or acting flaky). A few drew on the SF/Dungeons and Dragons mythos or cybergame references (one used his well-known out-of-class handle, Warlock),[22] such as were popular among the Legion of Doom and Masters of Deception hackers busted by Operation Sundevil (Sterling 1992): Knight Lightning, Phiber Optik, Acid Phreak.

Writing Infinite Loops and Future Bostons
If *The Hacker's Dictionary* and ethnographic investigations of linguistic usages open windows into not just the life worlds but philosophical attitudes and engineering-design pragmatics of several hacker, programmer, and computer scientist subcultures, the larger linguistic units of storytelling by such subculture members reflecting on their worlds may help sketch some of the broader and deeper dimensions of these worlds and perspectives. Indeed, storytelling is itself a central object of speculation, analysis, and design-curiosity for several of these subcultures (see, for instance, the weekly meetings of the Narrative Group at MIT's Media Lab [ni@media.mit.edu]). Three story collections provide first frames: *Infinite Loop: Stories about the Future by the People Creating It* (Constantine, ed., 1993), an anthology of twenty-seven short stories (eight by women) by programmers, systems analysts, and software engineers, not inappropriately published (as was Malamud's book) by a company that also produces software trade shows; *Future Boston* (D. Smith 1994); and *In the Cube* (D. Smith 1993), a science fiction collective project (with each writer contributing a different piece of a single story-world) by a more varied set of ten contributors (two women), including one from *Infinite Loop* and five other programmers and technical writers, a physicist, a multimedia artist, a financial consultant, and a writer.

The ethnographic fascination of these stories lies in the interplay between the texts and RL (real lives), especially in *Infinite Loop*. In contrast to stereotypes about nerds who have no emotional lives, or whose emotional lives are fueled largely by adolescent testosterone—not that such a subculture does not exist,[23] but there are many other more interesting groups,[24] including the turn by some who have suffered neurological diseases in their families to intensive research in cognitive science, linguistics, and artificial intelligence modeling (see Powers 1995)—these stories are about psychological and relational issues, about animating paradoxes and breakthroughs of apparent impossibilities that computer or cyborg futures provide as proleptic vehicles of current design thinking.

Pati Nagle's story "Pygmaleon 3.0," for instance, interplays fascinatingly with MIT Media Lab team leaders' descriptions of their projects. At the tenth anniversary celebration of the Media Lab (10/10/95), Pat Maes talked about the butler metaphor common in thinking about the design of software agents. Other Media Lab researchers described projects in perceptual computing (the programming of computers to recognize faces, emotions, gestures, and subtle changes of expression); smart rooms and the communication among smart objects so that, for instance, a vacuum cleaner knows not to turn itself on when someone is home, or could be told by a couch that it was too heavy to be pushed around. Even the fact that *Infinite Loop* is published by a company that produces trade shows was mirrored in Marvin Minsky's self-consciously and ironically identifying the manufacturers of the various robotic devices he talked about, identifying each manufacturer with a pause and a laugh line, "made by Hewlett-Packard . . . a sponsor of the Media Lab."

In Nagle's story, a single woman programmer is trying to negotiate the expectations of having to sleep with a boss who disgusts her in order to get ahead. Her condominium is fully managed by an operating system named Oz, who not only adjusts the lights and heat, brings her drinks, and talks to her, and whose programming can be overridden by her voice commands, but also monitors her emotional states and adjusts her environment according to her stress levels. One of the advertising catalogs displayed on her holographic television screen includes an extraordinarily responsive, self-learning male lover whom she decides to rent, "just to test out" how his operating system works. He is much more sophisticated than she expects, and he and Oz propose various ways of dealing with her boss. This is one of the few stories that incorporate the computer command structures into the story text.

Other stories involve psychological conundrums of holograms and implants that change personality or sensation (the commoditization of brands of personality, the mapping onto human players various animal sensory capabilities); of bioengineering (a woman has her dog, Riley, reengineered as a man and slowly trains him to do what she wants; this process is inter-twined with a budding relationship with a real man who leaves when the re-engineered Riley is delivered, providing a neatly ambiguous mediation by a woman on "what women want"); and the (im)possibilities of computer me-diation of illicit, impersonal sex without guilt. There are stories about rivalry between programmers and the feeling of omnipotence that computing can give; the dilemmas of parenting in a municipality that is free of computer viruses because it has outlawed personal computers but where they still exist illicitly; a parody of the San Francisco heavy metal, mechanical gladiatorial artist Mark Pauline (see Dery 1996) and what his work says about blood-shed among humans. There are stories about the fierce competition of the computer age, both about speeded-up work time (a hilarious version of the physics fantasy of being in two, or more, places at once, and the devastation and havoc this can wreak on family, body, and ability to survive economi-cally); as well as about a laid-off lead programmer at Boeing who, now a homeless woman, finds a stolen biological computer. (After a few false starts, she guesses the correct command to turn it on, "Boot!" Imagining its uses, she thinks of selling it for fabulous sums, starting her own company, and gaining new autonomy; but she decides what she really needs is emotional security, and takes it along to the homeless center for Sunday turkey din-ner.) There is a spoof of gadgets designed for the military-industrial com-plex (the true uses of which are as consumer tools for "personal discovery"), which simultaneously parodies the script style of thinking about life that programming can foster.

A lovely story about cyborgs used to reengineer the human species and our environment as the latter becomes increasingly a threat to the former has a world populated with nanobots that allow humans to process chlorophyll, nanotooters to regenerate aging bodies, nanoassemblers for building, nano-computers for designing. The hero works on a holographic design model of a bird to fix the ozone by breathing in oxygen and nitrogen and breathing out ozone and nitrogen. But the story is also a deft account of husband-wife interaction, in which she proposes a solution but he does not hear her, at the same time remembering an old design that triggers his insight: the solu-tions are formally the same, if technologically differently located, and so he gives her no credit.

Lois Gresh, the author of the story about the human effects of time com-pression, also has a wonderful story about a self-reproducing biological computer with a capacity-straining program called Nietzsche ("compiles so slowly you'll think you've shorted"), which she finally births into a separate biological computer. Nietzsche now needs more tasks to keep from "terminal boredom" and thus births a third computer, a Hasidic rabbi intelligence that begins debating with Nietzsche. Parodying programming and philosophy, and hinting at the diseases of cancer and malignant tumors (and attendant ethical issues) to which such biologies might be subject, the dilemmas of what seems at first a merely amusing and textured story are shadowed more darkly in the life tragedies of the human designers: Marge, who lost her only child, and Arnie, who lost his wife to cancer. They worry about the transfer of their creations to the medical establishment and speculate about their possible future roles as consultants watching over these AIS, more animal than machinelike. Woven throughout run the ethical dilemmas of life, in whatever form, "out of control."

If *Infinite Loop* is ethnographically fascinating for the interplay between story and contemporary RL, as in the "Pygmaleon 3.0" and Media Lab project resonances, the *Future Boston* stories provide potential for ethnographically located grounding in a real place and for implicating history and changing social dynamics (see also *Zodiac*, Neal Stephenson's 1988 ecological SF reality parody set in Boston). The armature of *Future Boston* has a standard SF or cyberpunk cast (new technologies embedded in a decaying environment and a stratified authoritarian governance caught between warring factions), and the plot is noir thriller. (A female detective who misses her father killed in the Great Flood is used to repress an uprising. The client, a hard-boiled professional female City Operator or Supervisor, is, in turn, desperate to find her kidnapped adopted daughter, whose fingers are being sent to her one by one by a revenge-seeking infiltrator of a school for the children of the Boston elite merchant families.) Boston is projected into a more multicultural society (the detective is Irish, the police chief is Italian, but elite merchant families have names like Nyo, Martinez, Mudandes, and Gutfreund) and is expanded also through multispeciation (especially with the linguistically distinctive Phner, and the recombinant, bioengineering Targive).

The epic frame is a futuristic parody of Boston history: a busy interplanetary spaceport, after secession from the United States (in a Pyrrhic replay of the American Revolution), after the arrival of the Loophole, through which various alien species have arrived, after a municipal mutiny (Civil War) and repressive use of a Great Flood to drown the mutineers. The sea has reclaimed much of the landfill, and Bostonians now live in a huge, 180-story cube, an enclosed and stratified environment with video-simulation windows. Unenclosed suburban towns exist across the water: Charlestown, Dorchester, and Cambridge, where MIT and Harvard still maintain marginal existences. The spaceport in the harbor is the access to the obligatory physics parody: the Loophole or "multiply-connected space-time topological anomalous region which a spaceship can traverse to travel from one place to another without crossing the intervening distance" (D. Smith 1994: 155).

But the Loophole is less access to a *Star Trek* fantasy of outward expansive space colonization and more an inward, implosive, historical reminder of being colonized and of the tragic Fall of the Phner, a parody of the biblical myths of origin, including a Tower of Babel reminder that language differences can carry alternative worldviews. The linguistic play continues to be characteristic and a meditation on grammatical-philosophical potentials.

The Phner have a language without verbs: instead they "use concepts that concatenate existence and time, words like destruction-imminent-but-necessary or existed-once-now-ended-and-memory-still-influences-events" (40). From an English language point of view, "they have trouble with verb tenses, time sequences and causality—before and after are almost the same word in Phner" (12). But they have acute memories, imitate others to perfection as communication devices, and so can act as the "sents of Boston" (17): "To the Phner, every spot of blood, every crumb of dirt, every wound and scar and broken bone tells a story" (19). This syntactical, memory, and sleuthing structure provides as well a kind of karmic-cosmic attitude toward life and death: deaths are never forgotten, yet they are placed in larger contexts that judge them as "artful" or not. "Phner can accelerate their time-sense for brief periods, react more quickly, move faster, think more clearly . . . a survival reflex that conjures up terrifying and sad memories of the Endless Fall" (after losing a war with the Sh'ik), but which "at the same time it can be . . . a terrific buzz."

The Phners' acute memories (a process of esfn') make them superb craftsmen of the reconstructed historic parts of town, and also a threat to art markets that depend on uniqueness, since Phner easily re-create objects as they were when first esfn'd. To the Phner, the notion of copies destroying value makes little sense because "no two objects are identical because they have unique histories" (a re-created object retains for them traces of its mode and time of re-creation). They consequently also have extremely skilled physicians, and from human points of view ghoulish interests in dissecting the dead to learn what they can. Phner are social animals who live in tightly packed "warrens" and have communal rituals that exercise the moral as well as psychological senses. Whatever one makes of this fantasy, it stands in for, acts as a token of, cultural differences premised on real epistemological and linguistic-structural differences, something rare in most science fiction (Ursula Le Guin being a notable other exception).

The Targive are a similar token, this time of recombinant biological potentials, which even if not worked out with any particular technical didacticism available through contemporary molecular biology, nonetheless marks out that conceptual terrain. They are a race of nomads who build citadels, basilica, cathedrals out of local forms of biological life, and who also produce various "mods" or modifications of local biological forms. Every Targive gift (punning no doubt both on the German "gift," which means poison, and on the oxymoron of tar, which sticks rather than being giveable, or which tars the gift receiver with unwanted side effects) "conceals a scorpion so only the desperate accept their offer" (41). For cleaning up Boston's effluents, they biodesigned a "clivus" that eats, digests, and transforms, helping bacteria dismantle the complicated man-made molecules of pollutants into ammonia, water, nitrogen, and carbon dioxide (91). The Targive can perform modifications on human brains as well, but at a serious cost, for they exact in tissue of their choosing a price for their gifts.

The world of this future Boston is filled with chairs made of Targive-modified jellyfish; bioelectronic blackbirds that act as eyes for the City Operator; holographic exercise environments in which one can fight off lizards or Zulu and Nubian warriors; "biodesign on a grand scale, micronics so small and powerful that a lint-sized chip could not only beat you at chess but insult you in Swahili all the while, truly independent servobots, artificial brain aids, field-based technology; the list went on endlessly. With them came vermin, bugs, bizarre foodstuffs, and a host of alien con artists, lunatics, political fanatics, demagogues, courtesans, smugglers, and rapscalawags. And the dread disease cities, which in the late 2030s killed a fifth of the City's population before the Targives designed a treatment and a vaccine" (156). Indeed, "It's part of City lore that . . . City Operators have Targive implants to help them interface better with the bots, eyes, spatiens, and Phneri, and with the half-biological City organism itself" (24). There are even jesters: the popcorn aliens who parody the world of buying and selling:

"Sell to you and sell for me! Cells of two and cells of three! Cells for yet a hundred indecisions, and for a hundred visions and revisions, before the toasting of a fake or spree. This has been dyed grue, the rarest color in the galaxy. . . . appears green until you buy it, then . . . it turns blue. . . . that's why grue is unique!" . . .

"I've got to go I'm hunting for someone."

"Why didn't you say so?" . . .

"I did say so. You weren't paying attention."

"You weren't charging attention! I didn't know I could buy it from you." . . . The popcorn grabbed the picture and immediately turned it upside down. "Yes, yes," he replied. "Absolutely distinctive hairline. I can certainly sell you to him."

"But you haven't got him."

"Oh but this is a futures contract."

In Brief (the Law)

Everything you know about intellectual property is wrong. . . . Intellectual property law cannot be patched, retrofitted, or expanded to contain digitalized expression anymore than real estate law might be revised to cover the allocation of broadcasting spectrum. — John Perry Barlow, "The Economy of Ideas"

It is difficult for intellectual property laws to keep pace with technology. When technological advances cause ambiguity in the law, courts rely on the law's purposes to resolve that ambiguity. However, when technology gets too far ahead of the law, and it becomes difficult and awkward to apply the old principles, it is time for reevaluation and change. — Lehman Working Group Preliminary Draft

Software is a machine whose medium of construction is text. — Randy Davis

Futures contracts, in the lively languages of the law, changing briefs for changing times: It is striking how often lawyers write about challenges of law and cyberspace in the tropes of radical breaks with the past, that precedents are multiple and ambiguous, that a choice of metaphor on the part of legislators or judges can make an extraordinary difference. Paula Samuelson et al. (1995) writing about copyright and patent law, Michael Froomkin (1995) writing about cryptography, privacy, First and Fourth Amendment rights, Judge Richard Sterns, in the 1994 case of MIT undergraduate David LaMacchia, writing a decision about wire fraud, copyright infringement, and system operator liability — all express concern that the law is inadequate to developments in the new medium.[25]

Courtroom and legislative committee provide adversarial grounds between plaintiff and defendant, but also between economic interests and societal ones, state and individual rights. Networked connectivity, accumulating data banks, encryption, and the economics of a shape-shifting technological medium have over the past fifteen years reframed the conceptual universes by which lawyers, judges, and law enforcement operate. In the struggle for comprehension and adjudication, legal language has been given a workout. Lively languages operate here as much as in literary or imaginative spheres; metaphor here is both a serious workhorse (on the basis of which precedent and analogical reason operate with quite profoundly different outcomes depending on the metaphor chosen) and a computer functionality that the law has fumbled in accommodating (e.g., conceptual metaphors as the modality in which software programs give behavioral coherence and wherein resides much of their value as user interfaces).

That the law operates by matching new situations and new technologies to older precedents through metaphors and analogical logic is not a new observation, but Michael Froomkin's 1995 essay "The Metaphor Is the Key" demonstrates how the choice of metaphor in the debates over cryptography can make a major difference.[26] If encryption is regarded as being like a car (vehicle for messages), then government demands for random inspection can be analogized to random checks on cars: escrowed keys might be like license plates or like photographs on a license; no warrant would be necessary (by the time a warrant is obtained, car or message is long gone), and one can check for whether messages are encrypted according to approved encryption systems, without necessarily looking at the message content. "If the car metaphor prevails," warns Froomkin, "there will be far fewer constitutional rights in cyberspace than if any other metaphor comes to dominate."

If, on the other hand, one regards the cyphers of encryption as a language, then the government argument that it must have the ability to decrypt would be analogous to imposing limits on the use of other languages than English and would be unconstitutional under the First, Fifth, and Fourteenth Amendments. Rejection of the language metaphor, warns Froomkin, can lead to undesirable consequences. The metaphor of a house "may provide protection depending on whether a court could compel production of [an encryption] key not committed to paper. If the court is unwilling to do this on Fifth Amendment grounds, strong cryptography would provide nearly unbreakable protection of private papers stored on a home computer."

These metaphors do not operate in a historical vacuum, and Froomkin suggests shifting concern away from Big Brother to Big Drugs in the rhetoric of the FBI's campaign to impose mechanisms that would allow the government to access encrypted messages.[27] In fact, while much of the press coverage of computer crime has been about hackers breaking into systems,[28] white-collar crime and misuse of data banks are much more serious sources of computer crime both in financial terms and invasion of privacy terms.[29] Encryption technologies can be used both to protect privacy and to make such crimes much easier, and thus the struggle is vigorously contested between those who fear anarchistic black markets in everything from body parts, kidnapping and assassination contracts, money laundering, extortion ("the four horsemen" of drugs, terror, money laundering, and pedophiles), as well as the breakdown of taxation and general law enforcement abilities of the state, and those who fear the imposition of police state controls including outlawing of privacy-enhancing encryption, imposition of national identity cards (to be used at point-of-sale terminals to collect taxes and monitor health and other statuses),[30] as well as the general growth of surveillance by employers, marketing, and other information entrepreneurs.[31]

"Regardless of how the Court decides to strike the balance," says Froomkin, "it will involve a process requiring decisions not compelled by any precedent. . . . to predict where the law . . . may be going and to suggest feasible alternatives, one needs to understand the concerns that are likely to influence [future decisions]" (845).

Similar kinds of metaphorical choices are debated in the still unsettled question of system operator liability: is s/he like a publisher, an editor, a bookstore, or a common carrier? If an editor, then more liability is likely to accrue; if a bookstore or common carrier, then s/he cannot be held responsible for the content of the books/messages.[32] System operators at the moment are caught between potential suits for libel by victims of defamatory statements on their systems, and suits for abridgment of free speech. Economic pressures mediate some of this: Prodigy monitors at least children's chat rooms for fear that parents will cancel subscriptions if they find their children being subjected to materials and solicitations they find offensive. Legislative and technical mediations are also now being proposed.[33]

The debates over intellectual property law—copyright, patent, trade secrets—are central to the economic incentive structure of the computer industry. A series of contradictory outcomes of major appellate and Supreme Court decisions (*Whelan v. Jaslow* [1986]; *Lotus v. Mosaic and Paperback* [1987–1990]; *Apple v. Microsoft and H-P* [1988–1992]; *Computer Associates v. Altai* [1992]; *Borland v. Lotus* [1997]) have sparked vigorous debate about whether copyright and patent laws are adequate to the new medium, and whether a sui generis law should be written as was done for computer chips in 1984. At issue is the confusion over whether software can be analogized to texts and literary productions (copyright), or to machines (patents), or—least likely given the relative ease of reverse engineering—to trade secrets. At issue as well is a temporally unfolding change in the nature of the software market, which is paralleled by changes in positions taken by the industry.

The first software patent was issued in 1968, but in the 1960s software was normally bundled with hardware, given away as something that made mainframes usable. A 1966 presidential commission chaired by J. W. Birkenstock, the head of IBM (which controlled 70 percent of the computer market), did not want software to be patentable: algorithms are laws of nature, and thus not patentable. In *Gottshalk v. Benson* (1972) IBM, Burroughs, and

Honeywell filed friends of the court briefs in which again they argued that the mathematical character of algorithms, even if they facilitate machine implementation, make them ineligible for patent protection. But by the 1980s a mass market began to emerge for software, and industry began to demand protection for a commodity that was expensive to develop but easy to copy. A 1978 presidential commission urged Congress to add software to the 1976 Copyright Protection Act because there was no patent protection, and this was done in a 1980 amendment to the act. But copyright is an uncomfortable fit for software: copyright is intended to promote diversity of literary production; software to be most useful requires standardization. Copyright is intended to prevent copying; every computer operating system integrally contains copying programs. Although there have been extensions of copyright protections from the original application to printing, reprinting, and vending of printed materials (to public performance rights for drama, music, and public display, analyzed by the 1976 law into five kinds of rights: reproduction, derivation, distribution, public performance, and public display), copyright seems to stretch the meanings of copying to various reductio ad absurdums. These have become the source of the contradictory appellate court decisions in the series of "look and feel" court cases of the late 1980s, and the impetus for new policy initiatives explored in the July 1994 Preliminary Draft Report (or Green Paper) of the National Information Infrastructure initiative (NII) working group chaired by Bruce Lehman, the commissioner of patents and trademarks and assistant secretary of commerce.[34]

In 1981 the case of *Diamond v. Diehr* reopened the patent system to software, adding to the confusion. Taking the position that patents can be issued for industrial processes controlled by computer programs (rubber curing, in this case), IBM immediately began filing patents on software, and after an influential article by Donald Chisum (1986) supporting the use of patents for software, the Patent and Trademarks Office began in 1989 to accept more and more applications. IBM files some two hundred a year, and there are as many as a thousand a year being filed, many in anticipation of their use for cross-licensing with other companies. Indeed, software is often written up as both a patent application and a copyright, since it is increasingly difficult to distinguish between implementations done through hardware or software: they can be done either way. Like copyright, the patent system also fits software poorly. Intended to encourage the making public of processes and methods of production in exchange for a seventeen-year protection, the time period for protection is the first problem, since the time cycles of software (and hardware) in the computer industry are much shorter. The search for "prior art" to demonstrate that one's patent is nonobvious and original is difficult and confusing, both because of the lack of technical expertise in the PTO and because of the complexity of programs and the difficulty of deciding which elements might constitute prior art. These problems open the door to endless litigation, since software development depends on incremental modification. Litigation becomes a means for raising entry barriers to small companies and embroiling big ones, but it works, arguably, in the favor of large companies with considerable legal resources.[35]

If both copyright and patent definitions are hard to apply to software, perhaps a sui generis law is required. This was the solution found in the 1984 Semiconductor Chip Protection Act, in which patentlike protection is given for two years automatically, and for eight years if the chip is registered. At the same time, the act acknowledges incremental design development, the right to reproduce and reverse engineer chip designs to test and analyze how they work. The industry wants competitors to make compatible chips, and the production process relies on second sourcing. But the semiconductor industry, unlike the software industry, has only a dozen or so large manufacturers, the barriers to entry are high, and it is very expensive to set up a production facility. Still, the argument can be made (Samuelson et al. 1995) that the current laws generate an unstable oscillation between overprotection and underprotection, because none of the categories of intellectual property apply neatly to software. At the time of *Whelan v. Jaslow* (1986), it seemed that there was underprotection and the need to encourage investment, so an expansive interpretation of copyright was pursued. At the time of *Computer Associates v. Altai* (1992), it was not just a different circuit court and a different reasoning process but a different time, when the market felt cramped by overprotection, and so a narrower definition of copyright was pursued.

It would be better, argue Samuelson et al. (1995), if one thought out ways to protect the actual value of computer software, rather than forcing poor analogies. The most important property of programs lies in their useful behavior, including the conceptual metaphors that give behavior coherence. Behavior can be "cloned" without appropriating the text of the software: that is, different codes can produce the same behavior. If what is of value in the market is the behavior, it misses the point to try to copyright the codes, which in fact are made up of incremental elements modified, but rarely directly copied, from various prior art sources.

The 1994 Green Paper is an interesting document against which to test out this line of argument. Although the paper claims that copyright law needs only "minor clarification amendment," what is revealing is its item-by-item puzzlement over what traditional legal concepts might mean in the new digital environment. It can be read rather the way a wickedly delighted psychoanalyst might look for hesitations, ambivalences, and contradictions in the Official Story and thereby find another quite contradictory one being told. (The Green Paper was succeeded by a 1995 White Paper, which according to many analysts tries to erase the telltale ambiguities in the Green Paper by omitting unfavorable legal precedents, and tilts the resolution in favor of already existing communications industries in an unsustainable attempt to extend the meaning of copyright to even such "copies" as the electronic repetitions in the machine memory in order to be able to display or send a document.)[36]

Photocopying, once an analogous new technology, the Green Paper begins, also once "caused apprehension among copyright owners," but thanks to the time, cost, and degradation of quality involved in copying, as well as court decisions denying application of "fair use" to Kinkos and other off-campus copy shops' production of anthologies for professors, print copyright rules still work reasonably well. The same holds for audiotape recording, even digital ones (as worked out under the Audio Home Recording Act of 1992). But digital integration of all forms of text, image, and sound information, done with speed, ease, and no loss of quality, makes it sometimes difficult to even tell what is distribution, what is reproduction, what is publication. Traditional copyright law depends on a definition of publication that requires a material object to change hands in contrast to a display or performance. How stable is the notion that browsing in another computer constitutes "fixing" of a new copy because for it to be displayed, it must be in RAM or the buffer? In *Playboy Enterprises v. Frena*, the court decided that unauthorized downloading of digitized images scanned from Playboy photographs constituted economic damage to Playboy Enterprises. However, the Green Paper notes that it remains unclear whether in fact Frena "distributed" the photographs, or subscribers "reproduced" them; furthermore, if subscribers are then liable for copyright infringement, it is unclear if Frena is liable as contributory. In the Playboy case, and a similar case concerning video games *(Sega Enterprises Ltd. v. MAPHIA)*, judgments were made, but the principles at issue are unclear when applied more generally to the liability of bulletin board sysops (system operators) if the latter are able to claim no knowledge of what is put on their electronic bulletin boards. A prominent 1994 court case dealing with these issues, that of an MIT undergraduate, David LaMacchia, was dismissed as unprosecutable under either copyright law (he did not himself either engage in uploading or downloading, nor did he profit, nor was he held liable as "contributory" to copyright infringement for telling people where to place and get pirated software)[37] or the wire fraud statutes often used by prosecutors when they need a vaguer general-purpose statute. The judge in the case noted that prosecution should not be used as a vehicle for writing laws where current legislation does not fit the new cyberworld, that if Congress wished LaMacchia-style activity to be made criminal, it needed to write legislation to that effect.

Moreover, the Green Paper continues, the new digital environment also creates problems for the "first sale doctrine" (that when one buys a book, one may resell it), for archival and library exemptions (which allow free use and limited reproduction rights), for rights of free transmission on receiving apparatuses like radios in a bar or beauty shop (which "will change as home equipment merges with other equipment"), and for licensing provisions allowing cable and satellite operators to retransmit copyrighted materials ("will need to be reviewed" as creative, communications, and computer entities continue to merge). More subtly yet, since copyright infringement does not depend on intent, and since it also need not be a literal copying, the ability to easily manipulate works in digital format leads to a whole raft of issues regarding infringement, reproduction, and derivative work. Among these issues, the Green Paper lists manipulating photographs (in which the input may be infringement, but the result may not be) and the resale or distribution of items from gray markets (legally produced for distribution abroad but not authorized for the U.S. market). "If an infringing literary work, for instance, was physically shipped into the United States in the form of a paper copy, a CD-ROM disk or even stored on a memory chip, then it could be an infringing importation if the above discussed conditions exist, but it would appear that Section 602, as currently written, could not be used to block the electronic transmission of such material" (238).

A more obvious and basic issue is that domestic law will be made increasingly ineffective unless at the same time an international or "global" information infrastructure and legal framework are constructed. This, the Commerce Department Green Paper notes, is not merely an issue of intellectual property rights ("When the globe is blanketed with digital information dissemination systems, a user in one country will be able to manipulate information resources in another country in ways that may violate that country's copyright laws"), but also a potential problem for commerce: doing "electronic business" over information superhighways will be difficult unless rules for protection (of rights, but also privacy, and security) and harmonization of legal structures are provided. The initial issue is the claim of the Software Business Association that its members lose billions of dollars each year in pirated software.

Harmonizing copyright systems means among other things coming to terms with at least two different moral understandings of the purpose of copyright: for Anglo-American law, the purpose is to protect authors' economic rights so that they will make their ideas publicly available in order to promote the progress of science and the arts; for European law, "moral rights" of authorship are not transferable and have to do with natural rights or rights of personhood. The American authors of the Green Paper, citing a Japanese study for legitimacy, say these moral rights may have to yield in the new digital world.

The Green Paper has relatively little to say about patent law, which is under siege by the digital revolution at least as much as if not more than copyright law. Indeed, it has little to say about the entire confusion of patent and copyright categories created in a series of important court decisions over the past fifteen years about the copyrightability and patentability of software (as well as the blurring or interchangeability between hardware and software), a confusion so severe that many (e.g., Barlow, Newell, Samuelson) suggest that a whole new intellectual framework may have to emerge. The Green Paper proposal timidly hints at this by proposing that "transmission" be elevated into an elaborated conceptual apparatus to deal with many of the issues listed here. It ends with an important reminder of two social issues fundamental to the conflicts among the major interest groups (academia, industry, programmers as a profession, and the state) — the basic purpose of the copyright law and the problem of access:[38]

> The Copyright Act exists for the benefit of the public. To fulfil its constitutional purpose, the law should strive to make the information contained in protected works of authorship freely available to the public. "Freely available," of course, does not necessarily mean "available free." The Working Group does not believe that authors should be required to donate access time to their works on-line, but some reasonable approach must be adopted to ensure that the economically disadvantaged in this country are not further disadvantaged or disenfranchised by the information revolution.

The Green Paper, in short, provides a preliminary site of contestation in the information revolution as well as a sense of the destabilizing effect on basic conceptual categories that this revolution is generating. It does so by looking not at language uses that celebrate, exacerbate, or elaborate on these instabilities (as for instance in a "pomo" playful theoretical exposé), but on the contrary at a conservative document unable to hide the contradictions;

the paper argues both that only minor clarifications and amendments are needed and that when technology gets too far ahead of the law, . . . it becomes difficult and awkward to apply the old principles."

This situation should not be taken as an argument in favor of a presumption that new technologies necessarily make old laws obsolete, as Laurence Tribe (1991) notes in regard to First and Fourth Amendment rights, but rather that one pay close attention to the values that the law — constitutional or statutory — is meant to foster. While the stress here has been on the instabilities of legal categories, language, and reasoning, the argument has been underpinned by a questioning of the economic dynamics, democratic access, and private liberties that are under pressure. Just as the legal system periodically needs to be reminded that the Fourth Amendment protects the privacy of people, not places, so too, in thinking about the economic restructuring that cyberspace is facilitating, one needs to consider the values of the human beings involved, the values placed in the exchange system.[39]

In Exchange

Nineteen ninety-two . . . signaled a sea change in competitive dynamics. . . . The importance of this transition reaches far beyond the participants in the [information technology] industry. . . . None of these industries are able to operate successfully within autarkic national boundaries. — David Yoffie, *Strategic Management in Information Technology*

Chips make me think of the eyesight of women in Singapore and Korea, going blind during the process of crafting the fiddly little wire; of "clean rooms" . . . in Silicon Valley and the Netherlands . . . perhaps it is time to have a less boring idea of the body right now — a body politic . . . the combination of telecommuting with the global factory has proved terrible for women . . . isolated in the "electronic cottage," . . . an easy way for a corporation to do legal "union busting" and bypass any particular state's labour regulations . . . Tayloristic intervention . . . monitoring of key strokes in data entry . . . timing breaks to go to the toilet. — Susan Leigh Star, *The Cultures of Computing*

Information . . . Like other such deep phenomena as light or matter, it is a natural host to paradox . . . helpful to understand light as being both a particle and a wave, an understanding of information may emerge in the abstract congruence of its several different properties. . . .

Information is an activity . . . is experienced, not possessed . . . has to move . . . is conveyed by propagation, not distribution . . . grow[s] in the usual fractal lattice like frost spreading on a window. . . .

Information is a life form . . . as in an oral tradition, digital information has no final cut. . . .

Information is a relationship. . . . Receiving information is often as creative an act as generating it. — John Perry Barlow, "The Economy of Ideas"

Just as in the law (intellectual property law, export controls, privacy, freedom of information) there is a claim that the new electronic media are undoing old assumptions, definitions, and regulatory mechanisms, so too there is a claim that the information economy operates by laws different from those of classical or marginal utility economics. It is in the details of the paradoxes of this new economy that the double ethnographic challenges reside: the challenges to produce credible ethnographic accounts of the concrete and detailed temporal changes in the political economy of cyberspace; the challenges to provide critical mirrorings in which the utopian and dystopian sides of the political economy can be screened in their partialities and contingencies. In public discourse at least, it is as if one side of the paradoxical structure cannot be seen while the other is being discussed.

On the one side, in the extreme, John Perry Barlow, Carver Mead, George Gilder, and others argue that the constraints of labor and capital are being removed thanks to a technology that increasingly operates on the level of the microcosm, the particle world of electrons and biological molecular processes, as miniaturization has moved down from circuit boards to the integrated circuit and faster and faster chips made out of sand (silicon), and as parallel processing allows computations to work as "out of control" self-organizing systems. On the other side, these processes have also been described as allowing for an intensification of the labor and capital processes described by nineteenth-century political economists (exchange of formally free labor through a mystified process of alienation and extraction of surplus value). Cycles of innovation and consolidation have plagued the computer industries (Hayes 1989; Yoffie 1994; Teitelman 1994). David Yoffie and his colleagues at the Harvard Business School put together a casebook on the informational technologies in 1994, arguing that almost all firms have a stake in the evolution of these technologies both as customers for the technologies themselves and arguably more importantly as a model for management in the twenty-first century. None of the IT industries can operate in autarkic national boundaries; all must be transnational. No market is big enough (not the United States or Europe) to support the costs of developing a digital switch or semiconductors; those that tried to remain national went bankrupt. Only in the 1990s did the promise of merging technologies actually happen, and this caused the disintegration of vertically integrated businesses. Computers and telecommunications began to merge; the difference between personal computers, workstations, minicomputers, and mainframes began to collapse. "Blurred firm boundaries" led to new corporate forms of shifting alliances. First movers had enormous advantages in capturing market share and setting standards, and this required willingness to cannibalize one's own business (offering new products that reduce sales on older ones). Others might argue (Aglietta 1976/1979) that these are but consolidations of a globalizing market, acting like earlier and more national or regional mechanisms, as in the postwar housing and automobile consumer markets, supported by socialization of credit and loan facilities.

A second such paradox is the separation in cyberspace between production and use. Office use of software and terminals (where the physical downside seems to be "only" carpal tunnel syndrome, eye strain, sometimes sick building problems, and a sterility of environment that makes the screen seem like life) is so far removed from the manufacturing of the chips in "clean rooms" (which generate hidden toxicities) that it is far too easy for many to forget the production processes when talking about cyberspace. A third paradox has to do with the inability of economic measures to show productivity gains through computerization (Teitelman 1994; Uchitelle 1996). A fourth paradox, often tacitly understood and regretted, is the still important role that military contracts seem to play in the computer worlds of corporate survival. The secrecy of the military contracts, and the ways in which the work is parceled out so that programmers need not know the end uses to which they are contributing, are not dissimilar from the studied displacements of attention away from the hazards of manufacturing chips.

Hayes's 1989 exposé of these hazards suggests an ethnographic method of "following the work processes": evacuations of facilities for toxic leaks, medical disabilities, the intentional disabling of occupational hazard indicators, and the lack of medical research on accumulating multiple chemical sensitivity syndromes. The semiconductor industry uses toxic gases (arsine, phosphine, diborane, and chlorine) to give electrical properties to microchips. Hydrofluoric and hydrochloric acids are used to harden and etch chips, to electroplate, and to retard oxidation of solder attaching chips to boards. Trichloroethane, methylene chloride, chloroform, and carbon tetrachloride are used as solvents (64–69). Inhaling hydrogen chloride from silicon tetrachloride leaks can form hydrochloric acid inside the body (65). By 1980, occupational illness rates for semiconductor workers were more than three times those of general manufacturing workers. In response, the Semiconductor Industry Association changed the way it recorded injuries and illnesses so as to show a two-thirds drop in occupational illness rates (65), and the Reagan administration cut funding for the Project on Health and Safety in Electronics, PHASE, a program that collected and publicized information for electronics workers on chemicals used in manufacturing(66). In 1986, faced with preliminary results of a survey of its workers in Hudson, Massachusetts, showing a twice normal miscarriage rate—39 percent among workers in wafer etching, 29 percent in wafer photolithography—Digital Equipment Corporation reacted by banning interviews with workers and announcing programs of pregnancy testing and transfers for women of child-bearing age. AT&T also mandated job transfers out of clean-room work for pregnant women (67). In 1988 a California Department of Health study found that pregnant women who drank tap water in Silicon Valley had twice as many miscarriages and had babies with four times as many birth defects as those who drank filtered water or no tap water; IBM and Fairchild settled a class action suit quietly out of court (24). The astronaut-like suits worn in clean rooms are designed not to protect workers from chemical toxicities but to protect the wafers from the particles human bodies throw off (67); similarly, laminar airflows and filters are designed to protect the chips by extracting particulates, not to protect the workers by extracting fumes. Describing the false sense of protection that suits, filters, and airflow can impart, Hayes comments, "The ambience is misleading in a distinctly modern (i.e., ambiguous) way."

Apart from acute dangers from spills and leaks, chemical toxicities can build up in the fatty tissues of the body and can induce "chemical hypersensitivity," meaning increasing sensitivity to chemicals in the everyday environment. This "chemically induced T-cell inadequacy" debilitates the immune system not unlike the virally induced AIDS. And yet the chemicals, techniques, and brand names of clean-room equipment are all protected as "trade secrets" and "proprietary information," and daily logs with evacuations, fume detector tapes, and injured worker dismissals are also kept secret and rarely reported in the press. Threshold limit values (TLVs) are set by professional organizations for monitoring systems, but there is no independent checking; in fact, according to a National Research Council/National Academy of Sciences study, there are no TLVs at all for 79 percent of 48,523 workplace chemicals (76). Immigrant women are often favored workers in Silicon Valley for clean-room work, and as these manufacturing jobs are outsourced abroad, it is often women who are new industrial labor entrants who perform the work there.

It is thus not only the so-called clean room that is misleading but the entire economy of the computer industry, which goes through a classic sort of labor reorganization while claiming to be part of a new economy that operates according to laws that are no longer constrained by scarcities of labor. And yet the ideology of descent into the microcosm, and the laws of a quantum economics, remains a vital spur to the imagination and to chip design, to the embedding of cyberspace into a changing world of scientific exploration and technological innovation, a world of quantum, optical, and DNA computers that can overcome current physical limits to computational speed, and that operate on new computing principles far removed from the sequential logics of mechanical Turing machines. At each turn, in each dimension of cyberspace—in time, in language, in place, in brief, and in exchange—there appears to be productive paradox. As Richard Powers puts it in *Galatea 2.0*, his novel exploring the intersection between the worlds of computer scientists and their own incapacities and psyches:

> "It went like this, but wasn't."
> . . . That's good. Lead with a paradox. Hook her. It's the traditional Persian fable opener.

Resituating Ethnography

The problem was that you didn't always know what you were seeing until later, maybe years later, that a lot of it never made it in at all, it just stayed stored there in your eyes.—Michael Herr, *Dispatches*

Ethics has been confined largely to the domains of doing, which include performative acts of a linguistic nature. . . . What might interest us here is the fact that responsibility no longer pivots on a notion of interiority.—Avital Ronell, "Video/Television/Rodney King: Twelve Steps beyond the Pleasure Principle"

Man is no longer man enclosed, but man in debt.—Gilles Deleuze, "Postscript on the Societies of Control"

Like a Möbius strip, we return to the beginning, to Hans Jonas's suggestion that not only are the law, the economy, language, place, and time challenged by our contemporary technological era, but there is even a claim on the new in ethics, in how we deal with one another, and that this implicates, relocates, and complicates ethnographic writing.

The ethnographic starting point in this essay is the pervasive expressions by practitioners in many fields that things are outrunning their conceptual categories, and that in the 1990s, unlike earlier more generalized debates about the "postmodern," this has become a concrete practical matter for the diverse institutions of society (law, economics, engineering). Among the institutional facets most developed in this essay have been the law ("In Brief") through dense casework sequences affecting economic, academic, and civil rights interests, and involving material effects of choices about metaphors, where practitioners feel under challenge of the new in ways that, they say, stretch their traditional employments of analogy and precedent. Economics ("In Exchange") too has practitioners, from business school case writers to technology writers, who claim that traditional categories are outrun. Here the discussion opens further into historical horizons of business cycles, industrial reorganizations, labor processes and transvaluations of ideas, labor and materials into producer and consumer goods. It also engages the ongoing dialectic between those processes and what at least since Marx have been called processes of fetishization, specterization, or virtualization of the economy, and to which there has been an interesting return of analysis in the 1990s (Leitch 1996), as well as some ethnographic work on the social effects (Stacey 1990; Star 1995; G. Mathews 2003). Parallel fields of discussion might be opened into psychology ("In Conscience"), both human-machine interfaces (e.g., Papert 1996; Turkle 1995; or Stone 1995) and artificial life, brain and cognitive psychology, or neuroscience; into popular culture, entertainment, and advertising ("In Play") as theaters of exploration and preparation, as well as voicings of things that cannot be said in less court-jester environments; and into sciences ("In-formation") such as molecular biology, where it has been argued that the imagery of the genome as an information science is both misleading and productive.[40] Most concrete is the section on building the infrastructure of connectivity around the world ("In Place"), captured also in the title of one of cyberspace's cheerleading journals, *Wired*. The laying of a third generation of fiber-optic cable from England to Japan is driven by competition between giant transnational business alliances that undo national PTT monopolies and regulatory controls (Stephenson 1996). The "sea change" arguments of "In Exchange" are thereby further strengthened.

The form of this essay attempts to capture on paper—a static medium—in a kind of freeze-frame, some of the dimensions and institutional facets of what a hypertextual ethnography with cross-linkages could accomplish. Ethnographies can be and already are (a few) being written in hypertext, multimedia, and CD-ROM formats that overcome the linearity of traditional writing and that might put interconnections into play more easily than simple text (e.g., Goldman-Segall 1990, 1995; Callison 2002). Some research and collaboration can be, and already is being, conducted through e-mail and on the Web. But at issue in the influence of these modalities—as with cinematic or filmic forms earlier in the twentieth century—is not merely the literal adoption of new technical possibilities but a new pedagogical regime, in the same way that much fiction writing in the twentieth century is acknowledged to draw on cinematic techniques (Cohen 1979). Language itself is foregrounded in much thinking about this new pedagogical regime, ranging from the puns, metaphors, and syntactic play that access and hold in juxtaposition differential epistemological standpoints, to narratives and institutionalized discourses that act as switches and circuits of thought, behavior, action, organization, and cultural forms. Space, time, and differential access are being rearranged, and not only in the so-called First World.[41]

Cyberspace is part of the reality in which all of us live, and much of it works behind the scenes. Jaron Lanier debunks the hype that "virtual reality" prostheses could be mistaken as more real than the physical world: "The virtual world only exists because of the magic of the way your nervous system makes things real when you interact with them. And the moment you start to space out or become lazy, the reality goes away and it just turns into a bunch of junk on your head" (1996: 43–44). So too there is much hype about cyberspace. But cyberspace continues to work behind the scenes when we space out, compiling our credit ratings, positioning our financial futures, restructuring our work lives and stratification systems, building new decentralized bureaucratic surveillance and security systems, providing scientific and pragmatic knowledges beyond ordinary perception, keeping us distracted and suspended in complex temporal loops of partial knowledges, interactions, and circulating debts that merge and interact beyond individual responsibilities and control. We cannot afford to abandon responsibility, and we must therefore build new social forms of reflexive modernization that can make such systemic complexity and interactivity accountable. Hence the turn in much contemporary philosophy to questions of ethics—ethics no longer seen as the realm primarily of individual doings—as the quotations from Jonas, Derrida, Herr, Ronell, and Deleuze signal.

Ethnographies are challenged to no longer dwell merely in romantic tropes of discovery but to ground, make visible and audible,[42] contending worlds of difference, to provide translation circuitry that recognizes its own relations to other circulating representations (M. Fischer 1993).

9

Calling the Future(s): Delay Call Forwarding

Fifty years ago, Winston Churchill gave the keynote address at MIT's 1949 Mid-century Convocation on the Social Implications of Scientific Progress and the place of the humanities and social sciences in the education of engineers and scientists (Burchard 1950). The calls then for something like a science, technology, and society perspective as central to the conduct of professional lives as well as for the basic education of citizens in a technological society have continued to repeat in the succeeding decades. Easy generalities (and even disagreements) about humanistic or civilizational values (about which much was said at that three-day convocation on the occasion of the inauguration of a new president of MIT) sit uncomfortably with empirical investigations into the operations of the sciences and engineering, their social worlds, the worlds they transform, and the worlds within which they unfold (about which almost nothing was said). Fifty years later, at the beginning of a new century and a new millennium, even if many of the pieties remain the same, the conditions of the university, the composition of the student bodies and faculties, and the nature of knowledge bases and their constituencies have shifted dramatically; and a field of science, technology, and society has begun to emerge which makes available for citizens and professionals just such empirical investigations as basic everyday knowledge.

Science, technology, and society (STS) might become a canary discipline (as in the canaries miners take into the mines to sniff out deadly gases, thereby showing where the mines need to be vented or reworked) for the twenty-first century: a bringing together of the sciences and technologies around which modernities have been built, together with the social sciences, arts, and humanities, which constitute the analytic understanding and cultural commentaries about the societies of (post)modernity. Between 1996 and 1998 three calls were placed at MIT's STS program for such a canary discipline which would be integrative, critical, technically competent, and culturally resonant.[1] The calls placed were (1) to begin a conversation about, or testing-contesting, the disciplinary tools of ethnography and history, visual studies and literature, national institution building and transnational policy competitions; (2) to internationalize the conversation around the changing roles of the university[2] and the technosciences[3] in a globalizing world (including the complications of exacerbating uneven, unjust development, as well as the proliferating and conflicting alternative modernities); and (3) to move the pedagogical sites of STS into engineering, medical, science, and law schools. As in real life (RL), the calls have been received and disseminated through old-fashioned switching boxes, ancient lines of connectivity, with much breakdown, derailing, static, and interference. Still, much was accomplished, and the following is an account of the pedagogical platform deployed during 1996–1997 and 1997–1998.

The attempt at "integrative" weaving is not only the effort to reconnect the five cultures (sciences, engineering, humanities, arts, social sciences). It is also to counter the specialization, compartmentalization, and even secrecy or lack of ability to communicate among subfields of science and components of big engineering projects, both to allow checks and balances to operate and also to prevent the privatization of moral judgment, the enfeeblement of public discussion, and discriminatory restriction of access to the hierarchies of power and knowledge. It is also to contribute to the creation of multilayered institutional abilities to recognize and negotiate the differing knowledges and needs of societies and social strata in different parts of the globalizing world.

Science and technology are often thought of as having a center-periphery structure. A focus on (and from) the peripheries can often also ipso facto be a focus on the histories of exchanges in scientific knowledges (e.g., the Kerala toddy tappers who provided the Portuguese materia medica/botanica compiler Garcia da Orta, and his Dutch successor Hendrik van Reede, with the knowledge that Linnaeus was trained at Leiden [Grove 1985]), on hierarchies and access to centers of calculation (e.g., strategies used by Japanese women physicists to get resources from their international mentors to circumvent their lack of leverage within the patriarchal Japanese system [Traweek 1992, 1995]), and on alternative genealogies of knowledges too often codified in textbook histories as universal, as if one could simply build science modularly in any place (a kind of naive trickle-down modernization theory of science) without attention to the embeddedness of sciences and technologies in both sociopolitical factors and cultural imaginaries. The scientists and politicians who built the elite science institutions of India, China, Russia, Brazil, and elsewhere in the post–World War II period were hyperaware of leveraging comparative advantages, of playing off one power against another, and of building particular kinds of niches. In India, there were rationales in physics for beginning with cosmic ray physics and radioastronomy, or in developmental biology with Drosophila experimental systems. Paying attention to these modes of development throws a general light on the challenges of building science institutions. It also sheds light on the contemporary struggles over international agreements and treaties regulating environmental issues, intellectual property rights, and similar differences among the inhabitants of "planet earth."

The question is thus raised whether STS should not be integrally woven into the technoscientific curriculum, as questioning counterpoint, as a recombinant reagent, rather than in the old imagery as marginal critic, idealistic vanguard, elitist irritant, off to the side, out of the way, easily dismissed. Five or so exemplars of such efforts are recounted here. Are these a better way to develop cultural critiques of the biosciences, bioengineering, and biomedicine than, for instance, the new discipline of "bioethics," whose socializations, formulations, and positionings institutionally and intellectually push it toward being part of the public relations legitimation for medical centers and corporations? Are these a better way to develop practical understandings for engineers and applied scientists of their roles in shaping contemporary institutions than simply adding to their curricula new courses in management or business?

The following account begins in the fashion of humanist indirection, with a pair of examples "to think with," drawn from historically changing visual fields. The second part of the chapter turns to an account of the modular core course around which this vision of STS has been attempted. The core course began with a workshop on new pedagogical tools developed at MIT — the Shakespeare Project (under Pete Donaldson),[4] the Japanese Star Festival Project (under Shigeru Miyagawa),[5] the Chinese documentary project, Gate of Heavenly Peace (under historian Peter Perdue and director Carla Hinton), and a film-teaching tool that allows students to reblock scenes, change camera angles, and experience what difference a flipped image might make (under Henry Jenkins) — and challenged the STS community to experiment with Web-based and other visual materials not just for documentation but for transforming the conceptual and access means of production. A number of such projects were initiated.[6]

At issue is not merely tools but perhaps what Michel Foucault might have recognized as an emergent new episteme, not totally divorced from older ones but reconfiguring them and us in new cultural, social, and material logics. To help keep the visual thread in mind, the logo for the STS program was designed for four years around visual puzzle-logics that pose some of the calls and challenges.[7]

The "visual thread" was one of three such threads that were woven through the course;[8] the analogue in the world was the third-generation fiber-optic cables that at the time were being laid around the globe, expanding the connectivity of the new technological infrastructure, at the same time challenging and forcing reorganization of the old national postal systems by new multinational telecommunications corporate structures.

I. *Las Meninas* and Robotic-Virtual Surgical Systems: The Visual Thread/Fiber-Optic Carrier

Thought Experiment

Images are often powerful emblematic, mise-en-scène, even mise-en-abyme,[1] ways of signaling parameters of arguments or mapping the strategic terrains of debate. Let me stage a thought experiment contrasting Michel Foucault's deployment of Diego Velázquez's *Las Meninas* for thinking about the transition to the modern period with a photograph of a computer- and robot-assisted virtual-reality surgical operating system as an emblem of the transition to the science-and-technology-based knowledge and action systems within which we increasingly live. I want to use the former to orient us toward history, the latter to orient us toward ethnography, as complementary techniques of data collection, analysis, comparison, and understanding. Situated at MIT, I want to draw my students into the rich worlds of the academic laboratories, start-up companies, hospitals, environmental regulatory agencies, and corporate research worlds that surround them as ethnographic sites. And I want to use the historical record as a set of "grounds" against which these contemporary settings can be contrasted and compared, both to show how our inherited "wisdoms" (philosophy and ethics included) may be quite bound to their historical contexts, and to temper the euphoria of the "new" with recognitions of significant predecessors.

As an ethnographer and anthropologist, I am primarily interested in having students and colleagues help me understand the emergent worlds we are living in—more interested, in this sense, in the image of the surgical lab than in *Las Meninas*. But as a social theorist and social scientist, I am equally interested in having my engineering and scientist students and colleagues help me understand the histories, the social, political, economic, material, and cultural contexts, which motivate and constrain their work, and for this, *Las Meninas* is as critical as the photo of the surgical lab.

Consider, then, these two images structured by similar geometries of diagonal gazes and views. One, a painting, *Las Meninas*, is a scene of representation, of a painter painting. It is a "metapicture," a mise-en-abyme, an "encyclopedia of pictorial self-reference, representing the interplay between the beholder, the producer, the object or model of representation as a complex cycle of exchanges and substitutions," a "figure of the entire episteme" or "system of knowledge/power" (Mitchell 1994: 58).[2] The other, a photograph taken in Ian Hunter's lab at MIT, is a scene of action, a microsurgical system for eye surgery, a digital virtual imaging technology to enhance the sensory and actuating capacities of a surgeon's eye and hand (Hunter 1995, 1997). Might the contrast between these two scenes be helpful in thinking about the changing role of the visual in contemporary culture, about "diagrammatic thinking" in the contemporary technosciences,[3] about the descent into the worlds beneath the visibility of the eye (nanotechnology, molecular and atomic structures, quantum worlds, microcinematography and scanning — PET, genome sequencing machines — that can make visible to the eye biological processes otherwise too slow or fast to see), and about the transitions that often go under the names "modernity" and "postmodernity"? Moreover, although the slide or photograph is itself a representation, the scene of technology-in-development evokes immediately Bruno Latour's caveats against the use of "representation" as our primary metalanguage for understanding visualization technologies, be they prosthetic tools (microsurgical systems) or markers of brain activity claimed to model neurological-cognitive processes (PET scans). Latour directs our attention to the different kinds of translations and mediations that go into the construction of visualization and cognition, the organizational and sociological mediations of relations of power, as well as the material tools of inscription and scaling. Perhaps even more trenchantly, the slide evokes Walter Benjamin's prescient and still useful explorations of the shift between dialectical images in advertising and technologically empowered mimetic faculties that place the viewer inside, rather than outside, the flow of image, sound, and other sensory channels.

Las Meninas and the Scene of Modernity

Velázquez's *Las Meninas* has often been used as an "object to think with" about changes in perspective, technologies, and epistemologies at the limen between the Renaissance and the modern period. Perhaps the most famous current such meditation is the opening chapter of Michel Foucault's *The Order of Things*, but of complementary importance are the reflections of Norbert Elias, Svetlana Alpers, William Mitchell, Jonathan Crary, and — in

27. *Las Meninas or The Family of Philip IV*, c. 1656 (oil on canvas), by Diego Rodriguez de Silva y Velázquez (1599–1660). Prado, Madrid, Spain / Bridgeman Art Library.

another register, deciphering the status and power relations depicted, as well as understanding the patronage relations under which the painting was produced — recent radiographic analyses of the painting (Nash 1997; Brown 1997; Randall 1997; Stolz 1997; World Reporter 1999).[4] Complementary as well are the differences between the discourse networks (Kittler 1985/1990) of the brush, pen, and moveable-type literacies of the eighteenth century, as opposed to the "machinic" discourse networks ("systems," "assemblages," "electronic/digital media") of the twentieth century.

For Foucault, and for Jonathan Crary, Velázquez's *Las Meninas* is an image in which one can diagram the shift philosophically from what Foucault calls the classical episteme to the rise of the humanist or modern episteme, or in Crary's more instrument-mediated framework from ways of knowing via the seventeenth-century camera obscura to ways of knowing via the eighteenth-century stereoscope. The camera obscura, like the perspective aid of the draftsman's grid, is part of a technology of geometric optics that "suppresses subjectivity."[5] That is, the person for whom the representation exists is never within the picture (never within the tables and grids for representing knowledge), is never able to see his or her own position as part of the representation. The knower's body is marginalized into a phantasm; and so, the argument goes, thereby is established a space of pure reason, a paradoxical space for a philosophy that seeks foundation in the subjective (Descartes's *cogito*, standing outside what is viewed) yet claims objective validity (surveying through a grid of measurement).[6] With the rise of the humanist sciences, Foucault and Crary suggest, knowers appear in an oscillating position as both object and subject of knowledge: a movement away from Descartes's cogito, first to Kant's oscillating locus of the transcendental ego, the synthetic a priori; then to Hegel's rich vocabulary of imagery for the process of reason;[7] and then in the twentieth century to Durkheim's sociologization of knowledge and Foucault's sociologized panoptical constructions accomplished through intersecting gazes used to both control populations and normalize individuals through self-discipline or internalization, which during the course of the twentieth century becomes increasingly diffused and pervasive. (In technology terms, the movement is from Jeremy Bentham's physical prison structure,[8] in which the prisoner can be seen but cannot see and so internalizes the sense of being continuously under surveillance whether or not actually being watched, to "invisible" credit, police, and bureaucratic systems of surveillance, and now networked information systems.) This twentieth-century play of gazes and views (virtual realities, simulations, data architectures) through computer-mediated calculations, models, animations, data banks, and graphic constructions is prefigured in these readings of the intersecting and mirrored gazes in *Las Meninas*, a retrospectively appreciated prolepsis (quite like Walter Benjamin's dialectical images as "flashes of insight" that arise around previous understandings recalled in new subsequent contexts, or Freud's Nachtraeglichkeit).

The stereoscope for Crary and physiology for Foucault are markers of these transitions. The binocular vision of the stereoscope, or the retinal afterimages used by the phenakistiscope, foregrounded the reconstructive role of the mind in perception. Physiology replaces models of the mind's sovereignty with models of sensory and brain functions that abstract, separate, reconstruct, and reintegrate.[9] In the nineteenth century and the twentieth, with the analog media of film and then television, point of view is located in real space, and the integrative functions work through multiple channels of montaged inputs — kinetic, temporal, as well as visual — what Walter Benjamin called "distracted" or scanning perception, reintegrating what has been torn apart and reconstituted in the editing room (the German word is *Zerstreuung*).[10] The shift more recently to computerized digital information technologies inserts the knower into a haptic, sensory point of view, enhancing sensory inputs below or beyond unmediated human "normal" capacities. Thus the surgical virtual-reality master-slave imaging technology pictured in Ian Hunter's lab allows a surgeon to perform delicate operations for which the human hand would be too unsteady, which amplify the micropressures so that the surgeon can have feedback by "feel." The various images of seeing (poster of the eye, virtual reality helmet worn by the surgeon, digitally manipulated slave that operates on the eye of the patient and gives feedback to the hand of the surgeon) perhaps constitute a play on the geometries of *Las Meninas*, but the important geometric points are actually now those inside the picture or inside the digital "machinery"; the manipulations sought are at a micro, nano, and molecular level, which the unassisted eye cannot see.

A first-approximation contrast is thus between an old-fashioned (but for ethical purposes not yet outmoded) Cartesian ego *(Las Meninas)* and a contemporary position within the structure of multiply and synaesthetically constituted understanding (physiologically, biochemically, psychologically, mechanically) where there is no ego in a fully sovereign position outside the frame.[11] Even if, as Svetlana Alpers stresses, Velázquez's *Las Meninas* "confounds a single reading because it depends on and holds in suspension two contradictory (but, to Velázquez's sense of things, inseparable) ways of understanding the relationship of a picture and of the viewer to the world" (Alpers 1983: 69–70), that of a mapping (à la the northern or Dutch style) and that of a point of view (à la the southern or Italian style), the multimedia sensorium invoked by the VR surgical tableaux pushes the scene of representation well beyond its early modern limits, well beyond merely the visual into an informatics which is also tactile, and beyond ordinary unassisted human capacities, a cyborgian environment. Alpers rightly draws attention to the instrumentation of lenses — microscopes, telescopes, mirrors, liquid-filled bottles reflecting jewels, eyeglasses — and the inquiries into the structure of the eye taken up by Kepler as key genealogies for our contemporary cyborgian prostheses, noting that quite a number of Dutch painters were sons of glassblowers, dealing in their own way with refracted light (70–79).

Norbert Elias extends the analyses of *Las Meninas* in yet another dimension. He sees Velázquez as providing one of the first important paintings of a post-Cartesian subjectivity, where the painter paints himself in full-length portrait, a divided self both exquisitely sensitive to the dilemmas of portraying the social positioning of others in the court around him and himself within that structure, a self that is both inside and outside, one that is self-aware as a social being.[12] (The radiographic analyses of the paintings by Nash and Brown provide further detailing to Elias's reading of the patronage and social relations figured in the painting.)

To recap: *Las Meninas* is used by Foucault, Crary, Mitchell, Alpers, and Elias (supported now also by the radiographic analyses of Nash and Brown) to think about the interface or transition between two epistemes, both of which coexist uneasily within the painting. For Foucault, the painting negotiates between two historical epistemes (the Renaissance's play of resemblances, allegories, symbolisms, similitudes, and resonances; and the modernist, Cartesian, graphical techniques of mappings, triangulations, and surveying). For Svetlana Alpers, the painting negotiates between two regional styles of seeing/painting, that of the Italian discovery of perspectival drafting, of viewing the world as if looking through a window; and that of the Dutch mapping, of viewing the world as a filled surface (Alpers 1983). For Elias, the painting negotiates between a Cartesian isolated ego, and a more modern subjectivity constituted by a series of techniques of distancing and mediation, of learning to see oneself as others see one, of the civilizing process of detachment and self-awareness of being a social self (Elias 1983).

The transition from this Cartesian ego has to do with a series of changes that are challenges to the nature of how we think ethically, how we perceive, and how we judge. The autonomous ego is not just a simplification or regulative ideal (perceptually, cognitively, sociologically, psychodynamically). The dilemma is a serious one: if we abandon the autonomous ego on descriptive grounds, what does this do to the notion of ethical responsibility as a regulative ideal, and who, or what organization, can then be held accountable? For this we need to turn to our second emblematic scene, and the questions that it raises about the unstable transition from, or oscillation back and forth between, modernist frameworks and the postmodern conditions of knowledge. A parallel set of questions could be raised about the Freudian ego, and they have been by anthropology, Frankfurt school critical theory, and some of the late-twentieth-century French theory about embodied-mimetic desire.[13] In both cases — that of the liable and ethically responsible agent as autonomous ego or as self-conscious Freudian self, and that of the accountable organization, corporate, civil, religious, or economic — part of the answer has to do with the techniques of self-reflexive and comparative judgment from a position inside the picture.

Virtual Reality Surgical Robotics and the Scene of Postmodernity

The picture of Ian Hunter's lab places the active agent, the surgeon, inside the components of an interactive system. It also takes us into the debates about computer-mediated informatics, simulations as research environments, and virtual reality enhancements of the human sensorium; and into the microworlds of nanotechnology, molecular engineering, and the space of emergent self-organizing systems. Most critically, it leads us to explore the shift into technologically empowered mimetic faculties: from viewing pictures as passive representations to interacting with visual gazes and views as communicative and as consequential for movement in the material world.

The picture of Ian Hunter's lab becomes a potential microcosm for planetary connectivity: third-generation fiber-optic cables, geostationary communication satellites, orbital satellites that monitor environment and security, world geodetic and geographic information systems for measurement and location, the new Raytheon-built surveillance system of ground, air, and satellite monitors for the Brazilian Amazon, Internet, satellite television, transnational film circuits and advertising. Or it becomes a macrocosm for Hunter's fantasy-goal of micromotion robots that might someday scavenge around inside our blood vessels, and for already available swallowable cameras to supplement colonoscopy. It becomes a mesocosm for the MIT Media Lab's vision of wearable, implantable, or injectable computers and smart appliances and materials. Most critically, it becomes one vehicle for including within perception an awareness of the multiple perceptual processes, the physiological heterogeneity of neurological, electrodynamic, and photonic inputs that cannot be contained within the space of the image, that overflow representations, both for the individual and for collectivities.

Walter Benjamin has become in recent years a renewed predecessor-facilitator for thinking about these challenges (Buck-Morss 1989, 1993; Miriam Hansen 1987, 1993; Mark Hansen 2000; Rabate 2002; Taussig 1992, 1993; Weigel 1996). Benjamin took film as the exemplary site in the early

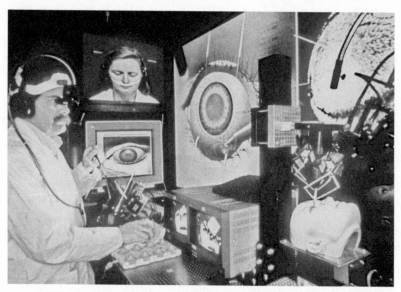

28. Ian Hunter in his lab at MIT: a robotic and virtual reality eye surgery system to enable finer haptic and visual feedback control than possible with a surgeon's unaided eye and hand. Photograph by Dr. Serge Lafontaine and Tilemachos Doukoglou.

twentieth century of the shift from the passive image of the photograph and the dialectical image of advertising to the movement of shocks in film sequences, each image coming in the wake of the aftershocks of the previous one, not unlike the physical, visual, sonic, and olfactory shocks of moving through a modern, heterogeneous urban mass of vehicles and pedestrians. As opposed to the hardening of the body, the fascist-modernist response, Benjamin and the surrealists first looked to technology as a way to provide the fragile human body with a looser network of protections, evoked by the humor and parody of Mickey Mouse as an icon of the technological, and of his ears as the reels of a film projector (Miriam Hansen 1993; Mark Hansen 2002; Rickels 1991). The cinema becomes a gymnasium of the senses, where the modernist, Freudian, reflective mode of processing trauma through the mystic pad of the psyche (repression, sublimation, displacement, secondary revision) is loosened, and instead the human physiology is retrained in a new technological environment. For Benjamin, this is an adjustment not just of the individual but also of the social collectivity. In World War I, "Human multitudes, gases, electrical forces were hurled . . . high-frequency currents coursed through the landscape . . . aerial space and ocean depths thundered with propellers" (quoted in Mark Hansen 2002: 254). Photography, radio, gramophone, and film in the interwar years proliferate the shock experience, the "spiral of sensory alienation, phantasmagoria, and violence" (Miriam Hansen 1993: 38) and require protection and intervention at those technologically innervated/embodied levels that are at least partly provided by the gaps, time lags, and disjunctions that new technologies produce.

This recognition of the human physiology always being in interactive coevolution with the technological media within which it operates helps undo the hypostatized fears about the "posthuman." As Catherine Waldby so nicely puts it, the phrase "posthuman" should be understood as "an effect of the slippage" in "naturalizing this network of production . . . moments of disjuncture which leave this technogenic network exposed and available for critical analysis" (Waldby 2000: 20). She is writing of the digital Visible Human Project and notes that it "is only one of many such moments, which are thrown up by abrupt innovations, and the lag between an innovation and its domestication." The critical challenge is to not just allow the coevolution of society and technology to be driven by market or totalizing political incentives, but to keep the relationship open to a rich diversity of interests, needs, desires, and democratic feedback mechanisms.

The picture of Ian Hunter's lab, then, can perhaps lead us to reflect on our current technoscientific life worlds as ones that increasingly draw their models from the submillimeter worlds of molecular biology, bioengineering, biochemistry, biophysics, and other growing interdisciplinary spaces that shift attention from modernist mechanics to postmodern biological and self-organizing complexities. These involve epistemological shifts, retraining the hands of surgeons, shifting from brute interventions to nurturing processes of repair and growth, using tools of informated touch. They involve these for medicine in dealing with bodies, but also for society in dealing with what Ulrich Beck has called "second-order modernization" or Jean-François Lyotard has called the "postmodern" conditions of knowledge.

Bodies: From Mechanics/Physics to Biology/Life Sciences
Down into the microworlds, extending the human sensorium. Twentieth-century physics already posed some of the counterintuitive challenges of modeling and visualizing the very small worlds of quantum mechanics (see Gilmore 1995 for an amusing contemporary spoof, and McCormmach 1982 for a novelization by a historian of physics of the difficult conceptual gestalt switch from classical to modern physics). These challenges exist on the levels of both theory and experimentation: high-energy physics has provided a fascinating methodological dialogue between "image and logic," between those most persuaded by capturing pictures of "golden events" (seeing is believing), and those most persuaded only by statistical patterns that through

redundancy confirm that what is seen is neither artifact of the instrument nor a chance fluke (Galison 1997). This dialogue has been materially embodied in changes in the instrumentation of experimental systems that allowed first one, then the other, style of confirmation to prevail (ibid.).

Today, however, molecular engineering provides a second kind of gestalt switch from the dominance of physics to biology, from a mechanical world, mechanical metaphors, and mechanical frames of reference, into a fascination with "biological machines, machines of nature," ecological interactions, biophysics, biochemistry, and processes of emergent complexity in micro- and nano-strategic terrains only newly available to human scrutiny and intervention, and requiring new tools between those developed by traditional physics and biology. Between the physics of the very small (individual photons hitting individual atoms) and biology at the cell level and above is a strategic terrain of "emergence" where proteins fold in various precise ways to form the machineries of life, where the difference in folding of beta amyloid might make the difference between having or not having Alzheimer's disease, and where not only can physicists help solve biological puzzles, but the self-organizing systems of biology might lead to understanding physics conundrums such as superconductivity. Says Robert Laughlin, winner of the 1998 Nobel Prize in physics, "Biology has provided physics with its new frontier"; and Hans Frauenhofer quips, "Ask not what physics can do for biology; ask what biology can do for physics" (Cook 2002).

On a slightly more macro-scale, computer-assisted surgical systems present some of the challenges of these new worlds. The Da Vinci Surgical System, developed by Intuitive Surgical of Mountain View, California, for instance, places the surgeon in an InSite™ 3-D Vision System and gives her or him remote-controlled EndoWrist™ instruments with seven degrees of freedom, and the promise, now confirmed by growing numbers of successful operations, that less-invasive cardiac and other surgeries can be done through tiny holes in the body. The surgeon operates at a remove from the patient's physical body inside a workstation and headset, coordinating and giving orders to assistants and nurses, and must learn an entirely new set of initially counterintuitive, counter physiologically trained motor skills (like the inverted or mirror geometry of learning to back up a trailer, but with each hand doing a different trailer): it is an exhausting and slow learning curve (Satava 2002). Other new surgical systems allow craniotomies to be performed by a neurosurgeon standing inside a large magnetic resonance imaging system with an overhead monitor refreshing and updating images of the operation's progress and guiding the surgeon's delicate work (Jolesz

1997, 1998; Grimson et al. 1999; Wells et al. 1996). A CyberKnife™ allows a 6MeV linear accelerator on a robot with six degrees of freedom to irradiate at a number of different angles to reduce X-ray dose to normal tissue. "Holomers" in the future may bring together digitized patient images and medical records for preoperation rehearsals and postoperation outcomes analysis (Satava 2002).

The slide of Ian Hunter's robotic virtual-reality eye surgery system captures some of these elements in a mise-en-scène that nicely parallels the geometric play of gazes in *Las Meninas*. Listening to Hunter provides a sense of how both the small scale and the effort to model biological rather than mechanical processes provide challenges for the biomedical engineer. He begins by quoting the punning quip of physicist Richard Feynman in 1959 that "there's plenty of room at the bottom," as an emblem for Hunter's own work in the "vast area of the submillimeter range . . . in building instrumentation, both sensing systems as well as actuators, that allow us to move . . . from hair in the millimeter range, to E. coli in the micrometer range, to nucleotides/amino acids in the nanometer range, and then down to the atomic level" (Hunter 1995). This is a world where both precision and speed matter:

> Quite often it turns out that perhaps you want to move over a millimeter range in the microworld, but you may want to position with the positioning resolution of a nanometer that you've got a displacement dynamic range of a million to one and that really raises some very interesting instrumentation challenges. And these challenges arise both at the actuator level — how do we construct actuators that can move accurately over this very large dynamic range — and also how can we build displacement transfuses and other sensors that allow us to determine where we are. Now I might add that we build devices that move by less than an angstrom down here (nanometer range) and one of the other instrumentation challenges that arises is how do we not only move with great precision, but how do we do it quickly, because it turns out that when you get down into this world, some things occur very rapidly. (Hunter 1995)

Nature's "actuators" range from the flagella of bacteria:

> — nature's only rotary motor . . . a proton actuator which actually spins up to three hundred revolutions per second. That is incredibly fast, and it propels this machine at fifteen body lengths per second. Now that's equivalent to taking an automobile, which is about, we'll say four meters long, and propelling it at sixty meters per second, or over 200 kilometers per hour in water. So it is really quite magnificent and quite humbling

. . . Now I like to think that this was a machine where early R&D started about 3,500 million years ago —

to ubiquitous actinmycin actuators:

Everything from fleas up utilize the actinmycin motor, probably developed about 550 million years ago. Consider the water flea, measuring a millimeter or two: It is a very impressive machine . . . I don't think there is any way by the time I die that we will have achieved artificially the ability to generate machines with the dimensions of one micrometer, but if we can generate autonomous life-like machines having total outside diameters perhaps of one millimeter which carry their own energy supply, their own effectively computing elements and sensors and actuators, I'll be very happy.

It's not just precision and speed, but there is a difference in design between the machines produced by the industrial revolution and the machines in nature:

At the molecular level the machinery that drives these huge machines [dinosaurs] is basically identical to that in a flea, in a mouse, and in your own muscles. . . . There is no reason, by analogy with nature, that one should not be creating large machines like this. If we consider the muscle cell itself, we see the equivalent of hundreds and hundreds of little molecular pistons, if you like . . . [showing a slide of a skeletal muscle fiber]. The diameter here is about 15 micrometers, and each of these muscle cells is made up of smaller entities, the myofibrils, which are a bundle of even smaller elements, the myafiliaments, which are really a bundle of individual molecules, and it is believed that every two micrometers or so we have about three hundred of these force generating elements here, the myacin heads, which reach out attached to the actin, generate about one kilo newton of force and moved by ten to fifteen nanometers. So we have a linear stepping motor here and what I find fascinating is that here down at this molecular level we have a machine where every two micrometers you have effectively a V300. So the way that nature has generated large machines is not just to scale things up, it basically instead uses a very large number of cooperating microelements.

A corollary is that the instrumentation to study at this scale is quite different from the world of large-scale robotics. Hunter really is on the trail of building micromotion robots that might someday scavenge around inside our blood vessels.

Quoting Hunter at length here is not meant uncritically to buy into all of his irrepressible enthusiasm, but rather to sketch worlds we are only beginning to explore. As the novelist Richard Powers warns in the context of another, similar, new technology: "In such a vat, people might create molecules to do anything. The team found itself staring at a universal chemical assembly plant at the level of the human cell. . . . The [capital to bankroll a biotech company] has been compounding forever, waiting for a chance to revenge its earnings" (1998: 355). The verb "revenge" is key here in his morally nuanced vision of processes of gain that redistribute in unexpected places their underside or counterpart losses. His novel *Gain* is built around such metaphors of the *pharmakon* (cure/poison): soap as peculiar filmic surfaces or interfaces that redistribute grime/clean, purity/pollution, germs/health; anesthetic agents of pain/comfort; cosmetics of beauty/biological action; pesticides of gardening/toxicity; capital as solvent/contractor; hype and advertising as illusion/creator of desire, possibility, and motivation; perhaps gain itself as playing across capital and Gaia; and chemistry as intentional/ unintentional human actions rearranging the inorganic and now the organic world.

If computer-integrated, virtual reality, and telesurgical systems integrate touch, vision, and informatics, they and other new visualization medical technologies (and their analogues in other fields) can shed light on the social and ethical issues entangled in developing informatics and simulation technologies. One of the important claims of contemporary visual technologies is that we can increasingly leave behind the "brute" technologies of the past with the assistance of progressively less invasive visualizing technologies. In biology in the past, many of the visual prostheses of science, such as the microscope, have often required fixing techniques that kill the object being observed. Visual techniques such as x rays or radioactive tags, in their early stages, involved danger both to the objects under observation and to the investigators and surroundings.

In medicine and the life sciences, the promise is to switch from brute technologies (the slash, burn, and poison cancer technologies of surgery, radiation, and chemotherapy) to less invasive surgeries, angiogenesis, tissue regeneration (albeit sometimes shifting the excruciating dilemmas of life and death to new places rather than eliminating death, pain, or suffering). New less invasive technologies are important in many fields: testing materials fatigue (e.g., of airplanes) rather than literally putting the airplane under stress; simulation models standing in for nuclear tests rather than actually setting off tests with their radioactive waste; teaching anatomy substituting the digitized Visible Human for dissection of scarce corpses (an ambiguous example given the mode of production of the Visible Humans and the debate over the relative merits of using these digitized cadavers versus hands-on experience).

The dangers of using "informed touch" data sets in these ways include an increasing shift from personhood that is more obviously under the control of their individual carriers, to unseen interactive data banks and doppelgängers. At least two decades of concern have focused on the dangers of credit, or medical risk, profiles that can be manipulated without the knowledge of "empirical individuals," affecting their life chances (through access to insurance, health care, employment, and to do so on population-based calculations for state or commercial reasons [Burnham 1983; Perin 1988; Garfinkle 2000]). Some more recent concern has been raised about the integration of medical records beyond the control of patients or individual doctors, and about the surgeon in the Ian Hunter or Da Vinci style surgical system being reduced from the center of control, judgment, and action to being a technician within a system governed by protocols of best practices, decision trees, cost concerns, and other inputs established elsewhere within the system. (This sort of reduction is under way in the field of psychiatry under the decision tree rules of managed care and insurance [Donald 2001].)

The Human Genome Project—and its successors with snps (single nucleotide polymorphisms), functional genomics, or proteonomic high-speed throughput machines; and in efforts by companies such as deCode, Ardais, or First Genomic Trust to link medical records, genetic information, and genealogies—is but the most recent of statistical databases that have been collected since the eighteenth century for use first by the state and now by corporations, first for economic and social policy and now for medical research and health care profits. Most critical is the increasing recognition that the Human Genome Project is not just a descriptive tool but a tool for reading ahead, projecting and shaping the decisions for constructing the future (functional genomics, personalized medicine, reformatting everyone into a matrix of potential patient-customers, and reworking the actuarial bases of insurance and biopolitical policies).

The promise is to be able to move from given worlds to literally writing new biologies with genetic, biochemical, proteonomic techniques, blocking or renewing biochemical pathways, reversing disease processes, regenerating tissue, enhancing capacities. These interventions can thereby also intensify ecological, developmental, and evolutionary dilemmas and questions. Such virtual technologies (on the verge, providing menus of alternative potentials that can be activated) are not altogether unlike the ancient Persian mythic idea of Jamshid's cup, that mystical wine cup in which the future is mirrored.

But today's transformed, informed touch version of Jamshid's cup is the fascination with the idea of *codes* such as the genetic code, of the increasing production of technology through *testing* alternative outcomes, and of scientific discovery through active writing with biological, chemical, and physical *experimental systems.*

Parallel to the genealogies of today's databases (with their potential powerful interlinkages, surveillance and control, discrimination and new forms of inequality) in the collection of social statistics and what Foucault traces as the development of biopolitics since the eighteenth century are the anatomy/dissection genealogies of contemporary virtual models of the body and the various scanning technologies of seeing into the body's interior more clearly than the scalpel permits (x rays, sonograms, magnetic resonance imaging or MRI, positron emission tomography or PET, computed tomography or CT, two-photon x rays). The increasing use of dissection since the eighteenth century involved a complicated ethical involvement with death ("To examine the causes of life, we must first have recourse to death," says Mary Shelley in *Frankenstein*), not least because cadavers were obtained from the hangman, connecting the worlds of public penal codes with the worlds of the surgeon, the worlds of the sheltered with those of the unquiet dead. The Visible Human Project is but the latest of these life's doubles or simulations, more real than the real, and disputably more practical.[14]

The complex social, ethical, and political entanglements are historically fascinating and constitute the grounds for democratic, socially responsible use of science and technology. Another eighteenth-century genealogy is also critical here: the debates about the two kinds of images: those that are in principle illustrations, substitutable for, or subsumable under, verbal arguments or descriptions, versus those that are in principle not describable verbally, but are constructions of objects in their own right.

With technologies like the Visible Human Project, genetic engineering, and many of the tools of molecular biology and biomedical engineering, we live now in a world of constructivism in the marked sense. Molecular biology, argues Hans-Jörg Rheinberger, has moved from a world of "discovery" to one where new knowledge is gained instead by literally "writing" with, or manipulating, genetic material. (An active molecular biologist as well as a leading historian of science, Rheinberger is also a translator into German of Jacques Derrida. Part of Rheinberger's interest in Derrida stemmed from Derrida's fascination in *Of Grammatology*, and in an unpublished year of seminars, with the work of molecular biologist François Jacob.) The physical sciences generally, argues Karin Knorr-Cetina, have moved from field sciences (the terrain of observation in situ) to laboratory sciences in which both nature and the social are reconfigured so as to be more efficiently manipulable. It is not only that one works, in biology, with DNA spliced by polymerase chain reaction (PCR) techniques, and, in physics, with particle streams generated in high-energy accelerators, that is, with reconfigured bits of nature. The laboratory teams, divisions of labor, and protocols of inquiry and repair are quite unlike the life worlds outside the laboratory. They too are reconfigured forms shaped to be generative of specified forms of output. Indeed, there is a three-stage transition from field sciences to laboratory sciences to simulation sciences. (*Las Meninas* in this sense stands in the transition between the first and second; Ian Hunter's lab between the second and the third.)

Simulations are technologies that can transcend linear reason, extending control over time and temporalities, introducing feedback loops, hypertextual linkages, and other touches of both hyperreality and the future-anterior, all features of the world that have been incorporated into the tool kits of those who wish to deal with a world of increasingly complex interactions.

Societies: From First-Order to Second-Order Modernities
Increasing global interaction with rigidly modern institutions leads, argues Ulrich Beck (1986/1992) among others, to a disjunction between the ways in which scientists experience the risks their manipulations generate, and the ways other groups of actors working with other configurations of the same materials experience risk. In the examples of industrial chemical accidents like Bhopal or Chernobyl, or the legacies of toxic wastes like Minamata or Love Canal, it has become routine for governments to deny that the accidents could have happened, or that their effects could be as serious as the injured populations claim, in part because of the disjunction between what is the case in the controlled conditions of a laboratory and what is the case in a production facility, as well as through pure denial and fear of the political and financial liabilities of owning up. Beck argues that we are now moving into a new social formation, a new phase of capitalist modernization, in which the production of risk takes on a heightened saliency, such that corporate strategies are involved in minimizing liability (which they do among other things by publicizing risks of alternatives to their own products, as in the case of the nuclear industry playing up the ozone hole), politicians feel that regulatory actions must be undertaken, and citizen groups increasingly demand oversight of both industry and government. Beck suggests these are among the forces that are moving society toward "reflexive" or "second-order" modernization: institutional forms that are no longer brittlely bu-

reaucratized along rational organizational chart lines but foster feedback from multiple perspectives and experiential positions.

Of critical importance to his account of "risk society" and "reflexive modernization" is the centrality of the sciences and their (recognition of) indeterminacies. Risks of radiation levels, toxins in the water and food, illness-causing bacteria and viruses, and so on are not available to ordinary perception. As with the surgical procedures in Ian Hunter's lab, science and instrumentation are necessary mediations; understanding their uses and limitations comes along with them. Risk, calculated probabilities, ambiguity, indeterminacy, and approximation models are part of this world. Moreover, the actuarial statistics on which accountability and liability for risk in the industrial era were based no longer apply in a world where strict causation is hard to determine amid multiple accretions of causalities, long-term effects are even harder to foresee, things cannot be tested before use, and thus the legal maxim "polluter pays" is hard to enforce.

Both Beck and Mark Poster (1990) sketch out different ways in which our currently emerging social formation may be quite different from that of our industrial, modern past. Beck points to social institutions that increasingly must coordinate complexly decentralized and multiple sources of information, thus negotiating among the partial and sometimes conflicting expertises and experiences of different segments of society—a set of institutions he calls reflexive modern, second-order modernization, or the second modernity, a modernization of the increasingly overly brittle, rationalized institutions of the first modernities. Poster looks to the media of communication as reworking the structures of social relations.

Drawing on the work of Marshall McLuhan, Walter Ong, and Jack Goody, Poster sketches out the heuristic contrasts through the three-stage transformations of self, culture, and social relations. In oral, face-to-face societies, the self is embedded in multiple, reinforcing communal relations, and language takes on dense mythic and symbolic sets of correspondences (not unlike Foucault's notion of the premodern episteme as composed around relations of similitude). Speech constitutes subjects and subjectivity as members of a community with all the warmth and coerciveness of shared experience and moral systems. With literacy, the argument goes, the self can be disembedded from its social relations, and analytic reason and autonomy of judgment can be fostered. Writing allows memory to be stored, externalized, and recalled for comparison and analysis. This is the period of the rational, autonomous ego hypostatized by Descartes. It is the period of representation, of sign systems, and correspondence theories of language. In contrast to speech, print constitutes subjects and subjectivity as rational, autonomous egos who can make judgments logically in relative isolation. Both Walter Ong and Poster suggest that electronically mediated culture—what Ong calls secondary oral culture—constructs the self, social relations, and reason in ways radically different as literacy reworks oral cultures.

Just as most cultures in the past millennium have been neither purely oral nor purely literate—rather, there has been a stratified literacy, with power being distributed differentially through access and control of these media—so too today, electronic media add a new layer of stratification and differential power. In contrast to face-to-face speech and print, Poster suggests, electronically mediated language replaces the community with dispersed interlocutors, undermines the referentiality necessary for the subjectivity of analytic literate egos, and instead invites subjects to try on alternative identities and masks. (The writer Samuel Delany [1998] makes an analogous point about the relation between literacy and analytic reason from the point of view of a postliterate, computer-mediated information society. He argues that we live not in an information society but in a misinformation society, precisely because misinformation is more simple and stable than information, and like Gresham's law of bad money driving out good money, misinformation easily drives out information. Print has the advantage, Delany argues, of stabilizing [mis]information so that it can be analyzed, compared, and evaluated. It lasts longer than the ephemeral or speeding flows of rumor, allegation, unchecked citation, or information simply out of context.)

Poster's most interesting chapter is on television ads as an instantiation of this argument about what he calls information society. Television ads, he says, ventriloquize audiences, simulate contexts, and interpellate viewers via constantly changing language games. No longer is it plausible to criticize ads as if viewers simplemindedly believed them (ads as falsehoods), or as if viewers are irrationally or subliminally manipulated (ads as playing on unconscious desire). Television ads are no longer representations or figures of realism. The commodity object in television ads is not the one viewers think they will take home ("prosaic, efficient, but forgettable"), but rather, as Poster puts it, "the television ad communicates at a level other than the instrumental which is placed in brackets" (1990: 63). It is rather the magical, desirable, exciting "white knight" of Johnson's floor wax, the hyperreal, or, with Baudrillard, the pleasure of the shift from economic categories (use or exchange values) to the play of signifiers which attracts attention and pleasure.

The point is not that there is no relation between the play of signifiers and the world of referents but rather that the old analytic, rational ego is no longer so singular as a previous generation of disciplinarians and moralists argued, that, for instance, informatics are generating doppelgänger personae for us in data banks (medical records, insurance records, credit records, etc.) that can be manipulated without our knowledge, that the information that constitutes our worlds flows around us in ways analogous to, yet different from, the capital flows that also abstract us from our exchange and production relations with one another. This too is not a sudden change but one that began at least with newspapers shifting from being organs of particular parties or points of view and printing long essays to being collages of bits of unconnected information juxtaposed in columns and boxes, "all the news that's fit to print" (Terdiman 1985).

To recap: Virtuality is not what is new in the visuality or virtual reality of the robotic surgical system. Virtuality is a feature of art. Art, Lévi-Strauss has suggested, is halfway between science and myth or magic. Myth builds structures with the remains of events through bricolage and metaphorical substitutions. If Clouet paints a lace collar that in reduced dimensions gives an intelligibility of a lace collar, science or engineering would instead build a loom to reproduce the lace, a metonymic process. Art usually operates through small-scale modeling (Michelangelo's painting on the Sistine Chapel ceiling is large, but not in relation to its subject, the End of Time; a larger-than-life statue may gain its aesthetic power from what appears from a distance as a large rock being cut down into human form). Even if there is not miniaturization in the dimensions of size, it works through art giving up dimensions (volume in painting, smell in sculpture). The compensation for the renunciation of sensible dimensions is the acquisition of intelligible ones. Art involves a kind of supplementarity, because there are always multiple solutions, such that the observer is presented with a set of permutations of which the given piece of art is but one, a choice which is a modification of the result to which another solution would have led (Lévi-Strauss 1962/1966: 22–30). What the line of thought from Benjamin adds is the movement from photograph to dialectical image to serial shocks to, and innervation of, the nervous system through the aftershocks of film images one upon the next in both cinema and other technologies of immersive moving pictures.

The virtual reality of the robotic surgical system may signal three quite different characteristics coming on-line: being able to manipulate the world at dimensions much smaller than normal human capacities of perception (haptic feedback, micro- and nano-dimensions); being able "to write" with biological materials; being able to nurture biological processes rather than destroy by intervening. There are sociological analogues of these scientific tool characterizations: being able to interact with the world through informated touch interfaces; being able to expand our technologically em-powered range of sensation, sense, and sensibility; being able to model and govern complexity both with dynamic matrices and with self-organizing simulations. Most critically, there are analogues in the arena of delibera-tive, democratic governance that are now being developed through patient groups, new social movements, citizen action organizations, and cross-national alliances, for which the Internet and other computer-networked infrastructures have provided the same kind of tipping point as Walter Benjamin saw in film early in the past century.

Reprise of Themes Carried on the Fiber-Optic: Ethnographic Challenges across Two Epistemologies of Science

What is the place of ethnography in this postmodern world of reflexive or second-order modernization? Ethnography has always been oriented toward the production of heuristically valuable social theory, drawing on — test-ing and contesting — older social theory grounded in older societal hori-zons, and claiming to build new theory empirically, comparatively, with at-tention to different worlds that languages and cultures produce, as well as to local social structures and their embedded (and conflictual) position in global systems. Anthropological ethnographies of science and technology — often in contrast to the "new sociology of science" monographs of the 1980s, and already by reflex from earlier ethnographic experiences in trac-ing out social formations — are attuned to the multiple perspectives nec-essary to gain an understanding of reconfigured sites such as the changed context of research in biology under conditions of venture capital fund-ing outpacing those of older public or academic sources (Gottweis 1998; Rabinow 1995; Werth 1994); the different class, religious, or cultural re-actions to amniocentesis predictions of Down's syndrome (Rapp 1990); or the feedback among media, clinic, laboratory, courtroom, and other sites in the circulation and mutation of scientific imagery, metaphors, and under-standings (Martin 1987, 1994; Dumit 1995). The role of the ethnographer is one less of explorer than of translator and facilitator of dialogue among segments of society, perhaps to improve communication, but also to clarify difference, interests, and issues at stake, particularly in the play of differ-ent (genres of) representations (ads, narratives, scenarios), social forms, and frames of ethics, accountability, and responsibility.

As a mnemonic for this I like the first approximation notion of "two kinds of science" or two epistemologies of science, working as necessary supplements to each other. Both Claude Lévi-Strauss (1962/1966) and Ulrich Beck provide variants of this notion. Call one narrative storytelling of experiences, while the other is the search for patterns and explanatory structures that are breaks with normal experience, that can only be arrived at through the prostheses of instruments, experiments, models, simulations, and other technological and scientific media.[15] This is, I think, more helpful than the more abstract and decontextualized philosopher's notion of an "analytic of finitude" as the tension between what is known "by society" at large over time and knowledge production from within bodies in particular times or places, even if the latter notions of "situated knowledge" fuse together the anthropologist Clifford Geertz's notions of "thick description" and "local knowledge."[16]

In the core course, each module had woven through it a visual thread; each module could be carried on the fiber-optic cable both live (ethnographically) and archivally (historiographically). Among the questions for each of the modules are the relation of the visual to temporalities and critique; to scenes of representation and virtual reality; to sociologies, psychologies, periodizations, and multiple worlds; and to politics, aesthetics, and ethics:

1. Temporalities and critique. Much of contemporary theory operates as a contrastive-comparative commentary on prior eras of modernity (postmodernity is a sender-receiver relationship between prior, contemporary, and emergent modernities, not, as some would have it, a forgetting of the past, any more than previous eras have selectively forgotten their pasts). In terms of theories about the visual, many of the contemporary arguments were presaged in the eighteenth century (Stafford 1996) and generate interesting questions about the difference between visualizations that are illustrative of verbal arguments versus ones that either are constructions difficult to put into words (the eighteenth-century sense) or are new simulated worlds with which we have had little prior experience (the late-twentieth-century sense). Epistemologically, one might ask, to use artificial intelligence lingo, whether there is a mode of "diagrammatic reasoning," different from grammatical-verbal logic (Glasgow, Narayan, and Chandrasekaran 1995). This historically conscious, doubled imagination of the visual between contemporary and past debates provides potentials for cultural critique, for redemption of utopian hopes attached to older worn-down technologies (as suggested by Walter Benjamin), but also for mapping the ways in which new visual technologies create a different sociological and even neurophysiological environment for perception, for reason, and for interaction. Such cultural critique is necessary to counter the process of erasure of history, politics,

and economy that some forms of simulation encourage, of reentering social responsibility, social and cultural accountability, and individual ethics.

2. Scenes of representation and virtual reality. We began with the now classic discussions of Velázquez's *Las Meninas* as a scene of the entry into the "modern," against a contemporary parallel scene — a virtual surgical robotics scene of entry into the "postmodern" — as a way of drawing us out of the books of the past and into the wet and dry laboratories of the present. Involved here are shifts both within the technosciences from field sciences, to lab sciences, to simulation sciences, but also within the larger institutional or sociological formations from those with which classical sociological theory dealt (Marx, Weber, Durkheim, Mannheim, Merton, Freud, the Frankfurt school of Adorno, Horkheimer, and Benjamin), to the kinds of formations that go under the names of reflexive modernization, postmodernity, late capitalism, and risk society and foreground the role of visual technologies or virtual ones in Deleuze's (1985) sense of multiplying the number of signifying systems that convey information. Culturally, Lyotard's idea of the "postmodern conditions of knowledge" points to a series of "inabilities" *(impouvoir)* to contain the incommensurabilities in our practices or agreements. This condition "ensures that the language one ends up with in thinking is never the same as the one from which one starts" (Rajchman 1998: 4), a condition that, as Lyotard memorably put it, means we tend nowadays not to deny but "to place in brackets" the old metanarratives that no longer provide the legitimation, certainty, or political will they were once able to mobilize. Increasingly we are pressed to pay attention not only to local contexts of knowledge but to the intensifying multiplicities of values and points of view that inhabit the same social spaces (Lyotard 1979/1984).

The visual provides key loci for many of these discussions: Lyotard stresses the difference between the figural and the textual, part of a family-of-resemblance set of problematics, analogous to the diagrammatic and grammatical of computer science, or the eighteenth-century visual as illustration versus visual as construction. Cinema and television are key exemplars for images that move: Deleuze stresses the multiplication of signifying dimensions that modern cinema, for example, deploys over pre–World War I "classical" cinemas; Virilio stresses the ways cinema and other visual technologies detach people from their traditional places, move them to the big city, and mark them for destruction in war; Poster stresses the way television models new relations among sender and audience, self and judgment, roles and communities; and Benjamin starts an ongoing discussion about the role of cinema and subsequent immersive technologies (simulators, robotic surgical systems, computer-assisted virtual experience [CAVE] rooms, pioneered at the University of Illinois and Brown University, and memorably novelized in Richard Powers's *Plowing the Dark*) as a tool of redisciplining and empowering the body, perception, and judgment, both on the individual and on the collective social level.

3. Sociologies, psychologies, periodizations, and multiple worlds. We began with the schematic arguments about the mode of information in contrast to previous communication modes (Poster 1990; see also Tyler 1978, 1987; Lee 1998), then complicated these a bit with efforts to think communication in terms of its machinic, material, and systemic assemblages (Kittler 1986, 1985/1990), as well as in the ways in which the figural and visual do not merely represent but index ways of thinking otherwise (Benjamin; Lyotard).[17] These arguments move from simple preliminary sociologies, historical periodizations, and psychologies toward more interesting multiple contemporary temporalities and spatialities. Involved are the arguments over the effects of the computer, film, and television, and the digitalization of information — the speed of disseminating fragments of information and altering images — on analytic abilities, notions of self, as well as constructions of sensibilities about society and community.

4. Politics, aesthetics, and ethics. In ecology and environmental issues, a number of the foregoing themes "organically" come together in an unavoidable matrix of questions about the interconnections between politics, aesthetics, and ethics. The shift of both sociologies and modalities of reason (the shift away from fetishizing the individual; the need for simulation to handle complexity) is put on clear display. Face-to-face public-sphere politics (grassroots organizing and its dilemmas), Internet connectivity, the state with its national and transnational regulatory politics — all reemerge as needed checks on, and potential synergies with, one another. Here are found arguments about the roles of images in creating a new sensitivity to environmental issues ("Planet Earth" satellite photos; "nuclear photographers" rephotographing the irradiated and toxic landscapes of the American West; techniques of mapping to track environmental problems). Here are also the older roles of visual imagery in written texts (such as Charles Darwin's skill in persuading readers of arguments through painting verbal pictures that they could "see," even though it would take another generation to provide the mechanisms of genetic reproduction that we now associate with the evolutionary synthesis (Krasner 1992). But even in the hardest of the natural sciences, such as high-energy physics, the struggle between logic and image (Galison 1997) reveals the competition between rival groups of scientists, research programs, and epistemological preferences. The law, similarly but differently than science, is another ethnographic site where images are ac-

cepted as skeptically as possible lest they mislead through their illusory per-
suasiveness (Mnookin 1999; Golan 1999; Dumit 1995). Indeed, one of the features of the postal relation between modernity and postmodernity is the use
of the cinema to train our senses to the "powers of the false" in what the
technologically naive viewer might experience as persuasive verisimilitude
(Deleuze 1985; Abbas 1992; see also chapter 7 in this volume).

II. Modules for a Science, Technology, and Society Curriculum: STS@the-Turn_[]ooo.mit.edu

In spring 1996, we held an off-campus faculty retreat, with the help of a team of professional facilitators, to consider proposals for restructuring the graduate program. The protocols for the ritual process of this retreat — and the various productive and unproductive tensions the retreat was designed to negotiate and overcome — can be read elsewhere (M. Fischer 1996). The results included an architecture for the graduate program composed of a modular core course to help forge the interdisciplinary ethos of the program; a second tier of foundation courses to provide in-depth disciplinary tools (historiography and historical methods, social theory and ethnographic methods, history of science, history of technology, and history of medicine); and a third tier of topical graduate seminars. A desire for practica was endorsed that would place graduate students in science and engineering laboratories to gain hands-on experience, especially for those who come into the program without such experience.

This cross-field desire extended in two more general directions: the positioning of STS vis-à-vis the discussions at MIT and elsewhere of the changing structure of education for engineers and applied scientists, and the changing relationships between ethnographers and their colleagues in the sciences and engineering (see M. Fischer 1995a; M. Fischer and Marcus 1999; and for a similar exploration at Virginia Tech, see Downey 1998).

The core course had several key functions, but most central was to construct a framework for cross-discipline intelligibility by identifying an evolving reference canon of texts to which first-year students would be introduced, and which advanced students and faculty would constantly rework with new commentary and insight. The emergent nature of this textual canon would be constantly renewed by placing emphasis on newly published texts each year that were helping to define the cutting-edge debates in the STS field, reading them in dialogue with older canonical texts. The core course was to frame substantive areas of expertise and inquiry as a plat-form for more detailed attention in advanced seminars, research programs, dissertations, and workshops.

Toward this end, the architecture of the core course was built around modules three to four weeks in length. Modules would allow more in-depth and cumulative discussion than a "parade of stars" class where each faculty would lead only a session or two. The agreement was that each module would be led by at least two faculty from differing disciplines. The point was to de-velop richly informed interdisciplinary discussions, that is, to learn how to ask questions and elicit complementary and troubling information across disciplines, to bring the systematic, rigorous techniques and tools of differ-ent disciplines to bear on the same substantive arenas. While modules might differ from year to year (in content, as well as rotating entirely different mod-ules), the original idea was to build on the foci of expertise of the program, and on key issues that a contemporary STS program should cover.

Modern biology, the computer revolution, and ecology and environmen-tal issues are at the top of the contemporary agenda as well as central re-search concerns across the MIT campus. Within the STS program in 1996, two of these (biology and computers) were central, and a third (environ-ment) a growing if as yet less powerful focal interest. In addition, it is hard to conceive of the twentieth century without the modern physics revolu-tions. These four areas — physics, biology, computers, environment — made a set of four relatively obvious modules for the second semester. Three other topics seemed equally obvious as first-semester introductions to the inter-disciplinary work of an STS program: the scientific revolution, bacteriology and the medical sciences, and technology.

First-Semester Modules: The Scientific Revolution; Bacteriology and Medical Sciences; Technology

"The Scientific Revolution" seemed a useful first module less because of its temporal priority or presumptive content (scientific methods, creation of modern scientific institutions, relations between science and nation-states), but because the seventeenth century had become within the world of STS a central arena for social theory and mutual borrowing between historians and anthropologists (e.g., Shapin and Schaffer 1985; Hallyn 1987/1990; Biagioli 1993; Newman 1994; the older work of Robert Merton [1938], who drew on Max Weber and Karl Mannheim, and whose arguments about the relation between democracy and science generated an important and continuing de-bate [on communist Russia, L. Graham 1972; on post-Mao China, H. Lyman

TABLE 1   Genres and threads, first semester modules

	Sci Rev	Medicine	Technology
GENRE			
Ethnography	*Shapin and Schaffer 1985*	*Fleck 1935*	Downey 1998
		Farmer 1992	Bucciarelli 1994
		Latour 1998	Kidder 1981
			Latour [1993] 1996
			Buderi 1996
Historiography	Newman 1994	Geison 1995	Graham 1998
	Biogioli 1993	J. Jones 1981	Huges 1998
	Foucault 1966/1970	Hammonds 1999	D. Hart 1998
	Merton 1938		Klein 1996
	Kuhn 1962		Smith 1979
			Alder 1999
			Fitzgerald 2000
			Endersby 1999
			Ellison 2000
Cultural Studies		Herzig 1998	Ronell 1989, 1994
			Haraway 1997
			Kittler 1985/1990
			Rickels 1991
THREAD			
Visual	Alpers 1983	Cartwright 1995	Stafford 1996
	Crary 1990	Avery 1997	Jones 1998
			Mnookin 1999
			Landecker 1999a
Literary	Banville 1976, 1981	Ghosh 1996	Powers 1998
			Latour [1993] 1996
			L. Marx 1964
			Williams 1990
Cross-Cultural	L. Graham 1972, 1998	Marglin 1990	Clancey 1999
	Miller 1996	Nicholas 1982	R. Hart 1997
	Lotfalian 1999	Benedict 1996	

Key to tables 1 and 2: Ethnographies and historiographic monographs are two of the basic disciplinary genres, juxtaposed like a double helix. Journalists' accounts often pioneer that territory; and autobiographies occasionally serve a similar function. Without claiming any completeness, the process of making charts of this sort is one way to begin to see where there are relative lacunae and relative density. Italics indicate crossover texts between anthropology and history.

TABLE 2   Genres and threads, second semester modules

	Physics	Biology	Computers and Society	Ecology and Environment
GENRE				
Ethnography	Collins 1974, 1975	Latour and Woolgar 1979	Dumit 1995	Crawford 1996
	Traweek 1988	Cambrosio and Keating 1995	MacKenzie 1995, 2001	Harr 1995
	Gusterson 1996	Fujimura 1996	Turkle 1995	Davis 1998
	Nowotny and Felt 1997	Martin 1987, 1994	Stone 1995	Lahsen 1998
	Knorr-Cetina 1999	Löwy 1996	Kelty 1999	*Reich 1991*
	McNamara 2001	Rabinow 1996, 1999		K. Fortun 2000
		Sunder Rajan 2002		
		Werth 1994		
Historiography	Galison 1987, 1997	Landecker 1999a	Emmeche 1994	White 1995
	Pickering 1995	Rheinberger 1997	Kelly 1994	Wildavsky 1995
	M. Jackson 1996	Kay 1993, 1999	Mindell 1996	Grove 1995
	Kelves 1978	Keller 1995		Shulman 1992
	Crease 1999	Kohler 1994		Bowler 1992
	Greco 1999	Abir-Am 1980, 1985, 1992		
	Westwick 2003	Gottweis 1998		
		Morange [1994] 1998		
		Judson 1979		
THREAD				
Visual	Nersessian 1995	Greisemer and Wimsatt 1989	Glasgow et al. 1995	Mizrahi 1990
	Cairus 1997	Lynch and Woolgar 1988	Hunter 1995	Nagatoni 1991
Literary	McCormmach 1982	Powers 1998	Coupland 1995	Powers 1998
	Lightman 1993	Djerassi 1989, 1994	Constantine 1993	Stephenson 1988
		Muske-Dukes 1993	Powers 1992	
		Bear 1985	Gibson 1984	
		Mawer 1998		
Cross-Cultural	Traweek 1988, 1992, 1995	Fujimura 1999	Gerovitch 1999	Reich 1991
		Sunder Rajan 2002		K. Fortun 2001
		Biehl 1999		
		Petryna 2002		

Several of the STS/HSST* dissertations that were in process and part of the discussions in the Core Course have now been finished and are listed here. Several of these are interdisciplinary, crossing the chart's genre categories: e.g., Clancey (1999), Landecker (1999a), Mnookin (1999). Others either comment upon language (Gerovitch 1999) or experiment with new media formats (Kelty 1999).

*History and Social Studies of Science and Technology (HSST) is the unwieldy official name of the STS graduate program at MIT, a joint program of STS, Anthropology, and History.

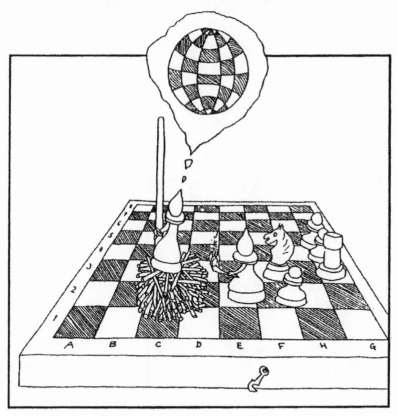

29. Scientific and cultural revolutions, then and now. Cartoon by Levon Abrahamian.

Miller 1996; on big-science physics and venture-capital-transformed biology in the 1990s, Galison 1997; Gottweis 1998; Rabinow 1996; Knorr-Cetina 1999]; and the older work of Thomas Kuhn [1962], which the so-called SSK "sociologists of science" in England claimed as their ancestor, sometimes to Kuhn's discomfort, and even more to the discomfort of some historians of other traditions of inquiry who also claimed Kuhn). We were able to begin our first year with a focal discussion on China enlivened with the presence of Wenkai He, a graduate student from China; Roger Hart, a postdoctoral fellow working on science in seventeenth-century China; Peter Perdue, our China historian; and Leo Lee, professor of Chinese language, literature, and culture. Their presence and participation made the arguments about science and political institutions do work cross-civilizationally, cross-historically, and across institutional and policy analysis.

More generally, the period of the scientific revolution(s) is also a central arena for discussions about the formation of disciplinary knowledges (Foucault 1966/1970; Blumenberg 1975/1987; Alpers 1983), as well as for some

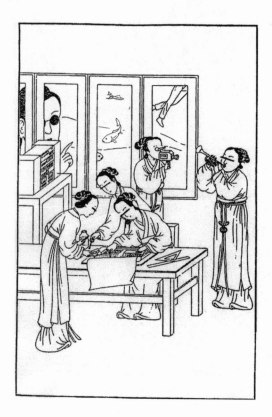

30. Cross-gender, cross-cultural, cross-temporal communications technologies. Image from Hong Kong performance group Zuni Icosahedron.

first-rate literary investigations (e.g., Banville 1976, 1981). The work of Biagioli (1993) on courtier science in Italy, R. Hart (1997) on the patronage of science in seventeenth-century China, Shapin and Schaffer (1985) on gentlemanly science in England, Latour (1988) and Gieson (1995) on public science in France, and Galison (1997) on the transition from craft to big science in Europe and the United States provides a schema for contrastive institutional social analysis (an analogue of comparative social structures or social organizational analysis in traditional social anthropology).

Simon Schaffer's notion of an eighteenth-century "period eye" built around virtuosi, curiosi, and savants (see also now Daston and Park 1998 on "wonder"; Findlen 1994 on early modern Italian museums), if pluralized, becomes a homophonic pun drawing attention to contrasting epistemes. Such period eyes (periodizations) point to a major problem in traditional accounts of the voyages of discovery of imperial and colonial sciences: the failure to (stereoscopically) include the "period eye" of the various native interlocutors, pilots, guides, informants, draftsmen, preparers of specimens to be sent back to "centers of calculation" in Europe. Michael Bravo (1998) invokes the dispute between the anthropologists Marshall Sahlins and Gananath Obeysekere over the apotheosis of Captain Cook to raise this crucial issue, and he argues that ethnography provides a tool in evaluating the degree to which genres of writing about early modern scientific encounters with other worlds can be disambiguated (see also Povinelli 2002; Fabian 2000; Taussig 1987).

A session on alchemy and science juxtaposed historiographic accounts — William Newman's account of George Starkey in Boyle's England, exploring the parallels between pharmacological and molecular biology patent protection effects on open science today and the protection of alchemical recipes in the seventeenth century, and Lawrence Principe's (1998) account of reproducing today alchemical experiments from the seventeenth century — with Michel Foucault's more synthetic and philosophical account in *The Order of Things* of the transition from the episteme of similitude to those of representation, supplemented ("recommended reading") by Marcel Detienne's (1977) structuralist account of how similitude worked in Greek mythology and Zimmerman's (1982) similar account for Hindu ecological texts.

A sequence of discussions thus proceeded from (1) social forms of science organization ("courtier science," "gentlemanly science") to (2) science and democracy (Shapin and Shafer; H. Lyman Miller; L. Graham) to (3) science and alchemy to (4) notions of epistemes, paradigms, and modest witness experimental systems (Kuhn 1962; Fleck 1935; Foucault 1966/1971).

The discussions of the scientific revolution(s) provided a locus where the presumptive division between the work of historians and anthropologists (and other social scientists) had already broken down. We had, within our program, some historians who claimed to be able to easily dismiss this work by sociologists and social historians, and so, I thought, what better way to initiate an interdisciplinary discussion than to publicly, in front of, and with students work out what was at stake?

The second module — on bacteriology, epidemics, and medical sciences — followed naturally. It would be hard to conceive of modern biology without its medical contexts (although again some of our historians of science have insisted on excluding history of medicine from the "status" of history of science), and it seemed that a key bridge between the "Sci Rev" discussions and a module on contemporary molecular biology and genetics could be the turn-of-the-century work in bacteriology and public health, where two or three other key texts do similar work as the texts for the Sci Rev module in bridging — or interrogating the different tools of inquiry in — the fields of history and anthropology/sociology: Ludwik Fleck's *Genesis and*

Development of a Scientific Fact (1935) and Bruno Latour's *The Pasteurization of France* (1988), together with Gerald Gieson's *The Private Science of Louis Pasteur* (1995), which last had drawn a vituperative attack from the crystallographer Marx Perutz in the pages of the *New York Review of Books* (1995, 1996).

Not only was Fleck's monograph the text that inspired Thomas Kuhn's *Structure of Scientific Revolutions* (1962). Reading Fleck's monograph along with Kuhn's text could disentangle Kuhn from some of the later readings that claimed Kuhn to be either a relativist or an antirelativist. More importantly Fleck's was a text that could have been written by a member of *L'Année sociologique*, the journal of Emile Durkheim's school of sociology. Fleck explicitly placed himself between the Durkheimians and the Vienna Circle logical positivists, who would later sponsor Kuhn (although bashers of "positivism" in the 1970s would misrepresent Kuhn as a reaction against Carnap and the Vienna Circle).[1] Here, then, was a text on the boundary between the philosophy of science, the sociology of science, and the history of science. Moreover, Fleck's life and career are deeply resonant with the ethical problems of science in the twentieth century. Not only did he happen to be on the right side in the sad story of the self-destruction of German and Central European science during the Nazi period, but he is a figure whose dedication and whose formulation of epistemological puzzles are again resonant in our own era of AIDS, mutating viral infectious agents, and illnesses whose definitions seem to change with every effort to place them under inspection (e.g., multiple chemical sensitivity syndrome, chronic fatigue syndrome).

The second module thus began with Fleck and the renewed discussions about Louis Pasteur and the rise of bacteriology over and against the hygienics movement (Latour 1988; Gieson 1995; Roll-Hansen 1982, 1983). It moved next into a reading together of ethnographic, political economy, and cultural accounts of AIDS (Farmer 1992; Treichler 1987; Hammonds 1999) and historical and anthropological accounts of previous epidemics around the globe (smallpox, cholera, diphtheria, plague), looking at both the scientific and the public sphere understandings of these epidemics, especially when complicated by cross-cultural, class and immigrant, or colonial contexts (e.g., Charles Rosenberg's [1992] dramatological model of responses to epidemics; Ralph Nicholas [1982] and Frederique A. Marglin [1990] on smallpox, the smallpox goddess, and the differential responses to variolation and British campaigns for vaccination in India; Evelynn M. Hammonds's work on the conflicts between different groups of professionals in "the search for perfect control" by bacteriologists, physicians, public health officials, politicians, and the media in the first public health campaigns in New York around diphtheria [Hammonds 1999] and Judith Waltzer Leavitt's [1996] account of Typhoid Mary; Carol Benedict [1996] on bubonic plague and demographic and economic growth in China, or more generally on populations, demography, and cross-cultural contact and imperialism [McNeill 1976; S. Watts 1997]).

This module was also a natural place to introduce problems of ethics in research, and the complications of ethics through legal and definitional shifts in meanings and in material incentives. We read, watched documentary video, and spoke about the Tuskegee syphilis experiment (J. Jones 1981), and about AIDS in Haiti (Farmer 1992) and the United States (Hammonds 1995; Treichler 1987), and used the class as a forum to explore a piece of Hannah Landecker's dissertation-in-progress on shifts in understandings of the HeLa immortal cell line from neutral tool for biological research to symbolic attractor of anxieties about race, miscegenation, and contagion, to symbolic attractor of competitions over patents and rights of patients versus those of clinical researchers, universities, and pharmaceutical companies (Landecker 1999a). The module also provided a quick and easy exercise in the contrast between (albeit historically important for generating public support for research) narratives of heroic scientist-geniuses (e.g., de Kruif 1926) versus sociological or anthropological and historical accounts.

The four sessions of this second module thus were on the construction of bacteriology as an "obligatory point of passage" for authoritative science; on the public sphere and scientific understandings and responses to epidemics; and on ethics and commodification in research with human populations. In all sessions, there was a productive interplay between ethnographic and historiographic methodologies.

The third introductory module interrogated ways of foregrounding technology. The ground was prepared in the two previous modules by the centrality of the roles of instrumentation, of technologies of communication, and of control over laboratories whose results are granted authority in both scientific and public arenas. But both the nature of the industrial revolution(s) and the cultural imaginaries invested in technologies — and, indeed, the epistemological and sociological implications of the historicized term "technology" itself, and its successors — should not be left to unexamined assumptions or background. Involved in the notion of "industrial revolutions" is a questioning of systemic interrelations across different parts of society, of periodizations and the structural social changes that modern societies have undergone, however unevenly, over the past three centuries. As in previous modules, sessions included presentations of graduate student work in progress, including bringing in experts from outside the program, notably

Ted Medcalfe's work on Fordism, capital accumulation, and commoditization, for which he brought along Michael Piore from the economics department and James Livingston from the Rutgers history department.

Technology is not just objects plus social organization; it is also powerfully invested with fantasies, aspirations, hopes, anxieties, and fears. Technological imaginaries are rich cultural fields of literary, philosophical, symbolic, and psychological production. The analysis of technological imaginaries is now producing some of the most exciting new work not only in STS (Haraway 1997; Latour 1993/1996) but also in German studies (Ronell 1989, 1994; Kittler 1985/1990, 1986/1999, 1997; Rickels 1991; Felderer 1998), French philosophy after 1968 (Deleuze and Guattari 1980/1987), postcolonial and Third World studies (Nandy 1988; Abraham 1998; Bayley 1996), feminism and film/media studies (Penley 1997; Cartwright 1995), and the study of visual and computer-mediated technologies (Turkle 1995; Dumit 1997, 1999, 2000).

Avital Ronell's *Telephone Book: Technology, Schizophrenia, Electric Speech* (1989), supplemented by her essays in *Finitude's Score* (1994), provided one touchstone text for the technology module to explore how one might analyze the cultural imaginaries of a set of technologies. Sections of the book range from fascinating biography (reading autobiographical and biographical canonical texts in their cultural and historical contexts) and wonderful accounts of the development of the telephone (e.g., the well-known nugget that Bell could hardly read the German of his Helmholtz "master text," could not make Helmholtz's experiments work, but could tinker from the diagrams, from experiments with human ears smuggled out of the Harvard medical school, as well as with magnets, electromagnets, diaphragms, and resonators; or the well-known tours to promote the technology that mixed seances and vaudeville). The chapters entitled "Watson," "Autobiography," "Tuning the Fork," "God's Electric Clerk," "The Bell Translator," "Micrographia," and "The Biography" provide rich and easy access and open up the imagination by paying close attention to the behavioral quirks of those approaching telephones for the first time (embarrassment, assuming telepathy is involved or that mediums might help transmission, forgetting to hang up). The brilliant opening pages ("Delay Call Forwarding") require students to do some close reading, registering a series of themes: (1) using technologies as "objects to think with,"[2] here the several telephonic technologies as "objects to think with" against Heidegger's philosophical laments about modernity, including (2) the ethical embedded in uses of technology, here not just the troubling failure of Heidegger to answer the call, or rather his choosing to only answer an early wrong number ("no such thing as a free call . . . accept the call . . . accept the charges"; and "Heidegger is not identical to National Socialism . . . operate as synecdoche . . . decryptage has become our task insofar as we are still haunted by National Socialism and threatened by its return from the future") but also "how to achieve a free relation to technology" ("disconnect, teach you to hang up, dial again"); (3) alternative hermeneutics, different ways of archiving information, registering and deciphering names, interpreting what's in the "telephone book"(s), here the Bible and the tradition of hermeneutics and ethics associated with Levinas, Benjamin, Derrida, and Kafka ("had already prefigured the dark side of the telephonic structure in *The Trial, The Castle,* and *The Penal Colony*"); (4) speech/communicative acts as ethical relations, here inserting interpretation into the ethical relation between self and other: Ronell and her brother, Alexander Graham Bell and his brother, technologies to aid the deaf; (5) speech/communicative acts as physical acoustics, as spiritual(ist) desire and as the uncanny in cultural interconnectivity, here relations between spiritualist circles and Thomas Watson (participant in table-tapping seances and a walking "catalogue of aversions" and neurotic phobias), sonic vibrations and various amplifiers (Bell), and the unconscious ("always a child left behind or the face of a distant friend").

Friedrich Kittler's (1990, 1999) reading of Bram Stoker's *Dracula* as a fable of the typewriter and the several readings now of Kafka and Nietzsche as embedded in the typewriter, railroad, telegraph, and postal technologies (e.g., Shapiro 1989) provide supplemental readings to Ronell's mode of cultural analysis and philosophical inquiry, as does Laurence Rickel's use of Mickey Mouse California (Mickey's ears = film projector reels) as the Frankfurt school's lite (utopian, pop) other to its portrait of Germany as dystopia of modernity. Sherry Turkle's *Life on the Screen* (1995) could be read here as a technology, and also is a bridge to the module on computers (as is Kittler's work), contrasting the ways we think and debate about computers as evocative and intimate objects in the 1990s with the ways we worried about them in the 1970s.

In the first two iterations of the technology module, different mixes of faculty provided different stresses on cultural analysis of technology versus social analysis of the industrial revolutions (early European classic models versus late Asian models, e.g., Stearns 1998). In both iterations, however, the attempt was to deal with the relationship between political economy and cultural formations, and also with the relationship between sociocultural theories about the technological and the social conditions from which they are produced. Thus one year we read Kristin Ross's *Fast Cars, Clean Bodies: Decolonization and the Reordering of French Culture* (1995), along with Henry

Ford's "autobiography" (referring back to Ronell's work on the autobiographies of Bell and Watson) and historian James Livingston's work (1994) on changing cultural ideologies and political economies in the United States since the Progressive era. Ross suggests parallels in the ways that theorists have framed the changes of culture and political economy in nineteenth-century France (Balzac, Marx, and Baudelaire on the emptying out of the countryside, new forms of employment and leisure, and the sense of living in two different worlds at once) and those of the 1950s and 1960s, culminating in the explosion of 1968 (Alain Touraine and the French intelligentsia's elevation of the transformations of "everyday life" to a conceptual terrain that had to be relearned, often from American films). Ross helps point up the ways in which the social sciences and structuralism were part of this process and the degree to which the *Annales* school of social history, whatever its other considerable virtues, was singularly unable to say much abiout modernity, and even less about modernization.

With Tom Hughes visiting for the second iteration, we examined the history of "systems" thinking from the early feedback model in the second edition of Thomas Malthus's Essay on Population, which is one of the first formulations of the demographic transition model, emerging out of the context of enclosures, Poor Laws, expansion of suffrage, marriage reform laws, reserve labor markets, and (later) underconsumption theories of imperialism justifying creation of colonial markets. "Systems theory" and "cybernetics" became central in the 1950s through the work of Norbert Weiner and Talcott Parsons in the context of fire-control systems, Keynesian economic management, Vassiley Leontiev's national input-output accounts, modernization theories for "new nations," and concumption and "postindustrial" and "post-productivist" models of "postscarcity" affluent societies. Tom Hughes's own work (1998) on large-scale engineering systems provided a lively juxtaposition to Loren Graham's (1998) comparisons of American, Soviet, and Chinese large-scale engineering in the context of increasing social complexity and pressures toward flexible, less centralized, more consultative or "reflexively modern" governance (Beck 1986; Lash and Urry 1994).

Second-Semester Modules:
Physics, Biology, Computers, Environment

The modules of the first semester were conceived as an introduction to central questions, methods, and approaches of an interdisciplinary STS inquiry. The second semester turned to modern physics, modern biology, computers, and environmental issues as four arenas that have transformed general consciousness, research strategies, and social institutions in this century. Pedagogically employing a double structure, they were intended retrospectively to build on the modules of the first semester, and prospectively to be platforms for the active research arenas in the STS program at MIT.

Module 4: Modern Physics
The physics module should in some way take up the questions of the transformed world that McCormmach's *Night Thoughts of a Classical Physicist* describes, the transformed philosophical and literary worlds that quantum mechanics and relativity stimulated (e.g., as alluded to in Alan Lightman's *Einstein's Dreams*), and the rise of big science, the military-industrial complex, and the nuclear state. In the first year, when I taught the module with Jed Buchwald, our stand-in for the claims of physicists for a role in the transformations of general cultural consciousness was to look at the so-called Forman thesis. Paul Forman (1971) attempted to locate the sudden appearance of "acausal quantum mechanics" after Germany's defeat in World War I in a wider Weimar culture hostile to reductions of the physical world to mechanical determinism. The various commentaries on this thesis provide a neat case study for a play of arguments about the relation between internal developments in physics versus physics being part of larger intellectual trends and interests, between localist versus internalist accounts of physics, among different models of how social constraints and resources can shape a technical field, and about how one draws discontinuities and continuities in historiographies. We then moved back into the nineteenth century to the establishment of the optical lens industry in Germany, exploring (as we had with George Starkey, Hobbes, and Boyle in the Sci Rev module and the bacteriologists in the Pasteurian module) the boundaries between artisanal skills and entrepreneurial protection of those skills (secrecy, patents, carefully controlled public "demonstrations," and standards), on the one hand, and university development of optical theory (open science, theoretical exploration versus empirical skill) (Jackson 1996).

In the second iteration of the course, I used Peter Galison's Image and logic (1997) to connect with the Technology and Sci Rev modules (from "courtier science" to seventeenth-century "gentlemanly science" to Pasteurian "public science") and to underscore the changing nature of scientific institutions.[3] Galison has some beautiful readings of the multiple lineages of instruments and contexts for theory. Using a variant of ethnographic thick description, he observes that laboratory objects are "dense with meaning": for example, C. T. R. Wilson's cloud chambers carry with them traces of their genealogies in meteorology, steam engines, photography, and atlas making;

Marietta Blau's invention of nuclear emulsions carries traces of social (marginalized women working in radiation institutes using simple technologies) and technical accents (x-ray film used in dentistry); and Cecil Powell's emulsion techniques, building upon Blau's work, drew upon the seismological networks and commercial film laboratories which kept their formulas from the scientists). Sociologically, Galison charts the transformation from craft physics to large collaborations, relations between theorists and experimentalists, engineers and physicists, and changing modes of authorship and assigning credit. He charts alternative histories: of the entities physicists claim exist (privileging experimental systems), of theories themselves (making experiments merely fallible proving grounds), or of instruments and practices. He traces the interplay between those physicist subcultures persuaded only by capturing events in (relatively) direct images versus those persuaded only by statistical arguments. These two traditions, image versus logic, have until recently played a seesaw game of one-upmanship, their relative credibility changing with innovations in instrumentation: cloud chambers, edged out by electronic counters, in turn upstaged by cloud chambers and nuclear emulsions, in turn edged out by newer electronics, large hydrogen bubble chambers, and microelectronics, until the 1980s, when the two traditions began to fuse with electronically generated computer-synthesized images (achieving, along the way, the discovery of W and Z particles). Galison argues for a recognition that subdisciplines and subcultures within physics communicate in pidgins and creoles, often nonverbal trading zone languages using instruments and practices, which themselves "function allusively," always linking the lab to other places and practices and keeping the play of explanations labile.

Karin Knorr-Cetina (1999) picks up the argument by contrasting high-energy physics' large-scale collaborations at transnational research facilities like CERN with small-team efforts in molecular biology. The former are communitarian social machineries, cyborgian superorganisms, preoccupied with sorting out signals from noise and with fending off loss of the empirical, fascinated with relations between simulation and the world. In sharp contrast, test bench molecular biology is a world of intensified competition for authorship and credit, of a disciplined concern with blind variation, natural selection, and the "good hands" of embodied experience and skill.

Gradually a small number of ethnographically rich accounts of doing physics (e.g., Traweek 1988; Collins 1974, 1975; Knorr-Cetina 1999) are emerging that are in conversation with historians of physics. Traweek's ethnographic study of Stanford's linear accelerator (SLAC) is particularly good on the ways that undergraduate, graduate, and postdoctoral training screens out those who do things according to the textbook and on mentor-disciple lineages across laboratories. In this and her subsequent work (1992, 1995), Traweek contrasts American and Japanese styles (e.g., the pleasure in and ideological valuing of tinkering by the Americans versus the industrial perfection of having instruments supplied by others in the Japanese setup, leading to misunderstandings and conflicts when Americans and Japanese work together in the same spaces). She charts local, national, and transnational social structures in physics (how Japanese women physicists mobilize international networks to leverage against male hierarchies in Japan; how peripheral countries are forced to have their experiments legitimized by metropole journals and institutions, and what their strategies are for moving upstream in the international exercise of dominance). Harry Collins delightfully documents how new experimental techniques are often hard to convey through the textual technologies of scientific articles and require face-to-face tutelage, transfer of local conditional knowledges, and embodied skills or tacit knowledge (Collins 1974, 1975). That such knowledges are in danger of being lost when generations of skilled engineers turn over is something that has been much discussed in engineering circles, particularly among builders of airplanes (Vincenti 1990), NASA space engineers (Funk 1993), and nuclear weapons designers (Gusterson 1999, McNamara 2001); hence, with the help of anthropologists, there is experimentation using video recording and the interviewing of older engineers to preserve what escapes technical manuals.

Among our own graduate students, Roberta Brawer offered her dissertation work on the anthropology of cosmology, a field composed of particle physicists and astrophysicists, as a methodological example for thinking through how to do ethnography in contemporary science studies.

At issue are not only the organization of government-funded-and-contracted big science establishments erected during the cold war and only now being superseded as the generation of the Manhattan Project has retired (Kevles 1978; Westwick 2003), but also the changes as biology and computer science replace physics as leading-edge sciences whose social organizational structures are different, even though the state spawns their infrastructures, as with the Internet (funded by the Defense Advanced Research Projects Agency [DARPA]) or the Human Genome Project (funded by the Department of Energy and Department of Health and Human Services).

Nuclear culture and the culture(s) of weapons designers (Weart 1988; Gusterson 1996) open into a large literature: histories of the bomb, novels of the secretive life among weapons designers (Silman 1990), photography of the nuclear landscape (M. Davis 1993; Mizrahi 1990; Nagatoni 1991), investigative journalism on the weapons laboratories (Broad 1985, 1992), histories of the antinuclear movement, A. G. Mojtabai's (1986) account of fundamentalist Christians in Abilene, Texas, the town where the final assembly of nuclear weapons was done — they blithely asserted that nuclear war was only one of the events of Armageddon and that the blessed would be raised in rapture above the conflicts of the last days and then be set down upon a paradisiacal earth.

Parallel work is gradually being done in places with different cultural armatures: first in Japan (Lifton 1967; Treat 1995), and now also in Ukraine (Petryna 1998, 2002), Israel (Cohen 1994), and India (Abraham 1998; Perkovitch 1999).

Research at the national laboratories and challenges in the different science organizational structures should link to the environmental module (radiation and toxic waste, the early work on ecology at Oak Ridge National laboratory) as well as to the biology and computer modules. The new computer simulation technologies that are supposed to replace physical nuclear tests or simulate new defense strategies are a testing ground for claims and realities of computer simulation and proof (MacKenzie 1995, 2001; Ghamari-Tabrizi 2000a, 2000b, 2001). Simulation models are central to climate-warming concerns (Lahsen 2001), physical limits of nonquantum computers (Milburn 1998), theoretical biology (Emmeche 1994), and reduction of error in high-risk, high-tech industries.

Module 6: Modern Biology
For a biology module, there is a richness of new ethnographies as well as histories that few of the other module topics can yet claim. Moreover, when we began the core course, we had four faculty members with expertises in the history of the biological sciences. We were arguably the most impressive site for the discussion of the contemporary history of molecular biology, genetics, developmental biology, neurobiology, and medicine in the country. In the three preceding years, we had hosted three Mellon workshops on the history of the life sciences, focusing on molecular biology (organized by Lily Kay and Charlie Wiener).

Lily Kay's *The Molecular Vision of Life* (1993), Emily Martin's *Flexible Bodies* (1994), Evelyn Fox Keller's *Figuring Life* (1995), Paul Rabinow's *Making PCR* (1996), and Donna Haraway's *Modest_Witness@Second_Millennium.FemaleMan©_Meets_OncoMouse™* (1997) provided one interesting preliminary grid for this module. In differing ways they present accounts of the emergence of new institutional settings, and of a new configuration of prestige and power among subfields of modern biology. Keller is concerned with the relative de-emphasis of embryology and developmental biology under the hegemonic rise of genetics over the course of the twentieth century and the reemergence of embryology and developmental biology in a quite changed world in which the body is experienced and interacted with quite differently, now as a "multimedia spectacle," visually available via gene tagging and fluorescent labels. Her story involves "trafficking across borders" of genetics and embryology, physics and biology (the entry of physicists into molecular biology in the post–World War II era), computer science and molecular biology, and between metaphors and rhetorics used by scientists to formulate both theories for themselves and proposals to nonscientists for funding (e.g., "the gene" or "gene action" and their changing referents over the course of the century), and the reworking of such understandings by experimental systems. Lily Kay provides an account of the rise of molecular biology under the funding umbrella of the Rockefeller Foundation, analyzing why the particular configuration of subfields at Caltech proved to be the most fertile ground for building this subfield among the six universities that were given the most funding in the 1930s to the 1950s. She places her work as well in a maturing historiographic field, evolving from insider accounts of intellectual history, to institutional and social histories, and accounts that weave together the science, the institutional histories, and the broader social and cultural politics of their times (Kohler 1994; Abir-Am 1980, 1985, 1992).

Emily Martin's books (1987, 1994) chart the trafficking across borders in a different way. She deploys anthropologists' ethnographic methods of tracking how metaphors, rhetorics, and understandings circulate among their several distinctive loci in the social world: scientific laboratories, clinics in different ethnic and class neighborhoods, the media (print, film) changing decade by decade. Like most anthropologists, she finds that people are not stupid or passive, that understandings of science do not divide into just lay and expert, and that probing understandings in different settings uncovers a great deal about how society is structured. More provocatively—and similarly to Keller's or Haraway's efforts to unpack the use of terms like "master molecule" or "gene action"—Martin notes, and then questions, the relations (reflection? synergy? "objective correlative"?) between the metaphors and rhetorics used in science and political economy—immunology and flexible capitalist accumulation, in the case of her second book.

Lily Kay's book on the history (and historiography) of DNA as the "code of life" (1999), Richard Doyle's (1997) book on the rhetorics of discourses in genetics since physicist Erwin Schrödinger's *What Is Life?* (1944), and Hans-Jörg Rheinberger's book (1997) on experimental systems take the analysis of scientific rhetorics in three quite different directions. Kay tracks the way information-theoretic language came into modern biology, initially promising a cryptographic solution to how combinations of four bases of DNA (in triplets) might specify, via RNA assembly, the permutations of twenty amino acids that produce myriads of proteins; and how biochemists (such as Marshall Nirenberg and Heinrich Matthei who "cracked" the code) had first eschewed this language but came to adopt it in order to be heard by their colleagues in molecular biology. Doyle, a rhetorician, unpacks selected moments in the same history in a very different way with different goals: he shows how discourses of "molecular biology" contain slippages and suggests that these lapses and slippages in logic are secreted in language as a "repository of the unthought of science" and continue to operate on a model of contagion as active forces on the thinking of scientists. At the simplest level this is an argument that exposes scientists' desire for univocal language, where terms can be fixed to mean exactly what they say, showing that, instead, language, texts, and rhetorics work as interfaces that keep in play those very ambiguities and slippages and function as critical features (not bugs) of language to keep scientists looking for new answers that are generative of new questions. More significantly, both Doyle and Kay push the analysis of rhetoric beyond the identification of metaphors in scientific discourses to the processes of semiosis and larger rhetorical resources carried in discourses (e.g., the desire for a postvital body that animates many usages in molecular biological discourses) and to the social and institutional fields of power that are rhetorically constructed and send thought and imagination on quests of their own, complicating the communication among contesting subfields of science.

Rheinberger, like Kay, takes us into the laboratory, extending earlier analyses of experimental systems (e.g., Kohler 1994 on the Drosophila experimental system; or, in physics, Galison 1987, 1997; Pickering 1995; or, in its nascent "modest witness" form of the seventeenth century, Shapin and Shafer 1985) and strategically using an experimental system in cancer research (developed between 1947 and 1963 at Paul Zamecnik's lab in the Massachusetts General Hospital) that was central for clarifying the mechanisms of protein synthesis and representing them as a cascade of steps in a metabolic reaction chain (Rheinberger 1997). This clarification made protein synthesis something that could be turned into a tool and that would lead to the genetic engineering revolution of the 1970s (identifying restriction enzymes, constructing recombinant plasmids, new DNA sequencing, and new techniques of electrophoresis, fluorescent probes, automated sequencing, and polymerase chain reaction amplification). Experimental systems work through differential reproduction, in an economy of displacement or difference, and so can behave as generators of surprises, of which the most interesting for historians and anthropologists are when things intended as mere substitutions or additions can reconfigure the system itself. At issue then is a network of actors, instruments, discourses, and, to use Donna Haraway's wonderful term, "material-semiotic objects," objects that through their materiality change the possibilities for and directions of semiosis.

Like Fleck, Rheinberger stresses the generativity of these sytems in producing surplus meanings beyond what may have been wanted, and so also the inscription of temporality. As Fleck famously asserted there can be no epistemology without history. Taking a cue from Jacques Derrida, Rheinberger emphasizes the degree to which we are now in the position of actually writing new "material-semiotic" objects with biological experimental systems. We are no longer just "understanding life" but "writing life," and this raises no longer just incremental philosophical, moral, and ethical issues (Habermas 2003). Rheinberger tracks the same pivotal period of shifts from biological chemistry to molecular genetics as Lily Kay's chapters on Gamov's cryptographic endeavors, and Nirenberg and Matthei's biochemical success, to crack the code. Like Galison's analysis of shifting pidgins and trading zones, Rheinberger looks to experimental systems as hybrid settings for creating the emergence of scientific objects ("epistemic things," "Galison's entities"). His historical thick description of a cancer-related in vitro system, based originally on rat liver tissue, ties in both to studies in the history of experimental systems and to the series of ethnographies covering laboratories that developed understandings of oncogenes (Fujimura 1996), interleukin molecules and the relation between clinical trials and experimental systems in laboratories (Löwy 1996), the trajectories of alternative cancer theories and therapies (Hess 1997b), monoclonal antibodies and hybridoma technology (Cambrosio and Keating 1995), and polymerase chain reaction or PCR (Rabinow 1996).

Rabinow's ethnography of the Cetus Corporation provides a strategic site for reconsidering the dramatically changed institutional and patronage environments from the 1970s to the 1990s. It is a site for highlighting four dimensions of a new power-knowledge nexus emerging around the new biotechnology institutions: (1) *Change in funding*. Although government funding (National Institutes of Health, National Science Foundation, and Department of Defense) for biomedical research replaced philanthropic foundations as the primary source of funding in the post–World War II period, with the goal of not only improving public health but also stimulating economic growth, by the 1980s venture capital began to become a major source of funding for biotechnology companies (Teitelman 1991).

(2) *Parapublic modes of scientists' self-regulation and containment of disrup-tive disputes.* These were signaled most clearly by the handling of concerns over recombinant DNA research in the 1970s. Concerns over waste disposal, escape of genetically engineered organisms from the laboratory, and eco-logical and evolutionary implications of transferring DNA from one species to another were handled by calling for a self-imposed moratorium; then, at the 1975 Asilomar Conference, regulatory controls were proposed that were made into NIH guidelines. By 1979, the debate over the safety of re-combinant DNA research had been contained (to resurface subsequently in Germany and Switzerland regarding bovine growth hormone), and as ex-perience accumulated, the NIH guidelines were gradually relaxed. (For com-parative notes on how German biotechnology has been even more carefully shielded from open public debate by parapolitical commissions, see Gott-weis 1998.) The so-called David Baltimore case provides materials for the reanalysis of problems of self-regulation in science, the management of accu-sations of fraud in large laboratories, and the dangers of politicization of whistle blowing (Kevles 1998). (3) *Market forces and the transformation of the symbolic distance of scientists from the market.* Venture capital became a named entity in the 1970s. The role of scientists, particularly biologists, was transformed from maintaining their symbolic capital by remaining distant from commercialization to being at the center of start-up companies as man-agers and directors of these new firms. Soon few biologists in leading aca-demic departments did not have commercial interests. The growth of federal grantsmanship was partly a training ground for managing large amounts of money and laboratories. But new biotechnology companies provided re-search funds without the time-consuming grant writing and reviewing and provided spaces for what seemed like greater research freedom as well as places to hire postdocs and to turn research efforts into real-world bene-fits. (4) *Legal changes.* There was also a transformation in the law surround-ing patents that further spurred the commercialization of biology and the making of knowledge into something less public and more closely guarded as intellectual property. In 1980 the Supreme Court ruled in the Chakra-barty case that new life forms could be patented ("anything made by man"). Ananda Chakrabarty, while working at General Electric, had created bacte-ria that could digest oil slicks by introducing new DNA plasmids into bacte-rial cells. Plant forms had been patentable since the 1930s, but such patents had limited impact due to the slowness of breeding new plant varieties and the organization of the seed industry. In the 1980s, the Patent and Trademark Amendment Act tried to make uniform patent policy out of the patchwork of previous policies in order to encourage licensing and industrial invest-

ment. Universities receiving federal research funds were now obligated to report any potentially patentable inventions. Failure to do so could result in rights reverting to the government. Biology patent applications immediately rose by 300 percent in 1980–84. The nature of publishing, even in academic environments, was transformed: you do not publish anything you have not patented first, in contrast to the traditional academic incentive structure of trying to publish as quickly as possible.

In his ethnography of Cetus, Rabinow outlined through interviews with its major scientists the attractiveness of working in this environment. But in 1990 much of Cetus and its PCR technology was bought by Hoffman-LaRoche (another part of Cetus, including its biological product IL-2, was sold at the same time to Chiron Corporation, which in turn was bought by Ciba-Geigy). These sales were part of a further shift in the institutional milieu whereby biotechnology companies found they could survive only by multiple alliances with large pharmaceutical firms. Part of this survival strategy has to do with capital and revenue flows, part also has to do with surviving expensive patent challenges.

Rabinow calls attention to the role of the scientist-manager who coordinates teams of technicians and scientists as well as to the shape-shifting objects of scientific production (compare Galison's "entities," Rheinberger's "epistemic objects"). PCR is alternatively a *technique* (whose provenance as prior art became the subject of a patent challenge by DuPont, citing the work of H. Gobind Korana on cloning), a *concept* (for which Kary Mullis won the Nobel Prize) having to do with the iteration process for amplification, an *experimental system* (designed and made to work by Henry Erlich and others), and a *kit* sold as a commodity by Cetus. Rabinow's subsequent book on a genome mapping project in France under Daniel Cohen begins to map further shifts in funding, patronage, and accountability among the state, industry, and patient groups. In this case only $1 million came from the state, while $80 million came from Hoffman-LaRoche, with additional funds from muscular dystrophy patients, who as stakeholders were also interested in being part of any regulatory process (Rabinow 1999).

Kaushik Sunder Rajan's STS dissertation (2002) follows the evolution of biocapital through competitions in the 1990s and the early twenty-first century to produce a map of the human genome and then maps of single nucleotide polymorphisms (SNPs). At issue are further shifts in the relations between public and private sector research (and in the internal restructuring of major pharmaceutical companies into "life sciences" or "pharmacogenomics" conglomerates); the role of new machines in changing the field of competition (as in the case of Celera forcing the field, including MIT's

Whitehead Institute, to buy new Perkins Elmer high throughput machines); the reorganization of intellectual property rights (as in the SNPs consortium, where major pharmaceutical companies agreed to contribute to open public knowledge bases, calculating that they could get larger returns on the downstream products and could thereby avoid costly upstream gridlock over patent fights and growing cross-licensing burdens); the ethical, legal, privacy, and efficacy challenges of recruiting patient pools and databanks needed in new forms of population-based biological research and promises of future personalized therapeutics; the creation of new software and informatics as themselves salable commodities (e.g., Ardais Corporation: First Genetic Trust); and the niche possibilities of research and commercial development in India as well as the United States. As with the earlier work of Kay, Doyle, and Rheinberger on the material-semiotic entities and epistemic objects of biologicals, part of Sunder Rajan's work on the production of contemporary biologicals, like Donna Haraway's recent work, attempts to locate their cultural imaginaries through promotional needs, conference symbolic spaces and rites, legal protections for "forward looking statements," and the like.

Haraway probes the cultural and ethical challenges in ways similar to our use of Ronell's *Telephone Book* in the technology module. Copyright, patent, trademark, and brand names, she points out in her resonant 1997 book title, are the "genders" (generic marks, "directional signals on maps of power and knowledge") of "asymmetrical, congealed processes which must be constantly revivified in law and commerce" in a world of transuranic elements and transgenic organisms. Like Doyle, she is interested in the "chimeras" and "wonderful bestiary" of new objects, and obligatory passage points in our technoscientific culture of cyborgs, chips, genes, bombs, fetuses, seeds, brains, ecosystems, and databases. These terms are cultural points of "implosion," which "bend our attention, warp our certainties, sustain our lives" and collapse categories that once were separate into one another. Like Rabinow, she is fascinated by changing legal and corporate structures, tracing the role of DuPont in synthetic organic chemistry (nylon), transuranic nuclear generation (building and running the Hanford reactors in Washington state), and genetic engineering. Like Martin, Haraway is fascinated by the multiple loci in which technoscientific objects and rhetorics circulate. Like Rheinberger, she is fascinated by experimental systems that are themselves hybrid settings and generate transforms of themselves in an ever-shifting generation of ethically, politically, and socially challenging new objects. Like Doyle, she is fascinated by the utopian and dystopian rhetorical grammars, not just metaphors but ever-productive semioses and grammatical processes of technoscience, now transmuting as well through the software programming and Internet address protocols (as indicated by the title of her 1997 volume).

Module 7: Computers and Society
The computer revolution module is one of the topic areas where MIT's STS Program has been adding strength, encompassing the ethnographic study of computer usage (Turkle 1995), the history of computing (Mindell 1996), the cultural studies of mediated technologies and computer-assisted imaging devices (Dumit 1995, 1997, 1999), and law, ethics, and social politics surrounding the Internet and cyberspace (chapter 8 in this volume).

As with physics and biology, there have been profound transformations: in computer science; in the simple and not-so-simple ways the Internet is changing the public sphere, the economy, and modes of "literacy" and knowledge; in the way users relate to computers and computer metaphors have infiltrated language and common sense (the sensus communis); in the speeding up of time and compression of space, not just in the real world but in the kinds of simulation modes that lead to new science and technological applications; and in the way in which computerization has become almost a biological medium for sciences such as nanotechnology and genomics (e.g., the increasing shift in biotech companies from producing physical biochemical products to producing data banks).

This module divides into four parts (or weeks): seeking maps or frameworks for reading and research in (1) ethnographies or empirical grounds for assessing these transmuting social worlds; (2) historiographies of the several fields of artificial intelligence, computer science, theoretical biology, et cetera; (3) cultural readings of this new technological arena; (4) political economy, law, and ethics driving the contingent outcomes, and the more difficult object of regulatory, market, and normative (or values we wish to build in) features of different architectures of these technologies (Lessig 1999, 2001).

1. Ethnographies. Given the pervasiveness of computer-mediated communication, and the ubiquity of ethnographic and sociological research (by anthropologists but also by others), it is surprising how few richly developed ethnographies of these worlds exist, and how much of what does exist is focused on the relatively narrow area of consumer entertainment, e-mail, or MUDS (multiuser domains). Still, there are a few ethnographic and journalistic studies of computer programmers (Hakken 1993); of producing equipment (albeit Kidder's [1981] still classic account is now equipment-wise, if not sociologically, generations old); of safety, health, gender, and minority

labor issues in production (Hayes 1989); and of effects on family and social structure of cottage, flextime niches for female heads of family (Stacey 1990), as well as of the workplace ecologies (Nordi and O'Day 1999; Schwarz 2002). The culture of hacking has attracted lively writing by Bruce Sterling (1992), Haffner and Markoff (1991), and many others and is of increasing interest as documents from a bygone age of panic among unprepared law enforcement agencies. Indeed, one of the most interesting aspects of the most sustained (over two decades) ethnographic corpus on cyberspace, by Sherry Turkle (1984, 1995), is its charting of dramatic historical shifts (1) in the thinking of computer scientists (e.g., from hierarchical, rule-governed procedures to distributed, modular play and testing) and (2) in the consciousness of users, philosophers, and children from anxiety about how humans are in principle different from machines (e.g., Dreyfus 1979) to intense interest in computers as evocative, interactive objects and interfaces.

2. Historiographies. This is a wonderful arena for STS-style historical studies of competing subfields, and cross-disciplinary alliances within the large arena of computer sciences (now the largest undergraduate major at engineering schools like MIT). An interestingly conceived STS course for a few years was called "Machines and Organisms" (taught by Evelyn Keller, Evelynn Hammonds, and David Mindell) which explored some of these cross-disciplinary nexuses. Among the most recent of these nexuses are the evolutionary possibilities of computers evolving "autopoetically," of allowing computers to evolve algorithms and "worlds" (artificial or a-life) both for what this teaches us about computer science and for the fields of chaos and complexity theory opened up as models for processes in biology, ecology, and the microworlds of quantum engineering and computing. There are obvious contact points here to the physics, biology, and ecology modules (Emmche 1994; Bear 1985; Hayes 1989; Kelly 1994) and to imaging technologies and their interpretation (Dumit 1995, 1997, 1999).

3. Cultural readings of technology. The cultural arena occupied by this module—literary, science fiction, film, journalism, popular science, advertising, and speculative writing by computer scientists themselves—is perhaps today the richest of all the modules, beginning with William Gibson's *Neuromancer* (1984), which popularized the word "cyberspace," and the obsessively reanalyzed film *Blade Runner* (and its difference from the book by Philip Dick, *Do Androids Dream of Electric Sheep?*, on which the film was based), and *Microserfs*, the novelistic account by Douglas Coupland (1995) of what it is like to work for Microsoft. Scott Bukatman, in *Terminal Identity* (1993), suggests that science fiction in this arena often exploits a distinctive writerly and playfully paradoxical style that requires active inferential work

by readers, and that indeed "it has fallen to science fiction to repeatedly narrate a new subject that can master cybernetic technologies," a kind of fort-da learning game. For the anthropologist, it is of interest to specifically locate, within the general efflorescence of this cultural reading of, and speculation about, cybertechnologies, those discourses that are, as a lovely collection is subtitled, "stories about the future by the people creating it" (Constantine 1993). Some of this writing is revealing of gendered (male) desires to escape the body (e.g., Hans Moravec for computer science, and not dissimilarly Wally Gilbert for genomics) and of age-graded (scientists toward the end of their careers) desires for immortality, but much of it pokes fun at the butler bots, agents, smart things, and paradoxical desires generated by software designers, providing mirror worlds set to reflect at useful oblique angles.

4. A final arena equally fast changing and equally fundamental is that of the political economy, law, and ethics debates over the kinds of architectures by which we wish to structure our future worlds. The stories of the shakeouts of the semiconductor industry (Yoffie 1994), for instance, are a window into the emergent global economy, and one of several ways this module is also an inquiry into the postmodern world, here at a material level quite different from the often purely metaphorical way in which the postmodern is discussed. While authors such as Gilder (1989) provide useful histories framed in terms of the transformations of the laws of economics by utopian thinking about a technology based on light, where value can be created for a time by giving things away for free, the other side is of classic labor reorganization, de-skilling, jobs lost, and disciplining of the labor force. The law is an important player in this economy through intellectual property (patent, copyright), as well as legislation about privacy, digital identity architectures, and encryption. Here it is important to recognize that not only does the law often lag behind technology, and sometimes new law must be written to fit new technological realities, but technologies are not "given," and can be designed in many different architectures (the subject of the "Law and Ethics on the Electronic Frontier" class, discussed hereafter).

Module 8: Ecology and Environmental Issues
"Ecology" is reemerging after a century of slightly shifting usages to become a word that indicates interconnectivities (both obvious and nonobvious), especially those between the natural environment, technologies, and social systems. Most simply, it is the methodological rule that "you cannot change only one thing," that is, a search device that allows you to follow the cascade of other things that also change with any initial change. As such, "ecology"

can serve as a set of mapping techniques for connectivities. It is thus a basic framework for approaches to environmental issues, a topic that has become a major initiative across the MIT campus, as it has elsewhere in society, as well as a slogan ("the greening of") for industry, management schools, government regulatory agencies, and politics. The STS Program has not yet formed a coherent set of teaching and research projects, although it has included a series of initiatives, including the "Down and Dirty" course/workshop described hereafter; a four-year Mellon workshop on environment and the humanities (Conway, Keniston, and Marx 1999) with an associated course; a course offered by Harriet Ritvo in environmental history; and two dissertation projects, one in Kerala (India), and one in Central Asia (Kazakhstan, Uzbekistan, Turkmenistan). The module is thus a potential platform for new initiatives.

We[4] divided the module into three parts: (1) landscapes, ecologies, and society; (2) extractions, markets, and environmental change; and (3) politics, environmental movements, and new grassroots and intermediate institutions or reflexively modernized social modes of governance.

1. The first part was framed by a review of Ulrich Beck's *Risk Society* and by an introduction to histories of ecology as field sciences of historical landscapes (Bowler 1992; Hoskins 1992; Bloch 1966; G. Good 1998); of colonial networks of apothecary and acclimatization gardens (Grove 1995), colonial forestry and meteorological knowledges (Grove 1997), and other modes of gaining ecological knowledge from peasants and others not usually acknowledged in professional histories of science (Koerner 1996); of efforts at agrarian intensification (Geertz 1963; Dumont 1957; Allen 1965; Gupta 1998); of efforts to trace radioactivity through food chains and the life worlds of American citizens (Bocking 1997); and of efforts to create a complete ecosystem in Biosphere I and II (Kelly 1994). At issue in all of these were notions of systematicities or the finding of unexpected interconnections; thresholds, feedback, and discontinuities of new succession patterns, and collapse; and the long historicity of human reworkings of the environment. It is quite noticeable that histories of the earth sciences seem quite naturally to include reflections on their own sociologies of knowledge: institutions, disciplinary formations, rival models, and their patrons.[5]

As a key text, we read Richard White's *The Organic Machine: The Remaking of the Columbia River* (1995), a beautiful account, among other things, of how changing technological efforts at controlling the river and salmon runs each time led to more complications. As a cultural counterpoint or supplement reminding students of a historical stratum of ecological knowledge carried by mythological armatures and narrative hermeneutics, I suggested we read at least Claude Lévi-Strauss's "The Myth of Asdiwal" (1960; see also Lévi-Strauss's 1972 lecture at Barnard on ecology and structuralism; Detienne 1977 on Greek mythological armatures for botany and zoology; and Zimmerman 1982, a similar effort for India). Selections from these texts not only provide histories of research programs, and of different conceptual structures for environments, landscapes, or ecologies, but can also serve to illuminate the presuppositions of empirical methods that historians, social scientists, and humanists use.

2. For the market and extractions segment, the key text was William Cronin's *Nature's Metropolis*, an account of the way in which the city of Chicago and its hinterland reworked each other. Cronin's book fits among other similar historical geographies from the spatial analysis tradition of the 1960s in geography (e.g., Haggett 1965; Berry and Marble 1968), the "radical geographers" of the 1980s and 1990s (Harvey 1985, 1989, 1996; Soja 1989; M. Watts 1983; M. Davis 1992, 1998), accounts of multinational corporations' extraction of resources from around the globe (Karliner 1997; Tsing 1993), and the environmental depredations of the military and nuclear industries (Shulman 1992; A. Wilson 1992: chap. 8; Kuletz 1998). An important complementary arena for analysis is the effort to change market incentives, and regulatory structures, so as to encourage Green production. Graham and Hartwell (1997) provide a first serious look at how regulatory incentives are working, and how one goes about doing the analysis that allows for the drafting of effective regulations and the evaluation of their effects beyond (non)compliance. That Graham's Harvard Center for Risk Analysis came under sharp questioning for its conflicts of interest affecting its studies (giving funders the answers they want) in the early days of the George W. Bush administration when Graham was nominated for a powerful national political appointment highlights the complications of work in these fields, and the importance of the third portion of the module.

3. For the third part, on politics and social movements, one of the central case studies in the "Down and Dirty" course, focusing on the problems in Woburn, Massachusetts, with leukemia clusters and their alleged causation by two drinking-water wells owned by the W. R. Grace and Beatrice Foods companies, provided an excellent way to examine grassroots environmental movements. *A Civil Action*, by journalist Jonathan Harr (1995), gives a riveting introduction by way of the court case but leaves out the citizen action group (now beginning its third decade of organizing), part of whose story can be found in Brown and Mikkelsen 1990. Comparative contexts

for both the court case and the difficult transformation of citizen concern into political action are provided in Michael Reich's (1991) cross-cultural set of three cases (Italy, Japan, the United States) and Kim Fortun's (1999) transnational ethnographic, multilocale analysis of "the second Bhopal disaster" and struggles over environmental justice and safety issues surrounding the chemical industry in both India and the United States. Crawford 1996 provides another richly textured account of the fight against a waste disposal site, involving Mississippi race politics, the environmental justice movement, and the interstate trade in toxic waste (a topic that in the nuclear industry has focused on Native American reservations [R. Hansen 1998]).

Wildavsky's *But Is It True: A Citizen's Guide to Environmental Health and Safety Issues* (1995) reviews the scientific reports that have fueled or damped public concerns since 1962, and illustrates the difficulties of decision making with inconclusive evidence. His message is the conservative one that mostly the suspicions cannot be proved, and money spent on banning these agents is misspent. In tandem, one might read Powell and Leiss 1997, on the dilemmas of communicating risks and appropriate solutions; Greife and Linsky 1995, which provides a manual for corporations on how to organize grassroots organizations for their own purposes; Helvag 1994, on the deceptive corporate "war against the Greens"; Safina 1997, for the struggles of fishermen and marine biologists over the management of fish reserves; Mayer and Ely 1998, on the dilemmas of the German Greens in turning social movement politics into party politics; and Sabel et al. 1999, on consolidating U.S. experiments with local governance linked to "rolling rule regime" national regulatory coordination.

Richard Powers's novel *Gain* (1998) provides a literary vehicle for some of these issues, including the kinds of math or statistics skills that individual citizens need to operate in such increasingly politicized, probabilistic, and statistically profiled information worlds.

Weft to the Core Course's Warp: Threads, Cross-School Courses

While this is not the place to explore the entire architecture of the STS graduate program envisioned at the spring 1996 retreat, the account of how the core course was intended to function as one part of a larger interweaving fabric would be incomplete without a brief thematization of three threads woven across the modules (visual, literary, and cross-cultural) and three calls for interdisciplinarity (across disciplines, across schools, and across the globalizing world).

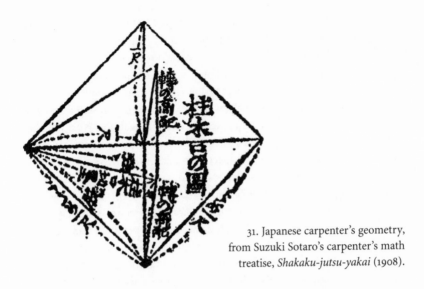

31. Japanese carpenter's geometry, from Suzuki Sotaro's carpenter's math treatise, *Shakaku-jutsu-yakai* (1908).

Visual, Literary, and Cross-Cultural Threads

1. The visual thread has already been articulated in the previous chapter. Several dissertation research projects of the time had a focus on the visual, notably Jennifer Mnookin's historical exploration of the forms of visual evidence—from charts to photographs to videos and animation reconstructions—that have gradually, and with careful hedging against their illusionary force for persuasive misleading, been allowed into the courts (Mnookin 1999); Hannah Landecker's chapters on microcinematography in her history of tissue culture in experimental biology in the twentieth century, and more generally the focus on making processes in the body visible (Landecker 1999a); Chris Kelty's work on informatics and software systems for managing diagnostic visuals that are important parts of how medical centers are trying to expand their patient catchment areas with telemedical technologies (Kelty 1999); and the Japanese building craftsmen's geometries, and the visual clues that helped construct early seismology, that figure in Greg Clancey's dissertation (Clancey 1999) on seismology and architecture (and that provided one year's STS logo).

2. The literary thread takes several forms, including (1) the partnering of historiographic and ethnographic accounts with novelists such as John Banville (1976, 1981, 1986, and 1987 for issues in the scientific revolutions module) or Richard Powers (1991, 1995, 1998) for the biology, computer, and technology modules; (2) the ethnographic use of creative writing by scientists and engineers as an access to their imaginaries (Constantine 1993);

(3) popular culture explorations, especially those that take on a "models of, models for"[6] function for the wider public sphere (Gibson 1994); (4) the exploration of different genres of writing (science journalism, scientists writing popular science books, scientists' autobiographies, biographies, institutional histories); (5) narrative techniques employed by professional historians and anthropologists; and (6) the analysis of metaphors, tropes, semiotics, and sociolinguistic pragmatics within scientific communications. We often held a first session of our colloquium as a book discussion, and a number of these focused on narrative techniques (McCormmach 1982; D. W. Cohen 1994; Cronin 1991; Latour 1993/1996, Powers 1998).

In writing an innovative history-of-technology dissertation that cuts across fields that are often radically separated, Gregory Clancey (1999) writes, "One can arrange a text analytically if speaking to an audience that accepts the terms of an analysis, and owns common analytical tools" (9); but if one is writing across fields, one often finds it useful to adopt a narrative form that can capture the historical realities where "chisel-wielding Japanese carpenters burst into a meeting of seismologists examining seismograms, architects find themselves dancing with politicians at a costume ball, zoologists declare themselves to be architectural historians, and seismologists turn out to be ethnographers" (10).

3. The cross-cultural thread began in the first module in 1996, as noted earlier, with a lively session on 1980s China and the Merton-Weber thesis, using Lyman Miller's *Science and Dissent in Post-Mao China* as a stimulus to discussion, and a chapter from Loren Graham's *Science and Philosophy in the Soviet Union* as a counterargument. In the room to help were four active researchers on China. For arguably the world's leading engineering university, one with an international faculty and student body, it would be anomalous for the sts Program to be exclusively focused on America and Western Europe. It is not that adding international expertise merely extends geographic or civilizational coverage. There are contributions to sts that can best be made by perspectives from other places than only those of the West. Graduate students in the sts Program have been working in India, China, Japan, Central Asia, the Middle East, and Latin America.

Cross-School Courses
One of the originary goals of sts programs in engineering schools around the country has always been to provide spaces for discussions of the sociocultural, historical, political, and ethical environments of doing science and engineering. The history of this ambition is interesting in its own right, but renewed debates about reforming the curriculum for engineers may dif-

fer from earlier debates. The nature of pedagogy itself is changing because of the changing nature of the technological worlds we inhabit. The speed and ability to access information also accelerate the changing relations between teachers' knowledge base and that of their students. This is perhaps not unlike the changing structure of Oedipal and patriarchal authority relations described for an earlier generation by Max Horkheimer and Theodor Adorno (1944/1969; Horkheimer 1972), where no longer do sons wait for fathers to give them access to land, and no longer does fathers' long experience in the fields translate into the knowledge that gives sons the skills they need in wage-, education-, and skill-based economies. Fathers look to sons for knowledge about computer-mediated society. In a course like "Law and Ethics on the Frontier" (http://mit.edu/6.085), young lawyers and engineers are capable of coming up to speed almost as fast as their professorial elders in part because they and their professors are changing the technologies and the laws as they go along. We are, in many arenas, in this together, so that, as Gary Downey puts it, "pedagogy becomes the model of and basis for research rather than the other way round" (1998); see again Geertz's "models of, models for."

Five STS courses illustrate variants on this modality of pedagogy: with the School of Engineering, the Medical School, the Law School, and the Media Lab.

"Down and Dirty: Technical Experts,
Citizens, Cleanup Controversies"
Designed as a workshop/course for STS and environmental engineering graduate students, taught by Charlie Wiener (historian) and Michael Fischer (anthropologist) with the support of Tina Voelker and Charles Harvey (both of the Parsons Lab at MIT's Civil and Environmental Engineering Department), the idea was to bring together technical experts, community activists, and government regulatory agencies involved particularly at two well-known Massachusetts sites: Woburn (a highly publicized drinking water contamination legal case and its possible connection to childhood leukemia) and Cape Cod (a military Superfund site at the Massachusetts Military Reservation, and its possible connection to elevated breast cancer rates). The course was intended to bring the field into the classroom, send students to the field, and allow actors in environmental negotiations to talk to each other in a neutral setting.

These were cases for thinking through the recent sociological and anthropological literature on risk society and reflexive or second-order modernization (Beck 1986/1992), how market forces and regulatory agencies can be

32. Boston's Big Dig, subject of electronic archive developed by Sara Wermeil. Photo source: Massachusetts Turnpike Authority. Overlaid graphic, *Three Body Problem*, as metaphor for complex systems such as the Big Dig, plotted by Babak Ashrafi. Layout: Ben Brophy. Conception: Michael Fischer.

leveraged, and how communities might establish mechanisms for learning from one another in dealing with both complex technical issues and everyday health care. For some of our visitors, it provided an unusual opportunity to learn about each other's backgrounds and a space to exchange perspectives outside the normal almost "scripted roles" of agonism and skepticism vis-à-vis one another on citizen advisory panels. For environmental engineering students who do technical work in sites such as Woburn or Winchester on issues of chemical transport (e.g., arsenic into the Mystic River system), the course was an opportunity to talk to people in these communities, sometimes even to help them formulate the appropriate technical questions, and to experience the larger contexts in which their technical work is or is not put to use.

"Social and Ethical Issues in the
Biosciences and Biotechnologies"
Taught at the Harvard Medical School for the joint MIT-Harvard Health, Science, and Technology (HST) Program, this is entering its sixth year as a formal course, and its eighth year as an ongoing workshop collaboration between myself and Byron and Mary-Jo Good of the Harvard Medical School's Department of Social Medicine. Intended to serve the three of us anthropologists (and a fourth colleague, Jim Weaver, an MIT biophysicist

who joined us for two years) as a vehicle for interviewing some of the leading bioscientists and bioengineers in the Boston area, the course also fulfills a social medicine requirement for HST medical students. The class has grown in size to some thirty-five medical students, M.D./Ph.D. students, and STS students, who bring to the table a wealth of their own experiences in a rapidly changing research and clinical environment.

We usually have two presentations specifically on the changing funding structures of medical science research and biotechnology. Most presentations are about technologies and basic sciences backstage, behind the therapeutic, clinical setting, and about how these come into the clinic and market. We probe for emergent ethical issues. We hope to draw into the discussion the different experiences that M.D./Ph.D. students have in the labs at MIT and the Harvard-associated hospitals versus the clinical settings at the Medical School and hospitals, as well as their experiences in industrial labs, and occasionally the venture capital or health investment worlds. We have been told by a number of our students that this is the place in the busy professional curriculum where social and ethical questions can be explored, where the cocoon experience of their intense technical and clinical training is exposed to outside contexts.

"Law and Ethics on the Electronic Frontier"
A joint STS course with the School of Engineering, taught by a varying staff under the leadership of Hal Abelson with the participation of Joanne Costello and myself, in 1998, this course was taught also jointly with Harvard Law School professors Larry Lessig and Jonathan Zittrain. Thirty MIT students and thirty Harvard Law students divide into teams of six, each team responsible for presenting the state of play today on issues such as encryption and digital signatures to how democratic structures might be enhanced. This is an extraordinarily fast changing arena. Even if the law does not change as fast as the technology, court cases have moved the legal playing field quite considerably from the time when the course began five years ago. The MIT students are often involved in managing and developing the technological changes—for example, working for the World Wide Web Consortium, or working on encryption technologies. Similarly the law students are often involved in clerking for firms, or doing work for law school professors, who are involved in both the litigation and the legislation. The setting up of teams in the class is intended to allow law students and engineers to teach one another the thought styles of the other discipline, but also to instill in engineers a sensibility about the trade-offs between technical standards and ethical, social, legal, and "policy" issues.

The course has evolved from a model, like that used in the Medical School course discussed earlier, of bringing in key actors—prosecutors, former heads of the National Security Agency or CIA, FBI computer crime agents, defense and civil liberties lawyers, software engineers from the creators of PGP, RSA, and PICS, a founder of Lotus and the Electronic Frontier Foundation—to a pedagogy of role playing and mutual teaching among engaged disciplines. In both models, the basic reading is of actual legal cases. In both models, most of the resources are accessed through a Web page, and discussions are held on-line in between class sessions. All of this cyberspace component of the course—except the on-line discussion—is available publicly. Final papers have been published on the Web, and the ethos of the paper writing is that they are contributions to the state-of-the art knowledge (http//:ai-swiss/mit/6.085).

"The Structure of Engineering Revolutions"
Taught in its first iteration with twenty-five students by David Mindell (a historian of computer technology) and Charles Lieserson (a computer scientist), this course is targeted primarily at, and fulfills a requirement for, fifth-year engineering students. It is intended to teach them to use the archival tools of a historian to understand the intricate social and political negotiations needed to complete a complex engineering project. This is part of a general mission of the School of Engineering to change the way engineers are educated.

"Loosely modeled on the famous 2.70/6.270 subjects at MIT where students receive a box of parts and have to build a robot, here students receive a box of documents, technical reports, drawings, technical artifacts, and engineers' names and addresses. From these diverse materials, they research and write a case history of an important technology, project, or company, taking into account its technical, political, and social dimensions. It is analogous to the case method of teaching in business schools, but instead of prepackaged cases, students research and write their own cases" (Mindell 1998: 2). Final project presentations were critiqued by experts from STS and Engineering faculties.

"Systems and the Self"
Taught by Sherry Turkle of STS and Mitch Resnick of the Media Lab, "Systems and the Self" is targeted both at students with computational backgrounds who have little vocabulary or opportunity to talk about their relationships with the objects they create except as obsessions or moneymaking ventures and at humanists who have little opportunity to experience what

it is like to create objects. Two sorts of relationships are focal: cognitive and affective. Students are asked to build objects and to write two papers, one about their own personal relationship with an object, either cognitive Piagetian ones, or affective Winnicottian ones; and another paper about other people's relations with objects. The Piagetian stance is that children (and all of us) use objects to develop thinking skills. Children, for instance, place the same objects repeatedly under the table and take them out to develop notions of permanence and continuity; or they learn the equivalence of geometric shapes, as in the famous experiments with a tall thin glass of water and a short wide one. The position of the MIT Media Lab (Marvin Minsky, Seymour Papert, Mitch Resnick, Sherry Turkle) has been that this learning process is enhanced not merely by manipulating objects but by actually making them ("constructivism"). The Winnicott affective questions are to ask why relationships with objects feel so compelling, and to provide a language for talking about affect via analogies with psychodynamic "transitional objects" (blankets, teddy bears) that children use to establish a sense of separate identity (music, sex, and motion are other transitional vehicles). The computer programmer who spends hours before a screen is encouraged to develop a language that can say much more than just being lost in an obsession or addiction. One student paper investigated the differences for diabetics of having insulin pumps embedded in their bodies (glucometers measuring blood sugar levels continuously and adjusting the insulin) versus pricking their fingers repeatedly during the day and thus exercising control over the levels of insulin supplied — this provides a concrete reality to contemporary fascination with, and fear of, becoming cyborgs. Another paper explored what would be acceptable as chips embedded in oneself: maybe yes for learning 6.001 (the basic computer programming course at MIT) or learning a language, but maybe no for engaging with Dostoyevsky; and how these different affective relationships relate to the question "What is it to feel human?"

From Papert's Logo program of building blocks for learning (learning how things work), to different styles of operating systems (learning to make the things do it your way), to cyborgian aids for self and social relations (from a diabetic's ability to self-administer appropriate insulin dosages, to wearable interactive computers, perhaps to chips embedded in the body), the positioning of the course is not just an intellectual exercise for MIT students but more like an architect's studio, where design work is being experimented with by those who will be designing the next generation of smart objects; it is also a place for teachers who actually put these ideas to work in community schools (e.g., Hooper 1998).

Other Pieces of the Fabric

STS at MIT also has an undergraduate program, and many of those courses also actively serve a cross-school pedagogy. Workshops provide further alternative forums for cross-school work. The Workshop on the Changing Conceptions of "Race" in the Histories of Biology, Medicine, Public Health, and Anthropology (run by Evelynn Hammonds and Everett Mendelsohn) is a joint MIT-Harvard working group (also hosting a Web site) investigating the ways in which race concepts have bedeviled in the past and continue to bedevil scientific and public sphere arguments and literatures even where race is disavowed as an analytic category. The Deep Water Archaeology Group, led by David Mindell, draws together engineers, archaeologists, and historians working on current projects in the Black Sea and elsewhere pioneering an emerging new kind of archaeology. The Control in Contexts: High Hazard Technologies in Operation workshop (led by anthropologist Constance Perin) involves engineers, historians of science and technology, sociologists and anthropologists, and has held sessions that contrasted safety cultures and risk management across different industries.

Legacy Worlds and Promissory Futures

The core course was an effort to provide a survey of the intellectual fields that make up STS, of the arenas of science and technology that have been transforming our intellectual, material, and social worlds, of the research arenas of the program, and of the basic vocabulary and genres of STS. Such vocabulary includes social, material, and literary technologies (Shapin and Schaffer 1985), managing public/private or skill/procedural techniques (Newman 1994; Biagioli 1993), points of obligatory passage and asymmetric and reversible ratios of power/legitimacy relations (Latour 1987, 1988), subculture rivalries (Hammonds 1999; Galison 1997), the semiotics and semiosis of cultural technologies (Ronell 1989; Haraway 1997), the circuits of knowledge dissemination and differential practical responses to technologies (Martin 1994; Traweek 1988), alternative histories of instruments, theories, entities, or sociologies and their pigeon languages and trading zones (Galison 1987), political economy changes surrounding patents, publishing, and regulation (Rabinow 1996; Gottweis 1998), experimental systems (Kohler 1994; Rheinberger 1997), transitional objects and alternative operating systems (Turkle 1995), alternative incentive structures and rational versus reflexive social institutions (Beck 1986), the procedural and organizational differences among the experimental sciences (Galison and Stump 1996; Knorr-Cetina 1999), not just differences among field, laboratory, and simulation sciences. Such genres include historiographic monographs, ethnographies, and also science journalistic books (which have often prepared the way for more academic genres); autobiographies (as a particular kind of source); biographies (with quite different functions and caveats for readers); literature, science fiction, documentary film and video (as genres of speculative and narrative reflection); and narrative popular film, popular science written by scientists, and photographic essays (as sources for circuits of discourse and image transformations).

On a larger sociological and cultural scale, the core course and the STS Program are part of a changing pedagogical regime. It makes sense that part of this shift should be toward courses that are placed in interdisciplinary settings across schools with students and faculty who together are deciphering the technoscientific worlds that they are at the same time engaged in helping to produce and modify, an almost Möbius strip–like structure of education. Perhaps the core course itself should undergo parallel changes, for instance, by seeking a new life as a platform that is more (inter)active in the form of a Web page document that can easily be updated and modified and shaped to other settings.[7] Modifications are potentially infinite and yet need to be constrained to achieve the purposes intended: I could easily imagine a biology module that would focus on the neurosciences — that increasingly interesting mix of imaging technologies, experimental systems, evolutionary speculation, and clinical interviewing. For the moment, however, I suspect, neither the histories nor the ethnographies are in place to easily create a module that would provide the methodological exemplars that could serve both as introduction to conceptual vocabulary, genres, and methods and as platforms from which to build better exemplars or complementary pieces of a mosaic of understandings. And yet the making of precisely such exemplars might be the work of an interdisciplinary group of students creating the next module.

At the public sphere level, this changing pedagogy is part of a pressure toward what Beck (1986/1992) calls secondary modernization or reflexive social institutions, or what Bill Readings (1996) calls an important new function for the university of learning to experiment in practical ways with social diversity (and institutional flexibility, not just ethnic identity politics diversity), including in and among the disciplines.

10

In the Science Zone: The Yanomami
and the Fight for Representation

Janus, the double-faced god of time and transitions (including war to peace, and exterior world to interior hearth), is perhaps chuckling at the paradoxes and dilemmas that bedevil anthropologists' efforts to defend and critique their studies of the Yanomami. The bedevilment lies at least in part in the fact that 1960s science and 1990s science are institutionally quite different enterprises. They are different along at least three axes: the ethics and institutional contexts of science; the way in which activists of all sorts, including scientists, become media players, complicating questions of who speaks for whom; and the palimpsest continuities and differences between the human biology research projects (population genetics, sociobiology, human genome diversity project, health and epidemiological transition) of the 1960s and the 1990s.

All three axes require attention to the importance of anthropology's interface with history on the one hand and biology on the other, and to an ethics of defending the Yanomami, science, and anthropology that depends on not turning the actors in any of these spheres into saints. The differences between the 1960s and the 1990s have to do as well with the increasing pressure for the participation by publics in decision making about scientific research that affects their welfare: a pressure toward accountability, if not transparency.

Three Axes of Difference from the 1960s to the 1990s

Ethics and the Representation of Science
The ethics of science — and the representations of science in both the epistemological (accuracy, reference, completeness) and political or stakeholders' senses — are no longer marginal issues left up to the sensibility of the researcher or expert. Across the sciences these are becoming matters for institutional review, efforts at transparency, and negotiations between pub-

lics and researchers over the propriety of research that involves people and publics.

Nowhere is this more focused than in the medical sciences, where there are long-standing morbidity and mortality rounds for surgical and other disciplines (routine collective reviews of adverse outcomes, instituted to minimize unnecessary error); institutional review boards (IRBS) for research approval (established in the aftermath of the Tuskegee syphilis experiment and the debate about human subjects research that began in the 1960s); ethics rounds that bring together surgeons, emergency room teams, intensive care teams, anesthesiologists, nurses, chaplains, and other disciplines, teams, and health care professionals to rethink cases where the interests of patients, doctors, and society are unclear (as in how to deal with organ donation); and hospital ethics committees to mediate conflicts between patients' rights to procedures (no matter the costs) and doctors' rights to refuse procedures when they feel futility and further suffering is all that would ensue.

Extensions of this institutional growth are developments in other fields. Citizen action panels (CAPs) are involved in monitoring the cleanup of toxic sites under U.S. Superfund legislation. International human rights law has a bearing on the ethics of clinical trials with issues of informed consent, return of benefit to research subjects, and dilemmas of playing on expectations where understandings of scientists and subject populations are quite different (see, for example, the five-part series in the *Washington Post* in December 2000, entitled "The Body Hunters," on First World–based medical research in China, Africa, and Latin America). There are issues of informed consent by volunteers in defenses against biological warfare (see Moreno 2000); negotiations over bioprospecting/piracy and patent law between North and South (including the right under GATT/WTO rules for countries to declare medical emergency rights to produce generic HIV/AIDS or other drugs if multinational companies refuse to sell at an affordable price); and in general various forums of deliberative democracy on policy issues.

For the discipline of anthropology, such ethical assessment and limit setting has a checkered history. The Ethics Committee of the American Anthropological Association was set up as a variant of such institutional review, at least for cases where putting research populations' lives at risk has been alleged. The trigger for setting up the Ethics Committee was during the Vietnam War when allegations were made that research on villagers was being turned over to security forces and villages were targeted for bombing ("the Laos affair"). At the same time there were allegations that anthropological research was being used for counterinsurgency interventions in Latin America ("Project Camelot"). And slightly later there were allegations that an anthropologist, by revealing "state secrets" about population control in China, was politicizing the discipline and endangering access to the field.

This third case was controversial, and since then it has proved increasingly difficult for the AAA to evaluate such allegations in politically charged fields in a discipline dedicated to examining the social bases of moral positions rather than enforcing any particular such position. Napoleon Chagnon's research among the Yanomami has been a long-running case of charges and countercharges that has been hard for the association to adjudicate without mounting a full-scale investigation with full legal ramifications, for which it has not been financially or institutionally set up to do.

That the ethics committee has always served to protect the association rather than research subjects may be true (Nugent 2001), even if many of those who helped get it established, such as David Schneider, did not have this in mind. IRBs too primarily protect their institutions from liability claims but in so doing can also protect research subjects. The larger point is that in many arenas of medical sciences, experimentation with human subjects, clinical trials, and so on, there is institutional development promoting both the defense of institutions and also accountability and creating—explicitly in the case of hospital ethics committees—spaces for negotiation.

Transparency and accountability are not necessarily easy to achieve. How to do so in a responsible manner that does not overly polarize controversial issues into battlefields but allows them to be negotiated and adjudicated over time—how to do this is on the political agenda today around the world in a way that was not the case thirty years ago; it is something that is unlikely to go away.

Research and the Media

A second axis of difference is that the media context of doing research among populations around the world is quite different. The Vietnam War is widely understood to have been the first televised war, and the effects of that visual access in the 1960s have an important legacy for the present, both in the increasing efforts by the military, governments, corporations, lobby groups (including scientists), and others to control information and public discourse and in the counterefforts by those who would provide counterimages and information. Since then, the world at large has become increasingly telemediatized: there is both increasing availability of footage, images, and textual information and increasing attempts to channel general understandings.

One of the tropes of writing anthropology and writing by journalists about anthropology must therefore inevitably give way: that of discovery and first contact. There continue, no doubt, to be places that are relatively isolated, but it is no longer credible to discount the archive of previous interactions of any locality with its larger geopolitical settings. The complaint about the lack of detailed attention to the long historical record — even where the trope is not first contact but interethnic friction after contact — is gradually coming to the fore in professional evaluations of the literature (see Viveiros de Castro 1996).

One of the disconcerting things about the anthropological writings about the Yanomami is how little attention is given to the long history (however poorly documented or understood) of contact with slavers, rubber tappers, miners, missionaries, state officials, military operations, journalists, nongovernmental organizations (NGOs), and others.

Brian Ferguson's 1995 compilation of what is known of the history of this region is an important start, but it too is framed oddly in a parochial anthropological discussion of 1960s theories of primitive warfare. An important and enduring part of this latter discussion is the hypothesis of the relationship between violence and location within trading networks, versus the relative merits of the hypothesis that violence is mainly related either to competition over women (and reproductive or genetic success) or an ecological device of spacing to ensure access to protein. (See now Ferguson's recent restatements in which he brings in other factors as well, including importantly social breakdown: B. Ferguson 2001a, 2001b.) Reading Ferguson together with the first-person accounts by the fifteen or so ethnographers of the Yanomami, plus accounts by missionaries, visitors, and others, does begin to build up a mosaic of understanding, including most importantly the observations by those who have visited repeatedly over long periods of time and who have a comparative sense of cycles, for instance, of disease (especially malaria), demography, as well as more direct interventions.

Alcida Ramos's 1995 account of malaria and depredations by miners in *Sanuma Memories* is one such important temporally comparative reflection, and the study by John Early and John Peters on the demography of eight Xilixama Yanomami villages since the 1930s is another, containing also some balanced evaluations of studies of particular groups vis-à-vis one another, including the studies of Chagnon, Ramos, and others. It is important for novice readers to have a good geographical map of the territory at hand (good cartography on both sides of the border exists, and although Yanomami frequently move their villages, ethnographers mark their locations on maps, and the history of movement can also be followed): this is a differentiated physical terrain, which has been difficult of access, but it is not one simplistically of a "dark" unknown territory.

To these considerations Patrick Tierney, in *Darkness in Eldorado* (2000), adds an important question: the degree to which the international media have been gulled into reporting periodic "first contact" stories that gain widespread audiences for portraits of primitives exoticized either by being particularly diseased or by being particularly warlike.

Part of the burden of this media thread is the degree to which such reports play into the legitimation of various policies of national governments (e.g., in denying or delaying long-promised land rights protection), international lending agencies, or NGOs (Alcida Ramos [1998] has an interesting chapter on the "hyper-real Indian," the Indian who has learned to play a kind of role for international NGOs that allow funding flows to occur, and a rich chapter more generally on Indian agency in interethnic contexts). That Indians should be sophisticated players in such games is neither surprising nor necessarily a bad thing. It does mean that narratives that do not allow for such agency on the part of Indians may well be suspect, and that one needs to look for the coalitions and mediators who allow such agency to be expressed on the national and international stage.

I think it is a general problem of anthropological writing that so much of it is written as if the archive of what is otherwise known of these populations can be ignored, in favor of the personal experience of an individual investigator, as if we were still nineteenth-century or early-twentieth-century explorers. Indeed, more twentieth-century than nineteenth-century, for as Johannes Fabian has shown in a lovely meditation on exploration fever, early explorations depended on large-scale caravan infrastructures and preexisting trade and political networks: they were hardly the work of individuals (Fabian 2000). In the twentieth century, when colonial and national structures were more established and travel was easier, it became easier as well for individuals to move about and imagine themselves as egoistic discoverers of new terrain. The ways in which this has become packaged as tourism or standardized as new versions of *Wanderjahr* journeys (the hippie trail from Istanbul to Katmandu in the 1960s, for instance, and similar if less frequent self-discovery/self-testing journeys into the Amazon to live with the Indians) have been the subject of a number of anthropological (and other) accounts.

Accounts of the archival, infrastructural, and media contexts have actually been sparse, despite the widespread commentary on the e-mail dissemination of the Terrence Turner and Leslie Sponsel memo warning the American Anthropological Association officers of the potential scandal that might occur with the publication of the Tierney book (summarizing the allegations in florid and surefire attention-grabbing fashion), and the astonishing extent that the news media for months contented themselves with reporting hearsay opinions based on this e-mail traffic.

More important are the questions raised by Hannah Arendt and others in the post–World War II period about the structure of mediated circuits of communication, the power of the mediated "lie" for state and institutional purposes, and especially of telling the truth in ways that ensure the truth will be treated as if it were not the case, the truth hidden in the open as in Edgar Allan Poe's "The Purloined Letter." In the case of the Yanomami, the truth hidden in the open is that the Yanomami have been and continue to be threatened by disease, miners, and the state's failure to live up to its land rights promises. Providing solutions to these problems is rarely part of media coverage and was totally absent in the media coverage of the Tierney case. How one breaks through such complacency should be on the political agenda for the coming decades. Escalating allegations of scandal obviously are not the way, but neither is business as usual in the media world of failing to track historical legacies, interests, infrastructures, and maneuvers into the present. (It is an interesting side note that, like Salman Rushdie in *The Satanic Verses* describing what would befall him, so too Tierney in *Darkness in El Dorado* describes the media campaigns organized against Napoleon Chagnon's enemies and some of the tactics of those campaigns. A few journalists, such as Charles Mann in *Science*, did track some of these media campaigns.)

These questions of media, infrastructure, and archives; of who speaks for whom as both corporate activists and NGO activists become sophisticated media players, as governments change policies, patronage networks, and front stage actors, as publishing and marketing become edited and mediated beyond author-message relations, and as groups of scientists themselves mount lobbying campaigns to shape the public arena; and of the power differentials between research communities in Brazil, Venezuela, and the United States — these are also questions about representation in its dual epistemological and stakeholder/political senses. As the world becomes more integrated and interactive, questions of how information is collected, packaged, and made available as part of social institutions of reflexive or second-order modernization (to use Ulrich Beck's terms) become more important and open to insistent questioning.

The New Genetics and Human Biology
Finally, a third important axis of difference has to do with the difference in our understandings of genetics and human biology between the 1960s and

the 1990s, with the ways in which large-scale research projects are mounted, and the relative power differentials of research communities in different countries to set agendas.

There are at least two or three sets of research projects that intersect here. First there were the multidisciplinary, multiperson, multiyear, multi-sited projects of social science. In anthropology there were quite a number of such regional research projects, including the Rhodes-Livingston Institute studies of the 1940s and 1950s, the comparative social anthropology projects of the Malinowski, Radcliffe-Brown, Evans-Pritchard, Daryll Forde seminars and their successors; and the modernization studies from the United States in the 1960s, 1970s, and 1980s.

Examples of the latter include the MIT Indonesia project in which Clifford Geertz got his start; the Cornell Peru project; the Harvard Chiapas project directed by Evon Vogt; the Ge and Central Brazil Project directed by David Maybury-Lewis and Roberto Cardoso de Oliveira; the UNESCO-funded project on race relations in Brazil involving Brazilian and U.S. sociologists and anthropologists, an interethnic friction project on relations between Indians and local non-Indian populations in Brazil; the Chicago-London Family Project in West Africa, the Caribbean, and the United States directed by Raymond Firth, Raymond Smith, and David Schneider; and the Chicago Islam and Social Change project directed by Leonard Binder and Fazlur Rahman (in the last two of which I was involved).

Second, there were also the originally primate-based field studies of animal behavior, out of which grew interdisciplinary projects on hunting and gathering societies that were thought in evolutionary terms to represent a stage between primate societies and human societies, such as the Harvard Project on the !Kung or San Bushman.

In genetics and human biological research, meanwhile, there were efforts to do population genetics both to trace historical migration patterns (Luca Cavalli-Sforza first in Italy on genetic drift and then globally in his *History and Geography of Human Genes*) and to understand demographic, disease, and genetic relatedness structures (examples include James Neel in the Amazon and in Africa; the interesting 1972 volume edited by G. A. Harrison and A. J. Boyce, which includes a contribution by Chagnon and another by Francisco Salzano; and more generally see Collins and Weiner 1977).

Some of these projects today have a second life with new technologies and have a palimpsest quality. Among these is the Human Genome Diversity Project (HGDP), which as the Brazilian anthropologist Ricardo Ventura Santos points out has an eerie quality in the Amazon. Brazilians, Venezuelans, and others around the world watched medical research in the 1960s collect blood, mucus, stool samples, et cetera, and now they see the collection repeated but with DNA samples (Santos 1998). Ironically, he points out, just as the United States is divesting museums and repatriating for burial collections of Native American bones, it is at the same time building up new biological collections of DNA. Collections for whom? There is a vigorous organization of Native North Americans, the Indigenous Peoples' Council on Biocolonialism, which is actively resisting the HGDP on the grounds that it may be science, but it is not science that is likely to have any benefits for them. The University of California at Berkeley sociologist Troy Duster is fond of pointing out that we have medical tests for cystic fibrosis among Caucasians, but none to test for it among Zuni populations, where its incidence is the same as in other populations.

Collections again move from the Amazon to North America—to the University of Michigan and Penn State in the 1960s, and to other repositories today—with the prospect today of being used by multinational pharmaceutical firms for profits that again may not accrue any short-term benefits (except in the general longer terms of "benefit to mankind") to the populations from whom the DNA is taken. The Yanomami are now contemplating a lawsuit against the U.S. government, perhaps for reparations for the use of their blood without informed consent, but at least to establish a legal requirement for a signed agreement before their DNA can be used further (www.proyanomami.org.br/voz.htm).[1]

Does a local population always have to benefit, or is there a place for presumed consent to collection of various sorts of data, which only after considerable processing can be turned into knowledge and products? The answers to these questions are not in, but they are today central questions publicly debated and politically negotiated—from Iceland's experiment to allow deCode Corporation to link data banks of medical records, genealogies, and DNA samples, to the Harvard-Millennium Pharmaceuticals project in China to collect DNA samples from populations in Anhui province—and are not easily swept under the carpet as they were in the 1960s, and as some of the players of the 1960s insist should still be the case. (Cavalli-Sforza, for instance, is said to have refused suggestions by Robert Cook-Deegan and others that the HGDP would run into problems if it did not include public participation avenues among those from whom it wished to take collections. The predicted trouble has occurred, if not yet quite as serious as what happened to Monsanto Corporation with its "Terminator" seeds.)

Again, these are questions of representation in both its senses, with the consent and participation of multiple populations always at issue.

Biology, Anthropology, and
Twenty-First-Century Sciences

The Scientific Generation Gap

It strikes me that much of the bombast that erupts in the United States every few years over Napoleon Chagnon's portrayal of the Yanomami as "fierce" (not merely like all of us using "fierceness" or *waitheri* to bluff our way along) has to do with generational passing ships in the night, the 1960s "old-timers" defensive that they did nothing wrong, and the 1990s practitioners insisting—in order to protect the very legitimacy of doing science—that what was done in the 1960s cannot be done today without consequences. As to whether Neel caused a measles epidemic in 1968, everyone on all sides—including even Tierney now—seems to agree that this is not within the scale of much plausibility, although as a theoretical possibility, there is always the slim chance of a mutation from using live viruses, as, under quite different circumstances and without causing an epidemic, we recently saw with the polio vaccine in the Caribbean (www.cdc.gov/mmmwr/;preview/mmwrhtl ml/mm4948a4.htm).

In other words, it would be more interesting, and more honest in terms of medical science, if we acknowledged the great challenges and uncertainties of vaccine development and did so in ways that do not disrupt the use of properly conducted public health vaccination campaigns, and on the contrary that increase the robustness of informed consent and legitimacy.

Tierney's speculations along the way are perhaps sometimes a convolution of the 1960s realities, the 1970s sociobiology debates, and the intense popular scrutiny of biomedical research that emerged during the 1990s. Neel in 1968, of course, cannot be held to ethical codes that have only been more fully institutionalized in more recent years (of informed consent, which in principle goes back to the Nuremberg Code in 1947, or the Helsinki Declaration in 1964; of return of benefit to research subjects that is part of the later revised Helsinki Declarations). However, a historical knowledge of what he and others did and failed to do in 1968 remains part of an important genealogy that still has continuing legacies in the structure of practices, incentives, abuses, and politics of science today. For instance, the donation of drugs near expiry by pharmaceutical companies to gain a tax write-off is not necessarily a bad thing, although it can lead to abuses if the drugs do not find timely and appropriate use.

In this case, the practice perhaps explains why Neel got doses of Edmonton B vaccine rather than the newer Schwartz (more attenuated) vaccine that was being introduced in the United States and was adopted by the Venezuelan government a few months later in 1968. In a letter to the missionary Robert Shaylor, dated 22 April 1968, Neel discusses the use of a vaccine that is "a little old," recommending the doubling of the recommended dosage and ignoring the label's recommendation not to use gamma globulin, and asking for feedback on how these administrations work, feedback useful for the pharmaceutical company and for Neel in obtaining more donations.

Similarly, that Neel talked to people in the National Communicable Disease Center in Atlanta about using the Edmonton B vaccine among a population that was likely to be vulnerable to particularly severe reactions to the vaccine does not necessarily guarantee appropriate use; recently both the Centers for Disease Control and the World Health Organization insisted that short-course direct-observation therapy (DOT) drug treatment as usual was still recommended for multi-drug-resistant tuberculosis in Russian prisons and elsewhere, when it was clear that this could only exacerbate the problem (Farmer 1999).

Again it would be more interesting and more honest to admit and study the challenges and dilemmas, not deny them as the rush to defend Neel and Chagnon has tried to do. It is worth noting, after all, that the same winter of 1968 saw a measles epidemic in Chicago that the new antiepidemic procedures in the United States failed to stop (Hardy et al. 1970). In other words, this was not just a period of science knowing what to do and doing it correctly and efficiently. It was a learning process. Neel and colleagues were quite aware that the high fevers and reactions that the Edmonton strain of vaccine was likely to cause were "even more likely among measles-free peoples," as a letter from team member William Centerwall on 9 January 1968 ("To Whom It May Concern") documents; Centerwall also asks that reports flow back comparing the reactions of vaccines prepared in egg versus in canine kidney cultures, as part of the ongoing efforts toward experimental understanding of these vaccines.

Sociobiology and Beyond
On the other hand, as anyone who reads his autobiography, and relevant published papers, will acknowledge (Neel 1994, 1970, 1980), it cannot be denied that Neel had an interest in sociobiology during the 1970s and was interested in finding a "gene" or an "index of innate ability" for "headmanship" which had something to do with reproductive success and strengthened immune systems against diseases in small populations.

Some scholars may differ on how central this was to Neel's work, and whether this was, as Terrence Turner remembers, already an interest in the 1960s or only became a side interest with the rise of sociobiology in the 1970s.

The general interest was clearly present early on, and the mix with violence as a key component may have been sharpened with Napoleon Chagnon's representations.

Chagnon worked with Neel first as a graduate student and then as a post-doctoral researcher; part of his job was to prepare the Yanomami to give blood, stool, and mucus samples, as well as genealogical information. He has been championed by sociobiologists such as E. O. Wilson and Irven De-Vore for his insistence on the connection between violence and reproduc-tive success, and even more recently by evolutionary psychologists such as Steven Pinker, who seems to know little anthropology and even less about the Yanomami but manages to be quoted on these topics by the *New York Times* (8 October 2000) nonetheless.

What seems to infuriate cultural anthropologists about sociobiologists is their insistence on extrapolating from quite interesting statistics of animal mating and investment in care of offspring patterns, and the various predic-tive models that can be made of these patterns, to the Vietnam War or the decisions of the Supreme Court. Many of us remember an astonishing film they helped produce in the 1970s called *Doing What Comes Naturally*, a film for high school students, which opened with a shot of young women's rear ends in tight hot pants, primate females presenting, and fighter jets taking off for Vietnam bombing runs. Doing what comes naturally? When premiered to the anthropology department at Harvard, a few such as Irv DeVore had the grace to be embarrassed, but E. O. Wilson and Robert Trivers were unre-pentant, the latter asserting that eventually even the decisions of the Supreme Court would be reduced to genetic patterns.

If this is science, well then of course most scientists are not scientific. But much of sociobiology has this wild extrapolating inferential structure, and no amount of breast-beating that it is scientific (or accusations that its critics are "antiscience") will make it so. Indeed, given that science can change quite rapidly (see for instance the observations by Cavalli-Sforza in the introduc-tion to his 1994 compendium on how DNA collections are likely to revise some of the earlier work, to which Neel's collections among the Yanomami, Makiritare, Xavante, and Kayapo contributed data sets for South America), the greatest legacies of sociobiology are not likely to be scientific, but their popular culture advertisements, which are in the end a fairly ethnocentric packaging of odds and ends from modern folk psychology about men liking to sow their wild oats and women trying to protect family.

For these reasons the best of the first-round commentaries produced on the Tierney affair are those which are couched in somewhat resigned his-torical terms: we have seen this before. See particularly Clifford Geertz's

"Life among the Anthros" (Geertz 2001); Marshall Sahlins's more combative "Guilty not as Charged" (Sahlins 2000); Greg Grandin's more geopolitical "Coming of Age in Venezuela" (Grandin 2000); Charles C. Mann's comprehensive "Anthropological Warfare," including a full two-page box "Preemptive Strike Sought to Discredit Book Before It Was Published" (Mann 2001); and the letter to the editor from Terence Turner after reading James Neel's field notes (Turner 2001). See now also the April 2001 issue of *Current Anthropology*, especially Fernando Coronil's comments on the protests in Venezuela against the Charles Brewer Carias, Cecilia Matos, and Chagnon alliance which aimed to create a privatized mining and biosphere on Yanomami land, and the failure of these protests to have much impact on discussions in the United States.

The sense of déjà vu with regard to the sociobiology debates is, however, quite a separate issue from the need for anthropology to engage with contemporary biology. The latter is proceeding quite robustly not via sociobiology, which, at least in its imperialistic reductionism to what today in a postgenomics/proteomics age is after all a rather midlevel and relatively single strand version of biology. Rather, the engagement of anthropology and biology is proceeding robustly through both medical anthropology and the synergy of anthropology and sts (science, technology, and society studies), where people trained in both biology and social science are bringing onto the front stage not only the corridor talk that scientists use to help form their fields of action but also the corporate strategies for biotechnologies that are shaping the directions science takes.

Public Participation and Informed Research

A third strand, once much stronger, and, as Monsanto's "Terminator" seed fiasco demonstrates, in need of renewed attention by scientists as well as corporations, government, and academics, is public participation by an informed citizenry. This is necessary at the very least to provide legitimacy and direction in terms of what society will countenance, but ideally to bring to the table not just laboratory sophistication but also ecological and experiential entailments, interactions, and consequences.

We need a robust institutional vision that deals with power, access, equity, and accountability. This need not hamper science, and it is arrogant for some scientists to think they can rule it out of court merely because it might. The investigation of the development of vaccines, of the human genome project, of strategies for both agricultural and medical biotechnologies (including the histories of human genetics in the Amazon)—these have an expanding place in American Anthropological Association meetings and should form an important component of practical civics more generally. So if there is an exasperated air to having to counter the sociobiologists yet again, there are also new dimensions to the discussion.

What is new is the gradual effort to move to the twenty-first-century sciences in the following ways:

1. Remapping what we know of the Yanomami in comprehensive terms — putting the villages on maps along with their neighbors and those they interact with, laying out the historical horizons; not allowing one village or one period of a few months to represent all of Yanomami history or culture, nor one ethnographer to be the only voice heard, nor only one research team's results.

2. Acknowledging the relation between the means of gathering data and the kinds of accounts produced from such gathering; not allowing the backstage of science to be unavailable to view or evaluation. This includes the backstage of the remarkable Tim Asch films, which were not just Andy Warhol set-up-a-camera-and-let-it-roll "cinema verité" affairs (something that was much debated in ethnographic film circles at the time, even if the sociobiologists deny the fact today). Asch himself was explicit about this, including when he wanted to remove his films from classrooms at the request of Yanomami who asked that if these films were to be shown to American students, they be shown along with other films that showed them as they are today and not as they "once were").

3. Acknowledging the political contexts in which we and the Yanomami live; not allowing them to represent the eternal primitive and we the Cartesian point of view; acknowledging the interests of the multinationals, the miners, the militaries of Brazil and Venezuela, the missionaries, the local entrepreneurs, the journalists, and the egos of individual anthropologists who wish to be seen as the only experts.

4. Understanding the power (both cognitive and commercial) of contemporary genetics, molecular biology, and pharmacogenomics in shaping research agendas; not allowing the categories and data of molecular biology to be confused with the categories and data of social usages (a good example is the somewhat contradictory — or better, imprecise — assertions that there is no such thing as "race," yet funding research for genes that affect particular groups defined in proxy terms for socially defined races or ethnic groups).

5. Acknowledging the institutional structures through which science operates and which are the subject of a struggle, on the one hand, to be opened to public inspection and, on the other, to be closed in the name of patent rights, and proprietary interests that are said to be (and in our current world are) the engines of innovation and progress.

None of these acknowledgments lessen the power, realism, or objectivity of science, nor do they make the world naively relativistic without standards of evaluation; on the contrary, they are the very substance of precision that allows for evaluation and scientific validity by acknowledging partiality, standpoint of knowledge, or relative relativism, and of the inescapable double meaning of representation in science as elsewhere.

Yanomami Studies Reevaluated

In a book on the Xavante at Etenitepa, another group among whom James Neel collected information, we can see features of a 1990s perspective that integrates and contextualizes the work of the 1960s. Written by Carlos E. A. Coimbra, Nancy M. Flowers, Francisco M. Salzano, and Ricardo V. Santos, *The Xavante in Transition: Health, Ecology, and Bioanthropology in Central Brazil* (2002) presents a diachronic historical account of the Xavante, one that acknowledges the epidemics, armed conflicts of the eighteenth and nineteenth centuries, and the Xavante response through increased mobility and migration and argues that there is "no way to regard the Xavante as a society until recently isolated from the political and economic processes that have been taking place for centuries in Brazil and beyond," even though the most recent and continuous contact began only in the 1940s (Coimbra et al. 2002).

In the case of the Xavante, the authors can trace a history from conflicts with gold miners in Goias in the eighteenth century, Indian raiding of towns, and efforts to settle them in secular mission villages. In the nineteenth century they migrated westward across the Araguaia River, where they were able to maintain isolation and hostility until the 1940s. Village splits and moves can be traced since then, as well as gradually increasing links with outsiders. These include a failed government project to mechanize rice growing on their land, and subsequent pursuit of resources beyond hunting, gathering, fishing, and planting in the forest. Recently they have allied with environmental groups to try to block the building of an inland waterway that would negatively affect their fishing and other wild resources.

The authors also provide a historical sketch of the several lines of research on human biology in the Amazon since the 1960s, noting particularly the work on population genetics by Neel and Salzano, and the work on the epidemiology of infectious and parasitic diseases by Francis L. Black and Roberto G. Baruzzi, and place these traditions of research in the context of 1990s work on the epidemiological transition profile of the Xavante that makes them today look more like impoverished and malnourished populations elsewhere, with the emergence of obesity, diabetes, and hypertension as serious concerns even as they are still plagued with infectious and parasitic diseases.

Etenitepa is the community that the social anthropologist David Maybury-Lewis described in an important and rich ethnography, *Akwe-Shavante Society*, and in a memoir, *The Savage and the Innocent*, based on fieldwork in 1957 and 1958. Neel and Francisco Salzano collected human biological data in 1962 with Maybury-Lewis's help and correlated them with genealogies Maybury-Lewis elicited. Flowers did more research in 1976 and 1977 on demography and human ecology. A linguist, Laura Graham, in the 1980s worked on oratory and leadership, and from 1990 to 1995, Coimbra, Santos, and Flowers and their students collected epidemiological and health data.

One can thus track the reversal of population decline and fears that Indians would disappear to recovery and growth of Indian populations in the 1980s, along with changing patterns of health, nutrition, disease, marriage, violence, and politics. In the context of the fierce debates over Chagnon's portrait of the Yanomami as somehow primordially and sociobiologically "the fierce people," the comments of these authors on the Xavante are interesting, linking depopulation to both disease and violence provoked by sorcery that targeted weaker factions and had effects on marriage patterns. (Many have noted that in the 1960s the Yanomami did not have the highest levels of violence among Amazonian groups.)

In the 1960s, development projects initiated by the military government in Brazil—highways, hydroelectric dams, mining, agricultural settlement— brought migration into the Amazon with severe consequences for many native groups, including the Yanomami. The point is not that the time of troubles for the Xavante is over but that changing historical contexts matter profoundly. In the debates about whether population collapse after epidemics was due to a lack of genetic diversity in small, relatively homogeneous populations, or whether social breakdown was a more important cause, Neel seems to have taken the latter side.

None of the Actors Were Saints, Nor Should We Champion Them as if They Were

James Neel was not a saint. He was an important founder of human genetics in the United States. He headed the U.S. organization evaluating the genetic effects of radiation on survivors of the atomic bomb in Japan, which collected biological data but did not provide medical care to survivors, many of whom were impoverished and ill.

Susan Lindee's chapter "No Treatment Policy" in her book about Neel and the Atomic Bomb Casualty Commission, *Suffering Made Real* (Lindee 1994), points out that this was part of the U.S. refusal to atone for the use of atomic weapons (providing treatment might be taken as admission of wrongdoing), and that there was resentment and protest over this policy, especially when Atomic Bomb Casualty Commission (ABCC) director John Morton in 1954 offered treatment for the twenty-three-member crew of the fishing boat *Lucky Dragon*, heavily irradiated by fallout from Bravo weapons tests at Bikini, and that this fueled rumors that Hiroshima and Nagasaki had been bombed as part of a biomedical experiment.

The United States should have provided care, and refusal of care would no longer be ethical under the current Helsinki Declarations. But, as Lindee points out, Neel was involved in the collection of epidemiological data, not experimentation or clinical trials with human subjects; and the only part of the research ethical code existing at the time that was violated was informed consent. Japanese researchers participated in, and in fact had initiated, the research. Families were asked permission for the body to be autopsied and studied, but this was in exchange for free cremation, for which many survivors otherwise had no money. It was under conditions of occupation, and people may have felt they had to give up the bodies. Even after the occupation, the offer of free cremation seems to have been sufficient inducement for many.

Neel acknowledged that the research in Japan would not, and did not, generate statistically significant information about the effects of radiation on the offspring of the survivors (i.e., detecting hereditary mutations, as opposed to more easily detected somatic mutations). The Nobel Prize–winning radiation geneticist H. J. Muller questioned the scientific usefulness of studies on survivors, but Neel and the AEC and other scientists thought it important to do these studies because of public demand for information and reassurance. And Neel was interested in the fact that Japanese populations practiced high rates of cousin marriage and what effects that practice might have on the circulation of deleterious genes (see his official report; see also Schull and Neel 1965; Neel 1994; Kevles 1985; Lindee 1994).

There were complaints about taking blood, organ, and tissue samples back to the United States, and not making them available to Japanese scientists who had pioneered radiation research in the 1920s, and especially that the U.S. researchers had used help from, but not fully acknowledged, the insights and suggestions of Tsuzuki Masao. (See also Lindee's 1999 article, where she softens her earlier observations, stressing the degree to which Japanese — unlike the case of Native American burial repatriations — were invested in the use of these remains for the future knowledge of all mankind.) As funding for the ABCC became threatened, there was increasing pressure from within the U.S. establishment for the return of the remains, which finally took place in 1973.

Neel's ideas about primitives were romantically naive — listen to his voice on the Tim Asch film *The Feast*, or read his autobiography, *Physician to the Gene Pool*, or his scientific publications on the Yanomami. He often fell (with occasional disclaimers) into first-contact tropes about our primitive ancestors, despite the fact that such understandings were disputed. In the 1966 "Man the Hunter" conference (proceedings of which were published in 1968; see Lee and DeVore 1968), Donald Lathrap and Claude Lévi-Strauss both took exception. Neel's submission of a paper to *Science*, "Lessons from a 'Primitive' People: Do Recent Data concerning South American Indians Have Relevance to Problems of Highly Civilized Communities?" (published in 1970), was criticized on these grounds by reviewers, as well as for not adequately laying out the limitations of the models he was adapting from Cavalli-Sforza. (Neel included these letters of criticism in the files deposited at the American Philosophical Society.) In the 1980s these sorts of criticisms against those who wanted to see contemporary hunter-gatherers as analogues of our primitive ancestors would become much sharper, as in Edwin Wilmsen's arguments regarding the Bushmen (Wilmsen 1989). Neel was a eugenicist of the sort the historian Daniel Kevles calls "reform eugenics" (a term that Susan Lindee also adopts in her book on Neel and Japan): that is, he was interested to remove disease-bearing genes through genetic counseling (Kevles 1985). He warned against prematurely experimenting on germ line genetic engineering because we do not know enough yet about biologically complex systems, but thought such experimentation would be put into practice (witness today the publicly expressed desire of researchers such as French Anderson). Neel speculated that primitive leadership structures were better than those in the "civilized" world, and this centered on his ideas about the selection for leadership genes as well as small population structures.

In the Amazon, Neel engaged in research projects of a sort that are being continued today with new technologies and slightly new wrappings. Some of these are being challenged with regard to their purpose, scientific productivity, and return of benefit to research populations, but others seem to be more grounded in the local needs and participation of the research subjects. Whether Neel could have provided more, or more effective, medical care at the time of the January–February 1968 epidemic is a perennial practical issue for scientific expeditions operating in the midst of severe illness:

The Report of the Medical Team of the Federal University of Rio de Janeiro on Accusations Contained in Patrick Tierney's "Darkness in El Dorado" points out that since Neel knew of serious outbreaks of measles before his arrival in the field, his planning for dealing with the medical emergencies could have been better. Although it is unlikely that he would have set up an experiment on the natural course of a measles epidemic, the report cites his collaborator Ryk Ward to the effect that he had intended to vaccinate Yanomami to measure their serum levels a year or two later. The report does fault him for not living up to the Helsinki Declaration rules for informed consent but admits that this was not unusual at the time. In any case, Neel returned repeatedly to the Amazon, and his concern for getting vaccines to the Yanomami did not stop when he left the field in 1968, though this was an individual effort, not part of a comprehensive public health campaign.

Neel wanted to collect information on how disease pressures had shaped human evolution, and so cared about immune responses, and thought he might have a chance to see human evolution at work by tracking antibody levels in Yanomami. It is perhaps unfair that Tierney hyperbolizes this into taking advantage of a measles epidemic as providing a "natural experiment," but there was an intense debate at the time about the dynamics of epidemics on unexposed populations, and this would have been grist to the mill. As it happens, Neel did stress the social breakdown that comes with epidemics as a major factor in the devastating mortality, against those who argued that it was due to the fact that their genetic makeup might not have had a chance to develop genes for resistance. The result, for better or worse, was the argument that the treatment of Indians should not be any different than for others: Edmonton B vaccine might cause severe reactions, but it would still save lives.

It is a fascinating history that is bowdlerized by turning it into simplistic hagiography of Neel. Skeptical readers of Neel's field notes, such as Terence Turner (2001), provide a useful check against the early rush by Susan Lindee and other historians of genetics to join with sociobiologists in defending Neel, and dismissing Tierney *tout court*, as Susan Lindee did at the American Anthropological Association meetings in November 2000, both accusing Tierney of basic violation of journalistic ethics, and applauding William Irons's suggestion that people not read Tierney's book for themselves.

Lindee has since moderated her views (in the April 2001 issue of *Current Anthropology*), calling Tierney's text "an unstable narrative [that] has provoked many of us to look at ethnographic and genetic practices with disturbing, if not novel, questions," while at the same time continuing to thoroughly impugn Tierney's credibility. Her view of Neel, however, has always been nuanced, and her 1994 book began with the still well taken observation that applies not only to Neel but also to many sociobiologists today: "I do think Neel and his colleagues struggled heroically to conduct their science in that neutral zone in which language, culture, and history do not exist, that is, in the realm of the idealized science that they learned in the course of their formal education. My text operates from the assumption that such a neutral zone does not exist, for anyone, at any time" (Lindee 1994: ix–x).

What might be quite useful is to have a detailed accounting of just what Neel's projects in the Amazon actually accomplished. I would expect three things. First, that there will be descriptive and suggestive, but few clear or definitive, findings about genetic drift that indicate directions of migration or provide models of disease among early Native Americans. For an example of one of a series of fascinating papers that tell us more about the development of methods and arguments for speculating about "microevolution" or migration and connectedness among groups, see the paper by Richard Spielman, Neel, and others that demolishes as an artifact of typological measures of distance a possible closer connection between the Yanomami and the Guaymi of Panama than with their neighbors (Spielman et al. 1979). Alcida Ramos, in the printed responses following the paper, archly remarks that the conclusion is an anticlimax, but that it is good at least to come to a negative conclusion about the methods (see also Cavali-Sforza's comments in his 1994 compilation). Major findings are said to include the fact that there is as much heterogeneity within villages as between them, and that there is marked local differentiation in gene frequencies among villages; whether this is "major" is a matter of opinion.

Second, when these health, demographic, and epidemiological data collected in the 1960s are integrated with newer findings, they may help give an important picture of changes over the past decades in health transition profiles, ecological change, and changing relations with the surrounding worlds (cf. Coimbra et al. 2002). Coimbra and his coauthors make no bones about the inefficiencies and failures of health services for the Xavante, but they draw attention to the physicians and research scientists who have remained engaged in trying to provide services, and this is an important story in thinking through ethics for the future.

Third, at least equally interesting could be a history of such a project fascinating for its ambitions and its difficulties: for example, the logistics of keeping temperature-sensitive materials, the changing formulas of how to preserve feces and other samples for analysis by the CDC and other labs, the preservation of samples in freezers at Michigan, later transferred to Penn State (and how these contributed to reanalyses over the years), and so on.

Tierney's wonderful image of big science pursued without much resistance—the image of Venezuelan air force cargo planes and helicopters delivering containers of biology research paraphernalia, ethnographic film equipment, and trade goods, landing on small round compounds in the jungle and conscripting half the villagers as porters—is perhaps a little overdone. But the difficult logistics of expeditions, making sure that airstrips were cleared, that gasoline drums and boats were available, and so on, are equally part of the story of expeditions under challenging Third World and tropical conditions, although the actual conditions may have been closer to Fabian's account of nineteenth-century Africa, with mission stations, local power brokers, and traders part of the landscape, and various sorts of resistance to be read between the lines.

Equally interesting in such an account would be the network of, and collaboration and competition among, laboratories and the sense of pioneering new methods: HLA typing and cytogenetics was just coming into use in the 1970s, and there are negotiations with Miguel Layrisse in Caracas about bringing down a Japanese team member to help with this, as well as discussions with Walter Bodmer in London and D. B. Amos at Duke about the techniques. Several labs at the NCDC and elsewhere helped with analysis, and there are discussions about collecting better soil samples for fungal analysis, and so on; there are negotiations not to overlap too much with a student of Lévi-Strauss, and concern that maybe he should be directed to work elsewhere; concerns by the missionaries that a graduate student not be sent too soon to an area they are just beginning to work in; concerns that Layrisse and Roche's own studies proceed collaboratively as well as independently. Neel's files reflect the various things that always arise in complicated projects: they record proudly that they can keep cells in nitrogen indefinitely with a high recovery rate, but then a technician made an error in making up the solution, resulting in loss of samples, so that they have to simply write up what they have analyzed so far on Rh results (Neel, letter to Miguel Layrisse in Caracas, 18 April 1968); or from the NCDC, Irving Kagan writes that a technician failed to code the blood slides with individuals names and so identities are lost, and only the statistical findings of pathogen traces can be reported (9 December 1968). In other words, it is not only the Yanomami who are fascinating in their activities and networks, but the researchers as well.

Neel worked with anthropologists and geneticists in Brazil as well as Venezuela, and it would be of interest to know how the growth of institutes such as the Venezuelan Institute for Scientific Investigation (IVIC) was affected by the collaboration; the power differentials and collaborative trade-offs in the research communities of Venezuela, Brazil, and the United States; and why there seems to have been more public turmoil and airing of dirty laundry between the missionaries, the Neel-Roche-Brewer-Layrisse collaborations, and Chagnon on the Venezuelan side of the border than on the Brazilian side, even given the pressures the Yanomami in Brazil were experiencing from the local elites, army, central government, and miners.

Perhaps the most intriguing of the various micromoves in the Neel story is that he seems to have had a forewarning about Tierney and so placed a copy of his field diary in a folder marked "Yanomamo 1968 Insurance," along with correspondence, in the archives at the American Philosophical Society in Philadelphia so that scholars would have easy access (Papers of James V. Neel, Archives of the American Philosophical Society, Philadelphia).

Patrick Tierney is obviously not a saint. He is a self-described activist-journalist, and a reformed Chagnon groupie. Converts are often a bit over-zealous. Still, he does what journalists often do: put together with great detail a vivid picture, much of which the principals in the story find wrong and misconceived but which sometimes puts a new set of questions on the public agenda. In this case, Tierney's primary achievement, I think, is to paint a panorama of how genetics, ethnography, and filmmaking (things that are normally compartmentalized as if they had nothing to do with one another) fit together into a volatile research project. He sets this in the context of the wider public perception of Indians, miners, and state militaries, in which the Indians are but the bit players who always get the short end of the stick, in an all-too-familiar soap opera of suffering served up to us by the news media diet of Third World tales of woe.

But the use of scandalous allegation, while effective in generating temporary publicity, is not a useful long-term strategy. This is especially so given the memory of 1960s allegations of efforts to kill Native Americans which were documented by Brazilian state officials and which went to trial (in 1969): state officials and landowners were accused of giving Indians "gifts" of clothing impregnated with disease organisms, including smallpox, chicken-pox, measles, and tuberculosis (clippings of news reports are also in Neel's files). Tierney perhaps got caught up in 1990s anxieties about new biological research along with the declassification of materials on radiation experiments in the Cold War period (Welsome 1999). (One of the media questions in the Tierney affair is why the reported early drafts of his book, which are said to have focused on the miners and environmental issues, were changed, and whether this had to do with the editorial and marketing decisions of his publishers, who would have been attuned to the 1990s anxieties about biomedical research, as opposed to the somewhat less immediate U.S. public concerns with miners and environments outside the United States.)

Over the past decades in Brazil and Venezuela, there has been plenty of corruption, opposition to Yanomami land rights from economic elites and state deputies in the state of Roraima as well as from the Brazilian army, and failure to keep mining and other operations in check. We have also seen the attempt by Charles Brewer Carians, Cecilia Matos, and Chagnon to turn Yanomami land in Venezuela into a privately owned mining and biosphere reservation. The task is to make these corruptions, oppositions, and failures accountable in ways that will make it increasingly more difficult for them to continue.

Napoleon Chagnon is not a saint. Everyone, probably even himself, agrees on that. He wrote a classic and sometimes funny account of a novice anthropologist's entry into the field full of fear and fantasy of "first contact." He is one of those academic egos who has pushed away as many of his students and colleagues as he has attracted, most notably the filmmaker Tim Asch. Often belligerent and full of waitheri, Chagnon has also had the grace to write an account of his falling out with Asch and has depicted his stormy relations with Neel (on the CD-ROM *Yanomamo Interactive: The Ax Fight*). The ethics of Chagnon's fieldwork, his battles against missionaries and other anthropologists over who protects and who harms the Yanomami, and his relationship with the Yanomami and the efforts to keep him banned from their land also raise many questions. The organization Cultural Survival, for instance, says: "The ways in which anthropologists portray the societies they study have consequences, sometimes serious consequences in the real world. Indigenous societies have all too often been maligned in the past, denigrated as savages and marginalized at the edges of the modern world and the modern societies in it. It is not therefore a trivial matter to insist on the fierceness of a people or to maintain that they represent an especially primitive stage in human evolution. Chagnon has not done this inadvertently to the Yanomami. On the contrary, he has done so deliberately, systematically, and over a long period of time, in spite of the remonstrances of his fellow anthropologists. We at Cultural Survival consider this to be not only bad science but also a bad example of harmful writing about an indigenous people" (www.cs.org/main.html).

Tim Asch no doubt was not a saint, though when I knew him, he was an engaging soul, who pioneered efforts to work with at least two well-known anthropologists. His film *The Ax Fight* bears repeated viewing, and the posthumous CD-ROM of it, *Yanomamo Interactive: The Ax Fight*, is a wonderful way to do so, with its introductory essays by Peter Beilla and Chagnon. The film is edited into five replays of the fight: chaotic first viewing with no explanation; efforts to get an explanation and to superimpose on the visuals kinship charts so that one can keep track of the players; explanation of the step-by-step escalation and de-escalation of the dispute; and a final replay of the opening sequence again without any voice-over or subtitling, intended to provide a now informed opportunity to view the fight with the kind of knowledge that would be available to the players.

However, to many students and audiences, the final sequence reinforces a sense of chaotic primitive savagery—a stark reminder of the need to use subtitles or other means to block reemergence of unreflective stereotypes, which can easily override seeing the patterned slow escalation by stages, intervention, and calming that the film intends to put on display. There is a posthumous lesson and analogy here for the continuing struggles over the representations of the Yanomami.

The Yanomami are, of course, also not saints. But as the Yanomami slowly begin to have spokesmen of their own, such as Davi Kopenawa, who travel abroad and are able to speak on the international stage, despite their relative lack of means (to buy air tickets and the like), their fragmentation into disparate villages, the still slow means of communication on the ground in the watersheds between the two mighty rivers, the Orinoco in Venezuela and the Amazon in Brazil, their voices will begin to help shift the power of representation away from those who make claims about them and in their name. (See Ramos's account of how Brazilian Indians have "instrumentalized exoticism and turned it into a decoy to first attract national attention and then put across their own message" and have learned to deploy Western rhetoric on human rights and environmental concerns in a world of interethnicity [Ramos 1998: 99, 135].) Yanomami are becoming bilingual, literate, trained in the use of microscopy, able to create a future-looking ethnicity (see Ramos in the *Current Anthropology* Forum, April 2001). As with the Kayapo, who have preceded the Yanomami in such efforts, this will not mean any lessening of internal or external political competition.

But surely acknowledging the passions, missteps, dilemmas, competitions, and lack of knowledge is a better way of defending the Yanomami, science, and anthropology than denying human form to their productions and insisting on an immaculate conception and purity of implementation of science, anthropology, and native population rights.

Epilogue: On Distinguishing Good and Evil in Emergent Forms of Life (Woodblock Print to Newspaper Illustration)

In the Yoshitoshi woodblock print on the cover of the paperback edition of this book, Lord Koremochi looks into the bowl, expecting to see the direct reflection of the beautiful woman standing by his side. Mirroring surfaces, however, reflect indirect and deeper truths. He sees instead a horned ogre. It is, of course, an age-old metaphor for distinguishing good from evil, superficial appearance from structural reality, and perhaps today technoscientific phantasmagoria from emergent forms of life.

That the print comes from a transitional period after the Meiji Restoration and the enforcement of modernist rationality seems apt to our own moment of debates about new technoscientific genies/demons garbed in the most beautiful of promises, desires, and passions. Will we, like Koremochi, have to draw our sword, as some in recent debates over cloning, gene therapy, and genetically modified foods have tried to suggest? Are our eyes, like those of Koremochi at the moment of the print, too heavy lidded with sleep to distinguish the dream world and the real? Or is it rather a moment of careful judgment, prudent decisions, and steady vigilance?

The geometry of gazes in the print might be compared with those in Velázquez's *Las Meninas* and in the photograph of the Ian Hunter virtual reality surgical system (see chapter 9.1). The anxieties and uncertainties being confronted in this woodblock print might be compared with the phantasmagoria and psychopathologies in the woodblock prints of chapter 4, but also in the films of chapters 3 and 7, the theater of politics of chapters 1 and 10, and the high-stakes experiments of chapter 5.

The print is from the series *Shingata Sanjurokkaisen* (Thirty-six ghosts), the last series completed by Yoshitoshi before he died. *Shingata* can be read as "new forms" of old ghost stories. It can also be pronounced *shinkei*,

33. Yoshitoshi woodblock print, c. 1870. Perceiving good and evil, appearance and reality, surface and deep structure. Print owned by Michael Fischer, photograph by Richard Chase.

"nerves," or the use of old ghost stories as projective vehicles for contemporary anxieties. The nervous system of emergent forms of life.

Yoshitoshi (1839–1892) was the last of the great *ukiyo-e* print artists, and one of the first of the popular newspaper illustrators. A student of Utagawa Kuniyoshi (d. 1861), Yoshitoshi began his apprenticeship in 1850. Kuniyoshi, in turn, was the third in a line of virtuoso masters of the Utagawa school founded by Toyoharu. One of the remarkable features of this school was the way in which Japanese, Chinese, and Western pictorial techniques cross-fertilized. Toyoharu transformed the flat aesthetic of the ukiyo-e, introducing depth perspective and spatial expansiveness, inspired both by Chinese landscape painting and by Dutch engravings. The ukiyo-e expanded in subjects from interior scenes, actor prints *(yakusha-e)*, and beautiful women prints *(bijin-ga)* to exterior scenes and many kinds of subjects.

Yoshitoshi's initial fame came with his series *Twenty-eight Murders* (1866–1867), reflecting the unrest of the years immediately preceding the Meiji Restoration. Rejected as too bloody by refined modernist commentators of the post-Meiji period, these prints were part of a popular obsession with blood and gore cultivated on the stage with Noh theater *shuramono* genre pieces depicting the fall of warriors into the realm of angry *shurado* (demigods), into hell, and with Kabuki live-action thrillers and horror stories.

Yoshitoshi's fame rose further with the fall of the shogunate and his eye-witness depiction of the Battle of Ueno (1868). His series *Hundred Warriors* (1868–1869) used medieval warrior stories to convey the unrest of his contemporary world.

In 1875 he became a staff artist for the newspaper industry, which was allowed now to expand after a period of censorship. He worked for the *Postal News, Masago Shimbun, Iroha Shimbun, Illustrated Liberal*, and *Lamp of Liberty*. Shinichi Segi says that Yoshitoshi's woodblock print work and this commercial work made him "the public eyes on the fighting of the Meiji Restoration" (Segi 1985). Like the WPA photographs of the Great Depression or the General Eisenhower–faciliated photographs of the 1945 liberation of the concentration camps, and the television camera of the Vietnam War, Yoshitoshi provided indelible and reverberating images and templates of the nerves and anxieties of his time. Roger Keyes says that Yoshitoshi's 1874 woodblock print of the assassination of Ii Naosuke at Edo Castle created a sensation, stirring up painful memories, rekindling passions, raising the untamed ghosts of the past that had never been laid to rest during the period of censorship and disciplined rationality of the first years of the Meiji Restoration (Keyes 1982: 130). Other prints included the incident of Japanese ships provoking attack and then taking the Korean fort on Koka Island (1875), the Satsuma Rebellion (1877), the Battle of Fushimi, which had initiated the civil war, and the series *Mirror of Famous Generals* (1878). By 1884 he had more than eighty apprentices working for him.

Ghost stories are entertainment, a means of nervous deep play, and a way to raise a ghost. They are told at Buddhist temples and graveyards, where it is customary to light one hundred candles, extinguishing them one by one after each ghost story is told, until the audience is huddled together in pitch black (Segi 1985). If the collective nervous system achieves a state of sufficient anxiety and fearful expectation, a ghost may appear.

Yoshitoshi's print pictured in figure 33, is titled *Taira no Koremochi Toga-kushi-yama ni akki o taijisu zu* (Koremochi of the Taira clan vanquishing the demons of Mount Togakushi).[1] It is a story that had been both a Noh play, *Momji-gari* (Maple-viewing picnic), and a Kabuki play with the same name adapted in the 1880s for Yoshitoshi's friend, the actor Ichikawa Danjuro IX.

One autumn morning in the tenth century, as the leaves of the maple are turning color, Lord Koremochi leaves Kyoto on a deer hunt. As he treks into the mountain forest above Kyoto, he comes upon a princess and her attendants picnicking in a maple grove. Invited to join in the drinking and dancing, eventually he falls into an intoxicated sleep. A messenger from Hachiman, the god of war, comes to Koremochi in a dream and warns that the princess is really Kijo, the demon of Mount Togakushi, and that she intends to kill him. The messenger gives Koremochi a sword and tells him to awake. He wakes with a start, sees the threat just in time, and runs the demon through with the magic sword (Stevenson 1983: 50).

This story line does not yet fill in the whys and wherefores of the passions, dreams, jealousies, desires, and vengeances that might put flesh and blood, nerves, and emergences into the narration. Like all good metaphoric vehicles, the tenor is left to our own discernments and deployments. The play of triangulation on the sake cup's mirror surface can lead to discernments of good and evil.

The sake itself, as well, can, like any *pharmakon*, both paralyze and speed the faculties of discernment. It too is the scene of struggle, a third space or virtual cave immersive environment of ogre/beauty, falsehood/truth, elixir/mirror, biochemical medium/symbolic operator, material/semiotic object.[2] In this work of indirection and cultural reweaving lie both emergent forms of life and cultural forms of critique.

Prologue

1 On the interplay between the hype and pragmatics of the Y2K problem, see further M. Fischer 1999b. As Donald MacKenzie notes, much of the estimated $400 billion spent worldwide represented system replacement and upgrading desirable on other grounds (2001: 8). MacKenzie's book *Mechanizing Proof* traces the history of attempting to find ways to allow automated verification of complex computer programs to avoid near catastrophes such as the 5 October 1960 nuclear attack false alarm, or the July 1962 error in a computerized system that forced the destruction of the *Mariner* interplanetary space probe. On hype and successful product development in the software and Internet economy, see Kelty 2001; on hype and genomics, biotechnology, and biocapitalism, see Sunder Rajan 2002; on the invisible work of maintaining networked, distributed offices, see Schwarz 2002; and on the failure of businesses despite efforts to recruit and enthuse constituents, see Latour 1993/1996.

2 Edward Said and Jacqueline Rose's slim volume *Freud and the Non-European* (2003) uncannily appeared, aptly as it were, as the present volume was being copyedited, just in time for a footnote here. Whatever one makes of Said's contribution to the many speculative interpretations of Freud's *Moses and Monotheism*, and Said's lovely invocations of "late style" as partial explanation, it is Rose's affiliative anecdote about Said, herself, the Vienna Philharmonic, and Vienna that reverberates here. In 2001, Vienna celebrated the centenary of Freud's *The Interpretation of Dreams*, and Edward Said was to give the annual Freud Memorial Lecture. It was canceled on grounds of "the political conflict in the Middle East." Rose's own lecture went on as planned, and the following day Simon Rattle conducted the Vienna Philharmonic Orchestra at the site of the Mauthausen concentration camp in "the first commemoration of the Holocaust in Austria." What was strangest, Rose says, was "the fact that my hosts seemed to want to talk, far more than about Freud and psychoanalysis, about the election of Haider and the resurgence of Austrian anti-Semitism (a traumatic resurgence, as one might say). To cancel Edward Said's lecture on political grounds in this context seems to me to be the saddest commentary on these anxieties and a missed opportunity, to say the least." The ironies and, even more, the psychic entanglements, obsessions, repetitions, blindnesses, and defensive aggressions constitute continuing deep play.

On trauma, identity processes, and exile, see also Fischer 1986, 1993.

1. Deep Play in Vienna

1   This chapter was originally presented on 27 September 2000 at the University of Vienna Opening Plenary Panel, Society for the Social Study of Science, and European Society for the Social Study of Science and Technology.

2   Many ancient Middle Eastern religions have two New Years, one in the fall and one in the spring. Mehregan, falling on the day Mehr of the month Mehr, is one of the six bimonthly seven-day festivals, or *gahambars*, that honor the annual cycle of rebirth and re-creation of the earth and the cosmos. I am fond of, and marked by, these different calendars, since I did some of my most formative fieldwork with the Zoroastrian, Jewish, Shiite, and Baha'i communities of Yazd, Iran (M. Fischer 1973).

3. Filmic Judgment and Cultural Critique

I thank Joao Biehl and Mazyar Lotfalian for commenting on drafts of this chapter, for insights and suggestions, and for general encouragement.

1   A'li 1985. For an analysis of these posters, see M. Fischer and Abedi 1990. That volume is organized into parts on oral, literate, and visual-media worlds.

2   Derrida plays on the German terms *Offenbarung* and *Offenbarkeit*, invoking primarily their theological and philosophical resonances; but these terms also raise questions (especially given the debate over religion in Iran) about religion, democracy, and the public sphere. The term used by Habermas is *Offentlichkeit* (1962/1989).

3   Quoted in Derrida 1996/1998: 55.

4   For an account of these debates, see M. Fischer 1980.

5   *International Film, Iranian Film Quarterly* 1999: 14.

6   See also the late-1990s documentary *Divorce Iranian Style*, by Kim Longinotto and Ziba Mir-Hosseini, which, while documenting both the continuing struggles of Iranian women and their ability to speak for themselves forcefully and volubly, has as its most affecting moment when the six-year-old daughter of the clerical judge sits on his empty seat, puts a cap on her head to imitate his turban, and proceeds to pronounce on all the reasons she would refuse to marry, mimicking the discourse of the adults in the court.

7   Engineer Mehdi Bazargan used the contrast between peep show and cinema to signify Iranian knowledge of the West of the generation at the turn of the century, and of his own generation of the pre–World War II era educated in Europe and America. I am indebted to Mazyar Lotfalian (1999) for recovering this metaphorical usage for me.

8   Walter Benjamin, "The Work of Art in the Age of Mechanical Reproduction," in Benjamin 1968.

9   The documentary film *Rosie the Riveter* deals explicitly both with this push of women back into the home and with some of the filmic propaganda used to help effect it (Friedan 1963).

5. Ethnographic Critique

I thank Joao Biehl, Hannah Landecker, and George Marcus for reading an earlier draft and making suggestions, traces of which they will recognize in the present version.

1 Printed first in 1956 in *L'Evolution psychiatrique*, vol. 1; translated by Alan Sheridan as "The Freudian Thing," in *Ecrits* (London: Tavistock, 1997), 145.

2 One can, of course, interrogate the idiosyncratic, social, and other forms of construction that go into making any description of reality. The point here is that this inquiry about the constitution of reality is a fundamental inquiry for ethnography in a way that is only backstage in advertising, advocacy, or business discourses. This is not to say that the formulators of these other discourses are not as sophisticated about what they are doing as are anthropologists, literary critics, ideology critics, and others. Indeed, such sophistication is increasingly part of the state of play in the real world. But their efforts are to veil such backstage understandings in order to deliver the message they wish to send, whereas arguably part of the mission of anthropology is to unveil such backstage understandings.

3 Similarly, if more generally, literary critic Wolfgang Iser (2000) suggests that ethnographies operate on a feedback principle of descriptively approximating reality, checking the descriptions, and then refining the approximations, in an ever more "closed" loop, "closer and closer" to reality. By contrast, novels, although often ethnographically and historically well researched, operate on a more "dissipative" and more "open" principle.

4 For example, Oron Catts and Ionat Zurr's work with tissue engineering in an effort to create "semi-living objects" that can help us think about the changing of cultures of production from manufacturing to growing, from throwaway consumption to Green, caring of ecologies of living objects. In their installation for the Ars Electronica Festival 2000, held in Linz, Austria, they made semi-living worry dolls, inspired by the traditional Guatemalan worry dolls, with cells grown over biodegradable polymers using the same techniques as medical researchers are using to create organs for patients, and hooked up to computers where installation visitors could type in their worries about these technologies (Catts, Zurr, and Ben-Ary 2000). They point out that an early effort to grow an ear for a child born without one, using a "nude mouse" (lacking T-cells, lacking an immune system) and creating a chimera of an ear growing on the back of a mouse with cartilage cells from the patient, was seen by many as grotesque, and hence there was a drive to artificial bioreactors to grow the cells on polymer matrices and in incubators rather than using mice so directly. Either way, the efforts to find the right polymer matrices that will not collapse, and to grow capillaries to support the tissue, are still unsolved problems. Catts and Zurr have found places as artists in residence at the Massachusetts General Hospital, as well as the Department of Anatomy and Human Biology at the University of Western Australia (Perth). Other bioartists include Joe Davis and Adam Zaretsky, artists in residence in the Biology Department at MIT, and Eduard Kac at the Art Institute in Chicago. One conceptual interface, or other end of a continuum, of this work — as was partly explicit in the Ars Electronica Festival, whose theme was "Next Sex, New Reproductive Technologies" — is with the work of anthropologists working with families with genetic disabilities, and shifting the understanding of both the genetics and social challenges from discourses of

normal/abnormal to ones of recombinant possibilities that require varied forms of caring (e.g., Ginsburg 2001; Rapp 1999). See now also S. Wilson 2002.

5 A series of the workshop papers are posted at http://meno.open.ac.uk/meno/ht97.html.

6 The figure of the old mole is from Hegel's *Lectures on the History of Philosophy* and Marx's *The Eighteenth Brumaire of Louis Napoleon*. As Ned Lukacher points out, it is in part a figure of waiting, of withdrawing or being driven (by the imperial eagle of ascendant state politics) underground during periods when politics are not "a viable alternative," of connecting through "passages" (Benjamin's term) legacies from the past into the present, of tracking the ways the past haunts the present. Lukacher points out how Balzac's novels operate as a kind of prefiguration for Marx's analysis, and he works out connections between literature, philosophy, and psychoanalysis. Lukacher analogizes Marx's analyses of nineteenth-century France to the Oedipus story in its various tellings, drawing on the performative effects of rumor/prophecy (Greek, *phatis*); the conflict between chthonian laws of family (psychosocial structures) and the more abstract, legislative, and procedural or bureaucratic powers of the state; and the recognition by Marx after 1848 that philosophy is "no longer a programmatic prescription for the future but rather a means of recognizing the detours and deferrals that must always be analyzed in retrospect," including the misrecognition by the peasants and petit bourgeoisie in the 1850s of their interests, conflating them with those of Louis Bonaparte. Antonio Negri and Michael Hardt in *Empire* attempt to sketch out the ways in which global flexible production regimes attract cycles of protest directed, but in discontinuous modes, in new variants of the nineteenth-century old mole. More precisely they "suspect that Marx's old mole has finally died" and has been replaced instead by the "infinite undulations of the snake" (Hardt and Negri 2000: 57). By this they wish to point to the apparent oddity that revolts today like Tiananmen Square, the Los Angeles riots, the strikes in Paris, and the Zapatistas in Chiapas do not seem to directly communicate with one another; there is not the continuity of cycles of proletarian struggles that emerged in nineteenth-century Europe, or the transnationally linked organization. Instead, in a kind of "paradox of incommunicability," these hypermediatized attacks on the global order are like ripples or sinuous movements, occasionally with tidal or typhoon force. I will suggest that a mutated or transgenic mole might be a better image: it is unclear that the old mole has died — Seattle and the environmental movements may yet construct the tunnels of the old mole — and yet it is the case that governance and politics, "the subject of labor," and the composition of the working, managerial, knowledge, and finance classes have changed, mutated, and recombinantly been reconfigured, and that new platforms and infrastructures have issued forth.

7 These are legacy terms from early-twentieth-century modernisms.

8 The abbreviation for Freiheits Partei Österreich, the party of Jörg Haider, which joined the Austrian government coalition in January 2000.

9 Ethnographically one might want to tease out some of the strands that the novel condenses: Austrian cultural critics often point out that contemporary right-wing politics almost never result in actual physical violence. Burning of guest worker hostels happens in Germany, but not in Austria. On the other hand, these same cultural critics underscore that because Austria did not undergo official de-Nazification as Germany did, xenopho-

bic and anti-Semitic verbal culture is socially acceptable (*Salon-fehig*) in ways that would be shocking in Germany. Indeed, some of the furor surrounding the rise of Jörg Haider and the FPÖ has to do precisely with the ambiguity of what the younger generation re-circulates unknowingly/knowingly from Nazi discourse. An oft-quoted anecdote about an FPÖ elected official is that at his electoral victory party he said, "Our honor is loyalty," and when a reporter asked if he was aware that was the slogan of the SS, he claimed he did not know. Similarly Haider tries to project an image of the casual/chic dressing, youthful sportsman (marathon runner, skier) of a new generation while playing on resentments and Nazi sentiments of his father's generation (they were good ordinary men; if Jewish victims of the Nazis are to be compensated, what about the Suddeten Deutsch forced out of Czechoslovakia after the war? Immigrants need not necessarily be deported, but they should stay in their place, segregated, "mit Anstendigkeit und Ordnung," proper and orderly, in the same way that reservations were made for the Slovenes and Slovaks after World War I). Note that the novel was published well before the FPÖ joined the government, provoking outrage and mild sanctions from the European Union. The novel tapped nicely into the logic of the situation, which continued to unfold. Thus the vertiginous effect (or Möbius effect) of reality seeming to follow or imitate fiction.

10   I'm indebted to Adrian Mathews for revealing this structuring of the relation between the mystic-love triangle in the novel and the Chaucer-era "testing tale" (in a 13 June 2000 conversation at the Au Chai de l'Abbaye on rue de Buci, a key site in Mathews's first novel). He points out there are clues in the text, including the "Green Chapel" chapter title (which, however, I cannot find, and may have been removed in favor of "an abandoned chapel"). But the parallels are quite amusing.

11   Both novels open with the weather and a funeral: in Greene, it is February, and the ground in Vienna's Zentralfriedhof (Central Cemetery) is so frozen that electric drills must be used; in Mathews's satirical counterpoint, because of global warming (meteorological, political), it is the first time it has snowed for seven years. Greene's novel is set at the beginning of the Cold War and in the border crossings of the Four Power occupation of Vienna; Mathews's is set after the Cold War in the border crossings of entrepreneurial biotechnology. The penicillin racket is not only the stealing from military hospitals, or only the growth of organized crime, but the dilution of the penicillin so that it becomes ineffective for the future. In both novels there is a romantic interest between the friend of the alleged deceased and his girlfriend or wife, and the plot revolves around the friend unraveling the oddities of the death to find that someone else is in the grave.

12   The cliché distinction in contemporary discussions is between therapy and enhancement, but the image here was parallel to the idea of a periodic table: a Sears catalog by which parents could attempt to select genetic modifications for their descendants. The extraordinary ads for the film GATTACA played on this thematic, though the film itself was less about this possibility than about establishing a dystopic totalitarian caste society in which molecular biology techniques of identifying people would become pervasive.

13   The degree to which there is or is not open space for debate and discussion is now being contested. At the Bio2000 Biotechnology Organization Conference, held in Boston, against which "biodevastation" demonstrations and counterconferencing were mounted,

organizers of the Bio2000 expressed frustration at debating scientifically poorly informed opponents, while insisting they were open to serious debate. The Council for Responsible Genetics, however, complained that their professionally accredited staff writer for GeneWatch was refused a press entry and told he could attend only if he paid the full fees (GeneWatch 2000, 13(2):12). Industry organizations have learned in many subtle, and not so subtle, ways to influence and shape both who of the media are given access and what gets openly circulated (Greife and Linsky 1995).

14 Adrian Mathews claims to like this identification but says it had not occurred to him. Oscar, for him, has to do with a bit of English cultural history: the oddity that since Oscar Wilde, the name has fallen into disuse. (Wilde is buried in the great Paris cemetery of Père Lachaise, which plays an important role in Mathews's first novel.)

15 "The Bitter Tears of Petra van Klimt." (I'm indebted here to Mathews for the identification.)

16 Adrian Mathews claims no longer to remember how he settled on this name, and not to know of Max Delbrück, and has no particular explanation for the name. I suspect another of these cases where the author had done a great deal of reading about molecular biology, so that the name lodged subliminally and structurally provided a neat reversal of trajectory.

17 A name that is phonemically resonant in several ways. Adrian Mathews says he originally thought of "Pinky" as a further homage to Graham Greene, whose *The Third Man* is a shadow text behind Mathews's novel. Sharkey also resonates with "shark" ("Sharks die if they do not keep moving: it is how they breathe"), a good name for a muckraking journalist, caught in several liminal worlds.

18 See Murakami's interviews with survivors of the Tokyo attack, exploring their post-traumatic stress and social responses, and also with members of the Aum Shinrikyo cult (Murakami 2000). On the Russian anthrax accident, cover-up, and exposure, see Guillemin 1999.

19 Compare the allegations in England (Mathews's native country) that Imutran — a leading biotechnology company involved in immunological experiments with genetically modified pigs for developing xenotransplantation of organs for humans — is circumventing Britain's strict rules by exporting genetically modified pigs for experiments conducted in Holland's Biomedical Primate Research Center in Rijswijk. Similarly Imutran pigs have been transported to xenotransplant researchers in Italy. Novartis, which owns Imutran, as well as the rights to cyclosporin, the immunosuppressant drug that has made allotransplants possible, is a multinational operating in many countries, and Imutran itself says that its collaborative experiments in Holland are not circumvention but merely conducting the collaborations it has with many international research groups. Given Europe's sensitivities about genetic engineering and human experimentation, these are somewhat charged issues, and the questions of harmonizing international standards are real ones. Herbert Gottweis in a study of Germany speaks of the use of parapolitical commissions to study technological issues as a way of *limiting* public debate, especially where there are issues of using biomedical research as a tool of national economic competitiveness (1998).

20 India's 1994 Transplantation of Human Organs Act made the selling of solid organs ille-

gal, allows the taking of organs from brain-dead cadavers, and forbids the gift of an organ from a live donor except parent, child, sibling, or spouse. Exceptions can be allowed by authorization committees in each state. The Madras/Chennai newsweekly *Frontline* did an article on how easy these committees could be circumvented (L. Cohen 1999: 136).

21 For the argument in favor of regulated but legal markets, see Radcliffe-Richards et al. 1998.

22 Originating in the famous comment of Robert Oppenheimer that when the physicists realized that the bomb was actually feasible, it became "too technically sweet" for them to stop.

23 The 1968 Harvard Brain-Stem Death Committee report that established this definition explicitly was tied to justifications regarding a shortage of organs and tissue and has slowly been accepted globally, in Japan, and in India with much hesitation. On Japan, see Lock 1994, 2002.

6. Autobiographical Voices and Mosaic Memory

1 As the careers of prominent physicists such as Lise Meitner (Rife 1999; Sime 1996), Marietta Blau (Galison 1997), and Herta Leng (the first tenured woman physicist at Rensselaer Polytechnic Institute) make clear, marginalization was an ever-present issue in the struggle for fame, recognition, and position. However, there is a danger of overwriting the experiences of one historical period with the ideological structures of a later one, as is illustrated in the reevaluations of Barbara McClintock's career (Keller 1983; Comfort 2001), and this danger is even greater when it is not just across different generations but across different cultural-institutional settings. The majority of women who went to the Albertsgasse Gymnasium in Vienna in the early decades of the twentieth century were expected to, and did, end up as successful professional women: physicians, professors, scientists, journalists, novelists. In one class of twenty-nine, for instance, of thirteen whose professions are known, there were three physicians, two lawyers, two art history professors, a chemist, a teacher, a journalist and translator, a well-known novelist (Elisabeth "Liesl" Freundlich), a famous social psychologist (Marie Jahoda), and a well-known geodesist (Irene Fischer).

2 For example, studies of women graduates of the University of Buenos Aires in the 1980s suggested that self-confident upper-class women did not pay attention to negative comments and slights felt by those from more working-class backgrounds.

3 Irene Fischer's detailed autobiography and history of the evolution of the field of geodesy between 1952 and 1977 proved to be unpublishable explicitly for this reason, according to Rutgers University Press's series on women and science, even though the manuscript contains a number of illuminating anecdotes about being a woman in male environments, from not being able to grade blue books for Leontiev when Harvard men found out they were being graded by a woman, to succeeding in being given closely held survey data from Latin American geodesists that would not be given formally to the U.S. government but would be given only personally to Fischer. The complaint of feminists that there are too few autobiographical role models of women in science proved in this case to be somewhat disingenuous. The autobiography is deposited in both longer and shorter (demanded by

Rutgers and several similar presses) versions at the Schlesinger Library at Radcliffe and the American Institute of Physics and has been made use of in Deborah Warner's account of the competitions to produce a global geodetic system (Warner 2000a, 2000b); see also Macdonald 2000.

But this is perhaps a comment not only on feminist publishing but also on the kinds of science autobiographies in general (also by men) that are allowed through the gatekeepers, such as the series of autobiographies published through the Sloan Foundation, which force the accounts into the genius tropes of the sort that are not particularly helpful to serious reflections on the history and development of the sciences and their institutional matrices between industry, government, and academia.

7. Post-Avant-Garde Tasks of Polish Film

1   On the romantic tropes of Polish resistance to the Austro-Hungarian, Russian, German, and Soviet dominations, see the conversations with Leszek Koczanowicz (M. Fischer 1993).

2   Malinowski is still remembered in Poland, though often as Stanislaw Witkiewicz's friend. In 1914 Witkiewicz went with Malinowski to Australia as photographer and draftsman. When the war broke out, as a holder of a Russian passport, Witkiewicz returned to Saint Petersburg and enlisted in an elite regiment, won battle distinction, and when the revolution came was elected commissar by his men. Malinowski, of course, held an Austrian passport and talked the British into letting him do fieldwork in the Trobriand Islands instead of interning him. On the era of folklore collection, national consolidation, and the struggles over unity, Ernest Gellner notes: "In the West, Ernest Renan perceptively pointed out how France was made, not by shared memories, but by a shared amnesia, and he opposed the intrusion of ethnology in politics: will, not ethnography, was to be the basis of the state. . . . But in the eastern half of Europe things were different. The Czechs, for instance, tried to buttress their own identity and existence by a medieval epic which was shown to be a forgery during the period when Malinowski was growing up. The Russians possess a similar piece of literature whose status continues to be disputed to this day. . . . There cannot be much serious doubt concerning the motives of his ahistoricism in anthropology" (Gellner 1988:175).

3   The usage is from Derrida (1972/1981); see also Johnson 1993: 154.

4   Protected under the communists because it contains the grave of Ferdinand LaSalle (social democrat founder), and later by the Catholics because it contains the grave of Edith Stein, the student of Edmund Husserl who became a nun and was later made a Catholic saint. The graveyard is full of well-known names—the historian Heinrich Graetz; Bismarck's eye doctor Hermann Cohn and his son, the writer Emil Cohen; Gustav Born (father of the physicist Max Born, and grandfather of the American pop singer Olivia Newton-John); the ancestors of American actor Peter Falk—and of poignant stories of historical turns of fortune: Edith Stein had an unhappy love affair with another Husserl student who became an SS officer. The parents of the chemist Fritz Haber, who invented the poison gas used in World War I, are buried next to a girl killed by poison gas. Neisser, the discoverer of the syphilis bacteria, lived in Breslau but like many rich folk was buried in his own gar-

den. Danziger, the Canadian historian of science, was born here, as was Bread and Puppet Theater founder Peter Schumann.

The grave iconography is stunningly varied. There are the standard Jewish symbols: hands parted in blessing, menorah, star of David. There are classical symbols: Greek drama masques, a Roman helmet (for soldiers such as Lt. Georg Sternberg, regiment 36, died 1917), urns. There are nineteenth-century Romantic symbols: cut tree trunks, broken pillars, chrysalis butterflies, weeping willows. And there are distinctive ones: a banker has his bank building carved in relief; the Kaufman mercantile family (Max, 1855–1893, was a cotton trader; Solomon financed artists like Liszt and Brahms) has a colorfully tiled Turkish-style pavilion mausoleum.

A second Jewish graveyard still in active use also exists in another part of town. The grand old synagogue near the center of town still stands, a dilapidated, unsteady ruin. It survived the war, only then to be destroyed by treasure hunters. A few poor Jews still live in the attached, decaying tenements.

5 The panorama is a painting 114 meters long, 15 meters high, mounted in a rotunda as an unbroken circle. The battle at Raclawice (forty kilometers from Cracow) was one of the last defenses of Poland's independence, but the insurrection was crushed by the Russians. Poland was partitioned in 1795, ceasing to exist as an independent entity until World War I. Patriots in Lvov, with Austrian permission, commemorated the battle, commissioning Jan Styka and Wojciech Kossak with seven assistants to paint the battle. It was a central attraction in Lvov until 1944, when a bomb hit the building. It was moved to Wroclaw, but in deference to the Russian overlords of the communist era, it was not displayed until 1980. Now restored and in a new building, it is again a tourist attraction. Most of the German population of Breslau was evacuated before the three-month-long siege by the Russians at the end of the war; most of the rest either fled with the retreating German army or were expelled later to Germany. The city was resettled with people from Poland's eastern regions, especially Lvov.

6 See Verenne 1985 on the metaphorical structure of Hegel's *Phenomenology of Spirit*, constructed through a *Galerie von Bildern* that work through *Er-innerungen*.

7 The zoo motif comes up again with a shot of a television series on animals and a male voice saying he doesn't want to run for office only on account of his television popularity, but that people actually asked him to run. This is a reference that many Poles find amusing. During the first open elections, two-thirds of the parliamentary seats were reserved for the Communist Party members, and one-third were open seats, but party members could also run for those. So the party tried to find popular individuals who had ties to the party. The director and vice director of the Wroclaw zoo, husband and wife, had run a popular television series on animals, and he became one of the popular figures tapped to run for an open seat. The couple had long been the subject of much joking and commentary for the analogies between their relationships and those they described about their animals, particularly the monkeys. If the political metaphors about monkeys and zoos and the politics of the elections are hardly subtle, nonetheless the self-parodic situation is quite funny.

8 On the quite different mode of using "ethnographic" footage in Chinese Fifth Genera-

tion films, see the essays in Berry 1991 and Gladney 1994. As Gladney points out, Tian Zhuangzhuang uses Tibetan footage and rituals to exoticize and sharpen alterity in order to critique urban Chinese society, rather than ethnographically attempting to generate understanding of, or provide points of identification with, Tibetan problems. But as others have argued, the minimalist dialogue, plot, and interpretive direction in Fifth Generation films did provide spaces of ambiguity and openness to alternative ideological stances that were previously not available in the overly didactic films of earlier filmmakers. Fifth Generation films were thus an important part of the cultural movements of the 1980s.

9   Born in 1948, Holland's mother was a Catholic journalist who joined the Polish underground and fought in the Warsaw uprising; her father was a prominent assimilated Jewish journalist whose parents died in the Warsaw ghetto and who escaped to fight in the Red Army. A committed communist, he saw Stalin as a historical necessity and argued after the war that anti-Semitism was finished. In 1961 he fell from a window to his death as either a suicide or a murder in the early days of an anti-Semitic purge. The parents divorced when Agnieszka was eleven, and her mother married another prominent Jewish journalist, Stanislaw Brodzki. Her own films include the 1991 *Europa, Europa* (about the true story of Solomon Perl, sent by his parents to the east to avoid the Nazis approaching from the west); the 1985 *Angry Harvest* (about the love-hate relationship between a Polish Catholic farmer and a Jewish woman whom he hides from the Nazis); *To Kill a Priest* (about the 1984 case of the Polish priest Jerzy Popieluszko); *Provincial Actors, The Fever, A Woman Alone* (about individuals trying to escape oppression); and her 1966 Prague film school thesis, *The Sin of God* (about a prostitute, tired of being abused by men, who asks God for a tender man; God gives her an angel, but she crushes him making love to him, and rebukes God). She studied in Prague because she had been refused admission to the Lodz film school; but she was able to return to Poland and work with Wajda during the 1970s. In 1981 she denounced the martial law and went into exile to Paris.

10   No Ukrainians lived in town. Ukrainians of this region paid for the mass killings of Poles further east in Ukraine at Wolyn, and for the operations of Ukrainian guerrillas who burned villages during the war. General Swierczewski commanded one of the two Polish armies organized in the Soviet Union to deal with the Ukrainians. (A veteran of the Spanish civil war, he is the General Goltz of Ernest Hemingway's *For Whom the Bell Tolls*.) Assassinated, he was elevated after World War II into a national hero after whom streets and schools were named. Leszek Koczanowicz notes that it was more useful to the Russians to elevate a Pole martyred by Ukrainians than by Germans. After the war, Action Vistula removed Ukrainians and the Lemkowie (Ruthenian) ethnic group to the west (Legnica, Wroclaw). The general in charge was then arrested. From 1956 to 1958 a few were allowed to return, and in the 1990s a political debate emerged about whether reparations should be considered. The Polish senate condemned the action, but many Poles want Ukraine to condemn the massacre of Poles at Wolyn before anything further is done.

11   These are cataloged by the Hebrew University in Jerusalem, and Stanislaw keeps in touch with former Jewish residents of Rymanov and their children.

12   Not only does the film underplay the resistance by both Poles and Jews, but no motivation

is established for Schindler, whereas Keneally, on the basis of interviews with survivors, repeatedly says that Oskar Schindler saw himself as a future witness. "You have to remember," says one survivor, "Oskar had a German side, but a Czech side too. He was the good soldier Schweik. He loved to foul up the system" (Keneally 1982: 233).

13 Wajda also made a movie version of Wyspianski's play.

8. Worlding Cyberspace

1 I adapt here for the infrastructure of cyberspace a phrase Derrida uses to describe the way in which "the closure of metaphysics" in philosophical discourses is used to unveil the limitations and inescapability of moves in philosophy (Derrida 1995: 80).

2 By spring 1995 the first successful experiment with a biological computer was no longer science fiction.

3 The notion of two necessary and complementary kinds of science has been broached in various ways by Lévi-Strauss (1962/1966), Lacan (1973/1977), Ulrich Beck (1986/1992), advocates of "social learning" participatory policy making (Rip, Misa, and Schott 1995), and others. As the Greg Bear epigraph and the first successful experiments with a biological computing illustrate, science fiction and popular culture can operate, as Lévi-Strauss describes "savage thought" more generally, as a proleptic or anticipation effect, "like a shadow moving ahead of its owner," partly through a systematizing of what is immediately presented to the senses, and partly through a bricolage style of working out logical possibilities (1962/1966: chap. 1).

4 On reflexive modernity, see Beck 1986/1992; Giddens 1991; Lash and Urry 1994. On empirical cases that support Beck's description of the dynamics of risk society, see Reich 1991; Brown and Mikkelsen 1990; on the agonism required to force honest disclosure, see Wiener 1999.

5 Thus, for example, while reform of the U.S. health care system foundered again in the political arena during the first two years of the Clinton administration, the market pushed ahead quite rapidly, totally reworking the nature of the health care system. Similarly, while the government seeds research in arenas such as the development of the Internet and the Human Genome project, the amount of money the private sector has to spend in these areas has dwarfed that of public monies.

6 See Ulrich Beck 1986/1992 for an elaboration of these formulations as well as those of shadowboxing and shell games by multinational corporations. At issue in these terms is not that the threats might not be real, but that one often does not know ahead of time, and that corporate strategies of investment and protecting against liability often involve publicizing alternative threats which make their product seem less of a risk (as in the publicizing of the ozone hole by the nuclear industry), or that new knowledge or accidents are liable to upset today's notions of prudent action, so that, in contrast to the negotiated contract relations after conflict between unions or communities and corporations in the nineteenth century and in contrast to the actuarial statistics on which rules of insurance accountability were made for traditional industrial risk, such stable frameworks seem less available in today's world of risk production, making corporate investment strategies

more volatile as well. See Beck's lovely passage comparing the specularity of risk today with the gods and demons of antiquity (73).

7   Or dreams that have effectiveness in the world, from Freenberg's reading of Ursula K. Le Guin's 1971 novel *The Lathe of Heaven* about a man whose dreams come true. The man tries to sleep as little as possible so as not to change the world too much, and goes to an unscrupulous psychiatrist who tries to turn these "effective dreams" into a tool for changing the world, but his posthypnotic suggestions, diffracted by the man's unconscious, never work the way the psychiatrist intends. The trick, says Feenberg, is to learn how to use effective dreaming in harmony with the complexity of the world, not to impose modern technology on the world (Feenberg 1995: 141–42).

8   On origin stories, see Serres 1991; for a technological example, see Ronell 1989. Alternative genealogies for contemporary computer and Internet cultures include cybernetic control systems, information theory, networking technologies (railroads, telegraph, water and sewage systems), and virtual reality sensory machinic assemblages (film, telephone, phonograph). On the pre–World War II development of cybernetics *avant la lettre*, see Mindell 1996; for a postwar history, see Edwards 1994. On the history of ARPA and the beginnings of the Internet, see Norberg and O'Neill 1996. On the history of networks as the political precursor for the struggles over the Internet, see Russell, McKnight, and Solomon 1995.

9   One thinks of Walter Benjamin's notion of "dialectical images" in which the technological object serves to remind subsequent generations of the difference between early liberatory hopes for the technology and the normalized subsequent uses. See Buck-Morss 1991; Mehlman 1993.

10 Consider the linear and hierarchical rule-governed modes of programming and modeling enforced in the 1970s, as opposed to the more intuitive and play-based styles of using the computer in the 1980s—and the fascination with user-friendly Macintosh-style metaphors for graphic interfaces, metaphors of self-organizing complexity, and small, multiple ("parallel processing") robots rather than large centralized computers.

11 For accounts of the struggles and competitions to establish networks in China, see Triolo and Lovelock 1996; on North Africa, see Danowitz, Nassef, and Goodman 1995. Egypt had 214 Internet hosts by 1995, and the state has supported not only university and government use but also the development of local PC assembly and software industries by creating demand in the state sector. The Ministry of Defense bought the first PCs locally assembled by the state-owned Banha Electronics Corporation. In Algeria, by contrast, a drive to computerize state firms in the 1980s and other uses of information technologies has slowed because of the current political unrest.

12 This is but a hint: Computers are called Acharya, Veda, Soochak . . . There are some Germanisms in *The New Hacker's Dictionary*: DAU (*Dummster Anzunehmender User*, "stupidest imaginable user") derived from engineering slang's GAU (*grosster anzunehmender Unfall*, "worst foreseeable disaster," as in nuclear plant core meltdown); but also borrowings such as "kluge," a patch, from the word for "clever"; and *gedanken thesis*, a pejorative and ironic contrast to physicists' usage of "gedanken experiment," lack of intuition about what is programmable, about what constitutes a clear specification of an algorithm. Rus-

sian via Yiddish makes some appearances in *The New Hacker's Dictionary*, and there are *kremvax* and *kgbvax*, fictitious USENET sites at the Kremlin announced on 1 April 1984, predating by six years the first genuine site in Moscow. Eventually Vadim Antonov had a real site named kremvax, which became an electronic center of anticommunist resistance during the failed coup of August 1991 (Raymond 1993: 252).

13 "The red sun is high, the blue low," Bukatman says, is a typical sentence that keeps the reader guessing until the final word signals a location diegetically far from earth, generically in an SF text. "The door dilated," or "Daddy married, a man this time," similarly keep one's assumptions flexible about the life worlds one is entering. New metaphors and terminologies are coined to capture emergent or possible combinatories, as in his title taken from Burroughs, "terminal identities," a double articulation of both the interface with the global electronic circulation of data and an end point or concrete machine that grounds the flight of electrons.

14 See the entry under "cyberpunk" in Raymond 1993: "Gibson's near-total ignorance of computers and the present-day hacker culture enabled him to speculate about the role of computers and hackers in the future in ways hackers have since found both irritatingly naive and tremendously stimulating" (129). See also Gibson's interview with Larry McCaffery (1986), in which he talks about influences (Thomas Pynchon, Robert Stone, Dashiell Hammett, William Burroughs), says that the language of *Neuromancer* that seems futuristic is actually from 1969 Toronto drug and biker slang, and admits, "Listen to me trying to explain this, it immediately becomes apparent that I have no grasp of how computers really work."

15 Unless otherwise noted, all jargon and definitions in this section are taken from Raymond 1993.

16 See also pyston, bogon, and inventing nonce particle names (cluon, futon, etc.). Pystons were elementary particles carrying the sinister force, with the probability of lossage being proportional to the number of pystons falling on a process; since pystons are generated by observers, demos tend to fail when many people watch. Now largely succeeded by bogon, whose antiparticle is a clutron or cluon, a unit of cluefulness. Futon is the elementary particle of randomness.

17 "Law and Ethics on the Electronic Frontier" is also the name of a course (6.095/STS095) at MIT—taught by Hal Abelson, Joanne Costello, Danny Weitzner, and myself—using, in addition to real-time class, an on-line signature-encrypted discussion, and a Web home page with readings and with links to various archives and information sources. In fall 1998 the MIT class joined forces with the Harvard Law School and Professors Larry Lessig and Jonathan Zittrain. Thirty law students and thirty engineers constituted the class. In spring 2002, a student paper challenging airport security screening scored some national publicity (Chakrabarti and Strauss). In fall 2002, Barbara Fox of Microsoft and Joe Pato of Hewlett-Packard helped teach the class, focusing attention on copyright, intellectual property, and security. See the course and exemplary student papers at http://swissnet.ai .mit.edu/6095/.

18 There is, however, a hacker underground and even institutional islands of hackerdom within IBM, acknowledged in Raymond 1993. Charles Andres allegedly even received a

letter of appreciation from the head of IBM's Thomas J. Watson Research Laboratories (Raymond 1993: 121).

19   ITS (Incompatible Time-Sharing System), influential operating system for PDP-6s and PDP-10s at MIT that generated much AI-hacker jargon; actual work shifted to newer machines after 1982, and the last ITS machine shut down at MIT in 1990, but the Royal Institute of Technology in Sweden maintains one in its computer museum (Raymond 1993: 243).

20   Multics was a late-1960s time-sharing operating system developed by MIT, GE, and Bell Labs, treating all devices uniformly as special files. After that consortium broke up, Ken Thompson and Dennis Ritchie in 1969 invented UNIX, "a weak pun on Multics," as an interactive time-sharing system that has become the most widely used multiuser general-purpose operating system in the world. Raymond comments that many see UNIX as the most important victory of hackerdom over industry opposition (1993: 427).

21   Year two of the class had the following: bitter, Boy, chopper, crab, durham, Dragon, hmm, Fox Muldor, Idless, interzone, kosmo, Kraken, krakpot, loki, Lyle, mercury, Motts, Nicki, Pik, Prophet, repeatloaf, satire@myplace.disorg, Seen, Smithers, spock, spot, student, Thoreau, vapor, will.

22   Wizards and warlocks being those empowered in various cybergames and MUDs to create and enforce rules. Or more generally, a wizard is "(1) a person who knows how a complex piece of software or hardware works . . . esp. someone who can find and fix bugs quickly in an emergency" and "(2) a person who is permitted to do things forbidden to ordinary people; one who has wheel privileges on a system" (Raymond 1993: 453).

23   For example, the FBI profile of hackers and crackers is one of young, introverted males who do not have outside interests. Enough publicity about computer crime has been disseminated that many young hackers who intend to go on to college quit cracking activities before their eighteenth birthday, when they would become liable to prosecution as adults, although they may continue as "mentors" to their juniors (Carol Covert, MIT, 3 October 1994). A more troubling subculture is that of virus writers (Korey Sandler, PC *Computing Magazine*, September 1994). These range from mischievous hackers to industrial saboteurs and disgruntled employees out for revenge, to Third World malcontents filled with resentment about a technology to which they can gain only partial access. Dark Avenger, for instance, was a Bulgaria-based (Bulgaria was the Soviet Union's Silicon Valley, but individuals did not have their own computers) individual who told a journalist that the United States might be able to deny him entry to the country but could not deny entry to his viruses.

24   Compare "A Portrait of J. Random Hacker" in Raymond 1993, which describes not only an older, university-educated age set but also the shift from the nerd stereotypes of the early 1970s to the "more whole earth than whole polyester" and more "mildly health-food faddish" than the junk food stereotype. See also the portrait of working for companies like Microsoft in Douglas Coupland's story "Microserfs" (1993) and subsequent novel (1995).

25   Decision dismissing the David LaMacchia case. LaMacchia had created a BBS in which people were encouraged to post and download pirated software, but since he himself did not profit from these activities, he could not be prosecuted under the Copyright Act; and

the Wire Fraud Act under which prosecutors tried him was, according to Judge Stern, too far afield to apply, since there was no fraud (deceit, misleading statements). Expressing widespread discontent with prosecutorial efforts to make public policy by stretching the law, Judge Stern said that if Congress wanted to criminalize activities such as LaMacchia's, it needed to write legislation to that effect. Rumor at MIT has it that there had been similar bulletin boards before which had come to system operator notice and had simply been shut down; this one was not noticed in time and through a series of procedural missteps was turned over to authorities outside the university, rather than simply being shut down as well.

26 The 1994–1995 debates over the Clipper Chip, initially a mandate that the telecommunications hardware sold in the United States accommodate a chip that would allow law enforcement officials, under court order supervision, the ability to wiretap the flow of digital information. The FBI argued for this in its fight against the "four horsemen" of drugs, terrorists, money launderers, and pedophiles. Opponents feared Big Brother more than Big Drugs.

27 Admiral Bobby Inman, former director of the National Security Administration and a professor of public affairs at the University of Texas, points out that among voters, crime trumps privacy issues (talk to Law and Ethics on Electronic Frontier class, MIT, fall 1994).

28 In 1988 Robert Morris Jr., a computer science student at Cornell and son of the chief computer scientist at the National Security Agency, was the first to be charged under the new 1986 Computer Fraud and Abuse Act (18 USC 1030) for having released an Internet worm, causing computers around the country to crash. The now famous Internet worm was the first of a series of highly publicized viruses that forced awareness on users that one ought not to leave systems unprotected. A parallel case in the same year, centered in Germany but breaching the computers of NASA, the Lawrence Livermore Berkeley Laboratory, several corporations, CERN, and with a Cold War angle, reinforced the public awareness. The German Chaos Club founded in the mid-1980s had publicized its own hacking feats as a way of warning the public that it should not naively put trust in the new technologies. Eventually caught by Clifford Stoll on the Lawrence Livermore Berkeley computer system, Chaos Club members were traced and prosecuted for selling information gained through computer hacking to East German agents under Russian KGB supervision. Since the information sold proved to be trivial, and the reason for selling less interest in helping the Russians than merely in getting money to continue hacking, the primary outcome was to increase awareness of the inadequacy of the German legal system to deal with cases of this sort. Meanwhile hacking and phreaking into the telephone system were becoming a sufficient nuisance that the FBI and Secret Service launched "Operation Sundevil" in 1988, arrested some teenagers in sting operations, and then in 1990 made an infamous and legally bungling raid on Steve Jackson Games in Austin, Texas, seizing the computers and disks of the company, allegedly in search of a document stolen from Bell South. In 1993 a suit by SJG against the Secret Service found the latter guilty of violating the provisions of the 1986 Electronic Communications Privacy Act. Still, the publicity of Operation Sundevil put a fright into many teens, who shut down their electronic bulletin boards, and more importantly helped the hacker underground around the electronic magazine

Phrack mature into a security-conscious, more legally savvy, and political subculture. In turn, the ignominy for the FBI and Secret Service of the procedural debacle of Operation Sundevil, and the 1991 simultaneous failure of telephone switches on both the East and West Coasts, resulted in the formation of a Computer Crime Squad within the FBI that recruited computer-knowledgeable agents. Meanwhile the use of the Internet had expanded so rapidly that while problems of vulnerability of the system itself remain, focus shifted to rules of use, encryption and privacy protection, commercial security, system operator liability, control of pornography, stalking, and other issues of shaping a public and civil arena.

29 Senators Leahy and Kyle, for instance, in proposing a modification to the Computer Fraud and Abuse Act, cite not only concerns about Dutch hackers who broke into the computers used in the Gulf War and NASA computers but also the abuse of privileges on government computers, snooping tax returns, selling confidential criminal histories from the National Crime Information Center, and breaching federal courthouse computers holding confidential records.

30 For the most elaborate account of the potential implications of cryptoanarchy, see May 1994. See also M. Miller 1994.

31 Concern about employer surveillance has been long-standing, both in monitoring work operations, in reading employee e-mail, and in compiling and selling database information. There are now companies that are expanding the capabilities of all these activities, including forensics companies that retrieve e-mail that companies or employees thought destroyed to be used in court cases. Lotus Marketplace was a program, withdrawn after public outcry, which would have given small businesses consumer profiles on millions of households. The U.S. Postal Service finances a significant part of its operations by selling change-of-address lists to direct marketers. And most recently, entrepreneurial sites on the Web are experimenting with ways of collecting transactional information from people who visit their sites and click on advertising promotions.

32 *Cubby v. CompuServe* (1991) held the system operator not liable for content on the system because CompuServe does not regularly monitor content and serves more like a common carrier (like the telephone system). In 1995 Prodigy was sued by a stockbrokerage, Stratton-Oakmont, in a $200 million libel suit, because Prodigy does do a certain amount of routine screening.

33 A series of bills were proposed in the House and Senate during 1995 to regulate content, criminalize "indecent" material, but also to prohibit content regulations. The World Wide Web Consortium has instead proposed a demand-side technical mechanism: a rating format for content to which users can attach filters developed on their own or by advocacy groups, or by groups like the Good Housekeeping Seal of Approval.

34 The NII is sometimes compared in scale and ambition to the 1960s space program, as well as in its own metaphoric name to the federal interstate highway infrastructure for encouraging the postwar economy. Lewis Branscomb and Brian Kahin (1964) suggest that it is very different in organizational form and dynamics. It is not managed by a single agency but rather is a "distributed program, minimally managed by interagency task forces," and it is propelled by rapid changes in commercial information technologies, in turn heavily

influenced by the entertainment and information services businesses. The question of whether or not there should be mechanisms to ensure universal service makes the comparison with the telephone system pertinent as well and foregrounds the role that intellectual property and regulatory law can play in shaping the economic direction of this new medium.

35 See the fascinating debate between Paul Heckel (1992) and Simpson Garfinkle, Richard Stallman, and Mitchell Kapor (1991).

36 The committee composition for the White Paper was heavily stacked with industries needed in any future lobbying effort for the proposal, and representatives of the public were marginalized. The Green Paper at least went through the motions of a more open set of hearings both physically around the country as well as soliciting feedback on-line.

37 See note 25.

38 For a critique of the stance of the report and its recommendations precisely in terms of these power balances, see Samuelson 1994.

39 Tribe writes about the way in which the court has abridged, expanded, and again abridged the constraints on wiretaps in *Olmstead v. U.S.* (1928), *Katz v. U.S.* (1964), and *Smith v. Maryland* (1976).

40 Compare the critiques of the Human Genome Project to those of Reagan's "Star Wars" Strategic Defense Initiative, both seen as technically improbable goals, yet mechanisms for generating new computational technologies and having powerful social effects. The promise of gene therapies and other medical interventions, even if further in the future than most realize or admit, is already having effects on employment practices, family planning, education, insurance, and in reworking notions of self, health, and disease. It has been argued that the influx of information theory concepts into biology in the 1950s and 1960s fostered a hegemonic role for molecular biology, occluding fields (at least temporarily) such as embryology and developmental biology, and that in the 1960s it even temporarily occluded the vital contributions of biochemistry (see Kay 1999; Keller 1995; Lewontin 1994; Nelkin and Tancredi 1989).

41 In India, for instance, the pioneering generation of S. Ramani (of the National Center for Software Technologies, a Ph.D. training ground, and ERNET), J. G. Krishnaya (early advocate of personal computers and the Macintosh instead of investment in mainframes at the computer center of the Indian Institute of Management and the Space Research Center, which shared the first mainframes in Ahmedabad in the 1970s and 1980s, and then founder of the Systems Research Institute, Pune, the first research and software developer for government, educational, and public sector development projects); Faqir C. Kohli (of Tata Consultancy Services, the largest and oldest employer and trainer of programmers and software engineers); and Narayan Murthy (of InfoSys, the first Indian software company listed on the Nasdaq stock exchange) are being replaced by a younger generation. The operating and economic environment has gone through at least three or four major reorganizations, beginning with liberalization in the early 1990s; body shopping, service contracting, and call center servicing for multinational and U.S. corporations in the mid-1990s; the rise and collapse of a dot.com bubble in the late 1990s; and, in the early twenty-first century, the gradual expansion into the export market of a few transnational

Indian firms such as Wipro and InfoSys, as well as the pilot experimentation domestically with entrepreneurial village computer kiosks to reduce the hold of middlemen on crop prices and on access to government forms and documents (see Kumar 2001; Kumar and Jhunjhunwala 2002; Rajora 2002). These are still new technologies in India, and in some ways the changing spatial and temporal connectivity and the differential access can be seen in heigtened dramatic form. In the mid-1990s there was considerable resistance to computerization in banks and government agencies, in part for fear of labor redundancy and in part for fear of managers that their knowledge and control would be quickly made obsolete. During the dot.com boom, young twenty-year-olds in Bangalore were earning salaries much higher than executives in old-line companies, allowing them to buy houses, cars, and appliances, thus upsetting the seniority and status hierarchies. Companies such as InfoSys built their own cable and satellite connectivity, not daring to rely on the slow and inefficient access through ERNET and the other state systems. India, it is often said, has a middle class the size of the U.S. population (some 300 million) that can afford computer and Internet access. But today, urban ISTD telephone entrepreneurs also have computer terminals for rent, making Internet access far more available than only through personal computers, corporate access, cybercafes, or upscale hotels. If villages can be connected, with high school students helping their elders make use of agricultural prices, government forms, agricultural extension help, and perhaps even primary medical consultation, the potential exists for rearranging agrarian life worlds.

42 "Worlding" draws on all three in quasi-Derridean *différance*: the auditory homophony with whirl, hinting at electron(ic) speed; the textual difference between ideational whirl and the grounding of the ethnographic world.

9. Calling the Future(s)

I take this chapter's subtitle, "Delay Call Forwarding," from Avital Ronell and mean to indicate with it the temporality of desire, constraint, blockage, and belatedness with which pedagogical goals are often installed (Ronell 1989: 1).

1 The initial formulations were worked out at a faculty retreat convened in spring 1996 for a modular core course, a three-tiered set of foundation and advanced or topical courses, supplemented by workshops, a communal colloquium partly keyed to the core course platform, and a cross-linking set of requirements in both anthropology and history. See http://web.mit/sts/documents, and M. Fischer 1996. After 1998, in addition to courses cotaught in the Schools of Engineering (David Mindell), Science (David Kaiser), and the joint MIT-Harvard Health Science and Technology Program (at the Harvard Medical School) (Michael Fischer), the program sponsored cross-school initiatives in technology and the self (under Sherry Turkle), the Center for Diversity (under Evelynn Hammonds), and agricultural and environmental history (under Deborah Fitzgerald and Harriet Ritvo). Several members of the faculty were also closely involved in the new program in Comparative Media Studies (led by Henry Jenkins and William Urrichio): Joe Dumit, Michael Fischer, and Susan Slyomivcs.

2 "The University in Ruins": Fifty years after the 1949 MIT convocation, the functions of

the university, and of technical training of engineers and technoscientists, again is under question. A lecturer in a course in the joint MIT and Harvard Medical School HST Program (a program training both M.D.'s and Ph.D.'s) put it this way: Many scientists in the biological sciences say they hope their research will benefit humankind; that is equivalent to saying they hope someone will make money from their research. Otherwise it cannot get into the marketplace and has no way to benefit humankind. This is not an isolated example of dramatic changes in the academy over the past decades and is most obvious in the biology/biotechnology nexus. But it surfaces in other ways as well, as in the call for a new "postmodern engineer" by Joel Moses, former dean of engineering and provost of MIT, and the efforts to design a new five-year undergraduate engineering degree that will not just provide technical skills but provide the contextual, communication, and political understandings that career engineers need (and in midcareer often tell the alumni office they did not get in their training). Some of this sounds repetitive over the past five decades, the call for the humanist engineer, the well-rounded engineer, the engineer who will not just work for the executive trained at Harvard, Yale, or Princeton but will himself or herself be a leader (as engineers were in the 1920s and 1930s). While the phraseology of such calls sounds repetitive, many analysts claim that deeper changes lie underneath.

In the widely discussed book *The University in Ruins*, the late Bill Readings, for instance, argues that the university is being set adrift from its past modernist mooring in cultural projects of maintaining the nation-state, in favor now of becoming transnational bureaucratic corporations regulated under administrative metrics of "excellence" and productivity. This is felt most starkly in money-strapped state universities, less so in capital-rich private universities; but Readings points to a pervasive shift in cultural sensibility, not just a market-driven or management-glib pragmatics. The word "ruins" is from Walter Benjamin and baroque aesthetics, referring to the layered remembrance of past aspirations that are still encoded within contemporary objects and institutions that have taken on quite different functionalities. Ruins may provide means for redemption of such past aspirations and need not be simply nostalgic signs, or evidence of decay. Readings wants to suggest that there are important new functions for universities to perform in today's world that go beyond the efficient transmission of information, that can be measured in student-consumer satisfaction surveys, or in scores on exams, or in numbers of faculty publications or patents held.

Most importantly, Readings argues, the university now provides a space for learning to live with socially supported diversity. The nineteenth-century idea of the university formulated by Fichte and Humboldt had to do with the cultivation of the citizen and the creation of a culture for the nation-state. Hence the focal importance of national literatures in the university. Even scientists thought of their pedagogies as inculcating a "culture of science" built on the analogy of the cultures being taught by historians and literature professors. The university was a space apart from society, an ideal public sphere where argumentation could be pure, in search of truth, uncomplicated by the pressures in the real public sphere of power and resources. Even if it wasn't quite so, this operated as the regulatory ideal. But today, Readings argues, the regulatory ideas are changing, increasingly attuning themselves to notions of competition, efficiency, and transfer of information and skills, rather than ideals of deferring decision, keeping inquiry open as long as possible, questioning the grounds on which people act in the real world. If, however, there is a danger of the university being absorbed into marketing and management ideals on the one side, another, more salutary absorption by the world is also occurring: the student bodies and faculties of universities are becoming open to a much more diverse set of people. The university is becoming, Reading argues, one of a number of social spaces where people are learning to deal with diversity. This, he says, is a positive and important function, even if it undermines the old regulatory ideal and assumption that the cultivated, university-educated citizen would be a universal rational ego, unmarked by identity politics, or the other modalities of difference that seem to be so much at issue in the contemporary world. His primary "canary" for watching these changes is the rise of cultural studies, a field that seems to want to replace literature where literature as the foundation of a nation-state culture is in ebb, but with the result that "culture" in cultural studies seems to have no referent, is a floating signifier that can point at almost anything.

But perhaps STS would be a different kind of canary, one showing how the university can reclaim the kinds of aspirations that James Killian proposed in 1949 for MIT in a situation where the calls are being renewed for integrated knowledges across engineering fields, the sciences, the social sciences, the arts and humanities. A ruin worthy of redemption, and of reworking for the contemporary era.

3   "Technoscience" is an odd-job word and signal of institutional change. It has been suggested (L. Marx 1997) that the word "technology" came into English usage in the 1840s as a neologism for a semantic space that had no lexical term. It had to do with designating railways, not just the locomotives, or just the locomotives and tracks, but the whole complicated material and social network, including the bureaucracy, the personnel, the financing, and telegraph lines for communication. Since then "technology" has been applied to almost anything, so that today one has the feeling that it has been entirely emptied of meaning by its overuse. Although in institutions such as MIT, distinctions are often sharply drawn between technology (what engineers do) and science (what scientists do), ever since at least the second industrial, and science-based, revolution (chemicals, steel, electricity) at the end of the nineteenth century, doing science has also involved relations with production of useable and marketable products ("applied science"). In the 1980s, particularly in biology, with the growth of biotechnologies, the boundaries between basic science and applied science became increasingly institutionally blurred. A range of new neologisms increasingly came to fill the semantic needs: biotechnology, bioengineering, technoscience, environmental science, and so on. It is useful to pay attention to these lexical indices of changing social and cultural configurations of relations among disciplines and among academia, market, state, and the military.

The term *techné* has been fetishized via Heidegger in recent years, and it might be worth reconsidering that his stress on the mathematization of the world, on calculability of standing reserves, as the "essence" of modern technology, which itself is not technological, is partly just a reflex of the second or "science-based" industrial revolution (chemistry, explosives, electricity, steel): the priority of science/theory/math to technology, which in today's biotechnology world is again being challenged, albeit in a different, more hybridized way, than in preindustrial artisanal modes of production (which Heidegger uses as his exemplar of *Herausfordern*, bringing forth). Heidegger had little of real social or political insight or concern, and his stress that poesis too is a kind of (also dangerous) techné is, as Jean-Michel Rabaté points out, quite indicative. The exemplar is the lyric poet Hölderlin, who attempted to catch the language of the gods and convey it to men and in the process went mad. So too techné, like poesis, is a revealing of (ontological) nature behind the (ontic) surface distractions of idle talk, curiosity, and ambiguity *(Gerede, Neugier, Zweideutigkeit)*. This is the difference between techné and the merely technical *(das Technische)*. It is in this context that Heidegger plays with three etymologies of *theorein* (theory) but ignores the classical Greek social and political meanings of the *theoros*, whose activity is theorein. The theoros was the observer, ambassador, official witness who traveled to see and report to the city in terms of its highest values, evaluating everyday deeds in terms of a sociopolitical sacred "theater." Heidegger sees a parallel between modern technology and Hölderlin, who went mad for gazing at the gods from too close, an activity fraught with danger, a deep play perhaps. But Heidegger's meditation, quite symptomatically, Rabaté suggests, ignores the social and political function (Rabaté 2002: 111–14). It's not much help to merely recognize that technology can be used for good or ill, if one is unable or unwilling to do the social and cultural analysis that using it for good would require. Hence, after all, the classical figures of Tiresias (blind insight) and Oedipus (seeing blindness). Mark Hansen, in a recent reconsideration of Heidegger's lifelong concern with modern technology as an obstacle to the revealing of Being, points out that Heidegger was fundamentally hampered by the contradiction that he wanted to distinguish modern technology and yet reduce it at the same time to an essence that was defined in terms of premodern forms of technology (Hansen 2000).

4   Under Shakespeare scholar Peter Donaldson, the archiving of all known video and film productions, and all folios, transforms the student's understanding of authorial function (was there one Shakespeare?), critical editions (does a single, stabilized original text have any meaning in this corpus?), and the differences in performances among directors and actors. It constitutes a concordance that allows lines and scenes from comparable texts and performances to be called up and compared easily. Students are able to import video clips into their papers to illustrate and demonstrate contrasts.

5   Linguist Shigeru Miyagawa, working with professional production help, has produced a new kind of language and culture learning tool. Beginning from the observation that even Berlitz-style intensive immersion does not use natural language flow, Miyagawa first returned to his Japanese hometown to film and interview residents about memories of life since World War II. A menu allows students to click on glosses, word-for-word translation, transcriptions in different writing systems, dictionaries, and contextual materials. Later this was enveloped with a mystery-quest story to draw students through branching further animations, pathways, and cultural materials. Finally, an interactive Web site was established to allow pen-pal relations to grow further.

6   Eric Sievers hosted a transnational site on environmental policies and data for Central Asia: information collected locally could be stored on the MIT server and accessed from Central Asia, providing a neutral safe haven (a tool of democratization). Hugh Gusterson

and Babak Ashrafi hosted a moderated discussion group on nuclear weapons stockpile policy, involving leading figures in the national laboratories as well as activists and others (an experiment again demonstrating the difficulties of this medium for charged arenas of contention). Sara Wermeil experimented with a Web site to collect archival materials on Boston's Big Dig, one of a series of Sloan Foundation–funded experiments at Stanford, UCLA, Berkeley, and MIT, none of which proved particularly successful for reasons that are themselves interesting to learn from: new media are not magically successful. One needs, above all, to learn how to insert these technologies into appropriate and themselves new social configurations, rather than expect old forms of interaction to easily adopt or adapt to new media (see now, several years later, the new effort at a history of science site under the direction of Babak Ashrafi: http://hrst.mit.edu). Several resource Web sites were also hosted: on race and science (organized by Evelynn Hammonds), on Russian science (organized by Slava Gerovitch). And there were several ethnographic video projects: Chris Kelty made a short video, differently clipped and performatively framed for varied conference audiences, on the biology laboratories of the Whitehead Institute at MIT; Aslihan Sanal made a short video on the MIT nuclear reactor used in experimental brain oncology. And Chris Kelty developed a dissertation that not only incorporated video clips but textually drew on the tactics of the new media.

7   The cartoon by Armenian anthropologist Levon Abrahamian ("The world may be round, but not in this case") has a double referent — to Giordano Bruno and the seventeenth-century struggles for a scientific revolution, but also to today's ethnic conflict (ethnic conflict in the Caucasus may be archaic and irrational, but at the moment it defines the world one must react in). As such it serves as a metaphor for STS against idealist visions of the philosophy of science divorced from how science and technology are actually done. The wonderful transform of a Ming dynasty woodcut shows five women using communication technologies (tape deck, newspaper, video). Another scene in the series is of these same five but in a medical operating theater, while outside the Tiananmen Square demonstrations can be seen through the windows. Done for the avant-garde Hong Kong performance troupe Zuni Isocahedron, this logo was intended to index the need for an STS program that can deal with science and technology around the world, attentive to its cultural localizations, politics, and production, not merely to the abstract mathematical residues that are said by some to be the "essence" of science.

The third logo (for 1997–1998) was an ideograph-like geometry diagram from a Japanese carpenter's math treatise, a reference to Greg Clancey's dissertation on seismology, architecture, and engineering across the force fields of Japan, Europe (Britain, Italy, and Germany), and the United States (Clancey 1999). The fourth logo (for 1998–1999) was a combined graph of the "three body problem" superimposed on a photograph of the Big Dig civil engineering project in Boston, referring to Sara Wermeil's experimental electronic archive on the Big Dig, and as a metaphor for the controlled "chaos" both in the mathematical sense and in the ordinary sense of a large-scale engineering project that requires political and community skills as well as engineering skills, the theme of several of our colloquiums, especially by Tom Hughes and Loren Graham comparing the Three Gorges project in China with the Big Dig in Boston.

8   A literary thread and a cross-cultural thread were the other two. For the literary thread, a novel was often used to start each term's colloquium series, and key novels were identified for each module of the core course. For the cross-cultural thread, local resources in the way of graduate students from, and faculty colleagues with specialties in, China, Russia, South Asia, the Middle East helped lead discussions. One particularly dramatic session on the old theme of the relation between science and democracy (Merton 1938 and Shapin and Schaffer 1985 on seventeenth-century England; L. Graham 1972, 1998, on Soviet science; Lyotard 1979/1984, Beck 1986/1992, and Gottweis 1998 on contemporary Europe; and H. Lyman Miller 1996 on 1990s China) involved Peter Perdue, our China historian; Leo Oufan Lee, the literature and cultural critic from Harvard; Roger Hart, a postdoctoral fellow and expert on math and science in seventeenth-century China; and Winke He, an sts graduate student from the People's Republic of China.

For the visual thread, care was taken to ensure that at least one or two of the weekly sts colloquiums each term focused attention on the visual thread. Art historian Caroline Jones talked about Francis Picabia and the psychodynamics of anxieties about technology in connection with the module on technology (C. Jones 1998). Performance artist Andor Carius talked about the sonic and visual as vehicles to elicit ethnographic commentary from physicists and engineers at the Tokomak fusion test reactor at Princeton. To record sounds inside the reactor, he needed to enroll engineers to design a new listening device (one cannot just drop a Sony tape recorder into plasma), thereby creating a new instrument for the engineers and physicists. Heat graphs were used to visually track the crashes and whistles of the plasma. Historian of science Robert Brain talked about mechanical observation in psychophysics and neoimpressionism in late-nineteenth-century France, connecting the scientific and the aesthetic. Media analyst and performer Sandy Stone talked about phantom limbs, prostheses, and their psychological projections (discovered with Civil War amputees) and the parallels involved in today's computer virtual realities. Ted Postal, our weapons analyst, showed dramatic videos that demonstrated by tracking trajectories on tape the ineffectiveness of the Patriot missile, thereby countering Pentagon propaganda. Eric Avery showed how printmaking could provide both visual and performance techniques of cultural critique of, and institutional therapy for, contemporary social traumas (see chapter 4 in this volume).

9.1. *Las Meninas* and Robotic Surgical Systems

1   See Dallenbach 1977/1989 for a historical survey of devices that go under this term (including Velázquez's *Las Meninas*), figures that include within themselves what they are depicting.

2   Mitchell (1994: 58–60) discusses a series of metapictures, including the originally anonymous Duck-Rabbit drawing from a humor magazine that Ludwig Wittgenstein raised to a philosophical icon and that became a key illustration in psychology; Foucault's use of *Las Meninas*, which transformed it from being merely a canonical painting; and Magritte's *Ceci n'est pas une pipe*.

3   The phrase refers both to the philosophical tradition of Foucault and Deleuze and to the

technical search in cognitive science for an alternative to propositional logic models both for constructing "intelligent machines" and for modeling human intelligence. See Glasgow, Narayan, and Chandrasekaran 1995.

4 In addition to being an exemplar par excellence for the notion of a mise-en-abyme in contemporary discussions, the recent x-ray research and art historical debates have made it also a meditation on "its exceptional there-not-there effect" (Stoz 1999). Not only do we stand where the mirrored king and queen stood as they suddenly entered, interrupting the work of the painting, making Velázquez look up. Not only, thus, is there the aporia of whether he looks at them from a respectful distance, or at us, acknowledging them but asserting the immortality of painting beyond their temporality. But now in addition our eyes can flip back and forth between two pictures on one canvas, an original dated 1656 and a radically reworked painting done around 1659. Since the eighteenth century, observers have wondered about the artist's seemingly anachronistic red cross of the Order of Santiago (the painting is dated 1656, but Velázquez was not knighted until 1658). The eighteenth-century Spanish court painter Antonio Palomino suggested that the cross had been added by King Philip himself. This story codes at least the fact that the knighthood could only have been given at Philip's specific decree, since Velázquez's mother was Portuguese, probably of Jewish origin. The recent x-ray studies and reinterpretations of the painting by Manuela Mena, the distinguished curator, and José Manuel Pita Andrade, the former director of the Prado Museum, suggest that the entire left side of the painting was reworked around 1659, eliminating a table and a red velvet curtain and reworking a figure of a young page holding a command baton (symbol of the infanta's future state power) into the familiar Velázquez holding a paintbrush. Studies of the brush strokes on the artist's chest indicate the black tunic and the cross were painted at the same time. The impetus for the reworking of the painting was the birth in 1657 of a male heir. The older painting was a state portrait anticipating the succession of the five-year-old Margarita (while the other infanta, Maria Teresa, was to be married to Louis XIV in hopes of concluding the long hostilities with France). Margarita is shown as a tiny imperious future queen, with a variety of symbols of state surrounding her (the command baton in the page's hand, a ring of power), two meninas or maids of honor tending to her (Maria Augustina Sarmiento with the cup, Isabel de Velasco bending attentively), two dwarfs (Maribarbola looks at us, Nicolasito Pertusato rouses a dog), two courtiers (José Nieto, a friend of Velázquez, on the stairway in the background; and the page). In the reworked painting, after the birth of Margarita's brother in 1657, the artist replaces the page, and the state portrait is converted into a court genre piece (or a mise-en-abyme of a painter painting, a chronicler of court life chronicling himself chronicling court life).

5 Rotman (1987: 43–44) points out that Snyder's 1985 reading of *Las Meninas*, which dismisses Foucault for having misrecognized the vanishing point—it is not within the mirror but rather near the elbow of the figure within the doorway—is a complement more than a refutation of Foucault's reading. Snyder says that the mirror cannot contain the reflections of the real king and queen standing in the foreground, but only a reflection of a reflection of them, an *ideal* of their royalty. Mirrors in the seventeenth century were metaphors for the ideal. Foucault is interested in the play of gazes, the construction of subjectivities.

As Rotman puts it, even if Foucault is technically wrong about the vanishing point, his insights remain about the sociological construction of subjectivities and about the organization of modern scenes of representation — where representation undertakes to represent itself — as being constructed around a void, around a disappearance of that which is its foundation.

6   See also Martin Jay 1993: 402–6.

7   See Donald Varene's 1985 tracking of Hegel's call for "a new mythology of Reason" through an epistemology of *Schein* (appearance), *Vorstellung* (placing before, representation), *Aufhebung* (lifting up, saving, from sense-certainties to concept), *verkehrte Welt* (inverted world of mirrors, cameras, and reason necessary to overcoming repetitive false certainties), and the use of humor and the trope of irony to dispel illusion. This vocabulary provides important starting points for Marx, Nietzsche, Freud, Benjamin, Husserl, Heidegger, and Foucault, among others. Descartes's *cogito*, of course, is a move toward this reflexive self-consciousness, but the philosophers' trinity of Descartes, Kant, and Hegel, from an anthropologist's point of view, although they can be productively read and reinvested in their contexts of political and social transformations, overly hypostatize the individual knower. Durkheim takes as his task the transformation of this tradition into a sociological one (most explicitly in *The Elementary Forms of Religious Life* [1912]).

8   Jeremy Bentham is conventionally credited with the philosophical formulation of the psychology of the Panopticon. His brother actually built the physical structure in Russia which provided the image for the metaphor.

9   Even if Descartes was an amateur anatomist, dealing in the fifth part of his *Discourse* with the structure of the heart and circulation of the blood, and recommending the reader first cut open some large animal and reach into the chest cavity to feel the heat of the body and the nature of blood, still Descartes dismisses the body as inessential, observing that a limb could be taken away without affecting the mind or soul, and recommending the experience of cutting open an animal mainly for those who do not know the force of a mathematical demonstration, who need to be persuaded by the theatricality of popular science demonstration. Descartes is barely modern in abstracting and textualizing knowledge; but he is otherwise decidedly not part of our post-nineteenth-century episteme — take away our hormonal, immune, neurological, or genomic systems, and Descartes's soul and reason also rapidly give way. For a lovely reading of Descartes and of Rembrandt's *The Anatomy Lesson*, see Barker 1995.

10 On the spatiality of Benjamin's use of *Zerstreuung*, and the physicality of Heidegger's use of the term, see S. Weber (1996: 91–93), who in turn draws on Derrida's analysis in "Psyche" (1987/1989b). See also Benjamin's notion of the cinema hall as a "gymnasium of the senses," where people collectively, by monitoring each other's reactions, learned how to process and react to this new montaged configuration of sensory inputs ("The Work of Art in the Age of Mechanical Reproduction," in Benjamin 1968).

11 One might object that the photographer is no more represented within the frame of the Ian Hunter laboratory image than is Velázquez as painter of *Las Meninas*. Technically, one might "save" the contrast by noting that the gazes within Velázquez's painting explicitly raise the question of point of view, whereas in the photograph the point of view issue is

"distributed" among various technological devices (camera, helmet, screen, patient under the robotic arm). Philosophically, I would perhaps rather say that this is one image that raises the poverty of Heidegger's notion of the technological picture of the world, which still depends on a Cartesian notion of totalization and refuses the crucial issue of the various agencies that need to be called to account in technological society. Heidegger can thus hide his Nazi-disappointed politics and refusal to acknowledge an ethical position for himself behind a claim that technology is to blame. As his various critics at the time (Walter Benjamin) and in later generations (Jacques Derrida, Avital Ronell) have noted, ethics do not disappear in technological society. For another account of the poverty of Heidegger's response to the fast-moving pace of technological destruction and reconstruction, see Samuel Weber's account of Heidegger's effort to rethink Descartes's cogito (S. Weber 1996: chap. 2).

12   I am indebted to Miles Ogborn (1995) for drawing attention to Elias's analysis of *Las Meninas* (the picture is on the cover of Elias's *Engagement und Distanzierung* [1983]). I see a greater continuity than does Ogborn between the analyses of Foucault, via Crary and Alpers, and those of Elias.

13   At least three traditions of thought are important to the transformation of Freud. In anthropology, Malinowski's *Sex and Repression in Savage Society* took the Freudian argument seriously: if family structure and early childhood are formative for psychological patterns, and the repression structure that generates social patterns of crime or other transgressions, then if family structure is quite different (as in a matrilineal lineage organization, rather than a patrilineal or cognatic bourgeois nuclear family structure), patterns of psychological development, crime, and mental illness should also be different. Gananath Obeyesekere's work in *Medusa's Hair* and *The Cult of the Goddess Pattini* pursues this line of thinking. A complementary line of thought is that of Adorno and Horkheimer, who argued that the Oedipus complex had been transformed by conditions of property and knowledge or skill that no longer passed down from father to son, but where sons were independent of fathers for access to income, and often (as today with computers) had more access to knowledge and skill than did their fathers, thus reversing traditional authority, power, idealization, and fantasy relations. Walter Benjamin explored the idea that the technological environment is a new training ground of the sensorium and reworks the nature of embodied-mimetic perception. Recent French theorists (Lacan, Lyotard, Foucault, Deleuze and Guattari, Irigaray, Cixous, Kristeva) have pursued these questions of desire, *jouissance*, and fantasy under conditions of a new technological environment.

14   The cadavers of a thirty-nine-year-old Texas male and a fifty-nine-year-old female have been very thinly sliced (1,800 slices for the male, 6,000 for the female) photographed, X-rayed, electronically digitized, and made available on the Internet by the National Library of Medicine. The goal is to provide a teaching and research tool that allows three-dimensional images of human anatomy, among other uses, to supplement and perhaps substitute for cadavers in medical school anatomy classes. Some of the ethical, psychological, feminist, and cultural issues surrounding this project have been analyzed by Thomas Csordas (2000), Lisa Cartwright (1998), and Catherine Waldby (2000). The artist-psychiatrist Eric Avery pushed Csordas and Cartwright to not overly sanitize their accounts and

visual presentations, and also to include the production process of people freezing the bodies and slicing them with a high-speed rotary saw (Conference at University of Wisconsin, Milwaukee 1997). Although initially the intent was to keep the identities of the cadavers anonymous, the press identified Joseph Paul Jernigan, executed in 1993 by the state of Texas by lethal injection for killing a man during a burglary.

15   The structuralist, linguistic, geological, and Marxist versions of this, as Lévi-Strauss argued in the 1960s, used a notion of deep versus surface structure. The model was grammatical speech: a native speaker can distinguish correct from incorrect sentences but not necessarily articulate the rules of grammar; the analyst can produce rules that in turn he can check with native informants. Actual performance of a speaker may not always match his or her competence (recognition of correct forms). Chomskian generative grammar was the project of producing the small number of rules that could generate an infinite number of correct utterances.

16   "Analytic of finitude" is a phrase from Foucault's *The Order of Things* (1966/1970: 303–43), drawing on a tradition of philosophical debate in Heidegger and Levinas; "situated knowledge" is a phrase popularized by Donna Haraway (1991) in an important essay that embraces the challenge of fitting together projects that may interrupt one another (socialism, feminism, and positive science, in her case); "standpoint epistemology" is a similar term proposed by the feminist philosopher Sandra Harding (1992). For "thick description" and "local knowledge," see Geertz 1973b, 1983.

17   There is a family of resemblance among the various explorations by, for instance, Freud, Benjamin, Lacan, Lyotard, Deleuze, Levinas, and Derrida, of the rich underside of the tapestries of controlled communication, that shows the threads or traces of other ways of thinking.

9.2. Science, Technology, and Society Curriculum

1   The historian of science Robert Cohen, in a conference on the (still narrowly conceived) legacy of the Vienna Circle, held at Harvard in spring 1997, noted that members of his generation of American philosophers of science never actually read much of the Vienna Circle, and so their downplaying of the deep relations between pragmatism, operationalism, and the Vienna Circle, and their ridiculing of one of the projects of the Vienna Circle that attempted to conceptually reconstruct the world from sense impressions and logical relations, by way of protocol sentences, was based on a kind of ignorance, a downplaying of the sociopolitical context of that project, and almost willful misreading. As Robert Westman and others have reclaimed from the historical record, Carnap commissioned Kuhn's *The Structure of Scientific Revolutions* and intended to include it in the Unity of Science publication series: it is more a conversation with, than a repudiation of, the Vienna Circle or Carnap. In any case, Carnap was only one of the several vying political and philosophical strands among the members of the Vienna Circle, from Neurath on the more socialist Left to Schlick on the more liberal Right, and from Carnap on the more analytic end to Schlick on the more pragmatist end.

2   An ordinary language phrase, resonant from Piaget and from Lévi-Strauss's *La Pensée Sau-*

vage (1962/1966), which has been elevated as a useful slogan at MIT in Seymour Papert's "constructivist" approach to learning, used effectively by Sherry Turkle in her studies of computers, adding to Papert's approach also psychological and psychodynamic dimensions from Piaget, from object relations theories, and from Lacan.

3 In the first iteration, my colleague refused to put Galison on the syllabus and did not want Foucault discussed. While I respect his own work and his opinions, and have been very pleased to learn from him, insofar as these were genuinely scholarly and principled objections, I would have preferred having had those objections dealt with in a careful professional way as topics for the class. Such negotiations between faculty of different disciplines was after all the contractual basis for the course. Similar problems arose with other faculty on occasion. The rationale in all cases for which books to discuss in class was either that they provided major conceptual frameworks used by one or another discipline or that they were important new books that were shaping the field of the present and future.

4 Deborah Fitzgerald, Harriet Ritvo, Charlie Weiner, and myself.

5 The encyclopedia *Sciences of the Earth* (G. Good 1998) — written by geodesists, geographers, geophysicists, oceanographers, historians, and even one contributor from an STS program in Japan, and two from history and philosophy of science programs in the British Commonwealth — includes entries on Michel Foucault, Imre Lakatos, historiography, sociological/constructivist approaches to geoscience, and entire sections on institutions and the study of the earth, and social perspectives and the earth. See also Bowler 1992 and Bocking 1997.

6 A phrase from Clifford Geertz's essay "Religion as a Cultural System" that became popular in anthropological analyses of symbol systems in the 1960s and 1970s (Geertz 1966, reprinted in Geertz 1973b).

7 MIT's open courseware initiative is now pursuing this suggestion for a wide array of courses.

10. In the Science Zone

I thank Joao Biehl, Joe Dumit, Susan Lindee, Mariza Peirano, Alcida Ramos, Jenny Reardon, and Ricardo Ventura Santos, as well as the anonymous *Anthropology Today* reviewer(s), for comments and suggestions on earlier versions of this essay.

1 The retrovirus HTLV IIc, said to be endemic among Brazilian Indians, including Yanomami and Kayapo, is today a subject of interest for the evolution of human retroviruses, as migration markers, as "social habit" markers, and for possible association with hematological (leukemia) and neurological (cerebellar ataxia) diseases. For a review of the field and bibliography, and a laconic note that "few strategic data have been produced regarding HTLV or HIV infection among Amazonian groups" because of the "difficulties in obtaining permits to perform studies within Indian communities," see R. Ishak, A. C. R. Vallinoto, V. N. Azevedo, and M. O. G. Ishak, "Epidemiological Aspects of Retrovirus (HTLV) Infection among Indian Populations in the Amazon Region of Brazil," *Cadernos de Saude Publica* 19(4), July/August 2003, <http://www.scielosp.org/scielo.php?script=sci_arttext&pid=S0102-311X2003000400013&lng=pt&nrm=iso&tlng=en>.

Epilogue

1 Stories about Koremochi stress his powers of discernment, reading signs, and using, as well as seeing through, disguises. He is said to have won the epithet "shogun" or "yogo shogun" by dramatically reversing his losses and near annihilation in land dispute battles with the Morotane clan. Having through contempt for his rivals left himself undefended, Koremochi realized at the last moment, thanks to the sound of surprised waterfowl (a frequent trope in medieval Japanese literature on war), that he and his party of twenty men were about to be overwhelmed by Fujiwara of the Morotane clan. Koremochi fought until dawn, ensured the escape of his wife and children, and then set fire to his residence. All his men died in the fighting, but he escaped, disguising himself in women's garb and hiding in the reeds. In a reverse and fatal presumption, Fujiwara, finding only charred, unidentifiable bodies, assumed that Koremochi was dead. Hearing of the attack, Koremochi's forces gathered, and Koremochi revealed himself to be alive. Instead of acceding to counsel of gathering strength and preparing a battle plan, Koremochi opted for an immediate surprise attack, rallying his men with the slogan that living in shame is much worse than a splendid death, and the call that they could join him or not. Fujiwara was killed, Koremochi's fame increased, and he lived to the age of seventy-nine. In a variant of the Noh and Kabuki story used by Yoshitoshi, it is said that Koremochi, when traveling over Mount Togakushi, saw through the disguise of a bandit dressed as a woman and killed him. (Thanks to Yasuko and John Dower for pursuing the entry on Taira no Koremochi in the *Dai Hyakka Jiten* [The Great Encyclopedia].)

2 In addition to Derrida's well-known meditation on the pharmakon in Plato's *Phaedrus*, see also the meditations on the elixir of the Zoroastrian high liturgy *yasna* rituals, the *soma* of the Vedas, and the associated legends of the Avesta (M. Fischer 2003: chap. 1). Jamshid's cup of the Shahnameh tradition is also an analogue of the sake cup here.

BIBLIOGRAPHY

Abbas, Ackbar. 1992. Review of *Cinema 1, 2*, by Gilles Deleuze. *Discourse* 14(3).
———. 1996. *Hong Kong Culture*. Minneapolis: University of Minnesota Press.
———. 1999. "On Fascination: Walter Benjamin's Images." *New German Critique* 48:43–62.
Abelson, Harold, and Gerald Jay Sussman, with Julie Sussman. 1985. *Structure and Interpretation of Computer Programs*. MIT Press.
Abir-Am, Pnina. 1980. "From Biochemistry to Molecular Biology: DNA and the Acculturated Journey of the Critic of Science Erwin Chargaff." *History and Philosophy of the Life Sciences* 2:3–60.
———. 1985. "Themes, Genres, and Orders of Legitimation in the Consolidation of New Scientific Disciplines: Deconstructing the Historiography of Molecular Biology." *History of Science* 23:74–117.
———. 1992. "The Politics of Macromolecules: Molecular Biologists, Biochemists, and Rhetoric." *Osiris* 7:164–91.
Abraham, Itty. 1998. *The Making of the Indian Atomic Bomb: Science, Secrecy, and the Postcolonial State*. London: Zed.
Abu-Lughod, Lila. 1986. *Veiled Sentiments: Honor and Poetry in a Bedouin Society*. Berkeley: University of California Press.
Adorno, Theodor, and Walter Benjamin. 1994/1999. *The Complete Correspondence, 1928–1940*. Cambridge: Harvard University Press.
Aglietta, Michel. 1976/1979. *A Theory of Capitalist Regulation*. London: New Left Books.
Ahtisaari, Marti, Jochen Fowein, and Marcelino Oreja. 2000. Report to the President of the European Court of Human Rights and the Council of the European Union. Paris.
Ajami, Fuad. 1986. *The Vanished Imam: Musa al-Sadr and the Shi'a of Lebanon*. Ithaca: Cornell University Press.
A'li, Abulfazl, ed. 1985. *The Graphic Art of the Islamic Revolution*. Tehran: Publications Division of the Art Bureau of the Islamic Propagation Organization.
Allen, Barbara. 1999. "Uneasy Alchemy: Dissonance, Resistance, Justice, and Change in Louisiana's Industrial Corridor." Ph.D. diss., Rensselaer Polytechnic Institute.
Allen, William. 1965. *The African Husbandman*. New York: Oxford University Press.
Alpers, Svetlana. 1983. *The Art of Describing: Dutch Art in the Seventeenth Century*. Chicago: University of Chicago Press.

Amayun, Milton B. 1981. "Assessment Report on the Health Care Program of World Vision in Las Dhure." 15 May. Typescript.

Anderman, Janusz. 1988. *The Edge of the World*. New York: Readers International.

Arlen, Michael. 1975. *Passage to Ararat*. New York: Farrar, Straus, and Giroux.

Aronowitz, Stanley. 1994. *The Jobless Future: Sci-Tech and the Dogma of Work*. Minneapolis: University of Minnesota Press.

Ash, Timothy Garten. 1993. *Inside the Magic Lantern*. New York: Pantheon.

Avery, Eric. 1980. Letters from Somalia, September–March 1981. Avery archives, Galveston, Texas.

———. 1982a. "Eric Avery and His Art." Interview by Inci Bowman. *Bookman* 9(7):3–9.

———. 1982b. Transcript of "Interview with Eric Avery," by Inci Bowman. 1 June.

———. 1983. "Hands Healing: A Photographic Essay." In *The Visual Arts and Medical Education*, ed. Geri Berg. Carbondale: Southern Illinois University Press.

———. 1990. "Creating Good Bone Culture." In *Reimagining America: The Arts of Social Change*, ed. Mark O'Brien and Craig Little. Philadelphia: New Society.

———. 1997a. "Art of Medicine/Medicine of Art." Colloquium, MIT Science, Technology, and Society Program, 1 December.

———.1997b. Class on Social and Ethical Issues in the Biosciences and Biotechnologies. MIT-Harvard Health Science and Technology Program, 2 December.

———. 1997c. *The Lost Art of Healing*. Installation, University of Wisconsin, Milwaukee. Video.

Bach, Fritz, et al. 1996. "Delayed Xenograft Rejection." *Immunology Today* 17(8): 379–84.

———. 1998. "Uncertainty and Xenotransplantation: Individual Benefit versus Collective Risk." *Nature Medicine* 4(2):141–44.

Banville, John. 1976. *Doctor Copernicus*. New York: Vintage.

———. 1981. *Kepler*. New York: Vintage.

———. 1986. *Mefisto*. London: Secker and Warburg.

———. 1987. *The Newton Letter*. New York: Godine.

Barker, Francis. 1995. *The Tremulous Private Body*. Ann Arbor: University of Michigan Press.

Barlow, John Perry. 1992a. "Crime and Puzzlement." http://www.feist.com/~fqdb/texts/cp.html.

———. 1992b. "Decrypting the Puzzle Palace." *Communications of the ACM* 35(7).

———. 1994. "The Economy of Ideas." *Wired* 2.03. http://www.musicwest.com/MW/95/Panelists/B/Barlow/economy.html.

———. 1995. "Property and Speech: Who Owns What You Say in Cyberspace." *Communications of the ACM* 38(12):19–22.

———. 1996. "Selling Wine without Bottles: The Economy of Mind on the Global Net." In *Clicking In: Hot Links to a Digital Culture*, ed. L. Leeson. Seattle: Bay Press.

Barnes, Barry, David Bloor, and John Henry. 1996. *Scientific Knowledge: A Sociological Analysis*. Chicago: University of Chicago Press.

Baudrillard, Jean. 1981/1994. *Simulation and Simulacra*. Ann Arbor: University of Michigan Press.

Bayly, C. A. 1996. *Empire and Information: Intelligence Gathering and Social Communication in India, 1780–1870*. New York: Cambridge University Press.

Bear, Greg. 1985. *Blood Music*. New York: Berkeley Publishing Group.

———. 1999. *Darwin's Radio*. New York: Ballantine Books.

Beck, Ulrich. 1986/1992. *Risk Society: Towards a New Modernity*. Thousand Oaks, Calif.: Sage.

———. 1991/1995. *Ecological Enlightenment*. Atlantic Highlands, N.J.: Humanities Press.

———. 1997/2000. *What Is Globalization?* London: Blackwell.

Benedict, Carol. 1996. *Bubonic Plague in Nineteenth Century China*. Stanford: Stanford University Press.

Benedikt, Michael. 1992. *Cyberspace: First Steps*. Cambridge: MIT Press.

Benjamin, Andrew, and Peter Osborne, eds. 1994. *Walter Benjamin's Philosophy*. New York: Routledge.

Benjamin, Walter. 1968. *Illuminations*. New York: Schocken.

———. 1996–1999. *Selected Writings*. Vols. 1 and 2. Cambridge: Harvard University Press.

———. 1999. *The Arcades Project*. Cambridge: Harvard University Press.

Benson, Harry. 1982. "Doctor Sees Life and Death. . . . Retreats to Art in San Ygnacio." *Zapata County News*, 14 October.

Berry, Brian, and Duane Marble. 1968. *Spatial Analysis: A Reader in Statistical Geography*. Englewood Cliffs, N.J.: Prentice-Hall.

Berry, Chris, ed. 1991. *Perspectives on Chinese Cinema*. London: British Film Institute.

Bhabha, Homi K. 1998. "Joking Aside: The Idea of a Self Critical Community." In *Modernity, Culture, and "the Jew,"* ed. Bryan Cheyette and Laura Marcus. Stanford: Stanford University Press.

Biagioli, Mario. 1993. *Galileo, Courtier: The Practice of Science in the Culture of Absolutism*. Chicago: University of Chicago Press.

———. 1996. "Etiquette, Interdependence, and Sociability in Seventeenth Century Science." *Critical Inquiry* 22(2): 193–238..

Biehl, Joao. 1999. "Other Life: AIDS, Biopolitics, and Subjectivity in Brazil's Zones of Social Abandonment." Ph.D. diss., University of California at Berkeley.

Biella, Peter, Napoleon Chagnon, and Gary Seaman. 1997. *Yanomamo Interactive: The Ax Fight*. CD-ROM. Orlando: Harcourt Brace.

Bloch, Marc. 1966. *French Rural History: An Essay on Its Basic Characteristics*. Berkeley: University of California Press.

Blumenberg, Hans. 1975/1987. *The Genesis of the Copernican World*. Cambridge: MIT Press.

Bocking, Stephen. 1997. *Ecologists and Environmental Politics*. New Haven: Yale University Press.

Bottigheimer, Ruth. 1987. *Grimm's Bad Girls and Bold Boys: The Moral and Social Vision of the Tales*. New Haven: Yale University Press.

Bowler, Peter. 1992. *The Norton History of the Environmental Sciences*. New York: Norton.

Brand, Stewart. 1987. *The Media Lab: Inventing the Future at MIT*. New York: Viking.

Branscomb, Anne Wells. 1994. *Who Owns Information? From Privacy to Public Access*. New York: Basic Books.

Branscomb, Lewis, and Brian Kahin. 1994. Information Infrastructure Course Syllabus.

Harvard Kennedy School of Government: Science, Technology, and Public Policy Program.

Bravo, Michael. 1998. "The Anti-anthropology of Highlanders and Islanders." *Studies in the History and Philosophy of Science* 29(3): 369–89.

Breyer, Stephen. 2000. "The Courts and Genetics." Presentation at "Genes and Society: The Impact of New Technologies on Law, Medicine, and Policy," Whitehead Policy Symposium, MIT, 10–12 May.

Broad, William. 1985. *Star Warriors: A Penetrating Look into the Lives of the Young Scientists behind Our Space Age Weaponry.* New York: Simon and Schuster.

———. 1992. *Teller's War.* New York: Simon and Schuster.

Brown, Jonathan. 1997. "Letter to the Editor: *Las Meninas.*" *Times Literary Supplement* (London), 18 April.

Brown, Phil, and Edwin J. Mikkelsen. 1990. *No Safe Place: Toxic Waste, Leukemia, and Community Action.* Berkeley: University of California Press.

Bucciarelli, Louis L. 1994. *Designing Engineers.* Cambridge: MIT Press.

Buck-Morss, Susann. 1991. *The Dialectics of Seeing: Walter Benjamin and the Arcades Project.* Cambridge: MIT Press.

———. 1993. "Dream World of Mass Culture: Walter Benjamin's Theory of Modernity and the Dialectics of Seeing." In *Modernity and the Hegemony of Vision*, ed. David Michael Levin. Berkeley: University of California Press.

Buderi, Robert. 1996. *The Invention That Changed the World.* New York: Simon and Schuster.

Bukatman, Scott. 1993. *Terminal Identities.* Durham: Duke University Press.

Bunzl, John. 1997. *Between Vienna and Jerusalem: Reflections and Polemics on Austria, Israel, and Palestine.* Frankfurt am Main: Peter Lang.

———. 2000. "Who the Hell Is Jörg Haider?" MS.

Burchard, John Ely. 1950. *Mid-century: The Social Implications of Scientific Progress.* Cambridge: MIT Press.

Burnham, David. 1983. *The Rise of the Computer State.* New York: Vintage.

———. 1996. *Above the Law.* New York: Macmillan.

Callison, Candis. 2002. "A Digital Assemblage: Diagramming Social Realities of Stikine Watershed." M.A. thesis, MIT.

Cambrosio, Alberto, and Peter Keating. 1995. *Exquisite Specificity: The Monoclonal Antibody Revolution.* New York: Oxford University Press.

Carius, Andor. 1996. "The Sounds of Plasma Physics." MIT Colloquium.

Carson, Rachel. 1962. *Silent Spring.* New York: Houghton-Mifflin.

Cartwright, Lisa. 1995. *Screening the Body: Tracing Medicine's Visual Culture.* Minneapolis: University of Minnesota Press.

———. 1998. "A Cultural Anatomy of the Visible Human project." In *Visible Woman: Imaging Technologies, Gender, and Science*, ed. Paula Treichler, Lisa Cartwright, and Constance Penley. New York: New York University Press.

Castells, Manuel. 1996. *Rise of the Network Society.* Malden, Mass.: Oxford University Press.

———. 1997. *The Power of Identity.* Malden, Mass.: Oxford University Press.

———. 1998. *End of Millennium.* Malden, Mass.: Oxford University Press.

Catts, Oron, and Ionat Zurr. 1998–2002. *Tissue Culture and Art Project.* http://www.tca
.uwa.edu.au/index.html.

Catts, Oron, Ionat Zurr, and Guy Ben-Ary. 2000. "Tissue Culture and Art(ificial) Wombs."
In *Next Sex, Ars Electronica—Ars Electronica Festival 2000,* ed. Gerfried Stocker and
Christine Schöpf. New York: SpringerWien-New York.

Cavalli-Sforza, Luca. 1994. *History and Geography of Human Genes.* Princeton: Princeton
University Press.

Cavazos, Edward, and Gavino Morin. 1994. *Cyberspace and the Law.* Cambridge: MIT Press.

Centers for Disease Control. 2000. "Public Health Dispatch: Outbreak of Poliomyelitis—
Dominican Republic and Haiti." *CDC MMWR Weekly* 49(48):1094, 1103. www.cdc.
gov/mnmwr/; preview/mmwrhtml/mm4948a4htm.

Chakrabarti, Samidh, and Aaron Strauss. 2002. "Carnival Booth: An Algorithm for Defeating
the Computer-Assisted Passenger Screening System." www.firstmonday.org/issues/
issues7_10/chakrabarti.

Chisum, Donald. 1986. "The Patentability of Algorithms." *University of Pittsburgh Law
Review* 47:959.

Chouhan, T. R. 1994. *Bhopal: The Inside Story: Carbide Workers Speak Out on the World's
Worst Industrial Disaster.* New York: Apex Press.

Clancey, Greg. 1999. "Foreign Knowledge or Art Nation, Earthquake Nation: Architecture,
Seismology, Carpentry, the West, and Japan, 1876–1945." Ph.D. diss., STS Program, MIT.

Clarke, Adele E. 1998. *Disciplining Reproduction.* Berkeley: University of California Press.

Cliff, Michelle. 1987. *No Telephone to Heaven.* New York: Dutton.

Coe, Sue. 1994. "Scenes from an AIDS Ward." *Village Voice* 34(8):19–23.

———. 1995. *Dead Meat.* New York: Four Walls, Eight Windows.

Cohen, David W. 1994. *The Combing of History.* Chicago: University of Chicago Press.

Cohen, Keith. 1979. *Film and Fiction: The Dynamics of Exchange.* New Haven: Yale University
Press.

Cohen, Lawrence. 1998. *No Aging in India: Alzheimer's, the Bad Family, and Other Modern
Things.* Berkeley: University of California Press.

———. 1999. "Where It Hurts: Indian Material for an Ethics of Organ Transplantation."
Daedalus 128(4):135–66.

Cohen, Marjorie B. 1997. "Letter to Fogg Print Fans." Fogg Art Museum, Harvard University.
15 August.

Cohen, Percy. 1968. *Modern Social Theory.* New York: Basic Books.

Cohen, Roger. 1993. "[Agnieszka] Holland without a Country." *New York Times Magazine,*
8 August, 28.

Coimbra, Carlos E. A., Nancy M. Flowers, Francisco M. Salzano, and Ricardo V. Santos.
2002. *The Xavante in Transition: Health, Ecology, and Bioanthropology in Central Brazil.*
Ann Arbor: University of Michigan Press.

Collins, Harry. 1974. "The TEA set: Tacit Knowledge and Scientific Networks." *Science
Studies* 4:165–86. Reprinted in *Science in Context,* ed. Barry Barnes and David Edge
(Cambridge: MIT Press, 1982).

———. 1975. "The Seven Sexes: A Study in the Sociology of a Phenomenon, or the

Replication of Experiments in Physics." *Sociology* 9:205–24. Reprinted in *Science in Context*, ed. Barry Barnes and David Edge (Cambridge: MIT Press, 1982).

Collins, Harry, and Trevor Pinch. 1993. *The Golem: What Everyone Should Know about Science*. New York: Cambridge University Press.

———. 1998. *The Golem at Large: What You Should Know about Technology*. New York: Cambridge University Press.

Collins, K. J., and J. S. Weiner. 1977. *Human Adaptability: A History and Compendium of Research in the International Biological Programme*. London: Taylor and Francis.

Comfort, Nathaniel C. 2001. *The Tangled Field: Barbara McClintock's Search for the Patterns of Genetic Control*. Cambridge: Harvard University Press.

Constantine, Larry, ed. 1993. *Infinite Loop: Stories about the Future by the People Creating It*. San Francisco: Miller Freeman.

Conway, Jill, Kenneth Keniston, and Leo Marx, eds. 1999. *Earth, Air, Fire, Water: Humanistic Studies of the Environment*. Amherst: University of Massachusetts Press.

Cook, Gareth. 2002. "Bio Envy: As Biology Picks up Steam and Money, Physicists Join the Juggernaut." *Boston Globe*, 13 August, D1, D3.

Cooke, Miriam. 1987. *War's Other Voices: Women Writers on the Lebanese Civil War*. New York: Cambridge University Press.

Coughlin, Kevin. 1997. "The Cutting Edge: Images and Maybe Sound Will Allow Surgeons to Enter the Brain without Second Thoughts." *Newark (N.J.) Star Ledger*, 8 September, 59, 62.

Coupland, Douglas. 1993. "Microserfs: Seven Days in the Life of Young Microsoft." *WIRED Online. HotWIRED* 2.01.

———. 1995. *Microserfs*. New York: Harper/Collins.

Crary, Jonathan. 1990. *Techniques of the Observer: On Vision and Modernity in the Nineteenth Century*. Cambridge: MIT Press.

Crawford, Colin. 1996. *Uproar at Dancing Rabbit Creek: Battle over Race, Class and the Environment*. Reading, Mass.: Addison-Wesley.

Critical Art Ensemble. 1994. *The Electronic Disturbance*. Brooklyn, N.Y.: Autonomia.

Cronin, William. 1991. *Nature's Metropolis*. New York: Norton.

Csordas, Thomas J. 2000. "Computerized Cadavers: Shades of Being and Representations in Virtual Reality." In *Biotechnology, Culture, and the Body*, ed. P. Brodwin. Bloomington: Indiana University Press.

Czajkowski, Jerzy. 1984. *Materialy Muzeum Budownictwa Ludowego w Sanoku*. Rzeszow: Rezeszowskie Zaklady Graficzne.

Dallenbach, Lucien. 1977/1989. *The Mirror in the Text*. Chicago: University of Chicago Press.

Daniel, E. Valentine. 1996. *Charred Lullabies: Chapters in an Anthropology of Violence*. Princeton: Princeton University Press.

Daniel, E. Valentine, and John Chr. Knudsen, eds. 1995. *Mistrusting Refugees*. Berkeley: University of California Press.

Danowitz, A. K., Y. Nassef, and S. E. Goodman. 1995. "Cyberspace across the Sahara: Computing in North Africa." *Communications of the ACM* 38(12):23–28.

Darnton, Robert. 1984. *The Cat Massacre and Other Episodes in French Cultural History*. New York: Basic Books.

Das, Veena. 1990. *Mirrors of Violence: Communities, Riots, and Survivors in South Asia*. Delhi: Oxford University Press.

———. 1995. *Critical Events*. Delhi: Oxford University Press.

———. 2000. "The Practice of Organ Transplants: Networks, Documents, Translations." In *Living with New Medical Technologies*, ed. Margaret Lock, Alberto Cambrosio, and Alan Young. New York: Cambridge University Press.

Daston, Lorrine, and Katharine Park. 1998. *Wonders and the Order of Nature, 1150–1750*. Cambridge: Zone/MIT Press.

Davis, Lee N. 1984. *Corporate Alchemists: Profit Takers and Problem Makers in the Chemical Industry*. New York: William Morrow.

Davis, Mike. 1992. *City of Quartz*. New York: Vintage.

———. 1993. "Dead West: Ecocide in Marlboro Country." *New Left Review*, no. 200.

———. 1998. *Ecology of Fear*. New York: Holt/Metropolitan.

Davis-Floyd, R., and J. Dumit, eds. 1998. *Cyborg Babies*. New York: Routledge.

Dearborn, Mary V. 1986. *Pocahontas' Daughters: Gender and Ethnicity in American Culture*. New York: Oxford University Press.

deCastro Lobos, Maria S., et al. [2001]. "Report of the Medical Team of the Federal University of Rio de Janeiro on the Accusations Contained in Patrick Tierney's *Darkness in El Dorado*." Unpublished report.

Dedrick, Jason, and Kenneth L. Kraemer. 1998. *Asia's Computer Challenge*. New York: Oxford University Press.

Deix, Manfred. 2000. *Deix: Good Vibrations, Eine Retrospective*. Kunst Haus Wien. Wien: Museums Betriebsgesellschaft.

de Kruif, Paul. 1926. *Microbe Hunters*. New York: Harcourt Brace.

Delany, Samuel. 1998. Transcript of discussion with Samuel Delany and Octavia Butler, MIT, 19 February. http://media-in-transition.mit.edu/science_fiction/. transcripts/butler_delany_index.html.

Deleuze, Gilles. 1983/1986. *Cinema 1: The Movement-Image*. Trans. Hugh Tomlinson and Barbara Habberjam. Minneapolis: University of Minnesota Press.

———. 1985/1989. *Cinema 2: The Time-Image*. Trans. Hugh Tomlinson and Robert Galeta. Minneapolis: University of Minnesota Press.

Deleuze, Gilles, and Félix Guattari. 1980/1987. *A Thousand Plateaus*. Trans. Brian Massumi. Minneapolis: University of Minnesota Press.

Delgado, Abelardo. 1982. "Stupid America." In *Chicano Poetry*, ed. Juan Bruce-Nova. Austin: University of Texas Press.

Derrida, Jacques. 1967/1974. *Of Grammatology*. Baltimore: Johns Hopkins University Press.

———. 1972/1981. *Disseminations*. Chicago: University of Chicago Press.

———. 1982/1988. *L'Oreille de l'autre: Otobiographies, transferts, traductions* (The ear of the other). Ed. and trans. Peggy Kamuf et al. New York: Schocken.

———. 1987/1989a. *Of Spirit*. Chicago: University of Chicago Press.

————. 1987/1989b. "Psyche: Inventions of the Other." In *Reading de Man Reading*, ed. L. Waters and W. Godzich. Minneapolis: University of Minnesota Press.

————. 1992/1995. *Points . . . Interviews, 1974–1994*. Stanford: Stanford University Press.

————. 1996/1998. "Faith and Knowledge: The Two Sources of 'Religion' at the Limits of Reason Alone." Ed. and trans. Samuel Weber. In *Religion*, ed. J. Derrida and G. Vattimo. Stanford: Stanford University Press.

————. 2001. "No Journalists Allowed!" In *Religion and Media*, ed. Hent de Vries and Samuel Weber. Stanford: Stanford University Press.

Dery, Mark. 1996. *Escape Velocity: Cyberculture at the End of the Century*. New York: Grove Press.

Detienne, Marcel. 1977. *The Gardens of Adonis*. New York: Humanities.

de Vries, Hent. 1999. *Philosophy and the Turn to Religion*. Baltimore: Johns Hopkins University Press.

Djerassi, Carl. 1989. *Cantor's Dilemma*. New York: Doubleday.

————. 1994. *The Bourbaki Gambit*. Athens: University of Georgia Press.

————. 1998. *NO*. Athens: University of Georgia Press.

Donald, Alisdair. 2001. "The Wal-Marting of American Psychiatry: An Ethnography of Psychiatric Practice in the Late Twentieth Century." *Culture, Medicine, and Psychiatry* 25(4):427–39.

Douglas, Mary, and Aaron Wildavsky. 1982. *Risk and Culture: An Essay on the Selection of Technical and Environmental Dangers*. Berkeley: University of California Press.

Downey, Gary Lee. 1998. *The Machine in Me: An Anthropologist Sits among Computer Engineers*. New York: Routledge.

Downey, Gary Lee, and Joseph Dumit, eds. *Cyborgs and Citadels: Anthropological Interventions in Emerging Sciences and Technologies*. Santa Fe: School for American Research Press.

Doyle, Richard. 1997. *On Beyond Living: Rhetorical Transformations of the Life Sciences*. Stanford: Stanford University Press.

Dreyfus, Hubert. 1979. *What Computers Can't Do*. New York: Harper and Row.

Dukes, Carol Muske. 1993. *Saving St. Germ*. Baltimore: Penguin.

Dumit, Joseph. 1995. "Mindful Images: Brains and Personhood in Biomedical America." Ph.D. diss., University of California at Santa Cruz.

————. 1997. "A Digital Image of the Category of the Person: PET Scanning and Objective Self-Fashioning." In *Cyborgs and Citadels*, ed. G. Downey and J. Dumit. Sante Fe: School of American Research.

————. 1999. "Objective Brains, Prejudicial Images." *Science in Context* 12(1):173–201.

————. 2000. "When Explanations Rest: 'Good-enough' Brain Science and the New Sociomedical Disorders." In *Living and Working with the New Biomedical Technologies*, ed. M. Lock, A. Young, and A. Cambrosio. Cambridge: Cambridge University Press.

Dumont, René. 1957. *Types of Rural Economy*. London: Methuen.

Durkheim, Emile. 1912. *The Elementary Forms of the Religious Life*. Trans. J. W. Swain. New York: Free Press.

Early, John, and John Peters. 2000. *The Xilixama Yanomami of the Amazon*. Gainesville: University Presses of Florida.

Edelson, Harriet. 1982. "Dr. Avery." *Houston Chronicle*, 17 August, sec. 7, p. 3.

Edwards, Paul. 1996. *The Closed World: Computers and the Politics of Discourse in Cold War America*. Cambridge: MIT Press.

Egger, Martin. 1993. "Hermeneutics and the New Epic of Science." In *The Literature of Science*, ed. M. W. McRae. Athens: University of Georgia Press.

Eisenstein, Sergei. 1949. *Film Form: Essays in Film Theory*. Ed. and trans. Jay Leyda. New York: Harcourt, Brace.

Elias, Norbert. 1982. *The Civilizing Process*. London: Blackwell.

———. 1983. *Engagement und Distanzierung*. Frankfurt am Main: Suhrkamp.

Emmeche, Claus. 1994. *The Garden in the Machine: The Emerging Science of Artificial Life*. Princeton: Princeton University Press.

Escobar, Arturo. 1994. *Encountering Development: The Making and Unmaking of the Third World*. Princeton: Princeton University Press.

Evans-Pritchard, E. E. 1937. *Witchcraft, Oracles, and Magic among the Azande*. Oxford: Clarendon Press.

Fabian, Johannes. 1983. *Time and the Other*. New York: Columbia University Press.

———. 1996. *Remembering the Present: Painting and Popular History in Zaire*. Berkeley: University of California Press.

———. 2000. *Out of Our Minds: Reason and Madness in the Exploration of Central Africa*. Berkeley: University of California Press.

Farmer, Paul. 1992. *AIDS and Accusation*. Cambridge: Harvard University Press.

———. 1999. "Responding to Outbreaks of Multidrug Resistant Tuberculosis." In *Tuberculosis: A Comprehensive International Approach*, ed. L. B. Reichman and E. S. Hershfield. New York: Marcel Dekker.

Feenberg, Andrew 1995. *Alternative Modernity: The Technical Turn in Philosophy and Social Theory*. Berkeley: University of California Press.

Felderer, Brigitte. 1996. *Wunschmaschine Welterfindung*. Vienna: Springer.

Ferguson, Brian. 1995. *Yanomami Warfare*. Santa Fe: School for American Research.

———. 2001a. "Materialist, Cultural, and Biological Theories on Why Yanomami Make War." *Anthropological Theory* 1(1):99–116.

———. 2001b. "100,000 Years of Tribal Warfare: History, Science, Ideology, and 'the State of Nature.' " *Journal of the International Institute* 8(3):1, 22–23.

Ferguson, James. 1990. *The Anti-Politics Machine: "Development," Depoliticization, and Bureaucratic Power in Lesotho*. New York: Cambridge University Press.

Findlen, Paula. 1994. *Possessing Nature: Museums, Collecting, and Scientific Culture in Early Modern Italy*. Berkeley: University of California Press.

Fischer, Claude. 1992. *America Calling: A Social History of the Telephone to 1940*. Berkeley: University of California Press.

Fischer, Eric. 1943. *The Passing of the European Age*. Cambridge: Harvard University Press.

Fischer, Irene K. [1979]. "Geodesy? What's That? My Personal Involvement in the Age-Old Quest for the Size and Shape of the Earth, with a Running Commentary on Life in a

Government Research Office." MS. Schlesinger Library, Radcliffe, Cambridge, Mass.; and Institute of Physics Library, New York.

Fischer, Michael M. J. 1973. "Zoroastrian Iran between Myth and Praxis." Ph.D. diss., University of Chicago.

———. 1980. *Iran: From Religious Dispute to Revolution.* Cambridge: Harvard University Press.

———. 1982. "Portrait of a Mullah: The Autobiography and Bildungsroman of Aqa Najafi-Quchani." *Persica* 10:223–57.

———. 1983. "Ethnicity and the Postmodern Arts of Memory." In *Writing Culture: The Poetics and Politics of Ethnography,* ed. J. Clifford and G. Marcus. Berkeley: University of California Press.

———. 1984. "Towards a Third World Poetics: Seeing the Persian Culture Sphere through Short Stories and Film." *Knowledge and Society* 5:171–241.

———. 1986. "Ethnicity and the Postmodern Arts of Memory." In *Writing Culture,* ed. James Clifford and George Marcus. Berkeley: University of California Press.

———. [1987]. "Torn Religions from Gandhi to Rajneesh: (Auto)biographical Call and Response in the Postmodern Age." MS.

———. [1990]. "Mirroring and the Construction of Indian Bourgeois Selves: (Auto)- biographical Explorations among Modern Jains." MS.

———. 1990. "Bombay Talkies, the Word and the World: Salman Rushdie's *Satanic Verses.*" *Cultural Anthropology* 5(2).

———. 1993. "Working through the Other: The Jewish, Spanish, Turkish, Iranian, Ukrainian, Lithuanian, and German Unconscious of Polish Culture; or One Hand Clapping: Dialogue, Silences, and the Mourning of Polish Romanticism." In *Late Editions 1: Perilous States,* ed. G. Marcus. Chicago: University of Chicago Press.

———. 1995a. "Eye(I)ing the Sciences and Their Signifiers (Language, Tropes, Auto- biographers): InterViewing for a Cultural Studies of Science and Technology." In *Technoscientific Imaginaries: Late Editions 2,* ed. G. Marcus. Chicago: University of Chicago Press.

———. 1995b. "Film as Ethnography and Cultural Critique in the Late Twentieth Century." In *Shared Differences: Multicultural Media and Practical Pedagogy,* ed. Diane Carson and Lester Friedman. Urbana: University of Illinois Press.

———. 1995c. "Starting Over: How, What, and for Whom Does One Write about Refugees? The Poetics and Politics of Refugee Film as Ethnographic Access in a Media-Saturated World." In *Mistrusting Refugees,* ed. E. V. Daniel and J. Knudsen. Berkeley: University of California Press.

———. 1996. "Whence From?—Where To? Prospectus for the 1996 Retreat. A Self-Study Document." http://stsfac.mit.edu/Core Course/Documents.

———. 1998. "Filmic Judgment and Cultural Critique." In *Recent Trends in Anthropological Theory and Ethnography,* ed. Dimitra Gefou-Madianou. Athens: Ellinika Grammata.

———. 1999a. "Calling the Future(s) with Ethnographic and Historiographic Legacy Disciplines: STS @ the Turn []ooo.mit.edu." In *Zeroing In on the Year 2000: Late Editions 8,* ed. G. Marcus. Chicago: University of Chicago Press.

———. 1999b. "If Derrida Is the Gómez-Peña of Philosophy, What Are the Genres of Social Science: The Y2K Computer Bug and Other Uncertainties, a Critical Simulation." In *Para-sites: Late Editions*, ed. G. Marcus. Chicago: University of Chicago Press.

———. 2000. "Before Going Digital/Double Digit/Y2000: A Retrospective of Late Editions." In *Zeroing In on the Year 2000: Late Editions 8*, ed. G. Marcus. Chicago: University of Chicago Press.

———. 2002. "After Twenty Years: Introduction to the 2002 Edition." In *Iran: From Religious Dispute to Revolution*. Madison: University of Wisconsin Press.

———. 2004. *Mute Dreams, Blind Owls, and Dispersed Knowledges: Persian Poesis in the Transnational Circuitry*. Durham: Duke University Press.

Fischer, Michael M. J., and Mehdi Abedi. 1990. *Debating Muslims: Cultural Dialogues in Postmodernity and Tradition*. Madison: University of Wisconsin Press.

Fischer, Michael M. J., and Stella Gregorian. 1993. "Six to Eight Characters in Search of Armenian Civil Society amidst the Carnivalization of History." In *Perilous States: Late Editions 1*, ed. George Marcus. Chicago: University of Chicago Press.

Fischer, Michael M. J., and George E. Marcus. 1999. Introduction to *Anthropology as Cultural Critique*. 2d ed. Chicago: University of Chicago Press.

Fleck, Ludwik. 1935. *Genesis and Development of a Scientific Fact*. Chicago: University of Chicago Press.

Forbes, Jill, and Michael Kelly, ed. 1995. *French Cultural Studies*. New York: Oxford University Press.

Ford, Henry [and Samuel Crowther]. 1925. *My Life and Work*. New York: Doubleday, Page.

Forester, Tom, and Perry Morrison. 1990. *Computer Ethics: Tales and Ethical Dilemmas in Computing*. Cambridge: MIT Press.

Forman, Paul. 1971. "Weimar Culture, Causality, and Quantum Theory, 1918–1927." *Historical Studies in the Physical Sciences*, 3:1–115.

Fortun, Kim. 2001. *Advocating Bhopal: Environmentalism, Disaster, New Global Orders*. Chicago: University of Chicago Press.

Fortun, Michael. 2000. "Iceland Cometh to Commercial Genomics: From the Individual as Biomass to the Nation as Database." Paper presented to the Society for the Social Study of Science, September, San Diego.

Fortun, Michael, and Herbert Bernstein. 1998. *Muddling Through: Pursuing Science and Truths in the 21st Century*. Washington: Counterpoint.

Foucault, Michel. 1963/1973. *The Birth of the Clinic*. New York: Vintage.

———. 1966/1970. *The Order of Things*. New York: Random House.

———. 1975/1977. *Discipline and Punish*. New York: Pantheon.

———. 1978. *The History of Sexuality*. Vol. 1. New York: Pantheon.

———. 1980. *Power/Knowledge*. New York: Pantheon.

Franklin, Sarah. 1997. *Embodied Progress: A Cultural Account of Assisted Conception*. London: Routledge.

Friedan, Betty. 1963. *The Feminine Mystique*. New York: Norton.

Friedman, Alan J., and Carol C. Donley. 1985. *Einstein: Man and Myth*. New York: Cambridge University Press.

Froomkin, A. Michael. 1995. "The Metaphor Is the Key: Cryptography, the Clipper Chip, and the Constitution." *University of Pennsylvania Law Review*.

Fujimura, Joan H. 1996. *Crafting Science: A Sociohistory of the Quest for the Genetics of Cancer*. Cambridge: Harvard University Press.

Funk, J. 1993. "Reflections of a Design Engineer at NASA: Interviews with M. M. J. Fischer." Tapes and Transcripts.

Galison, Peter. 1987. *How Experiments End*. Chicago: University of Chicago Press.

———. 1997. *Image and Logic: The Material Culture of Microphysics*. Chicago: University of Chicago Press.

Galison, Peter, and David J. Stump. 1996. *The Disunity of Science*. Stanford: Stanford University Press.

Garfinkle, Simpson. 2000. *Database Nation: The Death of Privacy in the Twenty-first Century*. Cambridge, Mass.: O'Reilly and Associates.

Garfinkle, Simpson, Richard Stallman, and Mitchell Kapor. 1991. "Why Patents Are Bad for Software." *Issues in Science and Technology*.

Gary, Romain. 1967/1968. *The Dance of Genghis Cohen*. New York: New American Library.

Gawande, Atul. 2002. *Complications: A Surgeon's Notes on an Imperfect Science*. New York: Henry Holt.

Geertz, Clifford. 1963. *Agricultural Involution*. Berkeley: University of California Press.

———. 1966. "Religion as a Cultural System." In *Anthropological Approaches to the Study of Religion*, ed. M. Banton. London: Tavistock.

———. 1973a. "Deep Play." In *The Interpretation of Culture*. New York: Basic Books.

———. 1973b. *The Interpretation of Culture*. New York: Basic Books.

———. 1983. *Local Knowledge*. New York: Basic Books.

———. 1995. *After the Fact*. Cambridge: Harvard University Press.

———. 2000. *Available Light*. Princeton: Princeton University Press.

———. 2001. "Life among the Anthros." *New York Review of Books*, 8 February, 18–22.

———, ed. 1963. *Old Societies and New States: The Quest for Modernity in Asia and Africa*. Glencoe, Ill.: Free Press.

Geison, Gerald L. 1995. *The Private Science of Louis Pasteur*. Princeton: Princeton University Press.

———. 1996. "Reply to Max Perutz." *New York Review of Books*, 4 April, 68–69.

Gellner, Ernest. 1988. "The Zeno of Cracow." In *Malinowski between Two Worlds*, ed. Roy Ellen, Ernest Gellner, Grazyna Kubica, and Janusz Mucha. London: Cambridge University Press.

GeneWatch. 2000. "GeneWatch Banned from Biotech Meeting." *GeneWatch* 13(2):12.

George, Timothy S. 2001. *Minamata: Pollution and the Struggle for Democracy in Postwar Japan*. Cambridge: Harvard University Press.

Gerovitch, Vyacheslav. 1999. "Speaking Cybernetically: The Soviet Remaking of an American Science." Ph.D. diss., MIT.

Ghamari-Tabrizi, Sharon. 2000a. "Simulating the Unthinkable: Gaming Future Wars in the 1950s and 1960s." *Social Studies of Science* 30(2):163–223.

———. 2000b. "The Reality Effects in Contemporary Defense Simulations." MS.

―――. 2001. "Why Is Validation of Defense Military and Simulation So Hard to Do?" Paper presented at the Society for the Social Study of Science, 1–4 Nov.

Ghosh, Amitav. 1996. *The Calcutta Chromosome*. Delhi: Ravi Dayal.

Gibson, William. 1984. *Neuromancer*. New York: Ace.

―――. 1986. "An Interview with." In *Across the Wounded Galaxies: Interviews with Contemporary American Science Fiction Writers*, by Larry McCaffrey. Urbana: University of Illinois Press.

Giddens, Anthony. 1990. *The Consequences of Modernity*. London: Cambridge University Press.

―――. 1991. *Modernity and Self-Identity: Self and Society in the Late Modern Age*. Stanford: Stanford University Press.

Giergerich, Steve. 2001. *Body of Knowledge: One Semester of Gross Anatomy, the Gateway to Becoming a Doctor*. New York: Scribner.

Gilder, George. 1989. *Microcosm: The Quantum Revolution in Microcosm: Economics and Technology*. New York: Simon and Schuster.

Gilmore, Robert. 1995. *Alice in Quantumland*. New York: Springer.

Gingrich, Andre. 2000. "A Man for All Seasons: An Anthropological Perspective on the Austrian Freedom Party's Cultural Politics." MS.

Ginsburg, Faye. 2001. "Enabling Disability, Rewriting Kinship: Accommodating Difference in Brave New Families." Harvard Medical School, Department of Social Medicine, Pettus Crowe Seminars on Ethical and Social Science Perspectives on the New Genetics.

Ginsburg, Faye, Lila Abu-Lughod, and Brian Larkin, eds. 2002. *Media Worlds: Anthropology on New Terrain*. Berkeley: University of California Press.

Gladney, Dru. 1994. "Tain Zhuangzhuang: The Fifth Generation, and Minorities Film in China." Typescript.

Glasgow, N., H. Narayan, and B. Chandrasekaran, eds. 1995. *Diagrammatic Reasoning*. Cambridge: MIT Press.

Golan, Tal. 1999. "Scientific Expert Testimony in Anglo-American Courts, 1782–1923." Ph.D. diss., University of California at Berkeley.

Golden, Marita. 1983. *Migrations of the Heart*. New York: Doubleday.

Goldman-Segall, Ricki. 1990. "Learning Constellations: A Multi-Media Ethnographic Research Environment Using Video Technology for Exploring Children's Thinking." Ph.D. diss., MIT.

―――. 1995. *The Global Forest*. Oracle CD-Rom. http://www.merlin.ubc.ca/ppl/ricki.html.

Good, Byron. 1994. *Medicine, Rationality, and Experience*. New York: Cambridge University Press.

Good, Gregory, ed. 1998. *Sciences of the Earth: An Encyclopedia of Events, People, and Phenomena*. Garland Encyclopedias in the History of Science. New York: Garland.

Good, Mary-Jo DelVecchio. 1994. "Oncology and Narrative Time." *Social Science and Medicine* 38(6):855–62.

―――. 1996. "L'Abbraccio biotechnico: Un invito al trattemento sperimentale." In *Il spaere della quarigole*, ed. Pino Donghi. Spoleto: Laterza.

―――. 1998. "Metaphors for Life and Society in Health and Illness and the Biotechnical

Embrace." Paper presented at the International Symposium on Health and Illness, Bologna, Italy.

―――. 1999. "Clinical Realities and Moral Dilemmas: Contrasting Perspectives from Academic Medicine in Kenya, Tanzania, and America." *Daedalus* 128(4):167–96.

Good, Mary-Jo DelVecchio, Irene Kuter, Simon Powell, Herbet C. Hoover Jr., Maria E. Carson, and Rita Lingood. 1995. "Medicine on the Edge: Conversations with Oncologists." In *Technoscientific Imaginaries: Late Editions 2*, ed. G. Marcus. Chicago: University of Chicago Press.

Goodwin, Jean M. 1993. *Human Vectors of Trauma: Historical Casebook and Clinical Manual.* Washington: Psychiatric Press.

Goody, Jack. 1977. *The Domestication of the Savage Mind.* New York: Cambridge University Press.

Goonasekere, Ratna Sunilantha Abhayawardana. 1986. "Renunciation and Monasticism among Jains of India." Ph.D. diss., University of California at San Diego.

Gottweis, Herbert. 1998. *Governing Molecules: The Discursive Politics of Genetic Engineering in Europe and the United States.* Cambridge: MIT Press.

Graham, John D., and Jennifer Kassalow Hartwell. 1997. *The Greening of Industry: A Risk Management Approach.* Cambridge: Harvard University Press.

Graham, Loren. 1972. *Science and Philosophy in the Soviet Union.* New York: Knopf.

―――. 1998. *What Have We Learned about Science and Technology from the Russian Experience.* Stanford: Stanford University Press.

Grandin, Greg. 2000. "Coming of Age in Venezuela." *The Nation*, 11 December.

Greek, C. Ray, and Jean Swingle Greek. 2000. *Sacred Cows and Golden Geese: The Human Cost of Experiments on Animals.* New York: Continuum.

Green, Arthur. 1979. *Tormented Master: A Life of Rabbi Nahman of Bratislav.* Birmingham: University of Alabama Press.

Greenberg, Mike. 1982. "Artist's Work Is Alive with Death." *San Antonio Express-News*, 14 November, sec. M, pp. 1, 8.

Greife, Edward, and Martin Linsky. 1995. *New Corporate Activism.* New York: McGraw Hill.

Greisemer, J. R., and W. Wimsatt. 1989. "Picturing Weismannism: A Case Study of Conceptual Evolution." In *What the Philosophy of Biology Is*, ed. M. Ruse. Dordrecht: Kluwer.

Grimson, W. Eric L., Ron Kikinis, Ferenc A. Jolesz, and Peter McL. Black. 1999. "Image-Guided Surgery." *Scientific American* 280(6):63–69.

Grove, Richard. 1995. *Green Imperialism.* New York: Oxford University Press.

―――. 1997. *Ecology, Climate, and Empire: Colonialism and Global Environmental History, 1400–1940.* Cambridge: White Horse Press.

Guattari, Félix. 1992/1995. *Chaosmosis: An Ethico-Aesthetic Paradigm.* Bloomington: Indiana University Press.

Guha, Ramachandra. 1989. *The Unquiet Woods: Ecological Change and Peasant Resistance in the Himalayas.* Delhi: Oxford University Press.

Guha, Ranajit, and Gayatri Chakravorty Spivak, eds. 1988. *Selected Subaltern Studies.* Delhi: Oxford University Press.

Guillemin, Jean. 1999. *Anthrax: The Investigation of a Deadly Outbreak*. Berkeley: University of California Press.

Gupta, Akhil. 1998. *Postcolonial Developments: Agricultural Culture in the Making of Modern India*. Durham: Duke University Press.

Gürses, Hakkan. 2000. "Österreich, einmal anders: Ein versuch, gemäss Kanzler Schuessels Vorschlag in abgerüsteter Sprache die 'Strasse' zu verteidigen." MS.

Gusterson, Hugh. 1996. *Nuclear Rites: A Weapons Laboratory at the End of the Cold War*. Berkeley: University of California Press.

―――. 2001. "The Virtual Nuclear Weapons Laboratory in the New World Order." *American Ethnologist* 28(1):417–37.

Habermas, Jürgen. 1962/1989. *The Structural Transformation of the Public Sphere*. Cambridge: MIT Press.

―――. 2003. *The Future of Human Nature*. Cambridge: Polity Press.

Haffner, Katie, and John Markoff. 1991. *Cyberpunk: Outlaws and Hackers on the Computer Frontier*. New York: Simon and Schuster.

Haggett, Peter. 1965. *Locational Analysis in Human Geography*. London: Edward Arnold.

Hakken, David. 1993. *Computing Myths, Class Realities*. Boulder, Colo.: Westview.

Hallyn, Fernand. 1987/90. *The Poetic Structure of the World: Copernicus and Kepler*. New York: Zone.

Hammonds, Evelynn M. 1995. "Missing Persons: Black Women and AIDS." In *Words of Fire: An Anthology of African-American Feminist Thought*, ed. Beverly Guy-Sheftall. New York: New Press.

―――. 1996. "When the Margin Is the Center: African-American Feminism(s) and 'Difference.'" In *Transitions, Environments, Translations*, ed. Joan Scott and Cora Kaplan. New York: Routledge.

―――. 1999. *Childhood's Deadly Scourge: The Campaign to Control Diphtheria, 1880–1930*. Baltimore: Johns Hopkins University Press.

Hansen, Mark. 2000. *Embodying Technesis: Technology beyond Writing*. Ann Arbor: University of Michigan Press.

Hansen, Miriam. 1987. "Benjamin, Cinema, and Experience." *New German Critique* 40:179–224.

―――. 1993. "Of Mice and Ducks: Benjamin and Adorno on Disney." *South Atlantic Quarterly* 92(1):27–61.

Hansen, Randall. 1998. "From Environmental Bads to Economic Goods: Marketing Nuclear Waste to American Indians." Ph.D. diss., University of Minnesota.

Haraway, Donna. 1989. *Primate Visions: Gender, Race, and Nature in the World of Modern Science*. New York: Routledge.

―――. 1991. *Simians, Cyborgs, and Women*. New York: Routledge.

―――. 1997. *Modest_Witness@Second_Millennium.FemaleMan©_Meets_OncoMouse™*. New York: Routledge.

Harding, Sandra. 1992. *Whose Science, Whose Knowledge? Thinking from Women's Lives*. Ithaca: Cornell University Press.

Hardt, Michael, and Antonio Negri. 2000. *Empire*. Cambridge: Harvard University Press.

Hardy, George, et al. 1970. "The Failure of a School Immunization Campaign to Terminate an Epidemic of Measles." *American Journal of Epidemiology*, 91(4):286–93.

Harr, Jonathan. 1995. *A Civil Action*. New York: Vintage.

Harrison, G. A., and A. J. Boyce, eds. 1972. *The Structure of Human Populations*. Oxford: Clarendon Press.

Hart, David M. 1998. *Forged Consensus: Science, Technology, and Economic Policy in the United States, 1921–1953*. Princeton: Princeton University Press.

Hart, Roger. 1997. "Proof, Propaganda, and Patronage: A Cultural History of the Dissemination of Western Studies in Seventeenth Century China." Ph.D. diss., University of California at Los Angeles.

Harvey, David. 1985. *Consciousness and the Urban Experience*. New York: Oxford University Press.

———. 1989. *The Condition of Postmodernity*. London: Blackwell.

———. 1996. *Justice, Nature, and the Geography of Difference*. London: Blackwell.

———. 2001. *Spaces of Capital*. New York: Routledge.

Hayes, Dennis. 1989. *Behind the Silicon Curtain*. Cambridge: South End Press.

Hayles, N. Katherine. 1990. *Chaos Bound*. Ithaca: Cornell University Press.

———. 1993. "The Seduction of Cyberspace." In *Rethinking Technologies*, ed. Verena Andermatt Conley. Minneapolis: University of Minnesota Press.

———. 1996. "Narratives of Artificial Life." In *Future Natural: Nature, Science, Culture*, ed. George Robertson et al. New York: Routledge.

Heckel, Paul. 1992. "Debunking the Software Patent Myths." *Communications of the ACM* 35(6):121.

Heilbron, John. 1985. "The Earliest Missionaries of the Copenhagen Spirit." *Revue d'histoire des sciences* 38:194–230.

Heims, Steve J. 1993. *Constructing a Social Science for Postwar America: The Cybernetics Group 1946–1953*. Cambridge: MIT Press.

Helmreich, Stephen. 1998. *Silicon Second Nature: Culturing Artificial Life in a Digital World*. Berkeley: University of California Press.

Helvag, David. 1994. *The War against the Greens*. Sierra Club.

Henderson, Kathryn. 1998. *On Line and on Paper: Visual Representations, Visual Culture, and Computer Graphics in Design Engineering*. Cambridge: MIT Press.

Hendry, John. 1980. "Weimar Culture and Quantum Causality," *History of Science* 18:155–80.

Hess, David. 1997a. *Can Bacteria Cause Cancer? Alternative Medicine Confronts Big Science*. New York University.

———. 1997b. *Science Studies*. New York: New York University Press.

Hoffman, Eva. 1993. *Exit into History*. New York: Viking.

Honwana, A. 1996. "Spiritual Agency and Self-Renewal in Southern Mozambique." Ph.D. thesis, SOAS, University of London.

Hooper, Paula Kay. 1998. "They Have Their Own Thoughts: Children's Learning of Computational Ideas from a Cultural Constructivist Perspective." Ph.D. diss., Program in Media Arts and Sciences, MIT.

Hoskins, W. G. 1992. *The Making of the English Landscape*. London: Hodder and Stoughton.

Horkheimer, Max. 1972. *Critical Theory*. New York: Herder and Herder.

Horkheimer, Max, and Theodor Adorno. 1944/1969. *Dialectic of Enlightenment*. New York: Herder and Herder.

Hughes, Alton. 1978. *Pecos: A History of the Pioneer West*. Seagraves, Tex.: Pioneer.

Hughes, Thomas. 1998. *Rescuing Prometheus*. New York: Pantheon.

Hunter, Ian. 1995. "Ophthalmic Microrobots and Surgical Simulator." Electrical Engineering Colloquium, MIT, 3 April.

———. 1997. "Microworld Engineering." Health, Science, and Technology (HST) class on Social and Ethical Issues in the Biosciences and Biotechnologies, STS 449/HST 930.

Hutchinson, Sharon. 1996. *Nuer Dilemmas: Coping with War, Money, and the State*. Berkeley: University of California Press.

Ikels, Charlotte. 1997. "Kidney Failure and Transplantation in China." *Social Science of Medicine* 44(9): 1271–83.

International Film, Iranian Film Quarterly. 1999. Vol. 6, no. 3.

Iser, Wolfgang. 2000. "What Is Literary Anthropology? The Difference between Explanatory and Exploratory Fictions." In *Revenge of the Aesthetic: The Place of Literature in Theory Today*, ed. Michael P. Clark. Berkeley: University of California Press.

Ito, Mizuko. 1994. "Cyborg Couplings in a Multi-User Dungeon." 4S meetings, New Orleans, 14 October.

Ivy, Marilyn. 1995. *Discourses of the Vanishing: Modernity, Phantasm, Japan*. Chicago: University of Chicago Press.

Jacob, François. 1987/1988. *The Statue Within: An Autobiography*. New York: Basic.

Jackson, Myles. 1996. "Buying the Dark Lines of the Solar Spectrum: Joseph von Frauenhofer's Standard for the Manufacture of Optical Glass. *Archimedes* 1.

Jahanshah, Javid. 1995. "Interests Conflict over Control of Internet Access." *Iran Business Monitor* 4(9):3.

Jahoda, Marie, Paul Lazarsfeld, and Hans Zeisel. 1933. *Die Arbeitslosen von Marienthal*. Leipzig: S. Hirzel. English translation: 1971. *Marienthal: The Sociography of an Unemployed Community*. Chicago: Aldine, Atherton.

Jameson, Fredric. 1991. *Postmodernism, or The Logic of Late Capitalism*. Durham: Duke University Press.

Jamison, P. K. 1994. "Medieval Empires and Hyperindustrial Consciousness: An Exploration of Transformative Identities and Biospheres in Western Toys." Paper, 4S meetings, New Orleans, 14 November.

Jardine, N., J. A. Secord, and E. C. Spary, eds. 1996. *Cultures of Natural History*. New York: Cambridge University Press.

Jasanoff, Sheila. 1995. *Science at the Bar: Law, Science, and Technology in America*. Cambridge: Harvard University Press.

Jasanoff, Sheila, et al. 1995. *Handbook of Science and Technology Studies*. Thousand Oaks, Calif.: Sage.

Jay, Martin. 1993. *Downcast Eyes: The Denigration of Vision in Twentieth-Century French Thought*. Berkeley: University of California Press.

Jerschina, Jan. 1988. "Polish Modernism and Malinowski." In *Malinowski between Two*

Worlds, ed. Roy Ellen, Ernest Gellner, Grazyna Kubica, and Janusz Mucha. London: Cambridge University Press.

Johnson, Christopher. 1992. *System and Writing in the Philosophy of Jacques Derrida*. New York: Cambridge University Press.

Jolesz, Ferenc. 1997. "Image-Guided Procedures and the Operating Room of the Future." *Radiology* 204(3):601–12.

———. 1998. "Image-Guided Surgery." Health, Science, and Technology (HST) class on Social and Ethical Issues in the Biosciences and Biotechnologies, STS 449/HST 930.

Jonas, Hans. 1984. *The Imperative of Responsibility: In Search of an Ethics for the Technological Age*. Chicago: University of Chicago Press.

Jones, Caroline. 1998. "The Sex of the Machine: Mechanomorphic Art, New Women, and Francis Picabia's Neurasthenia." In *Picturing Science, Producing Art*, ed. C. Jones and P. Galison. New York: Routledge.

Jones, James. 1981. *Bad Blood: The Tuskegee Experiment*. New York: Free Press.

Judson, Horace. 1979. *The Eighth Day of Creation*. New York: Simon and Schuster.

Kadvany, John. 2001. *Imre Lakatos and the Guises of Reason*. Durham: Duke University Press.

Kakar, Sudhir. 1981. *The Inner World: A Psychoanalytic Study of Childhood and Society in India*. 2d ed. New Delhi: Oxford University Press.

Kan, Alex, and Nick Hayes. 1994. "Big Beat in Poland." In *Rocking the State: Rock Music and Politics in Eastern Europe and Russia*, ed. Sabrina Petra Ramet. Boulder, Colo.: Westview Press.

Kapuscinski, Ryszard. 1985. *Shah of Shahs*. New York: Quartet.

Karliner, Joshua. 1997. *The Corporate Planet: Ecology and Politics in the Age of Globalization*. Sierra Club.

Kay, Lily. 1993. *The Molecular Vision of Life*. New York: Oxford University Press.

———. 1999. *Who Wrote the Book of Life? A History of the Genetic Code*. Stanford: Stanford University Press.

Keller, Evelyn Fox. 1983. *A Feeling for the Organism: The Life and Work of Barbara McClintock*. New York: W. H. Freeman.

———. 1995. *Refiguring Life*. New York: Columbia University Press.

———. 2002a. *The Century of the Gene*. Cambridge: Harvard University Press.

———. 2002b. *Making Sense of Life*. Cambridge: Harvard University Press.

Kelly, Kevin. 1994. *Out of Control: The Rise of NeoBiological Civilization*. Reading, Mass.: Addison-Wesley.

Kelty, Chris. 1999. "Scale and Convention: Programmed Language in Regulated America." Ph.D. diss., MIT.

———. 2001. "Final Report: Linux and Dot.com in Bangalore." Washington: National Science Foundation.

Keneally, Thomas. 1982. *Schindler's List*. New York: Simon and Schuster.

Kevles, Daniel J. 1978. *The Physicists: The History of a Scientific Community in Modern America*. New York: Knopf.

———. 1985. *In the Name of Eugenics*. New York: Alfred A. Knopf.

———. 1998. *The David Baltimore Case*. New York: Norton.

Keyes, Roger. 1982. "Courage and Silence: A Study of the Life and Color Woodblock Prints of Tsukioka Yoshitoshi 1839–1892." Ph.D. diss., Union for Experimenting Colleges and Universities, Cincinnati.

Kidder, Tracy. 1981. *Soul of a New Machine*. New York: Little, Brown.

Kijowski, Janusz. 1993. "The Dirty, the Cruel, and the Bad: Why Should People Want to See Our Films about Heroism and Suffering?" *Polityka* (Warsaw), 14 August, 11.

Kingston, Maxine Hong. 1981. *The Woman Warrior: Memoirs of a Girlhood among Ghosts*. New York: Alfred A. Knopf.

Kittler, Friedrich. 1985/1990. *Discourse Networks, 1800/1900*. Stanford: Stanford University Press.

———. 1986/1999. *Gramophone, Film, Typewriter*. Stanford: Stanford University Press.

———. 1997. *Literature, Media, Information Systems*. Amsterdam: G and B Arts International.

Klein, Hans K. 1996. "Institutions, Innovation, and Information Infrastructure: The Social Construction of Intelligent Transportation Systems in the U.S., Europe, and Japan." Ph.D. diss., Technology, Management, and Policy Program, MIT.

Kleinman, Arthur, Veena Das, and Margaret Lock, eds. 1997. *Social Suffering*. Berkeley: University of California Press.

Knebel, Fletcher. 1961. "The Predicament of Pecos, Texas: The Town That Made the Billie Sol Estes Scandal Possible." *Look*, 31 July, 75–82.

Koch, Robert. 1995. "The Case of Latour." *Configurations* 3:319–47.

Koerner, Lisbet. 1996. "Goethe and Botany." *Isis* 87.

———. 1999. *Linnaeus: Nature and Nation*. Cambridge: Harvard University Press.

Kohler, Robert. 1991. *Partners in Science: Foundations and Natural Scientists, 1900–1945*. Chicago: University of Chicago Press.

———. 1994. *Lords of the Fly: Drosophila Genetics and the Experimental Life*. Chicago: University of Chicago Press.

Kolata, Gina. 1994. "The Assault on 114,381 . . ." *New York Times*, 22 March.

Knorr-Cetina, Karin. 1995. "Laboratory Studies: The Cultural Approach to the Study of Science." In *Handbook of Science and Technology Studies*, ed. S. Jasanoff et al. Thousand Oaks, Calif.: Sage.

———. 1999. *Epistemic Cultures: How Science Makes Sense*. Cambridge: Harvard University Press.

Krall, Hanna. 1977/1986. *Shielding the Flame: An Intimate Conversation with Dr. Marek Edelman, the Last Surviving Leader of the Warsaw Uprising*. New York: Henry Holt.

Kramare, Chris. 1995. "A Backstage Critique of Virtual Reality." In *Cybersociety*, ed. S. G. Jones. Thousand Oaks, Calif.: Sage.

Krasner, James. 1992. *The Entangled Eye: Visual Perception and the Representation of Nature in Post Darwinian Narrative*. New York: Oxford University Press.

Kratz, Corinne A. 1990. "Amusement and Absolution: Transforming Narratives during Confession of Social Debts." MS.

Krieg, Kathryn C., and Jean M. Goodwin. 1993. "The Dora Syndrome: Attempts to Re-structure Childhood in Adult Victims of Childhood Abuse." In *Rediscovering Childhood Trauma*, ed. Jean M. Goodwin. Washington: Psychiatric Press.

Kuhn, Thomas. 1962. *The Structure of Scientific Revolutions*. Chicago: University of Chicago Press.

Kuletz, Valerie. 1998. *The Tainted Desert: Environmental and Social Ruin in the American West*. New York: Routledge.

Kumar, Richa. 2001. "The Internet in Indian Villages: A Survey of Rural Connectivity Projects." B.A. thesis, Georgetown.

Kumar, Richa, and Ashok Jhunjhunwala. 2002. "Taking Internet to Village: A Case Study of Project at Madurai Region." Madras: n-Logue Communications Pvt. Ltd. and TeNet Group of IIT Madras.

Lacan, Jacques. 1973/1977. *Ecrits: A Selection*. New York: Norton.

Lacoue-Labarthe, Philippe. 1998. *Typography: Mimesis, Philosophy, Politics*. Stanford: Stanford University Press.

Lahsen, Myanna. 1998. "Climate Rhetoric: Constructions of Climate Science in the Age of Environmentalism." Ph.D. diss., Rice University.

Lakatos, Imre. 1980. *Philosophical Papers: Mathematics, Science, and Epistemology*. London: Cambridge University Press.

Landecker, Hannah. 1999a. "Technologies of Living Substances: Tissue Culture and Cellular Life in Twentieth Century Biomedicine." Ph.D. diss., STS Program, MIT.

———. 1999b. "Between Beneficence and Chattel: The Human Biological in Law and Science." *Science in Context* 12(1): 203–25.

———. 2000. "Immortality In Vitro: A History of the HeLa Cell Line." In *Biotechnology and Culture*, ed. Paul Brodwin. Bloomington: University of Indiana Press.

Landzelius, Kyra, ed. 2003. *Going Native on the Net: Indigenous Cyber-Activism and Virtual Diasporas over the World Wide Web*. New York: Routledge.

Lanier, Jaron. 1994. "Quantum Pricing for Information." *Wired* 2.08:63–64.

———. 1996. "Interviewed by Lynn Hershman Leeson." In *Clicking In: Hot Links to a Digital Culture*, ed. L. Leeson. Seattle: Bay Press.

Lansing, Steven. 1991. *Priests and Programmers: Technologies of Power in the Engineered Landscape of Bali*. Princeton: Princeton University Press.

Lant, Antonia. 1991. *Blackout: Reinventing Women for Wartime British Cinema*. Princeton: Princeton University Press.

Lash, Scott, and John Urry. 1994. *Economies of Signs and Space*. Thousand Oaks, Calif.: Sage.

Latour, Bruno. 1987. *Science in Action*. Cambridge: Harvard University Press.

———. 1988. *The Pasteurization of France*. Cambridge: Harvard University Press.

———. 1990a. "Drawing Things Together." In *Representation in Scientific Practice*, ed. M. Lynch and S. Woolgar. Cambridge: MIT Press.

———. 1990b. "Postmodern? No, Simply Amodern: Steps towards an Anthropology of Science. An Essay Review." *Studies in the History and Philosophy of Science* 21:145–71.

———. 1993/1996. *Aramis, or The Love of Technology*. Cambridge: Harvard University Press.

———. 1999. *Pandora's Hope: Essays on the Reality of Science Studies*. Cambridge: Harvard University Press.

Latour, Bruno, and Steven Woolgar. 1979. *Laboratory Life*. Beverly Hills: Sage.

Lears, T. J. Jackson. 1981. *No Place of Grace: Antimodernism and the Transformation of American Culture, 1880–1920*. New York: Pantheon.

Leavitt, Judith Walzer. 1996. *Typhoid Mary: Captive to the Public Health*. Boston: Beacon.

Lee, Benjamin. 1998. *Talking Heads: Language, Metalanguage, and the Semiotics of Subjectivity*. Durham: Duke University Press.

Lee, Richard, and Irven DeVore, eds. 1968. *Man the Hunter*. Chicago: Aldine.

Lehman, Bruce, et al. 1994. "Intellectual Property and the National Information Infrastructure: A Preliminary Draft of the Report of the Working Group on Intellectual Property Rights." Washington: Department of Commerce, July 1994.

Leitch, Vincent. 1996. *Postmodernism: Local Effects, Global Flows*. Albany: State University of New York Press.

Lenoir, Timothy. 1997. *Instituting Science: The Cultural Production of Scientific Disciplines*. Palo Alto: Stanford University Press.

———. 2001. "The Virtual Surgeon: New Practices for an Age of Medialization." Paper presented at the Dibner Institute.

Lessig, Lawrence. 1999. *Code and Other Laws of Cyberspace*. New York: Basic Books.

———. 2001. *The Future of Ideas: The Fate of the Commons in a Connected World*. New York: Random House.

Levi-Montalcini, Rita. 1988. *In Praise of Imperfection: My Life and Work*. New York: Basic Books.

Lévi-Strauss, Claude. 1960. "La Geste d'Asdiwal." In *The Structural Study of Myth and Totemism*, ed. and trans. E. R. Leach. London.

———. 1962/1966. *La Pensée Sauvage/The Savage Mind*. Chicago: University of Chicago Press.

———. 1972. "Structuralism and Ecology." In *The View from Afar*, by Claude Lévi-Strauss. New York: Basic.

Lewontin, Richard C. 1994. "The Dream of the Human Genome." *New York Review of Books*.

Lifton, Robert Jay. 1967. *Death in Life: The Survivors of Hiroshima*. New York: Simon and Schuster.

Lightman, Alan. 1993. *Einstein's Dreams*. New York: Pantheon.

Lindee, Susan. 1994. *Suffering Made Real: American Science and the Survivors at Hiroshima*. Chicago: University of Chicago Press.

———. 1999. "The Repatriation of Atomic Bomb Victim Body Parts to Japan." *Osiris*, 2d ser., 13:376–409.

Livingston, James. 1994. *Pragmatism and the Political Economy of Cultural Revolution, 1850–1940*. Chapel Hill: University of North Carolina Press.

Lock, Margaret. 1994. "Contests with Death." In *Life and Death under High Technology Medicine*, ed. Ian Robinson. Manchester: University of Manchester Press.

———.2002. *Twice Dead: Organ Transplants and the Reinvention of Death*. Berkeley: University of California Press.

Lock, Margaret, Allan Young, and Alberto Cambrosio, eds. 2000. *Living and Working with the New Medical Technologies*. New York: Cambridge University Press.

Lotfalian, Mazyar. 1996. "A Tale of an Electronic Community." In *Late Editions 3: Connected: Engagements with Media*, ed. G. Marcus. Chicago: University of Chicago Press.

———. 1999. "Technoscientific Imaginaries: Muslims and the Culture of Curiosity." Ph.D. diss., Rice University.

Loundy, David. 1994. E-Law 2.0: Computer Information Systems Law and System Operator Liability Revisited. ftp://infolib.murdoch.edu.au/pub/subj/law/jnl/elaw/refereed/loundy.txt.

Lown, Bernard. 1996. *The Lost Art of Healing*. New York: Houghton-Mifflin.

Löwy, Ilana. 1996. *Between Bench and Bedside: Science, Healing, and Interleukin-2 in a Cancer Ward*. Cambridge: Harvard University Press.

Luckacher, Ned. 1986. *Primal Scenes: Literature, Philosophy, Psychoanalysis*. Ithaca: Cornell University Press.

Luria, S. E. 1984. *A Slot Machine, A Broken Test Tube—an Autobiography*. New York: Harper and Row.

Lynch, Michael, and Steve Woolgar, eds. 1988. *Representation in Scientific Practice*. Cambridge: MIT Press.

Lyon, David. 1994. *The Electronic Eye: The Rise of Surveillance Society*. Minneapolis: University of Minnesota Press.

Lyotard, Jean-François. 1979/1984. *The Postmodern Condition: A Report on Knowledge*. Minneapolis: University of Minnesota Press.

———. 1983/1988. *The Differend*. Minneapolis: University of Minnesota Press.

Macdonald, A. 2000. "Two Continents, One Meridian, Two Visionaries, One Goal." *Survey Review* 35(275):307–20.

MacKenzie, Donald. 1990. *Inventing Accuracy: A Historical Sociology of Nuclear Missile Guidance*. Cambridge: MIT Press.

———. 1995. *Knowing Machines*. Cambridge: MIT Press.

———. 2001. *Mechanizing Proof: Computing, Risk, and Trust*. Cambridge: MIT Press.

Malamud, Carl. 1993. *Exploring the Internet: A Technical Travelogue*. Englewood, Calif.: Prentice Hall.

Malkki, Liisa. 1995. *Purity and Exile: Violence, Memory, and National Cosmology among Hutu Refugees in Tanzania*. Chicago: University of Chicago Press.

Malthus, Thomas. 1803. *An Essay on the Principle of Population*. 2d ed. London: J. Johnson.

Malzberg, Barry. 1985. *The Remaking of Sigmund Freud*. New York: Random House.

Mann, Charles. 2001. "Anthropological Warfare." *Science* 291:416–21.

Marcus, George, ed. 1993. *Perilous States: Late Editions 1*. Chicago: University of Chicago Press.

———. 1995. *Technoscientific Imaginaries: Conversations, Profiles, and Memoirs. Late Editions 2*. Chicago: University of Chicago Press.

———. 1996. *Connected: Late Editions 3*. Chicago: University of Chicago Press.

———. 1997. *Cultural Producers in Perilous States: Late Editions 4*. Chicago: University of Chicago Press.

———. 1998. *Corporate Futures: Late Editions 5*. Chicago: University of Chicago Press.

———. 1999a. *Paranoia within Reason: Late Editions 6*. Chicago: University of Chicago Press.

———. 1999b. *Para-Sites: Late Editions 7*. Chicago: University of Chicago Press.

———. 1999c. *Zeroing In: Late Editions 8*. Chicago: University of Chicago Press.

Marcus, George E., and Michael M. J. Fischer. 1986. *Anthropology as Cultural Critique: An Experimental Moment in the Human Sciences*. Chicago: University of Chicago Press.

Marglin, Frederique Appfel. 1990. "Smallpox in Two Systems of Knowledge." in *Dominating Knowledge: Development, Culture, and Resistance*, ed. F. Marglin and S. Marglin. London: Oxford University Press.

Martin, Emily. 1987. *The Woman in the Body*. Boston: Beacon Press.

———. 1994. *Flexible Bodies: Tracking Immunity in American Culture from the Days of Polio to the Age of AIDS*. Boston: Beacon Press.

Marx, Leo. 1997. "Technology: The Emergence of a Hazardous Concept." *Social Research* 64(3):965–88.

Marx, Karl. 1928. *Capital*. London: Allen and Unwin.

———. 1971. *The Grundrisse*. New York: Harper and Row.

Massignon, Louis. 1975. *The Passion of al-Hallaj*. Trans. Herbert Mason. Princeton: Princeton University Press.

Mathews, Adrian. 1999. *Vienna Blood*. London: Jonathan Cape.

Mathews, Glenna. 2003. *Silicon Valley, Women, and the California Dream*. Stanford: Stanford University Press.

Mauss, Marcel. 1925/1954. *The Gift*. Glencoe: Free Press.

Mawer, Simon. 1998. *Mendel's Dwarf*. New York: Harmony Books.

May, Larry. 1980. *Screening Out the Past: The Birth of Mass Culture and the Motion Picture Industry*. New York: Oxford University Press.

May, Tim. 1994. The Cyphernomicon. http://www2.pro-ns.net/~crypto/cyphernomicon .html.

Maybury-Lewis, David. 1965. *The Savage and the Innocent*. Cleveland: World Publishing Company.

———. 1967. *Akwe-Shavante Society*. Oxford: Clarendon Press.

———. 2000. *The Politics of Ethnicity: Indigenous Peoples in Latin America*. Cambridge: Harvard University Press.

Mayer, Margit, and John Ely. 1998. *The German Greens: Paradox between Movement and Party*. Philadelphia: Temple University Press.

McCormmach, Russell. 1982. *Night Thoughts of a Classical Physicist*. Cambridge: Harvard University Press.

McHale, Brian. 1992. *Constructing Postmodernism*. New York: Routledge.

McLuhan, Marshall, and Quentin Fiore. 1967. *The Medium Is the Message*. New York: Random House.

McNamara, Laura. 2001. "Ways of Knowing about Weapons: The Cold War's End at the Los Alamos National Laboratory." Ph.D. diss., University of New Mexico.

McNeill, William. 1976. *Plagues and People*. New York: Anchor.

McRae, Murdo William. 1993. *The Literature of Science*. Athens: University of Georgia Press.

Mehlman, Jeffrey. 1993. *Walter Benjamin for Children: An Essay on His Radio Years*. Chicago: University of Chicago Press.

Merton, Robert K. 1938. *Science, Technology, and Society in Seventeenth Century England*. Bruges: Sant Catherine Press.

———. 1973. *The Sociology of Science*. Chicago: University of Chicago Press.

Milburn, Gerard. 1998. *The Feynman Processor: Quantum Entanglement and the Computing Revolution*. Reading, Mass.: Perseus.

Miller, H. Lyman. 1996. *Science and Dissent in Post-Mao China*. Seattle: University of Washington Press.

Miller, Michael. 1994. "The Effect of the Specter of Crypto Anarchy on the Evolution of Laws Governing Cyberspace." Paper for Law and Ethics on the Electronic Frontier, MIT, STS 095/6.095. http://www.swiss-ai.mit.edu.

Milosz, Czeslaw. 1977. "Stanislaw Ignacy Witkiewicz: A Writer for Today." In *Emperor of the Earth*. Berkeley: University of California Press.

Mindell, David. 1996. "Datum for Its Own Annihilation: Feedback, Control, and Computing, 1916–1945." Ph.D. diss., STS Program, MIT.

———. 2000. *War, Technology, and Experience aboard the USS Monitor, 1861–1863*. Baltimore: Johns Hopkins University Press.

Mitchell, William J. T. 1994. *Picture Theory: Essays on Verbal and Visual Representation*. Chicago: University of Chicago Press.

Mizrahi, Richard. 1990. *Bravo 20: The Bombing of the American West*. Baltimore: Johns Hopkins University Press.

Mnookin, Jennifer. 1999. "Images of Truth: Evidence, Expertise, and Technologies of Knowledge in the American Courtroom." Ph.D. diss., STS Program, MIT.

Mojtabai, A. G. 1986. *Blessed Assurance: At Home with the Bomb in Amarillo, Texas*. Boston: Houghton-Mifflin.

Morange, Michel. 1994/1998. *A History of Molecular Biology*. Cambridge: Harvard University Press.

Moravec, Hans. 1988. *Mind Children: The Future of Robot and Human Intelligence*. Cambridge: Harvard University Press.

Moreno, Jonathan. 2000. *Undue Risk: Secret State Experiments on Humans*. New York: W. H. Freeman.

Morris, Rosalind. 2000. *In the Place of Origins: Modernity and Its Mediums in Northern Thailand*. Durham: Duke University Press.

Morse, Philip. 1977. *In at the Beginnings: A Physicist's Life*. Cambridge: MIT Press.

Mottahedeh, Roy. 1985. *The Mantle of the Prophet*. New York: Random House.

Mukerjee, Chandra. 1990. *A Fragile Power: Scientists and the State*. Princeton: Princeton University Press.

Murakami, Haruki. 2000. *Underground: The Tokyo Gas Attack and the Japanese Psyche*. London: Harvill Press.

Naficy, Hamid. 1981. "Cinema as a Political Instrument." In *Continuity and Change in Modern Iran*, ed. M. Bonine and N. Keddie. Albany: State University of New York Press.

Nagatoni, Patrick. 1991. *Nuclear Enchantment*. Albuquerque: University of New Mexico Press.

Nandy, Ashis. 1988. "Science as a Reason of State." In *Science, Hegemony, and Violence*, ed. Ashis Nandy. New York: Oxford University Press.

———, ed. 1988. *Science, Hegemony, and Violence*. New York: Oxford University Press.

Nash, John. 1997. "How the Birth of a Son Altered 'Las meninas.'" *Times Literary Supplement* (London), 4 April.

Neel, James. 1970. "Lessons from a 'Primitive People': Do Recent Data Concerning South American Indians Have Relevance to Problems of Highly Civilized Communities?" *Science* 170:815–22.

———. 1980. "On Being Headman." *Perspectives in Biology and Medicine* 23:277–93.

———. 1994. *Physician to the Gene Pool*. New York: J. Wiley.

———. Papers. Archives of the American Philosophical Society, Philadelphia.

Neel, James, et al. 1970. "Notes on the Effect of Measles and Measles Vaccine in a Virgin Soil Population of South American Indians." *American Journal of Epidemiology* 91(4):418–29.

Nelkin, Dorothy, and Lawrence Tancredi. 1989. *Dangerous Diagnostics: The Social Power of Biological Information*. New York: Basic Books.

Nersessian, Nancy. 1995. "How Do Scientists Think? Capturing the Dynamics of Conceptual Change in Science." In *Diagrammatic Reasoning*, ed. J. Glasgow, N. H. Narayanan, and B. Chandrasekaran. Cambridge: MIT Press.

Newell, Allen. 1986. "The Models Are Broken, the Models Are Broken." *University of Pittsburgh Law Review* 47(4):1023–35.

Newman, William. 1994. *Gehennical Fire: The Lives of George Starkey, an American Alchemist in the Scientific Revolution*. Cambridge: Harvard University Press.

———. 2001. "The Alchemical Art-Nature Debate and the Fine Arts." Paper presented to the Dibner Institute.

Nicholas, Ralph. 1982. "The Goddess Sitala and Epidemic Smallpox in Bengal." *Journal of Asian Studies* 41(1):20–44.

Nilekani, Rohini. 1998. *Stillborn: A Medical Thriller*. New Delhi: Penguin.

Norberg, Arthur, and Judy E. O'Neill. 1996. *Envisioning Technology for the National Security State: A History of the Information Processing Techniques Office of the Department of Defense*. Baltimore: Johns Hopkins University Press.

Nordstrom, Carolyn, and Antonius C. G. M. Robben, eds. 1995. *Fieldwork under Fire: Contemporary Studies of Violence and Survival*. Berkeley: University of California Press.

Nowotny, Helga, and Ulrike Felt. 1997. *After the Breakthrough: The Emergence of High-Temperature Superconductivity as a Research Field*. New York: Cambridge University Press.

Nugent, Steven. 2001. "The Yanomami, Science, and Ethics." *Anthropology Today* 17(3):10–13.

Obeyesekere, Gananath. 1981. *Medusa's Hair: An Essay on Personal Symbols and Religious Experience*. Chicago: University of Chicago Press.

———. 1984. *The Cult of the Goddess Pattini*. Chicago: University of Chicago Press.

Ogborn, Miles. 1995. "Knowing the Individual: Michel Foucault and Norbert Elias on *Las Meninas* and the Modern Subject." In *Mapping the Subject*, ed. Steve Pile and Nigel Thrift. New York: Routledge.

Ong, Aiwa. 1987. *Spirits of Resistance and Capitalist Discipline: Factory Women in Malaysia.* Albany: State University of New York.

———. 1999. *Flexible Citizenship: The Cultural Logics of Transnationality.* Durham: Duke University Press.

Ong, Aiwa, and Donald Nonini, ed. 1997. *Underground Empires: The Cultural Politics of Modern Chinese Transnationalism.* New York: Routledge.

Ong, Walter. 1982. *Orality and Literacy: The Technologization of the Word.* New York: Methuen.

Osborne, Michael. 1994. *Nature, the Exotic, and the Science of French Colonialism.* Bloomington: Indiana University Press.

Ostriker, Alicia. 1986. *Stealing the Language: The Emergence of Women's Poetry in America.* Boston: Beacon.

Ötsch, Walter. 2000. *Haider Light: Handbuch für Demagogie.* Vienna: Czernin Verlag.

Ottomeyer, Klaus. 2000. *Die Haider Show: Zur Psychopolitik der FPÖ.* Klagenfurt: Drava Verlag.

Oulahan, Richard. 1962. "Scandal Hot as a Pistol." *Life* 52(22):78–94.

Ozan, Esra. 2001. "The Design of Turkish Web Sites." M.A. thesis, Istanbul Technical University.

Papert, Seymour. 1996. *The Connected Family.* Atlanta: Longstreet.

"Parched Land of the Dying." 1981. *Life,* April.

Parsons, Talcott. 1937. *The Structure of Social Action.* New York: McGraw-Hill.

———. 1951. *The Social System.* Glencoe: Free Press.

Penley, Constance. 1997. *NASA/TREK: Popular Science and Sex in America.* London: Verso.

Perin, Constance. 1988. *Belonging in America.* Madison: University of Wisconsin Press.

———. 2004. *Shouldering Risks: The Culture of Control in the Nuclear Power Industry.* Princeton: Princeton University Press.

Perlez, Jane. 1993. "Reburial Is Both a Ceremony and a Test for Today's Hungary." *New York Times,* 5 September, A18.

Perrow, Charles. 1984. *Normal Accidents: Living with High-Risk Technologies.* New York: Basic Books.

———. 1999. *Normal Accidents: Living with High-Risk Technologies.* With a new afterword and postscript on the Y2K problem. Princeton: Princeton University Press.

Perutz, Max. 1995. Review of *The Private Science of Louis Pasteur,* by Gerald Geison. *New York Review of Books,* 21 December.

———. 1996. "Reply to Geison." *New York Review of Books,* 4 April, 69.

Petryna, Adriana. 1995. "Sarcophagus: Chernobyl in Historical Light." *Cultural Anthropology* 10(2):196–220.

———. 1998. "A Technical Error: Measure of Life after Chernobyl." *Social Identities* 4(1).

———. 2002. *Life Exposed: Biological Citizens after Chernobyl.* Princeton: Princeton University Press.

Pickering, Andrew. 1995. *The Mangle of Practice.* Chicago: University of Chicago Press.

Piore, Michael, and Charles Sabel. 1984. *The Second Industrial Divide: Possibilities for Prosperity.* New York: Basic Books.

Plotkin, A. S. 1957. "Educational Godfather to Youth Being Buried from B.U. Today: Modest Avery Gave $5 Million." *Boston Globe*, 29 May, 1, 4.

Popper, Karl. 1985. *Unended Quest: An Intellectual Autobiography*. London: Open Court.

Porush, David. 1993. "Making Chaos: Two Views of a New Science." In *The Literature of Science*, ed. M. W. McRae. Athens: University of Georgia Press.

Poster, Mark. 1990. *The Mode of Information*. Chicago: University of Chicago Press.

———. 2001. *What's the Matter with the Internet*. Minneapolis: University of Minnesota Press.

Pound, Christopher. 1995. "Imagining In-Formation: The Complex Disconnections of Computer Networks." In *Late Editions 2: Technoscientific Imaginaries*, ed. G. Marcus. Chicago: University of Chicago Press.

———. 1996. "Framed, or How the Internet Set Me Up." In *Late Editions 3: Connected: Engagements with Media*, ed. G. Marcus. Chicago: University of Chicago Press.

Povinelli, Elizabeth. 2002. *The Cunning of Recognition: Indigenous Alterities and the Making of Australian Multiculturalism*. Durham: Duke University Press.

Powell, Douglas, and William Leiss. 1997. *Mad Cows and Mother's Milk: The Perils of Poor Risk Communication*. Montreal: McGill Queen's University Press.

Powers, Richard. 1991. *The Gold Bug Variations*. New York: William Morrow.

———. 1995. *Galatea 2.2*. New York: Farrar, Straus and Giroux.

———. 1998. *Gain*. New York: Farrar, Straus and Giroux.

———. 2000. *Plowing the Dark*. Farrar, Straus and Giroux.

Principe, Lawrence M. 1998. *The Aspiring Adept: Robert Boyle and His Alchemical Quest*. Princeton: Princeton University Press.

Pucci, Suzanne Rodin. 1990. "The Discrete Charm of the Exotic: Fictions of the Harem in Eighteenth-Century France." In *Exoticism in the Enlightenment*, ed. G. S. Rousseau and Roy Porter. Manchester: Manchester University Press.

Pynchon, Thomas. 1973. *Gravity's Rainbow*. New York: Viking.

Rabaté, Jean-Michel. 2002. *The Future of Theory*. Malden, Mass.: Blackwell.

Rabinow, Paul. 1996. *The Making of PCR*. Chicago: University of Chicago Press.

———. 1998. *French DNA*. Chicago: University of Chicago Press.

Rabinow, Paul, and Gisli Palsson. 1999. "Iceland: The Case of a National Human Genome Project." *Anthropology Today* 15(5):14–18.

Radcliffe-Richards, J., A. S. Daar, R. D. Guttman, R. Hoffenberg, I. Kennedy, M. Lock, R. A. Selb, and N. Tilney. 1998. "The Case for Allowing Kidney Sales." *Lancet*, 27 June, 1950–52.

Rajchman, John. 1998. "Jean-François Lyotard's Underground Aesthetics." *October* 86:3–18.

Rajora, Rajesh. 2002. *Bridging the Digital Divide: Gyandoot, the Model for Community Networks*. New Delhi: Tata McGraw-Hill.

Ramos, Alcida. 1995. *Sanuma Memories*. Madison: University of Wisconsin Press.

———. 1998. *Indigenism: Ethnic Politics in Brazil*. Madison: University of Wisconsin Press.

Rampton, Sheldon, and John C. Stauber. 2001. *Trust Us, We're Experts*. New York: Penguin Putnam.

Randall, Frederika. 1997. "A New Look at an Old Master." *Wall Street Journal*, 16 May.

Rapp, Rayna. 1993. "Accounting for Amniocentesis." In *Knowledge, Power, and Practice:*

The Anthropology of Medicine and Everyday Life, ed. Shirley Lindenbaum and Margaret Locke. Berkeley: University of California Press.

———. 1997. "Real Time Fetus: The Role of the Sonogram in the Age of Monitored Reproduction." In *Cyborgs and Citadels: Anthropological Interventions in Emerging Sciences and Technologies*, ed. G. L. Downey and J. Dumit. Santa Fe: School of American Research Press.

———. 1999. *Testing Women, Testing the Fetus: The Social Impact of Amniocentesis in America*. New York: Routledge.

Rappaport, Roy. 1968. *Pigs for the Ancestors: Ritual in the Ecology of a New Guinea People*. New Haven: Yale University Press.

Rasmussen, Nicolas. 1997. *Picture Control: The Electron Microscope and the Transformation of Biology in America, 1940–1960*. Stanford: Stanford University Press.

Raymond, Eric. 1993. *The New Hacker's Dictionary*. Cambridge: MIT Press.

Readings, Bill. 1996. *The University in Ruins*. Cambridge: Harvard University Press.

Reich, Michael. 1991. *Toxic Politics: Responding to Chemical Disasters*. Cornell University Press.

Rheinberger, Hans-Jörg. 1997. *Toward a History of Epistemic Things: Synthesizing Proteins in the Test Tube*. Stanford: Stanford University Press.

Rheingold, Howard. 1991. *Virtual Reality*. New York: Summit Books.

Rickels, Laurence. 1991. *The Case of California*. Baltimore: Johns Hopkins University Press.

Ricoeur, Paul. 1971. "The Model of the Text: Meaningful Action Considered as a Text." *Social Research* 38:529–62.

Rife, Patricia. 1999. *Lise Meitner and the Dawn of the Nuclear Age*. Boston: Burkhaeuser.

Ringland, Gill. 1998. *Scenario Planning*. New York: Wiley.

Rip, Arie, Thomas Misa, and John Schot, eds. 1995. *Managing Technology in Society: The Approach of Constructive Technology Assessment*. New York: St. Martin's.

Robinson, Walter. 1999. "When to Transplant: Ethical and Clinical Issues in the Treatment of Children and Adolescents with Cystic Fibrosis." Social Studies of Bioscience and Biotechnology, Harvard Medical School, HST class session, October 1999.

Roland, Alan. 1988. *In Search of Self in India and Japan: Toward a Cross-Cultural Psychology*. Princeton: Princeton University Press.

Roll-Hansen, N. 1982. "Experimental Method and Spontaneous Generation: The Controversy between Pasteur and Pouchet, 1859–64." *Journal of the History of Medicine and Allied Sciences* 34:273–92.

———. 1983. "The Death of Spontaneous Generation and the Birth of the Gene: Two Case Studies of Relativism." *Social Studies of Science* 13:481–519.

Ronell, Avital. 1989. *The Telephone Book*. Lincoln: University of Nebraska Press.

———. 1994. *Finitude's Score*. Lincoln: University of Nebraska Press.

Rose, Jacqueline. 2003. "Response to Edward Said." In *Freud and the Non-European*, by Edward Said. London: Verso.

Rosenberg, Charles. 1992. *Explaining Epidemics and Other Studies in the History of Medicine*. New York: Cambridge University Press.

Roskies, David. 1993. "The Last of the Purim Players: Itzik Manger." *Prooftexts* 13:211–35.

Ross, Kristin. 1995. *Fast Cars, Clean Bodies: Decolonization and the Reordering of French Culture*. Cambridge: MIT Press.

Rotenberg, Marc. 1994a. "Privacy and the National Information Infrastructure." *Educom Review* 29(2)50–51.

———. 1994b. "Privacy Protection." *Government Information Quarterly* 11(3):253–54.

Rotman, Brian. 1987. *Signifying Nothing: The Semiotics of Zero*. Stanford: Stanford University Press.

———. 1993. *The Ghost in Turing's Machine*. Stanford: Stanford University Press.

Rushdie, Salman. 1988. *The Satanic Verses*. London: Viking Press.

Russell, Neuman, Lee McKnight, and Richard Jay Solomon. 1995. *The Gordian Knot: Political Gridlock on the Information Highway*. Cambridge: MIT Press.

Sabel, Charles, Archon Fung, and Bradley Karkkainen. 1999. "Beyond Backyard Environmentalism." *Boston Review*, Oct.–Nov. http://bostonreview.mit.edu.BR 24.5/sabel.html.

Safina, Carl. 1997. *Song for the Blue Ocean*. New York: Henry Holt.

Sahlins, Marshall. 1972. *Stone Age Economics*. Chicago: Aldine.

———. 2000. "Guilty Not As Charged." *Washington Post*, 10 December.

Said, Edward. 1986. *After the Last Sky*. New York: Pantheon.

———. 2003. *Freud and the Non-European*. London: Verso.

Samuelson, Paula. 1988. "Is Copyright Law Steering the Right Course?" *IEEE Software*.

———. 1989. "Why the Look and Feel of Software User Interfaces Should Not Be Protected by Copyright Law." *Communications of the ACM* 32(5):563–72.

———. 1990. "Should Program Algorithms Be Patented?" *Communications of the ACM* 33(8)23–27.

———. 1994. "Legally Speaking: The NII Intellectual Property Report." *Communications of the ACM* 37.

Samuelson, Paula, Randall Davis, Mitchell D. Kapor, and J. H. Reichman. 1995. "A Manifesto Concerning the Legal Protection of Computer Programs." *Columbia Law Review* 94:2308.

Sanal, Aslihan. 2003. "Criminality Topos, Policy Shifts, and the Politics of Medical Institutional Change in the Turkish Transplant and Body Parts Trade." *Culture, Medicine, and Psychiatry* (forthcoming).

Santos, Ricardo Ventura. 1998. "Indigenous Peoples, the Atomic Bomb, and the HGDP: Reflections on Postwar Human Biology in/from Amazonia, 1960–2000." Working Paper, STS Program, MIT (revised version: "Indigenous Peoples, Postcolonial Contexts, and Genetic/Genomic Research in the Late Twentieth Century: A View from Amazonia," *Critique of Anthropology*, 2001).

Sassen, Saskia. 2001. *The Global City*. Princeton: Princeton University Press.

Satava, Richard M. 2002. "The BioIntelligence Age: Science after the Information Age." Presentation to the Center for Integration of Medicine and Innovative Technology (CIMIT) Forum, Massachusetts General Hospital, 23 April.

Schallack, Jason. 1997. *The Lost Art of Healing*. Video of the Eric Avery Installation at the Art History Gallery, University of Wisconsin–Milwaukee. Available at eavery@utmb.edu.

Scheper-Hughes, Nancy. 2000. "The Global Traffic in Human Organs." *Current Anthropology* 41(2).

Scholem, Gershom. 1956. *Shabbatai Sevi*. Trans. Zvi Werblovski. Princeton: Princeton University Press.

Schoonmaker, Sara. 2002. *High-Tech Trade Wars: U.S.-Brazilian Conflicts in the Global Economy*. Pittsburgh, Pa.: University of Pittsburgh Press.

Schull, William, and James Neel. 1965. *The Effects of Inbreeding on Japanese Children*. New York: Harper and Row.

Schwartz, Peter. 1996. *The Art of the Long View*. New York: Doubleday.

Schwarz, Heinrich. 2002. "Techno-Territories: The Spatial, Technological, and Social Reorganization of Office Work." Ph.D. diss., MIT.

Sclove, Richard. 1995. *Democracy and Technology*. New York: Guilford.

Sefer Rymanov. n.d. *The Rymanov Commemorative Book*. Jerusalem.

Segi, Shinichi. 1985. *Yoshitoshi: The Splendid Decadent*. Tokyo: Kodansha International.

Serres, Michel. 1980/1982. *The Parasite*. Baltimore: Johns Hopkins University Press.

———. 1991. *Rome: The Book of Foundations*. Chicago: University of Chicago Press.

Shah, Navalbhai. 1975. *Santabalji: Satupani Sagdandi* (Santabalji: Peripatetic Path to Saintliness). Ahmedabad, Gujurat.

Shapin, Steven, and Simon Schaffer. 1985. *Leviathan and the Air-Pump: Hobbes, Boyle, and the Experimental Life*. Princeton: Princeton University Press.

Shapiro, Gary. 1989. *Nietzschean Narrative*. Bloomington: Indiana University Press.

Sheehy, Sandy. 1997. "Healing Art." *Biomedical Inquiry* (spring–summer):8–15.

Shulman, Seth. 1992. *The Threat at Home: Confronting the Toxic Legacy of the U.S. Military*. Boston: Beacon Press.

Sigurdsson, Skulli. 1999. "Icelanders Opt Out of Genetic Database." *Nature* 400:708.

Silman, Roberta. 1990. *Beginning the World Again: A Novel of Los Alamos*. New York: Viking.

Sime, Ruth L. 1996. *Liese Meitner: A Life in Physics*. Berkeley: University of California Press.

Slade, Joseph, and Judith Yaross Lee. 1990. *Beyond the Two Cultures*. Iowa City: University of Iowa Press.

Smith, Adam. 1776. *An Inquiry into the Nature and Causes of the Wealth of Nations*. London: W. Strahan and T. Cadell.

Smith, David Alexander. 1993. *In the Cube: A Novel of Future Boston*. New York: Tor.

———, ed. 1994. *Future Boston*. New York: Tor.

Smith, Merritt Roe. 1977. *Harper's Ferry Armory and the New Technology*. Ithaca: Cornell University Press.

Snyder, Benson. 1972. *The Hidden Curriculum*. New York: Knopf.

Snyder, J. 1985. "Las Meninas and the Mirror of the Prince." *Critical Inquiry* 11:539–72.

Sobolewski, Tadeusz. 1993. "Feliks Edmundowsicz ze styropianu." *Kino*, June, 5–7.

———. 1993. "Rozmowy w Lubomierzu" [Discussion in Lubomierz]. *Kino*, December, 15–17.

Sobolewski, Tadeusz, et al. 1994. "Na jakie kino czekamy" [What Cinema Are We Waiting For?]. *Kino*, January, 20–25.

Sohrabi, Naghmeh. 1994. "Weapons of Propaganda, Weapons of War: Iranian Wartime Rhetoric, 1980–1988." B.S. thesis, Department of History, MIT.

Soja, Edward. 1989. *Postmodern Geographies: The Reassertion of Space in Critical Social Theory*. London: Verso.

Sokal, Alan. 1996. "Transgressing the Boundaries." *Social Text* 46–47:217–52.

Sorlin, Pierre. 1991. *European Cinema, European Societies, 1939–1990*. London: Routledge.

Spielman, Richard, et al. 1979. "The Evolutionary Relationship of Two Populations: A Study of the Guyami and the Yanomami." *Current Anthropology* 20(2):377–88.

Stacey, Judith. 1990. *Brave New Families*. New York: Basic Books.

Stafford, Barbara M. 1996. *Good Looking: Essays on the Virtue of Images*. Cambridge: MIT Press.

Star, Susan Leigh, ed. 1995. *The Cultures of Computing*. Boston: Blackwell.

Stauber, John C., and Sheldon Rampton. 1995. *Toxic Sludge Is Good for You: Lies, Damn Lies, and the Public Relations Industry*. Monroe, Me.: Common Courage Press.

Steingraber, Sandra. 1997. *Living Downstream*. New York: Vintage.

Stephenson, Neal. 1988. *Zodiac*. New York: Bantam.

———. 1996. "The Hacker Tourist Travels the World to Bring Back the Epic Story of Wiring the Planet." *Wired* 4.12:97–160.

Sterling, Bruce. 1992. *Hacker Crackdown: Law and Disorder on the Electronic Frontier*. New York: Bantam.

Stevenson, John. 1983. *Yoshitoshi's Thirty-six Ghosts*. Hong Kong: Weatherhill/Blue Tiger.

Stolz, George. 1999. "In Search of the White Knight." *ARTnews* 98(8). http://global.factiva.com/en/arch/display.asp.

Stone, Allucquére Rosanne. 1995. *The War of Desire and Technology at the Close of the Mechanical Age*. Cambridge: MIT Press.

Strathern, Marilyn. 1992. *Reproducing the Future*. New York: Routledge.

Subramanian, C. R. 1992. *India and the Computer: A Study of Planned Development*. Delhi: Oxford University Press.

Sunder Rajan, Kaushik. 2002. "Biocapital: The Constitution of Postgenomic Life." Ph.D. diss., STS Program, MIT.

———. 2003. "Genomic Capital: Public Cultures and Market Logics of Corporate Biotechnology." *Science as Culture* 12(1):87–121.

Taheri, Amir. 1986. *The Spirit of Allah: Khomeini and the Islamic Revolution*. Bethesda, Md.: Adler and Adler.

Tamas, G. M. 2000. "On Post Fascism: How Citizenship Is Becoming an Exclusive Privilege." *Boston Review*, summer, 42–45.

Tambiah, Stanley J. 1986. *Sri Lanka: Ethnic Fratricide and the Dismantling of Democracy*. Chicago: University of Chicago Press.

———. 1992. *Buddhism Betrayed? Religion, Politics, and Violence in Sri Lanka*. Chicago: University of Chicago Press.

———. 1996. *Leveling Crowds: Ethno-nationalist Conflicts and Collective Violence in South Asia*. Comparative Studies in Religion and Society 10. Berkeley: University of California Press.

Tatar, Maria. 1987. *The Hard Facts of the Grimms' Fairy Tales*. Princeton: Princeton University Press.

Taussig, Michael. 1980. *The Devil and Commodity Fetishism in South America*. Chapel Hill: University of North Carolina Press.

———. 1987. *Shamanism, Colonialism, and the Wild Man: A Study in Terror and Healing*. Chicago: University of Chicago Press.

———. 1992. *The Nervous System*. New York: Routledge.

———. 1993. *Mimesis and Alterity*. New York: Routledge.

Taylor, Mark. 1999. *The Picture in Question: Mark Tansey and the Ends of Representation*. Chicago: University of Chicago Press.

Teitelman, Robert 1991. *Gene Dreams: Wall Street, Academia, and the Rise of Biotechnology*. New York: Basic Books.

———. 1994. *Profits of Science*. New York: Basic Books.

Terdiman, Richard. 1985. *Discourse/Counter-Discourse*. Ithaca: Cornell University Press.

Tierney, Patrick. 2000. *Darkness in El Dorado: How Scientists and Journalists Devastated the Amazon*. New York: Norton.

Traweek, Sharon. 1988. *Beamtimes and Lifetimes*. Cambridge: Harvard University Press.

———. 1992. "Border Crossings: Narrative Strategies in Science Studies and among Physicists in Tsukuba Science City, Japan." In *Science as Practice and Culture*, ed. Andrew Pickering. Chicago: University of Chicago Press.

———. 1995. "Bachigai [Out of Place] in Ibaraki: Tsukuba Science City, Japan." In *Technoscientific Imaginaries: Late Editions 2*, ed. G. Marcus. Chicago: University of Chicago Press.

———. 1996. "Kokusaika (International Relations), Gaiatsu (Outside Pressure), and Bachigai (Being Out of Place)." In *Naked Science: Anthropologial Inquiry into Boundaries, Power, and Knowledge*, ed. Laura Nader. New York: Routledge.

Treat, John Wittier. 1995. *Writing Ground Zero: Japanese Literature and the Atomic Bomb*. Chicago: University of Chicago Press.

Treichler, Paula. 1987. "AIDS, Homophobia, and Biomedical Discourse: An Epidemic of Signification." *October* 43:31–70.

Treichler, Paula, Lisa Cartwright, and Constance Penley, eds. 1998. *The Visible Woman: Imaging Technologies, Gender, and Science*. New York: New York University Press.

Tribe, Laurence. 1991. "The Constitution in Cyberspace." Keynote address at the First Conference on Computers, Freedom, and Privacy. http://www.eff.or/legal/cyber_constitution.paper.

Triolo, Paul S., and Peter Lovelock. 1996. "Up, Up, and Away—with Strings Attached: China's Internet Development Has to Overcome Cultural, Regulatory, and Infrastructural Hurdles." *China Business Review*, November–December, 18–29.

Tsing, Anna L. 1993. *In the Realm of the Diamond Queen*. Princeton: Princeton University Press.

Turkle, Sherry. 1984. *The Second Self: Computers and the Human Spirit*. New York: Simon and Schuster.

———. 1994. "Why Do I Need to Get a 'Real Life' If My Life Is on the Internet?" Paper, 4s meetings, New Orleans, 14 October.

————. 1995. *Life on the Screen: Identity in the Age of the Internet*. New York: Simon and Schuster.

Turner, Terence. 1992. "Representing, Resisting, Rethinking: Historical Transformations of Kayapo Culture and Anthropological Consciousness." In *Colonial Situations*, ed. G. W. Stocking. Madison: University of Wisconsin Press.

————. 2001. Letter to the editor. *New York Review of Books*, 26 April, 69.

Tyler, Steven. 1978. *The Said and the Unsaid: Mind, Meaning, and Culture*. New York: Academic.

————. 1987. *The Unspeakable: Discourse, Dialogue, and Rhetoric in the Postmodern World*. Madison: University of Wisconsin Press.

Uchitelle, Louis. 1996. "Bit Player: What Has the Computer Done for Us Lately?" *New York Times*, 8 December, sec. 4, pp. 1, 4.

Ulmer, Gregory. 1994. *Heuretics: The Logic of Invention*. Baltimore: Johns Hopkins University Press.

Vaughan, Diane. 1997. *The "Challenger" Launch Decision: Risky Technology, Culture, and Deviance at NASA*. Chicago: University of Chicago Press.

Verene, Donald Phillip. 1985. *Hegel's Recollection: A Study of Images in the Phenomenology of Spirit*. Albany: State University of New York Press.

Vincenti, Walter. 1990. *What Engineers Know and How They Know It: Analytical Studies from Aeronautical History*. Baltimore: Johns Hopkins University Press.

Virilio, Paul. 1977/1986. *Speed and Politics*. New York: Columbia University Press.

————. 1984/1989. *War and Cinema: The Logics of Perception*. London: Verso.

————. 1993/1995. *The Art of the Motor*. Minneapolis: University of Minnesota Press.

Visvanathan, Shiv. 1985. *Organizing for Science: The Making of an Industrial Research Laboratory*. New Delhi: Oxford University Press.

————. 1988a. "Atomic Physics: The Career of an Imagination." In *Science, Hegemony, and Violence*, ed. Ashis Nandy. New York: Oxford University Press.

————. 1988b. "On the Annals of the Laboratory State." In *Science, Hegemony, and Violence*, ed. Ashis Nandy. New York: Oxford University Press.

Viveiros de Castro. 1996. "Images of Nature and Society in Amazonia." *Annual Review of Anthropology* 25:175–200.

Waldby, Catherine. 2000. *The Visible Human Project: Informatic Bodies and Posthuman Medicine*. New York: Routledge.

Warner, Deborah J. 2000a. "From Tallahassee to Timbuktu: Cold War Efforts to Measure Intercontinental Distances." *Historical Studies in the Physical and Biological Sciences* 30(2):393–416.

————. 2000b. "Political Geodesy: The First Department of Defense World Geodetic System." MS.

Watts, Michael. 1983. *Silent Violence: Food, Famine, and Peasantry in Northern Nigeria*. Berkeley: University of California Press.

Watts, Sheldon. 1997. *Epidemics and History: Disease, Power, and Imperialism*. New Haven: Yale University Press.

Weber, Max. 1968. *Economy and Society*. New York: Bedminister Press.

Weber, Samuel. 1996. *Mass Mediauras: Form, Technics, Media*. Stanford: Stanford University Press.

———. 2001. "Religion, Repetition, Media." In *Religion and Media*, ed. H. de Vries and S. Weber. Stanford: Stanford University Press.

Webster, Donovan. 1994. "Chips Are a Thief's Best Friend." *New York Times Magazine*, 18 September, 54–59.

Weigel, Sigrid. 1996. *Body- and Image-Space: Rereading Walter Benjamin*. London: Routledge.

Weiner, Charles. 1999. "Is Self-Regulation Enough Today? Evaluating the Recombinant DNA Controversy." *Health Matrix: Journal of Law and Medicine* 9(2):1–14.

Wells, W. M., W. E. I. Grimson, R. Kikinis, and F. A. Jolesz. 1996. "Adaptive Segmentation of MRI Data." *IEEE Transactions on Medical Imaging* 15(4):429–42.

Welsome, Eileen. 1999. *The Plutonium Files: America's Secret Medical Experiments in the Cold War*. New York: Dial Press.

Werbner, Richard. 1991. *Tears of the Dead: The Social Biography of an African Family*. Washington: Smithsonian.

———, ed. 1998. *Memory and the Postcolony*. London: Zed.

Werth, Barry. 1994. *The Billion Dollar Molecule: One Company's Quest for the Perfect Drug*. New York: Simon and Schuster.

Westwick, Peter J. 2003. *The National Labs: Science in an American System, 1947–1974*. Cambridge: Harvard University Press.

White, Richard. 1995. *The Organic Machine: The Remaking of the Columbia River*. New York: Hill and Wang.

Wiener, Norbert. 1956. *I Am a Mathematician: The Later Life of a Prodigy*. New York: Doubleday.

Wildavsky, Aaron. 1995. *But Is It True? A Citizen's Guide to Environmental Health and Safety Issues*. Cambridge: Harvard University Press.

Wilmsen, Edwin. 1989. *Land Filled with Flies*. Chicago: University of Chicago Press.

Wilson, Andrew. 1992. *The Culture of Nature*. London: Blackwell.

Wilson, Stephen. 2002. *Information Arts: Intersections of Art, Science, and Technology*. Cambridge: MIT Press.

Winston, Mark. 1997. *Nature Wars: People versus Pests*. Cambridge: Harvard University Press.

Wise, Steve. 1999. *Rattling the Cage*. Washington: Island Press.

Wittgenstein, Ludwig. 1969. *On Certainty*. Ed. G. E. M. Anscombe and G. H. von Wright. New York: Harper and Row.

Wodak, Ruth, and Richard Mitten. 1993. "On the Discourse of Prejudice and Racism: Two Examples from Austria." Center for Austrian Studies Working Paper 93–94. University of Vienna, April.

Wodak, Ruth, and Rudolf de Cillia. 1995. *Sprachenpolitik in Mittel- und Osteuropa*. Wien: Passagen Verlag.

Wodak, Ruth, et al. 1990. *"Wir sind alle unschuldige Täter!" Diskurshistorische Studien zum Nachkriegsantisemitismus*. Frankfurt am Main: Suhrkamp.

Wooley, Benjamin. 1992. *Virtual Worlds*. London: Blackwell.

World Reporter. 1999. "Velázquez Tests Show Self-Portrait Added to 'Las Meninas' at Later

Date." EFE News Service, World Reporter, Malaga, Spain, 9 Dec. http://global.factiva
.com/en/arch/display.asp.

Wurzer, Wilhem. 1990. *Filming Judgment*. New York: Columbia University Press.

Yoffie, David B. 1994. *Strategic Management in Information Technology*. Englewood Cliffs:
Prentice Hall.

Yoe, Mary Ruth. 1998. "[Jacqueline Bhabha and Robert H. Kirschner's] Human-Rights
Course Offers a Close Look at Worldwide Violations." *University of Chicago Magazine*
91(2):8–9.

Yukawa, Hideki. 1958. *Tabibto* [The Traveler]. Trans. L. Brown and Y. Yashida. Singapore:
World Scientific Publishing, 1982.

Zimmermann, Francis. 1982/1987. *The Jungle and the Aroma of Meats: An Ecological Theme in
Hindu Medicine*. Berkeley: University of California Press.

Zipes, Jack. 1983. *Fairy Tales and the Art of Subversion*. New York: Wildman Press.

Žižek, Slavoj. 1991. *Looking Awry: An Introduction to Jacques Lacan through Popular Cinema*.
Cambridge: MIT Press.

Zmarz Koczanowicz, Maria. 1993. "Postmodern Anxiety in Houston." *Kino*.

anthropologists (*continued*)
lary: Dumit; K. Fortun; Kelty; Lahsen;
Landecker; Latour; Lotfalian; E. Martin;
Sunder Rajan; Traweek
— *other ethnographers and sociologists*: Cambrosio and Keating, 351; Duster, 377;
Fujimura, 44, 49, 336, 351; Ghamari-
Tabrizi, 2, 348; M-J. DelV. Good, 33, 165,
166, 168; Jahoda, 30, 403n1; Lazersfeld, 30;
Löwy, 44, 351; Nandy, 200–201; Papert,
367, 423–24n2; Piaget, 367; Stacey, 303,
356; Turkle, 39, 49, 265, 269, 355, 356, 366–
67; Visvananthan, 200–202. *See also under*
STS concepts and vocabulary: Bucciarelli;
Collins; Knorr-Cetina; Star
anthropology: and biology, 381; challenges for, 3, 7–8, 38, 48, 57–58, 147, 176;
and Ethics Committee of the American
Anthropological Association, 371, 372; and
history, 334, 346, 370, 373–74, 383–84; and
regional, comparative, and team research,
376; and streams of representations, 22,
40, 58, 225–26, 257; as testing/constesting
philosophers, social theorists, historians,
psychologists, and novelists, 48, 147, 193,
196
anxieties and the social nervous system, 31, 51, 316–17, 395; ghost stories
(*shingata/shinkei*) as vehicles for modern
anxieties, 394; hospital poster as angst
factory, 157; Picabia and techno-anxieties,
419n8; primatology as screen for cultural
anxieties, 211
art circulation, 90; and art market, 12; and
cheap reproductions as interventions,
120, 127; and ephemeral art, 133, 134; and
Fogg Museum, 120; and Houston Contemporary Art Museum, 138; in Japan:
ukiyo-e prints, 394, Yoshitoshi prints and
newspaper illustrations, 395; and Mary
Ryan Gallery, 138; in medical and public
libraries, 110, 114; and Menil Museum,
121; in Mexico: calavera, 92, papel picado,

116, 118, retablo, 134; and Raimondi printmaking for the nascent bourgeois market,
120–21; of Southwest Indian paintings, 97;
and Wiener Kunsthaus, 31
artists: E. Avery, 18–19, 90–144, 419n8;
Beckman, *Morgue*, 135; Bingham, *Fur
Traders Descending the Missouri*, 18, 114;
Botticelli, *Birth of Venus*, 116, 118; Breughel, *The Harvesters*, 114; A. Carius and
tokomak fusion reactor, 419n8; Cézanne,
Great Bather, 134; S. Coe, 127; Copley,
Watson and the Shark, 18, 128; Deix, 31–32,
33; Desprez, *Chimera*, 130–31; Dürer, *Bath
House*, 134–35; Etienne, *De dissectione*, 110;
Gericault, *Raft of the Medusa*, 128; Goya,
Sleep of Reason, 116, 119, *The Third of May*,
116, 117; Holbein, 92, 114; Issenheim altarpiece, 132; M. Lasansky, 97; Magritte, *Ceci
n'est pas une pipe*, 419n2; Mapplethorpe,
18; E. Munch, 96, 104, 105, 106, 107;
neoimpressionsists and psychophysics,
419n8; nuclear photographers Mizrahi
and Nagatoni, 347; M. Pauline and mechanical gladiators, 286; Picabia and
techno-anxieties, 419n8; Picasso, *Demoiselles d'Avignon*, 116, 117; Piranesi, 94–95;
Posada, 92, 110, 114; Raimondi, *Massacre
of the Innocents*, 120–21; Rembrandt, *The
Storm on the Sea of Galilee*, 128; D. Rivera,
131; N. Rockwell, 18; A. Rush, 97, 105;
Tansey, *The End of Painting*, 71; M. Tracey,
121–23, 134; Velázquez, *Las Meninas*, 25,
309–14, 393, 419n2, 420nn4–5; Yoshitoshi,
393–95
autobiographies and life histories, 181, 192;
beginnings, 203; gatekeepers of, 403–4n3;
genres of, 179, 198, 224
— *and ethnicity*, 183–92; five modes of articulation, 184: A. Delgardo, 186; D. Der Havanessian, 186–87; M. H. Kingston, 182, 183,
184, 185; S. Rushdie, 190; G. Vizenor, 187
— *and religion*, 192–98; criteria of double-
voiced texts, 196; al-Hallai/Massignon, 21,

195; Santabalji/Navalbhai Shah, 21, 195;
Scholem/Green, 21, 195
— *and science*, 199–221; criteria of, 202: Darwin, 204; Einstein, 204; I. Fischer, 203,
207, 213–21; Levi-Moltancini, 199–200,
207, 213–15; S. Luria, 203; P. Morse, 203;
Newton, 204; Pasteur, 204; Popper, 202,
204; J. Watson, 199; N. Wiener, 203, 204,
216; Yukawa, 205–7
— *and technology*: Bell and T. Watson, 51,
342–43; H. Ford, 342, 344

bacteriology, 340; Chakrabarty and plasmid-
enhanced oil-eating bacteria, 352; Neisser
and discovery of syphilis, 404n4; Pasteur
and Pasteur Institutes, 43, 204, 340. *See
also under* STS concepts and vocabulary:
Fleck
biology and biomedicine, 6, 44, 45, 323,
340–41, 348–55, 425n2; and brain death,
175, 403n23; and computer-assisted surgical systems, 318; as deep play, 31, 33–34;
and embryology and developmental biology, 307, 349; and ethics, 33, 35, 341,
371, lab governance/investigation of fraud
(Baltimore case), 352; experimental systems in, 350–52, 353; and HeLa immortal
cell line, 341; and HLA markers, 147, 389;
human biology in 1960s vs. 1990s, 370;
Human Genome Diversity Project, 147,
376; Human Genome Project, 152, 322,
347, 413n40; microcinematography, 310;
neurobiology, 207, 213, 310, and Dante's
Ulysses, 214; and organ transplantation,
173–74, 402nn19–20; and patents, 353;
protein synthesis PCR and monoclonal
antibodies as tools for genetic engineering revolution, 45, 324, 350, 351, 353; and
recombinant DNA and containment regulations (Asilomar), 34, 170, 173, 352; and
vaccines, 35, 378–79; and xenotransplantation, 31, 33–34, 169–75. *See also* genetics:
genomics; geneticists

— *bioart*, 146, 399n4
— *biochemists*: Matthei, 350; Nirenberg, 350
— *biocolonialism* and bioprospecting, 371;
Indigenous Peoples' Council on Biocolonialism, 377
— *bioengineering*, 318, 323. *See also* surgical
systems
— *bioethics*, 164, 307
— *bioinformatics*, 322; and Visible Human
Project (*see under* visual thread)
— *biologists*: Amos, 389; Bach, 33, 170, 172;
F. Black, 383; Bodmer, 389; D. Cohen, 353;
S. Cohen, 200, 207, 336; W. Gilbert, 356;
Jacob, 323; Korana, 353; Levi-Montalcini,
21, 199, 203, 207, 208, 213–17; S. Luria,
203–4; H. J. Muller, 385; Rheinberger,
323, 350–51; Watson, 199; E. O. Wilson,
380; Zamecnik, 350. *See also* genetics:
geneticists
— *biopolitics, biopower, biosocialities, and
biological citizenship*, 49, 150, 159, 323
— *biotechnology companies*: Ardais, 322;
Celera, 167; Cetus, 45, 353; Chiron,
353; deCode, 152–53, 163, 322, 377; First
Genomic Trust, 322; Genzyme, 173;
Harvard-Millennium Pharmaceuticals,
377; Imutran, 173, 402n19; Vertex, 336;
pharmaceutical and life science companies:
Ciba-Geigy, 343; Hoffman-LaRoche, 153,
353; Novartis, 402n19; *research institutes
and universities*: California Institute of
Technology, 349; Harvard, 377; Michigan, 377, 388; Pennsylvania State, 377, 388;
Whitehead/MIT, 9, 152, 418n6
— *biowarfare*: anthrax in Russia, 402n18; and
deliberate infection of Brazilian Indians,
390; history of, 160, 390; informed consent
for research on, 371
botanists: Goethe, 47; da Orta, 307, Kerala
toddy tappers, 47, 307, Linnaeus, 47, 307,
van Reede, 307
Brazil: Central Ge Project, 376; DNA collection in the Amazon, 377, HTLV II, 424n1;

Brazil (*continued*)

Kayapo, 380, 392; organ transplantation, 174; race relations, 376; Raytheon satellite-airborne-ground monitoring system for the Amazon, 315; report of the medical team on accusations against Chagnon and Neel, 387; trials over deliberate 1960s infection of Indians, 390; Xavante activism, epidemiological transition, and history, 383–84. *See also* Yanomani

—*scientists and anthropologists*: Cardoso de Oliveira, 376; Coimbra, 376, 383–84, 388; Ramos, 373, 374, 388, 392; Salzano, 376, 383–84; Santos, 376–77, 383–84

calendars, 29

catacoustis, 91, 141

chemical industry, 47–48, 56, 321; DuPont, 353, 354; F. Haber, 404n4

China, 337, 362; DNA collection in Anhui Province, 377; documentary film project on, 307; Ming dynasty woodcut and avant-garde performance poster, 418; and organ transplantation, 174; population control in, 372; Three Gorges Project in, 418n7

cinema. *See* film

civil society, 3, 30; and civil defense drills, 15; and deliberative democracy tools, 4, 31, 170, 328, 360; impact of computerized public records on accountability, 265; Internet as platform for, 34, 159, 170; and parapolitical commissions, 402n19

class and stratification, 128, 181–82; and art, 120, 128; and information technologies, 263, 265; and medicine, 328; and science, 200, cross-class circulation of science and media ideas/metaphors, 349

comparative methods and understanding, 14, 188, 193; comparison involving at least three, 184, 196

computer hackers, 409n18; and gaming and wit, 155, 356, 410nn19, 21, 23, and 24

computers and IT networks, 355–57

—*biological computers*, 264, 407n2

—*computer-assisted*: surgical systems, 309, 315–16, 318–19, 321; virtual experience (CAVE), 13, 330–31

—*cryptography*: cryptoanarchy, 267, 291, 412n30; and secure networks, 20, 155–56, 162–63

—*as cyberspace*, 17, 23, 53, 261, 356

—gender and identity, 283; and styles of computer use, 269

—*as infrastructure*, 39, 52–54, 57, 264, 267, 304, 322; in Finland, 273; French Minitel, 267–68; Internet history, 267–73, 408nn8 and 11, 413n41

—*and language*, 273–84; *The Hacker's Dictionary*, 275, 277–84; Jargon File, 282; perception, 52–54, 264

—*and the law*, 290–298, 410–412; copyright, 293, 296–97; National Information Infrastructure Initiative, 293–97; patents, 293; Stallman and Free Software Foundation, 282

—and new social movements, 158–59

—and political economy, 270, 298–302, 355–56

—*as technologies of self and personhood*, 53, 322; face and emotion recognition, 285

—and toxicities in manufacture, 300–302, 356

—and Y2K bug, 1–2, 396n1

consciousness, 69; class (*see* class and stratification); *conscience collective*, 16, 40; cross-cultural, 64, 188, 198; gestalt switching, 419n2; Green, 265; historical, 12, 17, 21; locally infected global, 225; and physiology, 315

cross-cultural thread, 335–36, 362; "period eyes" as contrasting epistemes, 338

culture. *See also* deep play; nuclear cultures; postmodern; technologies: and cultural imaginaries/readings

—concept, 7

—*cultural critique*, 4, 12, 68, 69, 225, 396; and

ethnography (*continued*)
of, 58; and cyberspace, 262–63; and
ethnographic-collaborative voice, 149,
309, 333; and ethnographic sensibility, 2,
13; and ethnographic turn in Polish film,
225, 232–33; and film, 53, 69; multilocale
or multisited, 40, 56, 354; mutlivocal
and multi-audience, 40, 196; and novels,
399n3; as reality check, 146, 148; and science studies, 41, 44–48; as translation and
facilitator of dialogue, 328
European Union, 31, 32
expert cultures, 12, 24–25, 41–48

fantasy, desire, hype, and phantasmagoria:
148, 155, 166, 317, 393; advertising embrace,
166, 167; in biomedicine, 33, biotechnical
embrace, 165, 169, corruption of desire to
introduce world-class care, 165, narratives
of hope, 166; in computer science: desire
to escape the body, 357, Moravec, 275;
desire and jouissance, 422n13; ethics and
scandal publicities as fantasy formations,
164; phantasmic ecological threats, 265;
rescue and technocratic fantasies, 163. *See
also* hauntings and ghosts of the past
film, 52; as cultural critique, 69, 71, 88; Eisenstein, 53, 71, 234; and filmic judgment, 53,
68, 69; intertextuality of, 67, 79, 83, 84,
87; and moral codes, 65, 88; new forms of
perception or consciousness, 69–71, 81,
89; peep show vs. cinema as metaphor,
398n7; as revelatory of cultural struggles,
66, 81, 88; silent film and Kafka's novels,
158; social functions of, 71–72, 73; struggle
between Islam and Bollywood in immigrant consciousness, 190; struggles for
control over, 73–74, 76, 88; Tarkovsky,
234; virtuality vs. montage, 227–28
—*Balkan*: E. Kusterica, *Underground*, 67;
M. Manchevski, *Before the Rain*, 67, 256
—*Chinese Fifth Generation*, 234; and the
ethnographic, 405n8

—*French*: C. Lanzman, *Shoah*, 235; New
Wave, 227
—*Indian*: V. V. Chopra, *Mission Kashmir*, 67;
S. Kapur, *Phoolan Devi*, 67; M. Rathnam,
Bombay, 67; A. Sen, *Mr. And Mrs. Iyer*, 67
—*Iranian*: *abgushti* ("B films"), 74, 82, 88;
discursive dimensions of, 87–88; New
Wave, 61; statistics, 74; war films, 61, 82;
and work of interruption, 73; filmmakers:
Bani-Etemad, *Ru-sari Abi* (Blue-Veiled),
85; Beza'i, 83, *Bashu*, 72, 89; Darvish,
Kimia, 87; Davudnezad, *Niaz* (Need),
85, 89; Hatamikia, *Ajans Shishe-i* (The
Glass Agency), 86; Jalili, *A True Story*,
88; Kiarostami, 82; *Life and Nothing Else*,
83–84, 233, *Nema-ye Nazdik* (Close-Up),
53, 68, 77, 78, 83, *A Taste of Cherries*,
78–80, 88, *Through the Olive Trees*, 88;
Kiamiavi, *Moghul-ha*, 76–77, 84, *Where
Is My Friend's House*, 84; Longinotto and
Mir-Hosseni, *Divorce Iranian Style*, 398n6;
Makhmalbaf, 68, 82; *Boycott*, 82, 88, 89,
Bread and Vase, 82, *The Marriage of the
Blessed*, 77, 82, 84, 87, 88, 89, *Once Upon
a Time Cinema*, 82, 84, *The Peddler*, 77–
78, 82, 84, 88, 89, *A Time of Love*, 82, 89;
Mehrjui, 83, *Gav*, 75, 79, 84, *Leila*, 78, 89
—*Italian*, 227: Antonioni, *Blow Up*, 68
—*Polish*, 71; critics: Kijowski, 231–32, 235;
Sobolewski, 226, 230, 231, 233–34, 235, 246,
247, 254; filmmakers: Drygasa, *Listen to
My Cry*, 233; A. Holland, 235, 406n9; Kies-
lowski, 234; Konwicki, 234; M. Lozinski,
Eighty-nine Millimeters to Europe, 233,
Seven Jews from My Class, 233; P. Lozin-
ski, *Birthplace*, 233, 235; Piwowski, *Rejs*,
232; Wajda, *Korczak*, 235, *Man of Marble*,
235, and *The Wedding*, 407n13; Zmarz-
Koczanowicz, 21, 225–60, *Camera*, 253,
Democracy, 227, *Don't Trust the Politicians*,
227, 249, 251–52, *Edge of the World*, 227,
228–30, 231–32, 233, *Everyone Knows Who
Stands behind Whom*, 248–49, *Last Gypsy*

historians (*continued*)
50; Landecker, 39, 49, 335, 336, 341, 361; Lindee, 385, 386, 387; MacKenzie, 39, 44, 336; Mindel, 44, 335, 366, 368; Newman, 334, 339; Principe, 339; Rheinberger, 39, 44, 323, 350–51; Ritvo, 358; C. Rosenberg, 340; Shapin and Shaffer, 42, 334, 338, 339; Smith, 335; Stafford, 329; C. Weiner, 348, 363; L. White, 48; R. White, 47, 358–59; R. Williams, 335

history and historiography, 30, 335–36; Annales school, 49; and Central European small societies and minor literatures, 188; Subaltern Group, 188

Hoover, Herbert, 15

Huntington, Samuel, 7

Iceland, 152–153, 163, 322, 377

identity, 179; and feminism, 191

images and visualization: art images as debris, 105; dialectical, 225, 408n9, illustrations vs. constructions, representations vs. translations, 310, 323, 329; gestalt switch (Duck-Rabbit drawing), 419n2; golden events vs. statistical logic, 317–18, 331; logos for STS, 307, 418n7; mise-en-scène, mise-en-abyme, 309, 310; medical imaging instruments (PET, CT, MRI), 323; news images as generic vs. specific, 227, 255–57; skepticism of visual evidence in courts of law, 332, 361. *See also* visual thread: cartoons

India: computers and information technologies in, 41, 57, 273, 412n34, 413n41; ecological knowledges, 306, 339; and nuclear weapons, 348; and organ transplantation, 164–65; science policy of, 306–7; *social scientists* (*see under* anthropologists and ethnographers: V. Das, A. Gupta, A. Nandy, K. Sunder Rajan, S. Visvananthan)

industrial revolutions, 38, 40, 52, 341, 343

information technologies, 57; databases, 322. *See also* computers and IT networks

institutional therapy: and medical humanities, 139–41; and museums, 137–39; and process of working through resistances, 137, 138

Iran: early Internet use, 273. *See also* film: Iranian

Italy: and genetics, 376; and molecular biology, 21; and perspectival painting, 313–14; and presumed consent, 174; and Turin medical school, 216; and xenotransplantation, 402n19
—*scientists*: P. Levi (and Dante's Ulysses), 214; Levi-Montalcini, 21, 199, 203, 204, 207, 208, 213–15; S. Luria, 203

Jamshid's cup, 322–23, 425n2

Japan: Atomic Bomb Casualty Commission, 385; ghost stories (*shingata/shinkei*) as ritual process, 395, as vehicles for modern anxieties, 394; Internet beginnings in, 272; Kunio (modernist folklorist), 226; parables of judgment, 4, 393, 394, 396; style of physics contrasted with that in United States, 347; *ukiyo-e* prints of warrior stories as metaphors for contemporary unrest, 394; and uxorilineal naming, 206; and Web and Internet language-learning tools, 307, 417n3; and women physicists, 347; Yoshitoshi as printmaker, newspaper illustrator, and "public eyes on the Meiji Restoration," 395
—*scientists*: cytogenetics and HLA expert Venezuelans, 389; T. Masao (radiation researcher), 385; H. Yukawa, 203, 205–6

journalists: use of metaphors and tropes, 372, use of TRAC statistics, 265

on computers: engineers: Kidder, 44, 335, 355; hackers: Hafner and Markoff, 275; and justice system: Burnham, 265, 267, 322, 347, 359; third-generation fiber-optic global cable and PTT restructuring: Stephenson, 303

on environment: Crawford, 47, 360; Harr, 6; Shulman, 336, 359

on molecular biology: Teitelman, 300, 351; Werth, 328, 336

on physicists and nuclear weapons: Broad, 44, 348; Jungk, 200–201; radar: Buderi, 335

on Yanomami: C. Mann, 375, 381; Tierney, 34–36, 374, 375, 378, 380–81, 387, 389, 390–91

language and communication models, 32; behaviorist, symbolist, structuralist, poststructuralist models, 185; and computers, 273–84; correspondence theories of language, 325; cultural linguistics of Nazi discourse, 401n9; diversion (Bialik), 179, and *Mitteilbarkeit* (Benjamin), 63; hackish, 377–84; interlinguistic models, 182, 183, 192; scientific creoles and pidgin languages, 346

legal thread: challenges to polluter pays, 325; death penalty, 126–27; intellectual property rights, 218, 261, and patents in biology, 353; international human rights law and clinical trials, 371, 385, and genomics, 152; law and the Internet, 23, 290–98, 411n26, 412n29; law and organ transplantation, 403n21; role of courts in ethical plateaus of technoscience (Breyer), 9, 167

—*international declarations, conventions, protocols, treaties*: Helsinki Declarations, 378, 385; GATT/WTO, 371; Nuremburg Code, 378; UNESCO Universal Declaration on the Human Genome and Human Rights, 152

—U.S. legislation: Superfund, 371

literary thread, 335–36, 361, 419n8; anecdotes (*see* anecdotes); alternative narratives vs. laments, 191; and the ethnographic, 149 (*see also* ethnography); male vs. female

storytelling, 193; metaphors and rhetoric in the law, 291–92, in science, 349–50, 354–55; narratives of hope, 166, 247–48; novels (*see* novels); origin stories and genealogies, 266, 267, 345, 408n8, discovery and first-contact tropes, 372–73, 386, 391, genius tropes, 199, 341; role of literary forms in shaping and understanding technosciences, 149; romantic tropes, 404n4; the uncanny and hauntings in generational consciousness, 151, 225–26, 237, 238–39; wedding and funeral tropes, 246; writerly style of science fiction, 409n13; zoos and aquariums as political metaphor, 232, 405n7

—*literary critics*: Abbas, 332; Benjamin, 12, 13, 15, 18, 48, 52, 63, 64, 69, 70, 73, 90, 141, 142, 145, 225, 227, 315–16, 310, 315, 327, 328, 331, 408n9, 421n10; Bhabha, 4, 11, 15, 36, 163; Bukatman, 53, 265, 356, 409n13; Cacciari, 16; Delaney, 326; Donaldson, 417n4; Doyle, 349–50; Iser, 399n3; Jameson, 7; Kittler, 16, 50, 311, 331, 343; McHale, 265, 277; Ronell, 50, 51, 265, 342–43, 354, 414n1; Said, 189–90, 191, 223, 397

—*writers* (*see also* novels): Becket, 229; Celan, 12; Cixous, 16; Hedayat, 81, 226; Hemingway, 406n10; Jabès, 12; Joyce, 180; Kafka, 50, 229, 343; Poe, 375; Rushdie, 182, 190, 192, 375

media: Arendt and the mediated lie, 375; global telemedia circuits, 62, 234; *MIT Media Lab*: constructivism, 367; print and newspaper media, 394–95; typewriter/postal system and Kafka, Nietzsche, *Dracula*, 90, 343; and wearable computers, 305, 315; woodblock printmaking as mechanical reproduction, 120–21, 394. *See also* film; orality and literacy; photography; technologies: teletechnologies; virtuality; visual thread medicine, 339–41; medical humanities, 101; medical imaging, 310, 323; personalized, 322; VR surgical systems: da Vinci, 322, I. Hunter, 322. *See also* biology and biomedicine

Mexico: Chiapas, 376; Zapatistas, 400n6

Mickey Mouse, 316, 343

modernity and modernities, 39, 40–41, 181; *alternative*, 18, 55; and fundamentalisms, 192; Hispanic, 186; *lethal*, 163, fascism and the hardening of the body vs. Benjamin and coevolution/innervation of the techno-social body, 316–17, sites of evisceration of modernity, 4, 36; majoritarian/minor literatures and ideologies, 188, and film, 70, and folklore, 226, 404n2; *second-order (reflexive)*, 2, 12, 31, 317, 324–28, 344, 375, and biological and computer self-organizing complexity, 264, 309, 317; environmental issues as exemplars, 363–64; *and universities*, 414n2. *See also* postmodern

moral entrepreneurship, 2; moral traditions under reconstruction, 193

multidisciplinary research projects and expeditions, 35, 374, 376, 389, 390

nanotechnology, 310, 318–19, 327, 355; micromotion robots, 315, 320; nanobots, 286

nationalism: and folklore, 404n2; and universities, 414–15n2

neuroscience module, 369; neurobiology and neurochemistry, 213

novels (paired with ethnographies/histories in STS), 145, 148, 149, 163, 335–36; and anticipation effect, 401n9, 407n3; Balzac's novels and Marx, 400n6; Banville, *Dr. Kepler* and *Copernicus* (and the scientific revolution), 361; Bear, *Blood Music* (and Rabinow's *Making PCR*, Werth's *Million Dollar Molecule*, biotech startups), 147, 264, *Darwin's Radio* (retroviruses, AIDS, and public health response to pan-

demics), 147; Constantine, *Infinite Loop* (and Media Lab new technologies), 53, 284–87; Coupland, *Microserfs*, 53, 58, 356; Dick, *Do Androids Dream of Electric Sheep?*, 356; Djerassi, *Cantor's Dilemma*, *Bourbaki Gambit*, and *NO*, 336; Gary, *The Dance of Ghengis Cohen* (return of repressed Jewish ancestries), 163; Ghosh, *Calcutta Chromosome* (malaria, subaltern science, information retrieval, and global water management), 58, 147, 190; Gibson, 58, 275, 409n14, *Neuromancer*, 275; Grass, *The Rat* (laboratory rats, ecological research, toxic waste, death of forests), 147, *The Tin Drum* (and the genomic brave new world), 154; Greene, *The Third Man* (penicillin racket), 152, 401n11; Hasek, *The Good Soldier Schweik*, 14, 407n12; Kafka, *The Castle* (telephone), 343, *The Trial*, 151, 343; Kafka's novels and silent film, 158; Lightman, *Einstein's Dreams*, 345; Malzberg, *The Remaking of Sigmund Freud* (social relations in space flight, cryogenics), 149; Mathews, *Vienna Blood* (biowarfare, cryptography, genetic engineering, transnational evasion of institutional review boards, and Imutran), 146, 147, 150–64, 173; Mawer, *Mendel's Dwarf* (achondroplasia, biological gardens, molecular biology laboratories), 146; McCormmach, *Night Thoughts of a Classical Physicist* (and physics module), 317, 345; Nilekani, *Stillborn* (transnational clinical trials), 147, 165; Powers, 13, 361, *Gain* (cancer etiology, technology project management, and Latour's *Aramis*), 321, *Galatea 2.2* and *Plowing the Dark* (artificial intelligence, virtual reality, human-machine interfaces, information management), 13, 274, 331, *Gold Bug Variations* (and Kay's *Who Wrote the Book of Life*, molecular biology), 147; Pynchon, *Gravity's Rainbow* (determinism, probabilism, aesthetics of scientific styles, science and violence, and Galison's *Image and Logic*, Nandy's *Science, Hegemony and Violence*), 274; Rushdie, *Satanic Verses*, 182, 190, 192, 375; Smith, *Future Boston* and *In the Cube*, 58; Stoker, *Dracula* (and the typewriter), 50, 343

nuclear cultures, 347–48; Hanford nuclear reactor, 354; in Japan, 348; military nuclear waste, 336, 359; nuclear civil defense, 15; nuclear photographers, 347; nuclear war and Christian rapture, 348; nuclear waste market and Native American reservations, 360; nuclear weapons: in India, 348, in Israel, 348, simulated tests, 321, in United States, 347, 385; plasma physics and tokomak fusion reactor, 419n8; radiation research, 385, 390, nuclear reactor and brain oncology at MIT, 418n6; Three Mile Island, 6

orality and literacy, 180, 190, 325–27; and the Qur'an, 66–67, 197

parables: two Tablets of Moses, two sequences of Qur'anic revelation, 180
period eyes: as historical vs. cultural epistemes, 338
pharmacology: in eighteenth century, 43. *See also* biology and biomedicine: biotechnology companies
pharmakon, 321; and haoma/soma, 425n2; and sake cup, 396. *See also* Jamshid's cup
philosophical thread: Adorno, 11, 40,48, 158, 363; Agamben, 16; Arendt, 375; Blumenberg, 337; Carnap, 423n1; Deleuze and film, 70–71, 227–28, 330; Deleuze and Guattari, 16, 49, 50–51, 53, 188, 265; Derrida, 12, 16, 17, 54, 265, 278, and molecular biology, 323, and teletechnologies, 62, 261, 263; Descartes, 312, 314, 325, 421n9; Diderot, 222; Dilthey, 8, 16; Dreyfus, 356; Fichte, 38, 414n2; Foucault, 16, 25, 49, 307, 309, 310, 312, 325, 337, 339, 419n2,

424nn3 and 5; Habermas, 16, 351, 398n2; Hegel, 227, 312, 400n6, 405n6, 421n7; Heidegger, 12, 48, 51, 416n3, 422n11; Humboldt, 38, 415n2; Husserl, 404n4; Jonas, 51, 302; Kant, 312; Kuhn, 41, 335, 340, 423n1; Lacoue-Labarthe, 91; Lakatos, 203; Levinas, 10, 11, 12, 23, 37, 63, 73, *adieu/à Dieu*, 63; Luhmann, 16; Lyotard, 16, 40, 265, 267–68, 317, 330, 331, *differends*, 80, 268; and computers, 265, 267–68; Nietzsche, 50, 90, 180, 182, 187, 343; Peirce, 40; Popper, 202–4; Schlick, 30, 423n1; Serres, 186, 265; Vattimo, 16; Virilio, 70, 265, 330; Wittgenstein, 9, 37, 51, 176, 199, 419n2; Žižek, 70, 145

photography: *documentary*, 112, 125, on surgery and art, 104, 105, on use of space by the elderly, 101; *environmental*: on nuclear landscape, 347, on Planet Earth, 331; *photo-essay*: on refugees, 105, 108, 109, 124, use and abuse of, 108, 189–90

physics, 44, 317, 345–48; contrasted with molecular biology, 346; cultural genealogies of instruments, 345–46; generational turnover, 347; Japanese and U.S. styles contrasted, 347
—*physicists*: Bethe, 201; Blau, 346; Boltzman, 217; Bohr, 200, 279; Born, 404n4; Einstein, 200, 204, 217; Fermi, 200; Leng, 403n1; Meitner, 403n1; Oppenheimer, 33, 199, 200, 201, 403n22; Rabi, 238; Teller, 201; Yukawa, 203; S. Weinberg, 5

Poland: and *chocholi* dance, 231, 236; elections in, 229, 234, 251, 254, 405n7; film as cultural critique of, 225–60; media privatization scandals in, 253, and control of television, 255; and politics of laughter, 249–51; production of commercials for Russia, 253; and punk rock, 248, 250, 251, 252–53; romantic tropes as nationalist defense, 404n1; Solidarity's camera as metaphor, 253; and Yiddish folklore, 226. *See also* film: Polish

332, 361, in Hollywood (Hays Code), 65, in Iran, 65. *See also* image

— *Visible Human Project*, 317, 321, 322, 323, 422n14

— *visual imagery of texts*: in Darwin, 331; visual tableau, 203, mise-en-scène, 309, 310

— *visual literacy*, 101, 143; disturbing photos informed by art history, 104; Lazarus up from the dead and nursing, 105, 116; Michelangelo and surgery, 102

— *visual technologies*: computer-assisted virtual experience (CAVE), 330–31, simulations and informated touch, 310, 317, 321, 322, 328; icons, 21; inherently life-killing vs minimally invasive, 321; in medicine, 323, PET, 310; photography, 101, photo archives, 21; and the postmodern, 330

war: and theories of tribal warfare, 373; U.S. Civil War and phantom limbs, 419n8; Vietnam and television, 372, and sociobiology, 380; World War I, 316. *See also* films: Iranian — *Bashu, Glass Agency*, and *Marriage of the Blessed;* refugees

women in science: in Argentina, 403n2; M. Blau, 346, 403n1; I. Fischer, 21, 203, 215–21, 403nn1 and 3; in interwar Vienna, 403n1; in Japan, 347; H. Leng, 403n1; R. Levi-Montalcini, 21, 199, 203, 207, 208, 213–17; B. McClintock, 214, 403n1; L. Meitner, 403n1

Yanomami, 25; agency and "the hyperreal Indian," 374, 392, D. Kopenawa as spokesman, 392; T. Asch films of, 34, 382, 391–92; as deep play, 31, 34–35; demography of, 373; DNA and blood collection of, 380, 424n1; history of, 373; land rights of, 375, 391; lawsuit against United States, 377; and malaria, 373; *weitheri* (fierceness) of, 378, 391

Michael M. J. Fischer is a professor of anthropology and science and technology studies at the Massachusetts Institute of Technology. His previous books include *Iran: From Religious Dispute to Revolution*; *Debating Muslims: Cultural Dialogues in Postmodernity and Tradition*, coauthored with Mehdi Abedi; and *Anthropology as Cultural Critique: An Experimental Moment in the Human Sciences*, coauthored with George Marcus.

Library of Congress Cataloging-in-Publication Data
Fischer, Michael M. J.
Emergent forms of life and the anthropological voice /
Michael M. J. Fischer.
p. cm. Includes bibliographical references and index.
ISBN 0-8223-3225-6 (cloth : alk. paper)
ISBN 0-8223-3238-8 (pbk. : alk. paper)
1. Anthropology—Philosophy.   2. Anthropological ethics.
3. Visual anthropology.   4. Cross cultural communication.
5. Communication in anthropology.   I. Title.
GN33.F57 2003   301'.01—dc22   2003016427